Octane

# CLASSIC PRICE GUIDE

CLASSIC CAR
PRICE GUIDE
1945-2005

Octane editorial office
DENNIS PUBLISHING LTD
31-32 Alfred Place
London WC1E 7DP
Tel +44 (0)20 3890 3890
email info@octane-magazine.com

EDITORIAL
**Price guide editor** Peter Tomalin
**Assistant editor** Matthew Hayward
**Designer** Robert Hefferon
**Editorial director** James Elliott

ADVERTISING
**Advertising director** Sanjay Seetanah
**Account director** Sam Snow
**Account manager** Paul Landry
**Special projects** John Deverell
**Dealer account manager** Marcus Ross
**Email:** ads@octane-magazine.com
**Tel:** +44 (0)1628 510080
**Advertising production**
Mike Hills and Daniel Stark

MANAGEMENT
**Publishing manager** Holly Jerram
**Operations director** Robin Ryan
**MD of advertising** Julian Lloyd-Evans
**Newstrade director** David Barker
**Chief brand officer** Nicola Bates
**Chief executive** James Tye
**Company founder** Felix Dennis

MAGBOOK



ISBN 978-1-78106-726-0

LICENSING & SYNDICATION
To license or syndicate this content, please contact Nicole Creasey on +44 (0)20 3890 3998 or email nicole_creasey@dennis.co.uk



**Printed by Precision Colour Printing**

# Keeping calm – and carrying on driving

THIS TIME LAST YEAR the classic car market was holding its breath as we waited to find out when (indeed, if) Brexit would happen. Well, we now know the answer to that one – although its final shape is yet to be revealed. And now, a year later, coronavirus stalks the land, whole countries have been in lockdown and financial markets in turmoil. Next year? My money's on an asteroid.

In the early months of 2020, Brexit did appear to have re-energised much of the classic car scene, most specialists reporting increased activity, with more people looking to buy and sell cars, though this was yet to translate into an upsurge in values. It's certainly true that prices have yet to return to the levels of a few years ago. Some have slipped further, though most have remained more or less static over the last 12 months. What we do know is that they *will* pick up again eventually – and in the meantime we can still self-isolate in our classics!

We've given the guide a shake-up this year, extending the cut-off by five years to 2005 and bringing in dozens of cars that are thoroughly deserving of classic status – and worthy of consideration for your next purchase. Cars like the wild TVR Sagaris (above), sublime Aston DB9 and thrilling Ferrari F430, as well as affordable icons like the Ford Focus RS and Renault Sport Clio.

Also new this year, we've asked our experts to come up with ten cars that are conspicuously good value right now and which should prove a decent long-term investment as well as a great ownership proposition. Asteroids permitting.

Peter Tomalin, Price Guide editor

# MARKET WATCH

Just as Brexit had started to reboot the market, coronavirus brought new uncertainty. After a quiet 2019, it now looks as though 2020 will see most values remain on hold. Here's our review of recent market trends

**REMEMBER NORMAL LIFE?** It's getting trickier to recall the time when our biggest concern was the cost of taking the family to the Goodwood Revival. We'll get back there eventually, of course, though it may take a little time...

Meanwhile, our network of specialists and marque gurus have been trying to make sense of it all and give us a snapshot of the classic car market as it stood in the early summer of 2020, always accepting that events are moving rapidly, and in sometimes unexpected directions.

Aston specialist Nick Mee told us there had been more sales activity in early 2020 than a year previously, though a lot of it was very price-sensitive. One interesting trend in the Aston world, he observed, was the differing fortunes of the DB-era cars and those from the later, V8 period of hand-built models. While DB4s and the like had seen their values softening in the last year or two, cars like the classis V8 Vantages of the late '70s and '80s, along with the supercharged Vantage of the '90s, were holding firm.

'It has to be a generational thing,' said Mee. 'There's a whole generation of buyers coming through now whose pin-up cars when they were young were these V8 Vantages, V600s and so on, and now they've reached the age when they can buy those cars.'

In the Ferrari world, James Cottingham of DK Engineering reported that business was reasonably good, though values had remained pretty static, with a number of notable exceptions. The gorgeous 250 GT Berlinetta Lusso has seen prices for the best examples creep ever upwards, the very best now commanding £1.5m-plus, and it's a similar story with the ultra-rare 500 Superfast. 'The best are now easily £2m-plus, and I wouldn't be surprised to see one fetch £2.5m,' said Cottingham.

Of the more modern exotics, the 1980s 288 GTO continues to fly, the best now fetching as much as £3m – around twice as much as a comparable F40. It's a numbers game at this level – just 272

ASTON PARROTT

**Above**
The way we were in 2019: here at the Classic Motor Hub, Bibury, and below at Hampton Court

CLASSIC MOTOR HUB

ASTON PARROTT

AML

GTOs were built, compared with 1315 F40s. That sort of rarity also works in favour of the Enzo – a new entry into our guide this year. The fact just 400 were built keeps demand high, and that's reflected in our guide price of £2.5m for an excellent car.

'There are buyers,' said BMW specialist Munich Legends' Dan Norris, 'and there are deals to be done. But they are very price-sensitive. It's definitely a buyer's market. Over the last year there's been a real blunting of values at the top end – the 2002 Turbo, for example, has taken a hit, nice examples down £15k in the last 12-18 months from £105K to £90k.'

The M1 supercar, is another example of this blunting, Dan pegging values back from £650k to £500k for an excellent car. 'I'm convinced the M1 has still got long-term legs,' he told us, 'but it is symptomatic of what's happening in the market at the moment.'

One BMW that's bucking current trends is the late-80s 325i Sport, the six-cylinder sports saloon closing the gap on the more celebrated E30 M3 of the same period. 'There's not many around, they're right-hand drive, unlike the M3, and people are paying big money for the best ones – as much as £50k,' said Norris.

Most specialists we spoke to reported more interest in buying and selling, and more conversations taking place, though these were not always translating into sales and even less into higher prices. 'Most values are flat,' confirmed Richard Norris of Classic Alfa, though one exception was the iconic Giulia Sprint GTA, the best of which are now fetching £300k. Of the more affordable Alfas, the pretty '70s and '80s Alfetta GT and GTV are also on the rise, as prices for the earlier 105-series GTVs move out of reach for many enthusiasts.

Very much still within reach, their values having slipped in the last 12 months, are the handsome Alvises of the 1960s, the TD, TE and TF coupés. With hand-built bodies in aluminium, straight-six engines and leather-lined interiors, think of them as Aston DB4 alternatives at around a tenth of the price, says Ian Simpson of specialists Red Triangle.

Staying at the more affordable end, the original Fiat 500 continues to gain value, top examples now fetching £20,000. But be wary, says Tony Castle-Miller of Italian car specialists Middle Barton Garage, 'there are lots of bad ones around for £6000-£7000.' In a largely static market, one Fiat that has suddenly hits its stride is the late-60s, early-70s 124 Coupé and its Spider sibling. Sharp lines, lively twin-cam power and numbers decimated by corrosion mean surviving Coupés can now reach as high as £17,500, while the delectable little Spider can command as much as £25k.

Talking of trends, Matt Guilliard-Watts of Jensen specialists Cropredy Bridge reckons his market is in a transitional period. 'We're seeing a changing clientele,' he reports, 'with fewer speculators and investors and a return to enthusiasts. Interestingly, they tend to be quite a lot pickier about cars and specs than the former group!'

Lotus specialist Paul Matty reports that the 340R and the Exige S1 have both taken a bit of a hit in the last 12 months after the market got a little carried away with their investment potential. Lotuses generally are holding their values, though there has been an upsurge in interest – and values – for the V8-engined Esprits, while the previously rather underrated Elan M100 is gradually building a following.

'This year started with a lot more enthusiasm and positivity than last year ended,' reports Andy Heywood of McGrath Maserati, although increased interest has not meant that cars have been changing hands for more money. In fact McGrath report that most Maserati values are down by around 10%, in some cases more, and especially those for good and average cars.

In the Jaguar world, XKs and E-types seem to have peaked; the fastest climbers now are saloons, 'particularly the early XJ6 and XJ12s,' says Graham Searle of the Jaguar Enthusiasts' Club. 'XJ40s are also becoming sought-after, particularly very good 4.0-litres.

'My particular favourite, the Series 1 XJ6, could be one to watch as the appreciation of this mould-breaking car continues to grow. The following Series 2 and Series 3 models are picking up and it is getting harder to find a very good Series 3, the best of them being the later Jaguar V12/Daimler Double Six.'

JLR

In the Japanese classics market, Tristan Longden, director of Torque GT, reports an increased interest in lesser-known models as buyers search for the unique and unusual. Also in demand are the Mazda RX7 and Nissan Silvia S15 Spec R, though the latter is becoming scarce. 'Demand has remained pretty strong across the spectrum but we're probably seeing a slight drop off in the £100k+ cars,' says Longden. 'Limited production numbers, special editions or even a rare colour can be the difference.'

And finally, in times of crisis, a Land Rover can be an appealing proposition. The early series models (such as the S1 above) have long been seriously collectable, and now interest is moving to their successors, the '80s and '90s Defender models; still very affordable and just the thing for times of trouble!

Until next year...

# *Your guide to the Classic Car Price Guide*

## THE SPEC TABLES

**Performance:** We have tried to obtain independent road test data, but where this has not been possible, we have quoted manufacturer data
**Engine:** Plain English descriptions covering capacity, fuelling and cylinder count. Where there are several versions of the same model, we have identified which variation is described in the spec.
**Power and torque:** Quoted directly from the manufacturer in DIN standard. German (PS), American (SAE) and Japanese (JIS) figures have been converted to bhp where possible.
Torque is UK-standard lb ft.
**Drivetrain:** FWD: Front-wheel drive
RWD: Rear-wheel drive
AWD: All-wheel drive
**Transmission:** The standard gearbox package, detailing the number of forward speeds and whether it's manual or auto.
**Structure:** The car's construction type, be it monocoque, separate chassis, backbone, or race-style carbonfibre tub.
**Weight:** Manufacturer-quoted kerbweight in kg wherever possible, although throughout the years car makers have changed the way they report weight, and some quoted figures may include a full tank of fuel, or even the driver's weight. All figures, therefore, must be taken as a guide only.

## PRICE DEFINITIONS

**Launch price:** The UK launch price wherever it is possible to quote. For model ranges, we quote the price of the entry-level car unless indicated. For cars not officially imported into the UK, no price is applicable (N/A). In cases where cars were imported via a third-party concessionaire, theirs is the price we have quoted.
**Excellent:** The value of a car in excellent all-round condition, where there is unlikely to be any expenditure required. Original factory-fresh condition, or a high-standard restoration, but not necessarily concours. NOTE: concours cars, or those with specific historic significance, may be worth considerably more.
**Good:** Sound, useable and presentable cars that you would be happy to drive on a regular basis. Not perfect, and may need some cosmetic or minor mechanical work, but a representative example of the breed, and one you would be happy to display at an owners' club meeting.
**Average:** Running cars, but ones with plenty of issues that need sorting. Most will have MOTs but might need work to get through the next one. For anything built before around 1980, chances are they will need welding or other refurbishment.
**Project:** Often cars that have been unused for a long period of time, generally those needing substantial work to get back on the road or through the next MOT.

COURTESY OF RM SOTHEBY'S

# AUCTION WATCH

**The world is changing, and so is the way we buy cars, including at auction. Here's what the market has been doing over the last 12 months**

IT'S FAIR TO SAY the face of the classic car market has changed hugely over the past two years, and during 2019 in particular we saw a continued shift in the expectations of both buyers and sellers. While we should never rely on the auctions alone to get a full picture of what's going on, it can give us a good steer on the general mood of the market, not to mention recent trends.

There's no way to sugarcoat the fact that, for many in the trade, 2019 was a bit of a lacklustre year. The challenging market conditions of 2018 continued to disappoint in many areas, while growth – where it can be found – has been small. General values of some market leaders have continued to slip back, and while the very top of the market is still very much its own entity, 2019 certainly saw fewer blockbusters at the top international auctions. That meant the number of top-end Ferraris, Astons and Mercedes-Benz cars actually selling at auction remained lower, resulting in the continued shift towards lower sale totals and fewer record prices throughout 2019.

As 2019 progressed, though, the market adapted to this new state of affaird. We started to see slightly lower estimates, more sensible reserves and as a consequence far fewer 'no sale' results. The market has started to find its level again.

This means that cars are selling at their correct values and helping to give a clearer picture of where the market really is. As it turns out, most cars are very much still in demand – but it's definitely a buyers' market. People are no longer willing to pay top prices for anything but the very best.

Driven by fresh blood in the scene, enthusiasm for younger classics is at an all-time high, too. The most valuable auction car of 2019 was the 'LM Specification' 1994 McLaren F1 (left), which sold for $19,805,000 at RM Sotheby's Monterey sale. The F1 might be a law unto itself, but it's difficult to imagine anything that isn't Italian and from the 1960s occupying this spot four or five years ago. RM sold a total of 69 cars above the $1m threshold in 2019, contributing five of the most valuable top ten cars sold at auction. This put its global sales total 'over $400m' against a high of $526m in 2017.

Gooding & Company ended the year with sales totalling $147 million and 32 million-dollar-plus cars, although it managed this with just three US auctions. Its top seller was also at Monterey, the $9,905,000 1958 Ferrari 250 GT LWB California Spyder.

That's the top end. There's a slightly different picture emerging elsewhere, especially in the UK. As the market for more usable modern classics continues to grow, auction houses catering to this end of the market have flourished amid difficult conditions. Classic Car Auctions is one good example of this, thriving throughout 2019 with bigger sales and as demand for affordable modern classics soars. It's an area of the market that Bonhams has also been keen to enter with its new Bicester Heritage-based offshoot, MPH. In an effort to further focus Bonhams towards the top end, MPH targets the more mainstream.

We've seen significantly more volume and interest in online auctions, too, a trend that we would expect to continue further into the next decade. While eBay remains a favourite at the lower end of the market, more traditional and specialist online-only auction houses have seen huge growth in the last year.

One well-established player is The Market, which reported its best year ever in 2019, with total sales of £3.6 million. Since it was founded in June 2019, the Collecting Cars online auction platform has racked up well over £3m in sales, focusing on modern classics.

With far lower overheads, thanks to lower transport costs and venue hire fees, these online platforms can offer better value for buyers and sellers, even if they come without the buzzing atmosphere of a live salesroom. Even some of the traditional auction houses have been successfully holding 'online only' auctions with increased frequency, including the offerings from H&H and RM Sotheby's. Expect this trend to continue, even post-Covid...

MONTEREY 2019 / DARIN SCHNABEL COURTESY OF RM SOTHEBY'S

# TEN HOT TIPS

**With the help of our network of specialists and marque gurus, we've selected ten cars that should prove a solid investment**

## TVR GRIFFITH 500

The '90s Griffith offers old-school driver appeal, timeless good looks and thunderous performance – commodities as prized today as ever. Best bet, according to Simon Bartlett of Fernhurst TVR, is the 1996-2000 Griffith 500. Values have taken a hit in the last 12 months, so you can pick up a very presentable example for £25k and a really first-class one for £35k.

## MGB GT V8

If you can't afford an Aston or an E-type but you want a quick, refined British classic, then the Rover V8-engined B GT is one of the most underrated cars out there, reckons MG specialist Malcolm Gammons. 'You can get a good car for £25k and a really excellent one for £35k but at that sort of money they're still undervalued and a solid investment,' he says.

## LOTUS ELISE SERIES 2

Trailing the S1 price-wise but in many ways a much better car – better built, more spacious and easier to live with. 'K-series cars are good, but the Toyota-engined cars from '04 onwards are totally reliable,' says Lotus guru Paul Matty. His pick of the range: the 134bhp 'S' with the five-speed gearbox.'Such a lovely little car and £20-22k gets a really nice one,' says Matty.

## BMW E12 M535i

Though it wasn't badged as an M5, this was really the car where the whole M thing was seeded. 'It's just so cool,' says Munich Legends' Dan Norris. 'Quad headlamps, Recaros, M1 steering wheel, dog-leg 'box, limited-slip diff, big brakes... It gives so much feedback. And it's rare, with probably only around 450 left.' £30k buys a tidy car, £45k a real cracker.

## ASTON MARTIN VANQUISH MK1

Values of the '90s supercharged Vantage have been flying for some time now. We expect the car that replaced it as the Aston flagship, the mk1 Vanquish, to join those ranks in due course. The last model to be hand-built at Newport Pagnell (before the recent 'Continuation' cars), it looks good value right now, particularly the early non-S version, at £70-£90k.

## ALFA ROMEO MONTREAL

A real slice of Italian exotica at a fraction of the price of most contemporary Ferraris. 'Values topped out in 2018 and, if anything, have dropped back 10% in 2019,' say specialists Classic Alfa. 'So a good time to buy one of these still-underrated Alfas, which with a few mods can be made into an entertaining, fast, touring GT.' £55k buys the best right now.

## PEUGEOT 504 COUPÉ AND CABRIOLET

Like owning an Italian classic, but without the price tag: in the context of other Pininfarina-built coupés and convertibles from the late '60s, this gorgeous Peugeot is still a bargain. Europe is usually the place to find a good 504. Budget £10k for a half-decent V6 Coupé, roughly double that for a Cabriolet. Even prettier four-cylinder cars are even cheaper.

## RENAULT SPORT CLIO 172 CUP

Ten years ago, your go-to cheap French hot hatch was the Peugeot 205 GTI. If you're in need of a cheap track toy now, it's hard to find anything better than one of these Clios. Numbers of tidy original cars are diminishing as a result, so finding a good example – especially the pre-facelift 172 – is getting harder by the day. Values only going one way.

## HONDA INTEGRA TYPE-R (DC2)

A genuine Japanese icon, the DC2 is one of the finest front-drive performance cars ever built: addictive 8500rpm red line, brilliant chassis and excellent manual 'box. Prices have passed £10k for the best, but you can still find very usable examples from the £6k mark. UK cars are desirable, but late-spec Japanese-market cars are also highly sought-after.

## FORD FOCUS RS MK1

The fast Ford market can be a tricky thing to predict, but it's hard to deny that the limited-run mk1 Focus RS is still a bit of a bargain. It remains a usable, fun and great looking cult classic, and while super-low-mileage cars can be expensive, if you're happy to buy a car with more than 80k on the clock, there's a shrinking pool of sensibly priced cars from about £12k.

# ABARTH

FOUNDED as a hillclimb and sports car racing team in 1950, Carlo Abarth's company expanded into producing tuning equipment and engines for various Fiats alongside its own racing models. Such was the cachet of the name that Fiat was glad to have its products branded with the Abarth badge. Its best-known and arguably most fun creations were the tiny and giant-killing Fiat 500- and 600-based models. After a flirtation with Simca, Abarth was taken over by Fiat in 1971 and continued to denote performance models, although it became little more than a trim level during the 1990s and 2000s. In more recent years it has been relaunched as a separate division by Fiat.

## ABARTH Fiat 750 Zagato

Carlo Abarth's 750 Zagato GT first appeared at the Geneva Motor Show in 1956 and immediately caused a storm. The pretty little coupé and roadster were based on the Fiat 500's running gear, but powered by a tuned version of the Abarth 747cc engine in high-compression form, delivering 44bhp. Later versions were available with a twin-cam head that made enough power to take the featherweight sports car to a top speed of 118mph and on to success in motor sport, including a class win on the Mille Miglia in 1957. Highly prized.

### SPECIFICATIONS

| | |
|---|---|
| **Years produced:** | 1957-1961 |
| **Performance:** | 0-60mph: 15.8sec<br>Top speed: 95mph |
| **Power & torque:** | 44bhp/44lb ft |
| **Engine:** | Normally aspirated 747cc four cylinder, petrol, carburettor, 8 valves |
| **Drivetrain:** | Rear-engine RWD |
| **Structure:** | Separate chassis |
| **Transmission:** | Four-speed manual |
| **Weight:** | 535kg |

### PRICE GUIDE

| | |
|---|---|
| **Launch price:** | £2248 |
| **Excellent:** | £125,000 |
| **Good:** | £100,000 |
| **Average:** | £80,000 |
| **Project:** | £50,000 |

## ABARTH Fiat 850/1000

The Abarth-converted Fiat 850 and 1000 were front-running European Group 2 Touring Cars, winning the championship on several occasions. Their combination of grip, performance and low price made them highly desirable club-level competition cars, with the fastest examples easily topping 115mph. They remain popular with historic racers – and, appropriately, they are far better suited to the track than they are the road. Expensive and desirable today, the 1000 Corsa is still the car to beat in the 1000cc category.

### SPECIFICATIONS

| | |
|---|---|
| **Years produced:** | 1960-1970 |
| **Performance:** | 0-60mph: 7.0sec (1000TC Corsa)<br>Top speed: 118mph |
| **Power & torque:** | 112bhp/65lb ft |
| **Engine:** | Normally aspirated 982cc four cylinder, petrol, carburettor, 8 valves |
| **Drivetrain:** | Rear-engine RWD |
| **Structure:** | Monocoque |
| **Transmission:** | Five-speed manual |
| **Weight:** | 583kg |

### PRICE GUIDE

| | |
|---|---|
| **Launch price:** | Not sold in UK |
| **Excellent:** | £95,000 |
| **Good:** | £70,000 |
| **Average:** | £50,000 |
| **Project:** | £30,000 |

## ABARTH Simca 1300/2000 GT

French company Simca had close ties with Fiat, so when it was looking for a sporty new model to improve its image it was only natural it should turn to Abarth. Starting with the Simca 1000 as a base, Abarth conceived the pretty and extremely potent 1300 GT, which used a bespoke 136bhp twin-cam engine mounted in the tail and highly aerodynamic bodywork. The 1300 GT and its 1600 and 2000 successors (the latter producing 200bhp and reckoned to be capable of 168mph) scored many wins on the track, and are much prized.

### SPECIFICATIONS

| | |
|---|---|
| **Years produced:** | 1962-1965 |
| **Performance:** | 0-60mph: 6.8sec (1300 GT)<br>Top speed: 142mph |
| **Power & torque:** | 136bhp/97lb ft |
| **Engine:** | Normally aspirated 1288cc four cylinder, petrol, carburettor, 8 valves |
| **Drivetrain:** | Rear-engine RWD |
| **Structure:** | Monocoque |
| **Transmission:** | Six-speed manual |
| **Weight:** | 635kg |

### PRICE GUIDE (2000 GT in brackets)

| | |
|---|---|
| **Launch price:** | Not sold in UK |
| **Excellent:** | £260,000 (£350,000) |
| **Good:** | £200,000 (£250,000) |
| **Average:** | £170,000 (£180,000) |
| **Project:** | £85,000 (£110,000) |

## ABARTH Fiat 595/595SS/695SS

Carlo Abarth cut his performance car teeth on the rear-engined Fiat 500, producing some of Italy's finest pocket rockets. Although based on one of the slowest cars you could buy, the Abarth was every inch a Mini Cooper rival during the 1960s, with the bored-out 695 version packing a 40bhp punch. Abarths feature extrovert styling and, on the right road, will give much more powerful cars a real run for their money. Very rare and relatively valuable in the UK, and well worth seeking out if you like your thrills served on the raw side.

### SPECIFICATIONS

| | |
|---|---|
| **Years produced:** | 1963-1971 |
| **Performance:** | 0-60mph: N/A<br>Top speed: N/A |
| **Power & torque:** | 30bhp/33lb ft |
| **Engine:** | Normally aspirated 593cc twin, petrol, carburettor, 4 valves |
| **Drivetrain:** | Rear-engine RWD |
| **Structure:** | Separate chassis |
| **Transmission:** | Four-speed manual |
| **Weight:** | 500kg |

### PRICE GUIDE

| | |
|---|---|
| **Launch price:** | N/A in UK |
| **Excellent:** | £50,000 (£60,000 for 695SS) |
| **Good:** | £37,500 (£45,000) |
| **Average:** | £27,500 (£35,000) |
| **Project:** | £17,500 (£22,500) |

## ABARTH
## Fiat 124 Rally Spider

Homologation special based on 1800-engined 124 Spider. There's extra power from twin Weber carbs and new exhaust manifold – the last ones even being offered with an optional 16-valve head – and the stiffened shell was fitted with lightweight glassfibre bonnet and boot and alloy door skins. All got a rollcage and permanent hardtop. Independent rear suspension improved handling and one won the 1972 European Rally Championship. Pure road-going cars almost impossible to find these days. Prices flying, say specialists Middle Barton Garage.

**SPECIFICATIONS**

| | |
|---|---|
| **Years produced:** | 1972-1975 (1013 in total) |
| **Performance:** | 0-60mph: 7.5sec<br>Top speed: 118mph |
| **Power & torque:** | 128bhp/117lb ft |
| **Engine:** | Normally aspirated 1756cc four cylinder, petrol, carburettor, 8 valves |
| **Drivetrain:** | Front-engine RWD |
| **Structure:** | Monocoque |
| **Transmission:** | Five-speed manual |
| **Weight:** | 939kg |

**PRICE GUIDE**

| | |
|---|---|
| **Launch price:** | N/A |
| **Excellent:** | £120,000 |
| **Good:** | £75,000 |
| **Average:** | £50,000 |
| **Project:** | £35,000 |

# AC

BRITAIN'S OLDEST independent car marque, AC – for Auto Carriers – built its first three-wheeled passenger vehicle in 1907. It gradually moved upmarket; four-wheeled vehicles appeared in 1913 and, after WW1, the company expanded into sports cars. It continued after the next war as a struggling specialist manufacturer, even going back to three-wheelers, until it hit paydirt with the Cobra in 1962, its Ace roadster fitted with Ford V8 engines by US racing god Carroll Shelby. The marque limped through the 1970s and '80s with models such as the ME3000 but still exists today - the current AC Cars, led by Alan Lubinsky, builds updated Cobras in South Africa with a 6.2-litre, GM-sourced V8.

## AC
## 2-litre

After WW2 ended, AC resumed the building of low-volume quality cars with this gently sporting 2.0-litre saloon. A four-door was added to the range for 1953, by which time the already ageing triple-carb AC engine's output had risen from 74bhp to 85bhp. Bodies are aluminium over a wood frame and steel chassis; suspension also harks back to days past with solid axles and transverse leaf springs at each end of the car. At least the dampers are hydraulic: an AC first. Cable rear brakes are fitted to early cars, with an all-hydraulic system from 1951.

**SPECIFICATIONS**

| | |
|---|---|
| **Years produced:** | 1947-1958 (1284 in total) |
| **Performance:** | 0-60mph: 19.9sec<br>Top speed: 80mph |
| **Power & torque:** | 74bhp/105lb ft |
| **Engine:** | Normally aspirated 1991cc straight six, petrol, carburettor, 12 valves |
| **Drivetrain:** | Front-engine RWD |
| **Structure:** | Separate chassis |
| **Transmission:** | Four-speed manual |
| **Weight:** | 1222kg |

**PRICE GUIDE**

| | |
|---|---|
| **Launch price:** | £1277 |
| **Excellent:** | £15,000 |
| **Good:** | £10,000 |
| **Average:** | £4500 |
| **Project:** | £2000 |

## AC
## 2-Litre DHC/Buckland

Straightforward drophead version of the saloon was only in production a year, so few were built and all went for export – though most were still right-hand drive. You are more likely to come across one of the Buckland tourers, whose bodies were built by a coachbuilder of that name. These were a lot prettier, with more rounded lines and a fold-flat windscreen. Later examples also got cutaway doors for an even more sporting look, though mechanically they were identical to the saloons. Quite hard to find, and gently rising values reflect that.

**SPECIFICATIONS**

| | |
|---|---|
| **Years produced:** | 1949-1956 |
| **Performance:** | 0-60mph: 19.9sec<br>Top speed: 80mph |
| **Power & torque:** | 74bhp/100lb ft |
| **Engine:** | Normally aspirated 1991cc straight six, petrol, carburettor, 12 valves |
| **Drivetrain:** | Front-engine RWD |
| **Structure:** | Separate chassis |
| **Transmission:** | Four-speed manual |
| **Weight:** | 1320kg |

**PRICE GUIDE**

| | |
|---|---|
| **Launch price:** | Not known |
| **Excellent:** | £32,500 |
| **Good:** | £19,000 |
| **Average:** | £12,000 |
| **Project:** | £6000 |

## AC
## Ace (AC engine)

Designed to raise AC's post-war profile, and to tap into America's new-found enthusiasm for Brit sports cars. The simple but pretty aluminium body clothed a tube-frame chassis with all-independent suspension that gave excellent handling and stole a march over rivals like Jaguar – even if it was by transverse leaf springs. Finned aluminium drum brakes gradually gave way to discs around 1958. Only the engine disappointed. It was AC's own, but had been in production since the 1920s; output grew from 85bhp to 105bhp, but the car needed more.

**SPECIFICATIONS**

| | |
|---|---|
| **Years produced:** | 1951-1962 (223 in total) |
| **Performance:** | 0-60mph: 9.5sec<br>Top speed: 112mph |
| **Power & torque:** | 85bhp/110lb ft |
| **Engine:** | Normally aspirated 1991cc straight six, petrol, carburettor, 12 valves |
| **Drivetrain:** | Front-engine RWD |
| **Structure:** | Separate chassis |
| **Transmission:** | Four-speed manual |
| **Weight:** | 762kg |

**PRICE GUIDE**

| | |
|---|---|
| **Launch price:** | £1439 |
| **Excellent:** | £220,000 |
| **Good:** | £165,000 |
| **Average:** | £120,000 |
| **Project:** | £70,000 |

## AC
## Aceca-AC

Introduced for 1955, the Aceca was a grand touring coupé version of the Ace, offering more luxury than the roadster that fully justified its extra cost. The basic chassis followed the lines of the Ace, but with heavier-duty main rails, an extra crossmember and rubber mountings for the differential to reduce the amount of road noise transmitted to the cabin. For similar reasons, glassfibre front and rear bulkheads were used. Rather than the tubes of the Ace, doors and tailgate were wood-framed in the traditional manner. Rarity helps keep values strong.

**SPECIFICATIONS**

| | |
|---|---|
| **Years produced:** | 1954-1963 (151 in total) |
| **Performance:** | 0-60mph: 13.4sec<br>Top speed: 102mph |
| **Power & torque:** | 85bhp/110lb ft |
| **Engine:** | Normally aspirated 1991cc straight six, petrol, carburettor, 12 valves |
| **Drivetrain:** | Front-engine RWD |
| **Structure:** | Separate chassis |
| **Transmission:** | Four-speed manual |
| **Weight:** | 890kg |

**PRICE GUIDE**

| | |
|---|---|
| **Launch price:** | £1439 |
| **Excellent:** | £120,000 |
| **Good:** | £90,000 |
| **Average:** | £60,000 |
| **Project:** | £40,000 |

## AC
## Ace-Bristol

From 1956, those who had criticised the Ace for its lack of power got an answer (though it was to be the first of many): Bristol's 'six' of similar capacity was bought in. Of slightly newer and more sophisticated design, most were supplied in 128bhp spec, though a few were delivered with 125 or even 105bhp. The better Bristol gearbox was also used, with overdrive a popular option. They were sold at a price premium alongside other Aces and one was driven to the 1959 Le Mans 24 Hours, winning the 2.0-litre class and finishing seventh overall. Highly prized today.

**SPECIFICATIONS**

| | |
|---|---|
| **Years produced:** | 1956-1962 (463 in total) |
| **Performance:** | 0-60mph: 9.1sec<br>Top speed: 118mph |
| **Power & torque:** | 125bhp/123lb ft |
| **Engine:** | Normally aspirated 1971cc straight six, petrol, carburettor, 12 valves |
| **Drivetrain:** | Front-engine RWD |
| **Structure:** | Separate chassis |
| **Transmission:** | Four-speed manual |
| **Weight:** | 894kg |

**PRICE GUIDE**

| | |
|---|---|
| **Launch price:** | £2011 |
| **Excellent:** | £280,000 |
| **Good:** | £220,000 |
| **Average:** | £170,000 |
| **Project:** | £100,000 |

## AC
## Aceca-Bristol

In line with the Ace, a Bristol-engined version of the Aceca was added from 1956. Though markedly more expensive than the AC-engined car, it was a much better performer and outsold the lesser car, with 169 leaving the factory. As with all Acecas, you get details such as two rows of four louvres in the bonnet, burr walnut instrument surrounds and glovebox lid, and hinged rear side windows to aid ventilation. Though the car was directly related to the Ace, and had a similar nose and grille, no body panels are the same on both cars. Values holding.

**SPECIFICATIONS**

| | |
|---|---|
| **Years produced:** | 1956-1963 (169 in total) |
| **Performance:** | 0-60mph: 10.3sec<br>Top speed: 115mph |
| **Power & torque:** | 105bhp/123lb ft |
| **Engine:** | Normally aspirated 1971cc straight six, petrol, carburettor, 12 valves |
| **Drivetrain:** | Front-engine RWD |
| **Structure:** | Separate chassis |
| **Transmission:** | Four-speed manual |
| **Weight:** | 895kg |

**PRICE GUIDE**

| | |
|---|---|
| **Launch price:** | £1722 |
| **Excellent:** | £150,000 |
| **Good:** | £120,000 |
| **Average:** | £80,000 |
| **Project:** | £40,000 |

## AC
## Greyhound

Stylish and dignified four-seat big brother to the Aceca, also panelled in aluminium and fitted with all the same engine choices, though in reality most ordered used the Bristol straight-six, either in 2.0- or 2.2-litre form. No more than three are thought to have received the Zephyr 2.6. Despite a change to coil springs for independent suspension, handling isn't a match for the Aceca and, although only a quarter as many were built as the smaller car, they have never set the market alight in the same way and can be bought for about half as much.

**SPECIFICATIONS**

| | |
|---|---|
| **Years produced:** | 1959-1963 (83 in total) |
| **Performance:** | 0-60mph: 12.7sec<br>Top speed: 104mph |
| **Power & torque:** | 125bhp/132lb ft |
| **Engine:** | Normally aspirated 1971cc straight six, petrol, carburettor, 12 valves |
| **Drivetrain:** | Front-engine RWD |
| **Structure:** | Separate chassis |
| **Transmission:** | Four-speed manual |
| **Weight:** | 991kg |

**PRICE GUIDE**

| | |
|---|---|
| **Launch price:** | £2891 |
| **Excellent:** | £60,000 |
| **Good:** | £48,000 |
| **Average:** | £35,000 |
| **Project:** | £16,000 |

## AC
## Ace RS 2.6

Introduced in 1961 and originally a Ruddspeed conversion – hence the 'RS' – this used the cheap and cheerful 2.6-litre six-cylinder engine from a MkII Ford Zephyr. Depending on which state of tune the customer ordered, output could be up to 170bhp (Stage 3, with aluminium head and triple Webers). Even in that most potent form it was still cheaper then the Bristol-engined Ace. Now up to Ace-Bristol prices, only 37 were built and they're recognised by a new nose and grille that would soon adorn Cobras – along with a further eight Aceca coupés.

**SPECIFICATIONS**

| | |
|---|---|
| **Years produced:** | 1961-1963 (37 in total) |
| **Performance:** | 0-60mph: N/A<br>Top speed: 120mph |
| **Power & torque:** | 100bhp/133lb ft |
| **Engine:** | Normally aspirated 2553cc straight six, petrol, carburettor, 12 valves |
| **Drivetrain:** | Front-engine RWD |
| **Structure:** | Separate chassis |
| **Transmission:** | Four-speed manual |
| **Weight:** | 813kg |

**PRICE GUIDE**

| | |
|---|---|
| **Launch price:** | Not known |
| **Excellent:** | £250,000 |
| **Good:** | £200,000 |
| **Average:** | £150,000 |
| **Project:** | £85,000 |

## AC
# Cobra 260/289

Carroll Shelby's big idea outsold the Ace it was based on, with most sold in the US and none in the UK until 1964. The first 75 used 4.2-litre Ford V8s; those and the next 51 4.7 versions had cam-and-peg steering; after that it was much improved rack-and-pinion. Standard smallblock Cobras have flat faces to their flared arches, though there were 27 AC 289s (no Cobra in name) built from mid-1966 with the big-arched Cobra 427 bodyshell and coil-sprung chassis. Note: the mk2 289 can now fetch as much as a 427, as it is eligible for all historic events.

**SPECIFICATIONS**

| | |
|---|---|
| **Years produced:** | 1961-1965 (673 in total) |
| **Performance:** | 0-60mph: 5.5sec<br>Top speed: 138mph |
| **Power & torque:** | 271bhp/269lb ft |
| **Engine:** | Normally aspirated 4727cc V8, petrol, carburettor, 16 valves |
| **Drivetrain:** | Front-engine RWD |
| **Structure:** | Separate chassis |
| **Transmission:** | Four-speed manual |
| **Weight:** | 952kg |

**PRICE GUIDE**

| | |
|---|---|
| **Launch price:** | £2454 |
| **Excellent:** | £600,000 (add 40% for 289 mk2) |
| **Good:** | £420,000 |
| **Average:** | £280,000 |
| **Project:** | £170,000 |

## AC
# Cobra 427

A complete reworking of the Cobra's chassis was required for the installation of Ford's 'big block' 7.0-litre V8s, most of which were the 427ci in various states of tune, though some were sold with smaller-bore/longer-stroke 428ci engines. Chassis tubes were larger, with more crossmembers, and suspension was unequal-length wishbones with coil springs. The body changed, with bulging wings to cover much larger tyres. The ultimate Cobra, and the 31 427 S/C (Semi Competition) models are particularly sought-after and valuable.

**SPECIFICATIONS**

| | |
|---|---|
| **Years produced:** | 1965-1967 (413 in total) |
| **Performance:** | 0-60mph: 4.2sec<br>Top speed: 165mph |
| **Power & torque:** | 410bhp/480lb ft |
| **Engine:** | Normally aspirated 6997cc V8, petrol, carburettor, 16 valves |
| **Drivetrain:** | Front-engine RWD |
| **Structure:** | Separate chassis |
| **Transmission:** | Four-speed manual |
| **Weight:** | 1147kg |

**PRICE GUIDE**

| | |
|---|---|
| **Launch price:** | Not known |
| **Excellent:** | £900,000 |
| **Good:** | £650,000 |
| **Average:** | £450,000 |
| **Project:** | N/A |

## AC
# 428/428 Convertible

Heavy-hitter from Thames Ditton uses a six-inch-extended Cobra chassis clothed in bodywork – steel this time – by Frua from Turin. Passing resemblance to Frua's Maserati Mistral, but only handles and door-glass frames are shared. Engine is the 7.0-litre Ford Galaxie V8 used in some Cobras, but the 428. The cost of the bodies and shipping chassis to and from Italy meant prices were 20% higher than for Astons and Jensens. The AC wasn't special enough to justify that and only 51 coupés and 29 Convertibles were sold in six years.

**SPECIFICATIONS**

| | |
|---|---|
| **Years produced:** | 1967-1973 (80 in total) |
| **Performance:** | 0-60mph: 5.4sec<br>Top speed: 145mph |
| **Power & torque:** | 345bhp/462lb ft |
| **Engine:** | Normally aspirated 7010cc V8, petrol, carburettor, 16 valves |
| **Drivetrain:** | Front-engine RWD |
| **Structure:** | Separate chassis |
| **Transmission:** | Three-speed automatic |
| **Weight:** | 1483kg |

**PRICE GUIDE**

| | |
|---|---|
| **Launch price:** | £4250 |
| **Excellent:** | £120,000 (add 50% for Convertible) |
| **Good:** | £75,000 |
| **Average:** | £47,500 |
| **Project:** | £35,000 |

## AC
# 3000ME

An attempt to lift sales by building something more affordable saw AC mid-mounting a Ford V6 transversely over a custom-made transmission. That was one problem: the engine's heavy weight and less-than-sporting output meant only 120mph. Delays in reaching production meant the 3000ME was pitched against the similarly-priced Lotus Esprit. Those volume sales never materialised, with only around 100 built, including a short-lived revival in 1984-85 when licensed to a Scottish factory. Good survival rate and a keen following.

**SPECIFICATIONS**

| | |
|---|---|
| **Years produced:** | 1979-1985 (100 approx in total) |
| **Performance:** | 0-60mph: 8.5sec<br>Top speed: 120mph |
| **Power & torque:** | 138bhp/192lb ft |
| **Engine:** | Normally aspirated 2994cc V6, petrol, carburettor, 12 valves |
| **Drivetrain:** | Mid-engine RWD |
| **Structure:** | Glassfibre body/backbone chassis |
| **Transmission:** | Five-speed manual |
| **Weight:** | 1128kg |

**PRICE GUIDE**

| | |
|---|---|
| **Launch price:** | £12,432 |
| **Excellent:** | £15,000 |
| **Good:** | £12,000 |
| **Average:** | £8000 |
| **Project:** | £4250 |

## AC
# Cobra MkIV

The arrival of the Cobra MkIV heralded a new era for AC. The Hurlock family passed on the rights of the marque to Brian Angliss, who had been building Autokraft Cobra replicas for years, using much of the original '60s tooling. When they became ACs, these cars were lauded for their high levels of build quality and retention of the original's spirit. Most cars have subsequently had their '80s-era dashboards replaced by '60s replicas, and are good value considering the spiralling values of '60s examples. Add 50% for rare 'Lightweight' version.

**SPECIFICATIONS**

| | |
|---|---|
| **Years produced:** | 1983-1989 (450 approx in total) |
| **Performance:** | 0-60mph: 5.3sec<br>Top speed: 134mph |
| **Power & torque:** | 320bhp/385lb ft |
| **Engine:** | 4942cc V8, petrol, electronic fuel injection, 16 valves |
| **Drivetrain:** | Front-engine RWD |
| **Structure:** | Separate chassis |
| **Transmission:** | Five-speed manual |
| **Weight:** | N/A |

**PRICE GUIDE**

| | |
|---|---|
| **Launch price:** | £25,000 |
| **Excellent:** | £100,000 |
| **Good:** | £72,500 |
| **Average:** | £57,500 |
| **Project:** | £40,000 |

# ALFA ROMEO

WHAT STARTED life as Anonima Lombardo Fabbrica Automobili (ALFA) in 1910 in a factory bought from Darracq was taken over by Nicolo Romeo in 1915. Thus began one of the great marques in motoring history. Its original glory days were the 1930s, when Alfa Romeos were among the best cars money could buy. Post-war survival drove them downmarket, but the spirit remained with fine ranges of coupés and spiders to complement the saloons. Sadly that wasn't enough and when financial losses piled too high in the '80s, Fiat headed off a bid from Ford to take control in 1987. In recent times the marque has seen a resurgence with cars like the 8C supercar and the rapid Giulia sports saloon.

## ALFA ROMEO Giulietta Sprint

Unusually it was the coupé version of the Giulietta line that appeared first. The floorpan would prove adaptable, as the sheer number of variations that subsequently appeared bears testimony to, but for many this remains the most desirable of the mainstream factory cars. The Bertone-styled coupé was treated to a range of exciting twin-cams; even the original 1290cc version packed a respectable 65bhp. Later Veloce and SS models boasted outputs up to 100bhp. Expect to pay a large premium for Veloce models, especially on a 750-series car.

**SPECIFICATIONS**

**Years produced:** 1954-1962 (27,142 in total)
**Performance:** 0-60mph: 13.0sec
Top speed: 101mph
**Power & torque:** 80bhp/72lb ft
**Engine:** Normally aspirated 1290cc four cylinder, petrol, carburettor, 8 valves
**Drivetrain:** Front-engine RWD
**Structure:** Monocoque
**Transmission:** Four-speed manual
**Weight:** 860kg

**PRICE GUIDE**

**Launch price:** £2261
**Excellent:** £50,000
**Good:** £35,000
**Average:** £25,000
**Project:** £10,000

## ALFA ROMEO Giulietta Spider

The Spider was designed by Pininfarina and was an object lesson in Italian style and understatement. It's still great to drive in all forms, and remains in demand today. As with the rest of the family, rust was (and is) a serious factor in its survival rate, and the condition of the bodywork and chassis are of paramount importance. They have few mechanical issues, and just about all the mechanical parts are readily available off-the-shelf, so they're not difficult to run. Again, you pay a premium for Veloce models, say specialists Classic Alfa.

**SPECIFICATIONS**

**Years produced:** 1955-1962 (17,096 in total)
**Performance:** 0-60mph: 11.8sec
Top speed: 113mph
**Power & torque:** 80bhp/72lb ft
**Engine:** Normally aspirated 1290cc four cylinder, petrol, carburettor, 8 valves
**Drivetrain:** Front-engine RWD
**Structure:** Monocoque
**Transmission** Four-speed manual
**Weight:** 860kg

**PRICE GUIDE**

**Launch price:** £2116
**Excellent:** £55,000
**Good:** £40,000
**Average:** £25,000
**Project:** £12,000

## ALFA ROMEO Giulietta Berlina

These saloons might have hit the market during the mid-1950s, but they enjoyed an advanced specification and were built with the sporting driver in mind. In typical Alfa style, the Berlina started out powered by a modest engine, but with each new season, or so it seemed, a more powerful variation was shoehorned in. The pick of the crop ended up being the 75bhp Ti version, which ticked all of the important sporting saloon boxes. Sadly, the survival rate is very low, with the main culprits being damp climates and rabid rust.

**SPECIFICATIONS**

**Years produced:** 1955-1963 (39,057 in total)
**Performance:** 0-60mph: 17.7sec
Top speed: 98mph
**Power & torque:** 63bhp/69lb ft
**Engine:** Normally aspirated 1290cc four cylinder, petrol, carburettor, 8 valves
**Drivetrain:** Front-engine RWD
**Structure:** Monocoque
**Transmission:** Four-speed manual
**Weight:** 870kg

**PRICE GUIDE**

**Launch price:** £1726
**Excellent:** £15,000
**Good:** £10,000
**Average:** £4000
**Project:** £2000

## ALFA ROMEO Giulietta/Giulia Sprint Speciale

The Series 101 Giulietta was the first Alfa to be made available in Sprint Speciale form but, when the 105-Series Giulia followed on in 1962, these SS series Alfas really came into their own. With power from a 1570cc twin-cam, performance from these coupés was something rather special. The chances of finding an unrestored car these days are quite slim, but when they do turn up, they still command strong values. Today, these are the Giulias with the good looks that everyone wants, a fact reflected in their very strong values.

**SPECIFICATIONS**

**Years produced:** 1957-1962 (1366/1400 in total)
**Performance:** 0-60mph: 11.2sec
Top speed: 122mph
**Power & torque:** 106bhp/83lb ft
**Engine:** Normally aspirated 1290cc four cylinder, petrol, carburettor, 8 valves
**Drivetrain:** Front-engine RWD
**Structure:** Monocoque
**Transmission:** Five-speed manual
**Weight:** 785kg

**PRICE GUIDE**

**Launch price:** £2721
**Excellent:** £95,000
**Good:** £60,000
**Average:** £40,000
**Project:** £20,000

## ALFA ROMEO 2000/2600 Spider

Although there's a strong family resemblance to the Giulietta, the six-cylinder 2000/2600 harks back to the previous-generation Alfa Romeo 1900. The elegant styling was by Touring and its high price was justified by its 2+2 seating layout, detachable hardtop and five-speed gearbox. Performance was seriously improved with the arrival of the 2.6-litre version in 1962. 'Not the greatest of Alfas to drive,' say Classic Alfa, 'but continuing to climb in value as people recognise the fine styling and the value of the Touring Superleggera association.'

### SPECIFICATIONS

| | |
|---|---|
| **Years produced:** | 1958-1965 (2255 in total) |
| **Performance:** | 0-60mph: 10.9sec<br>Top speed: 124mph |
| **Power & torque:** | 145bhp/156lb ft |
| **Engine:** | Normally aspirated 2584cc straight six, petrol, carburettor, 12 valves |
| **Drivetrain:** | Front-engine RWD |
| **Structure:** | Monocoque |
| **Transmission:** | Five-speed manual |
| **Weight:** | 1257kg |

### PRICE GUIDE

| | |
|---|---|
| **Launch price:** | £2979 |
| **Excellent:** | £90,000 |
| **Good:** | £60,000 |
| **Average:** | £35,000 |
| **Project:** | £20,000 |

## ALFA ROMEO Giulia Spider

Exquisite looks by Pininfarina but now using the 1600 Giulia engine. Amongst the production of predominantly LHD about 400 factory RHD cars were finally made using the pretty Giulietta Spider shape. Rust is a serious issue, especially with the RHD cars due to the UK climate, and they suffer from it even more readily than the coupes and saloons. But engine and gearbox are strong with good support from a network of specialists. The last hurrah of the 101-series, but none the worse for that, and all versions are good to drive.

### SPECIFICATIONS

| | |
|---|---|
| **Years produced:** | 1962-1965 (10,341 in total) |
| **Performance:** | 0-60mph: 11.8sec<br>Top speed: 106mph |
| **Power & torque:** | 91bhp/80lb ft |
| **Engine:** | Normally aspirated 1570cc four cylinder, petrol, carburettor, 8 valves |
| **Drivetrain:** | Front-engine RWD |
| **Structure:** | Monocoque |
| **Transmission:** | Five-speed manual |
| **Weight:** | 960kg |

### PRICE GUIDE

| | |
|---|---|
| **Launch price:** | £1729 |
| **Excellent:** | £50,000 |
| **Good:** | £40,000 |
| **Average:** | £25,000 |
| **Project:** | £10,000 |

## ALFA ROMEO 2000/2600 Sprint

The 2600 Sprint was the ultimate incarnation of the twin-cam straight-six. Very much a grand tourer, the coupé lacked the agility of its smaller cousins, despite its sports car looks, but the torquey engine made this a car for covering continents, with prodigious straight-line pace. It wa also significant as one of Giorgetto Giugiaro's first designs, laying the foundations for a significant career ahead. Unlike more mainstream Alfas, parts for the 2600 Sprint are not so readily available. After rising steadily for years, values have levelled off.

### SPECIFICATIONS

| | |
|---|---|
| **Years produced:** | 1962-1966 (700/6999 in total) |
| **Performance:** | 11.7sec<br>Top speed: 117mph |
| **Power & torque:** | 145bhp/156lb ft |
| **Engine:** | Normally aspirated 2584cc straight six, petrol, carburettor, 12 valves |
| **Drivetrain:** | Front-engine RWD |
| **Structure:** | Monocoque |
| **Transmission:** | Five-speed manual |
| **Weight:** | 1361kg |

### PRICE GUIDE

| | |
|---|---|
| **Launch price:** | £2806 |
| **Excellent:** | £25,000 |
| **Good:** | £15,000 |
| **Average:** | £10,000 |
| **Project:** | £5000 |

## ALFA ROMEO Giulia Sprint GT/Veloce

A car with a strong following, the 'step front' Giulia coupé is always in demand because of its good looks, driving experience and ease of tuning. Values have increased significantly in recent years, bolstered by the desirability of the GTA. When launched, the twin-cam 1600 versions were quick from the box, but subsequent versions (1750 and 2000) added even more excitement to the mix. The advice is to go for the example with the best body you can find and worry about the mechanicals after that, as parts availability is excellent.

### SPECIFICATIONS

| | |
|---|---|
| **Years produced:** | 1964-1967 (21,850 in total) |
| **Performance:** | 0-60mph: 11.2sec<br>Top speed: 107mph |
| **Power & torque:** | 92bhp/87lb ft |
| **Engine:** | Normally aspirated 1570cc four cylinder, petrol, carburettor, 8 valves |
| **Drivetrain:** | Front-engine RWD |
| **Structure:** | Monocoque |
| **Trans:** | Five-speed manual |
| **Weight:** | 905kg |

### PRICE GUIDE

| | |
|---|---|
| **Launch price:** | £1650 |
| **Excellent:** | £45,000 |
| **Good:** | £28,000 |
| **Average:** | £15,000 |
| **Project:** | £6000 |

## ALFA ROMEO Giulia 1300/1600 Ti/Super

The boxy 105-Series Giulia might not look like the most exciting saloon on the planet, but underneath that plain-Jane exterior beats the heart of a truly sporting saloon. Given the lusty twin-cam engines, five-speed gearbox and well set-up chassis, it's easy to see why Alfa was so annoyed by the way its cars were depicted being outrun by the Mini-Coopers in *The Italian Job*. 'The hipster's choice!' say Classic Alfa. 'Values strong due to both the high prices being asked for the coupés and also due to a new wave of interest in their boxy but cool '60s styling.'

### SPECIFICATIONS

| | |
|---|---|
| **Years produced:** | 1962-1971 (836,323 in total) |
| **Performance:** | 0-60mph: 11.8sec<br>Top speed: 117mph |
| **Power & torque:** | 92bhp/108lb ft |
| **Engine:** | Normally aspirated 1570cc four cylinder, petrol, carburettor, 8 valves |
| **Drivetrain:** | Front-engine RWD |
| **Structure:** | Monocoque |
| **Transmission:** | Five-speed manual |
| **Weight:** | 1016kg |

### PRICE GUIDE

| | |
|---|---|
| **Launch price:** | £1659 |
| **Excellent:** | £20,000 |
| **Good:** | £15,000 |
| **Average:** | £8000 |
| **Project:** | £4000 |

## ALFA ROMEO
### Giulia TZ/TZ-2

Created as a replacement for the gorgeous Giulietta SZ, the Zagato-styled TZ and TZ-2 continued that car's glorious looks and race-bred handling. The TZ nomenclature stands for '*Tubolare Zagato*', denoting the car's tubular chassis. It was powered by Alfa's twin-cam with up to 170bhp, and its suspension was a sophisticated all-independent set-up – in other words, here was a true thoroughbred. The TZ-2 (pictured left) was the first Alfa with a glassfibre body (ten were built that way) and had even more dramatic styling. Incredibly desirable now.

**SPECIFICATIONS**

| | |
|---|---|
| **Years produced:** | 1963-64/1965-66 (120/50 in total) |
| **Performance:** | 0-60mph: 6.8sec<br>Top speed: 152mph |
| **Power & torque:** | 170bhp/122lb ft |
| **Engine:** | Normally aspirated 1570cc four cylinder, petrol, carburettor, 8 valves |
| **Drivetrain:** | Front-engine RWD |
| **Structure:** | Spaceframe |
| **Transmission:** | Five-speed manual |
| **Weight:** | 630kg |

**PRICE GUIDE (TZ-2 in brackets)**

| | |
|---|---|
| **Launch price:** | N/A in UK |
| **Excellent:** | £1,250,000 (£2,500,000+) |
| **Good:** | £750,000 (£2,000,000) |
| **Average:** | N/A |
| **Project:** | N/A |

## ALFA ROMEO
### Giulia Sprint GTA

The GTA might look like your standard Sprint GT, but it makes extensive use of aluminium body panels. The reason for this was simple – the GTA was built for racing and, wherever possible, weight-saving was applied. The A in its name means *Alleggerita*, Italian for 'lightened', and even the sump, cam cover, timing cover and clutch housing were replaced by featherweight magnesium alloy items. Values still climbing, say specialists Classic Alfa, and you will pay even more for a car with period Autodelta history. Deduct 20% for a 1300 GTA Junior.

**SPECIFICATIONS**

| | |
|---|---|
| **Years produced:** | 1965-1969 |
| **Performance:** | 0-60mph: N/A<br>Top speed: 115mph |
| **Power & torque:** | 115bhp/105lb ft |
| **Engine:** | Normally aspirated 1570cc four cylinder, petrol, carburettor, 8 valves |
| **Drivetrain:** | Front-engine RWD |
| **Structure:** | Monocoque |
| **Transmission:** | Five-speed manual |
| **Weight:** | 820kg |

**PRICE GUIDE**

| | |
|---|---|
| **Launch price:** | £2128 |
| **Excellent:** | £300,000 |
| **Good:** | £225,000 |
| **Average:** | £175,000 |
| **Project:** | £120,000 |

## ALFA ROMEO
### 1600 Duetto/1750 Spider

Forever associated with Dustin Hoffman in *The Graduate*. The pretty little Pininfarina-styled roadster appeared in 1966 as the final genuinely new variant on the 105-Series platform and was marked out by its enclosed headlamps and boat-tail rear end. Powered by the 1570cc twin-cam, it was a gem to drive with great handling, sharp steering and excellent all-round disc braking. It wasn't around for long though: after only 18 months, the 1600 was succeeded by the more potent 1750. Values have started to climb again, say Classic Alfa.

**SPECIFICATIONS**

| | |
|---|---|
| **Years produced:** | 1966-1971 (15,026 in total) |
| **Performance:** | 0-60mph: 13.2sec (1600)<br>Top speed: 102mph |
| **Power & torque:** | 110bhp/101lb ft |
| **Engine:** | Normally aspirated 1570cc four cylinder, petrol, carburettor, 8 valves |
| **Drivetrain:** | Front-engine RWD |
| **Structure:** | Monocoque |
| **Transmission:** | Five-speed manual |
| **Weight:** | 990kg |

**PRICE GUIDE**

| | |
|---|---|
| **Launch price:** | £1749 (1600) |
| **Excellent:** | £50,000 |
| **Good:** | £35,000 |
| **Average:** | £20,000 |
| **Project:** | £8000 |

## ALFA ROMEO
### Giulia GT Junior

Due to the complexity of the 105-Series Giulia range the easiest way of relating to the GT Junior is to think of it as the entry-level model. That means it initially came with a 1300cc engine and simplified interior, and gave sporting Italians the chance to own a Giulia Sprint GT lookalike without the fiscal implications. Over time it was developed in parallel with the larger-engined cars and, in 1970, it lost its characteristic step-front. In 1972 a 1600cc Junior was introduced to close the gap in the range to the 2000cc GTV. Values holding firm at present.

**SPECIFICATIONS**

| | |
|---|---|
| **Years produced:** | 1966-1977 (92,053 in total) |
| **Performance:** | 0-60mph: 11.1sec<br>Top speed: 109mph |
| **Power & torque:** | 103bhp/104lb ft |
| **Engine:** | Normally aspirated 1290cc four cylinder, petrol, carburettor, 8 valves |
| **Drivetrain:** | Front-engine RWD |
| **Structure:** | Monocoque |
| **Transmission:** | Five-speed manual |
| **Weight:** | 990kg |

**PRICE GUIDE**

| | |
|---|---|
| **Launch price:** | £1749 |
| **Excellent:** | £25,000 |
| **Good:** | £15,000 |
| **Average:** | £10,000 |
| **Project:** | £3000 |

## ALFA ROMEO
### Tipo 33 Stradale

As 1960s supercars go, the 33 Stradale is possibly the most special of all. Although its V8 displaced a 'mere' 2-litres, the lightly detuned racing engined pushed out an impressive 227bhp, giving the 700kg car an exceptionally healthy power-to-weight ratio. But the 33 Stradale is a racing car for the road. Its body was built by Franco Scaglione, the final assembly was by Autodelta and, with only 18 made, these cars take rare-and-exclusive to another level. Tipo 33s almost never come up for sale, so coming up with a definitive value is almost impossible.

**SPECIFICATIONS**

| | |
|---|---|
| **Years produced:** | 1967-1969 (18 in total) |
| **Performance:** | 0-60mph: 6.5sec<br>Top speed: 162mph |
| **Power & torque:** | 227bhp/152lb ft |
| **Engine:** | Normally aspirated 1995cc V8, petrol, fuel injection, 16 valves |
| **Drivetrain:** | Mid-engine RWD |
| **Structure:** | Spaceframe |
| **Transmission:** | Six-speed manual |
| **Weight:** | 700kg |

**PRICE GUIDE**

| | |
|---|---|
| **Launch price:** | N/A in UK |
| **Excellent:** | £8,000,000+ |
| **Good:** | £6,000,000+ |
| **Average:** | N/A |
| **Project:** | N/A |

## ALFA ROMEO
### 1750/2000 GTV

To ally itself with the launch of the 1750 Berlina, the Giulia Sprint was facelifted to become the 1750 GTV coupé. It retained the original GT1300/GT Junior 1.6 bodyshell but gained a quad-headlight front end and cleaner external trim details (as well as losing the step-front). The revised interior was an ergonomic improvement, although purists prefer the older design. The 1779cc four cylinder was now the base power unit for the non-Junior line, meaning lusty performance. These later models are considered the easiest to live with. Values holding steady.

**SPECIFICATIONS**

**Years produced:** 1967-1969 (44,269/37,459 in total)
**Performance:** 0-60mph: 11.2sec
Top speed: 118mph
**Power & torque:** 122bhp/137lb ft
**Engine:** Normally aspirated 1779cc four cylinder, petrol, carburettor, 8 valves
**Drivetrain:** Front-engine RWD
**Structure:** Monocoque
**Trans/weight:** Five-speed manual/1040kg

**PRICE GUIDE**

**Launch price:** £2248
**Excellent:** £48,000
**Good:** £30,000
**Average:** £18,000
**Project:** £7000

## ALFA ROMEO
### 1750/2000 Berlina

With Alfa Romeo's new model development concentrating on the 'Sud and Alfetta, the mid-range Giulia saloon was treated to a front and rear makeover and relaunched to become the 1750/2000 Berlina. Although the styling (by Pininfarina) was considered unimaginative, it retained the outgoing car's roomy interior and boot, as well as the driver's car credentials that made the original so appealing. An updated interior and dashboard made the car feel more modern. The top-of-the-range 2000cc version with 132bhp was a genuine sports saloon.

**SPECIFICATIONS (1750)**

**Years produced:** 1967-1977 (101,883 in total)
**Performance:** 0-60mph: 10.8sec
Top speed: 116mph
**Power & torque:** 122bhp/139lb ft
**Engine:** Normally aspirated 1779cc four cylinder, petrol, carburettor, 8 valves
**Drivetrain:** Front-engine RWD
**Structure:** Monocoque
**Transmission:** Five-speed manual
**Weight:** 1110kg

**PRICE GUIDE**

**Launch price:** £1898
**Excellent:** £8500
**Good:** £4500
**Average:** £2000
**Project:** £800

## ALFA ROMEO
### Spider 1750/2000 S2

Alfa couldn't leave its cars alone during the 1960s and '70s. After just three years in production, the 1750 Spider Veloce was given a major restyle, the boat-tail giving way to the more aerodynamic Kamm tail. It made the Spider look less streamlined but more modern. In 1972 the 1750 engine was upgraded to the final-incarnation 2000cc unit. There were also cut-price 1600 Junior versions. Given what is happening with the 'roundtail' cars, these Series 2s represent excellent value and a sound investment, say specialists Classic Alfa.

**SPECIFICATIONS**

**Years produced:** 1969-1982 (42,406 in total)
**Performance:** 0-60mph: 8.8sec
Top speed: 123mph
**Power & torque:** 131bhp/134lb ft
**Engine:** Normally aspirated 1962cc four cylinder, petrol, carburettor, 8 valves
**Drivetrain:** Front-engine RWD
**Structure:** Monocoque
**Transmission:** Five-speed manual/1040kg

**PRICE GUIDE**

**Launch price:** £2439
**Excellent:** £25,000
**Good:** £15,000
**Average:** £7000
**Project:** £2500

## ALFA ROMEO
### 1300/1600 Junior Z

An appealing Italian 'bitza' that somehow transcends the sum of its parts. Created by Zagato using the chassis from the Spider and normal GT Junior mechanicals, the Junior Zagato was an arresting-looking coupé that added real variety to the Alfa Romeo line-up. The sloping front and Kamm tail were certainly a world apart from the well-crafted classicism of the rest of the Giulia-derived cars, but no less appealing for it. It was lighter and more aerodynamic than the standard cars so it was usefully quicker too.

**SPECIFICATIONS**

**Years produced:** 1970-1975 (1108/402 in total)
**Performance:** 0-60mph: 11.5sec
Top speed: 118mph
**Power & torque:** 125bhp/115lb ft
**Engine:** Normally aspirated 1570cc four cylinder, petrol, carburettor, 8 valves
**Drivetrain:** Drivetrain: front-engine RWD
**Structure:** Monocoque
**Trans/weight:** Five-speed manual/950kg

**PRICE GUIDE**

**Launch price:** Not known
**Excellent:** £35,000
**Good:** £22,000
**Average:** £15,000
**Project:** £8000

## ALFA ROMEO
### Montreal

Appeared at Expo '67 in Montreal, Canada, (hence the name) as a concept car, and proved so popular that the company decided to turn it into a production reality. Hurried production meant using ordinary 105-series suspension, resulting in a car whose handling didn't really match it's race-car-based V8. However, today a few modifications make it an entertaining, fast, touring GT. Values topped out in 2018 and have dropped a little over the last 12 months, say specialists Classic Alfa. A good time to buy one of these still underrated Alfas.

**SPECIFICATIONS**

**Years produced:** 1970-1977 (3925 in total)
**Performance:** 7.6sec
Top speed: 137mph
**Power & torque:** 200bhp/173lb ft
**Engine:** Normally aspirated 2593cc V8, petrol, carburettor, 16 valves
**Drivetrain:** Front-engine RWD
**Structure:** Monocoque
**Transmission:** Five-speed manual
**Weight:** 1267kg

**PRICE GUIDE**

**Launch price:** £5077
**Excellent:** £55,000
**Good:** £40,000
**Average:** £30,000
**Project:** £15,000

HHW 607G
636 UYN

## ALFA ROMEO
### Alfetta

Alfa Romeo's first new big saloon of the '70s marked something of a departure from its predecessors. Boasting a new platform that would last for well over two decades, all the ingredients were there for a great sporting saloon: a range of twin-cam engines and a transaxle gearbox for perfect weight distribution. Build quality was variable, with the earliest cars the most solidly assembled, but a bigger problem was corrosion. Rare today, not fully understood, and perhaps more deserving of its own accolades than being known as the saloon that begat the GTV.

**SPECIFICATIONS (2000)**

| | |
|---|---|
| **Years produced:** | 1972-1984 (450,000 in total) |
| **Performance:** | 0-60mph: 9.7sec<br>Top speed: 115mph |
| **Power & torque:** | 122bhp/129lb ft |
| **Engine:** | Normally aspirated 1962cc four cylinder, petrol, carburettor, 8 valves |
| **Drivetrain:** | Front-engine RWD |
| **Structure:** | Monocoque |
| **Transmission:** | Five-speed manual |
| **Weight:** | 1080kg |

**PRICE GUIDE**

| | |
|---|---|
| **Launch price:** | £2649 |
| **Excellent:** | £4000 |
| **Good:** | £2500 |
| **Average:** | £1000 |
| **Project:** | £500 |

## ALFA ROMEO
### Alfasud

When it went on sale in 1972, the Alfasud rewrote the small-car book. Given that Alfa Romeo had no experience of small, front-driven cars, the sheer dynamic excellence of the flat-four powered 'Sud came as a shock. However, Alfasud was also a government-led experiment in the redistribution of manufacturing (a new factory was built near Naples, where the workforce was unskilled in car-making). Customers found their new 'Suds would rust, or fall to pieces. Today good examples are prized but are also quite hard to find. A flawed gem.

**SPECIFICATIONS (1.5)**

| | |
|---|---|
| **Years produced:** | 1972-1983 (387,734 in total excluding Ti) |
| **Performance:** | 0-60mph: 11.8sec<br>Top speed: 103mph |
| **Power & torque:** | 93bhp/96lb ft |
| **Engine:** | Normally aspirated 1490cc flat four, petrol, carburettor, 8 valves |
| **Drivetrain:** | Front-engine FWD |
| **Structure:** | Monocoque |
| **Transmission:** | Five-speed manual |
| **Weight:** | 885kg |

**PRICE GUIDE**

| | |
|---|---|
| **Launch price:** | £1399 |
| **Excellent:** | £5500 |
| **Good:** | £3500 |
| **Average:** | £1750 |
| **Project:** | £700 |

## ALFA ROMEO
### Alfetta GT 1.8/GTV 2000

It was left to Bertone to create a suitably handsome coupé from Alfetta underpinnings. It was originally launched as the Alfetta GT in 1779cc twin-cam form, and a 1.6GT joined the range in 1976 – along with the GTV 2000. With a full 2.0 litres under the bonnet, it delivered effortless performance, accompanied by the rorty soundtrack you would expect from an Alfa. Prone to rust at the time, but most surviving examples should have been properly rebuilt. All models now on the increase due to the high prices of 105-series GTVs and the rarity of good examples.

**SPECIFICATIONS (GTV)**

| | |
|---|---|
| **Years produced:** | 1973-1987 (31,267 in total) |
| **Performance:** | 0-60mph: 9.7sec<br>Top speed: 113mph |
| **Power & torque:** | 122bhp/123lb ft |
| **Engine:** | Normally aspirated 1779cc four cylinder, petrol, carburettor, 8 valves |
| **Drivetrain:** | Front-engine RWD |
| **Structure:** | Monocoque |
| **Transmission:** | Five-speed manual |
| **Weight:** | Five-speed manual/1048kg |

**PRICE GUIDE**

| | |
|---|---|
| **Launch price:** | N/A |
| **Excellent:** | £15,000 |
| **Good:** | £7500 |
| **Average:** | £3500 |
| **Project:** | £1000 |

## ALFA ROMEO
### Alfasud Sprint

The Italians have always been great at turning innocuous-looking family saloons into great sporting coupés. So when Alfa Romeo turned the rather good 'Sud into a usable small sporting car, the results were predictably sparkling. Styling was handled by Giugiaro, and to many the Sprint successfully eclipsed the already desirable GTV. It was especially rapid in twin-carb Veloce form, but any example will reward the enthusiastic driver. An iffy 1980s facelift did it no favours, though, and fans prefer the crisp original.

**SPECIFICATIONS**

| | |
|---|---|
| **Years produced:** | 1976-1990 (96,450 in total) |
| **Performance:** | 0-60mph: 10.0sec<br>Top speed: 105mph |
| **Power & torque:** | 84bhp/89lb ft |
| **Engine:** | Normally aspirated 1490cc flat four, petrol, carburettor, 8 valves |
| **Drivetrain:** | Front-engine FWD |
| **Structure:** | Monocoque |
| **Transmission:** | Five-speed manual |
| **Weight:** | 915kg |

**PRICE GUIDE**

| | |
|---|---|
| **Launch price:** | £3999 |
| **Excellent:** | £4000 |
| **Good:** | £3750 |
| **Average:** | £1100 |
| **Project:** | £600 |

## ALFA ROMEO
### Alfa Six

Strangely appealing today for those with a penchant for automotive losers, but the Alfa Six is a car the Arese company would rather choose to forget. It was ready for production by the mid-1970s, but the oil crisis and Alfa Romeo's enfeebled cashflow situation meant that the launch was continually delayed. When it arrived, the Six underwhelmed – its engine was magnificent, but the duff dynamics, narrow body and obvious Alfetta styling overtones let it down. Maybe a handful left in the UK now, so bask in its rarity if you find one, but don't pay over the odds.

**SPECIFICATIONS**

| | |
|---|---|
| **Years produced:** | 1979-1987 (12,070 in total) |
| **Performance:** | 0-60mph: 9.8sec<br>Top speed: 130mph |
| **Power & torque:** | 160bhp/157lb ft |
| **Engine:** | Normally aspirated 2492cc V6, petrol, electronic fuel injection, 12 valves |
| **Drivetrain:** | Front-engine RWD |
| **Structure:** | Monocoque |
| **Transmission:** | Five-speed manual (opt. auto) |
| **Weight:** | 1480kg |

**PRICE GUIDE**

| | |
|---|---|
| **Launch price:** | £11,900 |
| **Excellent:** | £2000 |
| **Good:** | £1250 |
| **Average:** | £850 |
| **Project:** | £500 |

## ALFA ROMEO
## Alfetta GTV6

As big Alfa saloons go, the Six was not a huge success, but we owe the existence of one of the best-sounding Alfa Romeos to the failed executive saloon, which donated its wonderful V6 engine to the Alfetta GTV. Running a new Bosch fuel injection system, the V6's power was up to 160bhp, giving the GTV6 a very useful power hike. As with the Alfetta GT and GTV before it, a good GTV6 was a great car in the bends – especially as it finally had the power to exploit it. Prices firmly on the up as good examples are very rare in the UK, say Classic Alfa.

### SPECIFICATIONS

| | |
|---|---|
| **Years produced:** | 1980-1987 (279,821 in total) |
| **Performance:** | 0-60mph: 8.8sec<br>Top speed: 130mph |
| **Power & torque:** | 160bhp/157lb ft |
| **Engine:** | Normally aspirated 2492cc V6, petrol, electronic fuel injection, 12 valves |
| **Drivetrain:** | Front-engine RWD |
| **Structure:** | Monocoque |
| **Transmission:** | Five-speed manual |
| **Weight:** | 1210kg |

### PRICE GUIDE

| | |
|---|---|
| **Launch price:** | £9495 |
| **Excellent:** | £12,000 |
| **Good:** | £7500 |
| **Average:** | £2000 |
| **Project:** | £1000 |

## ALFA ROMEO
## Alfa 33

Much was expected of the 33. It was supposed to build on the best bits of the Alfasud, to create a formidable new family car for the slick '80s. Instead, it failed to move on the game at all – even if the styling hinted that this was a much more upmarket offering. As it was, the wedge from Naples sold slowly and despite a welter of improvements throughout its life, stubbornly refused to realise its potential. As a driver's car, it's marred by a weird driving position but, for the family, it's an excellent proposition, thanks to its roomy cabin. Cheap and characterful now, but a 'Sud betters it.

### SPECIFICATIONS (1.5)

| | |
|---|---|
| **Years produced:** | 1983-1994 |
| **Performance:** | 0-60mph: 11.8sec<br>Top speed: 108mph |
| **Power & torque:** | 85bhp/69lb ft |
| **Engine:** | Normally aspirated 1490cc flat four, petrol, carburettor, 8 valves |
| **Drivetrain:** | Front-engine FWD |
| **Structure:** | Monocoque |
| **Transmission:** | Five-speed manual |
| **Weight:** | 890kg |

### PRICE GUIDE

| | |
|---|---|
| **Launch price:** | £5690 |
| **Excellent:** | £2000 |
| **Good:** | £1000 |
| **Average:** | £650 |
| **Project:** | £350 |

## ALFA ROMEO
## Spider 2000 S3/S4

The final restyle of the Spider took place at the beginning of 1990 – and Pininfarina was given the honour of preparing the Spider for its final days. The car was rounded off with smoother bumpers and slimmer rear light clusters. By this point the Spider was almost 30 years old, but the new fuel-injected engines, along with power-assisted steering, prolonged its life for three years. North American sales of the S4 Spider remained strong right to the end, with more than 75% of the production run ending up in the US.

### SPECIFICATIONS

| | |
|---|---|
| **Years produced:** | 1982-1993 (18,456 in total) |
| **Performance:** | 0-60mph: 9.2sec<br>Top speed: 119mph |
| **Power & torque:** | 120bhp /117lb ft |
| **Engine:** | Normally aspirated 1962cc four cylinder, petrol, electronic fuel injection, 8 valves |
| **Drivetrain:** | Front-engine RWD |
| **Structure:** | Monocoque |
| **Transmission:** | Five-speed manual |
| **Weight:** | 1110kg |

### PRICE GUIDE (S4, for S3 deduct 25%)

| | |
|---|---|
| **Launch price:** | £15,950 |
| **Excellent:** | £12,000 |
| **Good:** | £8000 |
| **Average:** | £5000 |
| **Project:** | £2500 |

## ALFA ROMEO
## 75 V6/3.0 V6

Launched on Alfa Romeo's 75th anniversary, the 75 was a mixture of Giulietta and Alfa 90. Alfa engineered the car to use a transaxle and this gave it almost perfect 50:50 weight distribution. That, coupled with the melodic V6 engine, made the 75 one of the most desirable sporting saloons of the 1980s. The styling was done in-house, following on from the Alfa 33, which had a similar square headlamp and grille arrangement. The 75 also came with a reasonable amount of equipment as standard, but power steering was extra.

### SPECIFICATIONS (3.0)

| | |
|---|---|
| **Years produced:** | 1985-1992 |
| **Performance:** | 0-60mph: 7.5sec<br>Top speed: 137mph |
| **Power & torque:** | 187bhp/181lb ft |
| **Engine:** | Normally aspirated 2959cc V6, petrol, electronic fuel injection, 12 valves |
| **Drivetrain:** | Front-engine RWD |
| **Structure:** | Monocoque |
| **Transmission:** | Five-speed manual |
| **Weight:** | 1160kg |

### PRICE GUIDE

| | |
|---|---|
| **Launch price:** | £11,649 |
| **Excellent:** | £2400 |
| **Good:** | £1800 |
| **Average:** | £850 |
| **Project:** | £350 |

## ALFA ROMEO
## SZ/RZ

First conceived as a design study in 1987, the Sprint Zagato caused such a sensation that, in 1989, Alfa launched a production version at the Geneva Motor Show. Based on a heavily modified 75, the SZ had the performance (and sound) to back up its sporty yet unconventional looks. Its ability to hang on in bends really made the SZ special – it could generate 1.1*g* of cornering force. The RZ (Roadster Zagato) was produced from 1992 until the end of 1993. Only 284 were made. Values of both have edged up slowly in recent years but have yet to really take off.

### SPECIFICATIONS

| | |
|---|---|
| **Years produced:** | 1989-1994 (998 in total) |
| **Performance:** | 0-60mph: 6.9sec<br>Top speed: 153mph |
| **Power & torque:** | 210bhp /181lb ft |
| **Engine:** | Normally aspirated 2959cc V6, petrol, electronic fuel injection, 24 valves |
| **Drivetrain:** | Front-engine RWD |
| **Structure:** | Monocoque |
| **Transmission:** | Five-speed manual |
| **Weight:** | 1260kg |

### PRICE GUIDE

| | |
|---|---|
| **Launch price:** | £40,000 |
| **Excellent:** | £45,000 |
| **Good:** | £35,000 |
| **Average:** | £25,000 |
| **Project:** | N/A |

## ALFA ROMEO
### GTV 2.0/3.0 V6

Launched in 1995, the front-drive GTV filled a coupé-shaped gap in Alfa Romeo's 1990s line-up, effectively replacing the rear-drive GTV and GTV6. It's among the most striking cars of its era, with wedgy Pininfarina coachwork. A 2.0-litre, four-cylinder Twin Spark engine was offered initially, with Alfa's familiar 3.0-litre 'Busso' V6 joining in 1997. The GTV and equivalent Spider convertible also marked a step up in quality for Alfa and a fully galvanised body keeps rust at bay. A 2003 facelift brought newer 2.0 JTS and 3.2 V6 engines.

**SPECIFICATIONS**

**Years produced:** 1995-2005
**Performance:** 0-60mph: 6.7sec (V6)
Top speed: 149mph
**Power & torque:** 221bhp/199lb ft
**Engine:** Normally aspirated 2959cc V6, petrol, fuel injection, 24 valves
**Drivetrain:** Front-engine FWD
**Structure:** Monocoque
**Transmission:** Five/six-speed manual
**Weight:** 1415kg

**PRICE GUIDE (V6 in brackets)**

**Launch price:** £21,351 (£27,795)
**Excellent:** £5000 (£7000)
**Good:** £3000 (£5000)
**Average:** £1500 (£2000)
**Project:** £500 (£1000)

## ALFA ROMEO
### 156/147 GTA

Alfa's 156 sports saloon was a world-beater when it was launched in 1998, and the 3.2-litre 'Busso' V6-engined GTA offered the full-on Junior Italian supersaloon experience. Changes included bigger wheels, bodykit and leather Recaros, while multi-link suspension and super-quick steering assured deft handling. Based on the same platform, the 147 GTA soon became the go-to tyre-smoking hot hatch. Neither sold in big numbers, and many have been broken for spares, so good ones are on the up. Optional Q2 LSD helps dynamics hugely.

**SPECIFICATIONS**

**Years produced:** 2001-2004
**Performance:** 0-60mph: 6.0sec (147 GTA)
Top speed: 153mph
**Power & torque:** 246bhp/221lb ft
**Engine:** Normally aspirated 3179cc V6, petrol, electronic injection, 24 valves
**Drivetrain:** Front-engine FWD
**Structure:** Monocoque
**Transmission:** Six-speed manual/six-speed semi-auto
**Weight:** 1410kg

**PRICE GUIDE**

**Launch price:** £22,500 (147 GTA)
**Excellent:** £12,000
**Good:** £9000
**Average:** £7000
**Project:** £3000

# ALLARD

SYDNEY ALLARD founded the marque that bore his name in 1936, with his first car being based on a Ford V8. The first bespoke Allards came along in 1945, still with Ford V8 engines but now with very distinctive long-nosed bodies. Always competition-orientated, Allards remained rather idiosyncratic and dramatic-looking until the 1950s when a series of roadsters – the K3, Palm Beach and JR – came out, sporting four- and six-cylinder engines as well as V8s. Demand plummeted as rivals produced cheaper, faster, better-looking alternatives. The firm ended up modifying Ford Anglias until 1966 when a fire destroyed the factory. Sydney Allard died at home the same night

## ALLARD
### L/M

If you enjoy your Allard-shaped kicks with the kids in the back seats then the Allard L and M are just the ticket. Effectively just a K1 with a six-inch wheelbase stretch (to 112in) and a pair of occasional seats in the rear, the additional model in the Allard line-up proved surprisingly popular. The M added some civilities such as coil-sprung suspension (from 1949) and a column gearchange. Although most UK cars were fitted with Ford Pilot engines, many were shipped overseas without a powertrain, leaving the owner to chose a suitable local engine.

**SPECIFICATIONS**

**Years produced:** 1946-1950 (191/500 in total)
**Performance:** 0-60mph: 15.2sec
Top speed: 82mph
**Power & torque:** 85bhp/N/A
**Engine:** Normally aspirated 3622cc V8, petrol, carburettor, 16 (side) valves
**Drivetrain:** Front-engine RWD
**Structure:** Separate chassis
**Transmission:** Three-speed manual
**Weight:** 1396kg

**PRICE GUIDE**

**Launch price:** £1151
**Excellent:** £55,000
**Good:** £40,000
**Average:** £24,000
**Project:** £14,000

## ALLARD
### K1/K2

Allard's first post-war sports car was a leap forward. Although it looked ungainly (a subsequent family trait) it was a great car to drive, proving very effective in competition. The technical make-up might have been simple, with a box-section frame, transverse leaf springs and a steel body, but careful chassis development was the key. The fitment of a powerful V8 engine (from the Ford Pilot) delivered plenty of effortless performance. The end result was a charismatic English sports car that has a loyal following to this day. Add c10% for K2.

**SPECIFICATIONS**

**Years produced:** 1946-1951 (151/119 in total)
**Performance:** 0-60mph: 13.6sec
Top speed: 102mph
**Power & torque:** 85bhp/150lb ft
**Engine:** Normally aspirated 3622cc V8, petrol, carburettor, 16 valves
**Drivetrain:** Front-engine RWD
**Structure:** Separate chassis
**Transmission:** Three-speed manual
**Weight:** 1118kg

**PRICE GUIDE**

**Launch price:** £1277
**Excellent:** £95,000
**Good:** £67,500
**Average:** £45,000
**Project:** £30,000

# ALLARD
## P1

Derived from the M 'drophead coupé', the Allard P1 was a hard-topped two-door saloon that broke with tradition for the marque. Although marketed as something of a gentleman's carriage, the P1 couldn't disguise its competition roots, making it an appealing proposition for enthusiastic drivers. Sydney Allard drove one to victory in the 1952 Monte Carlo Rally, making him the only person in the history of the event to win the event in a car bearing his own name. Today, the P1 continues to be well regarded by enthusiasts. Prices on the rise.

**SPECIFICATIONS**

| | |
|---|---|
| **Years produced:** | 1949-1951 (559 in total) |
| **Performance:** | 0-60mph: 15.2sec<br>Top speed: 85mph |
| **Power & torque:** | 85bhp/150lb ft |
| **Engine:** | Normally aspirated 3622cc V8, petrol, carburettor, 16 valves |
| **Drivetrain:** | Front-engine RWD |
| **Structure:** | Separate chassis |
| **Transmission:** | Three-speed manual |
| **Weight:** | 1372kg |

**PRICE GUIDE**

| | |
|---|---|
| **Launch price:** | £1277 |
| **Excellent:** | £35,000 |
| **Good:** | £26,000 |
| **Average:** | £18,000 |
| **Project:** | £9000 |

# ALLARD
## J2/J2X

The most celebrated of all the Allards and, despite their rarity, the most likely to come onto the market. In the UK, the J2 came with either the 3.6-litre V8 from the Ford Pilot or a 4.4-litre Mercury unit. In the US, enthusiastic owners fitted a whole range of V8 powerplants. Suspension was more sophisticated than the earlier cars', ensuring excellent handling, and the J2 enjoyed a successful racing career on both sides of the Atlantic. In 1952, Allard introduced the J2X, with the engine pushed further forward, partly to allow more legroom (hence X for extended).

**SPECIFICATIONS**

| | |
|---|---|
| **Years produced:** | 1950-1954 (173 total – 90 J2, 83 J2X) |
| **Performance:** | 0-60mph: 8.6sec (J2)<br>Top speed: 111mph |
| **Power & torque:** | 120bhp/221lb ft |
| **Engine:** | Normally aspirated 4375cc V8, petrol, carburettor, 16 valves |
| **Drivetrain:** | Front-engine RWD |
| **Structure:** | Separate chassis |
| **Transmission:** | Three-speed manual |
| **Weight:** | 914kg |

**PRICE GUIDE**

| | |
|---|---|
| **Launch price:** | £1277 |
| **Excellent:** | £275,000 |
| **Good:** | £230,000 |
| **Average:** | £160,000 |
| **Project:** | £100,000 |

# ALLARD
## K3

Altogether more sophisticated than its earlier relatives, the K3 was Allard's attempt at appealing to more sophisticated buyers with luxuries such as a one-piece bonnet and wide bench seat that was supposed to accommodate the entire family. This being Allard's supposedly softer option, Americans were the target. Problem was, Stateside buyers were looking for the exact opposite in their English sports cars, and so the K3's market failure was disappointing. But it was a pretty car, especially by Allard's standards. Values have been climbing.

**SPECIFICATIONS**

| | |
|---|---|
| **Years produced:** | 1952-1955 (62 in total) |
| **Performance:** | 0-60mph: N/A<br>Top speed: 85mph |
| **Power & torque:** | 85bhp/150lb ft |
| **Engine:** | Normally aspirated 3622cc V8, petrol, carburettor, 16 valves |
| **Drivetrain:** | Front-engine RWD |
| **Structure:** | Separate chassis |
| **Transmission:** | Three-speed manual |
| **Weight:** | 1181kg |

**PRICE GUIDE**

| | |
|---|---|
| **Launch price:** | £1713 |
| **Excellent:** | £110,000 |
| **Good:** | £75,000 |
| **Average:** | £55,000 |
| **Project:** | £35,000 |

# ALPINE

SOCIÉTÉ ANONYME des Automobiles Alpine was born in 1954, the brainchild of competition driver Jean Rédélé. It used Renault underpinnings with attractive glassfibre coupé bodies on top, leading to 1962's definitive A110, which remained in production until 1977 and turned Alpine into France's leading sports car maker. Alpine was always closely tied with Renault, which took over in 1974. This era also saw the striking A310, which in time evolved into the GTA and A610. From 1994 the Dieppe factory was given over to building Renaults, but today the marque is being revived. The all-new A110, inspired by the '60s classic, has earned rave reviews and could yet have a positive effect on values.

# ALPINE
## A110

Jean Rédélé branched out into building competition-style cars based on Renault running gear in 1956 with the A106. The car proved so effective (winning its class in the 1956 Mille Miglia) that production blossomed as keen drivers clamoured to get hold of their own. By the time the A110 hit the market in 1962 the formula was pretty much perfected with a glassfibre body fixed to Renault 8 Gordini running gear, making for a seriously effective rally weapon. Ex-works cars can be £200k-plus, but all are highly prized today, says specialist Chris Rabbets.

**SPECIFICATIONS**

| | |
|---|---|
| **Years produced:** | 1962-1977 (7500 in total) |
| **Performance:** | 0-60mph: 7.1sec (1600S)<br>Top speed: 132mph |
| **Power & torque:** | 138bhp/117lb ft |
| **Engine:** | Normally aspirated 1565cc four cylinder, petrol, carburettor, 8 valves |
| **Drivetrain:** | Rear-engine RWD |
| **Structure:** | Glassfibre body/backbone chassis |
| **Transmission:** | Five-speed manual |
| **Weight:** | 625kg |

| | 1300 | 1600S |
|---|---|---|
| **Launch price:** | N/A in UK | N/A in UK |
| **Excellent:** | £68,000 | £120,000 |
| **Good:** | £50,000 | £90,000 |
| **Average:** | £35,000 | £60,000 |
| **Project:** | £20,000 | £40,000 |

## ALPINE
## A310

Bringing the Alpine family firmly into the 1970s, the A310 was developed from the rear-engined A110 GT4, but civilised to such an extent that it could be used as a day-to-day road car. The wedge styling was certainly striking, and the glassfibre body was as light and aerodynamic as Alpine tradition demanded. Powered by the Renault 17TS high-output 1605cc engine, it could easily top 125mph. Never officially imported into the UK, and as with the A110 all are left-hand drive. Prices have slipped a little in the last 12 months.

**SPECIFICATIONS**

| | |
|---|---|
| **Years produced:** | 1971-1976 (2349 in total) |
| **Performance:** | 0-60mph: 8.1sec<br>Top speed: 131mph |
| **Power & torque:** | 127bhp/108lb ft |
| **Engine:** | Normally aspirated 1605cc four cylinder, petrol, carburettor, 8 valves |
| **Drivetrain:** | Rear-engine RWD |
| **Structure:** | Glassfibre body/backbone chassis |
| **Transmission:** | Five-speed manual |
| **Weight:** | 940kg |

**PRICE GUIDE**

| | |
|---|---|
| **Launch price:** | N/A in UK |
| **Excellent:** | £35,000 |
| **Good:** | £28,000 |
| **Average:** | £20,000 |
| **Project:** | £8000 |

## ALPINE
## A310 V6

Alpine was rapidly moving upmarket and the scale of its ambition was reflected in the A310 V6. Introduced in 1976, it slotted in the range above the four-cylinder car, which was discontinued shortly afterwards. Powered by the 2664cc Douvrin V6, co-developed by Renault and Peugeot, the latest Alpine developed 150bhp in the rortiest fashion possible. However, despite the excellent soundtrack, the car wasn't fast enough, nor did it have the right badge to woo Porsche buyers at the time. Values have levelled off after climbing steeply.

**SPECIFICATIONS**

| | |
|---|---|
| **Years produced:** | 1977-1985 (9276 in total) |
| **Performance:** | 0-60mph: 7.6sec<br>Top speed: 137mph |
| **Power & torque:** | 150bhp/150lb ft |
| **Engine:** | Normally aspirated 2664cc V6, petrol, carburettor, 12 valves |
| **Drivetrain:** | Rear-engine RWD |
| **Structure:** | Glassfibre body/backbone chassis |
| **Transmission:** | Five-speed manual |
| **Weight:** | 1016kg |

**PRICE GUIDE**

| | |
|---|---|
| **Launch price:** | N/A in UK |
| **Excellent:** | £35,000 |
| **Good:** | £28,000 |
| **Average:** | £20,000 |
| **Project:** | £15,000 |

## ALPINE
## GTA V6

The GTA (GT in France) was a very effective update of the A310 V6. Although the basic layout was shared with the older car, the slippery new glassfibre body and expanded PRV V6 engine gave the standard model (which boasted 160bhp) a top speed of nearly 140mph. However, the GTA's main forte was its handling. Despite – or partly because of – the overhung rear engine, it provided huge lateral grip and near-flat cornering. Sales in the UK were pitiful and as a marketing exercise for Renault it was a huge failure. Buy one today and enjoy the attention.

**SPECIFICATIONS**

| | |
|---|---|
| **Years produced:** | 1984-1989 (1366 LHD, 212 RHD) |
| **Performance:** | 0-60mph: 7.5sec<br>Top speed: 139mph |
| **Power & torque:** | 157bhp/163lb ft |
| **Engine:** | Normally aspirated 2849cc V6, petrol, carburettor, 12 valves |
| **Drivetrain:** | Rear-engine RWD |
| **Structure:** | Glassfibre body/backbone chassis |
| **Transmission:** | Five-speed manual |
| **Weight** | 1140kg |

**PRICE GUIDE**

| | |
|---|---|
| **Launch price:** | £19,040 |
| **Excellent:** | £11,000 |
| **Good:** | £8000 |
| **Average:** | £4000 |
| **Project:** | £2000 |

## ALPINE
## GTA V6 Turbo

When launched, the GTA Turbo became France's fastest-ever production car. With a power output of nearly 200bhp from its 2.5-litre V6 engine, shared with the Renault 25, its top speed pushed 150mph. Pricing in the UK was ambitious and the GTA went head-to-head with the Porsche 911 and Lotus Esprit. These more established cars continued to overshadow the French upstart, outselling it comfortably. Few RHD cars remain in the UK (fewer than 40) but in recent years a number of left-hookers have been imported. Terrific value.

**SPECIFICATIONS**

| | |
|---|---|
| **Years produced:** | 1985-1991 (3641 LHD, 370 RHD) |
| **Performance:** | 0-60mph: 6.3sec<br>Top speed: 149mph |
| **Power & torque:** | 197bhp/214lb ft |
| **Engine:** | Turbocharged 2458cc V6, petrol, fuel injection, 12 valves |
| **Drivetrain:** | Rear-engine RWD |
| **Structure:** | Glassfibre body/backbone chassis |
| **Transmission:** | Five-speed manual |
| **Weight:** | 1190kg |

**PRICE GUIDE**

| | |
|---|---|
| **Launch price:** | £23,635 |
| **Excellent:** | £15,000 |
| **Good:** | £9000 |
| **Average:** | £5000 |
| **Project:** | £3000 |

## ALPINE
## A610

The GTA's successor reverted to traditional Alpine naming conventions - though it didn't do much good for sales: annual sales in the UK never amounted to more than a few dozen. That was a shame, because the A610 was a fine driver's car with bags of character and ability. Visible changes included pop-up headlamps and revised body panels, while the engine was up from 2.5 to 3 litres, gaining a handy 50bhp, and the chassis was stiffer, though today you need to watch out for rust. Intriguing alternative to a 911, and prices rising. Very best can be up to £40k.

**SPECIFICATIONS**

| | |
|---|---|
| **Years produced:** | 1992-1995 (750 LHD, 67 RHD) |
| **Performance:** | 0-60mph: 5.4sec<br>Top speed: 160mph |
| **Power & torque:** | 250bhp/258lb ft |
| **Engine:** | Turbocharged 2975cc V6, petrol, fuel injection, 12 valves |
| **Drivetrain:** | Rear-engine RWD |
| **Structure:** | Glassfibre body/backbone chassis |
| **Transmission:** | Five-speed manual |
| **Weight:** | 1420kg |

**PRICE GUIDE**

| | |
|---|---|
| **Launch price:** | £37,980 |
| **Excellent:** | £28,000 |
| **Good:** | £20,000 |
| **Average:** | £15,000 |
| **Project:** | £7000 |

# ALVIS

FOUNDED in 1919, the Alvis name reputedly came from a design of piston: 'al' from 'aluminium' and 'vis' meaning 'strong' in Latin. Its 12/50 and 12/60 models were notable early designs and it was also a pioneer of front-wheel-drive during the 1920s. It built a range of imposing and progressive sports models during the 1930s but adopted a one-model policy after the war. In 1955, Swiss firm Graber penned a new and very handsome body and the TC108G, TD21 , TE21 and TF21 that followed were noted for their arresting appearance, especially the final stacked-headlamp cars. Competitor Rover took over the firm in 1965 and, from 1967, Alvis was confined to making military machines.

## ALVIS TA14

Despite the fact that the TA14 was merely a mildly modified version of the 1938 12/70, it was Alvis's post-war best-seller – explained by the traditional styling. It also means cart springs and mechanically operated brakes, though you get a slightly wider track and longer wheelbase. The engine was bored out by an extra 50cc, but extra weight means this high-quality car can manage only 75mph. There were quite a few special bodies about, and it's these – particularly the Tickford and Carbodies dropheads – that are most sought-after.

### SPECIFICATIONS

| | |
|---|---|
| **Years produced:** | 1946-1950 (3311 in total) |
| **Performance:** | 0-60mph: 22.2sec<br>Top speed: 74mph |
| **Power & torque:** | 65bhp/95lb ft |
| **Engine:** | Normally aspirated 1892cc four cylinder, petrol, carburettor, 8 valves |
| **Drivetrain:** | Front-engine RWD |
| **Structure:** | Separate chassis |
| **Transmission:** | Four-speed manual |
| **Weight:** | 1422kg |

### PRICE GUIDE

| | |
|---|---|
| **Launch price:** | £893 |
| **Excellent:** | £18,000 |
| **Good:** | £15,000 |
| **Average:** | £11,000 |
| **Project:** | £5000 |

## ALVIS TA21/TC21

The cabin was carried over from the TA14, but rounded wings and faired-in headlamps added a hint of modernity. Brakes are hydraulic and there's independent coil-sprung front suspension, but the big change is under the bonnet. Alvis's all-new 3.0-litre engine – with twin carbs on all but the first few – is tough and torquey as well as smooth and quiet. By the time the TA evolved into the TC21/100 'Grey Lady' in 1953, higher compression meant 100bhp... and just about 100mph. Specialists Red Triangle say to add 30-40% for Graber-bodied versions.

### SPECIFICATIONS

| | |
|---|---|
| **Years produced:** | 1950-1955 (2074 in total) |
| **Performance:** | 0-60mph: 16.5sec<br>Top speed: 86mph |
| **Power & torque:** | 90bhp/147lb ft |
| **Engine:** | Normally aspirated 2993cc straight six, petrol, carburettor, 12 valves |
| **Drivetrain:** | Front-engine RWD |
| **Structure:** | Separate chassis |
| **Transmission:** | Four-speed manual |
| **Weight:** | 1518kg |

### PRICE GUIDE

| | |
|---|---|
| **Launch price:** | £1598 |
| **Excellent:** | £35,000 |
| **Good:** | £29,000 |
| **Average:** | £23,000 |
| **Project:** | £8000 |

## ALVIS TA21/TC21 DHC

Even though it looked distinctly pre-war, the TA21 was the first post-war Alvis to feature a brand new chassis. The coachwork was by Tickford, and it was heavily influenced by the earlier TA14 Cabriolet. The new chassis and 90bhp engine gave the car hugely improved dynamics and driveability. The updated TC21 was unveiled in 1953 and the addition of twin SU carburettors boosted the existing 2993cc engine to 100bhp. Both TA21 and TC21 featured independent front suspension and remained unchanged for years. Great value, say Red Triangle.

### SPECIFICATIONS

| | |
|---|---|
| **Years produced:** | 1950-1955 |
| **Performance:** | 0-60mph: 16.5sec<br>Top speed: 86mph |
| **Power & torque:** | 90bhp/147lb ft |
| **Engine:** | Normally aspirated 2993cc straight six, petrol, carburettor, 12 valves |
| **Drivetrain:** | Front-engine RWD |
| **Structure:** | Separate chassis |
| **Transmission:** | Four-speed manual |
| **Weight:** | 1448kg |

### PRICE GUIDE

| | |
|---|---|
| **Launch price:** | £1822 |
| **Excellent:** | £60,000 |
| **Good:** | £48,000 |
| **Average:** | £35,000 |
| **Project:** | £18000 |

## ALVIS TA14 Drophead Coupé

With a design that originated in the '30s, the TA14 was never intended to be break new ground, merely to re-start Alvis production following the war. The Cabriolet was introduced alongside the saloon, and two drophead bodies were offered from the start – one by Tickford and the other by Carbodies. All versions featured the same front-end treatment, and the interior had high-quality leather seats and a wooden dashboard. The single-carburettor pushrod engine wasn't powerful, but it was smooth, and suited the touring-car nature of the TA14.

### SPECIFICATIONS

| | |
|---|---|
| **Years produced:** | 1946-1950 |
| **Performance:** | 0-60mph: 22.2sec<br>Top speed: 74mph |
| **Power & torque:** | 65bhp/95lb ft |
| **Engine:** | Normally aspirated 1892cc four cylinder, petrol, carburettor, 8 valves |
| **Drivetrain:** | Front-engine RWD |
| **Structure:** | Separate chassis |
| **Transmission:** | Four-speed manual |
| **Weight:** | 1447kg |

### PRICE GUIDE

| | |
|---|---|
| **Launch price:** | £893 |
| **Excellent:** | £38,000 |
| **Good:** | £29,000 |
| **Average:** | £20,000 |
| **Project:** | £11,000 |

THE BEST
BOLT-ON UPGRADE
FOR YOUR CLASSIC
HWB 685J
The best classic car experience is just a new set of tyres away. Vintage Tyres stocks new tyres in traditional tread patterns for cars from the 1890s to the 1990s. Let us help you to bolt on the best upgrade for your classic.
EST. 1962
VINTAGE TYRES
FOR CARS AND BIKES FROM THE 1890s TO THE 1990s
Branches at Beaulieu and Bicester
Trustpilot
01590 612261
sales@vintagetyres.com
www.vintagetyres.com

## ALVIS
### TB21

In 1950 Alvis had launched the TB14, a low-slung roadster based on the TA14 chassis and engine but most notable for its odd, pear-shaped grille. It was a huge flop and lasted just a year. Its replacement, the TB21, had a more conventional grille and was widely admired. It used the same chassis as the TA21 and was also fitted with the TA21's 90bhp engine, giving it sprightly performance. However, it was expensive and – perhaps more to the point – up against the much sexier Jaguar XK. The result: a mere 31 cars were produced, which helps keep values strong.

#### SPECIFICATIONS

| | |
|---|---|
| **Years produced:** | 1952 (31 in total) |
| **Performance:** | 0-60mph: N/A<br>Top speed: 95mph |
| **Power & torque:** | 90bhp/150lb ft |
| **Engine:** | Normally aspirated 2993cc straight six, petrol, carburettor, 12 valves |
| **Drivetrain:** | Front-engine RWD |
| **Structure:** | Separate chassis |
| **Transmission:** | Four-speed manual |
| **Weight:** | 1283kg |

#### PRICE GUIDE

| | |
|---|---|
| **Launch price:** | £1598 |
| **Excellent:** | £57,000 |
| **Good:** | £40,000 |
| **Average:** | £25,000 |
| **Project:** | £15,000 |

## ALVIS
### TD21

The handsome TD21 was bodied by Park Ward, based loosely on the short-lived TC 108G that was styled by Swiss coachbuilder Graber and built in Loughborough by bus-maker Willowbrook from 1956-57. Front brakes were discs, and all but the first few TDs got an uprated 115bhp engine. A four-speed Austin-Healey gearbox was employed, with the option of a three-speed auto. The Series II, from October '62, has all-wheel disc brakes and a ZF five-speed 'box. Spectacular value at the moment, say specialists Red Triangle, particularly the saloons.

#### SPECIFICATIONS

| | |
|---|---|
| **Years produced:** | 1958-1963 (1070 in total) |
| **Performance:** | 0-60mph: 13.9sec<br>Top speed: 104mph |
| **Power & torque:** | 115bhp/152lb ft |
| **Engine:** | Normally aspirated 2993cc straight six, petrol, carburettor, 12 valves |
| **Drivetrain:** | Front-engine RWD |
| **Structure:** | Separate chassis |
| **Transmission:** | Four-speed manual/three-speed auto |
| **Weight:** | 1495kg |

#### PRICE GUIDE (Drophead in brackets)

| | |
|---|---|
| **Launch price:** | £2766 |
| **Excellent:** | £38,000 (£95,000) |
| **Good:** | £28,000 (£80,000) |
| **Average:** | £18,000 (£65,000) |
| **Project:** | £8000 (£35,000) |

## ALVIS
### TE/TF21

Distinguished from its TD predecessor by those stacked twin headlamps that were *so* fashionable in the early 1960s, the TE gained a new cylinder head that lifted output to 130bhp. Both saloon and drophead were available, and it's the latter that makes serious money today. Power steering was a desirable option from 1965, but Alvis saved the best for last: just 106 TFs were built, and they come with a triple-carb 150bhp engine, improved gearbox and uprated suspension. Red Triangle advise adding 30-40% for Graber-bodied cars.

#### SPECIFICATIONS

| | |
|---|---|
| **Years produced:** | 1963-1967 |
| **Performance:** | 0-60mph: 12.5sec<br>Top speed: 112mph |
| **Power & torque:** | 130bhp/172lb ft |
| **Engine:** | Normally aspirated 2993cc straight six, petrol, carburettor, 12 valves |
| **Drivetrain:** | Front-engine RWD |
| **Structure:** | Separate chassis |
| **Transmission:** | Five-speed manual/three-speed auto |
| **Weight:** | 1473kg |

#### PRICE GUIDE (Drophead in brackets)

| | |
|---|---|
| **Launch price:** | £2775 |
| **Excellent:** | £45,000 (£120,000) |
| **Good:** | £32,000 (£85,000) |
| **Average:** | £26,000 (£65,000) |
| **Project:** | £12,000 (£38,000) |

# ARMSTRONG SIDDELEY

SIDDELEY was founded in 1902 and, after various partnerships, was taken over by the Armstrong Whitworth Development Company in 1919. The new Armstrong-Siddeley combine specialised in large luxury machines (although it did market a smaller 12hp model). In the week WW2 ended, it launched the patriotically-named Lancaster saloon and Hurricane drophead coupés, soon followed by the Typhoon and Whitley variants. The Sapphire 346 of 1952 brought power steering to British cars for the first time, but the smaller and awkwardly styles 234 and 236 models were a failure and contributed to the decision to end car production after a merger with Bristol in 1960.

## ARMSTRONG SIDDELEY
### Hurricane DHC

As part of a two-pronged attack on the world's car markets, Armstrong Siddeley introduced this stylish two-door drophead. Using the same chassis and running gear as the Lancaster, it was stodgy to drive, but the styling set it apart from its pre-war counterparts: flush-fitting headlights and faired-in front wings (from the Lancaster) were up-to-the-minute. The 70bhp 1991cc overhead-valve engine was carried over from the pre-war 16hp, but was rugged and torquey, offering easy 50mph cruising in those restrained times.

#### SPECIFICATIONS

| | |
|---|---|
| **Years produced:** | 1946-1949 (2606 in total) |
| **Performance:** | 0-60mph: 29.9sec<br>Top speed: 75mph |
| **Power & torque:** | 75bhp/107lb ft |
| **Engine:** | Normally aspirated 2309cc straight six, petrol, carburettor, 12 valves |
| **Drivetrain:** | Front-engine RWD |
| **Structure:** | Separate chassis |
| **Transmission:** | Four-speed manual |
| **Weight:** | 1412kg |

#### PRICE GUIDE

| | |
|---|---|
| **Launch price:** | £1151 |
| **Excellent:** | £19,000 |
| **Good:** | £14,000 |
| **Average:** | £6500 |
| **Project:** | £3750 |

## ARMSTRONG SIDDELEY Lancaster

It might have been the company's first post-war car, but underneath the Lancaster's skin beat the heart of a pre-war car. Despite that, it can justifiably be described as Britain's first all-new post-war car, appearing on the market the same week hostilities ceased in Europe. The 2.0-litre saloon was hardly groundbreaking but, with torsion bar suspension, hydromechanical brakes and a four-speed all-synchromesh gearbox, it was comfortable and easy to drive. Dignified and refined it might have been, but it suffered badly from rust.

**SPECIFICATIONS**

**Years produced:** 1946-1952 (3597 in total)
**Performance:** 0-60mph: 29.7sec
Top speed: 75mph
**Power & torque:** 70bhp/N/A
**Engine:** Normally aspirated 1991cc straight six, petrol, carburettor, 12 valves
**Drivetrain:** Front-engine RWD
**Structure:** Separate chassis
**Transmission:** Four-speed manual
**Weight:** 1527kg

**PRICE GUIDE**

**Launch price:** £1151
**Excellent:** £12,000
**Good:** £8000
**Average:** £4500
**Project:** £2250

## ARMSTRONG SIDDELEY Typhoon Coupé

The Typhoon is the entry-level version of the Hurricane, but that doesn't stop it having an appeal all of its own. Just like its Hurricane/Lancaster brethren it features a front suspension set-up of surprising sophistication: independent with longitudinal torsion bars, along with a more traditional rear set-up of a live axle and leaf springs. The driving experience is stately and dignified, befitting of its upright styling. But the steel-and-aluminium bodywork is corrosion-prone and tough to restore. Continues to have a following.

**SPECIFICATIONS**

**Years produced:** 1946-1953 (1701 in total)
**Performance:** 0-60mph: 29.7sec
Top speed: 78mph
**Power & torque:** 70bhp/109lb ft
**Engine:** Normally aspirated 1991cc straight six, petrol, carburettor, 12 valves
**Drivetrain:** Front-engine RWD
**Structure:** Separate chassis
**Transmission:** Four-speed manual
**Weight:** 1351kg

**PRICE GUIDE**

**Launch price:** £1214
**Excellent:** £15,000
**Good:** £11,000
**Average:** £6500
**Project:** £3000

## ARMSTRONG SIDDELEY Whitley

Once the great export drive was under way, Armstrong Siddeley was instantly building a car that it considered more than suitable for the Colonies. More imposing styling was the key to its appeal, with an updated nose and roofline to distance it from the Lancaster. It wasn't the new recipe that the British car industry needed, although it did prove a big seller. Underneath it was a familiar story, powered by the familiar 2.3-litre straight six that saw service in the last of the previous generation of models. It was big and comfortable, too.

**SPECIFICATIONS**

**Years produced:** 1950-1954 (2582 in total)
**Performance:** 0-60mph: 19.0sec
Top speed: 80mph
**Power & torque:** 75bhp/107lb ft
**Engine:** Normally aspirated 2309cc straight six, petrol, carburettor, 12 valves
**Drivetrain:** Front-engine RWD
**Structure:** Separate chassis
**Transmission:** Four-speed manual
**Weight:** 1430kg

**PRICE GUIDE**

**Launch price:** £1247
**Excellent:** £12,500
**Good:** £9000
**Average:** £4500
**Project:** £2250

## ARMSTRONG SIDDELEY Sapphire 346

When it appeared, it could have been easy to conclude that the 346 was just another rebody of the pre-war models, such was the timidity of its design. However, it was entirely new underneath, featuring a fresh suspension set-up of coil springs at the front and leaf springs at the back. It received a new engine, too – a lusty 3.4-litre six that was powerful enough to push the the 346 to 95mph, a significant step forward. But compared with the opposition it was too unwieldy for mass appeal. All of that said, values have been rising in recent times.

**SPECIFICATIONS**

**Years produced:** 1952-1958 (8187 in total)
**Performance:** 0-60mph: 13sec
Top speed: 100mph
**Power & torque:** 150bhp/185lb ft
**Engine:** Normally aspirated 3435cc straight six, petrol, carburettor, 12 valves
**Drivetrain:** Front-engine RWD
**Structure:** Separate chassis
**Transmission:** Four-speed manual
**Weight:** 1575kg

**PRICE GUIDE**

**Launch price:** £1728
**Excellent:** £14,500
**Good:** £9500
**Average:** £5500
**Project:** £2000

## ARMSTRONG SIDDELEY Sapphire 234/236

Despite sharing a name with the bigger 346, this Sapphire was less appealing thanks to the 236 being powered by a 2.3-litre engine previously seen on the Whitley and Lancaster/Hurricane, and the 234 by a smaller version of the 346's power unit. Both cars failed to make an impression on the market, selling disastrously – and you'll be hard-pressed to find one now, thanks to their relative lack of appeal compared with the 346 and the Star Sapphire. Best known for being a contributing factor in Armstrong Siddeley's closure. Values slowly edging upwards.

**SPECIFICATIONS**

**Years produced:** 1955-1958 (803/603 in total)
**Performance:** 0-60mph: 15.5sec
Top speed: 97mph
**Power & torque:** 120bhp/139lb ft
**Engine:** Normally aspirated 2290cc four cylinder, petrol, carburettor, 8 valves
**Drivetrain:** Front-engine RWD
**Structure:** Separate chassis
**Transmission:** Four-speed manual
**Weight:** 1360kg

**PRICE GUIDE**

**Launch price:** £1599
**Excellent:** £14,000
**Good:** £9250
**Average:** £5250
**Project:** £1750

## ARMSTRONG SIDDELEY
### Star Sapphire

Star by name, star by nature. Although it looked rather similar to the Sapphire 346, the Star Sapphire was in an entirely different league as far as driving pleasure was concerned. It received a lusty 4.0-litre straight-six that could deliver genuine 100mph performance – and, finally, the four-speed all-synchromesh gearbox was joined by the option of a Rolls-Royce Hydramatic auto transmission that made driving this swift saloon genuinely easy. Even today, a well-sorted Star Sapphire will surprise other people on the road. Values on the up.

**SPECIFICATIONS**

| | |
|---|---|
| Years produced: | 1958-1960 (980 in total) |
| Performance: | 0-60mph: 15.7sec<br>Top speed: 100mph |
| Power & torque: | 145bhp/230lb ft |
| Engine: | Normally aspirated 3990cc straight six, petrol, carburettor, 12 valves |
| Drivetrain: | Front-engine RWD |
| Structure: | Separate chassis |
| Transmission: | Four-speed manual |
| Weight: | 1778kg |

**PRICE GUIDE**

| | |
|---|---|
| Launch price: | £2646 |
| Excellent: | £17,500 |
| Good: | £13,000 |
| Average: | £7500 |
| Project: | £3250 |

# ASTON MARTIN

LIONEL MARTIN and Robert Bamford built the first Aston Martin in 1914, the 'Aston' coming from the Aston Clinton hillclimb. From this small acorn grew one of Britain's best-loved sports car marques. The golden era for the manufacturer began in 1948 when industrialist David Brown took over; the iconic DB series cars were fast, beautiful, desirable and expensive. After Brown sold up in 1972, Aston Martin had a number of owners while the long-lived V8 range kept the firm afloat. Ford's takeover in 1987 led to a period of stability and new models such as the DB7 and Vanquish. In 2014 a partnership with Mercedes-AMG was announced, the first fruit of which was the all-new DB11.

## ASTON MARTIN
### DB2/DB2 Drophead

While the 2-Litre of 1948 has become retrospectively known as the DB1, the DB2 of 1950 was the first officially to wear the initials of owner David Brown. The chassis was largely the same as for the 2-Litre, but the curvaceous fastback body with an imposingly long bonnet was fresh and graceful, and would inspire Aston's styling for two decades. The 2.6-litre twin-cam engine was a WO Bentley design for Lagonda and gave the DB2 decent performance, especially in 121mph 'Vantage' form from 1951. Dropheads are sought-after, but all values are down this year.

**SPECIFICATIONS**

| | |
|---|---|
| Years produced: | 1950-1953 (513 in total) |
| Performance: | 0-60mph: 11.2sec<br>Top speed: 116mph |
| Power & torque: | 105bhp/125lb ft |
| Engine: | Normally aspirated 2580cc straight six, petrol, carburettor, 12 valves |
| Drivetrain: | Front-engine RWD |
| Structure: | Superleggera |
| Transmission: | Four-speed manual |
| Weight: | 1207kg |

**PRICE GUIDE (Drophead in brackets)**

| | |
|---|---|
| Launch price: | £1920 |
| Excellent: | £200,000 (£270,000) |
| Good: | £150,000 (£200,000) |
| Average: | £120,000 (£150,000) |
| Project: | £70,000 (£90,000) |

## ASTON MARTIN
### DB2/4 & Drophead

The '4' tacked onto the DB2's title denoted that this reworking of the theme could now fit four people… at a squeeze. The 2+2 seating was made more habitable by a higher roofline and opening rear screen – perhaps so those in the back could escape if it became too tight! The extra weight affected performance, so a boost to 3 litres in 1954 took power to 140bhp. Around 130 Dropheads were built. The Mk2 of 1955 incorporated a rear-end restyle and a stronger rear axle, and also introduced the rare 'notchback' hardtop version (just 34 built).

**SPECIFICATIONS**

| | |
|---|---|
| Years produced: | 1953-1957 (764 in total) |
| Performance: | 0-60mph: 10.5sec<br>Top speed: 119mph |
| Power & torque: | 125bhp/139lb ft |
| Engine: | Normally aspirated 2580cc straight six, petrol, carburettor, 12 valves |
| Drivetrain: | Front-engine RWD |
| Structure: | Superleggera |
| Transmission: | Four-speed manual |
| Weight: | 1257kg |

**PRICE GUIDE (Drophead in brackets)**

| | |
|---|---|
| Launch price: | £2622 |
| Excellent: | £180,000 (£200,000) |
| Good: | £140,000 (£160,000) |
| Average: | £100,000 (£140,000) |
| Project: | £50,000 (£70,000) |

## ASTON MARTIN
### DB MkIII/MkIII Drophead

Really the third series of DB2/4, but Aston dropped the 2/4 nomenclature for its 1957-1959 range of saloons and dropheads. The most noticeable change was a more tapering front end topped by a neater grille, there were vertical rear lights and the body was tidied. Mechanically, the engine rose marginally in capacity but was made a lot stronger and more powerful at 162bhp. Aston claimed 214bhp was possible with the competition-tuned triple-carb version, but this was probably exaggerated. Values have softened in last year.

**SPECIFICATIONS**

| | |
|---|---|
| Years produced: | 1957-1959 (551 in total) |
| Performance: | 0-60mph: 9.3sec<br>Top speed: 119mph |
| Power & torque: | 162bhp/180lb ft |
| Engine: | Normally aspirated 2922cc straight six, petrol, carburettor, 12 valves |
| Drivetrain: | Front-engine RWD |
| Structure: | Superleggera |
| Transmission: | Four-speed manual |
| Weight: | 1270kg |

**PRICE GUIDE (Drophead in brackets)**

| | |
|---|---|
| Launch price: | £3076 |
| Excellent: | £275,000 (£400,000) |
| Good: | £200,000 (£300,000) |
| Average: | £150,000 (£200,000) |
| Project: | £90,000 (£140,000) |

## ASTON MARTIN
## DB4/DB4 Convertible

The definitive Aston shape was born with the DB4 of 1958. It was massively over-engineered with a hefty chassis and new all-alloy 240bhp DOHC engine of 3.7 litres (but capable of being expanded beyond if needed). But what really grabbed the headlines was the stunning Touring Superleggera body. It was formed of aluminium panels laid over a frame of steel tubes, making the car strong but also light. Early 'Series 1' cars are highly prized, but the super-rare Convertibles (just 70 built) are the most valuable of all. Prices have stalled for now.

**SPECIFICATIONS**

| | |
|---|---|
| **Years produced:** | 1958-1963 (1183 in total) |
| **Performance:** | 0-60mph: 8.5sec<br>Top speed: 141mph |
| **Power & torque:** | 240bhp/240lb ft |
| **Engine:** | Normally aspirated 3670cc straight six, petrol, carburettor, 12 valves |
| **Drivetrain:** | Front-engine RWD |
| **Structure:** | Superleggera |
| **Transmission:** | Four-speed manual with overdrive/auto |
| **Weight:** | 1361kg |

**PRICE GUIDE (Convertible in brackets)**

| | |
|---|---|
| **Launch price:** | £3980 |
| **Excellent:** | £500,000 (£1,000,000) |
| **Good:** | £400,000 (£800,000) |
| **Average:** | £325,000 (£700,000) |
| **Project:** | £225,000 (£500,000) |

## ASTON MARTIN
## DB4 GT

With an eye on motorsport, the DB4 GT was created for the 'gentleman racer' of the day. With its wheelbase shortened by five inches, it was designed to compete head-on with the SWB Ferraris. Less length meant less weight and the twin-plug engine meant more power (302bhp), so it was a fast machine. The faired-in headlamps would later be adopted as standard on the DB5. The most thrilling and driver-focused of all the David Brown-era Astons – especially in Zagato guise (see below) – and that's reflected in today's stratospheric prices.

**SPECIFICATIONS**

| | |
|---|---|
| **Years produced:** | 1959-1961 (81 in total) |
| **Performance:** | 0-60mph: 6.4sec<br>Top speed: 152mph |
| **Power & torque:** | 302bhp/278lb ft |
| **Engine:** | Normally aspirated 3670cc straight six, petrol, carburettor, 12 valves |
| **Drivetrain:** | Front-engine RWD |
| **Structure:** | Superleggera |
| **Transmission:** | Four-speed manual |
| **Weight:** | 1277kg |

**PRICE GUIDE**

| | |
|---|---|
| **Launch price:** | £4534 |
| **Excellent:** | £2,500,000 |
| **Good:** | £2,000,000 |
| **Average:** | N/A |
| **Project:** | N/A |

## ASTON MARTIN
## DB4 GT Zagato

The rarest, most beautiful and most desirable of all post-war Astons. With the shortened chassis and highly tuned engine of the DB4 GT (but with an even higher compression ratio), and clothed in even lighter aluminium bodywork of quite exquisite proportions (the work of a young Ercole Spada), today Zagatos command vast sums. Incredible to tell, then, that the original planned run of 25 was reduced to 20 because of lack of take-up. The unused chassis numbers were eventually recycled in the 1990s with the Sanction II and III cars, which totalled a further six.

**SPECIFICATIONS**

| | |
|---|---|
| **Years produced:** | 1960-1963 (20 in total - see text) |
| **Performance:** | 0-60mph: 6.1sec<br>Top speed: 154mph |
| **Power & torque:** | 314bhp/278lb ft |
| **Engine:** | Normally aspirated 3670cc straight six, petrol, carburettor, 12 valves |
| **Drivetrain:** | Front-engine RWD |
| **Structure:** | Superleggera |
| **Transmission:** | Four-speed manual |
| **Weight:** | 1225kg |

**PRICE GUIDE**

| | |
|---|---|
| **Launch price:** | £5470 |
| **Excellent:** | £10,000,000+ |
| **Good:** | N/A |
| **Average:** | N/A |
| **Project:** | N/A |

## ASTON MARTIN
## DB5/DB5 Convertible

Had not a certain James Bond turned it into the most famous car in the world, the DB5 would be viewed as another evolution of the DB4. However, *Goldfinger* made stars of both the car and its maker. Four litres of potent power – 282bhp as standard, 314bhp for the Vantage – and long, lean looks meant the legend was largely justified. Disc brakes were now on each wheel, and all but the very earliest cars had five gears – less entertaining were the autos. Again, Convertibles (just 123 of which were made) command a huge premium.

**SPECIFICATIONS**

| | |
|---|---|
| **Years produced:** | 1963-1966 (1186 in total) |
| **Performance:** | 0-60mph: 8.1sec<br>Top speed: 141mph |
| **Power & torque:** | 282bhp/288lb ft |
| **Engine:** | Normally aspirated 3995cc straight six, petrol, carburettor, 12 valves |
| **Drivetrain:** | Front-engine RWD |
| **Structure:** | Superleggera |
| **Transmission:** | Four/five-speed manual |
| **Weight:** | 1346kg |

**PRICE GUIDE (Convertible in brackets)**

| | |
|---|---|
| **Launch price:** | £4249 |
| **Excellent:** | £700,000 (£1,300,000) |
| **Good:** | £600,000 (£1,000,000) |
| **Average:** | £500,000 (£850,000) |
| **Project:** | £400,000 (£700,000) |

## ASTON MARTIN
## DB6/DB6 Volante

A longer wheelbase meant the DB6 could seat four, although only the two up-front enjoyed real comfort. The higher roofline, split bumpers and more aerodynamic Kamm tail were the main identifying points. Extra civilisation was offered in the form of power steering, air-con and a limited-slip diff and, as was the Aston way, there was a more powerful Vantage version boasting 325bhp (add up to 20%). The Mk2, from 1969, was distinguished by flared arches and commands around 25% more. Even more valuable is the Volante (just 178 built).

**SPECIFICATIONS**

| | |
|---|---|
| **Years produced:** | 1965-1970 (1567 in total) |
| **Performance:** | 0-60mph: 6.5sec<br>Top speed: 148mph |
| **Power & torque:** | 325bhp/290lb ft |
| **Engine:** | Normally aspirated 3995cc straight six, petrol, carburettor, 12 valves |
| **Drivetrain:** | Front-engine RWD |
| **Structure:** | Spaceframe |
| **Transmission:** | Five-speed manual/three-speed auto |
| **Weight:** | 1474kg |

**PRICE GUIDE (Volante in brackets)**

| | |
|---|---|
| **Launch price:** | £4998 |
| **Excellent:** | £300,000 (£750,000) |
| **Good:** | £250,000 (£650,000) |
| **Average:** | £200,000 (£550,000) |
| **Project:** | £150,000 (£450,000) |

# ASTON MARTIN
## DBS/DBS V8

A new stylist – William Towns – meant a completely new look for Aston and an eye on the US market. The four-seater DBS was designed for a new V8, but it wasn't ready in time so the car used the DB6's 4.0-litre six with an uprated Vantage option, though the extra weight knocked performance back. The magnificent 5.3-litre V8 engine arrived in 1969, transforming the DBS into a genuine 160mph GT, though the six-cylinder continued until 1973 as the entry-level Aston. Six and eight-cylinder cars are valued similarly today.

**SPECIFICATIONS**

| | |
|---|---|
| **Years produced:** | 1967-1973 (1301 in total) |
| **Performance:** | 0-60mph: 6.0sec (V8)<br>Top speed: 162mph |
| **Power & torque:** | 315bhp/400lb ft |
| **Engine:** | Normally aspirated 5340cc V8, petrol, fuel injection, 16 valves |
| **Drivetrain:** | Front-engine RWD |
| **Structure:** | Monocoque |
| **Transmission:** | Five-speed manual/three-speed auto |
| **Weight:** | 1724kg |

**PRICE GUIDE**

| | |
|---|---|
| **Launch price:** | £5500 |
| **Excellent:** | £170,000 |
| **Good:** | £110,000 |
| **Average:** | £100,000 |
| **Project:** | £50,000 |

# ASTON MARTIN
## V8/V8 Volante

If the 1960s was Aston's golden era, the glow faded in the '70s. David Brown sold the firm in 1972, resulting in the DB initials being dropped and the V8's front end being restyled with single lights, a smaller grille and a few more curves. The engine's troublesome fuel injection was soon dropped in favour of four Weber carbs, with a large bonnet bulge to clear them. Later cars had a new electronic fuel injection system (the EFi models). There was also a Volante version, introduced in 1978, the values of which have rocketed in the last few years.

**SPECIFICATIONS**

| | |
|---|---|
| **Years produced:** | 1972-1990 (2012 in total) |
| **Performance:** | 0-60mph: 7.2sec<br>Top speed: 146mph |
| **Power & torque:** | 320bhp/360lb ft |
| **Engine:** | Normally aspirated 5340cc V8, petrol, carburettor, 16 valves |
| **Drivetrain:** | Front-engine RWD |
| **Structure:** | Monocoque |
| **Transmission:** | Five-speed manual/three-speed auto |
| **Weight:** | 1814kg |

**PRICE GUIDE (Volante in brackets)**

| | |
|---|---|
| **Launch price:** | N/A |
| **Excellent:** | £150,000 (£250,000) |
| **Good:** | £120,000 (£220,000) |
| **Average:** | £80,000 (£150,000) |
| **Project:** | £35,000 (£75,000) |

# ASTON MARTIN
## V8 Vantage/Volante

Hailed as 'Britain's first supercar,' the Vantage version of the AM V8 was tuned to a truly formidable 438bhp. The dash to 60mph took just 5.4sec; top speed was 170mph. Visually, the car could be distinguished by a blanked-off grille and bonnet scoop. Most potent of all was the X-pack version, which commands a hefty premium. There was also a mechanically identical but heavily body-kitted Volante soft-top Values of all are strong, but most sought-after is the more subtle 'PoW' version of the Vantage Volante, which can fetch up to £600,000.

**SPECIFICATIONS**

| | |
|---|---|
| **Years produced:** | 1977-1989 (429 in total) |
| **Performance:** | 0-60mph: 5.4sec<br>Top speed: 170mph |
| **Power & torque:** | 438bhp/400lb ft |
| **Engine:** | Normally aspirated 5340cc V8, petrol, fuel injection, 16 valves |
| **Drivetrain:** | Front-engine RWD |
| **Structure:** | Monocoque |
| **Transmission:** | Five-speed manual |
| **Weight:** | 1818kg |

**PRICE GUIDE (add c10% for X-pack)**

| | |
|---|---|
| **Launch price:** | £20,000 |
| **Excellent:** | £400,000 |
| **Good:** | £300,000 |
| **Average:** | £275,000 |
| **Project:** | £125,000 |

# ASTON MARTIN
## V8 Zagato & Convertible

Looking to reignite an old alliance, Aston had Zagato rebody a lightened, shortened V8 chassis. The result divided opinion; gone were the luscious curves of Zagato's Aston DB4 GT of the 1960s and in their place were brutal straight lines. But while the looks weren't to all tastes, the performance was scintillating, and with only 87 ever built, including 37 convertibles, the V8 Zagato has real appeal to Aston collectors. Convertibles tend to fetch less, except for the rare Vantage Volante version, which matches coupé prices. Rarity should help future values.

**SPECIFICATIONS**

| | |
|---|---|
| **Years produced:** | 1986-1989 (87 in total) |
| **Performance:** | 0-60mph: 5.0sec<br>Top speed: 186mph |
| **Power & torque:** | 432bhp/395lb ft |
| **Engine:** | Normally aspirated 5340cc V8, petrol, fuel injection, 16 valves |
| **Drivetrain:** | Front-engine RWD |
| **Structure:** | Monocoque |
| **Transmission:** | Five-speed manual |
| **Weight:** | 1650kg |

**PRICE GUIDE (Convertible in brackets)**

| | |
|---|---|
| **Launch price:** | £87,000 |
| **Excellent:** | £450,000 (£295,000) |
| **Good:** | £350,000 (£200,000) |
| **Average:** | £200,000 (£150,000) |
| **Project:** | N/A |

# ASTON MARTIN
## Virage/Virage Volante

After 20 years of the V8 saloon, even Aston was forced to concede that it was time for a change – the Virage, the final blast of the original V8 concept. A bold and imposing new body was designed by Royal College of Art tutors John Heffernan and Ken Greenley, and slotted over the existing V8 chassis. Despite the old-fashioned underpinnings, the car still looked sufficiently sleek and modern to revitalise Aston Martin for the 1990s. Values are finally starting to rise. The 500bhp 6.3 version is prized, and the Volantes, as ever, attract a premium.

**SPECIFICATIONS**

| | |
|---|---|
| **Years produced:** | 1989-1995 (365 in total) |
| **Performance:** | 0-60mph: 6.8sec<br>Top speed: 157mph |
| **Power & torque:** | 330bhp/350lb ft |
| **Engine:** | Normally aspirated 5340cc V8, petrol, electronic fuel injection, 32 valves |
| **Drivetrain:** | Front-engine RWD |
| **Structure:** | Monocoque |
| **Transmission:** | Five-speed manual/three-speed auto |
| **Weight:** | 1948kg |

**PRICE GUIDE (Volante in brackets)**

| | |
|---|---|
| **Launch price:** | £120,000 |
| **Excellent:** | £70,000 (£120,000) |
| **Good:** | £50,000 (£80,000) |
| **Average:** | £35,000 (£50,000) |
| **Project:** | £17,500 (£25,000) |

## ASTON MARTIN
### Vantage/V8 Coupé

There was a clear appetite for a faster Virage, and in 1993 came the full-house Vantage version with a twin-supercharged V8 providing 550bhp and 550lb ft of torque – at the time the most powerful production engine in the world. In 1998 came the V600, with an additional 50bhp – enough to propel this near-two-ton monster to a reported 200mph. Add around 20% for these. A final run of 40 'Le Mans' editions brought production to 279 (a mint Le Mans now commands £500k-plus). Also look out for the non-blown V8 Coupé, which shared much of the Vantage's styling.

**SPECIFICATIONS**

| | |
|---|---|
| **Years produced:** | 1993-2000 (279 in total) |
| **Performance:** | 0-60mph: 4.6sec<br>Top speed: 186mph |
| **Power & torque:** | 550bhp/550lb ft (V550 version) |
| **Engine:** | Twin-supercharged 5340cc V8, petrol, electronic fuel injection, 32 valves |
| **Drivetrain:** | Front-engine RWD |
| **Structure:** | Monocoque |
| **Transmission:** | Five-speed manual |
| **Weight:** | 2020kg |

**PRICE GUIDE V550 (V8 Coupé in brackets)**

| | |
|---|---|
| **Launch price:** | £185,000 |
| **Excellent:** | £200,000 (£110,000) |
| **Good:** | £135,000 (£85,000) |
| **Average:** | £100,000 (£55,000) |
| **Project:** | N/A (£27,000) |

## ASTON MARTIN
### DB7/DB7 Volante

Aston couldn't survive building handfuls of handbuilt supercars; a more affordable 'entry-level' model was needed. Ford, who had bought a majority share in AML in 1988, knew this and in 1993 launched the Ian Callum-styled DB7 – evoking memories of the 1960s line of DB cars – with a supercharged 3.2-litre straight-six and a steel monocoque that had its origins at Jaguar (also Ford-owned at the time). The DB7 was a huge success, sales eventually topping 7000 across all versions, and today it's a tempting entry-point to AM ownership.

**SPECIFICATIONS**

| | |
|---|---|
| **Years produced:** | 1993-1999 (2451 incl Volante) |
| **Performance:** | 0-60mph: 5.8sec<br>Top speed: 157mph |
| **Power & torque:** | 335bhp/361lb ft |
| **Engine:** | Supercharged 3228cc straight six, petrol, electronic injection, 32 valves |
| **Drivetrain:** | Front-engine RWD |
| **Structure:** | Monocoque |
| **Transmission:** | Five-speed manual/three-speed auto |
| **Weight:** | 1700kg |

**PRICE GUIDE (Volante in brackets)**

| | |
|---|---|
| **Launch price:** | £78,500 |
| **Excellent:** | £35,000 (£40,000) |
| **Good:** | £27,000 (£32,000) |
| **Average:** | £20,000 (£25,000) |
| **Project:** | £12,500 (£15,000) |

## ASTON MARTIN
### DB7 Vantage & Volante

In 1999 the DB7 stepped up a division when the Vantage appeared with a brand new 5.9-litre V12. It was an instant hit, sales of the i6 model drying up almost overnight. A Volante version with an electrically operated soft-top followed in 2000. Good value today, but prices have been hardening for the best examples. There was also a run-out GT coupé model with an extra 15bhp and a sportier chassis set-up. The GT and its GTA auto-gearbox sibling command a substantial premium, the best now fetching c£70k.

**SPECIFICATIONS**

| | |
|---|---|
| **Years produced:** | 1999-2003 (c4500 in total) |
| **Performance:** | 0-60mph: 4.9sec<br>Top speed: 185mph |
| **Power & torque:** | 420bhp/400lb ft |
| **Engine:** | Normally aspirated 5935cc V12, petrol, electronic injection, 48 valves |
| **Drivetrain:** | Front-engine RWD |
| **Structure:** | Monocoque |
| **Transmission:** | Six-speed manual/five-speed auto |
| **Weight:** | 1770kg |

**PRICE GUIDE (Volante in brackets)**

| | |
|---|---|
| **Launch price:** | £92,500 (£101,950) |
| **Excellent:** | £40,000 (£47,000) |
| **Good:** | £35,000 (£40,000) |
| **Average:** | £27,000 (£30,000) |
| **Project:** | N/A |

## ASTON MARTIN
### Vanquish (mk1)

Aston's flagship car in the early Noughties and the last to be built at Newport Pagnell (until the recent run of 'Continuation' models). Also the first to explore the wide use of aluminium in its main structure. Early cars had 460bhp; the Vanquish S appeared in 2004, with an increase in power to 520bhp, better brakes and a more sporting suspension set-up. In between there was a Sport Dynamic Pack ('SDP') which introduced many of the chassis improvements, and whose values today sit somewhere between the two models.

**SPECIFICATIONS**

| | |
|---|---|
| **Years produced:** | 2001-2007 (2578 in total) |
| **Performance:** | 0-60mph: 4.5sec<br>Top speed: 190mph |
| **Power & torque:** | 460bhp/400lb ft |
| **Engine:** | Normally aspirated 5935cc V12, petrol, electronic injection, 48 valves |
| **Drivetrain:** | Front-engine RWD |
| **Structure:** | Monocoque |
| **Transmission:** | Six-speed automated manual |
| **Weight:** | 1835kg |

**PRICE GUIDE (Vanquish S in brackets)**

| | |
|---|---|
| **Launch price:** | £160,000 (£174,000) |
| **Excellent:** | £90,000 (£130,000) |
| **Good:** | £80,000 (£115,000) |
| **Average:** | £70,000 (£100,000) |
| **Project:** | N/A |

## ASTON MARTIN
### DB9 & Volante

Effectively the successor to the DB7 Vantage, the DB9 was a landmark car for Aston, being the first to be built around the so-called 'VH' aluminium patform that would underpin a whole new generation of cars, and also the first to be built in the new factory at Gaydon. Quick, capable and timelessly stylish, it was an instant hit and still has immense appeal today. Note: in 2008 there was a round of revisions that included a boost in power to 470bhp – these later cars will fetch more money than the prices shown here.

**SPECIFICATIONS**

| | |
|---|---|
| **Years produced:** | 2004-2016 |
| **Performance:** | 0-60mph: 4.9sec<br>Top speed: 185mph |
| **Power & torque:** | 450bhp/420lb ft |
| **Engine:** | Normally aspirated 5935cc V12, petrol, electronic injection, 48 valves |
| **Drivetrain:** | Front-engine RWD |
| **Structure:** | Monocoque |
| **Transmission:** | Six-speed manual/six-speed auto |
| **Weight:** | 1710kg |

**PRICE GUIDE (Volante in brackets)**

| | |
|---|---|
| **Launch price:** | £103,000 (£115,000) |
| **Excellent:** | £40,000 (£45,000) |
| **Good:** | £35,000 (£40,000) |
| **Average:** | £30,000 (£35,000) |
| **Project:** | N/A |

# AUDI

AUGUST HORCH chose Audi as a name for his 1909 company because 'Horch' in German means 'hark', which equates to 'Audi' in Latin. In its early years, the marque became best-known for its luxurious and sporting big-engined cars, joining with the Wanderer, DKW and Horch firms to form Auto Union in 1932, leading to the four-ring logo. Largely dormant after WW2 because its factories were in East Germany, Auto Union was bought by Volkswagen in 1964 and the relaunched Audi brand started building front-wheel-drive cars. It came into its own in the 1980s with advanced models such as the 4wd Quattro, which saw great success in rallying. Today, Audi is one of the world's foremost prestige brands.

## AUDI 100 Coupé S

The 100 saloon was a bit like the school swot; useful to know but ultimately quite dull to be around. However, when shorn of its sensible suit and clothed in an Aston DBS-like coupé bodyshell, it suddenly started to look a little more interesting. Although never a massive seller when new, the 100S Coupé is one of those cars that became more desirable with the passage of time, as classic car enthusiasts warmed to its styling combined with thorough German engineering.That turned it into something of a cult car, with prices to match.

**SPECIFICATIONS**

| | |
|---|---|
| **Years produced:** | 1970-1976 (30,687 in total) |
| **Performance:** | 0-60mph: 10.8sec<br>Top speed: 118mph |
| **Power & torque:** | 112bhp/118lb ft |
| **Engine:** | Normally aspirated 1871cc four cylinder, petrol, carburettor, 8 valves |
| **Drivetrain:** | Front-engine RWD |
| **Structure:** | Monocoque |
| **Transmission:** | Four-speed manual |
| **Weight:** | 1082kg |

**PRICE GUIDE**

| | |
|---|---|
| **Launch price:** | £2418 |
| **Excellent:** | £20,000 |
| **Good:** | £15,000 |
| **Average:** | £10,000 |
| **Project:** | £3000 |

## AUDI 80 (B1)

Audi's first 80 was a bold step into the '70s, even if much of the engineering that underpinned it was familiar. FWD was hardly new to a company rooted in DKW and NSU, but the EA827 engine was advanced in its day – and would live on well into the 21st century. The 80 was light and efficient, and wore a sharp Gandini-penned suit. Owner VW benefited from Audi by badge-engineering the 80 to become the Passat – the car that made Wolfsburg's long wished-for move away from its air-cooled past. Double these prices for a'74/75 GTE, but all B1s are currently on the up.

**SPECIFICATIONS**

| | |
|---|---|
| **Years produced:** | 1972-1978 (1,103,766 in total) |
| **Performance:** | 0-60mph: 11.0sec<br>Top speed: 104mph |
| **Power & torque:** | 75bhp/70lb ft |
| **Engine:** | Normally aspirated 1588cc four cylinder, petrol, carburettor, 8 valves |
| **Drivetrain:** | Front-engine FWD |
| **Structure:** | Monocoque |
| **Transmission:** | Four-speed manual |
| **Weight:** | 855kg |

**PRICE GUIDE**

| | |
|---|---|
| **Launch price:** | £1275 |
| **Excellent:** | £8250 |
| **Good:** | £5000 |
| **Average:** | £3750 |
| **Project:** | £2500 |

## AUDI 80/quattro (B2)

When it came to facelifting the 80, it was up to Giugiaro to make it look like a more substantial car. He did such a good job that it became difficult to tell it apart from the 100. Like its predecessor, the 80 was light and efficient so, when it was fitted with a 1.6-litre fuel-injection engine, it was transformed into a genuinely quick sporting saloon. It was facelifted again in 1984, with smoother styling and a posher interior – and the five-cylinder cars became 90s. Getting sought-after now, and values are rising – especially for the quattro AWD version.

**SPECIFICATIONS**

| | |
|---|---|
| **Years produced:** | 1978-1986 (1,680,146 in total) |
| **Performance:** | 0-60mph: 12.1sec<br>Top speed: 104mph |
| **Power & torque:** | 85bhp/86lb ft |
| **Engine:** | Normally aspirated 1588cc four cylinder, petrol, carburettor, 8 valves |
| **Drivetrain:** | Front-engine FWD/AWD |
| **Structure:** | Monocoque |
| **Transmission:** | Five-speed manual |
| **Weight:** | 910kg |

**PRICE GUIDE (quattro in brackets)**

| | |
|---|---|
| **Launch price:** | £4650 |
| **Excellent:** | £4950 (£11,000) |
| **Good:** | £3500 (£7000) |
| **Average:** | £2000 (£4500) |
| **Project:** | £1300 (£2000) |

## AUDI 200

Audi continued its habit of producing new model designations by upping the power and equipment levels on a cooking model – in this case by adding a turbocharger to the 100 to create the 200. The new model was priced to compete with the BMW 528i and could easily outgun what was considered the pacesetter of the class. And it wasn't restrained – its quad headlamps looked brutal, while the chintzy velour-clad interior took some getting used to. A rare beast, and far more characterful than the car it was based on. '5T' turbo version is worth most.

**SPECIFICATIONS**

| | |
|---|---|
| **Years produced:** | 1979-1982 |
| **Performance:** | 0-60mph: 7.5sec<br>Top speed: 125mph |
| **Power & torque:** | 170bhp/195lb ft |
| **Engine:** | Turbocharged 2144cc five cylinder, petrol, electronic fuel injection, 10 valves |
| **Drivetrain:** | Front-engine FWD |
| **Structure:** | Monocoque |
| **Transmission:** | Five-speed manual |
| **Weight:** | 1260kg |

**PRICE GUIDE (5T in brackets)**

| | |
|---|---|
| **Launch price:** | £12,500 |
| **Excellent:** | £6500 (£10,500) |
| **Good:** | £4750 (£7000) |
| **Average:** | £3200 (£4950) |
| **Project:** | £1250 (£2250) |

## AUDI
# Quattro

Developed as a low-volume homologation special for rallying, with four-wheel drive and 200bhp of turbocharged power, the Quattro became a performance icon. Yet despite its motorsport pedigree, it was always civilised on the road. RHD and a slightly larger engine came in 1983, with the controversial digital dashboard (which you'll either love or hate) arriving the following year. Earliest cars ('80-81, lhd), identified by quad headlamps, are most sought-after: the experts at classic-audi.co.uk reckon the very best can be worth up to 50% more.

### SPECIFICATIONS
**Years produced:** 1980-1989 (11,452 in total)
**Performance:** 0-60mph: 7.1sec
Top speed: 137mph
**Power & torque:** 200bhp/210lb ft
**Engine:** Turbocharged 2144cc five cylinder, petrol, electronic fuel injection, 10 valves
**Drivetrain:** Front-engine AWD
**Structure:** Monocoque
**Transmission:** Five-speed manual
**Weight:** 1300kg

### PRICE GUIDE
**Launch price:** £14,500
**Excellent:** £30,000
**Good:** £20,000
**Average:** £15,000
**Project:** £8500

## AUDI
# Coupé/Coupé quattro

Six months after the Quattro burst onto the scene, Audi launched its lower-powered FWD sister car onto the market. Although the Coupé shared its doors and basic body with the Quattro, its slimline wheelarches and slimmer wheels meant that no-one was going to confuse the pair. A facelift in 1984 saw the Coupé's square-rigged styling softened with the arrival of wrap-around bumpers and plastic sill extensions. Solid, dependable, and desirable in top condition, with plenty of retro kudos. Parts are getting hard to come by, and quattro drivetrain components are pricey.

### SPECIFICATIONS
**Years produced:** 1980-1989 (174,687 in total)
**Performance:** 0-60mph: 9.1sec
Top speed: 122mph
**Power & torque:** 136bhp/126lb ft
**Engine:** Normally aspirated 2144/2226cc five cylinder, petrol, mechanical fuel injection
**Drivetrain:** Front-engine FWD/AWD
**Structure:** Monocoque
**Transmission:** Five-speed manual
**Weight:** 1050kg

### PRICE GUIDE (quattro in brackets)
**Launch price:** £7475
**Excellent:** £5000 (£10,000)
**Good:** £3500 (£7000)
**Average:** £1750 (£3500)
**Project:** £950 (£1750)

## AUDI
# 100/200/quattro (C3)

The trouble with the Audi 100 is that it looks too modern for its own good. It's hard to believe that the cigar-shaped executive dates back to 1982, but then it redrew the map when it arrived on the scene. Pioneering use of flush glass and an aerodynamic shape meant that the 2.2-litre version could outpace a Rover 3500 but use 30% less fuel. The 100 is still reasonably common thanks to tough build and a galvanised shell from 1985, but the 200 is endangered – a shame given its 140mph potential. Values currently holding steady, say the guys at classic-audi.co.uk.

### SPECIFICATIONS (200 Turbo)
**Years produced:** 1982-1991 (1,078,443 in total)
**Performance:** 0-60mph: 7.4sec
Top speed: 143mph
**Power & torque:** 182bhp/186lb ft
**Engine:** Turbocharged 2226cc five cylinder, petrol, fuel injection, 10 valves
**Drivetrain:** Front-engine FWD/AWD
**Structure:** Monocoque
**Transmission:** Five-speed manual
**Weight:** 1410kg

### PRICE GUIDE
**Launch price:** £8772
**Excellent:** £4500
**Good:** £3250
**Average:** £2250
**Project:** £1000

## AUDI
# 90/90 quattro

The 90 was proof positive that, as the '80s progressed, Audi was becoming increasingly ambitious. Despite being a facelift of a six-year-old car, this rebadged 80 was considered by Audi to be a credible rival to the BMW 3-Series and Mercedes-Benz 190 – and it was *just* good enough thanks to its warbling five-pot and the quattro's grippy four-wheel-drive handling. Plush interiors and Coupé-style bodykits certainly differentiated the 90 from its Plain Jane sister car, but whether that justified premium pricing was a different matter. Rare now, but the 90 has a small following.

### SPECIFICATIONS
**Years produced:** 1984-1987
**Performance:** 0-60mph: 9.7sec
Top speed: 122mph
**Power & torque:** 136bhp/137lb ft
**Engine:** Normally aspirated 2226cc five cylinder, petrol, electronic fuel injection, 10 valves
**Drivetrain:** Front-engine FWD/AWD
**Structure:** Monocoque
**Transmission:** Five-speed manual
**Weight:** 1150kg

### PRICE GUIDE (quattro in brackets)
**Launch price:** £12,500
**Excellent:** £5000 (£9000)
**Good:** £3500 (£6000)
**Average:** £2500 (£4000)
**Project:** £1500 (£2000)

## AUDI
# Sport Quattro

By 1984, the Quattro's best Group B rallying days were behind it. It was simply too big and heavy to compete with the flighty new Peugeot 205T16 – so, as a riposte, Audi lopped 20cm from the original car's wheelbase, and installed a 20-valve head on its turbo five. The rally cars met with moderate success, while the road versions proved quick if costly. They're rare and valuable now though – the best examples can fetch £400,000 and upwards – but there are many fakes out there, so make sure you're looking at a real one. The upright Audi 80 windscreen is a giveaway.

### SPECIFICATIONS
**Years produced:** 1983-1985 (214 in total)
**Performance:** 0-60mph: 4.8sec
Top speed: 155mph
**Power & torque:** 302bhp/243lb ft
**Engine:** Turbocharged 2133cc five cylinder, petrol, mechanical fuel injection, 20 valves
**Drivetrain:** Front-engine AWD
**Structure:** Monocoque
**Transmission:** Five-speed manual
**Weight:** 1000kg

### PRICE GUIDE
**Launch price:** N/A in UK
**Excellent:** £450,000
**Good:** £350,000
**Average:** N/A
**Project:** N/A

# AUDI V8

Audi was all about being upwardly mobile during the '80s, and no car it produced better embodied its ambition than the V8. Although clearly based on the 100/200, it was powered by an all-new 3.6-litre V8 and underpinned by a capable quattro drivetrain. Typically, it was also crammed with all the technology that Audi could stuff in – much of which caused problems for hapless owners down the line. It was an admirable first go at a top-line motor, but the V8 wasn't a success, and that makes it a rarity – yet one worth seeking out if you like your barges lesser-spotted.

**SPECIFICATIONS**

| | |
|---|---|
| **Years produced:** | 1988-1993 (21,564 in total) |
| **Performance:** | 0-60mph: 7.6sec<br>Top speed: 152mph |
| **Power & torque:** | 247bhp/251lb ft |
| **Engine:** | Normally aspirated 3562cc V8, petrol, electronic fuel injection, 32 valves |
| **Drivetrain:** | Front-engine AWD |
| **Structure:** | Monocoque |
| **Transmission:** | Five/six-speed manual |
| **Weight:** | 1710kg |

**PRICE GUIDE**

| | |
|---|---|
| **Launch price:** | £40,334 |
| **Excellent:** | £7000 |
| **Good:** | £5000 |
| **Average:** | £3000 |
| **Project:** | £1000 |

# AUDI Quattro 20v

The Audi Quattro was supposed to fade quietly out of production in 1988. However massive demand – especially from the UK – ensured that the old favourite remained in production long after the 80/90/Coupé from which it was derived had disappeared from the scene. To celebrate its stay of execution, Audi shoehorned in the 20-valve five-cylinder engine from the 200 and upped the output to a more-than-useful 220bhp. Of all the Quattros, these last-of-line 20v examples are by far the best to drive – and quickest to boot. Prices holding firm.

**SPECIFICATIONS**

| | |
|---|---|
| **Years produced:** | 1989-1991 (931 in total) |
| **Performance:** | 0-60mph: 6.3sec<br>Top speed: 141mph |
| **Power & torque:** | 220bhp/228lb ft |
| **Engine:** | Turbocharged 2226cc five cylinder, petrol, electronic fuel injection, 20 valves |
| **Drivetrain:** | Front-engine AWD |
| **Structure:** | Monocoque |
| **Transmission:** | Five-speed manual |
| **Weight:** | 1300kg |

**PRICE GUIDE**

| | |
|---|---|
| **Launch price:** | £32,995 |
| **Excellent:** | £60,000 |
| **Good:** | £50,000 |
| **Average:** | £40,000 |
| **Project:** | £20,000 |

# AUDI S2/RS2

The S2 Coupé (1990-95) was a high-performance version of the B3-series 80, designed to replace the Quattro 20v and inheriting its powertrain, if not its star quality. There was also an Avant estate version, which famously spawned the RS2 (left) – the first of Audi's 'RS' models. Partner Porsche squeezed 315bhp from the five-cylinder turbo engine, fettled the chassis, and supplied the huge vented disc brakes. The RS2's unique blend of performance, practicality and discreet but purposeful style makes it a genuine landmark car, reflected in high prices.

**SPECIFICATIONS (RS2)**

| | |
|---|---|
| **Years produced:** | 1994-1995 (2891 in total) |
| **Performance:** | 0-60mph: 4.8sec<br>Top speed: 163mph |
| **Power & torque:** | 315bhp/302lb ft |
| **Engine:** | Turbocharged 2226cc five cylinder, petrol, electronic fuel injection, 20v |
| **Drivetrain:** | Front-engine AWD |
| **Structure:** | Monocoque |
| **Transmission:** | Six-speed manual |
| **Weight:** | 1595kg |

**PRICE GUIDE (S2 Avant/S2 Coupé/RS2)**

| | |
|---|---|
| **Launch price:** | £32,560/£30,033/£45,705 |
| **Excellent:** | £15,000/£18,000/£50,000 |
| **Good:** | £12,000/£14,000/£35,000 |
| **Average:** | £10,000/£12,000/£30,000 |
| **Project:** | £5000/£6000/£15,000 |

# AUDI TT mk1

Concept-car looks and well-proven Audi/VW mechanicals made the TT a global hit. With 178bhp or 222bhp turbocharged four-cylinder engines, two- or four-wheel drive, and coupé or convertible body styles, there's plenty of choice. Later variants included a 3.2-litre V6, and the first appearance of VW/Audi's twin-clutch 'DSG' transmission. Most sought-after is the lightweight 237bhp quattro Sport model (2005) with its fixed-back Recaro seats (and no rear seats), the best examples of which can command £12k-plus.

**SPECIFICATIONS**

| | |
|---|---|
| **Years produced:** | 1999-2006 (c274,000 in total) |
| **Performance:** | 0-60mph: 6.1sec (225 version)<br>Top speed: 150mph |
| **Power & torque:** | 222bhp/206lb ft |
| **Engine:** | Turbocharged 1781cc four cylinder, petrol, electronic injection, 20 valves |
| **Drivetrain:** | Front-engine 4WD/FWD |
| **Structure:** | Monocoque |
| **Transmission:** | Six-speed manual/six-speed DSG |
| **Weight:** | 1395kg |

**PRICE GUIDE (225/V6 3.2/Sport)**

| | |
|---|---|
| **Launch price:** | £29,650/£29,355/£31,995 |
| **Excellent:** | £5000/£7500/£12,000 |
| **Good:** | £4000/£5000/£10,000 |
| **Average:** | £2000/£3500/£8000 |
| **Project:** | £1000/£1500/£4000 |

# AUDI RS4

Successor to the RS2, and built by Audi's new performance division, quattro GmbH, the RS4 was faster still, thanks to its Cosworth-developed, 375bhp twin-turbo V6. Mated to the latest quattro 4wd and stability systems, it delivered stunning performance in a practical package (it was only sold as an estate, or Avant in Audi-speak). Though the top speed was officially limited to 160mph, journalists on the launch found they were hitting 175mph-plus on the autobahns. Contemporary S4 model uses the same engine but in 261bhp form.

**SPECIFICATIONS**

| | |
|---|---|
| **Years produced:** | 1999-2001 (6030 in total) |
| **Performance:** | 0-60mph: 4.7sec<br>Top speed: 160mph (limited) |
| **Power & torque:** | 375bhp/324lb ft |
| **Engine:** | Twin-turbocharged 2671cc V6, petrol, electronic injection, 30 valves |
| **Drivetrain:** | Front-engine 4WD |
| **Structure:** | Monocoque |
| **Transmission:** | Six-speed manual |
| **Weight:** | 1620kg |

**PRICE GUIDE**

| | |
|---|---|
| **Launch price:** | £46,500 |
| **Excellent:** | £27,500 |
| **Good:** | £20,000 |
| **Average:** | £15,000 |
| **Project:** | N/A |

# AUSTIN

FOUNDED IN Longbridge, Birmingham in 1905, Herbert Austin's car company grew to become one of Britain's industrial powerhouses. Its early, troubled years came to an end with the hugely-popular Austin Seven of 1922, arguably the UK's first people's car. After WW2, Austin became the dominant partner in BMC, and the successful and forward-thinking models continued; not least the best-selling Mini. Economic conditions saw BMC becoming part of British Leyland in 1968 and led to troubled times symbolised by such models as the Maxi and Allegro. The 1980 Metro was a much-needed sales triumph, but the Austin name was dropped in 1987 by the then Rover Group.

## AUSTIN A40 Devon/Dorset

Austin's first step into the brave new world of flush-mounted headlamps and front-hinged doors was a raging success, with over a quarter of a million built. It's also notable for first using what would come to be known as the BMC B-series engine, here in its smallest capacity. There's still a separate chassis with hydro-mechanical brakes, but independent front suspension makes it a decent drive. Dorset is merely a two-door version of the Devon, nearly all of which went for export. More hot-rodded than standard examples survive in the UK.

**SPECIFICATIONS**

**Years produced:** 1947-1952 (289,897 in total)
**Performance:** 0-60mph: 34.8sec
Top speed: 67mph
**Power & torque:** 40bhp/57lb ft
**Engine:** Normally aspirated 1200cc four cylinder, petrol, carburettor, 8 valves
**Drivetrain:** Front-engine RWD
**Structure:** Separate chassis
**Transmission:** Four-speed manual
**Weight:** 965kg

**PRICE GUIDE**

**Launch price:** £403
**Excellent:** £5500
**Good:** £3700
**Average:** £1750
**Project:** £800

## AUSTIN A125/A135

The Sheerline was Austin's first post-war flagship car, even if its design dated back to the 1930s. The first model, designated A110, was powered by a 3.5-litre straight six, but this was soon upgraded to four litres to become the A125 – the iconic luxury car without the price. Offered in both saloon and limousine versions, these big bruisers became synonymous with the undertaking world, as well as a mainstay on mayoral fleets. Not sophisticated, nor good to drive, but effective and surprisingly popular on the classic car scene.

**SPECIFICATIONS**

**Years produced:** 1947-1956 (9000/1910 in total)
**Performance:** 0-60mph: 19.4sec
Top speed: 81mph
**Power & torque:** 125bhp/N/A
**Engine:** Normally aspirated 3990cc straight six, petrol, carburettor, 12 valves
**Drivetrain:** Front-engine RWD
**Structure:** Separate chassis
**Transmission:** Four-speed manual
**Weight:** 2000kg

**PRICE GUIDE**

**Launch price:** £1277
**Excellent:** £12,500
**Good:** £7500
**Average:** £4250
**Project:** £1750

## AUSTIN A70 Hampshire

Just like an Austin Devon, only larger (the easiest way to tell them apart is the Hampshire's rear 'skirts'). It's a tall car, designed for people who wore hats, and you can seat three abreast on both front and rear seats, making it just the thing for those extended family trips to Goodwood. The 2.2-litre engine is an overhead-valve unit carried over from the Austin 16 – strong on torque but short on gearing, so they fly up hills but run out of steam above 60mph. Probably as well – the steering's not great and half-mechanical brakes need careful setting up.

**SPECIFICATIONS**

**Years produced:** 1948-1950 (35,261 in total)
**Performance:** 0-60mph: 21.5sec
Top speed: 82mph
**Power & torque:** 64bhp/96lb ft
**Engine:** Normally aspirated 2199cc four cylinder, petrol, carburettor, 8 valves
**Drivetrain:** Front-engine RWD
**Structure:** Separate chassis
**Transmission:** Four-speed manual
**Weight:** 1270kg

**PRICE GUIDE**

**Launch price:** £608
**Excellent:** £6500
**Good:** £5000
**Average:** £2750
**Project:** £800

## AUSTIN A90 Atlantic

Quirky styling that looks more interesting now than it did to Americans in 1948. That was the car's target market but the US had cheaper options with bigger engines, and a row of chrome strips down the bonnet fooled nobody into thinking it was a Pontiac. At least the Atlantic's big four-pot found fame a little later in the Austin-Healey 100. Convertible version was launched before fabric-topped coupé, but stayed in production for only two years. By the end, in 1952, Austin had managed to shift slightly less than 8000 of them. Values currently becalmed.

**SPECIFICATIONS**

**Years produced:** 1948-1952 (7981 in total)
**Performance:** 0-60mph: 16.6sec
Top speed: 91mph
**Power & torque:** 88bhp/140lb ft
**Engine:** Normally aspirated 2660cc four cylinder, petrol, carburettor, 8 valves
**Drivetrain:** front-engine RWD
**Structure:** Separate chassis
**Transmission:** Four-speed manual
**Weight:** 1359kg

**PRICE GUIDE (Convertible in rackets)**

**Launch price:** £953
**Excellent:** £23,500 (£33,000)
**Good:** £15,000 (£20,000)
**Average:** £7500 (£11,000)
**Project:** £3500 (£4000)

## AUSTIN A40 Sports

The aluminium body is by Jensen and mounted to an Austin Devon chassis. Fun as these soft-tops are, 'Sports' is maybe pushing the idea a little too far. Still, with the help of twin carbs and larger inlet valves, the Devon engine's power was raised from 40bhp to 46bhp, so a genuine 80mph was possible. Also, to lend credibility, one was driven to victory in the 1956 RAC Rally Ladies' Cup, beating various Fords and an MGA in the process. Column-shift gearchange from 1952 is less desirable, and despite low build numbers there are still quite a few about.

**SPECIFICATIONS**

**Years produced:** 1950-1953 (4011 in total)
**Performance:** 0-60mph: 25.6sec
Top speed: 80mph
**Power & torque:** 46bhp/61lb ft
**Engine:** Normally aspirated 1200cc four cylinder, petrol, carburettor, 8 valves
**Drivetrain:** Front-engine RWD
**Structure:** Separate chassis
**Transmission:** Four-speed manual
**Weight:** 695kg

**PRICE GUIDE**

**Launch price:** £818
**Excellent:** £14,500
**Good:** £10,500
**Average:** £5000
**Project:** £3000

## AUSTIN A70 Hereford

This was the Hampshire's replacement, and in keeping with Austin's styling policy it's very much an inflated Somerset. Indeed, it can be difficult to tell those two cars apart when they're not side-by-side: they even share the same doors and rear wings. For at-a-glance recognition look out for the raised pressing around the front wheelarches and the full-width 'whiskers' below the grille. There's an improvement in power, but 68bhp is still disappointing from 2.2 litres. They are also quite thirsty, and you don't buy one for its handling.

**SPECIFICATIONS**

**Years produced:** 1950-1954 (50,421 in total)
**Performance:** 0-60mph: 21.4sec
Top speed: 81mph
**Power & torque:** 68bhp/116lb ft
**Engine:** Normally aspirated 2199cc four cylinder, petrol, carburettor, 8 valves
**Drivetrain:** Front-engine RWD
**Structure:** Separate chassis
**Transmission:** Four-speed manual
**Weight:** 1280kg

**PRICE GUIDE**

**Launch price:** £687
**Excellent:** £6500
**Good:** £4600
**Average:** £2300
**Project:** £700

## AUSTIN A30/A35

Austin's answer to the Morris Minor was lighter and more compact, but with a steering box and part-hydraulic, part-rod brakes, it doesn't feel as advanced. At first A30s came with an 803cc engine and four doors. A two-door was added in late 1953. The more usable A35 replaced it in 1956, armed with more power from the 948cc A-series engine. Visually the changes included a painted grille and a much larger rear window. Saloon production ceased in 1959, but the van went on as late as 1968, with 1098cc, then 848cc, powerplants.

**SPECIFICATIONS**

**Years produced:** 1951-1968 (527,000 in total)
**Performance:** 0-60mph: 30.1sec
Top speed: 72mph
**Power & torque:** 34bhp/50lb ft
**Engine:** Normally aspirated 948cc four cylinder, petrol, carburettor, 8 valves
**Drivetrain:** Front-engine RWD
**Structure:** Monocoque
**Transmission:** Four-speed manual
**Weight:** 685kg

**PRICE GUIDE**

**Launch price:** £507
**Excellent:** £7000
**Good:** £5000
**Average:** £3000
**Project:** £1000

## AUSTIN A40 Somerset

The successor to the Devon ensured Austin kept on churning out large numbers of quality saloons for the masses. The styling is more bulbous, but the separate chassis is much the same as before, though this time the brakes are low-maintenance hydraulics. There's another couple of bhp from the 1200cc engine, though they still won't quite hit the national speed limit. Not particularly collectible, except for the convertible version: rare in any condition, the good ones command strong money – currently double those of saloons.

**SPECIFICATIONS**

**Years produced:** 1952-1954 (173,306 in total)
**Performance:** 0-60mph: 31.6sec
Top speed: 69mph
**Power & torque:** 42bhp/62lb ft
**Engine:** Normally aspirated 1200cc four cylinder, petrol, carburettor, 8 valves
**Drivetrain:** Front-engine RWD
**Structure:** Separate chassis
**Transmission:** Four-speed manual
**Weight:** 1000kg

**PRICE GUIDE**

**Launch price:** £728
**Excellent:** £5500
**Good:** £3000
**Average:** £1500
**Project:** £600

## AUSTIN A40/A50/A55 Cambridge

Austin took a big step forward with its 1954 Cambridge saloons, finally adopting monocoque construction for its mid-sized cars. Bottom of the pile was the A40, which used the 1200cc 42bhp engine from the Somerset, while the A50 had the newly-enlarged 1489cc B-series unit and 50bhp. Customers spending the extra money for the Deluxe version were treated to additional chrome and leather. The A55 succeeded both types in 1957, with a bigger boot, fledgling fins and a larger back window. In van and pick-up form, these models lasted until 1971.

**SPECIFICATIONS**

**Years produced:** 1954-1958 (299,500 in total)
**Performance:** 0-60mph: 28.8sec
Top speed: 74mph
**Power & torque:** 50bhp/74lb ft
**Engine:** Normally aspirated 1489cc four cylinder, petrol, carburettor, 8 valves
**Drivetrain:** Front-engine, RWD
**Structure:** Monocoque
**Transmission:** Four-speed manual
**Weight:** 1118kg

**PRICE GUIDE**

**Launch price:** £650
**Excellent:** £5000
**Good:** £3250
**Average:** £1500
**Project:** £750

## AUSTIN
## A90/A95/A105 Westminster

Although it looked like a glammed-up version of the Cambridge, it shared only the same doors as its smaller sibling. The 2.6-litre C-series put out a mere 85bhp, meaning performance was leisurely. This was addressed with the A95 and A105 of 1956, the former getting 92bhp, the latter 102bhp. Together with its lower suspension, standard overdrive and two-tone paint, the A105 was almost sporty, with a top speed approaching 100mph. For the ultimate in Westminster appeal, there was a Vanden Plas version, dripping with leather.

**SPECIFICATIONS**

| | |
|---|---|
| **Years produced:** | 1954-1959 (60,367 in total) |
| **Performance:** | 0-60mph: 19.8sec<br>Top speed: 90mph |
| **Power & torque:** | 92bhp/130lb ft |
| **Engine:** | Normally aspirated 2639cc straight six, petrol, carburettor, 12 valves |
| **Drivetrain:** | Front-engine RWD |
| **Structure:** | Monocoque |
| **Transmission:** | Four-speed manual |
| **Weight:** | 1100kg |

**PRICE GUIDE**

| | |
|---|---|
| **Launch price:** | £792 |
| **Excellent:** | £9000 |
| **Good:** | £5750 |
| **Average:** | £2250 |
| **Project:** | £1200 |

## AUSTIN
## Metropolitan

Never actually badged an Austin, the Metropolitan was originally made solely for Nash in America, which wanted a small car but had no experience of building one. This explains the bumper-car-like American styling. On sale in the UK from 1957, the car had by then been given the 1489cc B-series in place of the original 1200. One strange quirk is the three-speed gearbox, an A50 four-speed with the slot for first blanked off. Both hardtop and convertible versions were made, and about equal numbers of each survive in the UK.

**SPECIFICATIONS**

| | |
|---|---|
| **Years produced:** | 1954-1956 |
| **Performance:** | 0-60mph: 22.4sec<br>Top speed: 70mph |
| **Power & torque:** | 42bhp/58lb ft |
| **Engine:** | Normally aspirated 1200cc four cylinder, petrol, carburettor, 8 valves |
| **Drivetrain:** | Front-engine RWD |
| **Structure:** | Monocoque |
| **Transmission:** | Three-speed manual |
| **Weight:** | 810kg |

**PRICE GUIDE (Convertible in brackets)**

| | |
|---|---|
| **Launch price:** | N/A |
| **Excellent:** | £13,500 (£17,000) |
| **Good:** | £9500 (£11,000) |
| **Average:** | £4750 (£5500) |
| **Project:** | £2000 (£2500) |

## AUSTIN
## A30/35 Countryman

Introduced in September 1954 – so you won't find many A30 versions – the Countryman is a tiny estate created by fitting back seats, a full headlining and two-piece sliding rear side windows to the A30 van. Many vans have since been converted to look like a Countryman (an okay alternative, but don't pay the Countryman premium for one of these). As a giveaway, many conversions use fixed side windows and fail to remove the van's vent roof. Also, only the A30 and early A35 versions have van-style indent pressings in the doors. Values currently edging up.

**SPECIFICATIONS**

| | |
|---|---|
| **Years produced:** | 1954-1962 |
| **Performance:** | 0-60mph: 31.0sec<br>Top speed: 73mph |
| **Power & torque:** | 34bhp/50lb ft |
| **Engine:** | Normally aspirated 948cc four cylinder, petrol, carburettor, 8 valves |
| **Drivetrain:** | Front-engine RWD |
| **Structure:** | Monocoque |
| **Transmission:** | Four-speed manual |
| **Weight:** | 749kg |

**PRICE GUIDE**

| | |
|---|---|
| **Launch price:** | £541 |
| **Excellent:** | £8000 |
| **Good:** | £5500 |
| **Average:** | £3500 |
| **Project:** | £1500 |

## AUSTIN
## A40 Farina

The unassuming Austin A40 Farina is one of the marque's most significant models ever. Why? Well it was the first Pininfarina-styled BMC car, the first 'two-box' design and, in Countryman estate form with a split tailgate, has a claim to fame as one of the first hatchbacks. The 1958 car that would inform so many future models was mainly Austin A35 underneath its Italian suit, even down to the inferior hydro-mechanical brakes. Fortunately, these were changed to hydraulic on the 1961 MkII, while 1962 saw a 1098cc A-series slotted in. Values holding.

**SPECIFICATIONS**

| | |
|---|---|
| **Years produced:** | 1958-1967 (364,064 in total) |
| **Performance:** | 0-60mph: 27.1sec<br>Top speed: 82mph |
| **Power & torque:** | 48bhp/60lb ft |
| **Engine:** | Normally aspirated 948cc four cylinder, petrol, carburettor, 8 valves |
| **Drivetrain:** | Front-engine RWD |
| **Structure:** | Monocoque |
| **Transmission:** | Four-speed manual |
| **Weight:** | 761kg |

**PRICE GUIDE**

| | |
|---|---|
| **Launch price:** | £639 |
| **Excellent:** | £5500 |
| **Good:** | £3500 |
| **Average:** | £1750 |
| **Project:** | £650 |

## AUSTIN
## Gipsy

The failure of the Champ might have been ringing in its ears, but that didn't stop Austin having another go at building a Land Rover beater. The second time around, it produced a car that many casual observers thought was Solihull's latest product. The Gipsy was available with a petrol or diesel engine and offered with two wheelbases. It had an all-steel body, and innovative Moulton Flexitor suspension, but these weren't big enough advantages to tempt people out of their Land Rovers. Rust claimed many, but values of the survivors are strong.

**SPECIFICATIONS**

| | |
|---|---|
| **Years produced:** | 1958-1968 (21,208 in total) |
| **Performance:** | 0-60mph: N/A<br>Top speed: 65mph |
| **Power & torque:** | 62bhp/102lb ft |
| **Engine:** | Normally aspirated 2199cc four cylinder, petrol, carburettor, 8 valves |
| **Drivetrain:** | Front-engine AWD |
| **Structure:** | Separate chassis |
| **Transmission:** | Four-speed manual |
| **Weight:** | 1010kg |

**PRICE GUIDE**

| | |
|---|---|
| **Launch price:** | N/A |
| **Excellent:** | £10,000 |
| **Good:** | £6000 |
| **Average:** | £3500 |
| **Project:** | £1500 |

## AUSTIN
### A99/A110 Westminster

Pininfarina's finest BMC moment was the 1959-'68 Westminster series; the larger canvas suited the angular lines and resulted in a suitably prestigious machine. A twin-carb C-series engine pumped up to 3 litres coupled with a three-speed transmission allowed stately progress with reasonable haste if pushed. Servo-assisted front disc brakes added to the enjoyment. 1961's A110 was even better, but the ultimate Westminster was the MkII of 1964, which gained four gears for the model's final four years of production.

**SPECIFICATIONS**

**Years produced:** 1959-1968 (41,250 in total)
**Performance:** 0-60mph: 14.4sec
Top speed: 98mph
**Power & torque:** 103bhp/165lb ft
**Engine:** Normally aspirated 2912cc straight six, petrol, carburettor, 12 valves
**Drivetrain:** Front-engine RWD
**Structure:** Monocoque
**Transmission:** Four-speed manual/three-speed auto
**Weight:** 1530kg

**PRICE GUIDE**

**Launch price:** £1149
**Excellent:** £8000
**Good:** £4750
**Average:** £2000
**Project:** £1000

## AUSTIN/MORRIS
### Cambridge/Oxford

Pininfarina styled the Austin Cambridge A55/A60 and Morris Oxford V/VI for the 1960s and turned in a smart job. As fins were fashionable, the Farina twins wore them, but their underpinnings were much the same as with the previous Cambridge. The 1489cc motors struggled to shift these heavy models but, in 1961, the engine was enlarged to 1622cc for the A60 and Oxford VI. BMC badge engineering was at its height, and resulted in Wolseley, Riley and MG versions, too. Values for Morris and Austin very similar, although the former lived two years longer.

**SPECIFICATIONS (A55)**

**Years produced:** 1959-1969/1971 (426,500/296,255 total)
**Performance:** 0-60mph: 23.0sec
Top speed: 78mph
**Power & torque:** 52bhp/82lb ft
**Engine:** Normally aspirated 1489cc four cylinder, petrol, carburettor, 8 valves
**Drivetrain:** Front-engine RWD
**Structure:** Monocoque
**Transmission:** Four-speed manual
**Weight:** 1118/1054kg

**PRICE GUIDE**

**Launch price:** £802
**Excellent:** £4500
**Good:** £3000
**Average:** £1250
**Project:** £600

## AUSTIN/MORRIS
### 1100/1300/1300GT

BMC badge engineering ran rampant with the 1100/1300 range, Alec Issigonis' extension of his Mini concept using front-wheel drive, front disc brakes, interconnected Hydrolastic fluid suspension and a Tardis-like interior. Performance was lively thanks to the A-series engines, in 1098cc and (from 1967) 1275cc sizes, and handling came close to Mini standards. All rusted ferociously. Great to drive, though 1100s are undergeared for the motorway. Vinyl-roofed GT (pictured) had twin-carb 70bhp 1275cc engine, lifting the top speed to 93mph.

**SPECIFICATIONS**

**Years produced:** 1963/1962-1974 (1,200,00 in total)
**Performance:** 0-60mph: 17.3sec (1300)
Top speed: 87mph
**Power & torque:** 60bhp/69lb ft
**Engine:** Normally aspirated 1275cc four cylinder, petrol, carburettor, 8 valves
**Drivetrain:** Front-engine FWD
**Structure:** Monocoque
**Transmission:** Four-speed manual
**Weight:** 776kg

**PRICE GUIDE (GT in brackets)**

**Launch price:** £593 (£910)
**Excellent:** £3500 (£7000)
**Good:** £1850 (£3500)
**Average:** £1100 (£2000)
**Project:** £400 (£800)

## AUSTIN/MORRIS
### 1800/2200

After the Mini and 1100/1300 range, the 1800/2200 models were expected to complete Alec Issigonis' successful hat-trick of BMC front-wheel-drive cars. But they didn't – and that was down to building the new car around the MGB-tune B-series engine, which Issigonis exploited to make a larger car than was necessary. Despite the 1800 winning the Car of the Year award in 1964, sales were disappointing. Over-engineered and with Hydrolastic suspension, the ungainly looks and austere interior counted against them. Best had with power steering.

**SPECIFICATIONS (1800)**

**Years produced:** 1964-1975/1966-1975 (315,000 in total)
**Performance:** 0-60mph: 17.1sec
Top speed: 90mph
**Power & torque:** 85bhp/90lb ft
**Engine:** Normally aspirated 1798cc four cylinder, petrol, carburettor, 8 valves
**Drivetrain:** Front-engine FWD
**Structure:** Monocoque
**Transmission:** Four-speed manual
**Weight:** 1200kg

**PRICE GUIDE**

**Launch price:** £769
**Excellent:** £3500
**Good:** £1800
**Average:** £1000
**Project:** £350

## AUSTIN
### 3-Litre

After the handsome Westminster, the 3-Litre – its 1967 replacement – was a big disappointment. Big was the operative word, but being saddled with the centre section of the 1800/2200 with a long bonnet and boot tacked on either end did not make it attractive. The cabin was massive, but at the expense of much of the usual luxury and traditional design that buyers expected in a car of this class. Rear-wheel drive and a 2.9-litre engine shared with the MGC gave reasonable performance, yet prestige was lacking... thus, so were sales.

**SPECIFICATIONS**

**Years produced:** 1968-1971 (9992 in total)
**Performance:** 0-60mph: 15.7sec
Top speed: 100mph
**Power & torque:** 124bhp/163lb ft
**Engine:** Normally aspirated 2912cc straight six, petrol, carburettor, 12 valves
**Drivetrain:** Front-engine RWD
**Structure:** Monocoque
**Transmission:** Four-speed manual
**Weight:** 1524kg

**PRICE GUIDE**

**Launch price:** £1418
**Excellent:** £6500
**Good:** £3350
**Average:** £1750
**Project:** £1000

# AUSTIN-HEALEY

RACER AND engineer Donald Healey built cars from 1945 onwards, but real success eluded him until his Healey 100 of 1952 was noticed by Austin boss Leonard Lord. Austin agreed to build the Healey, using its mechanical parts and, thus, Austin-Healey as a marque was formed, intended as a sort of Austin-centric version of MG. The 'Big' Healeys – the 100, 100/6 and 3000 models – were later joined by the smaller Austin-Healey Sprite, a small, cheap and cheerful roadster. Things soured with the formation of British Leyland in 1968; the 3000 came to an end the same year and the Sprite continued until 1971, when the Austin and Healey deal was finally cancelled.

## AUSTIN-HEALEY 100/100M

What was originally the Healey 100 became the Austin-Healey 100 overnight when Leonard Lord of BMC saw it at the 1952 London Motor Show and liked it enough to offer to build it, with the four-cylinder 2660cc engine from the A90 Atlantic. The USA took the 100 to its heart, and the car was an instant success there, while a race programme led to the legendary 100S. Specialist Jon Scott-Nelson reckons on adding a 10% premium for the BN2 version, while the rare, high-performance M version (110bhp, bonnet straps, etc) can fetch up to £200k.

**SPECIFICATIONS**

**Years produced:** 1953-1956 (c15,000 in total)
**Performance:** 0-60mph: 10.3sec
Top speed: 103mph
**Power & torque:** 90bhp/144lb ft
**Engine:** Normally aspirated 2660cc four cylinder, petrol, carburettor, 8 valves
**Drivetrain:** Front-engine RWD
**Structure:** Separate chassis
**Transmission:** Three-speed with overdrive
**Weight:** 975kg

**PRICE GUIDE (100M in brackets)**

**Launch price:** £1064
**Excellent:** £90,000 (£200,000)
**Good:** £60,000 (£150,000)
**Average:** £40,000 (£120,000)
**Project:** £30,000 (£70,000)

## AUSTIN-HEALEY 100S

Created so the marque could have a greater visibility in motorsport than a handful of works cars would allow, 50 examples of the 100S were built, of which only six stayed in the UK. The 'S' refers to the Sebring 12-hour race in Florida, where a prototype finished a surprise third in 1954. Based on the 100, the 100S had a stiffer chassis and more aluminium body panels. Brakes were discs front and rear. The engines had the same capacity but a different block casting and aluminium Weslake head. Larger SU carburettors were fitted and the result was 132bhp.

**SPECIFICATIONS**

**Years produced:** 1954-1955 (50 in total)
**Performance:** 0-60mph: 7.8sec
Top speed: 119mph
**Power & torque:** 132bhp/168lb ft
**Engine:** Normally aspirated 2660cc four cylinder, petrol, carburettor, 8 valves
**Drivetrain:** Front-engine RWD
**Structure:** Separate chassis
**Transmission:** Four-speed manual
**Weight:** 873kg

**PRICE GUIDE**

**Launch price:** Special order only
**Excellent:** £700,000+
**Good:** £600,000
**Average:** £500,000
**Project:** N/A

## AUSTIN-HEALEY 100/6

The success of the 100 convinced BMC it had a bright future, but the Austin four-cylinder engine was due to cease manufacture in 1956. No problem: the Westminster's 2639cc straight-six took its place. In fact the heavier unit sapped performance until a new cylinder head and manifolds boosted power to 117bhp. Other changes included an oval grille and 2+2 seating, although the latter wasn't particularly well regarded and was dispensed with after just two years. Longbridge-built cars are rarer and tend to be more soughtafter and hence worth slightly more.

**SPECIFICATIONS**

**Years produced:** 1956-1959 (14,436 in total)
**Performance:** 0-60mph: 12.9sec
Top speed: 103mph
**Power & torque:** 102bhp/142lb ft
**Engine:** Normally aspirated 2639cc straight six, petrol, carburettor, 12 valves
**Drivetrain:** Front-engine RWD
**Structure:** Separate chassis
**Transmission:** Four-speed with overdrive
**Weight:** 1105kg

**PRICE GUIDE**

**Launch price:** £1144
**Excellent:** £70,000
**Good:** £45,000
**Average:** £35,000
**Project:** £20,000

## AUSTIN-HEALEY 3000 MkI/MkII

The first generation of the 'Big' Healey arrived in 1959, when the C-series engine from the 100/6 was upgraded to three litres. Although there was no change of styling, the mechanical alterations – more power, a better gearbox and disc brakes on the front – were thought significant enough to merit the change of model designation. The option of 2+2 seating was reintroduced. The MkII, introduced in 1961, brough a curved front windscreen, a more user-friendly hood and 2+2 seating as standard. Tri-carb two-seater 'BN7' particularly prized.

**SPECIFICATIONS**

**Years produced:** 1959-1962 (29,276 in total)
**Performance:** 0-60mph: 11.2sec (MkI)
Top speed: 111mph
**Power & torque:** 117bhp/149lb ft
**Engine:** Normally aspirated 2912cc straight six, petrol, carburettor, 8 valves
**Drivetrain:** Front-engine RWD
**Structure:** Separate chassis
**Transmission:** Four-speed manual with overdrive
**Weight:** 1143kg

**PRICE GUIDE (BN7 tri-carb in brackets)**

**Launch price:** £1159
**Excellent:** £70,000 (£120,000)
**Good:** £50,000 (£90,000)
**Average:** £35,000 (£70,000)
**Project:** £20,000 (£35,000)

## AUSTIN-HEALEY Sprite MkI

The original Sprite was a cheap and cheerful mass-produced sporting convertible that was also tremendous fun. Cheeky looks – those 'frogeye' headlamps were initially planned to be retractable until it was realised that would put the price up – distracted from the fact that underneath the skin the car was mainly a blend of Austin A35 and Morris Minor. However, that still meant entertaining performance. Prices today, still climbin, are out of all proportion to the budget origins; these are now dear machines in more ways than one!

### SPECIFICATIONS

| | |
|---|---|
| **Years produced:** | 1958-1961 (48,987 in total) |
| **Performance:** | 0-60mph: 20.5sec<br>Top speed: 86mph |
| **Power & torque:** | 43bhp/52lb ft |
| **Engine:** | Normally aspirated 948cc four cylinder, petrol, carburettor, 8 valves |
| **Drivetrain:** | Front-engine RWD |
| **Structure:** | Monocoque |
| **Transmission:** | Four-speed manual |
| **Weight:** | 602kg |

### PRICE GUIDE

| | |
|---|---|
| **Launch price:** | £669 |
| **Excellent:** | £25,000 |
| **Good:** | £20,000 |
| **Average:** | £15,000 |
| **Project:** | £8000 |

## AUSTIN-HEALEY Sprite MkII/III/IV

The 1961 MkII was an effort to modernise the Sprite. Though it took away much of the car's character, it was still affordable and enjoyable, and at least passengers now had an opening boot. From 1962, there was a bigger 1098cc engine plus front disc brakes, but buyers had to wait until the MkIII of 1964 for door handles and winding windows. The MkIV of 1966 brough the 1275cc engine and near-100mph potential. Production finished in 1971 with the end of BMC's arrangement with Healey, but the Sprite's MG Midget sibling soldiered on until 1979.

### SPECIFICATIONS

| | |
|---|---|
| **Years produced:** | 1961-1971 (c80,000 in total) |
| **Performance:** | 0-60mph: 20.0sec<br>Top speed: 85mph |
| **Power & torque:** | 46bhp/53lb ft |
| **Engine:** | Normally aspirated 948cc four cylinder, petrol, carburettor, 8 valves |
| **Drivetrain:** | Front-engine RWD |
| **Structure:** | Monocoque |
| **Transmission:** | Four-speed manual |
| **Weight:** | 700kg |

### PRICE GUIDE

| | |
|---|---|
| **Launch price:** | £670 |
| **Excellent:** | £9000 (up to £11,000 for MkII) |
| **Good:** | £6500 |
| **Average:** | £4000 |
| **Project:** | £1750 |

## AUSTIN-HEALEY 3000 MkIII

The final version of the Big Healey appeared in 1964. Although the looks remained largely the same, this was the most powerful Austin-Healey ever, its 148bhp output making for a top speed of 121mph. The Phase 2 versions had revised rear suspension which improved handling. However, the end was nigh for the Healey and the final car was built in March 1968. Many mourned its passing, and its replacement, the MGC, failed to impress buyers in the same way. Values have levelled off, making a MkIII good value, says Jon Scott-Nelson.

### SPECIFICATIONS

| | |
|---|---|
| **Years produced:** | 1964-1968 (17,712 in total) |
| **Performance:** | 0-60mph: 9.8sec<br>Top speed: 121mph |
| **Power & torque:** | 148bhp/165lb ft |
| **Engine:** | Normally aspirated 2912cc straight six, petrol, carburettor, 12 valves |
| **Drivetrain:** | Front-engine RWD |
| **Structure:** | Separate chassis |
| **Transmission:** | Four-speed manual with overdrive |
| **Weight:** | 1180kg |

### PRICE GUIDE

| | |
|---|---|
| **Launch price:** | £1108 |
| **Excellent:** | £90,000 |
| **Good:** | £75,000 |
| **Average:** | £55,000 |
| **Project:** | £27,250 |

# BENTLEY

BENTLEY

THE FIRST Bentley appeared at the 1919 London Motor Show and, within a few years, the cars had become the darlings of rich playboys who delighted in taking them racing. Brooklands and Le Mans were two of the famous venues dominated by the marque. But, in 1931, Bentley was bought by Rolls-Royce and its sporting glories started to fade. Although there were glorious moments such as the 1952-1955 R-type Continental, eventually the cars became little more than badge-engineered RRs. In the 1980s, though, the marque re-emerged from the shadow of its parent, with more emphasis on performance. Now owned by VW, Bentleys are once again sporting and individualistic machines.

## BENTLEY MkVI

The first of the postwar Bentleys was also the first with a steel body as standard, although many buyers still took the coachbuilding route. Its chassis was quite advanced for the time, with independent front suspension, servo brakes, a four-speed gearbox and the very useful centralised chassis lubrication system. The 4526cc (4566cc from 1951) straight six gained a reputation for sturdiness; not so the standard body which, despite its painstaking handbuilt construction, showed an unfortunate tendency to rust. Values holding.

### SPECIFICATIONS

| | |
|---|---|
| **Years produced:** | 1946-1955 (5201 in total) |
| **Performance:** | 0-60mph: 15.2sec<br>Top speed: 100mph |
| **Power & torque:** | N/Q/N/Q |
| **Engine:** | Normally aspirated 4526cc straight six, petrol, carburettor, 12 valves |
| **Drivetrain:** | Front-engine RWD |
| **Structure:** | Separate chassis |
| **Transmission:** | Four-speed manual |
| **Weight:** | 1816kg |

### PRICE GUIDE

| | |
|---|---|
| **Launch price:** | £2997 |
| **Excellent:** | £55,000 |
| **Good:** | £40,000 |
| **Average:** | £20,000 |
| **Project:** | £10,000 |

# BENTLEY R-Type

With the standard steel body fitted, the 1952-1955 R-Type looked a lot like the MkVI – something the marque's traditional customers no doubt approved of. However, there was extra grace to the design thanks to the more flowing lines and a capacious boot. The same 4566cc straight-six engine as on the MkVI continued, but with the option of a four-speed auto from 1952. For 1953 there was a dashboard revamp, but the most exciting developments with the R-Type were saved for the Continental models. Values remain strong, say specialists Hillier Hill.

**SPECIFICATIONS**

| | |
|---|---|
| **Years produced:** | 1952-1955 (2320 in total) |
| **Performance:** | 0-60mph: 15.0sec<br>Top speed: 101mph |
| **Power & torque:** | N/Q/N/Q |
| **Engine:** | Normally aspirated 4566cc straight six, petrol, carburettor, 12 valves |
| **Drivetrain:** | Front-engine RWD |
| **Structure:** | Separate chassis |
| **Transmission:** | Four-speed manual/three-speed auto |
| **Weight:** | 1816kg |

**PRICE GUIDE**

| | |
|---|---|
| **Launch price:** | £4474 |
| **Excellent:** | £65,000 |
| **Good:** | £40,000 |
| **Average:** | £25,000 |
| **Project:** | £10,000 |

# BENTLEY R-Type Continental

HJ Mulliner's Bentley Continental variant of the R-Type was pure automotive art. Looking far more modern than its 1952 origins, the sublime fastback shape, with the back wheels concealed by the curvaceous rear wings, was constructed from light alloy. The streamlined shape and lower weight helped the performance, as did the 4887cc engine that found its way into the final cars, with a top speed of nigh-on 120mph; far faster than the saloon versions. Hugely expensive now – concours cars regularly breach the £1m barrier.

**SPECIFICATIONS**

| | |
|---|---|
| **Years produced:** | 1952-1955 (208 in total) |
| **Performance:** | 0-60mph: 13.8sec<br>Top speed: 117mph |
| **Power & torque:** | N/Q/N/Q |
| **Engine:** | Normally aspirated 4566cc straight six, petrol, carburettor, 12 valves |
| **Drivetrain:** | Front-engine RWD |
| **Structure:** | Separate chassis |
| **Transmission:** | Four-speed manual/three-speed auto |
| **Weight:** | 1651kg |

**PRICE GUIDE**

| | |
|---|---|
| **Launch price:** | £7608 |
| **Excellent:** | £1,000,000+ |
| **Good:** | £750,0000+ |
| **Average:** | £500,000+ |
| **Project:** | £350,000+ |

# BENTLEY S1 saloon

As striking as the S1 certainly was, it was also the Rolls-Royce Silver Cloud with a different grille and badges. However, gone were the traditional pre-war looks as in came a very sleek integrated body built out of aluminium alloy. The straight-six engine was enlarged to 4887cc and improved brakes and front suspension were adopted, with a power-steering option from 1956. Bentleys outsold their Rolls-Royce counterparts, so are generally cheaper than their Spirit of Ecstasy cousins. Values holding firm, say specialists Hillier Hill

**SPECIFICATIONS**

| | |
|---|---|
| **Years produced:** | 1955-1959 (3072 in total) |
| **Performance:** | 0-60mph: 14.2sec<br>Top speed: 101mph |
| **Power & torque:** | N/Q/N/Q |
| **Engine:** | Normally aspirated 4887cc straight six, petrol, carburettor, 8 valves |
| **Drivetrain:** | Front-engine RWD |
| **Structure:** | Separate chassis |
| **Transmission:** | Four-speed manual/three-speed auto |
| **Weight:** | 1880kg |

**PRICE GUIDE**

| | |
|---|---|
| **Launch price:** | £4669 |
| **Excellent:** | £65,000 |
| **Good:** | £35,000 |
| **Average:** | £20,000 |
| **Project:** | £10,000 |

# BENTLEY S1 Continental

While there was nothing that scaled the heights of the R, the Continental S-Types – constructed by a variety of different builders – were almost universally elegant. Most special are the 151 fastbacks by HJ Mulliner, followed by the 99 Park Ward coupés, and both Mulliner and James Young weighed in with four-door versions. Special permission needed to be obtained from Rolls-Royce for these to be built. The most innovative S1s were made by Hooper, and Franay and Graber did one each. A small number of dropheads accompanied the coupés.

**SPECIFICATIONS**

| | |
|---|---|
| **Years produced:** | 1955-1959 (431 in total) |
| **Performance:** | 0-60mph: 12.9sec<br>Top speed: 119mph |
| **Power & torque:** | N/Q/N/Q |
| **Engine:** | Normally aspirated 4887cc straight six, petrol, carburettor, 12 valves |
| **Drivetrain:** | Front-engine RWD |
| **Structure:** | Separate chassis |
| **Transmission:** | Three-speed auto/four-speed manual |
| **Weight:** | 1930kg |

**PRICE GUIDE**

| | |
|---|---|
| **Launch price:** | £6127 |
| **Excellent:** | £450,000-£1,000,000+ depending on body |
| **Good:** | £375,000 |
| **Average:** | £270,000 |
| **Project:** | £150,000 |

# BENTLEY S2 saloon

By 1959 it was time to replace the Rolls-Royce/Bentley straight-six inlet-over-exhaust-valve engines, and what better than a chunky V8 for a company with its eyes on the American market? The 6230cc unit installed in the S2 was smoothly powerful and transformed the Bentley into a silky grand tourer that could waft around all day. Power-steering and automatic transmission were standard fitments, but there was very little to distinguish an S2 from an S1 visually. Drophead coupé and Continental versions were also built.

**SPECIFICATIONS**

| | |
|---|---|
| **Years produced:** | 1959-1962 (1863 in total) |
| **Performance:** | 0-60mph: 11.5sec<br>Top speed: 113mph |
| **Power & torque:** | N/Q/N/Q |
| **Engine:** | Normally aspirated 6230cc V8, petrol, carburettor, 16 valves |
| **Drivetrain:** | Front-engine RWD |
| **Structure:** | Separate chassis |
| **Transmission:** | Three-speed auto/four-speed manual |
| **Weight:** | 1981kg |

**PRICE GUIDE**

| | |
|---|---|
| **Launch price:** | £5661 |
| **Excellent:** | £65,000 |
| **Good:** | £35,000 |
| **Average:** | £20,000 |
| **Project:** | £10,000 |

## BENTLEY
## S2/S3 Flying Spur

Continental chassis were intended just for two-door Bentleys but, in 1957, HJ Mulliner was given special dispensation to build variations with four doors. These graceful cars were christened Flying Spurs and featured bigger boots than their more racy-looking two-door counterparts. The same changes made to the S2 and S3 saloons were also applied to the Flying Spur, so in 1959 there came the 6230cc V8 engine and, for 1962, twin headlamps were adopted. These final cars were considered the most handsome of the bunch.

### SPECIFICATIONS

**Years produced:** 1959-1965
**Performance:** 0-60mph: 12.3sec
Top speed: 120mph
**Power & torque:** N/Q/N/Q
**Engine:** Normally aspirated 6230cc V8, petrol, carburettor, 16 valves
**Drivetrain:** Front-engine RWD
**Structure:** Separate chassis
**Transmission:** Three-speed automatic
**Weight:** 1981kg

### PRICE GUIDE

**Launch price:** £6127
**Excellent:** £175,000
**Good:** £120,000
**Average:** £85,000
**Project:** £45,000

## BENTLEY
## S3 saloon

Hullabaloo surrounded the Bentley S3 of 1962-'65 because of its twin headlamps. There were other, less revolutionary touches as well in the form of restyled front wings, a lower bonnet line and improved appointments inside. Mechanically, some of the criticisms were answered with a higher-compression V8 engine and more effective power-steering. Alongside the saloons were the usual long-wheelbase version, a drophead coupé and some startling Continental creations that made intriguing use of the double light units.

### SPECIFICATIONS

**Years produced:** 1962-1965 (1286 in total)
**Performance:** 0-60mph: 11.5sec
Top speed: 113mph
**Power & torque:** N/Q/N/Q
**Engine:** Normally aspirated 6230cc V8, petrol, carburettor, 16 valves
**Drivetrain:** Front-engine RWD
**Structure:** Separate chassis
**Transmission:** Three-speed automatic
**Weight:** 2077kg

### PRICE GUIDE

**Launch price:** £6127
**Excellent:** £70,000
**Good:** £45,000
**Average:** £25,000
**Project:** £15,000

## BENTLEY
## T1/T2

1965's T-series was exactly the same as the Rolls-Royce Silver Shadows save for some minute details. This was the first of the marque to have unitary construction, which made it more difficult for coachbuilders to magic up alternative versions. Disc brakes featured on all wheels, as did self-levelling suspension. The V8 engine increased to 6750cc in 1970, while the T2 of 1977 had plastic bumpers, a revised dashboard and sharper rack-and-pinion steering. Values are firm, say specialists Hillier Hill, particularly for early 'Chippendale' dashboard cars.

### SPECIFICATIONS

**Years produced:** 1965-1980 (1712 in total)
**Performance:** 0-60mph: 10.9sec
Top speed: 115mph
**Power & torque:** N/Q/N/Q
**Engine:** Normally aspirated 6230cc V8, petrol, carburettor, 16 valves
**Drivetrain:** Front-engine RWD
**Structure:** Monocoque
**Transmission:** Three-speed automatic
**Weight:** 2113kg

### PRICE GUIDE

**Launch price:** £6496
**Excellent:** £50,000+
**Good:** £30,000
**Average:** £15,000
**Project:** £6000

## BENTLEY
## Corniche

The Rolls-Royce Shadow/Bentley T-series soon spawned two-door coupé and convertibles models, which became known officially as Corniches from 1971. These were Britain's most expensive cars at the time, with the mechanical layout of the Shadow but even more lavish levels of equipment. Bentley versions weren't popular when new, but their rarity now makes them very desirable, say specialists Hillier-Hill, with values pulling away from Shadow/T-series saloons. Dropheads, known as Continentals from 1984, command up to a third more.

### SPECIFICATIONS

**Years produced:** 1971-1987
**Performance:** 0-60mph: 9.7sec
Top speed: 126mph
**Power & torque:** N/A
**Engine:** Normally aspirated 6750cc V8, petrol, carburettor, 16 valves
**Drivetrain:** Front-engine RWD
**Structure:** Monocoque
**Transmission:** Three-speed automatic
**Weight:** 2184kg

### PRICE GUIDE

**Launch price:** £11,556
**Excellent:** £90,000+
**Good:** £70,000
**Average:** £40,000
**Project:** £20,000

## BENTLEY
## Mulsanne/Eight Saloon

Rolls-Royce continued to build Bentleys as badge-engineered models with the Mulsanne of 1980 (left). Named after the famous Le Mans straight, its alterations over the Silver Spirit included a black radiator insert and sports seats. The Eight, of 1984, departed further from the Rolls' appearance, though. The single rectangular headlamps were replaced by twin circular ones, and a mesh radiator grille was fitted along with a front spoiler. It was enough to set the car apart from the Rolls-Royce and help kick-start a revival of interest in Bentley.

### SPECIFICATIONS

**Years produced:** 1980-1992 (2039 in total)
**Performance:** 0-60mph: 9.6sec
Top speed: 119mph
**Power & torque:** N/Q/N/Q
**Engine:** Normally aspirated 6750cc V8, petrol, carburettor, 16 valves
**Drivetrain:** Front-engine RWD
**Structure:** Monocoque
**Transmission:** Three-speed automatic
**Weight:** 2226kg

### PRICE GUIDE

**Launch price:** £49,629
**Excellent:** £22,000
**Good:** £15,000
**Average:** £8000
**Project:** £3000

## BENTLEY
## Turbo

Sales of Bentleys had fallen so low during the T-series era that Rolls-Royce considered axing the marque. Fortunately, the decision was taken to make the Winged B cars stand out instead. The renaissance started with the Mulsanne Turbo of 1982. While the looks didn't differ much from the equivalent Rolls, attached to the 6750cc V8 engine was a Garrett AiResearch turbocharger that increased power by 50%. The Turbo R of 1985 (left) brought even more power and better roadholding, too. Prices have levelled-off. Still terrific value.

**SPECIFICATIONS**

**Years produced:** 1982-1998 (4815 in total)
**Performance:** 0-60mph: 6.7sec (Turbo R)
Top speed: 135mph
**Power & torque:** 328bhp/486lb ft (Turbo R)
**Engine:** Turbocharged 6750cc V8, petrol, electronic fuel injection, 16 valves
**Drivetrain:** Front-engine RWD
**Structure:** Monocoque
**Transmission:** Four-speed automatic
**Weight:** 2234kg

**PRICE GUIDE (Turbo R in brackets)**

**Launch price:** £58,613 (£79,397)
**Excellent:** £20,000 (£40,000)
**Good:** £15,000 (£25,000)
**Average:** £8000 (£10,000)
**Project:** £3000 (£5000)

## BENTLEY
## Continental R/T

In a nod to the most beautiful Bentley of them all, the first Continental since 1966 used the R suffix to recall memories of the R-type. The name wasn't taken in vain for this was also the first individually-styled Bentley since the Sixties. Launched in 1991, the glossy coupé looks were substantially more streamlined than the contemporary Bentley saloons and the usual V8 engine was boosted in power. Expect to pay more for the higher performance Continental S and Continental T versions. A convertible, the Azure, was launched in 1995.

**SPECIFICATIONS**

**Years produced:** 1991-2002 (c1300 produced)
**Performance:** 0-60mph: 6.2sec
Top speed: 152mph
**Power & torque:** 355bhp/450lb ft
**Engine:** Turbocharged 6750cc V8, petrol, electronic fuel injection, 16 valves
**Drivetrain:** Front-engine RWD
**Structure:** Monocoque
**Transmission:** Four-speed automatic
**Weight:** 2280kg

**PRICE GUIDE**

**Launch price:** £175,000
**Excellent:** £100,000+
**Good:** £55,000
**Average:** £30,000
**Project:** £18,000

## BENTLEY
## Arnage/Red Label

Introduced in spring 1998, the Arnage replaced the Mulsanne and Turbo R. In place of the old 6.75-litre pushrod V8, it had a new, BMW-sourced 4.4-litre V8, re-engineered by Cosworth with twin turbos. This light, compact unit endowed the Arnage with decent performance and handling, but it was slightly anaemic, and after VW took control of Bentley it decided to offer the old V8 again. This 'Red Label' version was introduced in October 1999. With a huge 619lb ft of torque, it quickly overshadowed the BMW-powered car.

**SPECIFICATIONS**

**Years produced:** 1998-2009 (c8000 in total)
**Performance:** 0-60mph: 5.9sec (Red Label)
Top speed: 155mph
**Power & torque:** 400bhp/619lb ft
**Engine:** Turbocharged 6750cc V8, petrol, electronic fuel injection, 16 valves
**Drivetrain:** Rear-engine RWD
**Structure:** Monocoque
**Transmission:** Four-speed automatic
**Weight:** 2520kg

**PRICE GUIDE**

**Launch price:** £149,000
**Excellent:** £30,000
**Good:** £20,000
**Average:** £15,000
**Project:** £7000

## BENTLEY
## Continental GT

First all-new car following VW's purchase of Bentley, the Continental GT sold on a scale never before seen at Crewe. It was no longer hand-built and the underpinnings were shared with the VW Phaeton limo, but that didn't put buyers off. With a twin-turbo 6-litre W12 and 4wd, the Conti GT was massively fast, while its £110k price opened it up to a whole new audience. The first-gen cars were in production until 2011, the GTC convertible arriving in '06 (expect to pay a £10k+ premium for a GTC). Buy carefully – big bills await the unwary.

**SPECIFICATIONS**

**Years produced:** 2003-2011 (first generation)
**Performance:** 0-60mph: 4.8sec
Top speed: 200mph
**Power & torque:** 552bhp/479lb ft
**Engine:** Twin-turbocharged 5998cc W12, petrol, electronic injection, 48 valves
**Drivetrain:** Front-engine 4WD
**Structure:** Monocoque
**Transmission:** Six-speed automatic
**Weight:** 2350kg

**PRICE GUIDE**

**Launch price:** £110,000
**Excellent:** £35,000
**Good:** £25,000
**Average:** £15,000
**Project:** N/A

# BERKELEY

BERKELEY WAS a caravan manufacturer until it diversified into tiny glassfibre sportscars designed by Lawrence Bond (of Bond car fame). Twin-cylinder motorcycle engines provided more than enough power for these very lightweight machines; the 50bhp B105 of 1959 could top 100mph. The most successful was the three-wheeled T60, of which 1830 were built between 1959 and 1960. However, the lure to customers of rivals like the Austin-Healey Sprite meant that the firm went bankrupt in 1961, although a new incarnation of it built a handful of T60s in the 1990s, using motorcycle engines. Meanwhile, the original Berkeley factory found employment making women's underwear...

## BERKELEY SA322/SE328

Sporting cars don't come much more minimalist than this – an Anzani two-stroke twin powered this glassfibre-bodied two-seater to a top speed of 65mph. Not fast, but certainly fun, and surprisingly popular during the boomtime 1950s. When seen away from other cars, the 322 and 328 look well-proportioned and ahead of their time, but the tiny size makes them a singular choice for the adventurous fans in real life. Cheap to fuel, cheap to buy, and easy to work on, these Berkeleys make great sense, and have a real following today.

**SPECIFICATIONS**

| | |
|---|---|
| **Years produced:** | 1956-1958 (146/1272 in total) |
| **Performance:** | 0-60mph: 38.3sec<br>Top speed: 65mph |
| **Power & torque:** | 15bhp/16lb ft |
| **Engine:** | Normally aspirated 322cc twin cylinder, petrol, carburettor |
| **Drivetrain:** | Front-engine FWD |
| **Structure:** | Monocoque |
| **Transmission:** | Three-speed manual |
| **Weight:** | 280kg |

**PRICE GUIDE**

| | |
|---|---|
| **Launch price:** | £575 |
| **Excellent:** | £9000 |
| **Good:** | £5500 |
| **Average:** | £2300 |
| **Project:** | £1250 |

## BERKELEY Sport SE492

First real update to the series saw power boosted by the fitment of a three-cylinder Excelsior motorcycle engine. The car was now considerably quicker, topping out at 80mph, a feat proved in motor sport when Giovanni Lurani found success running a team of three (with his own design of hardtop) in the Italian 750cc GT class of racing. The pinnacle of Berkeley's success was when Lorenzo Bandini scored a win in the 1958 Monza 12-hour race. A Foursome four-seater was also introduced, proving the flexibility of Lawrie Bond's original design.

**SPECIFICATIONS**

| | |
|---|---|
| **Years produced:** | 1957-1959 (666 in total) |
| **Performance:** | 0-60mph: 21.8sec<br>Top speed: 80mph |
| **Power & torque:** | 30bhp/36lb ft |
| **Engine:** | Normally aspirated 492cc three cylinder, petrol, carburettor |
| **Drivetrain:** | Front-engine FWD |
| **Structure:** | Monocoque |
| **Transmission:** | Four-speed manual |
| **Weight:** | 318kg |

**PRICE GUIDE**

| | |
|---|---|
| **Launch price:** | £650 |
| **Excellent:** | £12,000 |
| **Good:** | £7000 |
| **Average:** | £4000 |
| **Project:** | £1500 |

## BERKELEY T60

Lop a wheel off the 322/328 and you're left with the T60 – a three-seat microcar that is just as much fun to drive as its four-wheel counterparts. Designed by Lawrie Bond, who went on to build cars under his own name, the three-wheeler lightweight was incredibly fun to drive in the right circumstances, and remains so to this day. Berkeley even managed to squeeze a rear seat into some of the last models off the line, and had it not been for the collapse of the parent company, many more than 1830 might have been built.

**SPECIFICATIONS**

| | |
|---|---|
| **Years produced:** | 1959-1960 (1830 in total) |
| **Performance:** | 0-60mph: N/A<br>Top speed: 60mph |
| **Power & torque:** | 18bhp/22lb ft |
| **Engine:** | Normally aspirated 328cc twin cylinder, petrol, carburettor |
| **Drivetrain:** | Front-engine FWD |
| **Structure:** | Monocoque |
| **Transmission:** | Four-speed manual |
| **Weight:** | 280kg |

**PRICE GUIDE**

| | |
|---|---|
| **Launch price:** | £400 |
| **Excellent:** | £10,000 |
| **Good:** | £5500 |
| **Average:** | £2750 |
| **Project:** | £1300 |

## BERKELEY B95/B105

The evolution of the Berkeley was rapid and unabated, with the B95 and B105 the ultimate examples of the breed. Power was from a high-compression Royal Enfield Constellation parallel-twin, putting out 50bhp and pushing the car to a top speed of more than 100mph on the 105 model. Roadholding was excellent, as the chassis was easily capable of handling the extra power. However, as sound as the concept was, the Berkeley twins lost out in the market compared with the Austin-Healey Sprite and ended up selling disappointingly.

**SPECIFICATIONS**

| | |
|---|---|
| **Years produced:** | 1959-1961 (200 in total) |
| **Performance:** | 0-60mph: 17.2sec<br>Top speed: 105mph |
| **Power & torque:** | 50bhp/45lb ft |
| **Engine:** | Normally aspirated 692cc twin cylinder, petrol, carburettor, 4 valves |
| **Drivetrain:** | Front-engine FWD |
| **Structure:** | Monocoque |
| **Transmission:** | Four-speed manual |
| **Weight:** | 363kg |

**PRICE GUIDE**

| | |
|---|---|
| **Launch price:** | £628 |
| **Excellent:** | £13,000 |
| **Good:** | £7750 |
| **Average:** | £4500 |
| **Project:** | £2000 |

# BITTER

RACING DRIVER and car importer Erich Bitter was intrigued by a 1969 Opel concept he saw at the Frankfurt Motor Show. A deal was struck with Opel, and Bitter GMBH was formed, with Erich Bitter's reinterpretation of the Opel CD as its main product. The cars were actually constructed by Baur. After 395 had been built, the firm switched its attention to the more affordable SC in 1979, which was again Opel-based but had a coupé body designed by Bitter himself (although it did look awfully like the Ferrari 365 GT4 2+2). Convertibles and saloons followed, but Bitter failed in 1989. In 2007, it announced a comeback with a new car, the Vero, but it struggled to sell and was canned in 2012.

## BITTER CD

The Bitter CD started life as a styling study by Opel shown at the Frankfurt Motor Show in 1969 – and it was so well received that the company considered putting the Diplomat-engined coupé into production. However, it was down to former racing driver Erich Bitter to turn it into production reality in 1973 – just in time for the oil crisis. Despite the unpromising Opel platform and Chevrolet V8, the CD is a great car to drive, and an excellent long-distance tourer. The Baur-built bodies are prone to rusting, but many of the 395 cars built survive in the hands of enthusiastic owners.

**SPECIFICATIONS**

| | |
|---|---|
| **Years produced:** | 1973-1979 (395 in total) |
| **Performance:** | 0-60mph: 9.4sec<br>Top speed: 130mph |
| **Power & torque:** | 230bhp/314lb ft |
| **Engine:** | Normally aspirated 5354cc V8, petrol, carburettor, 16 valves |
| **Drivetrain:** | Front-engine RWD |
| **Structure:** | Monocoque |
| **Transmission:** | Three-speed automatic |
| **Weight:** | 1724kg |

**PRICE GUIDE**

| | |
|---|---|
| **Launch price:** | N/A in UK |
| **Excellent:** | £60,000 |
| **Good:** | £47,000 |
| **Average:** | £30,000 |
| **Project:** | £10,000 |

## BITTER SC

The SC is said to offer the best of both worlds – rugged and capable GM engineering (this time the Opel Senator's platform) combined with glamorous Italianate styling. Initially the bodies were built by OCRA, but production was switched to ILCA after just 79 SCs were completed. Power didn't initially match the looks, but an upgraded 3.9-litre engine righted the situation. Rust was the enemy with these cars, and sadly sales weren't great, and by the late 1980s the SC's failure almost bankrupted Erich Bitter. Values have softened for this underrated German tourer.

**SPECIFICATIONS**

| | |
|---|---|
| **Years produced:** | 1979-1989 (458 in total) |
| **Performance:** | 0-60mph: 7.4sec<br>Top speed: 142mph |
| **Power & torque:** | 210bhp/257lb ft |
| **Engine:** | Normally aspirated 3848cc straight six, petrol, carburettor, 12 valves |
| **Drivetrain:** | Front-engine RWD |
| **Structure:** | Monocoque |
| **Transmission:** | Three-speed automatic |
| **Weight:** | 1350kg |

**PRICE GUIDE**

| | |
|---|---|
| **Launch price:** | £26,950 |
| **Excellent:** | £23,000 |
| **Good:** | £17,000 |
| **Average:** | £10,000 |
| **Project:** | £3000 |

# BIZZARRINI

SPORTS CARS FOR the connoisseur, these were the creation of Giotto Bizzarrini, a former Alfa Romeo and Ferrari engineer who was heavily involved in the latter's legendary 250GTO. After leaving Ferrari in 1961, he worked on the Lamborghini V12 engine and Iso's Grifo project. In 1964, Bizzarrini SpA was formed, its first car being launched two years later. Based on the competition Grifo A3C, it was called the 5300 Strada. The firm's most famous design was the P538S, which raced at Le Mans. Only around 160 Bizzarrinis were built before production ceased in 1969. Giotto continued working as a consultant, producing prototypes and building replica P538s.

## BIZZARRINI GT Strada 5300

Taking the vast wealth of experience gained at Alfa Romeo and, more importantly, Ferrari, Giotto Bizzarrini set about creating the delectable GT Strada. Effectively a modified lightweight Iso Grifo clothed in a stunning and extremely low-line Giugiaro-styled set of clothes, this was a fully paid-up member of the supercar elite. As is the case with the Iso Grifo, the GT Strada is powered by a Chevrolet V8, which endows it with a very favourable power-to-weight ratio. A challenging car for gifted drivers, offered with glassfibre or aluminium body.

**SPECIFICATIONS**

| | |
|---|---|
| **Years produced:** | 1965-1969 (149 in total) |
| **Performance:** | 0-60mph: 6.4sec<br>Top speed: 165mph |
| **Power & torque:** | 365bhp/376lb ft |
| **Engine:** | Normally aspirated 5354cc V8, petrol, carburettor, 16 valves |
| **Drivetrain:** | Front-engine RWD |
| **Structure:** | Separate chassis |
| **Transmission:** | Four-speed manual |
| **Weight:** | 1252kg |

**PRICE GUIDE**

| | |
|---|---|
| **Launch price:** | N/A |
| **Excellent:** | £600,000 |
| **Good:** | £450,000 |
| **Average:** | £350,000 |
| **Project:** | N/A |

# BMW

BAYERISCHE MOTOREN Werke was an aviation manufacturer banned from building aircraft after World War One. So, it turned to motorcycles and cars; its first automobile was an Austin Seven copy named the Dixi. From that, BMW moved onto its own very fine sports and touring cars including the lovely 328. Turbulent times followed the end of World War Two, with BMW coming close to bankruptcy and turning to Isetta and 600 bubble cars to help sustain it. The 'Neue Klasse' models from 1961 saved the firm, and it's continued to flourish ever since. Today's BMWs are highly respected and capable machines, while the products of the M division are top-drawer drivers' cars.

## BMW 501

Starting from near enough the ground up, BMW worked quickly to design, develop and launch the brand new 501 from its new factory in Munich. But what an impressive fresh beginning – the saloon and roadsters were impressively styled (hence the nickname 'Baroque Angel'), refined, expensive and luxurious. Initially powered by pre-war 326 engine, upgraded to 2.1 litres in 1955. Considering Germany was recovering from the effects of WW2, it was probably a case of too much, too soon, but these grand cars put BMW firmly on the map.

**SPECIFICATIONS**

| | |
|---|---|
| **Years produced:** | 1952-1958 (8936 in total) |
| **Performance:** | 0-60mph: 17.2sec<br>Top speed: 95mph |
| **Power & torque:** | 73bhp/80lb ft |
| **Engine:** | Normally aspirated 1971cc straight six, petrol, carburettor, 16 valves |
| **Drivetrain:** | Front-engine RWD |
| **Structure:** | Separate chassis |
| **Transmission:** | Four-speed manual |
| **Weight:** | 1270kg |

**PRICE GUIDE (saloon)**

| | |
|---|---|
| **Launch price:** | N/A |
| **Excellent:** | £60,000 |
| **Good:** | £40,000 |
| **Average:** | £25,000 |
| **Project:** | £15,000 |

## BMW 501 V8/502/2600/3200

Even during the 1950s, BMW had cottoned on to the creation of more desirable models simply by adding larger engines. It was a policy that would serve the company well for generations to come. Just like its six-cylinder counterpart, the V8 was available in saloon, coupé and cabriolet forms. As the years passed, the engine was expanded to its ultimate 3.2-litre form with an impressive 160bhp. But in cash-starved '50s and early '60s Germany, few buyers stumped up and bought a BMW. Cabrios attract a huge premium – the best command £200k-plus.

**SPECIFICATIONS**

| | |
|---|---|
| **Years produced:** | 1954-1963 (13,044 in total) |
| **Performance:** | 0-60mph: 15.2sec<br>Top speed: 103mph |
| **Power & torque:** | 105bhp/95lb ft |
| **Engine:** | Normally aspirated 2581cc V8, petrol, carburettor, 16 valves |
| **Drivetrain:** | Front-engine RWD |
| **Structure:** | Separate chassis |
| **Transmission:** | Four-speed manual |
| **Weight:** | 1334kg |

**PRICE GUIDE (saloon)**

| | |
|---|---|
| **Launch price:** | N/A |
| **Excellent:** | £60,000 |
| **Good:** | £40,000 |
| **Average:** | £30,000 |
| **Project:** | £15,000 |

## BMW 503

Based on the impressive 501, BMW's 503 coupé sported an exciting new bodystyle penned by Albrecht Goertz. It introduced a new era of modernism for the marque, but at a hefty price that few could afford. It drove as well as it looked, too, with a top speed of nearly 120mph. The 503 coupé and its convertible sibling were designed primarily for the American market, but sadly, it was far too expensive to take off, and a mere 412 were built. The outcome pushed BMW to the edge of bankruptcy, but that rarity has seen values soar in recent years.

**SPECIFICATIONS**

| | |
|---|---|
| **Years produced:** | 1955-1959 (412 in total) |
| **Performance:** | 0-60mph: 12sec<br>Top speed: 118mph |
| **Power & torque:** | 162bhp/163lb ft |
| **Engine:** | Normally aspirated 3168cc V8, petrol, carburettor, 16 valves |
| **Drivetrain:** | Front-engine RWD |
| **Structure:** | Separate chassis |
| **Transmission:** | Four-speed manual |
| **Weight:** | 1501kg |

**PRICE GUIDE (Cabrio in brackets)**

| | |
|---|---|
| **Launch price:** | £4801 |
| **Excellent:** | £250,000 (£400,000+) |
| **Good:** | £200,000 (£300,000) |
| **Average:** | £175,000 (£250,000) |
| **Project:** | £75,000 (£150,000) |

## BMW ISETTA 250/300

Although universally admired, BMW's luxury cars were selling slowly. So the decision to acquire the licence to build the Isetta proved to be an inspired piece of lateral thinking by the company's management. The Isetta was just what was needed, and as the effects of the Suez crisis started to hit, and petrol became a rare commodity, suddenly the motorcycle-engined car that could achieve 50mpg all day long made a great deal of sense. Front-hinged door and three-wheeled handling were questionable, but buyers loved them... and still do.

**SPECIFICATIONS**

| | |
|---|---|
| **Years produced:** | 1955-1965 (161,728 in total) |
| **Performance:** | 0-60mph: N/A<br>Top speed: 60mph |
| **Power & torque:** | 13bhp/11lb ft |
| **Engine:** | Normally aspirated 297cc twin cylinder, petrol, carburettor, 4 valves |
| **Drivetrain:** | Rear-engine RWD |
| **Structure:** | Separate chassis |
| **Transmission:** | Four-speed manual |
| **Weight:** | 350kg |

**PRICE GUIDE**

| | |
|---|---|
| **Launch price:** | £415 |
| **Excellent:** | £25,000 |
| **Good:** | £20,000 |
| **Average:** | £15,000 |
| **Project:** | £7000 |

## BMW 507

Launched alongside the 503 Coupé, the 507 was – and still is – one of the most beautiful convertibles in the world. The aluminium-bodied roadster was built on a shortened 502 chassis and powered by the same V8, which produced 150bhp and gave the 507 a fair turn of speed. Despite its beauty, its high price and lack of an established image hampered sales – a mere 252 were made, at a significant loss. Which, of course, contributes to such strong values today. John Surtees' personal car sold for £3.8 million in 2018 – a world record for a BMW sold at auction.

**SPECIFICATIONS**

| | |
|---|---|
| **Years produced:** | 1956-1959 (252 in total) |
| **Performance:** | 0-60mph: 9.5sec<br>Top speed: 124mph |
| **Power & torque:** | 150bhp/174lb ft |
| **Engine:** | Normally aspirated 3168cc V8, petrol, carburettor, 16 valves |
| **Drivetrain:** | Front-engine RWD |
| **Structure:** | Separate chassis |
| **Transmission:** | Four-speed manual |
| **Weight:** | 1330kg |

**PRICE GUIDE**

| | |
|---|---|
| **Launch price:** | £4201 |
| **Excellent:** | £2,500,000+ |
| **Good:** | £2,000,000 |
| **Average:** | N/A |
| **Project:** | N/A |

## BMW 600

Following on from the original Isetta, the BMW 600 was a logical upward extension of the theme to capture buyers who'd grown out of their original bubble cars. The front-opening door remained in place, but the new car was larger, with an extra side door for rear passengers, a more powerful 582cc BMW flat-twin motorcycle engine and – most importantly – four wheels. It was usefully quicker than the original Isetta, but still crude for the price tag, being only marginally cheaper than a Beetle. Today, however, as with all bubbles, it's on the rise.

### SPECIFICATIONS

| | |
|---|---|
| **Years produced:** | 1957-1959 (34,813 in total) |
| **Performance:** | 0-60mph: N/A<br>Top speed: 63mph |
| **Power & torque:** | 19.5bhp/29lb ft |
| **Engine:** | Normally aspirated 582cc twin cylinder, petrol, carburettor, 4 valves |
| **Drivetrain:** | Rear-engine RWD |
| **Structure:** | Separate chassis |
| **Transmission:** | Four-speed manual |
| **Weight:** | 510kg |

### PRICE GUIDE

| | |
|---|---|
| **Launch price:** | £676 |
| **Excellent:** | £25,000 |
| **Good:** | £18,000 |
| **Average:** | £13,000 |
| **Project:** | £6000 |

## BMW 700 coupé/cabriolet

The 700 actually first appeared in coupé form, and although it looked a little awkward thanks to its sloping roofline, it proved just the right product for BMW. As the company's first unitary construction car, the 700's technical significance is oft-overlooked thanks to its rear-engined layout. The Sports model gained 10bhp thanks to twin carburettors and a high-compression engine, and it's these ones that buyers really want today. Open-topped cabriolet is often overlooked, but is just as much fun as its coupé counterpart.

### SPECIFICATIONS

| | |
|---|---|
| **Years produced:** | 1959-1965 (11,166/2592 in total) |
| **Performance:** | 0-60mph: 33.7sec<br>Top speed: 75mph |
| **Power & torque:** | 32bhp/37lb ft |
| **Engine:** | Normally aspirated 697cc twin cylinder, petrol, carburettor, 4 valves |
| **Drivetrain:** | Rear-engine RWD |
| **Structure:** | Monocoque |
| **Transmission:** | Four-speed manual |
| **Weight:** | 640kg |

### PRICE GUIDE

| | |
|---|---|
| **Launch price:** | N/A |
| **Excellent:** | £25,000 |
| **Good:** | £15,000 |
| **Average:** | £10,000 |
| **Project:** | £5000 |

## BMW 1500/1600/1800/1800ti

Another pivotal model in BMW's history. The 700 might have saved the company from bankruptcy, but the 'Neue Klasse' 1500 came from nowhere and struck a chord with West Germany's emerging middle class, selling hugely and returning BMW to profitability. Under the well-judged Michelotti skin, the 1500 boasted an up-to-the-minute specification, including unitary construction, disc brakes, independent suspension and a smooth 1.5-litre overhead-cam engine. Continually upgraded, transforming into the 2000 in 1966.

### SPECIFICATIONS (1500)

| | |
|---|---|
| **Years produced:** | 1961-1972 (c.200,000 in total) |
| **Performance:** | 0-60mph: 13.1sec<br>Top speed: 93mph |
| **Power & torque:** | 80bhp/87lb ft |
| **Engine:** | Normally aspirated 1499cc four cylinder, petrol, carburettor, 8 valves |
| **Drivetrain:** | Front-engine RWD |
| **Structure:** | Monocoque |
| **Transmission:** | Four-speed manual |
| **Weight:** | 1043kg |

### PRICE GUIDE (ti in brackets)

| | |
|---|---|
| **Launch price:** | N/A |
| **Excellent:** | £12,000 (£27,000) |
| **Good:** | £8000 (£20,000) |
| **Average:** | £5000 (£15,000) |
| **Project:** | £2000 (£3000) |

## BMW 2000/2000ti/2000tii

The 2000 was the ultimate evolution of the 1500/1800cc saloon car line. The medium-sized model seemed its most appealing with the bored-out four cylinder under the bonnet, especially in fuel-injection Tii form, which packed a useful 135bhp. Interesting to drive and a bit of a handful in the wet, the 2000 set the tone for the next generations of BMW's mid-sized saloons – sporting and satisfying. Survival rate in the UK is low although they are still fairly commonplace in Germany, so that would be your first place to look when buying.

### SPECIFICATIONS

| | |
|---|---|
| **Years produced:** | 1966-1972 (113,074 in total) |
| **Performance:** | 0-60mph: 12.4sec<br>Top speed: 104mph |
| **Power & torque:** | 100bhp/116lb ft |
| **Engine:** | Normally aspirated 1990cc four cylinder, petrol, carburettor, 8 valves |
| **Drivetrain:** | Front-engine RWD |
| **Structure:** | Monocoque |
| **Transmission:** | Four-speed manual |
| **Weight:** | 1130kg |

### PRICE GUIDE (ti/tii in brackets)

| | |
|---|---|
| **Launch price:** | £1777 |
| **Excellent:** | £12,000 (£25,000) |
| **Good:** | £8000 (£18,000) |
| **Average:** | £5000 (£12,000) |
| **Project:** | £2000 (£3000) |

## BMW 2000C/CS

BMW's 'Neue Klasse' range had proved an instant and substantial hit in Germany; and just as the Rover and Triumph 2000s had revolutionised the executive class here in the UK, the BMW equivalent changed the face of the market there. Easily the most appealing was the CS version, a pillarless coupé by Wilhelm Hofmeister. The Karmann-built bodies were pretty, but weren't immune to rust, and have now almost disappeared from the scene. Find a good one and cherish it – BMW's future success was mapped out here.

### SPECIFICATIONS

| | |
|---|---|
| **Years produced:** | 1966-1969 (11,720 in total) |
| **Performance:** | 0-60mph: 12.0sec<br>Top speed: 110mph |
| **Power & torque:** | 120bhp/123lb ft |
| **Engine:** | Normally aspirated 1990cc four cylinder, petrol, carburettor, 8 valves |
| **Drivetrain:** | Front-engine RWD |
| **Structure:** | Monocoque |
| **Transmission:** | Four-speed manual |
| **Weight:** | 1150kg |

### PRICE GUIDE

| | |
|---|---|
| **Launch price:** | £2950 |
| **Excellent:** | £17,500 |
| **Good:** | £12,000 |
| **Average:** | £6000 |
| **Project:** | £2000 |

## BMW 1602/1502

With the 'Neue Klasse' doing the business in the executive market, BMW repeated the trick in the small saloon sector with its '02 series models. Despite their relatively high prices, the smaller-engined cars in the '02 range were popular entry-level models, turning on a generation of drivers to BMW ownership – and today, they still enjoy a healthy following. Overshadowed somewhat by the pocket-rocket 2002, the 1502/1602 can be satisfying to own in their own right – if you can find one that isn't riddled with rust. Values holding steady.

**SPECIFICATIONS**

**Years produced:** 1966-1977 (324,320 in total)
**Performance:** 0-60mph: 14.5sec
Top speed: 96mph
**Power & torque:** 85bhp/91lb ft
**Engine:** Normally aspirated 1574cc four cylinder, petrol, carburettor, 8 valves
**Drivetrain:** Front-engine RWD
**Structure:** Monocoque
**Transmission:** Four-speed manual
**Weight:** 920kg

**PRICE GUIDE**

**Launch price:** £1298
**Excellent:** £10,500
**Good:** £6500
**Average:** £4000
**Project:** £2500

## BMW 1602/2002 cabriolet

The Baur-built 1600 cabriolet appeared on the market a year after the popular saloon, and looked like another sure-fire hit for BMW. But the four-seater was sold at a significant price premium over its tin-top counterpart, and lacked body rigidity, blunting its driver appeal considerably. However, those ills were put right by the 2002, which featured a beefed-up structure, with roll-over bar and targa panels. The addition of the potent 1990cc hemi-headed unit no doubt helped the driving experience, and today both cars have a healthy following.

**SPECIFICATIONS**

**Years produced:** 1967-1975 (1682/2272 in total)
**Performance:** 0-60mph: 12.0sec
Top speed: 107mph
**Power & torque:** 100bhp/116lb ft
**Engine:** Normally aspirated 1990cc four cylinder, petrol, carburettor, 8 valves
**Drivetrain:** Front-engine RWD
**Structure:** Monocoque
**Transmission:** Four-speed manual
**Weight:** 1040kg

**PRICE GUIDE**

**Launch price:** £1948
**Excellent:** £15,500
**Good:** £12,500
**Average:** £7000
**Project:** £3500

## BMW 2800 CS/CSA

With a straight six under the bonnet and sharper front-end styling, the BMW CS coupé came of age. The 2.8-litre engine developed 150bhp, which gave the handsome CS a maximum speed of 120mph – more in the up-gunned CSA. But speed wasn't this car's major trick, and neither was its elegant styling – the firm and well-controlled suspension blessed it with first-rate handling and long-distance comfort. Mercedes-Benz had met its match, and BMW was now considered a key player in the luxury car market. Values have crept up in the wake of the iconic CSL.

**SPECIFICATIONS (CSA)**

**Years produced:** 1968-1975 (9399 in total)
**Performance:** 0-60mph: 8.3sec
Top speed: 124mph
**Power & torque:** 168bhp/173lb ft
**Engine:** Normally aspirated 2788cc straight six, petrol, carburettor, 12 valves
**Drivetrain:** Front-engine RWD
**Structure:** Monocoque
**Transmission:** Four-speed manual
**Weight:** 1290kg

**PRICE GUIDE**

**Launch price:** £4997
**Excellent:** £27,500
**Good:** £22,000
**Average:** £17,000
**Project:** £7500

## BMW 2500/2800/3.0/3.3

With the compact saloon market cornered, BMW turned its attention to the luxury car sector and came up with the New Six. It looked like an upscaled version of the '02 Series, but that was no bad thing considering the strong identity Wilhelm Hofmeister had carved out for the niche. On the road, the 2500 and its larger-engined derivatives were also true to the marque, with all the power and poise you could need in a saloon. Indeed, the 3.0Si and 3.3Li were in many ways the foreunners of the M5, says Munich Legends' Dan Norris, and values reflect this.

**SPECIFICATIONS**

**Years produced:** 1968-1977 (217,635 in total)
**Performance:** 0-60mph: 9.0sec
Top speed: 127mph
**Power & torque:** 180bhp/255lb ft
**Engine:** Normally aspirated 2494cc straight six, petrol, carburettor, 12 valves
**Drivetrain:** Front-engine RWD
**Structure:** Monocoque
**Transmission:** Four-speed manual
**Weight:** 1295kg

**PRICE GUIDE (3.0Si/3.3Li in brackets)**

**Launch price:** £2197
**Excellent:** £12,000 (£32,000/£55,000)
**Good:** £9000 (£25,000/£40,000)
**Average:** £6000 (£18,000/£30,000)
**Project:** £2500 (£10,000/£20,000)

## BMW 2002 saloon

The 2002 was introduced a couple of years after the 1502/1602 and ended up cementing the series' reputation as the car to beat in the sporting saloon sector. The 2-litre M10-series engine was essentially a bored-out version of the old 1.8-litre unit, producing 100bhp in standard form and proving an absolute gem. With 120bhp, the twin-carburettor Ti version was more exciting, but also a real handful on challenging roads. A 2002 that hasn't rusted too badly is one of the most sensible ways of owning an early-'70s sporting saloon.

**SPECIFICATIONS**

**Years produced:** 1971-1975 (2517 in total)
**Performance:** 0-60mph: 12.0sec
Top speed: 107mph
**Power & torque:** 100bhp/116lb ft
**Engine:** Normally aspirated 1990cc four cylinder, petrol, carburettor, 8 valves
**Drivetrain:** Front-engine RWD
**Structure:** Monocoque
**Transmission:** Four-speed manual
**Weight:** 1040kg

**PRICE GUIDE**

**Launch price:** £1948
**Excellent:** £15,000
**Good:** £10,000
**Average:** £7000
**Project:** £2000

## BMW
# 2002tii

One of Europe's finest Q-cars of its era, the fuel-injection 2002Tii could crack 120mph on the autobahn and drive sideways on the merest whiff of throttle. Retaining all the strengths of the rest of the '02 series cars, the Tii has justifiably gone on to become a legend. However, like all '02s, it can suffer from extensive corrosion, while the Kugelfischer injection system can be tricky to set up. That said, a cult following means these cars are in demand and command a healthy premium over their less-glamorous counterparts.

**SPECIFICATIONS**

**Years produced:** 1971-1975 (38,701 in total)
**Performance:** 0-60mph: 10.0sec
Top speed: 120mph
**Power & torque:** 130bhp/131lb ft
**Engine:** Normally aspirated 1990cc four cylinder, petrol, mechanical fuel injection, 8 valves
**Drivetrain:** Front-engine RWD
**Structure:** Monocoque
**Transmission:** Four-speed manual; Five-speed optional
**Weight:** 1010kg

**PRICE GUIDE**

**Launch price:** £2299
**Excellent:** £35,000
**Good:** £25,000
**Average:** £17,000
**Project:** £9000

## BMW
# 2000/2002 Touring

Following the success of the 'New Class' saloons and cabriolets, BMW introduced another body style to the 02 line-up in April 1971. The three-door 2000 Touring (rebadged 2002 Touring from December 1972) was designed to combine the practicality of an estate car with the driving appeal of a sports coupe, rather like the contemporary Reliant Scimitar GTE. Fitted with the highly regarded 2.0-litre M10 engine, it could accelerate from 0-60 in a very respectable 11sec, while fully independent suspension and front disc brakes gave it handling to match.

**SPECIFICATIONS**

**Years produced:** 1971-1974
**Performance:** 0-60mph: 11.0sec
Top speed: 107mph
**Power & torque:** 100bhp/116lb ft
**Engine:** Normally aspirated 1990cc four cylinder, petrol, carburettor, 8 valves
**Drivetrain:** Front-engine RWD
**Structure:** Monocoque
**Transmission:** Four-speed manual
**Weight:** 1040kg

**PRICE GUIDE**

**Launch price:** c£2000
**Excellent:** £7500
**Good:** £5250
**Average:** £3250
**Project:** £1300

## BMW
# 3.0CS/CSi

Although outwardly similar to the 2800, the 1971 3.0CS had an uprated chassis and braking set-up. The excellent roadholding of the former model was easily surpassed, and unlike the smaller cars in the range, snap-oversteer was rare. The fuel-injected CSi passed the 200bhp mark, making it a paid-up member of the performance car elite, with a top speed of 139mph and 0-60mph time under 8sec. Dan Norris of Munich Legends says values have taken a hit in the last 12 months, but still a smart alternative to the vastly more expensive CSL.

**SPECIFICATIONS**

**Years produced:** 1971-1975 (19,207 in total)
**Performance:** 0-60mph: 7.5sec
Top speed: 139mph
**Power & torque:** 200bhp/200lb ft
**Engine:** Normally aspirated 2986cc straight six, petrol, electronic fuel injection, 12 valves
**Drivetrain:** Front-engine RWD
**Structure:** Monocoque
**Transmission:** Four-speed manual
**Weight:** 1270kg

**PRICE GUIDE**

**Launch price:** £6199
**Excellent:** £55,000
**Good:** £45,000
**Average:** £35,000
**Project:** £25,000

## BMW
# 3.0CSL

As homologation specials go, the BMW CSL is perhaps the most memorable. Featuring lightweight aluminium panels, a spartan interior and Plexiglas side windows, the CSL was brilliant on road *and* track. UK models retained the luxury interior of the standard cars, taking away some of the raw appeal – but buyers still loved them. Buy carefully today – there are bad examples around – but the best are really flying. Meanwhile the 3.2-litre bewinged 'Batmobile', of which only 39 were made, now commands £250k-plus – if the history checks out.

**SPECIFICATIONS**

**Years produced:** 1972-1975 (1096 in total)
**Performance:** 0-60mph: 7.5sec (3.2 'Batmobile')
Top speed: 138mph
**Power & torque:** 206bhp/195lb ft
**Engine:** Normally aspirated 3153cc straight six, petrol, mechanical fuel injection, 12 valves
**Drivetrain:** Front-engine RWD
**Structure:** Monocoque
**Transmission:** Four-speed manual
**Weight:** 1270kg

**PRICE GUIDE**

**Launch price:** £6399
**Excellent:** £155,000
**Good:** £110,000
**Average:** £90,000
**Project:** £55,000

## BMW
# 2002 Turbo

For thrill-seekers who could afford one, the BMW 2002 Turbo was the coolest car in town in the mid-70s. It was Europe's first turbocharged production model, and like all the earliest cars to sport a blower, the 2002 Turbo was prodigiously powerful – and suffered from massive turbo lag. Not for the faint-hearted! Only 1672 were built, and values reflect that, but Munich Legends' Dan Norris cautions that they're not an easy car to own, requiring constant fettling. You also need to beware replicas. Values have softened in last 12-18 months.

**SPECIFICATIONS**

**Years produced:** 1973-1974 (1672 in total)
**Performance:** 0-60mph: 8.0sec
Top speed: 130mph
**Power & torque:** 170bhp/177lb ft
**Engine:** Turbocharged 1990cc four cylinder, petrol, mechanical fuel injection, 8 valves
**Drivetrain:** Front-engine RWD
**Structure:** Monocoque
**Transmission:** Four-speed manual/five-speed manual
**Weight:** 1080kg

**PRICE GUIDE**

**Launch price:** £2433
**Excellent:** £90,000
**Good:** £65,000
**Average:** £50,000
**Project:** £30,000

## BMW
# 316/318/320/323i (E21)

The BMW 3-Series became the performance saloon to beat the moment it exploded onto the market in 1975. Four-cylinder M10-powered versions weren't quick, but were dependable. However, the straight-six cars with fuel injection were electrifying, especially in the wet! The 323 is the enthusiast's choice, but make sure you get a car with a limited-slip differential; the handling's especially challenging without it. Rare now thanks to the number that were crashed (and the usual rust issues), but survivors enjoy a growing cult status among younger enthusiasts.

**SPECIFICATIONS**

| | |
|---|---|
| **Years produced:** | 1975-1983 (1,364,039 in total) |
| **Performance:** | 0-60mph: 12.9sec (316)<br>Top speed: 100mph |
| **Power & torque:** | 90bhp/90lb ft |
| **Engine:** | Normally aspirated 1574cc four cylinder, petrol, carburettor, 8 valves |
| **Drivetrain:** | Front-engine RWD |
| **Structure:** | Monocoque |
| **Transmission:** | Four-speed manual |
| **Weight:** | 1020kg |

**PRICE GUIDE (323i in brackets)**

| | |
|---|---|
| **Launch price:** | £2799 |
| **Excellent:** | £15,000 (£23,000) |
| **Good:** | £10,000 (£15,000) |
| **Average:** | £7000 (£10,000) |
| **Project:** | £5000 (£6000) |

## BMW
# 633/628/635CSi

The 6-Series coupé replaced the CS range in 1976. The key BMW selling points of sharp steering, keen dynamics and strong performance were all intact, but many customers bemoaned the styling of the new car, which was less pretty. More of a grand tourer than the CS, the 6-Series was generally more refined and easier to live with. The 633 and 628 are generally passed over for the superior 635CSi, which recaptured more of the old CS/CSL magic and whose values are climbing fast. One to watch, but beware rust and potential high running costs.

**SPECIFICATIONS**

| | |
|---|---|
| **Years produced:** | 1976-1989 (c30,000 in total) |
| **Performance:** | 0-60mph: 8.0sec (635CSi)<br>Top speed: 138mph |
| **Power & torque:** | 218bhp/228lb ft |
| **Engine:** | Normally aspirated 3453cc straight six, petrol, electronic fuel injection, 12v |
| **Drivetrain:** | Front-engine RWD |
| **Structure:** | Monocoque |
| **Transmission:** | Five-speed manual |
| **Weight:** | 1475kg |

**PRICE GUIDE (635CSi in brackets)**

| | |
|---|---|
| **Launch price:** | £13,980 |
| **Excellent:** | £13,000 (£35,000) |
| **Good:** | £6500 (£25,000) |
| **Average:** | £3000 (£17,000) |
| **Project:** | £1000 (£7000) |

## BMW
# M1

The original M car, the M1 was created for Group Five racing, but thanks to delays in development which led to BMW taking control of body production (when partner Lamborghini couldn't deliver its side of the bargain), it arrived late and never fulfilled its racing potential. The styling by Giugiaro was spot-on, as was its chassis and race-bred 24-valve six, but after a run of 456, production of the era's most drivable supercar came to a halt. 'There's been a real blunting of values at the top end,' say Munich Legends, 'but the M1 still has long-term legs.'

**SPECIFICATIONS**

| | |
|---|---|
| **Years produced:** | 1979-1980 (456 in total) |
| **Performance:** | 0-60mph: 6.5sec<br>Top speed: 163mph |
| **Power & torque:** | 277bhp/243lb ft |
| **Engine:** | Normally aspirated 3453cc straight six, petrol, mechanical fuel injection, 24 valves |
| **Drivetrain:** | Mid-engine RWD |
| **Structure:** | Spaceframe |
| **Transmission:** | Five-speed manual |
| **Weight:** | 1300kg |

**PRICE GUIDE**

| | |
|---|---|
| **Launch price:** | £37,570 |
| **Excellent:** | £500,000+ |
| **Good:** | £300,000+ |
| **Average:** | N/A |
| **Project:** | N/A |

## BMW
# M535i (E12)

Although not strictly an M5, the BMW Motorsport division's first sporting 5-Series was still a fine driver's car and remains underrated. Shoehorning the 635CSi's engine into the compact 5-Series shell resulted in a seriously rapid sports saloon, although thanks to the Alpina-inspired chin spoiler and stripes, the world knew all about it. The M535i was offered with a limited-slip diff and close-ratio gearbox, and shared its pin-sharp steering with the rest of the range. Very few right-hand-drive cars left, so if you want one (especially a really good one), get in quick.

**SPECIFICATIONS**

| | |
|---|---|
| **Years produced:** | 1979-1981 (1410 in total) |
| **Performance:** | 0-60mph: 8.0sec<br>Top speed: 140mph |
| **Power & torque:** | 218bhp/229lb ft |
| **Engine:** | Normally aspirated 3453cc straight six, petrol, electronic fuel injection, 12 valves |
| **Drivetrain:** | Front-engine RWD |
| **Structure:** | Monocoque |
| **Transmission:** | Five-speed manual |
| **Weight:** | 1465kg |

**PRICE GUIDE**

| | |
|---|---|
| **Launch price:** | £13,705 |
| **Excellent:** | £45,000 |
| **Good:** | £30,000 |
| **Average:** | £18,000 |
| **Project:** | £10,000 |

## BMW
# 3-Series (E30)

In the E30-generation 3-Series, BMW created one of the iconic cars of the '80s. Powered by a range of M40 four-pots and M20 straight-sixes, such was the depth of the engineering that any 3-Series rewarded its owner with an immense sense of well-being. That's why they sold over two million – many of which seem to be still in use, and performing brilliantly! The convertible is effortlessly cool; also prized is the rapid 320is. As a starter classic – a car that still looks cool and drives well – an E30 takes some beating, especially in six-cylinder form.

**SPECIFICATIONS (318i)**

| | |
|---|---|
| **Years produced:** | 1982-1991 (2,339,520 in total) |
| **Performance:** | 0-60mph: 10.9sec<br>Top speed: 114mph |
| **Power & torque:** | 103bhp/107lb ft |
| **Engine:** | Normally aspirated 1766cc four cylinder, petrol, electronic fuel injection, 8 valves |
| **Drivetrain:** | Front-engine RWD |
| **Structure:** | Monocoque |
| **Transmission:** | Five-speed manual |
| **Weight:** | 1000kg |

**PRICE GUIDE**

| | |
|---|---|
| **Launch price:** | N/A |
| **Excellent:** | £15,000 |
| **Good:** | £12,000 |
| **Average:** | £9000 |
| **Project:** | £4000 |

## BMW
## M535i (E28)

The second-generation M535i followed the same formula as the original. Created by installing the 218bhp 635CSi engine into the E28-gen 5-Series body, it provided similarly strong performance but was far more polished. The deep front spoiler remained, which was at odds with the unadorned (and more powerful) M5. Recaro seats and a limited-slip differential remained options. Just like the original, many have now rusted away. As Munich Legends' Dan Norris says, 'a good one is a great way to nearly own an M5!' Values currently holding.

### SPECIFICATIONS

| | |
|---|---|
| **Years produced:** | 1984-1987 (45,655 in total) |
| **Performance:** | 0-60mph: 6.9sec<br>Top speed: 143mph |
| **Power & torque:** | 218bhp/224lb ft |
| **Engine:** | Normally aspirated 3430cc straight six, petrol, electronic fuel injection, 12 valves |
| **Drivetrain:** | Front-engine RWD |
| **Structure:** | Monocoque |
| **Transmission:** | Five-speed manual |
| **Weight:** | 1391kg |

### PRICE GUIDE

| | |
|---|---|
| **Launch price:** | £13,745 |
| **Excellent:** | £25,000 |
| **Good:** | £20,000 |
| **Average:** | £12,000 |
| **Project:** | £5000 |

## BMW
## M5 (E28)

The first fully M-Sport 5-Series repeated the formula of stuffing a powerful engine under the bonnet of the well-proportioned 5-Series. This time, the full-fat 24-valve 286bhp M1 engine created a super-saloon par excellence, and unlike the M535i – which looked every bit the road racer – the M5 was discreet to the point of anonymity. Canny owners even removed the badges. With just 187 RHD cars built, the E28 M5 has long gained legend status, though values have slipped a little this past year after a period of real growth.

### SPECIFICATIONS

| | |
|---|---|
| **Years produced:** | 1984-1987 (2145 in total) |
| **Performance:** | 0-60mph: 7.0sec<br>Top speed: 156mph |
| **Power & torque:** | 286bhp/251lb ft |
| **Engine:** | Normally aspirated 3452cc straight six, petrol, electronic fuel injection, 24 valves |
| **Drivetrain:** | Front-engine RWD |
| **Structure:** | Monocoque |
| **Transmission:** | Five-speed manual |
| **Weight:** | 1250kg |

### PRICE GUIDE

| | |
|---|---|
| **Launch price:** | £21,805 |
| **Excellent:** | £75,000 |
| **Good:** | £48,000 |
| **Average:** | £30,000 |
| **Project:** | £25,000 |

## BMW
## M635CSi

Another 1980s sporting classic was created when BMW hit on the bright idea of fitting the 286bhp M-Power engine from the mid-engined M1 into the 635CSi body. With stiffened suspension and improved damping, as well as a standard limited-slip differential, it was a sublime package, with masses of all-round ability. Values are significantly higher than non-M-Sport coupés, though they've dipped just recently. Look out for fakes and ropey, rusty ones (lots are), and remember the M-Sport engine costs a lot more to fix when it goes wrong.

### SPECIFICATIONS

| | |
|---|---|
| **Years produced:** | 1984-1989 (5803 in total) |
| **Performance:** | 0-60mph: 6.5sec<br>Top speed: 158mph |
| **Power & torque:** | 286bhp/246lb ft |
| **Engine:** | Normally aspirated 3453cc straight six, petrol, electronic fuel injection, 24 valves |
| **Drivetrain:** | Front-engine RWD |
| **Structure:** | Monocoque |
| **Transmission:** | Five-speed manual |
| **Weight:** | 1505kg |

### PRICE GUIDE

| | |
|---|---|
| **Launch price:** | £32,195 |
| **Excellent:** | £75,000 |
| **Good:** | £50,000 |
| **Average:** | £30,000 |
| **Project:** | £20,000 |

## BMW
## 3-Series convertible (E30)

After the Baur cabriolets with their bulky roll-over structures, the in-house 3-Series convertible – which used a strengthened windscreen surround instead – looked an incredibly clean design. And in a marketplace dominated by cluttered-looking convertibles, the E30 soft-top did very well indeed. It was available with a variety of engine options; the 318i version was the most popular in the UK, although the 325i came a close second. Fun to drive, reliable and cheap to run, they're a great 'starter classic' with values currently holding firm.

### SPECIFICATIONS

| | |
|---|---|
| **Years produced:** | 1985-1993 (143,425 in total) |
| **Performance:** | 0-60mph: 8.4sec (325i)<br>Top speed: 135mph |
| **Power & torque:** | 169bhp/167lb ft |
| **Engine:** | Normally aspirated 2494cc straight six, petrol, electronic fuel injection, 12 valves |
| **Drivetrain:** | Front-engine RWD |
| **Structure:** | Monocoque |
| **Transmission:** | Five-speed manual |
| **Weight:** | 1090kg |

### PRICE GUIDE

| | |
|---|---|
| **Launch price:** | £11,590 |
| **Excellent:** | £25,000 |
| **Good:** | £17,500 |
| **Average:** | £10,000 |
| **Project:** | £5000 |

## BMW
## M3 (E30)

Conceived to compete in Group A Touring Cars, the M3 was one of a rare breed of BMW homologation specials, as most M-cars were designed solely for the road. The 2.3-litre S14 engine was loosely based on the venerable M10 'four' and produced 192bhp straight from the box. However, it was developed throughout its life, and late Evo and Sport versions were pushing out 238bhp. In short, a brilliant sports saloon. Really good M3s are rare (particularly non-special editions) and provenance is everything. Evo 2 the smart buy at c£85k for a really good car.

### SPECIFICATIONS (Evo Sport)

| | |
|---|---|
| **Years produced:** | 1986-1990 (17,184 in total) |
| **Performance:** | 0-60mph: 6.5sec<br>Top speed: 154mph |
| **Power & torque:** | 238bhp/177lb ft |
| **Engine:** | Normally aspirated 2467cc four cylinder, petrol, electronic fuel injection, 16 valves |
| **Drivetrain:** | Front-engine RWD |
| **Structure:** | Monocoque |
| **Transmission:** | Five-speed manual |
| **Weight:** | 1200kg |

### PRICE GUIDE (Evo Sport in brackets)

| | |
|---|---|
| **Launch price:** | £22,750 |
| **Excellent:** | £60,000 (£150,000) |
| **Good:** | £45,000 (£90,000) |
| **Average:** | £30,000 (N/A) |
| **Project:** | £20,000 (N/A) |

## BMW
## Z1

The Z1 was initially a concept at the 1987 Frankfurt Motor Show, but buyers were soon clamouring to buy one. Most notable for its doors, which drop into the sills, it bristled with advanced design features and weight-saving touches, though with the same engine as the 325i it was no ball of fire considering its high price. Diminishing interest from buyers saw BMW halt production with 8000 built. Only 50 official UK imports, but more have been shipped in. Plastic body doesn't rust but can crack, so check carefully, and some parts are hard to find. Buy with care!

**SPECIFICATIONS**

| | |
|---|---|
| **Years produced:** | 1988-1991 (8000 in total) |
| **Performance:** | 0-60mph: 9.0sec<br>Top speed: 136mph |
| **Power & torque:** | 170bhp/164lb ft |
| **Engine:** | Normally aspirated 2494cc straight six, petrol, electronic fuel injection, 12 valves |
| **Drivetrain:** | Front-engine RWD |
| **Structure:** | Steel tub/plastic panels |
| **Transmission:** | Five-speed manual |
| **Weight:** | 1290kg |

**PRICE GUIDE**

| | |
|---|---|
| **Launch price:** | £36,925 |
| **Excellent:** | £40,000 |
| **Good:** | £30,000 |
| **Average:** | £25,000 |
| **Project:** | £15,000 |

## BMW
## 520/525/530/535i (E34)

The arrival of the sleek C2-generation Audi 100 caught BMW napping. Suddenly, its beautifully engineered but very upright E28 saloons looked old-hat. The E34-gen 5-Series launched in 1987 certainly put that right and created a look that would remain with BMW until into the 21st century. A wide range of engines was used, VANOS variable valve timing and 24-valve heads becoming standard fare for the sixes. The 535i Sport model was particularly well-regarded. Also look out for the excellent 540i. Quick, poised, beautifully built, a good one is still a joy to both own and drive.

**SPECIFICATIONS**

| | |
|---|---|
| **Years produced:** | 1987-1996 (1,333,412 in total) |
| **Performance:** | 0-60mph: 7.4sec (535i)<br>Top speed: 141mph |
| **Power & torque:** | 211bhp/225lb ft |
| **Engine:** | Normally aspirated 3430cc straight six, petrol, electronic fuel injection, 24v |
| **Drivetrain:** | Front-engine RWD |
| **Structure:** | Monocoque |
| **Transmission:** | Five-speed manual/four-speed auto |
| **Weight:** | 1450kg |

**PRICE GUIDE (535i/540i in brackets)**

| | |
|---|---|
| **Launch price:** | £34,480 (535i Sport) |
| **Excellent:** | £10,000 (£15,000) |
| **Good:** | £7000 (£8000) |
| **Average:** | £3500 (£4000) |
| **Project:** | £1000 (£2000) |

## BMW
## M5 (E34)

The E34-generation took the M5 squarely into the 1990s with modernised styling and a smooth new interior. The fabulous straight six received various modifications to boost power to 315bhp, pushing the top speed to a limited 155mph. The M5's balance and pace were something rivals struggled to match. In the latter half of 1991, engine capacity was increased to 3.8 litres, lifting power to 340bhp, in which form the M5 represents a pinnacle of the supersaloon genre. LHD-only Touring estate is rare and desirable. On all, beware high running costs.

**SPECIFICATIONS**

| | |
|---|---|
| **Years produced:** | 1988-1995 (11,098 in total) |
| **Performance:** | 0-60mph: 6.5sec<br>Top speed: 155mph |
| **Power & torque:** | 315bhp/265lb ft |
| **Engine:** | Normally aspirated 3535cc straight six, petrol, electronic fuel injection, 24 valves |
| **Drivetrain:** | Front-engine RWD |
| **Structure:** | Monocoque |
| **Transmission:** | Five-speed manual |
| **Weight:** | 1720kg |

**PRICE GUIDE (Touring in brackets)**

| | |
|---|---|
| **Launch price:** | £31,295 |
| **Excellent:** | £35,000 (£50,000+) |
| **Good:** | £25,000 (£40,000) |
| **Average:** | £15,000 (£25,000) |
| **Project:** | £6000 (£12,000) |

## BMW
## 325i Sport (E30)

Regarded as a yuppie's plaything at the time, but now seen as the ultimate evolution of Hofmeister's seminal designs of the '60s, BMW's small saloon lent itself well to every engine installed, but the ultimate 2.5-litre straight-six offered the biggest dose of thrills. The Sport model's slightly out-of-place bodykit lessened its Q-car appeal, but that wailing engine, controllable rear-biased handling and all-round quality made this the sports saloon to beat. Dan Norris at Munich Legends says if you can't stretch to an M3, a 325i Sport is a viable alternative. Values currently flying.

**SPECIFICATIONS**

| | |
|---|---|
| **Years produced:** | 1989-1991 |
| **Performance:** | 0-60mph: 7.5sec<br>Top speed: 140mph |
| **Power & torque:** | 169bhp/164lb ft |
| **Engine:** | Normally aspirated 2494cc straight six, petrol, electronic fuel injection, 12 valves |
| **Drivetrain:** | Front-engine RWD |
| **Structure:** | Monocoque |
| **Transmission:** | Five-speed manual |
| **Weight:** | 1147kg |

**PRICE GUIDE**

| | |
|---|---|
| **Launch price:** | £17,250 |
| **Excellent:** | £50,000 |
| **Good:** | £30,000 |
| **Average:** | £17,000 |
| **Project:** | £9000 |

## BMW
## 325i Touring (E30)

No-one who bought a BMW 3-Series Touring did so thinking this 'estate' was a practical hold-all. What they were getting was a stylish and driveable alternative to a hot hatchback – one that just happened to have 168bhp and rear-wheel drive. A 325iX four-wheel-drive version was also offered, but only in left-hand-drive form – and as a consequence, few made it into the UK. Of all the 'cooking' E30s, the Touring has the most timeless appeal, and still commands a healthy premium over the saloons. As with all '80s BMWs, there is a gulf between the values of excellent and shabby examples.

**SPECIFICATIONS**

| | |
|---|---|
| **Years produced:** | 1988-1991 |
| **Performance:** | 0-60mph: 8.5sec<br>Top speed: 135mph |
| **Power & torque:** | 169bhp/164lb ft |
| **Engine:** | Normally aspirated 2494cc straight six, petrol, electronic fuel injection, 12 valves |
| **Drivetrain:** | Front-engine RWD |
| **Structure:** | Monocoque |
| **Transmission:** | Five-speed manual |
| **Weight:** | 1270kg |

**PRICE GUIDE**

| | |
|---|---|
| **Launch price:** | £17,250 |
| **Excellent:** | £9000 |
| **Good:** | £5500 |
| **Average:** | £3000 |
| **Project:** | £1500 |

## BMW 850/840

A push upmarket for BMW, the 8-series was a true measure of the company's confidence by the late '80s. Powered by BMW's first V12 engine, the 850CSi was quick and effortlesss. But because sales were slow during the recession of the early '90s, BMW also introduced lower-priced V8 versions. These are also well worth considering, especially the 840Ci with its 4.4-litre V8. In fact 850CSi values have taken a hit recently as buyers have become aware of high running costs and patchy parts availability. Only go for the very best, advises Munich Legends' Dan Norris.

### SPECIFICATIONS

| | |
|---|---|
| **Years produced:** | 1989-1999 (31,062 in total) |
| **Performance:** | 0-60mph: 6.0sec (850)<br>Top speed: 155mph (limited) |
| **Power & torque:** | 380bhp/398lb ft |
| **Engine:** | Normally aspirated 5576cc V12, petrol, electronic fuel injection, 24 valves |
| **Drivetrain:** | Front-engine RWD |
| **Structure:** | Monocoque |
| **Transmission:** | Six-speed manual |
| **Weight:** | 1780kg |

### PRICE GUIDE (850CSi in brackets)

| | |
|---|---|
| **Launch price:** | £77,500 |
| **Excellent:** | £35,000 (£55,000) |
| **Good:** | £25,000 (£35,000) |
| **Average:** | £15,000 (£25,000) |
| **Project:** | £10,000 (£12,000) |

## BMW M3 (E36)

The second M3 was a different animal to the E30 1980s original, with a straight-six in place of the fizzy four, suaver styling and a more refined demeanour. Power was originally 286bhp, later 321bhp, in which form the M3 raced to 60mph in 5.4sec. Initially only a coupé, saloon and convertible versions appeared in 1994. The uprated GT is worth looking out for. The E36 M3 lacks the cachet of the E30 but is a fine car in its own right and well-loved examples are sure to become sought-after. Limited editions like the Imola fetch big money; Evo now up to c£35k. Avoid SMG clutchless gearbox.

### SPECIFICATIONS

| | |
|---|---|
| **Years produced:** | 1992-1998 (11,098 in total) |
| **Performance:** | 0-60mph: 5.4sec<br>Top speed: 157mph |
| **Power & torque:** | 321bhp/258lb ft |
| **Engine:** | Normally aspirated 3201cc straight six, petrol, electronic fuel injection, 24v |
| **Drivetrain:** | Front-engine RWD |
| **Structure:** | Monocoque |
| **Transmission:** | Five-speed manual |
| **Weight:** | 1460kg |

### PRICE GUIDE

| | |
|---|---|
| **Launch price:** | £32,450 |
| **Excellent:** | £30,000 |
| **Good:** | £25,000 |
| **Average:** | £12,000 |
| **Project:** | £7000 |

## BMW 3-Series (E46)

BMW's 3-Series makes significant steps forward with every new iteration, but as the last 3-series penned before Chris Bangle's Marmite 'flame surfacing' took hold, many regard the E46-gen cars as a highlight. From turgid 316i, through frugal 320d and 330d to sonorous 330i, and offered in saloon, coupé, convertible and Touring variants, there's an E46 for everyone. Straight-sixes are most appealing, particularly the 328i and later 330i. Club Sports are worth looking out for, but avoid clunky SSG sequential gearbox.

### SPECIFICATIONS

| | |
|---|---|
| **Years produced:** | 1998-2007 |
| **Performance:** | 0-60mph: 6.8sec (328i)<br>Top speed: 149mph |
| **Power & torque:** | 190bhp/206lb ft |
| **Engine:** | Normally aspirated, 2793cc, straight six, electronic injection, 24 valves |
| **Drivetrain:** | Front-engine RWD |
| **Structure:** | Monocoque |
| **Transmission:** | Five-speed manual |
| **Weight:** | 1465kg |

### PRICE GUIDE

| | |
|---|---|
| **Launch price:** | £25,040 |
| **Excellent:** | £5000 |
| **Good:** | £2500 |
| **Average:** | £1300 |
| **Project:** | £600 |

## BMW Z3/M Roadster

The Z3 arrived as part of a 1990s roadster boom kicked off by the Mazda MX-5. Like Mazda, BMW went down the retrospective route with the Z3, the car's design an homage to roadsters of old. Basic 1.9s lack the bite to match the styling's bark. The 2.8 and later 3.0 are better, with a tuneful straight-six up front. The M Roadster featured an E36 M3 engine and swollen bodywork, making it a sort of modern-day Cobra. Most prized are '01/02 cars with the 'S54' engine from the E46 M3, which can fetch £25k and more.

### SPECIFICATIONS

| | |
|---|---|
| **Years produced:** | 1995-2002 |
| **Performance:** | 0-60mph: 5.3sec (M Roadster)<br>Top speed: 155mph |
| **Power & torque:** | 325bhp/258lb ft |
| **Engine:** | Normally aspirated 3246cc straight six, petrol, electronic injection, 24 valves |
| **Drivetrain:** | Front-engine RWD |
| **Structure:** | Monocoque |
| **Transmission:** | Five-speed manual |
| **Weight:** | 1450kg |

### PRICE GUIDE (M Roadster in brackets)

| | |
|---|---|
| **Launch price:** | £28,120 (£40,595) |
| **Excellent:** | £7000 (£18,000) |
| **Good:** | £4000 (£13,500) |
| **Average:** | £2500 (£10,000) |
| **Project:** | £1000 (N/A) |

## BMW M5 (E39)

The E39-gen M5 is one of BMW's best-loved M cars, and it isn't hard to see why. Handsome styling is matched to a superb, 394bhp 4.9-litre V8 that made it the browniest super-saloon available on its debut in 1998. It also had a well-balanced chassis and was the last M5 to feature a manual gearbox in the UK. The E39 M5 is now firmly established as one of the greats, but it's vital to ensure any example you buy has been maintained impeccably. Can suffer from electronic glitches, and high-milers (100k+) are best avoided.

### SPECIFICATIONS

| | |
|---|---|
| **Years produced:** | 1998-2003 (20,482 in total) |
| **Performance:** | 0-60mph: 4.8sec<br>Top speed: 155mph |
| **Power & torque:** | 394bhp/369lb ft |
| **Engine:** | Normally aspirated 4941cc V8, petrol, electronic injection, 32 valves |
| **Drivetrain:** | Front-engine RWD |
| **Structure:** | Monocoque |
| **Transmission:** | Six-speed manual |
| **Weight:** | 1795kg |

### PRICE GUIDE

| | |
|---|---|
| **Launch price:** | £59,995 |
| **Excellent:** | £45,000+ |
| **Good:** | £35,000 |
| **Average:** | £20,000 |
| **Project:** | £8000 |

## BMW Z3 M Coupe

Known as the 'breadvan', the M Coupe's styling remains divisive. For some, the long bonnet and sharply truncated tail are just too disproportionate; for others, the squat stance and practicality of the shooting-brake rear are exactly why it appeals. The 'S50' straight-six from the E36 M3 (updated to the superior 'S54' unit when the E46 M3 arrived in 2001), offers more than enough power and a fine soundtrack. Challenging to drive, and not the best-built BMW, it does have a following though values have dipped in the last 12 months.

**SPECIFICATIONS**

**Years produced:** 1998-2003 (c9000 in total)
**Performance:** 0-60mph: 4.3sec
Top speed: 155mph
**Power & torque:** 325bhp/258lb ft
**Engine:** Normally aspirated 3246cc straight six, petrol, electronic injection, 24 valves
**Drivetrain:** Front-engine RWD
**Structure:** Monocoque
**Transmission:** Five-speed manual
**Weight:** 1450kg

**PRICE GUIDE ('S54' version in brackets)**

**Launch price:** £40,595
**Excellent:** £32,000 (£40,000)
**Good:** £20,000 (£30,000)
**Average:** £15,000 (£25,000)
**Project:** £5000 (£7500)

## BMW M3 (E46)

An evolution of the E36-gen M3, so behind the blistered arches and quartet of tailpipes, a BMW Motorsport-fettled in-line-six still took pride of place. The 3.2-litre delivered its 338bhp with a metallic rasp and was paired to a beautifully balanced chassis. A six-speed SMG II automated manual was optional but purists prefer the six-speed manual, many also favouring the ride and handling on the standard 18in alloy wheels over the optional 19s. Carbon-clad CSL is rare and pricey; CS arguably the best of all worlds.

**SPECIFICATIONS**

**Years produced:** 2000-2006
**Performance:** 0-60mph: 5.1sec
Top speed: 155mph
**Power & torque:** 338bhp/269lb ft
**Engine:** Normally aspirated 3246cc straight six, petrol, electronic injection, 24 valves
**Drivetrain:** Front-engine RWD
**Structure:** Monocoque
**Transmission:** Six-speed manual
**Weight:** 1495kg

**PRICE GUIDE (M3/CS/CSL)**

**Launch price:** £39,340
**Excellent:** £25,000/£35,000/£65,000
**Good:** £19,000/£27,500/£40,000
**Average:** £12,000/£22,000/£35,000
**Project:** £8000/--/--

## BMW Z8

A fleeting appearance in the James Bond film *The World Is Not Enough* did little justice to the pretty, Henrik Fisker-styled Z8. Dropping the contemporary M5's V8 drivetrain into a classically styled drop-top that echoed the immortal 507 was a neat move, and limited production means it's a strong performer on today's market. Launched in 1999 for £80,000, values of the aluminium-bodied, hand-finished roadster never really dipped. Bought mostly by collectors in the US, all are left-hand drive and few cover many miles.

**SPECIFICATIONS**

**Years produced:** 1999-2003 (5703 in total)
**Performance:** 0-60mph: 4.5sec
Top speed: 155mph
**Power & torque:** 394bhp/369lb ft
**Engine:** Normally aspirated 4941cc V8, petrol, electronic injection, 32 valves
**Drivetrain:** Front-engine RWD
**Structure:** Monocoque
**Transmission:** Six-speed manual
**Weight:** 1585kg

**PRICE GUIDE**

**Launch price:** £80,000
**Excellent:** £190,000
**Good:** £150,000
**Average:** N/A
**Project:** N/A

## BMW M5 (E60)

The E39 may be the sweet spot in the M5 story, but the E60 that replaced it was one mighty machine, with a stupendous 5-litre V10 (unique to the M5 and the M6 coupé sibling that followed) and a seven-speed SMG paddleshift gearbox. Top speed was limited to 155mph but could be raised to 190mph if the buyer selected the M-driver's package. Last of the big naturally aspirated M5s, but running costs are steep and fuel consumption is eye-watering. Touring estate version is a real cult car, but in all cases avoid high-milers.

**SPECIFICATIONS**

**Years produced:** 2005-2010 (20,589 in total)
**Performance:** 0-60mph: 4.7sec
Top speed: 155mph (limited)
**Power & torque:** 501bhp/383lb ft
**Engine:** Normally aspirated 4999cc V10, petrol, electronic injection, 40 valves
**Drivetrain:** Front-engine RWD
**Structure:** Monocoque
**Transmission:** Seven-speed automated manual
**Weight:** 1830kg

**PRICE GUIDE**

**Launch price:** £61,775
**Excellent:** £28,000
**Good:** £20,000
**Average:** £15,000
**Project:** £5000

# BOND

BOND STARTED life in 1948 with very spartan three-wheeler Minicars, the brainchild of founder Lawrie Bond. Although the Minicar continued until 1966, Bond diversified into more mature machines such as the 875 – three wheels and glassfibre bodywork – and the GT, which was a four-wheeled sports coupé using parts from the Herald bin. When Triumph moved on to the more powerful Vitesse, so did Bond, with the less visually appealing Equipe 2-Litre. The takeover by Reliant in 1970 killed off all these models, but the Bond name continued on the wacky Bug, a wedge-shaped three-wheeler designed purely for fun. Which is why it came only in bright tangerine...

## BOND
## Minicar three-wheeler

At the end of WW2 cars were at a premium, so engineer Lawrie Bond came up with a budget three-wheeler Britain could afford. The Bond Minicar was poverty motoring in the extreme: no roof, no doors, brakes only at the rear and precious little suspension. Its single-cylinder two-stroke 122cc motorcycle engine started life with just 5bhp, but gave 40mph and a claimed 104mpg. Minicars gradually became more refined and powerful, until production ended in 1966. The final Mark G had a roof, doors and hydraulic brakes.

**SPECIFICATIONS**

| | |
|---|---|
| **Years produced:** | 1948-1966 (24,484 in total) |
| **Performance:** | 0-60mph: N/A<br>Top speed: 50mph |
| **Power & torque:** | 5-12bhp/N/A |
| **Engine:** | Normally aspirated 122cc, single cylinder two-stroke, petrol, carburettor |
| **Drivetrain:** | Front-engine FWD |
| **Structure:** | Monocoque, then separate chassis |
| **Transmission:** | Chain drive |
| **Weight:** | 140kg |

**PRICE GUIDE**

| | |
|---|---|
| **Launch price:** | £199 |
| **Excellent:** | £6000 |
| **Good:** | £3500 |
| **Average:** | £1500 |
| **Project:** | £700 |

## BOND
## GT 2+2/GT4S

In 1963, Bond expanded into the world of specialist sportscars – with four wheels. But the full quotient of wheels still didn't fulfil the firm's claims that this was 'the most beautiful car in the world', although this glassfibre coupé on a Triumph Herald chassis was a neat enough effort. Initially the engine was the 1147cc from the Triumph Spitfire, which rose to 1296cc in 1967 when the Spitfire expanded. The improved GT4S of 1964 had four headlamps, a boot that actually opened and greater headroom that helped to up comfort levels. Add 25% for the GT4S.

**SPECIFICATIONS**

| | |
|---|---|
| **Years produced:** | 1963-1970 (2949 in total) |
| **Performance:** | 0-60mph: 20.0sec<br>Top speed: 91mph |
| **Power & torque:** | 67bhp/67lb ft |
| **Engine:** | Normally aspirated 1147cc four cylinder, petrol, carburettor, 8 valves |
| **Drivetrain:** | Front-engine RWD |
| **Structure:** | Separate chassis |
| **Transmission:** | Four-speed manual |
| **Weight:** | 737kg |

**PRICE GUIDE**

| | |
|---|---|
| **Launch price:** | £822 |
| **Excellent:** | £4300 |
| **Good:** | £2600 |
| **Average:** | £1400 |
| **Project:** | £500 |

## BOND
## Equipe 2-litre

Having built a Herald-based sports coupé, it was only logical that Bond would try something similar with the Vitesse chassis. The result, in 1967, was the Equipe GT, also known as the 2-Litre. The styling of the glassfibre/steel-panelled vehicle was totally different to Bond's previous version; more square-rigged and heavier. However, the extra weight didn't matter too much, as the additional power of the Triumph straight six (95bhp at first, 104bhp from 1968) gave adequate performance, with 100mph eventually obtainable.

**SPECIFICATIONS**

| | |
|---|---|
| **Years produced:** | 1967-1970 (1432 in total) |
| **Performance:** | 0-60mph: 10.7sec<br>Top speed: 102mph |
| **Power & torque:** | 95bhp/117lb ft |
| **Engine:** | Normally aspirated 1998cc straight six, petrol, carburettor, 12 valves |
| **Drivetrain:** | Front-engine RWD |
| **Structure:** | Separate chassis |
| **Transmission:** | Four-speed manual |
| **Weight:** | 914kg |

**PRICE GUIDE**

| | |
|---|---|
| **Launch price:** | £1096 |
| **Excellent:** | £6000 |
| **Good:** | £4000 |
| **Average:** | £1750 |
| **Project:** | £800 |

## BOND
## Bug 700E

This funky and fun three-wheeler was built for pure entertainment purposes by Reliant, Bond's new owner. A cheesy car for a cheesy decade, its Ogle Design-styled wedge shape gave the two passengers access via the pull-forward canopy. The only colour officially available was a very vibrant tangerine. The engines were Reliant: a 700cc unit offering 29bhp, and 31bhp on the ES model, followed by a 748cc offering 32bhp in 1973. Utterly mad, but the classic car world is all the richer for bizarre machines such as these. Values holding firm.

**SPECIFICATIONS**

| | |
|---|---|
| **Years produced:** | 1970-1974 (2270 in total) |
| **Performance:** | 0-60mph: 23.2sec<br>Top speed: 76mph |
| **Power & torque:** | 29bhp/35lb ft |
| **Engine:** | Normally aspirated 700cc four cylinder, petrol, carburettor, 8 valves |
| **Drivetrain:** | Front-engine RWD |
| **Structure:** | Separate chassis |
| **Transmission:** | Four-speed manual |
| **Weight:** | 394kg |

**PRICE GUIDE**

| | |
|---|---|
| **Launch price:** | £629 |
| **Excellent:** | £9500 |
| **Good:** | £7000 |
| **Average:** | £4500 |
| **Project:** | £2500 |

# BORGWARD

IN 1929, car radiator manufacturer Carl Borgward became a director of Hansa Lloyd AG; gradually this company became just Borgward. Its stylish models were typified by the large and sleek-looking 2400, which was the first European car to have its own automatic transmission, and the pretty Isabella, of 1954 to 1961, which was named after the founder's wife. Well over 200,000 were sold, thanks to the looks and the car's reputation for being almost bulletproof. Problems elsewhere in the conglomerate that Borgward was a part of led to bankruptcy in 1961, even though the company itself was still making money. Borgward himself died just two years later.

## BORGWARD
### Isabella TS saloon

A superbly-engineered car that was a revelation in its day. Alloy-head 1500 engine puts out an impressive 75bhp, which Ford only just surpassed eight years later with the Cortina GT, and no Cortina ever enjoyed the Isabella's independent rear suspension. Before he became a Vauxhall tuning guru, Bill Blydenstein successfully raced one in the 1950s. Brakes are another strong point and even the four-speed column change is a delight to use. Thanks to a strong following in the car's native Germany, parts supply is almost total.

**SPECIFICATIONS**

| | |
|---|---|
| **Years produced:** | 1954-1961 (202,862 in total) |
| **Performance:** | 0-60mph: 16.0sec<br>Top speed: 95mph |
| **Power & torque:** | 75bhp/85lb ft |
| **Engine:** | Normally aspirated 1493cc four cylinder, petrol, carburettor, 8 valves |
| **Drivetrain:** | Front-engine RWD |
| **Structure:** | Separate chassis |
| **Transmission:** | Four-speed manual |
| **Weight:** | 1080kg |

**PRICE GUIDE**

| | |
|---|---|
| **Launch price:** | £1124 |
| **Excellent:** | £9000 |
| **Good:** | £6500 |
| **Average:** | £4000 |
| **Project:** | £1250 |

## BORGWARD
### Isabella coupé

Generally considered to be Carl Borgward's masterpiece, the Isabella coupé was initially conceived as an image-booster for the firm. The 2+2 oozes class, has a decent turn of speed and handles tidily with its all-independent coil-sprung suspension and rear swing axles. The unburstable engines even run happily on unleaded fuel without any alteration. A cabriolet version was also built, but these are much rarer. However, the drop-tops are very highly thought of in Germany, and can easily fetch twice the price of a coupé.

**SPECIFICATIONS**

| | |
|---|---|
| **Years produced:** | 1955-1961 |
| **Performance:** | 0-60mph: 16.9sec<br>Top speed: 81mph |
| **Power & torque:** | 60bhp/79lb ft |
| **Engine:** | Normally aspirated 1493cc four cylinder, petrol, carburettor, 8 valves |
| **Drivetrain:** | Front-engine RWD |
| **Structure:** | Separate chassis |
| **Transmission:** | Four-speed manual |
| **Weight:** | 1080kg |

**PRICE GUIDE**

| | |
|---|---|
| **Launch price:** | £1874 |
| **Excellent:** | £27,000 |
| **Good:** | £18,000 |
| **Average:** | £12,000 |
| **Project:** | £5000 |

# BRISTOL

WITH SPARE production capacity after the end of the war, the Bristol Aeroplane Company decided to enter the car-making business and acquired the rights to pre-war BMWs. Its early cars were stylish, streamlined, fast and luxurious, and Bristols gained a reputation for being expensively handmade in small numbers for well-heeled customers. Chrysler V8s were introduced with the 407 of 1961. Thereafter it was a story of gradual evolution, with the exception of the 200mph gullwing-door Fighter in 2004. Rescued from administration in 2011, a new model, the Bullet speedster, was revealed in 2016, but none is believed to have been delivered and the company entered liquidation in March 2020.

## BRISTOL
### 400

Bristol Cars was formed when the Bristol Aeroplane Company joined forces with Frazer-Nash's parent company, AFN. Before the war, AFN was the concessionaire for BMW in the UK, so after Bristol took possession of BMW's designs, AFN was the natural choice for a build partner. The 400 was the first fruit of the combined companies' efforts, and was clearly based on a mixture of the pre-war BMW 326 (chassis) and 327/80 (body). Many changes were made – and aeroplane levels of build quality were a clear benefit. Values currently steady.

**SPECIFICATIONS**

| | |
|---|---|
| **Years produced:** | 1946-1949 (700 in total) |
| **Performance:** | 0-60mph: 14.7sec<br>Top speed: 94mph |
| **Power & torque:** | 80bhp/96lb ft |
| **Engine:** | Normally aspirated 1971cc straight six, petrol, carburettor, 12 valves |
| **Drivetrain:** | Front-engine RWD |
| **Structure:** | Separate chassis |
| **Transmission:** | Four-speed manual |
| **Weight:** | 1118kg |

**PRICE GUIDE**

| | |
|---|---|
| **Launch price:** | £2374 |
| **Excellent:** | £100,000 |
| **Good:** | £75,000 |
| **Average:** | £40,000 |
| **Project:** | £30,000 |

## BRISTOL
### 401/403

Building on the promise of the 400, the 401 was introduced initially for export markets only. Its handsome, more modern styling was developed largely in the wind tunnel and had an extremely good drag coefficient for the time. It was a look way ahead of its time, merely let down by a lack of power. This shortcoming was put right five years later, with the appearance of the 403 – and a welcome upgrade to 100bhp. Bristols were well crafted, which helps keep them surprisingly usable today – reflected in strong values of both models.

**SPECIFICATIONS**

| | |
|---|---|
| **Years produced:** | 1949-1955 (950 in total) |
| **Performance:** | 0-60mph: 15.1sec<br>Top speed: 97mph |
| **Power & torque:** | 85bhp/107lb ft (401) |
| **Engine:** | Normally aspirated 1971cc straight six, petrol, carburettor, 12 valves |
| **Drivetrain:** | Front-engine RWD |
| **Structure:** | Separate chassis |
| **Transmission:** | Four-speed manual |
| **Weight:** | 1224kg |

**PRICE GUIDE**

| | |
|---|---|
| **Launch price:** | £3214 |
| **Excellent:** | £70,000/£85,000 |
| **Good:** | £50,000/£60,000 |
| **Average:** | £45,000/£50,000 |
| **Project:** | £30,000/£30,000 |

## BRISTOL
### 404

The 404 had a shorter chassis married to an exquisitely styled two-door coupé bodyshell. But it was not without problems. There was the small issue of price (it cost twice as much as a Jaguar XK120) and a lack of ultimate power compared with its Coventry rival. The aluminium body and ash frame have caused problems for owners in later years. But for all its flaws, the 404's looks at least allowed it to break away from its Teutonic forebears. It is now one of the most collectable Bristols, with dropheads being particularly sought-after.

**SPECIFICATIONS**

| | |
|---|---|
| **Years produced:** | 1953-1955 (52 in total) |
| **Performance:** | 0-60mph: N/A<br>Top speed: 110mph |
| **Power & torque:** | 105bhp/123lb ft |
| **Engine:** | Normally aspirated 1971cc straight six, petrol, carburettor, 12 valves |
| **Drivetrain:** | Front-engine RWD |
| **Structure:** | Separate chassis |
| **Transmission:** | Four-speed manual |
| **Weight:** | 1039kg |

**PRICE GUIDE**

| | |
|---|---|
| **Launch price:** | £3543 |
| **Excellent:** | £230,000 |
| **Good:** | £165,000 |
| **Average:** | £100,000 |
| **Project:** | £50,000 |

## BRISTOL
### 405

This saloon was effectively a long-wheelbase version of the 404 (it had four doors) and it went on to score significantly more commercial success. Unlike the 404, which, through its extensive use of wood in its construction, has a low survival rate, the 405 has fared much better over the years. That's mainly because most of the wood in the body is *above* the waistline – a boon in damp climes. It was a pretty four-door GT that was crying out for more power. Interesting trivia fact: a 405 was the daily driver of Sir Paul Smith for many years.

**SPECIFICATIONS**

| | |
|---|---|
| **Years produced:** | 1954-1956 (340 in total) |
| **Performance:** | 0-60mph: N/A<br>Top speed: 110mph |
| **Power & torque:** | 105bhp/123lb ft |
| **Engine:** | Normally aspirated 1971cc straight six, petrol, carburettor, 12 valves |
| **Drivetrain:** | Front-engine RWD |
| **Structure:** | Separate chassis |
| **Transmission:** | Four-speed manual with overdrive |
| **Weight:** | 1230kg |

**PRICE GUIDE (DHC in brackets)**

| | |
|---|---|
| **Launch price:** | £3189 |
| **Excellent:** | £75,000 (£230,000) |
| **Good:** | £50,000 (£165,000) |
| **Average:** | £40,000 (£100,000) |
| **Project:** | £30,000 (£50,000) |

## BRISTOL
### 406

The 406 ended up being the last Bristol to be powered by the BMW-derived straight six, but the first of a long line of cars that would use essentially the same body, with a series of running updates. In terms of power, the 406 had no more than the 405, despite its engine being enlarged to 2.2 litres, and performance with this large body was predictably leisurely. The brakes were improved, though, featuring discs front and rear, and the back suspension got a Watt linkage. More would come with the arrival of the V8-powered cars.

**SPECIFICATIONS**

| | |
|---|---|
| **Years produced:** | 1958-1961 (292 in total) |
| **Performance:** | 0-60mph: N/A<br>Top speed: 106mph |
| **Power & torque:** | 105bhp/129lb ft |
| **Engine:** | Normally aspirated 2216cc straight six, petrol, carburettor, 12 valves |
| **Drivetrain:** | Front-engine RWD |
| **Structure:** | Separate chassis |
| **Transmission:** | Four-speed manual with overdrive |
| **Weight:** | 1365kg |

**PRICE GUIDE**

| | |
|---|---|
| **Launch price:** | £4494 |
| **Excellent:** | £75,000 |
| **Good:** | £50,000 |
| **Average:** | £30,000 |
| **Project:** | £18,000 |

## BRISTOL
### 407/408/409/410

Changes in the ownership of Bristol Cars meant that it was now a separate entity to the aeroplane manufacturer. A Chrysler V8 was installed under the long bonnet of the 406, giving the elegant sporting saloon the performance to match its looks. With a top speed of over 125mph, the Bristol became a credible alternative to Aston Martin and Jaguar. American muscle under the bonnet also meant improved parts and support. The 410 added power steering for improved manoeuvrability and is today particularly sought-after.

**SPECIFICATIONS**

| | |
|---|---|
| **Years produced:** | 1961-1969 (88/83/74/82 in total) |
| **Performance:** | 0-60mph: 8.8sec<br>Top speed: 130mph |
| **Power & torque:** | 250bhp/340lb ft |
| **Engine:** | Normally aspirated 5211cc V8, petrol, carburettor, 16 valves |
| **Drivetrain:** | Front-engine RWD |
| **Structure:** | Separate chassis |
| **Transmission:** | Three-speed automatic |
| **Weight:** | 1600kg |

**PRICE GUIDE (410 in brackets)**

| | |
|---|---|
| **Launch price:** | £4848 |
| **Excellent:** | £75,000 (£85,000) |
| **Good:** | £50,000 (£55,000) |
| **Average:** | £35,000 (£40,000) |
| **Project:** | £20,000 (£20,000) |

## BRISTOL
### 411

Considered by Bristol aficionados to be the best of the V8-powered 400 Series cars, the 411 appeared at the end of the 1960s, still looking understated and elegant. This version sported a 6.3-litre version of the Chrysler Type B V8 engine and could effortlessly top 140mph after sprinting from 0-60mph in seven seconds. It might not have been the ideal power unit during the oil crisis of the early '70s, but Bristol continued to sell cars to its loyal customers while those around went under. The last of the 'classic' Bristol line before '70s styling cues took over.

**SPECIFICATIONS**

| | |
|---|---|
| **Years produced:** | 1969-1976 (600 in total) |
| **Performance:** | 0-60mph: 7.0sec<br>Top speed: 140mph |
| **Power & torque:** | 335bhp/335lb ft |
| **Engine:** | Normally aspirated 6556cc V8, petrol, carburettor, 16 valves |
| **Drivetrain:** | Front-engine RWD |
| **Structure:** | Separate chassis |
| **Transmission:** | Three-speed automatic |
| **Weight:** | 1712kg |

**PRICE GUIDE (series 1-5)**

| | |
|---|---|
| **Launch price:** | £8793 |
| **Excellent:** | £80,000-£100,000 |
| **Good:** | £40,000-£55,000 |
| **Average:** | £30,000 |
| **Project:** | £15,000 |

THE MARKET
90% sale rate in 2020 so far
BEWARE OF IMITATORS.......
JOK 605N
The UK's most successful auction house
New classic & collectable auctions going live daily
No buyers' fees, only 5% + vat sellers' fees

## BRISTOL
### 412

Even maestros have a bad day. That could explain the square-looking Zagato styling of the 412. But despite being launched during the blackest days of the '70s with a gigantic V8 engine, the 412 continued to sell for Bristol, even building up a modest waiting list. The quality was as deep rooted as ever, and the chassis was straight from the tried-and-tested 411, although the targa roof panel was a genuine innovation for the company. The 6.6-litre V8 was downsized to 5.9 litres in the late '70s, but the grunt remained intact.

**SPECIFICATIONS**

| | |
|---|---|
| **Years produced:** | 1975-1980 |
| **Performance:** | 0-60mph: 7.4sec<br>Top speed: 140mph |
| **Power & torque:** | 335bhp/N/A |
| **Engine:** | Normally aspirated 6556cc V8, petrol, carburettor, 16 valves |
| **Drivetrain:** | Front-engine RWD |
| **Structure:** | Separate chassis |
| **Transmission:** | Three-speed automatic |
| **Weight:** | 1715kg |

**PRICE GUIDE**

| | |
|---|---|
| **Launch price:** | £14,584 |
| **Excellent:** | £48,000 |
| **Good:** | £35,000 |
| **Average:** | £19,000 |
| **Project:** | £5000 |

## BRISTOL
### 603/Britannia

In the late 1970s, Bristol started offering a two-model range: the 412 for those looking for open-topped motoring, and the 603, an elegantly-styled fastback with saloon levels of interior accommodation. It was an interesting mix, and one that ensured the firm's survival into the '80s. Under that new aluminium body lay the same basic separate chassis found in the 412 (and its predecessors), and it was none the worse for this. By now, Bristol was positively delighted with its image of exclusivity, and had a number of high-profile fans – notably writer LJK Setright – in its ranks.

**SPECIFICATIONS**

| | |
|---|---|
| **Years produced:** | 1976-1982 |
| **Performance:** | 0-60mph: 8.6sec<br>Top speed: 140mph |
| **Power & torque:** | 335bhp/270lb ft |
| **Engine:** | Normally aspirated 5898cc V8, petrol, carburettor, 16 valves |
| **Drivetrain:** | Front-engine RWD |
| **Structure:** | Separate chassis |
| **Transmission:** | Three-speed automatic |
| **Weight:** | 1783kg |

**PRICE GUIDE**

| | |
|---|---|
| **Launch price:** | £19,661 |
| **Excellent:** | £35,000 |
| **Good:** | £25,000 |
| **Average:** | £15,000 |
| **Project:** | £5000 |

## BRISTOL
### Beaufighter convertible

An interesting one, this, as although it was yet another revision of the continuously-evolving model line, the Beaufighter had rather more (undisclosed) power than the 412 it was based upon. The secret was, of course, turbocharging – which by the time the Beaufighter appeared, everyone was getting in on. Although Bristol was coy about power figures, or lending out test cars, the performance had leapt forwards – 0-60mph in 5.9 seconds with a top speed of 150mph. If a Bentley Turbo R is a little 'obvious', then a Beaufighter (or a Brigand) could be for you.

**SPECIFICATIONS**

| | |
|---|---|
| **Years produced:** | 1980-1993 |
| **Performance:** | 0-60mph: 5.9sec<br>Top speed: 150mph |
| **Power & torque:** | c.400bhp/N/A |
| **Engine:** | Turbocharged 5898cc V8, petrol, carburettor, 16 valves |
| **Drivetrain:** | Front-engine RWD |
| **Structure:** | Separate chassis |
| **Transmission:** | Three-speed automatic |
| **Weight:** | 1746kg |

**PRICE GUIDE**

| | |
|---|---|
| **Launch price:** | £37,999 |
| **Excellent:** | £50,000 |
| **Good:** | £35,000 |
| **Average:** | £19,000 |
| **Project:** | £5000 |

## BRISTOL
### Brigand

It was inevitable the turbocharged version of the Chrysler V8 that was so praised by Beaufighter customers would find its way into the Britannia. And just as it did with the targa-topped car's upgrade, Bristol re-named its coupé, launching the freshly-boosted Brigand as a brand new car. Considering the chassis and suspension set-up originated from the late 1940s – albeit with countless changes – it's remarkable that it was still able to cope with an additional 20% of power. Specialist help is readily available, most notably from Bristol itself.

**SPECIFICATIONS**

| | |
|---|---|
| **Years produced:** | 1982-1993 |
| **Performance:** | 0-60mph: 5.9sec<br>Top speed: 150mph |
| **Power & torque:** | N/A/N/A |
| **Engine:** | Turbocharged 5898cc V8, petrol, carburettor, 16 valves |
| **Drivetrain:** | Front-engine RWD |
| **Structure:** | Separate chassis |
| **Transmission:** | Three-speed automatic |
| **Weight:** | 1746kg |

**PRICE GUIDE**

| | |
|---|---|
| **Launch price:** | £46,843 |
| **Excellent:** | £42,500 |
| **Good:** | £27,500 |
| **Average:** | £15,000 |
| **Project:** | £5000 |

## BRISTOL
### Blenheim

The final evolution of the Type 603 two-door saloon that had been launched in 1976, the 1990s Blenheim introduced such refinements as multi-port fuel injection to the familiar Bristol formula, and a new four-speed automatic from the Blenheim 2 onwards. The 5.9-litre Chrysler engine continued to serve, now minus the turbocharger, and underneath the mildly updated bodywork, all was much as before. Old before its time, the Blenheim somehow soldiered on, selling in microscopic numbers, until the company went into administration in 2011.

**SPECIFICATIONS**

| | |
|---|---|
| **Years produced:** | 1993-2011 |
| **Performance:** | 0-60mph: 7.2sec<br>Top speed: 141mph |
| **Power & torque:** | N/A/N/A |
| **Engine:** | Naturally aspirated 5898cc V8, petrol, fuel injection, 16 valves |
| **Drivetrain:** | Front-engine RWD |
| **Structure:** | Separate chassis |
| **Transmission:** | Three-speed/four-speed automatic |
| **Weight:** | N/A |

**PRICE GUIDE**

| | |
|---|---|
| **Launch price:** | £109,980 |
| **Excellent:** | £60,000 |
| **Good:** | £45,000 |
| **Average:** | £28,000 |
| **Project:** | £10,000 |

## BRISTOL Fighter

An unexpected twist to the Bristol story came in 2004 with the gullwing-doored, V10-engined Fighter. The engine was a mildly reworked version of the V10 from the Chrysler Viper and it gave the aluminium and carbonfibre-bodied Fighter supercar levels of performance, but in a relatively tall and narrow body that actually made it more practical than most. Very few were sold; possibly as many as 15. Specialists SLJ Hackett say that values have climbed steadily in recent years, and the very best might now fetch £250,000-plus.

**SPECIFICATIONS**

**Years produced:** 2004-2011 (c15 in total)
**Performance:** 0-60mph: c4.0sec
Top speed: c200mph
**Power & torque:** 525bhp/525lb ft
**Engine:** Normally aspirated 7996cc V10, petrol, electronic injection, 20 valves
**Drivetrain:** Front-engine RWD
**Structure:** Steel backbone/carbon and alloy body
**Transmission:** Six-speed manual/four-speed auto
**Weight:** 1600kg

**PRICE GUIDE**

**Launch price:** £229,125
**Excellent:** £225,000
**Good:** £200,000
**Average:** N/A
**Project:** N/A

# BUGATTI

THERE HAVE been a number of Bugatti incarnations. The original French company, founded by the Italian-born industrial designer Ettore Bugatti in 1909, was famed for the beauty and quality of cars such as the 1920s Type 35 racer and the massive Type 41 'Royale'. After Ettore's death in 1947 the company struggled and eventually ceased trading. The Bugatti name was later ressurected, first in the early 1990s by Italian entrepreneur Romano Artioli, who built a new factory in Modena to build the EB110 supercar, and, after this company collapsed, by the Volkswagen group, who acquired the brand in 1998. Today's Bugattis are built at Molsheim, as were Ettore's originals.

## BUGATTI EB110

Romano Artioli's short-lived Italian reincarnation of Bugatti produced a car worthy of the badge in the form of the EB110, named in celebration of Ettore Bugatti's 110th birthday. It boasted a carbonfibre tub, four-wheel drive and a 553bhp 3.5-litre V12 with five valves per cylinder and four turbos. When the company went under, German race specialist Dauer built a handful more cars from parts. Lighter, more powerful (603bhp) Super-Sport (just 30 of which were built) could fetch as much as double the prices shown here.

**SPECIFICATIONS**

**Years produced:** 1991-1995 (139 in total)
**Performance:** 0-60mph: 3.5sec
Top speed: 212mph
**Power & torque:** 553bhp/451lb ft
**Engine:** Quad-turbocharged 3500cc V12, petrol, electronic injection, 60 valves
**Drivetrain:** Mid-engine 4WD
**Structure:** Carbonfibre tub/carbon and alloy body
**Transmission:** Six-speed manual
**Weight:** 1620kg

**PRICE GUIDE**

**Launch price:** £285,000
**Excellent:** £800,000
**Good:** £700,000
**Average:** £600,000
**Project:** N/A

## BUGATTI Veyron 16.4

The first Bugatti of the Volkswagen group era was so far in advance of other supercars that a new term, 'hypercar', was coined by the motoring press. The Veyron name was in honour of pre-war Bugatti racer Pierre Veyron (16.4 representing the number of cylinders and the four turbochargers for the magnificent 8-litre W16 engine). When the Veyron was officially clocked at 253.81mph, it became the fastest production road car the world had yet seen. In 2009, a convertible version, the Grand Sport, was launched, limited to 150 units.

**SPECIFICATIONS**

**Years produced:** 2005-2011 (450 in total)
**Performance:** 0-60mph: 2.4sec
Top speed: 253.81mph
**Power & torque:** 987bhp/922lb ft
**Engine:** Quad-turbocharged 7993cc W16, petrol, electronic injection, 64 valves
**Drivetrain:** Mid-engine 4WD
**Structure:** Carbonfibre tub and body
**Transmission:** Seven-speed dual-clutch automatic
**Weight:** 1888kg

**PRICE GUIDE**

**Launch price:** £1,065,000
**Excellent:** £1,200,000
**Good:** £1,000,000
**Average:** £900,000
**Project:** N/A

# CATERHAM

WHEN LOTUS stopped building its basic Seven sports car in 1973, the rights were acquired by Caterham Cars, a Kent-based Lotus dealer. So the firm has now built the Seven for many times longer than the 16 years chalked up by its creator. The original 1950s styling may be sacred, but elsewhere the car has been comprehensively updated, with Vauxhall, Ford and Rover mechanicals. Caterham dabbled with something different in the 1990s but the pretty 21, with its expanded bodywork, proved not to be a success and only 48 were built between 1995 and 1999. The company has stuck doggedly with the Seven ever since, and in recent years has developed a popular line in low-powered 'retro' versions.

## CATERHAM
### Seven

When Colin Chapman took Lotus upmarket in the early 1970s, he sold the rights to the Seven to dealer Caterham Cars, which quickly returned the sporting icon to production and has never looked back. The tubular steel chassis bodied in aluminium has remained almost unchanged, although engines (traditionally Ford, for a while Vauxhall, and from the early '90s chiefly Rover K-series) have come and gone. Prices depend on condition and spec rather than age and mileage – all you have to do is decide how much performance you can handle.

**SPECIFICATIONS**

| | |
|---|---|
| **Years produced:** | 1974-present |
| **Performance:** | 0-60mph: 7.7sec (Ford 1.6)<br>Top speed: 99mph |
| **Power & torque:** | 84bhp/96lb ft |
| **Engine:** | Normally aspirated 1598cc four cylinder, petrol, carburettor, 8 valves |
| **Drivetrain:** | Front-engine RWD |
| **Structure:** | Spaceframe |
| **Transmission:** | Four/five-speed manual |
| **Weight:** | 518kg |

**PRICE GUIDE**

| | |
|---|---|
| **Launch price:** | £2887 |
| **Excellent:** | £15,000+ |
| **Good:** | £12,000 |
| **Average:** | £8000 |
| **Project:** | £5000 |

# CHEVROLET

ONE OF the great American marques, often immortalised in song, Chevrolet was founded in 1911 by Billy Durant and Louis Chevrolet. Profits from the firm allowed Durant to buy General Motors in 1917, and thus Chevy became a major constituent of GM. It was soon the US's best-selling brand, building over a million cars annually by 1927. Designs in the 1950s were futuristic and powerful, with Chevy V8s becoming a legend in their own right. The glassfibre Corvette sportscar made a similar name for itself – as did the later Corvair, but for all the wrong, safety-related reasons. Recent times have been turbulent, but Chevrolet still remains the archetypical American car maker.

## CHEVROLET
### Corvette C1

Conceived as an image-builder, the Corvette was built in glassfibre because that was the quickest and cheapest way to get it into production. Only 300 were completed in 1953, all hand-built; these now command more than double the prices for '54/55 'Vettes. Most of this first series of Corvettes used a 3.8-litre straight six, and all but seven of the paltry 700 built in 1955 had a new 4.3-litre V8. The low numbers were because GM still had plenty of '54 Corvettes left to sell and nearly pulled the plug. Now, of course, these models are very collectible.

**SPECIFICATIONS**

| | |
|---|---|
| **Years produced:** | 1953-1955 (4640 in total) |
| **Performance:** | 0-60mph: 11.0sec<br>Top speed: 107mph |
| **Power & torque:** | 150bhp/172lb ft |
| **Engine:** | Normally aspirated 3859cc straight six, petrol, carburettor, 12 valves |
| **Drivetrain:** | Front-engine RWD |
| **Structure:** | Separate chassis |
| **Transmission:** | Two-speed automatic |
| **Weight:** | 1227kg |

**PRICE GUIDE (1953 model in brackets)**

| | |
|---|---|
| **Launch price:** | N/A |
| **Excellent:** | £75,000 (£230,000) |
| **Good:** | £57,000 (£160,000) |
| **Average:** | £40,000 (£100,000) |
| **Project:** | £25,000 (£75,000) |

## CHEVROLET
### Bel Air coupe

These are the cars that best encapsulate the optimistic era of '50s America, the dawn of rock 'n' roll, and any number of roadside diners. The Bel Air tag generically attached to them is actually the range-topping trim level – there was also the One-Fifty and Two-Ten. A radical departure from previous dull and dumpy Chevrolets, the models' body styling was updated each year with ever-growing fins, and this was the car that introduced the small-block Chevy V8 engine, in 1955. Straight-six versions were also available.

**SPECIFICATIONS**

| | |
|---|---|
| **Years produced:** | 1955-1957 |
| **Performance:** | 0-60mph: 9.7sec<br>Top speed: 105mph |
| **Power & torque:** | 180bhp/260lb ft |
| **Engine:** | Normally aspirated 4344cc V8, petrol, carburettor, 16 valves |
| **Drivetrain:** | Front-engine RWD |
| **Structure:** | Separate chassis |
| **Transmission:** | Three-speed automatic |
| **Weight:** | 1515kg |

**PRICE GUIDE**

| | |
|---|---|
| **Launch price:** | £2326 |
| **Excellent:** | £40,000 |
| **Good:** | £24,000 |
| **Average:** | £12,000 |
| **Project:** | £6000 |

## CHEVROLET
### Bel Air convertible

As ever, it's the soft-top in the range that brings in the big money. Added to that, all the 1955-1957 convertibles were sold in range-topping Bel Air trim. Of the three years – which has led to devotees referring to these cars as 'Tri-Chevys' – the 1957 incarnation is the most popular, and therefore most expensive. Not only do you get more chrome and bigger fins, but there was a larger V8, with tuning options all the way up to fuel injection as used in the Corvette. Although never officially marketed in the UK, plenty have found their way here over the years.

**SPECIFICATIONS**

| | |
|---|---|
| **Years produced:** | 1955-1957 |
| **Performance:** | 0-60mph: 9.7sec<br>Top speed: 106mph |
| **Power & torque:** | 180bhp/260lb ft |
| **Engine:** | Normally aspirated 4638cc V8, petrol, carburettor, 16 valves |
| **Drivetrain:** | Front-engine RWD |
| **Structure:** | Separate chassis |
| **Transmission:** | Three-speed automatic |
| **Weight:** | 1550kg |

**PRICE GUIDE**

| | |
|---|---|
| **Launch price:** | N/A |
| **Excellent:** | £67,000 |
| **Good:** | £40,000 |
| **Average:** | £25,000 |
| **Project:** | £15,000 |

## CHEVROLET
### Corvette C1

This is the version that started the Corvette legend, thanks to the input of two men. Bill Mitchell turned it from good-looking into gorgeous and Zora Arkus-Duntov added power. By early '57 even the carburetted version (now 4.7 litres) was up from 195bhp to as high as 270bhp. In place of the old two-speed auto, a manual gearbox was now standard. The optional Rochester fuel-injection 'Fuelie' versions introduced in 1957 attract a 20-25% premium. 1958-62 models worth around 10% more; 290hp variant carries a big premium.

**SPECIFICATIONS**

| | |
|---|---|
| **Years produced:** | 1956-1962 (9806 in total) |
| **Performance:** | 0-60mph: N/A<br>Top speed: 119mph |
| **Power & torque:** | 195bhp/260lb ft |
| **Engine:** | Normally aspirated 4344cc V8, petrol, carburettor, 16 valves |
| **Drivetrain:** | Front-engine RWD |
| **Structure:** | Separate chassis |
| **Transmission:** | Four-speed manual |
| **Weight:** | 1227kg |

**PRICE GUIDE (290bhp model in brackets)**

| | |
|---|---|
| **Launch price:** | N/A |
| **Excellent:** | £75,000 (£110,000) |
| **Good:** | £42,000 (£68,000) |
| **Average:** | £25,000 (£35,000) |
| **Project:** | £15,000 (£20,000) |

## CHEVROLET
### Corvair

The Corvair was conceived as General Motors' answer to the rising tide of imports flowing into the USA by the late-'50s. The characterful rear-engined air-cooled saloon was as far removed from the Detroit norm as it comes, and for its brief production run, the first-generation model sold very well indeed. However, its unpredictable handling and rearward weight bias incurred the wrath of safety campaigner Ralph Nader, who declared it 'Unsafe at any speed'. The two-door coupé has a cult following, and the Monza turbo (1962-1964) is now quite collectible.

**SPECIFICATIONS**

| | |
|---|---|
| **Years produced:** | 1960-1964 (1,271,089 in total) |
| **Performance:** | 0-60mph: 14.4sec<br>Top speed: 101mph |
| **Power & torque:** | 80bhp/125lb ft |
| **Engine:** | Normally aspirated 2296cc flat six, petrol, carburettor, 12 valves |
| **Drivetrain:** | Rear-engine RWD |
| **Structure:** | Separate chassis |
| **Transmission:** | Four-speed manual |
| **Weight:** | 1095kg |

**PRICE GUIDE**

| | |
|---|---|
| **Launch price:** | N/A |
| **Excellent:** | £12,000 |
| **Good:** | £8000 |
| **Average:** | £5000 |
| **Project:** | £3000 |

## CHEVROLET
### Corvette Sting Ray C2

Everything but the engine and box were changed for this new version of the 'Vette, power steering and independent rear suspension were useful advances and the Corvette now came as a coupé or convertible. More of the latter were sold, and prices are now roughly the same as for coupés. Sting Rays from 1964 are worth around 20% less than quoted, thanks to not having the '63 coupés' split rear window, or the later cars' disc brakes. From 1965 a 'big-block' 6.5-litre V8 was added; these, and fuel-injection cars, attract 30-50% more than quoted.

**SPECIFICATIONS**

| | |
|---|---|
| **Years produced:** | 1963-1967 (117,966 in total) |
| **Performance:** | 0-60mph: 6.2sec<br>Top speed: 142mph |
| **Power & torque:** | 360bhp/352lb ft |
| **Engine:** | Normally aspirated 5354cc V8, petrol, carburettor, 16 valves |
| **Drivetrain:** | Front-engine RWD |
| **Structure:** | Separate chassis |
| **Transmission:** | Three/four-speed manual |
| **Weight:** | 1377kg |

**PRICE GUIDE**

| | |
|---|---|
| **Launch price:** | £3323 |
| **Excellent:** | £70,000 |
| **Good:** | £45,000 |
| **Average:** | £27,000 |
| **Project:** | £10,000 |

## CHEVROLET
### Camaro

The Camaro was General Motors' response to the success of the Ford Mustang, and a very good response it was, too. The 'Coke bottle' styling of the coupé body for this first generation of Camaros was spot-on for the time, yet still looks good today, and this was the perfect home for exploiting Chevrolet's range of ever-more-powerful V8 engines. You'll need to pay more for any that come with an 'SS' performance upgrade package, and really big amounts for those with the initials 'Z28' attached. These excite the serious collectors.

**SPECIFICATIONS**

| | |
|---|---|
| **Years produced:** | 1967-1969 |
| **Performance:** | 0-60mph: 9.1sec<br>Top speed: 125mph |
| **Power & torque:** | 325bhp/410lb ft |
| **Engine:** | Normally aspirated 6470cc V8, petrol, carburettor, 16 valves |
| **Drivetrain:** | Front-engine RWD |
| **Structure:** | Separate chassis |
| **Transmission:** | Two/three-speed auto/four-speed manual |
| **Weight:** | 1403kg |

**PRICE GUIDE (SS/Z28 in brackets)**

| | |
|---|---|
| **Launch price:** | N/A |
| **Excellent:** | £25,000 (£45,000/£75,000) |
| **Good:** | £17,000 (£30,000/£56,000) |
| **Average:** | £9000 (£18,000/£28,000) |
| **Project:** | £5000 (£6500/£12,500) |

## CHEVROLET
### Corvette Stingray C3

Based on the Mako Shark II concept, the Corvette's late-'60s makeover is largely defined by its long, pointed nose and fat tyres – at 8in wide for 1969, they were the largest on any car at the time. Coupés started to outsell convertibles, so the latter are now worth around 25% more. Once again, engines come in a variety of small- and big-block options, with outputs ranging from 300-435bhp. Our prices are for the former – expect double for the latter and fill the gap with anything in between. Emissions regulations put the squeeze on power from 1971.

**SPECIFICATIONS**

| | |
|---|---|
| **Years produced:** | 1968-1972 (133,449 in total) |
| **Performance:** | 0-60mph: 7.2sec<br>Top speed: 135mph |
| **Power & torque:** | 370bhp/370lb ft |
| **Engine:** | Normally aspirated 5733cc V8, petrol, carburettor, 16 valves |
| **Drivetrain:** | Front-engine RWD |
| **Structure:** | Separate chassis |
| **Transmission:** | Four-speed manual |
| **Weight:** | 1402kg |

**PRICE GUIDE**

| | |
|---|---|
| **Launch price:** | £3432 |
| **Excellent:** | £30,000 |
| **Good:** | £19,000 |
| **Average:** | £9500 |
| **Project:** | £5000 |

## CHEVROLET
### Camaro

For 1970, a brand new monocoque body saw the car become an independent model line in its own right. It was offered with four-, six- and V8 engines spanning 95-375bhp, so there really was a Camaro for every American. As the 1970s progressed, the car became fatter, slower and weighed down with anti-smog equipment. The Z28 was the top of the heap, and is the most collectable of all Camaros – but not exactly rare, with 250,000 built. Badge-engineered Pontiac Firebird was more widely known in Europe thanks to numerous film appearances.

**SPECIFICATIONS**

| | |
|---|---|
| **Years produced:** | 1970-1981 (1,811,973 in total) |
| **Performance:** | 0-60mph: 7.5sec<br>Top speed: 125mph |
| **Power & torque:** | 360bhp/360lb ft |
| **Engine:** | Normally aspirated 6573cc V8, petrol, carburettor, 16 valves |
| **Drivetrain:** | Front-engine RWD |
| **Structure:** | Monocoque |
| **Transmission:** | Four-speed manual |
| **Weight:** | 1617kg |

**PRICE GUIDE (Z28 in brackets)**

| | |
|---|---|
| **Launch price:** | N/A |
| **Excellent:** | £13,000 |
| **Good:** | £7500 |
| **Average:** | £4000 |
| **Project:** | £2000 |

## CHEVROLET
### Corvette C4/ZR-1

After taking a year out to solve production problems, Chevrolet came back with an all-new and vastly improved Corvette in 1984. Sadly, the 'Vette's image was blunted by styling which – when compared with what had gone before – was clean and tidy rather than wild and rebellious. Fans welcomed the return of a convertible version in 1986, now worth around 40% more than a coupé, The real collectible arrived in 1990, though, in the shape of the 375bhp ZR-1 coupé. Lotus was involved in developing its all-aluminium four-cam V8 and the handling settings.

**SPECIFICATIONS**

| | |
|---|---|
| **Years produced:** | 1984-1996 (366,227 in total) |
| **Performance:** | 0-60mph: 6.0sec<br>Top speed: 155mph |
| **Power & torque:** | 245bhp/340lb ft |
| **Engine:** | Normally aspirated 5733cc V8, petrol, electronic fuel injection, 16 valves |
| **Drivetrain:** | Front-engine RWD |
| **Structure:** | Chassis and glassfibre body |
| **Transmission:** | Six-speed manual |
| **Weight:** | 1523kg |

**PRICE GUIDE (ZR-1 in brackets)**

| | |
|---|---|
| **Launch price:** | £28,757 |
| **Excellent:** | £12,000 £18,000) |
| **Good:** | £10,000 (£15,000) |
| **Average:** | £7500 (£12,000) |
| **Project:** | £5000 (£9000) |

## CHEVROLET
### Corvette C5/Z06

Despite still having an OHV engine and rear leaf spring, the C5-gen Corvette was surprisingly advanced. Beneath the sheet-moulded composite body was a new all-aluminium LS1 'small block' V8, rear-mounted transaxle gearbox and stiffer new hydroformed box-frame structure. There was even a stability system and the option of a head-up display. In 2001 came the Z06 version, successor to the ZR-1, with 385bhp (later 405bhp), uprated suspension and 0-60 in just 4sec. Both versions were – and are – performance bargains.

**SPECIFICATIONS**

| | |
|---|---|
| **Years produced:** | 1997-2004 (248,715 in total) |
| **Performance:** | 0-60mph: 4.7sec (C5)<br>Top speed: 175mph |
| **Power & torque:** | 345bhp/356lb ft |
| **Engine:** | Normally aspirated 5700cc V8, petrol, electronic fuel injection, 16 valves |
| **Drivetrain:** | Front-engine RWD |
| **Structure:** | Chassis and composite body |
| **Transmission:** | Six-speed manual |
| **Weight:** | 1493kg |

**PRICE GUIDE (Z06 in brackets)**

| | |
|---|---|
| **Launch price:** | £37,625 |
| **Excellent:** | £14,500 (£28,000) |
| **Good:** | £12,500 (£22,000) |
| **Average:** | £10,000 (£15,000) |
| **Project:** | £7500 (£10,000) |

# CHRYSLER USA

THIS MARQUE was founded by Walter Chrysler in 1925 out of the remnants of the Maxwell Motor Company, and had already overseen the launch of the well-received six-cylinder Chrysler automobile the previous year. The new company soon became associated with good-value products, and flourished during the 1930s when such things mattered. The firm was grown along the lines of GM, and soon incorporated Dodge, Plymouth, De Soto, Fargo and – after the war – Valiant and Imperial. It hit trouble in the 1970s, biting off more than it could chew in Europe, before being rescued by the Minivan in 1984. More financial woes in the 2000s led to a merger with Fiat in 2014.

## CHRYSLER
### C-300

Currently going through an image renaissance, the 'Letter-series Chryslers' are as desirable now as they were when new. The C-300 hardtop is where the phenomenon began, and where the US musclecar race began, thanks to the installation of a 300bhp Hemi (it's here where the C-300 got its name from). Virgil Exner styled the model magnificently, with few of the excesses of later US musclecars. The development of the C-300 is reputed to have been $100 million, which is a lot for such a short production run, but worth every penny as a halo product.

**SPECIFICATIONS**

| | |
|---|---|
| **Years produced:** | 1955 (3825 in total) |
| **Performance:** | 0-60mph: 9.0sec<br>Top speed: 125mph |
| **Power & torque:** | 300bhp/400lb ft |
| **Engine:** | Normally aspirated 5426cc V8, petrol, carburettor, 16 valves |
| **Drivetrain:** | Front-engine RWD |
| **Structure:** | Separate chassis |
| **Transmission:** | Three-speed automatic |
| **Weight:** | 1921kg |

**PRICE GUIDE**

| | |
|---|---|
| **Launch price:** | N/A |
| **Excellent:** | £75,000 |
| **Good:** | £45,000 |
| **Average:** | £25,000 |
| **Project:** | £15,000 |

## CHRYSLER 300F/300F Cabriolet

Five years on from the C-300, and the musclecar wars were in full flight. And once again, Chrysler continued to set the pace with its 'Wedge' engine pushing out 375bhp, making the 300 the king of quarter-mile strip. As well as the three-speed auto, the 300F buyer could also specify a four-speed manual as supplied by Pont-à-Mousson, for even quicker getaways. Well equipped, plush and surprisingly advanced – with a unitary body. Available as a coupe or convertible, and extremely popular as a club racer back then, it is now revered as one of the most desirable of all musclecars.

**SPECIFICATIONS**

| | |
|---|---|
| Years produced: | 1960 (964/248 in total) |
| Performance: | 0-60mph: 7.0sec<br>Top speed: 135mph |
| Power & torque: | 375bhp/450lb ft |
| Engine: | Normally aspirated 6746cc V8, petrol, carburettor, 16 valves |
| Drivetrain: | Front-engine RWD |
| Structure: | Monocoque |
| Transmission: | Three-speed automatic |
| Weight: | 2201kg |

**PRICE GUIDE (Cabriolet in brackets)**

| | |
|---|---|
| Launch price: | N/A |
| Excellent: | £65,000 (£130,000) |
| Good: | £47,000 (£85,000) |
| Average: | £32,000 (£55,000) |
| Project: | £20,000 (£40,000) |

## CHRYSLER Viper/GTS

An 8-litre V10 is always going to be amusing. The Viper, launched under Chrysler's Dodge brand, recalled the Cobra of the early '60s. Indeed, Cobra inventor Carroll Shelby drove a prototype as pace car for the 1991 Indy 500. With a GRP body over a tubular steel frame, a hefty kerbweight of 1490kg (despite no roof or even side glass) and no ABS or traction control, it was pretty crude and not very agile. Better was the second-gen GTS coupé introduced in 1996: lighter, stiffer, with power up from 400 to 450bhp and a top speed of 186mph.

**SPECIFICATIONS**

| | |
|---|---|
| Years produced: | 1992-2002 (c17,000 in total) |
| Performance: | 0-60mph: 4.7sec (RT/10)<br>Top speed: 166mph |
| Power & torque: | 400bhp/465lb ft |
| Engine: | Normally aspirated 7997cc V10, petrol, electronic injection, 20 valves |
| Drivetrain: | Front-engine RWD |
| Structure: | Separate chassis, GRP body |
| Transmission: | Six-speed manual |
| Weight: | 1493kg |

**PRICE GUIDE (GTS in brackets)**

| | |
|---|---|
| Launch price: | £59,500 |
| Excellent: | £37,000 (£45,000+) |
| Good: | £30,000 (£40,000) |
| Average: | £25,000 |
| Project: | N/A |

# CITROËN

CITROËN STARTED life in 1919 as a builder of worthy but ultimately dull machines. And then came the revolutionary Traction Avant in 1934 with front-wheel drive and svelte modern styling. That established Citroën as a free-thinking radical and the firm lived up to the hype with subsequent creations such as the utilitarian 2CV and the Hydropneumatic wonders that were the Goddess-like DS, the Maserati-engined SM, the futuristic CX and the novel GS. A takeover by Peugeot in 1975 killed off some of Citroën's quirkiness – although 1989's XM was in the marque's best mad traditions – but individuality and daring have returned again in recent years... thankfully!

## CITROËN Traction Avant

Before the Traction Avant, Citroën was just another European manufacturer of worthy but dull cars. The Traction's arrival in 1934 changed all that. It was a revolutionary machine, Europe's first mass-produced front-wheel-drive car of monocoque construction. Independent suspension and some very sleek bodies were also part of its chic cocktail; there was simply nothing like it at the time and its rivals wouldn't catch up for years. Initial cars had 1303cc engines and the range gradually expanded to include the popular 1911cc.

**SPECIFICATIONS**

| | |
|---|---|
| Years produced: | 1934-1957 (760,000 in total) |
| Performance: | 0-60mph: 23.4sec<br>Top speed: 72mph |
| Power & torque: | 56bhp/91lb ft |
| Engine: | Normally aspirated 1911cc four cylinder, petrol, carburettor, 8 valves |
| Drivetrain: | Front-engine FWD |
| Structure: | Monocoque |
| Transmission: | Three-speed manual |
| Weight: | 1143kg |

**PRICE GUIDE**

| | |
|---|---|
| Launch price: | £573 |
| Excellent: | £18,000 |
| Good: | £13,500 |
| Average: | £6500 |
| Project: | £2500 |

## CITROËN 2CV

Envisaged as a car to motorise the French peasant population, the 2CV went on to become a true world car. The deceptively simple appearance belied a car that was very clever, with interconnected suspension and a tough air-cooled twin-cylinder engine. The simply-constructed body was considered ugly when the car was launched in 1948, leading to nicknames such as Tin Snail and Duck. But it was that quirky styling that helped win the 2CV a legion of followers, and it stayed in production for 42 years. Increasingly prized today.

**SPECIFICATIONS**

| | |
|---|---|
| Years produced: | 1948-1960 |
| Performance: | 0-60mph: N/A<br>Top speed: 49mph |
| Power & torque: | 9bhp/17lb ft |
| Engine: | Normally aspirated 375cc twin, petrol, carburettor, 4 valves |
| Drivetrain: | Front-engine FWD |
| Structure: | Separate chassis |
| Transmission: | Four-speed manual |
| Weight: | 682kg |

**PRICE GUIDE**

| | |
|---|---|
| Launch price: | £565 |
| Excellent: | £12,000 |
| Good: | £8000 |
| Average: | £4000 |
| Project: | £1750 |

## CITROËN DS19/ID19

The Citroën DS is one of the most extraordinary cars ever created. Its 'goddess' name – '*Déesse*' in French – was entirely justified because it looked like it was from another world. The shape was like nothing else, while Hydropneumatics controlled the self-levelling suspension, brakes, clutch and power steering, with the ride height adjustable from inside the car. Only the old 1911cc engine was carried over from the Traction Avant. The budget-conscious ID19 appeared a year after the DS19 and had conventional brakes and steering. Values holding firm.

**SPECIFICATIONS**

| | |
|---|---|
| **Years produced:** | 1955-1975 |
| **Performance:** | 0-60mph: 22.1sec<br>Top speed: 88mph |
| **Power & torque:** | 75bhp/101lb ft |
| **Engine:** | Normally aspirated 1911cc four cylinder, petrol, carburettor, 8 valves |
| **Drivetrain:** | Front-engine FWD |
| **Structure:** | Monocoque |
| **Transmission:** | Four-speed manual |
| **Weight:** | 1237kg |

**PRICE GUIDE**

| | |
|---|---|
| **Launch price:** | £1486 |
| **Excellent:** | £19,000 |
| **Good:** | £12,000 |
| **Average:** | £500 |
| **Project:** | £2000 |

## CITROËN DS Décapotable

While a few European coachbuilders decapitated DSs, it was the guillotine work of Henri Chapron that was considered the most stylish and elegant – so much so that Citroën added his cars to its catalogue in 1961. The mechanical layout and the various upgrades over the years mirrored those of the saloons, but the looks were far more eye-catching, with the open-top, two-door format and long, sloping tail giving a characteristically elegant look. But at twice the price of the saloon, the cabriolet needed to be special. Add 25% for later 23 EFIs.

**SPECIFICATIONS**

| | |
|---|---|
| **Years produced:** | 1958-1973 (1365 in total) |
| **Performance:** | 0-60mph: 15.5sec<br>Top speed: 100mph |
| **Power & torque:** | 83bhp/98lb ft |
| **Engine:** | Normally aspirated 1911cc four cylinder, petrol, carburettor, 8 valves |
| **Drivetrain:** | Front-engine FWD |
| **Structure:** | Monocoque |
| **Transmission:** | Four-speed manual |
| **Weight:** | 1235kg |

**PRICE GUIDE**

| | |
|---|---|
| **Launch price:** | Special order only |
| **Excellent:** | £165,000 |
| **Good:** | £120,000 |
| **Average:** | £80,000 |
| **Project:** | £55,000 |

## CITROËN DS19 Safari

The Citroën DS Safari, introduced in 1958, was one of the most competent estate cars ever produced. As well as swallowing luggage it was also a seven-seater in ordinary form, but the Familiale version had three rows of seats and could accommodate eight. The Hydropneumatic suspension came into its own on the load-lugging DS as, however much you packed in the back, the car would always stay level. Safaris had the same engine options as the DS saloon and adopted the same shark-like front end in 1967. Values slowly edging upwards.

**SPECIFICATIONS**

| | |
|---|---|
| **Years produced:** | 1959-1975 |
| **Performance:** | 0-60mph: 19.4sec<br>Top speed: 88mph |
| **Power & torque:** | 66bhp/98lb ft |
| **Engine:** | Normally aspirated 1911cc four cylinder, petrol, carburettor, 8 valves |
| **Drivetrain:** | Front-engine FWD |
| **Structure:** | Monocoque |
| **Transmission:** | Four-speed maual |
| **Weight:** | 1260kg |

**PRICE GUIDE**

| | |
|---|---|
| **Launch price:** | £1745 |
| **Excellent:** | £22,000 |
| **Good:** | £13,000 |
| **Average:** | £5250 |
| **Project:** | £2000 |

## CITROËN Ami 6/8/Super

Citroën produced several 2CV-based cars, with the Ami being one of the more fascinating. The styling was strange even by French standards, especially the original 6 model, which had a reverse-rake window emulating the Ford Anglia 105E. A 602cc 20bhp engine provided reasonable performance and the Ami was better appointed inside than the 2CV. A redesign in 1969 brought the Ami 8, with a more conventional (and more boring) slope to the rear window. The ultimate Ami was the Super of 1972, with the GS's flat four. All have a following.

**SPECIFICATIONS**

| | |
|---|---|
| **Years produced:** | 1961-1978 (1,840,159 in total) |
| **Performance:** | 0-60mph: 17.1sec<br>Top speed: 88mph |
| **Power & torque:** | 26bhp/31lb ft |
| **Engine:** | Normally aspirated 602cc twin, petrol, carburettor, 4 valves |
| **Drivetrain:** | Front-engine FWD |
| **Structure:** | Separate chassis |
| **Transmission:** | Four-speed manual |
| **Weight:** | 673kg |

**PRICE GUIDE**

| | |
|---|---|
| **Launch price:** | £824 |
| **Excellent:** | £4800 |
| **Good:** | £2500 |
| **Average:** | £1600 |
| **Project:** | £750 |

## CITROËN DS 20/21/23

The DS deserved better engines than those from the Traction Avant, and from 1965, it started to get them. That year, the DS21 was launched with a 2175cc engine offering 109bhp. After a successful restyle in 1967 – with swivelling headlamps within a shark-like nose – the DS19 was replaced by the DS20 (1985cc and 90bhp). But it was in the 1970s that the Goddess reached its ultimate evolution, with a 2347cc engine, to create the DS23. Subsequently with fuel injection, it produced 141bhp. Add 10% for fuel-injected cars. Prices still rising.

**SPECIFICATIONS**

| | |
|---|---|
| **Years produced:** | 1966-1974 |
| **Performance:** | 0-60mph: 10.4sec<br>Top speed: 120mph |
| **Power & torque:** | 100bhp/121lb ft |
| **Engine:** | Normally aspirated 2175cc four cylinder, petrol, carburettor, 8 valves |
| **Drivetrain:** | Front-engine FWD |
| **Structure:** | Monocoque |
| **Transmission:** | Four-speed manual |
| **Weight:** | 1280kg |

**PRICE GUIDE**

| | |
|---|---|
| **Launch price:** | £1977 |
| **Excellent:** | £35,000 |
| **Good:** | £24,000 |
| **Average:** | £10,000 |
| **Project:** | £4000 |

# CITROËN Dyane 4/6

The Dyane was intended to replace the 2CV... but the Tin Snail was too much of a survivor. So this upgraded and restyled 2CV went on sale alongside the model it was designed to supersede. The chassis was the same with a 425cc twin for the 4 and a 602cc powerhouse for the 6, and the more angular looks were still closely 2CV-related, even down to the full-length canvas sunroof. The Dyane was clearly an update of the original design, with the addition of a hatchback, but it was dropped five years before the car it was meant to oust.

**SPECIFICATIONS**

| | |
|---|---|
| **Years produced:** | 1967-1985 (1,443,583 in total) |
| **Performance:** | 0-60mph: 30.8sec<br>Top speed: 70mph |
| **Power & torque:** | 32bhp/31lb ft |
| **Engine:** | Normally aspirated 602cc twin, petrol, carburettor, 4 valves |
| **Drivetrain:** | Front-engine FWD |
| **Structure:** | Separate chassis |
| **Transmission:** | Four-speed manual |
| **Weight:** | 600kg |

**PRICE GUIDE**

| | |
|---|---|
| **Launch price:** | £549 |
| **Excellent:** | £4500 |
| **Good:** | £2000 |
| **Average:** | £1200 |
| **Project:** | £450 |

# CITROËN SM

The 1968 marriage of Citroën and Maserati led to the birth of a highly individualistic coupé. The SM took DS technology, threw in a Maserati V6 and was finished off with a swooping body that was uniquely Citroën, but also looked prestigious. Utterly original and technologically advanced, this idiosyncratic car demanded care and developed a reputation for fragility, which harmed sales. When Citroën was taken over by Peugeot in 1975, the SM was one of the first casualties, despite late production being shunted to Ligier. Very best are sought-after.

**SPECIFICATIONS**

| | |
|---|---|
| **Years produced:** | 1970-1975 (12,920 in total) |
| **Performance:** | 0-60mph: 8.8sec<br>Top speed: 135mph |
| **Power & torque:** | 168bhp/170lb ft |
| **Engine:** | Normally aspirated 2670cc V6, petrol, fuel injection, 12 valves |
| **Drivetrain:** | Front-engine FWD |
| **Structure:** | Monocoque |
| **Transmission:** | Five-speed manual |
| **Weight:** | 1450kg |

**PRICE GUIDE**

| | |
|---|---|
| **Launch price:** | £5480 |
| **Excellent:** | £50,000 |
| **Good:** | £35,000 |
| **Average:** | £17,000 |
| **Project:** | £8000 |

# CITROËN SM Chapron Mylord

The DS Décapotable by Chapron has entered into the realms of super-valuedom yet, with 1365 built, it's positively common campared with his next Citroën-based open-top: the SM Mylord. This curiously named car (which was obviously inspired by the British gentry) was only available to special order and, due to its high cost, a mere seven were built in total. But what a fantastic looking convertible! Thanks to the SM's inherent strength, it's taken to the conversion very well indeed. Highly desirable, with values to match.

**SPECIFICATIONS**

| | |
|---|---|
| **Years produced:** | 1970-1975 (7 in total) |
| **Performance:** | 0-60mph: 8.8sec<br>Top speed: 135mph |
| **Power & torque:** | 168bhp/170lb ft |
| **Engine:** | Normally aspirated 2670cc V6, petrol, fuel injection, 12 valves |
| **Drivetrain:** | Front-engine FWD |
| **Structure:** | Monocoque |
| **Transmission:** | Five-speed manual |
| **Weight:** | N/A |

**PRICE GUIDE**

| | |
|---|---|
| **Launch price:** | N/A |
| **Excellent:** | £300,000+ |
| **Good:** | £250,000 |
| **Average:** | N/A |
| **Project:** | N/A |

# CITROËN SM Chapron Opéra

Making a saloon out of one of Europe's sleekest coupés might have seemed like an odd undertaking for Chapron, but it's one that worked remarkably well. The long nose of the donor car is balanced well by the lengthened rear end although, by contemporary standards, it resulted in a huge car, well over five metres in length. The work undertaken on the Opéra and Mylord was put to good use in the 1972 Presidential limousine – a hugely lengthened open-topped SM. It was so good that it remained in service well into the 1990s.

**SPECIFICATIONS**

| | |
|---|---|
| **Years produced:** | 1970-1975 (8 in total) |
| **Performance:** | 0-60mph: 8.8sec<br>Top speed: 135mph |
| **Power & torque:** | 168bhp/170lb ft |
| **Engine:** | Normally aspirated 2670cc V6, petrol, fuel injection, 12 valves |
| **Drivetrain:** | Front-engine FWD |
| **Structure:** | Monocoque |
| **Transmission:** | Five-speed manual |
| **Weight:** | N/A |

**PRICE GUIDE**

| | |
|---|---|
| **Launch price:** | N/A |
| **Excellent:** | £175,000+ |
| **Good:** | £125,000 |
| **Average:** | N/A |
| **Project:** | N/A |

# CITROËN GS/GSA/Birotor

Citroën brought its big-car Hydropneumatic technology to the small-car market with 1970's GS. It looked like a scaled-down blend of DS and SM, with motive power from a 1015cc air-cooled flat-four engine. The interior looked like it had borrowed its controls from a spaceship and, naturally, there was self-levelling suspension. The car became a hatchback as the GSA in 1979, but in the process gained ugly plasic bumpers and a 1980s-generic dashboard. Rare Birotor version features Wankel rotary engine and is quite sought-after today.

**SPECIFICATIONS (GS Club)**

| | |
|---|---|
| **Years produced:** | 1970-1979/1985 (2,473,150 GS and GSA) |
| **Performance:** | 0-60mph: 16.2sec<br>Top speed: 92mph |
| **Power & torque:** | 55bhp/52lb ft |
| **Engine:** | Normally aspirated 1015cc flat four, petrol, carburettor, 8 valves |
| **Drivetrain:** | Front-engine FWD |
| **Structure:** | Monocoque |
| **Transmission:** | Four-speed manual |
| **Weight:** | 880kg |

**PRICE GUIDE (Birotor in brackets)**

| | |
|---|---|
| **Launch price:** | £1001 |
| **Excellent:** | £4200 (£22,000) |
| **Good:** | £2150 (£15,000) |
| **Average:** | £1300 (£8000) |
| **Project:** | £500 (N/A) |

## CITROËN CX

Enthusiasts generally refer to 1974's CX as the last of the true Citroëns because it was the final model launched before Peugeot took over. A technological tour de force with typically innovative and individualistic sleek looks, the CX featured the usual hydraulics controlling many aspects of the car plus Varipower self-centring steering, which took a little getting used to. The interior was simply mad, although from 1985, Series 2 cars had traditional instrumentation and colour-coded bumpers. Engines extended from 2.0-litre petrol to 2.5-litre diesel.

**SPECIFICATIONS (2200)**

**Years produced:** 1974-1990 (1,034,489 in total)
**Performance:** 0-60mph: 9.7sec
Top speed: 114mph
**Power & torque:** 115bhp/131lb ft
**Engine:** Normally aspirated 2165cc four cylinder, petrol, carburettor, 8 valves
**Drivetrain:** Front-engine FWD
**Structure:** Monocoque
**Transmission:** Five-speed manual
**Weight:** 1245kg

**PRICE GUIDE (add 20% for Prestige)**

**Launch price:** £3195
**Excellent:** £5000
**Good:** £2700
**Average:** £1500
**Project:** £600

## CITROËN 2CV6

Although probably the world's best minimalist car, the 2CV became increasingly luxurous. These terms are relative, of course, and additions to the car that motorised a generation of French farmers included improved interior trim and a slightly uprated engine. The best features remained – the loping ride, comfortable seats and pull-back roof – and that helped maintain sales for what had become a cult car even during its production run. Finally laid to rest in 1990, the Citroën 2CV's place in society is assured – as are its values, currently holding firm.

**SPECIFICATIONS**

**Years produced:** 1978-1990
**Performance:** 0-60mph: 32.4sec
Top speed: 71mph
**Power & torque:** 26bhp/29lb ft
**Engine:** Normally aspirated 602cc twin, petrol, carburettor, 4 valves
**Drivetrain:** Front-engine FWD
**Structure:** Separate chassis
**Transmission:** Four-speed manual
**Weight:** 560kg

**PRICE GUIDE**

**Launch price:** £899
**Excellent:** £8000
**Good:** £4000
**Average:** £1850
**Project:** £750

## CITROËN BX

Launched under the Eiffel Tower at the end of 1982, the BX was a clever fusion of Peugeot rationalism and Citroën individualism. Despite being idiosyncratically styled by Marcello Gandini and blessed with drum dials and paddle switchgear, the BX was sold on the back of an advertising campaign that played on its easy-to-service nature. Sales started slowly but, following the arrival of facelifted models (and round dials) in 1986, then the turbodiesels and GTi model, they picked up massively. Survivors have thinned out, and banger status will soon be behind the BX.

**SPECIFICATIONS (16TRS)**

**Years produced:** 1982-1994 (2,315,739 in total)
**Performance:** 0-60mph: 10.8sec
Top speed: 109mph
**Power & torque:** 94bhp/101lb ft
**Engine:** Normally aspirated 1580cc four cylinder, petrol, carburettor, 8 valves
**Drivetrain:** Front-engine FWD
**Structure:** Monocoque
**Transmission:** Five-speed manual
**Weight:** 960kg

**PRICE GUIDE (Mk2 in brackets)**

**Launch price:** £4790
**Excellent:** £2750 (£2000)
**Good:** £1500 (£1200)
**Average:** £1000 (£750)
**Project:** £350 (£250)

## CITROËN CX GTi/GTi Turbo

Finally matching high performance to dramatic looks, 1977's CX GTi was Citroën's return to grand touring after the demise of the SM. Using the DS23's fuel-injected 2347cc engine gave 128bhp and a 120mph top speed, while the cars could be identified by their special alloy wheels, blacked-out trim and more sports-orientated interiors. In 1984 Citroën made things even more frantic with the CX GTi Turbo, rated at 168bhp. A long time in the shadow of the DS, the CX is now being recognised as one of the great Citroëns. Values currently holding steady.

**SPECIFICATIONS**

**Years produced:** 1984-1989
**Performance:** 0-60mph: 8.2sec
Top speed: 129mph
**Power & torque:** 166bhp/217lb ft
**Engine:** Turbocharged 2499cc four cylinder, petrol, electronic fuel injection, 8 valves
**Drivetrain:** Front-engine FWD
**Structure:** Monocoque
**Transmission:** Five-speed manual
**Weight:** 1490kg

**PRICE GUIDE**

**Launch price:** £6530
**Excellent:** £7500
**Good:** £4500
**Average:** £2000
**Project:** £1000

## CITROËN BX 4TC

Group B has a lot to answer for. And although we all remember the amazing Audi Quattros, Peugeot 205T16s and Ford RS200s, cusriosities like the Citroën BX 4TC have been almost forgotten. This apathy is mainly down to Peugeot's decision to downgrade the 4TC project before its first competitive rallying season in 1986. In its first events, the 4TC proved less than competitive, hampered by its poor weight distribution and unreliability. 200 were built, but the company bought back as many as it could, making this one of the rarest Group B cars. Now highly prized.

**SPECIFICATIONS**

**Years produced:** 1985-1986 (200 in total)
**Performance:** 0-60mph: 7.1sec
Top speed: 138mph
**Power & torque:** 200bhp/217lb ft
**Engine:** Normally aspirated 2141cc four cylinder, petrol, electronic fuel injection, 16 valves
**Drivetrain:** Front-engine AWD
**Structure:** Monocoque
**Transmission:** Five-speed manual
**Weight:** 1280kg

**PRICE GUIDE**

**Launch price:** N/A
**Excellent:** £75,000
**Good:** £60,000
**Average:** £50,000
**Project:** N/A

# CITROËN Visa GTi

As unlikely hot hatches go, the Visa GTi is probably top of the list. When the original Visa appeared in 1978, it married odd styling with rational Peugeot underpinnings to create a spacious, comfortable and totally conventional small 'big' car. Sporting it was not. Yet the boys from Citroën decided it would be good for them to install the hot little 1.6-litre from the 205GTi. The resulting car was quick, comfortable and surprisingly capable. Early models had 105bhp, upgunned to 115 in 1988. Quad headlamps look cool, too. If you can find one, snap it up, cosset it and enjoy.

**SPECIFICATIONS**

**Years produced:** 1985-1988
**Performance:** 0-60mph: 9.1sec
Top speed: 109mph
**Power & torque:** 105bhp/99lb ft
**Engine:** Normally aspirated 1580cc four cylinder, petrol, mechanical fuel injection, 8 valves
**Drivetrain:** Front-engine FWD
**Structure:** Monocoque
**Transmission:** Five-speed manual
**Weight:** 890kg

**PRICE GUIDE**

**Launch price:** £5899
**Excellent:** £4500
**Good:** £2000
**Average:** £1000
**Project:** £600

# CITROËN AX GT/GT5

The lightweight AX was transformed into a latter-day Mini-Cooper when given the sporting treatment. 'Rocky Marciano' was how the advertisers described it, and they had a point: it was a featherweight that packed a giant-killing punch. Despite being powered by a carb-fed 1.4-litre packing a mere 85bhp, the GT could sprint to 60mph in 8.4 seconds, and stay with the hot hatch grandees on the twisty stuff. Flimsy interior was a bit of a turn-off for some, but a constant source of delight for others. Has gained a growing following after years in the doldrums.

**SPECIFICATIONS**

**Years produced:** 1987-1993
**Performance:** 0-60mph: 8.4sec
Top speed: 110mph
**Power & torque:** 85bhp/86lb ft
**Engine:** Normally aspirated 1360cc four cylinder, petrol, carburettor, 8 valves
**Drivetrain:** Front-engine FWD
**Structure:** Monocoque
**Transmission:** Five-speed manual
**Weight:** 722kg

**PRICE GUIDE**

**Launch price:** £7914
**Excellent:** £5500
**Good:** £3000
**Average:** £1700
**Project:** £1000

# CITROËN BX 16 Valve

Perhaps one of the performance car surprises of the '80s, given the base car's utter lack of go-faster pretension. But when Citroën slotted in an all-aluminium engine pumping out 160bhp, beefed up the suspension and tacked on a bodykit, a sporting express was created. With a top speed of 135mph and 0-60mph in comfortably under 8sec, the BX could trade punches with far more expensive cars, but despite being relatively good value, sales were disappointing after an initial flurry. Most have gone, having fallen prey to the engine-swap brigade.

**SPECIFICATIONS**

**Years produced:** 1987-1993 (15,440 in total)
**Performance:** 0-60mph: 7.4sec
Top speed: 135mph
**Power & torque:** 160bhp/133lb ft
**Engine:** Normally aspirated 1905cc four cylinder, petrol, electronic fuel injection, 16 valves
**Drivetrain:** Front-engine FWD
**Structure:** Monocoque
**Transmission:** Five-speed manual
**Weight:** 1070kg

**PRICE GUIDE**

**Launch price:** £12,300
**Excellent:** £4000
**Good:** £2500
**Average:** £1700
**Project:** £1000

# CITROËN XM

Pity the XM: it had so much to live up to, following on from the DS and CX. In an age of PSA rationality, infusing it with the individuality of its forebears was always going to be challenging. Yet the fluid-suspended, computer-controlled XM managed that arduous task with considerable aplomb. Firmer-riding than Citroëns of old, the XM was still a magic carpet compared with executive class rivals. A wide range of normally aspirated and turbocharged petrols and diesels were offered during its ten-year life, and there was also a capacious estate version.

**SPECIFICATIONS (V6 24v)**

**Years produced:** 1989-2000 (333,775 in total)
**Performance:** 0-60mph: 7.5sec
Top speed: 146mph
**Power & torque:** 200bhp/192lb ft
**Engine:** Normally aspirated 2975cc V6, petrol, electronic fuel injection, 24 valves
**Drivetrain:** Front-engine FWD
**Transmission:** Five-speed manual
**Weight:** 1475kg

**PRICE GUIDE**

**Launch price:** £14,499
**Excellent:** £4500
**Good:** £2750
**Average:** £1250
**Project:** £500

# CITROËN Xantia/Xantia Activa

Once seen as a mark of Citroën's descent into mediocrity, the Xantia is finally earning plaudits as a dependable modern classic still possessed of some of Citroën's quirkiness of old. This is most apparent in the familiar hydropneumatic suspension, dubbed Hydractive. In 1994, the concept was built upon with the Xantia Activa. Additional hydraulics acted as active anti-roll bars, granting the Xantia cornering abilities to embarrass many modern vehicles. Imported left-hand-drive V6 Activas can fetch £5k-plus.

**SPECIFICATIONS**

**Years produced:** 1993-2001
**Performance:** 0-60mph: 9.2sec (Activa)
Top speed: 131mph
**Power & torque:** 145bhp/173lb ft
**Engine:** Turbocharged 1998cc four cylinder, petrol, electronic injection, 8 valves
**Drivetrain:** Front-engine FWD
**Structure:** Monocoque
**Transmission:** Five-speed manual
**Weight:** 1426kg

**PRICE GUIDE**

**Launch price:** £18,350 (Activa)
**Excellent:** £3000
**Good:** £1850
**Average:** £900
**Project:** £350

# CLAN

CLAN WAS created by Paul Haussauer after leaving Lotus in 1970. The factory was set-up in his former employer's stamping ground of Norfolk and, joined by Lotus man John Frayling, the team designed a composite-bodied sports car that would run on Hillman Imp power. The all-aluminium engine was light, and parent company Chrysler guaranteed continued supplies. Production started slowly, because of component supply problems – a shame because press reveiws were ecstatic about the car's performance and efficiency. Died in 1974 (along with most of the UK kit-car industry, due to taxation changes), only to make a brief return in the mid-80s.

## CLAN Crusader

So much more than a kit car, the Clan Crusader was an exercise in lightness and efficiency, while proving that the Hillman Imp's Coventry Climax engine really was something special. It was a classic '70s British sports car – glassfibre body, off-the-shelf engine and gearbox, all clothed in a wedge-shaped body. It was pricey, at 40% more than an MG Midget, but the Crusader was electric to drive, and the material choice for the bodywork means the survival rate is rather good. The engine is well-supported in the tuning community, too.

**SPECIFICATIONS**

**Years produced:** 1971-1974 (315 in total)
**Performance:** 0-60mph: 12.5sec
Top speed: 100mph
**Power & torque:** 51bhp/52lb ft
**Engine:** Normally aspirated 875cc four cylinder, petrol, carburettor, 8 valves
**Drivetrain:** Rear-engine RWD
**Structure:** Glassfibre body/backbone chassis
**Transmission:** Four-speed manual
**Weight:** 578kg

**PRICE GUIDE**

**Launch price:** £1399
**Excellent:** £5000
**Good:** £3250
**Average:** £1650
**Project:** £950

# DAF

DAF WAS A Dutch truck and trailer maker that decided to branch out into car design with its two-cylinder 600cc Daffodil of 1958. This was considered innovative because of its Variomatic belt-drive transmission, which meant it was just as fast in reverse as it was forwards. Good sales led to more powerful variants as well as the Michelotti-penned 44 of 1966; four-cylinder engines followed in 1967 as did rather cute-looking coupés. Volvo, which had been buying shares since the 1970s, took over fully in 1975, badged the current DAF 66 as one of its own models and went onto launch the belt-drive Volvo 300 series in 1976, which had initially been conceived as a DAF.

## DAF 600/750/Daffodil/33

The Van Doorne brothers had enjoyed good times building trucks, and concluded that they could do the same in the car industry. Their first car, the 600 – with its air-cooled two-cylinder engine – looked like an unexceptional addition to the mini-car market. But there was technical novelty in the transmission, a continuously variable automatic device that relied on V-section rubber bands to match engine and road speed. And that meant the driver had the choice of two gears, forward and reverse. How easy was that?

**SPECIFICATIONS (33 De Luxe)**

**Years produced:** 1959-1975 (312,367 in total)
**Performance:** 0-60mph: 28.5sec
Top speed: 70mph
**Power & torque:** 32bhp/42lb ft
**Engine:** Normally aspirated 746cc twin, petrol, carburettor, 4 valves
**Drivetrain:** Front-engine RWD
**Structure:** Monocoque
**Transmission:** CVT automatic
**Weight:** 670kg

**PRICE GUIDE**

**Launch price:** N/A
**Excellent:** £2500
**Good:** £1750
**Average:** £750
**Project:** £300

## DAF 44/46/55/66/Volvo 66

With the DAF car business off to a flying start, the company decided to launch a larger stablemate to the 33. The Michelotti-styled 44 had its wheelbase extended by 8in and, the following year, it received the four-cylinder Renault power unit to become the 55, the company's largest-engined product yet. Continuously evolved during its life, but always exclusively offered with the CVT gearbox; received a chunkier front end in 1973, and it was in this form that the 66 was re-badged a Volvo in 1975. Remained in production as a Volvo until 1980.

**SPECIFICATIONS (33 De Luxe)**

**Years produced:** 1966-1975 (510,786 in total)
**Performance:** 0-60mph: 14.9sec
Top speed: 87mph
**Power & torque:** 43bhp/62lb ft
**Engine:** Normally aspirated 1108cc four cylinder, petrol, carburettor, 8 valves
**Drivetrain:** Front-engine RWD
**Structure:** Monocoque
**Transmission:** CVT automatic
**Weight:** 787kg

**PRICE GUIDE**

**Launch price:** N/A
**Excellent:** £2200
**Good:** £1600
**Average:** £750
**Project:** £300

## DAF
## Marathon

The 55 was a big step forward for the Dutch firm. It used a Renault water-cooled four-cylinder engine that offered a huge improvement in performance, even if the characteristic hum of the older model was gone. To celebrate its success in the London-Sydney Marathon, DAF introduced a Marathon upgrade kit, boosting power, handling and roadholding. It was an immediate success and soon became a fully-fledged production model. Renault parts commonality means that availability is good, and the club has excellent back-up.

**SPECIFICATIONS**

| | |
|---|---|
| **Years produced:** | 1968-1972 |
| **Performance:** | 19.4sec<br>Top speed: 90mph |
| **Power & torque:** | 63bhp/63lb ft |
| **Engine:** | Normally aspirated 1108cc four cylinder, petrol, carburettor, 8 valves |
| **Drivetrain:** | Front-engine RWD |
| **Structure:** | Monocoque |
| **Transmission:** | CVT automatic |
| **Weight:** | 810kg |

**PRICE GUIDE**

| | |
|---|---|
| **Launch price:** | £1050 |
| **Excellent:** | £3850 |
| **Good:** | £2000 |
| **Average:** | £1200 |
| **Project:** | £500 |

# DAIMLER

THE BRITISH DAIMLER is unrelated to the German one; it was founded in 1897 after obtaining a licence to use Gottlieb Daimler's name. Royal patronage gave its early models an enviable reputation, with the marque specialising in luxury machines. It merged with BSA in 1910, leading to some incredibly flamboyant and imposing machines when Sir Bernard and Lady Docker were in overall charge. However, after the Second World War, Daimler found itself struggling and was taken over by rival company Jaguar in 1960. While some individuality was retained for a while, eventually by the late 1960s the Daimler name became little more than a trim level to distinguish top-flight Jags.

## DAIMLER
## DB18 Special Sports

With the DB18 saloons and convertibles representing the sportier side of Daimler, the 1948 Special Sports version of the type was a step closer to the wild side. Twin carburettors helped squeeze 85bhp from the 2522cc six-cylinder engine. Barker was responsible for most of the bodies and its design featured a rear passenger seat facing sideways, thus making the car a three-seater. Hooper weighed in with the heavier 'Empress' saloon style, although alloy-on-ash construction for both machines helped keep performance up.

**SPECIFICATIONS**

| | |
|---|---|
| **Years produced:** | 1948-1953 (608 in total) |
| **Performance:** | 0-60mph: 23.3sec<br>Top speed: 84mph |
| **Power & torque:** | 85bhp/N/A |
| **Engine:** | Normally aspirated 2522cc six cylinder, petrol, carburettor, 12 valves |
| **Drivetrain:** | Front-engine RWD |
| **Structure:** | Separate chassis |
| **Transmission:** | Four-speed manual |
| **Weight:** | 1650kg |

**PRICE GUIDE**

| | |
|---|---|
| **Launch price:** | £2560 |
| **Excellent:** | £40,000 |
| **Good:** | £30,000 |
| **Average:** | £18,000 |
| **Project:** | £10,000 |

## DAIMLER
## Conquest Roadster

Daimler's first attempt at an out-and-out sports car was the Conquest-based, aluminium-bodied Roadster of 1953. Much sleeker and lower than any previous car from the company it was a somewhat bizarre-looking creation; this was thanks to Daimler trying to retain the style of the big saloons, which didn't lend itself to the hunkered-down format. After 65 had been made from 1953 to 1955, it was dropped, but then came back from 1956 to 1957. Only another 54 managed to find homes second time around. Incredibly rare today.

**SPECIFICATIONS**

| | |
|---|---|
| **Years produced:** | 1953-1957 (119 in total) |
| **Performance:** | 0-60mph: 14.5sec<br>Top speed: 101mph |
| **Power & torque:** | 100bhp/N/A |
| **Engine:** | Normally aspirated 2443cc six cylinder, petrol, carburettor, 12 valves |
| **Drivetrain:** | Front-engine RWD |
| **Structure:** | Separate chassis |
| **Transmission:** | Four-speed manual |
| **Weight:** | 1219kg |

**PRICE GUIDE**

| | |
|---|---|
| **Launch price:** | £1673 |
| **Excellent:** | £40,000 |
| **Good:** | £30,000 |
| **Average:** | £20,000 |
| **Project:** | £10,000 |

## DAIMLER
## Conquest/Century

The Consort gave way to the Conquest in 1953. Well, it actually gave way to Daimler's badge-engineered version of the Lanchester 14, which was what the Conquest actually was. The Damiler was an improvement on its sister model though – thanks to a bigger engine with two extra cylinders – while its compact size gave it pleasing performance and handling. But for those who wanted a little more performance there was the Century drophead coupé, so called because of the 100bhp afforded by its alloy-head twin-carb engine.

**SPECIFICATIONS**

| | |
|---|---|
| **Years produced:** | 1953-1958 (9620 in total) |
| **Performance:** | 0-60mph: 24.3sec<br>Top speed: 82mph |
| **Power & torque:** | 75bhp/N/A |
| **Engine:** | Normally aspirated 2433cc six cylinder, petrol, carburettor, 12 valves |
| **Drivetrain:** | Front-engine RWD |
| **Structure:** | Separate chassis |
| **Transmission:** | Four-speed manual |
| **Weight:** | 1397kg |

**PRICE GUIDE**

| | |
|---|---|
| **Launch price:** | £1511 |
| **Excellent:** | £9000 |
| **Good:** | £6500 |
| **Average:** | £3500 |
| **Project:** | £1500 |

## DAIMLER 104/Majestic

Although the 1954 Daimler 104 looked very much like the Regency it replaced, the structure was bulked up, the brakes were improved and the 3468cc six-pot engine was granted more power. A special version was the Lady's Model, with a more 'feminine' interior including walnut veneer, satin chrome, picnic gear and, of all things, a gold-propelling pencil! 50 customers bought one. In 1958, the body put on considerable weight to become the Majestic. The bigger 3794cc engine pitched it directly against Jaguar.

### SPECIFICATIONS

| | |
|---|---|
| **Years produced:** | 1955-1962 (1399 in total) |
| **Performance:** | 0-60mph: 15.4sec<br>Top speed: 100mph |
| **Power & torque:** | 137bhp/N/A |
| **Engine:** | Normally aspirated 3468cc six cylinder, petrol, carburettor, 12 valves |
| **Drivetrain:** | Front-engine RWD |
| **Structure:** | Separate chassis |
| **Transmission:** | Four-speed manual |
| **Weight:** | 1880kg |

### PRICE GUIDE

| | |
|---|---|
| **Launch price:** | £2672 |
| **Excellent:** | £19,500 |
| **Good:** | £12,000 |
| **Average:** | £7000 |
| **Project:** | £2500 |

## DAIMLER SP250

The final all-new sports car to be offered by Daimler, and the most interesting of all. With its glassfibre body and 2.5-litre V8 engine, the SP250 was quick and agile. It was originally called 'Dart', but Chrysler forced Daimler to drop the name. There were problems – the glassfibre used to crack, and the handling wasn't as good as it should have been – and, following Jaguar's takeover of Daimler, the appealing roadster was on borrowed time, as it was considered a rival to the E-type. Numbers are low, and that helps to keep values strong.

### SPECIFICATIONS

| | |
|---|---|
| **Years produced:** | 1959-1964 (2650 in total) |
| **Performance:** | 0-60mph: 10.2sec<br>Top speed: 121mph |
| **Power & torque:** | 140bhp/155lb ft |
| **Engine:** | Normally aspirated 2548cc V8, petrol, carburettor, 16 valves |
| **Drivetrain:** | Front-engine RWD |
| **Structure:** | Glassfibre body/separate chassis |
| **Transmission:** | Four-speed manual |
| **Weight:** | 940kg |

### PRICE GUIDE

| | |
|---|---|
| **Launch price:** | £1395 |
| **Excellent:** | £55,000 |
| **Good:** | £40,000 |
| **Average:** | £30,000 |
| **Project:** | £15,000 |

## DAIMLER Majestic Major

What was most majestic and major about 1960's Majestic Major was its engine... Daimler's new 4561cc V8 with hemispherical combustion heads, designed by Edward Turner. An impressive 220bhp gave a top speed of 120mph, making the Majestic Major a superb luxury express and one that was easy to drive thanks to automatic transmission and power steering. The bodywork remained largely unchanged from the standard Majestic, save for a longer boot. For 1961 there was a two-ton limousine version, which was dubbed a '120mph funeral taxi'.

### SPECIFICATIONS

| | |
|---|---|
| **Years produced:** | 1960-1968 (1180 in total) |
| **Performance:** | 0-60mph: 10.3sec<br>Top speed: 119mph |
| **Power & torque:** | 220bhp/283lb ft |
| **Engine:** | Normally aspirated 4561cc V8, petrol, carburettor, 16 valves |
| **Drivetrain:** | Front-engine RWD |
| **Structure:** | Separate chassis |
| **Transmission:** | Four-speed manual |
| **Weight:** | 1778kg |

### PRICE GUIDE

| | |
|---|---|
| **Launch price:** | £2995 |
| **Excellent:** | £27,500 |
| **Good:** | £19,500 |
| **Average:** | £13,000 |
| **Project:** | £5000 |

## DAIMLER 2.5-litre/V8-250

1959's Mk2 was the archetypal Jaguar saloon of the era; Daimler's version dropped the 2548cc V8 from the SP250 roadster under the bonnet. The two suited each other well with the handsome and curvaceous body complemented by the smooth and sophisticated power source. Arguably, the Daimler was a nicer car to drive than the Jaguar thanks to the engine's light weight and the eight cylinders endowing it with silky flexibility. Just imagine what it would have been like with the 4561cc version of the V8 instead. Good value compared with a Mk2 Jag.

### SPECIFICATIONS

| | |
|---|---|
| **Years produced:** | 1962-1969 (17,620 in total) |
| **Performance:** | 0-60mph: 13.8sec<br>Top speed: 112mph |
| **Power & torque:** | 140bhp/155lb ft |
| **Engine:** | Normally aspirated 2548cc V8, petrol, carburettor, 16 valves |
| **Drivetrain:** | Front-engine RWD |
| **Structure:** | Monocoque |
| **Transmission:** | Four-speed manual |
| **Weight:** | 1473kg |

### PRICE GUIDE

| | |
|---|---|
| **Launch price:** | £1786 |
| **Excellent:** | £25,000 |
| **Good:** | £17,500 |
| **Average:** | £12,000 |
| **Project:** | £5000 |

## DAIMLER Sovereign

There was probably a very good case for the 1966-69 Sovereign – the badge-engineered version of Jaguar's big 420 – making use of the existing 4.5-litre Daimler V8 engine to power it. Unfortunately, Jaguar didn't hear it, and so the Sovereign came out with the same 4235cc six-cylinder XK engine as the 420. Not that this made it a bad car, but it took away some Daimler distinctiveness as the only different touches were a fluted grille, the 'D' bonnet mascot, 'Daimler' on the cam cover and assorted badges.

### SPECIFICATIONS

| | |
|---|---|
| **Years produced:** | 1966-1969 (5700 in total) |
| **Performance:** | 0-60mph: 9.9sec<br>Top speed: 123mph |
| **Power & torque:** | 245bhp/283lb ft |
| **Engine:** | Normally aspirated 4235cc straight six, petrol, carburettor, 12 valves |
| **Drivetrain:** | Front-engine RWD |
| **Structure:** | Monocoque |
| **Transmission:** | Four-speed manual |
| **Weight:** | 1575kg |

### PRICE GUIDE

| | |
|---|---|
| **Launch price:** | £2121 |
| **Excellent:** | £20,000 |
| **Good:** | £15,000 |
| **Average:** | £10,000 |
| **Project:** | £3000 |

## DAIMLER Sovereign S1-S3

The Sovereign name was re-used for the Daimler version of the XJ6, introduced in 1969. As with the original Sovereign, any 'Daimlerisations' were confined to the most minor of details; the traditional fluted grille and Daimler badges here, there and everywhere. Original engine options were either the 2.8- or 4.2-litre XK six (4.2 today worth c20% more); by now Daimler's wonderful V8 engine – which might have suited the Sovereign so well – had ceased production. The Sovereign name continued through the S2 and 3 versions of the XJ until 1987.

**SPECIFICATIONS**

**Years produced:** 1969-1987 (55,435 in total)
**Performance:** 0-60mph: 8.8sec (4.2-litre)
Top speed: 124mph
**Power & torque:** 173bhp/227lb ft
**Engine:** Normally aspirated 4235cc six cylinder, petrol, carburettor, 12 valves
**Drivetrain:** Front-engine RWD
**Structure:** Monocoque
**Transmission:** Four-speed (+O/D)/Three-speed auto
**Weight:** 1537kg

**PRICE GUIDE (4.2)**

**Launch price:** £2356
**Excellent:** £25,000
**Good:** £17,000
**Average:** £8000
**Project:** £2000

## DAIMLER Double Six saloon

Jaguar took its XJ saloon to new heights with its new and exciting V12 engine from 1972. The Daimler variant revived a title that had last been used in 1938, that of the Double Six. This created one of the better luxury cruisers of the era, a worthy rival for BMW, Mercedes-Benz and even Rolls-Royce. The V12 may have been terribly thirsty, but it was also terribly fast and refined too, while Vanden Plas versions had even more opulence. After Series 1-3, there were Double Six versions of the XJ40 (in 1993) and the X305-generation XJ which ran from '94-97.

**SPECIFICATIONS**

**Years produced:** 1972-1979 (16,608 in total)
**Performance:** 0-60mph: 7.4sec
Top speed: 146mph
**Power & torque:** 265/285bhp to 304/350lb ft
**Engine:** Normally aspirated 5343cc V12, petrol, carburettor, 24 valves
**Drivetrain:** Front-engine RWD
**Structure:** Monocoque
**Transmission:** Three-speed auto
**Weight:** 1760kg

**PRICE GUIDE**

**Launch price:** £3849
**Excellent:** £20,000
**Good:** £12,000
**Average:** £8000
**Project:** £2000

## DAIMLER 4.2 Coupé

Announced in 1973, the Daimler Coupé – a short-wheelbase, pillarless variation on the XJ6/Sovereign saloon theme – seemed to have a lot going for it. The lines were even more handsome than those of the standard saloons and the truncated length added a sporty aura. However, when the Coupé finally made it into production in 1975, as a Series 2 model, it had a difficult life. Build quality was poor and the black vinyl roofs sported by each model were allegedly there to hide imperfections. Just 1598 were made before a halt was called in 1977.

**SPECIFICATIONS**

**Years produced:** 1975-1977 (399 in total)
**Performance:** 0-60mph: 8.8sec
Top speed: 124mph
**Power & torque:** 173bhp/227lb ft
**Engine:** Normally aspirated 4235cc six cylinder, petrol, carburettor, 12 valves
**Drivetrain:** Front-engine RWD
**Structure:** Monocoque
**Transmission:** Four-speed manual/three-speed auto
**Weight:** 1689kg

**PRICE GUIDE**

**Launch price:** £5590
**Excellent:** £32,000
**Good:** £17,000
**Average:** £12,000
**Project:** £4000

## DAIMLER Double Six Coupé

As with the Sovereign saloons, Jaguar's V12 engine also made its way into the Daimler-badged Coupés. One of the rarest of all Daimlers – just 407 were made from 1975 to 1977 – this 285bhp 5343cc pillarless and shortened sophisticate had wonderful looks with a top speed of nearly 150mph. Unfortunately, all this couldn't quite make up for the supply and quality problems that bedevilled it during its short life. This was a model that deserved a fate better than befell it. Rarity makes them even more exclusive than the 1855 Jaguar versions made.

**SPECIFICATIONS**

**Years produced:** 1975-1977 (407 in total)
**Performance:** 0-60mph: 7.6sec
Top speed: 148mph
**Power & torque:** 285bhp/301lb ft
**Engine:** Normally aspirated 5343cc V12, petrol, carburettor, 24 valves
**Drivetrain:** Front-engine RWD
**Structure:** Monocoque
**Transmission:** three-speed auto
**Weight:** 1835kg

**PRICE GUIDE**

**Launch price:** £6959
**Excellent:** £40,000
**Good:** £27,000
**Average:** £20,000
**Project:** £5000

# DATSUN/NISSAN

JAPANESE CAR-MAKER D.A.T. was founded by the team of Den, Aoyama and Takeuchi in 1914. In 1931, one of its smaller cars was christened the Datson; when the Nissan conglomerate took over in 1933, it tweaked the name to Datsun, to honour the sun on the Japanese flag. Some of its early cars were copies of British Austins – including the Seven – but in the 1950s and '60s it started building its own designs. Much attention in the US and Europe was garnered by its sporty Fairlady and 240Z models, and Datsuns came to sell strongly across the world. However, in 1986, the badge was dropped in those export markets and all models have been badged as Nissans ever since.

# DATSUN
## Fairlady

The Sports Fairlady, to give the car its export name, was proof that the fledgling Japanese motor industry was willing to follow Western design themes. The sports car closely resembled an MGB, but it was underpinned by a crude ladder-frame chassis, and had leaf springs at the rear. It might not sound that promising, but the Fairlady looked good and sold well in the USA – and it's from there that most of the UK and European examples have originated. The best model to have is the 2.0-litre five-speed version. Add 15% – if you can find one.

**SPECIFICATIONS**

**Years produced:** 1962-1969
**Performance:** 0-60mph: 8.3sec
Top speed: 125mph
**Power & torque:** 150bhp/138lb ft
**Engine:** Normally aspirated 1982cc four cylinder, petrol, carburettor, 12 valves
**Drivetrain:** Front-engine RWD
**Structure:** Separate chassis
**Transmission:** Five-speed manual
**Weight:** 910kg

**PRICE GUIDE**

**Launch price:** N/A in UK
**Excellent:** £15,000
**Good:** £10,000
**Average:** £4500
**Project:** £2500

# DATSUN
## 240Z

Here's where it all began. The first in what has become the world's best sports car line, the Datsun 240Z had success written all over it from day one. The looks were spot on, thanks to styling input from Albrecht Goertz, and performance from its rorty straight six was ample. Being a Datsun, reliability was a given, but the agile, tail-happy handling was a pleasant surprise. During its five-year run, over 150,000 were produced, but survivors are now seriously collectible. Rust has been its main enemy, so be careful when buying. Prices currently steady.

**SPECIFICATIONS**

**Years produced:** 1969-1974 (622,649 inc 260Z in total)
**Performance:** 0-60mph: 8.3sec
Top speed: 125mph
**Power & torque:** 151bhp/146lb ft
**Engine:** Normally aspirated 2393cc six cylinder, petrol, carburettor, 12 valves
**Drivetrain:** Front-engine RWD
**Structure:** Monocoque
**Transmission:** Five-speed manual
**Weight:** 1025kg

**PRICE GUIDE**

**Launch price:** £2288
**Excellent:** £25,000
**Good:** £13,000
**Average:** £7500
**Project:** £3500

# DATSUN
## Cedric 260C

The large and conventionally engineered Cedric 260C was Datsun's first foray into the UK executive sector when it arrived here in 1973. Given that the brash and Transatlantic-looking saloon was up against Rover and Triumph's 2000 models, it's no surprise that the 260C (as it was called here) failed to catch on. Its main selling points were generous equipment, given reliability and a low list price. Today, the 260C and imported Glorias have gained quite a following, Japanese car enthusiasts can't get enough of them, and they're prepared to pay well.

**SPECIFICATIONS (260C)**

**Years produced:** 1971-1976
**Performance:** 0-60mph: 11.3sec
Top speed: 109mph
**Power & torque:** 151bhp/188lb ft
**Engine:** Normally aspirated 2565cc six cylinder, petrol, carburettor, valves
**Drivetrain:** Front-engine RWD
**Structure:** Monocoque
**Transmission:** Five-speed manual
**Weight:** 1350kg

**PRICE GUIDE**

**Launch price:** N/A
**Excellent:** £7000
**Good:** £3000
**Average:** £1200
**Project:** £750

# DATSUN
## 260Z

Despite adding power and equipment to the mix, the Datsun 260Z has always lived in the shadow of its older brother. Two-seat models looked as good as the original, but the introduction of the 2+2 with a12-inch longer wheelbase and reprofiled roofline diluted appeal despite being a lot more useful. Performance for the two-seater car is similar to the 240Z's and, because prices are lower, they are excellent value. Sold half as many as the first Z-car, and survival rate is poor – mainly because, like all '70s Datsuns, it rusted appallingly. Values firm.

**SPECIFICATIONS**

**Years produced:** 1974-1978 (total: see 240Z)
**Performance:** 0-60mph: 8.8sec
Top speed: 127mph
**Power & torque:** 162bhp/152lb ft
**Engine:** Normally aspirated 2565cc six cylinder, petrol, carburettor, 12 valves
**Drivetrain:** Front-engine RWD
**Structure:** Monocoque
**Transmission:** Five-speed manual
**Weight:** 1164kg

**PRICE GUIDE**

**Launch price:** £2896
**Excellent:** £18,500
**Good:** £13,500
**Average:** £6000
**Project:** £2000

# DATSUN
## Cedric 260C (330)

Large Datsuns failed to capture the imagination of British executive car buyers during the 1970s. It was hoped that the 1976 260C would turn the tide, but a combination of duff dynamics and tacky image (and interiors) saw the 260C continue to be a showroom ornament through the strife-torn '70s. The facelift gave the 260C more style, even if it looked too American – but it certainly looks good now. The pillarless coupé was never imported into the UK new, but a few have subsequently been imported, and are popular with those who like '70s Orientals.

**SPECIFICATIONS (260C)**

**Years produced:** 1976-1979
**Performance:** 0-60mph: 11.3sec
Top speed: 109mph
**Power & torque:** 151bhp/188lb ft
**Engine:** Normally aspirated 2565cc six cylinder, petrol, carburettor, 12 valves
**Drivetrain:** Front-engine RWD
**Structure:** Monocoque
**Transmission:** Five-speed manual/three-speed auto
**Weight:** 1350kg

**PRICE GUIDE**

**Launch price:** N/A
**Excellent:** £8000
**Good:** £3500
**Average:** £1200
**Project:** £750

# DATSUN
## Bluebird 160/180B

The Bluebird 710 series rode on the crest of Datsun's big push into the UK, and its follow-up, the 810 or 180B, really sold well. Although the road-testers did their best to disparage the 180B for its vague damping and steering, customers loved its keen pricing and standard-fit radio/cassette. The 180B SSS Coupé suffered, like all Datsuns of the time, from fussy styling, and failed to attract Capri and Manta buyers. But today it's the pillarless two-door rather than the four-door saloon that people want – and examples continue to be imported into the UK.

**SPECIFICATIONS**

| | |
|---|---|
| **Years produced:** | 1976-1979 |
| **Performance:** | 0-60mph: 10.9sec (180B Coupe)<br>Top speed: 106mph |
| **Power & torque:** | 95bhp/103lb ft |
| **Engine:** | Normally aspirated 1770cc four cylinder, petrol, carburettor, valves |
| **Drivetrain:** | Front-engine RWD |
| **Structure:** | Monocoque |
| **Transmission:** | Five-speed manual |
| **Weight:** | 1035kg |

**PRICE GUIDE**

| | |
|---|---|
| **Launch price:** | N/A |
| **Excellent:** | £6000 |
| **Good:** | £3200 |
| **Average:** | £1350 |
| **Project:** | £1000 |

# DATSUN
## 240K Skyline

Although the Skyline had been around in Japan since 1957, when it was introduced by defunct manufacturer Prince, the UK had to wait until the '70s to see what had become Datsun's big GT. When unveiled in 1978, the straight six-powered 240K was distinguished by its American-inspired styling but, following a series of damning road tests that criticised its sloppy handling and excessive thirst, it failed to sell. Datsun quietly pulled the plug, and few remain as a result. A number have since been imported, riding high on the Skyline GT-R cult and vibrant scene for Japanese classics.

**SPECIFICATIONS**

| | |
|---|---|
| **Years produced:** | 1978-1981 (576,797 in total) |
| **Performance:** | 0-60mph: 11.0sec<br>Top speed: 109mph |
| **Power & torque:** | 127bhp/132lb ft |
| **Engine:** | Normally aspirated 2393cc six cylinder, petrol, mechanical fuel injection, 12 valves |
| **Drivetrain:** | Front-engine RWD |
| **Structure:** | Monocoque |
| **Transmission:** | Five-speed manual |
| **Weight:** | 1266kg |

**PRICE GUIDE**

| | |
|---|---|
| **Launch price:** | £6001 |
| **Excellent:** | £20,000 |
| **Good:** | £14,000 |
| **Average:** | £8000 |
| **Project:** | £3500 |

# DATSUN/NISSAN
## 280ZX

Symbolic of the Z-car's descent into middle-aged spread, the 280ZX was far less appealing than the car it replaced. Longer, wider, heavier and uglier, the new 2.8-litre car was very much a boulevardier rather than a full-blooded sports car. Equipment levels were lavish, and power steering, all-round disc brakes and semi-trailing arm rear suspension were further refinements that cast the Z-car very much in the luxury car sector. Despite being panned when new, it sold well in the USA and is still in demand as a modern, useable classic car.

**SPECIFICATIONS**

| | |
|---|---|
| **Years produced:** | 1978-1983 (414,358 in total) |
| **Performance:** | 0-60mph: 8.3sec<br>Top speed: 117mph |
| **Power & torque:** | 140bhp/149lb ft |
| **Engine:** | Normally aspirated 2753cc six cylinder, petrol, electronic fuel injection, 12 valves |
| **Drivetrain:** | Front-engine RWD |
| **Structure:** | Monocoque |
| **Transmission:** | Five-speed manual |
| **Weight:** | 1272kg |

**PRICE GUIDE**

| | |
|---|---|
| **Launch price:** | £8103 |
| **Excellent:** | £6500 |
| **Good:** | £4200 |
| **Average:** | £2000 |
| **Project:** | £1000 |

# NISSAN
## Silvia

The Silvia name was familiar to North American and Asian buyers, but was new to Britain in 1984. And when it was launched, the Silvia was a breath of fresh air in a stagnating coupé market. With a turbocharged 1.8-litre engine and RWD, it was huge fun to drive thanks to its keen, direct steering and firm, well-controlled suspension. Considering the 1984 300ZX was such a disappointment, this was a welcome return to form for Nissan. Not many left in the UK as most succumbed to rust, but those that remain are cherished.

**SPECIFICATIONS**

| | |
|---|---|
| **Years produced:** | 1984-1989 |
| **Performance:** | 0-60mph: 8.1sec<br>Top speed: 125mph |
| **Power & torque:** | 133bhp/141lb ft |
| **Engine:** | Turbocharged 1009cc four cylinder, petrol, electronic fuel injection, 8 valves |
| **Drivetrain:** | Front-engine RWD |
| **Structure:** | Monocoque |
| **Transmission:** | Five-speed manual |
| **Weight:** | 1150kg |

**PRICE GUIDE**

| | |
|---|---|
| **Launch price:** | £11,870 |
| **Excellent:** | £4500 |
| **Good:** | £2750 |
| **Average:** | £1000 |
| **Project:** | £600 |

# NISSAN
## 300ZX Turbo

A sharp new look for the 1984 Nissan 300ZX failed to add any excitement to the Z-car line, despite it being all-new under the skin, and the first in the line to feature a V6 engine. The familiar-looking styling was more aerodynamic than before, boasting a drag co-efficient of just 0.30. In the UK, it was the first to be fitted with a turbo, which delivered lots of straight-line pace if not finesse. Handling was firmer than the Datsun 280ZX's, but still not good enough for the 300ZX to be considered a sports car in the traditional sense of the word.

**SPECIFICATIONS**

| | |
|---|---|
| **Years produced:** | 1984-1989 |
| **Performance:** | 0-60mph: 7.1sec<br>Top speed: 147mph |
| **Power & torque:** | 226bhp/246lb ft |
| **Engine:** | Turbocharged 2960cc V6, petrol, electronic fuel injection, 12 valves |
| **Drivetrain:** | Front-engine RWD |
| **Structure:** | Monocoque |
| **Transmission:** | Five-speed manual |
| **Weight:** | 1324kg |

**PRICE GUIDE**

| | |
|---|---|
| **Launch price:** | £16,996 |
| **Excellent:** | £5000 |
| **Good:** | £4000 |
| **Average:** | £2000 |
| **Project:** | £800 |

## NISSAN Sunny ZX Turbo

Nissan's 1986 Sunny range was hardly a memorable addition to the Escort class. Known as the Pulsar just about everywhere else in the world, the competent FWD hatchback became a driving school favourite, because it was so easy to operate. The ZX coupé had one distinction over the car it was based on: it was a head-turner. Sadly, the looks were deceiving, because that promising styling wasn't realised on the road. Poor ride and handling could be forgiven on the low-powered version, but the turbocharged car with 135bhp could be a real handful.

**SPECIFICATIONS**

**Years produced:** 1987-1991 (1,900,000 in total)
**Performance:** 0-60mph: 8.3sec
Top speed: 128mph
**Power & torque:** 135bhp/141lb ft
**Engine:** Turbocharged 1809cc four cylinder, petrol, fuel injection, 8 valves
**Drivetrain:** Front-engine FWD
**Structure:** Monocoque
**Transmission:** Five-speed manual
**Weight:** 1070kg

**PRICE GUIDE**

**Launch price:** £11,696
**Excellent:** £2750
**Good:** £1500
**Average:** £1000
**Project:** £400

## NISSAN Skyline GT-R

When the R32 GT-R came to Europe, it made serious waves. Capable of lapping the Nürburgring faster than a Porsche 928GTS, this triumph of technology over breeding created a new breed of cult Japanese sports cars. The car was conceived for Group A racing, and featured four-wheel drive, four-wheel steering and a turbocharged RB20 straight six. In Europe, the Skyline GT-R failed to sell in huge numbers, but gained a giant-killing reputation that subsequent R33 and R34 maintained. Values rising rapidly, but unmodified versions are few and far between. Add 50% for Spec V.

**SPECIFICATIONS**

**Years produced:** 1989-1994 (43,706 in total)
**Performance:** 0-60mph: 5.6sec (R32)
Top speed: 156mph
**Power & torque:** 276bhp/260lb ft
**Engine:** Twin turbocharged 2569cc straight six, petrol, fuel injection, 8 valves
**Drivetrain:** Front-engine FWD
**Structure:** Monocoque
**Transmission:** Five-speed manual
**Weight:** 1430kg

**PRICE GUIDE (R32)**

**Launch price:** N/A in UK
**Excellent:** £30,000
**Good:** £22,000
**Average:** £13,000
**Project:** £7500

## NISSAN Silvia 200SX

When the 200SX arrived on the scene in 1989 it seemed that Nissan had rediscovered its sports car mojo, which was apparently lost at the end of the 260Z production run in 1978. With 197bhp on tap and an expoitable RWD chassis, it was an excellent driver's car – and thanks to old-fashioned good looks, it was also desirable in the showroom. Nissan had no trouble selling all it could import, and it remained popular until it went out of production. Has gone on to enjoy a successful afterlife thanks to the drifting scene. Unmolested examples rare. Values on the up.

**SPECIFICATIONS**

**Years produced:** 1989-1996 (1,081,200 in total)
**Performance:** 0-60mph: 7.0sec
Top speed: 146mph
**Power & torque:** 197bhp/195lb ft
**Engine:** Turbocharged 1998cc four cylinder, petrol, fuel injection, 16 valves
**Drivetrain:** Front-engine RWD
**Structure:** Monocoque
**Transmission:** Five-speed manual
**Weight:** 1270kg

**PRICE GUIDE**

**Launch price:** £16,996
**Excellent:** £5750
**Good:** £3000
**Average:** £1500
**Project:** £1000

## NISSAN 300ZX Turbo (Z32)

The '90s generation Z-car (known as the Z32) made a clean break stylistically from its predecessors. Not only was the body competely new, but under the bonnet was now a twin-turbo 3-litre V6, giving a very serious 280bhp, dropping the 0-60 time to just 6sec. Like the previous three generations of Z-car, the 300ZX was offered as a two-seater or 2+2, and it was packed with high-tech hardware, such as 'HICAS' four-wheel steering. It lived on in Japan until 2000, and today you'll find many Japanese imports, often with automatic gearboxes, at very tempting prices.

**SPECIFICATIONS**

**Years produced:** 1989-1996 (164,170 in total)
**Performance:** 0-60mph: 6.0sec
Top speed: 155mph (limited)
**Power & torque:** 280bhp/275lb ft
**Engine:** Twin-turbocharged 2960cc V6, petrol, fuel injection, 24 valves
**Drivetrain:** Front-engine RWD
**Structure:** Monocoque
**Transmission:** Five-speed manual/four-speed auto
**Weight:** 1590kg

**PRICE GUIDE**

**Launch price:** £34,600
**Excellent:** £6000
**Good:** £4000
**Average:** £3000
**Project:** £1000

## NISSAN Figaro

Blending retro style with modern underpinnings, the Figaro was developed by Nissan's special projects group, which also created the S-Cargo van. Based on the contemporary Micra hatchback, with styling inspired by the 1960s Datsun Fairlady, the Figaro was originally sold only in Japan but has since proved a popular import to the UK. The inside was similarly retro, while standard equipment included leather seats, air conditioning and a CD player. UK owners are well-served by a small network of specialists and parts suppliers.

**SPECIFICATIONS**

**Years produced:** 1991 (20,000 in total)
**Performance:** 0-60mph: 12.0sec
Top speed: 106mph
**Power & torque:** 75bhp/78lb ft
**Engine:** Turbocharged 987cc four cylinder, petrol, fuel injection, 8 valves
**Drivetrain:** Front-engine FWD
**Structure:** Monocoque
**Transmission:** Three-speed automatic
**Weight:** 810kg

**PRICE GUIDE**

**Launch price:** N/A in UK
**Excellent:** £6000
**Good:** £4000
**Average:** £3000
**Project:** £1000

## NISSAN
### 350Z

Hoping to capture some of the 240Z's magic, this coupé (and later convertible) sports car was an affordable rear-wheel-drive hero to many. Powered by a gutsy 276bhp 3.5-litre V6 from launch, it was upped to 297bhp in 2006 and increased to 309bhp with the much-improved 'High Response' engine from 2007. Becoming a bit of a bargain in the last few years, beware of cheap or modified cars. Prices for well-maintained and low-mileage cars offer good value, but add up to 20% for special editions, such as the GT4 edition (pictured) and later HR cars.

**SPECIFICATIONS**

| | |
|---|---|
| **Years produced:** | 2002-2008 |
| **Performance:** | 0-60mph: 5.9sec<br>Top speed: 155mph |
| **Power & torque:** | 276bhp/268lb ft |
| **Engine:** | Normally aspirated 3498cc V6, petrol, electronic fuel injection, 24 valves |
| **Drivetrain:** | Front-engine RWD |
| **Structure:** | Monocoque |
| **Transmission:** | Six-speed manual/five-speed automatic |
| **Weight:** | 1525kg |

**PRICE GUIDE**

| | |
|---|---|
| **Launch price:** | £24,000 |
| **Excellent:** | £10,000 |
| **Good:** | £8,000 |
| **Average:** | £6000 |
| **Project:** | £3500 |

# DELOREAN

JOHN Z DELOREAN was an all-American high-flying car industry hero. At General Motors he'd made it to the sixth floor at a famously young age, thanks to the success of his GTO muscle car. However, he wanted to produce top-flight sports cars, and that ambition eventually forced him to cut loose. In the early '70s, he started work on a new gullwing sports car and, thanks to Italdesign, Lotus and the British government, managed to get the DMC-12 into production in Dunmurry, Northern Ireland, in 1981. However, the car sold poorly, and the company went bankrupt the following year – following allegations that DeLorean was selling drugs, a charge of which he was acquitted in court.

## DELOREAN
### DMC-12

John DeLorean set out to build his own vision of a sports car in the late 1970s and, on paper, it must have looked amazing. It featured a low-slung and pointy Giugiaro design, brushed steel outer skin, gullwing doors and a fuel-injection 2849cc V6 engine mounted 911-style at the rear. Unfortunately, the 1981 reality turned out to be less stimulating. The car was so heavy that the V6 struggled to offer sporty performance and the handling remained dodgy even after Lotus had done its best. Fairly high build numbers keep prices at moderate levels.

**SPECIFICATIONS**

| | |
|---|---|
| **Years produced:** | 1981-1982 (c10,000 in total) |
| **Performance:** | 0-60mph: 9.6sec<br>Top speed: 130mph |
| **Power & torque:** | 130bhp/153lb ft |
| **Engine:** | Normally aspirated 2849cc V6, petrol, electronic fuel injection, 12 valves |
| **Drivetrain:** | Rear-engine RWD |
| **Structure:** | Backbone chassis/glassfibre core |
| **Transmission:** | Five-speed manual |
| **Weight:** | 1244kg |

**PRICE GUIDE**

| | |
|---|---|
| **Launch price:** | £10,674 |
| **Excellent:** | £30,000 |
| **Good:** | £22,500 |
| **Average:** | £14,000 |
| **Project:** | £10,000 |

# DE TOMASO

ARGENTINEAN FORMER racing driver Alejandro de Tomaso moved to Italy in the late '50s and started to build racing cars. In 1967, De Tomaso branched out into production cars with the Mangusta. Like most subsequent models this was powered by a Ford V8 engine. The company's staple product, the Pantera, followed in 1970, and was soon joined by the Deauville and Longchamps. In the '70s De Tomaso acquired Maserati and Innocenti, which ended selling the Mini across Europe, though the former was sold off in 1993. Production in fits and starts since, including V8-powered Guarà and Bigua, and a relaunch in 2011 with a luxury saloon/crossover.

## DE TOMASO
### Vallelunga

First displayed at the 1964 Turin Show, the De Tomaso Vallelunga was a mid-engineered pioneer. It was a racer for the road, powered by a Ford Cortina engine with a Hewland transaxle, the glorious-looking was shaped in aluminium at the Fissore coachworks. Only three were were built before De Tomaso transferred the contract to Ghia, and these later cars were finished in glassfibre. Torsional rigidity was lacking, and that compromised handling and refinement. After a run of 55, the sweet little Vallelunga was dropped in favour of the Mangusta.

**SPECIFICATIONS**

| | |
|---|---|
| **Years produced:** | 1964-1968 (55 in total) |
| **Performance:** | 0-60mph: 6.0sec<br>Top speed: 155mph |
| **Power & torque:** | 135bhp/112lb ft |
| **Engine:** | Normally aspirated 1498cc four cylinder, petrol, carburettor, 16 valves |
| **Drivetrain:** | Mid-engine RWD |
| **Structure:** | Separate chassis |
| **Transmission:** | Five-speed manual |
| **Weight:** | 500kg |

**PRICE GUIDE**

| | |
|---|---|
| **Launch price:** | N/A in UK |
| **Excellent:** | £250,000 |
| **Good:** | £175,000 |
| **Average:** | £100,000 |
| **Project:** | N/A |

## DE TOMASO Mangusta

De Tomaso married the cancelled Ford 70P racing car programme with a rejected Iso design proposal by Giugiaro to create the Mangusta – the company's very first supercar. Essentially a racing car for the road with svelte styling, it was quite tricky to drive quickly and extremely difficult to live with. But that doesn't stop it being great today – and although values have seriously lagged behind those of the supercar opposition, the very best examples can now fetch upwards of £200k. That's only right for what is a truly stunning supercar.

**SPECIFICATIONS**

| | |
|---|---|
| **Years produced:** | 1967-1972 (400 in total) |
| **Performance:** | 0-60mph: 6.0sec<br>Top speed: 155mph |
| **Power & torque:** | 305bhp/392lb ft |
| **Engine:** | Normally aspirated 4727cc V8, petrol, carburettor, 16 valves |
| **Drivetrain:** | Mid-engine RWD |
| **Structure:** | Separate chassis |
| **Transmission:** | Five-speed manual |
| **Weight:** | 1322kg |

**PRICE GUIDE**

| | |
|---|---|
| **Launch price:** | Special order only |
| **Excellent:** | £200,000 |
| **Good:** | £125,000 |
| **Average:** | £80,000 |
| **Project:** | £50,000 |

## DE TOMASO Deauville

It seemed like a good idea at the time, and had there been any justice, more Deauvilles might have found their way into owners' hands. As it was, it was a big failure. De Tomaso set out to create its own XJ6, but without the complexity. So in went the Pantera's Detroit V8, and had BL not been in dire straits itself, the company's lawyers may well have been knocking on the door over the matter of the Deauville's styling. Despite the market not wanting it then, it's an interesting classic today, and well worth a look, should the opportunity arise.

**SPECIFICATIONS**

| | |
|---|---|
| **Years produced:** | 1970-1989 (355 in total) |
| **Performance:** | 0-60mph: 6.4sec<br>Top speed: 143mph |
| **Power & torque:** | 330bhp/325lb ft |
| **Engine:** | Normally aspirated 5763cc V8, petrol, carburettor, 16 valves |
| **Drivetrain:** | Front-engine RWD |
| **Structure:** | Monocoque |
| **Transmission:** | Five-speed manual/three-speed auto |
| **Weight:** | 1814kg |

**PRICE GUIDE**

| | |
|---|---|
| **Launch price:** | £8992 |
| **Excellent:** | £30,000 |
| **Good:** | £22,000 |
| **Average:** | £14,000 |
| **Project:** | £5500 |

## DE TOMASO Pantera

De Tomaso learned a lot of lessons with the Mangusta, so when it came to creating a new supercar for Ford to sell in the USA, it made sure the car was a lot more habitable. The reworked chassis ensured there was a lot less rearward weight bias and, therefore, snap oversteer wasn't an inevitable consequence of a bungled corner. The interior was roomier, and had standard air-con. However, quality and reliability were poor and, when Ford withdrew its support, De Tomaso had to go it alone with the Pantera. Values rising smartly.

**SPECIFICATIONS**

| | |
|---|---|
| **Years produced:** | 1971-1985 |
| **Performance:** | 0-60mph: 6.2sec<br>Top speed: 159mph |
| **Power & torque:** | 330bhp/325lb ft |
| **Engine:** | Normally aspirated 5763cc V8, petrol, carburettor, 16 valves |
| **Drivetrain:** | Mid-engine RWD |
| **Structure:** | Monocoque |
| **Transmission:** | Five-speed manual |
| **Weight:** | 1411kg |

**PRICE GUIDE**

| | |
|---|---|
| **Launch price:** | £6996 |
| **Excellent:** | £95,000 |
| **Good:** | £70,000 |
| **Average:** | £42,500 |
| **Project:** | £20,000 |

## DE TOMASO Longchamp

Having failed with the Deauville, De Tomaso went and repeated the concept with its Longchamp. Again, it was a case of producing an Italian version of another manufacturer's car – this time, the Mercedes-Benz 450SLC – going down the same road to do so. Again, sales were non-existent, mainly because there was simply no demand, and the quality just wasn't there. Once De Tomaso took a controlling interest in Maserati, it tried again with the car, rebadging it the Kyalami (complete with Maserati V8). Similar apathy ensued.

**SPECIFICATIONS**

| | |
|---|---|
| **Years produced:** | 1972-1989 (409 in total) |
| **Performance:** | 0-60mph: 6.4sec<br>Top speed: 149mph |
| **Power & torque:** | 330bhp/325lb ft |
| **Engine:** | Normally aspirated 5763cc V8, petrol, carburettor, 16 valves |
| **Drivetrain:** | Front-engine RWD |
| **Structure:** | Monocoque |
| **Transmission:** | Five-speed manual/three-speed auto |
| **Weight:** | 1814kg |

**PRICE GUIDE**

| | |
|---|---|
| **Launch price:** | £9945 |
| **Excellent:** | £35,000 |
| **Good:** | £22,000 |
| **Average:** | £10,000 |
| **Project:** | £6000 |

## DE TOMASO Pantera GT5/GT5S

De Tomaso didn't give up on the Pantera. The firm toughened it up, offered a 300bhp entry model, and rejigged the Tom Tjaarda styling with flared arches and wider wheels wearing Pirelli P7s to give it near-Countach levels of road presence. The days of big sales were gone, but somehow the Pantera survived like this into the 1990s by receiving a number of facelifts along the way. Its survival and subsequent appreciation are a credit to the original design, and testament to the effectiveness of an Italian supercar powered by Detroit muscle. Values holding.

**SPECIFICATIONS**

| | |
|---|---|
| **Years produced:** | 1985-1991 (10,000 approx in total) |
| **Performance:** | 0-60mph: 5.2sec<br>Top speed: 146mph |
| **Power & torque:** | 350bhp/330lb ft |
| **Engine:** | Normally aspirated 5763cc V8, petrol, carburettor, 16 valves |
| **Drivetrain:** | Mid-engine RWD |
| **Structure:** | Monocoque |
| **Transmission:** | Five-speed manual |
| **Weight:** | 1491kg |

**PRICE GUIDE**

| | |
|---|---|
| **Launch price:** | £41,410 |
| **Excellent:** | £65,000 |
| **Good:** | £42,000 |
| **Average:** | £30,000 |
| **Project:** | £15,000 |

# ELVA

ELVA STARTED out as a specials manufacturer set-up by Frank Nichols and based in Bexhill, Sussex. Its first car was completed in 1955, based on a combination of Ford power, Standard suspension and a hand-fabricated chassis, and known as the Mk1. It soon established itself as quite a force in club level competition. The Mk1 was subsequently developed with more sophisticated suspension set-ups and esoteric (Coventry Climax) engines, and sold well in the USA. Unfortunately, financial problems beset Elva in 1961, when the government refused to support the company's proposed growth plans. Although it continued until 1965, Nichols meanwhile sold the operation to Ken Sheppard.

## ELVA Courier

Created by Frank Nichols for racing, the Courier was a quintessential English specialist car that married low weight, great handling and excellent performance in a low-cost package. Nichols sold the project to Trojan, which introduced an improved version in 1962. In MkIII form, the Courier received a number of small changes to its chassis as well as a roomier cockpit. However, sales dried up following the Trojan takeover and production ceased in 1968 after a final fling with a stylish coupé version. Competition cars command up to 50% more.

**SPECIFICATIONS**

**Years produced:** 1958-1961 (500 in total)
**Performance:** 0-60mph: 12.7sec
Top speed: 98mph
**Power & torque:** 72bhp/77lb ft
**Engine:** Normally aspirated 1489cc four cylinder, petrol, carburettor, 8 valves
**Drivetrain:** Front-engine RWD
**Structure:** Glassfibre body/separate chassis
**Transmission:** Four-speed manual
**Weight:** 453kg

**PRICE GUIDE**

**Launch price:** £725
**Excellent:** £23,500
**Good:** £17,000
**Average:** £11,000
**Project:** £6000

## ELVA Elva-BMW GT160

The GT160 marked a massive change in direction for Elva when it was launched in 1964 – and it had the ingredients for success, had events not overtaken it. Trojan, Elva's parent company, was pulling out of car manufacture and, even though the Trevor Fiore-styled GT160 looked promising, a mere three were built. It was built on a Mk7S racing chassis and, with the prototype pushing out 182bhp, performance was impressive. One was entered at the Le Mans 24 Hours in 1965, where it proved to be the fastest British car. Incredibly rare and highly prized.

**SPECIFICATIONS**

**Years produced:** 1964 (3 in total)
**Performance:** 0-60mph: 6.9sec
Top speed: 140mph
**Power & torque:** 185bhp/150lb ft
**Engine:** Normally aspirated 1991cc four cylinder, petrol, carburettor, 8 valves
**Drivetrain:** Front-engine RWD
**Structure:** Glassfibre body/separate chassis
**Transmission:** Four-speed manual
**Weight:** 559kg

**PRICE GUIDE**

**Launch price:** N/A
**Excellent:** £80,000
**Good:** £65,000
**Average:** N/A
**Project:** N/A

# FACEL VEGA

FACEL VEGA – handily shortened from the cumbersome 'Forges et Ateliers de Construction de l'Eure et Loire' – was a French coachbuilder before, in 1954, it branched out into cars. The company only existed for ten years but, in that decade, it built some extraordinary machines with lashings of luxury and powerful Chrysler V8 engines. They were also expensive so, in 1959, the company attempted something more competitively priced in the form of the four-cylinder Facellia. It was unreliable and even Volvo P1800 and Austin-Healey 3000 engines couldn't save the car or the company. Facel Vega went bust in 1964, toppled by the many warranty claims against it.

## FACEL VEGA FV/FVS

Facel started out by building bodies for other manufacturers before going it alone in 1954 with a De Soto-engined car called the Vega. Once the car became established, the company rebranded itself Facel Vega, and the car became the FVS. From the original 4.5-litre V8, the FVS moved to 5.4-litre Chrysler power, which gave an impressive 330bhp. To rein in all that power, a brake servo was fitted in 1957, and disc brakes were an option the following year. It was a simple recipe and the quality was there, as was the driving experience. Highly prized

**SPECIFICATIONS**

**Years produced:** 1954-1958 (352 in total)
**Performance:** 0-60mph: 9.6sec
Top speed: 134mph
**Power & torque:** 330bhp/430lb ft
**Engine:** Normally aspirated 5801cc V8, petrol, carburettor, 16 valves
**Drivetrain:** Front-engine RWD
**Structure:** Separate chassis
**Transmission:** Two-speed auto/four-speed manual
**Weight:** 1863kg

**PRICE GUIDE**

**Launch price:** £4726
**Excellent:** £175,000
**Good:** £120,000
**Average:** £85,000
**Project:** £55,000

## FACEL VEGA
### Excellence

It was France's flagship limousine for six glorious years, and although the Excellence was far from perfect, it oozed charisma. Facel Vega created the Excellence by extending the FVS wheelbase by 20in and creating an all-new body. It was a fantastic-looking limousine, with clap-hands doors and panoramic windscreen, but the lack of a B-pillar caused structural issues in later life. Once again, Chrysler V8 power ensured ample performance (and thirst), and simpler restorations. A desirable prestige saloon, not just for Francophiles.

**SPECIFICATIONS**

| | |
|---|---|
| **Years produced:** | 1958-1964 (152 in total) |
| **Performance:** | 0-60mph: 11.0sec<br>Top speed: 120mph |
| **Power & torque:** | 335bhp/380lb ft |
| **Engine:** | Normally aspirated 5905cc V8, petrol, carburettor, 16 valves |
| **Drivetrain:** | Front-engine RWD |
| **Structure:** | Separate chassis |
| **Transmission:** | Three-speed auto |
| **Weight:** | 1956kg |

**PRICE GUIDE**

| | |
|---|---|
| **Launch price:** | N/A |
| **Excellent:** | £160,000 |
| **Good:** | £110,000 |
| **Average:** | £80,000 |
| **Project:** | £40,000 |

## FACEL VEGA
### HK500

The FVS was uprated in 1959 with a 360bhp 6.3-litre engine, making it one of the most powerful cars in Europe. Even with the power boost, the all-drum brake set-up was standard kit on the HK500 – not what you would necessarily want in a car with such prodigious straight-line performance. Despite that, it was a perfect flagship for the French car industry, even if the overall dynamics of the HK500 lagged behind the styling and straight-line performance. Chrysler power, steering and transmissions mean that parts supply is good. Rare, expensive and hard to find now.

**SPECIFICATIONS**

| | |
|---|---|
| **Years produced:** | 1958-1961 (490 in total) |
| **Performance:** | 0-60mph: 9.7sec<br>Top speed: 130mph |
| **Power & torque:** | 360bhp/400lb ft |
| **Engine:** | Normally aspirated 5905cc V8, petrol, carburettor, 16 valves |
| **Drivetrain:** | Front-engine RWD |
| **Structure:** | Separate chassis |
| **Transmission:** | Four-speed manual |
| **Weight:** | 1829kg |

**PRICE GUIDE**

| | |
|---|---|
| **Launch price:** | £4726 |
| **Excellent:** | £200,000 |
| **Good:** | £150,000 |
| **Average:** | £110,000 |
| **Project:** | £65,000 |

## FACEL VEGA
### Facellia

Facel Vega needed to up its production volumes to make up the shortfall in its third-party body supply business. As the 'affordable' second model, the Facellia was to help the firm expand while allowing it to continue producing V8-powered supercars. The 1.6-litre twin-cam engine had an impressive specification, but the 115bhp it made wasn't enough for anything other than average performance, and it wasn't reliable enough either. A great concept marred in the execution, with gorgeous HK500-like styling and still prized by enthusiasts today.

**SPECIFICATIONS**

| | |
|---|---|
| **Years produced:** | 1960-1964 (1767 in total) |
| **Performance:** | 0-60mph: 11.9sec<br>Top speed: 106mph |
| **Power & torque:** | 115bhp/106lb ft |
| **Engine:** | Normally aspirated 1647cc four cylinder, petrol, carburettor, 8 valves |
| **Drivetrain:** | Front-engine RWD |
| **Structure:** | Separate chassis |
| **Transmission:** | Four-speed manual |
| **Weight:** | 1153kg |

**PRICE GUIDE**

| | |
|---|---|
| **Launch price:** | £2582 |
| **Excellent:** | £50,000 |
| **Good:** | £35,000 |
| **Average:** | £23,000 |
| **Project:** | £10,000 |

## FACEL VEGA
### Facel II

Continuing Facel Vega's policy of regular updates, the HK500 remained in production for only two years, moving over for the Facel II. The new car featured sharper styling and an even more powerful Chrysler V8, now offerng 390bhp and finally allowing the French supercar to top a genuine 150mph. However, the chassis and steering were simply not good enough to control all this power, marring what was an extremely appealing package. Despite all that, a very cool car today, especially as it's the last in the line of big V8 Facel Vegas.

**SPECIFICATIONS**

| | |
|---|---|
| **Years produced:** | 1961-1964 (183 in total) |
| **Performance:** | 0-60mph: 8.4sec<br>Top speed: 129mph |
| **Power & torque:** | 355bhp/380lb ft |
| **Engine:** | Normally aspirated 6286cc V8, petrol, carburettor, 16 valves |
| **Drivetrain:** | Front-engine RWD |
| **Structure:** | Separate chassis |
| **Transmission:** | Four-speed manual |
| **Weight:** | 1842kg |

**PRICE GUIDE**

| | |
|---|---|
| **Launch price:** | £4879 |
| **Excellent:** | £300,000 |
| **Good:** | £250,000 |
| **Average:** | £175,000 |
| **Project:** | £100,000 |

## FACEL VEGA
### Facel III

Amazingly, when it came to replacing the Facel II, the idea of increasing power and opulence was thrown out of the window as the company adopted a clean-sheet policy for its new car. The Facel III was powered by a 1780cc Volvo engine, and delivered the sort of performance that was ample for most drivers. It sold well, too, as it managed to retain all the dignity and style of the V8 cars in a more manageable package. However, the company was already in trouble when it launched and, despite its relative success, it failed to halt the inevitable.

**SPECIFICATIONS**

| | |
|---|---|
| **Years produced:** | 1963-1964 |
| **Performance:** | 0-60mph: N/A<br>Top speed: N/A |
| **Power & torque:** | 108bhp/N/A |
| **Engine:** | Normally aspirated 1780cc four cylinder, petrol, carburettor, 8 valves |
| **Drivetrain:** | Front-engine RWD |
| **Structure:** | Separate chassis |
| **Transmission:** | Four-speed manual |
| **Weight:** | 1089kg |

**PRICE GUIDE**

| | |
|---|---|
| **Launch price:** | N/A |
| **Excellent:** | £45,000 |
| **Good:** | £30,000 |
| **Average:** | £19,000 |
| **Project:** | £10,000 |

# FERRARI

ONE OF THE towering figures in the history of motoring, Enzo Ferrari was first and foremost a race team leader, and it was to finance his racing cars that he first turned to road car production in 1947 with the V12-powered 166. Some afficionados consider the V12 cars to be the only 'real' Ferraris, though that's an increasingly outmoded view, with V6- and V8-engined cars having long gained classic status. In 1969 the company joined the Fiat empire, but kept its strong identity, Enzo himself retaining influence right up to his death in 1988, aged 90. Now independent again, the company he created remains as strong as ever, still racing in F1, and still creating hugely desirable road cars.

## FERRARI 166

Although Enzo Ferrari set up his own car company in 1940, it wasn't until 1947 that he launched the racing 125. Subsequently available with Touring bodies, they proved to be wonderful machines when partnered with Gioacchino Colombo's jewel-like V12 engine. The 125s were 1.5-litres, while the true road-going 166 was introduced with a 2.0-litre. Available with Pinin Farina, Bertone, Ghia, Vignale and Allemano bodies to complement the most widely known by Touring. Racing credentials were thoroughly proven at Le Mans, where it won in 1949.

### SPECIFICATIONS

| | |
|---|---|
| **Years produced:** | 1947-1953 (71 in total) |
| **Performance:** | 0-60mph: 9.5sec<br>Top speed: 106mph |
| **Power & torque:** | 110bhp/120lb ft |
| **Engine:** | Normally aspirated 1995cc V12, petrol, carburettor, 24 valves |
| **Drivetrain:** | Front-engine RWD |
| **Structure:** | Tubular frame |
| **Transmission:** | Four-speed manual |
| **Weight:** | 980kg |

### PRICE GUIDE (road cars)

| | |
|---|---|
| **Launch price:** | N/A |
| **Excellent:** | £3,500,000+ |
| **Good:** | £2,500,000 |
| **Average:** | £1,500,000 |
| **Project:** | £950,000 |

## FERRARI 195

A logical and useful update of the 166 that cemented Ferrari's position at the pinnacle of motor sport and road car production. The V12 had been bored out and, in the hottest versions with a trio of carburettors, was capable of delivering 180bhp. The Inter model was the car you bought for the road, while the Sport was the one you raced. As with the 166, the 195 was available with a number of coachbuilt bodies, all in aluminium, including by Ghia and Pinin Farina, though Touring and Vignale tend to be the most sought-after.

### SPECIFICATIONS (195 Inter)

| | |
|---|---|
| **Years produced:** | 1950-1952 (27 in total) |
| **Performance:** | 0-60mph: 8.0sec<br>Top speed: 115mph |
| **Power & torque:** | 130bhp/130lb ft |
| **Engine:** | Normally aspirated 2341cc V12, petrol, carburettor, 24 valves |
| **Drivetrain:** | Front-engine RWD |
| **Structure:** | Tubular frame |
| **Transmission:** | Four-speed manual |
| **Weight:** | 950kg |

### PRICE GUIDE (road cars)

| | |
|---|---|
| **Launch price:** | N/A |
| **Excellent:** | £1,200,000+ |
| **Good:** | £900,000 |
| **Average:** | £700,000 |
| **Project:** | £600,000 |

## FERRARI 212

The 195's V12 was once again bored out, this time to 2562cc – or 212cc per cylinder, hence the name. Power and torque were improved, most notably to improve all-round flexibility. Ferrari's reputation continued to rise as the 212's competition victories were racked up. The 212 was an important Ferrari in the USA, where the Export model sold well. Also available in 212 Inter form, which meant road spec, and these cars received a lengthened 98.5in wheelbase. Still essentially based on the Type 166 and available with a myriad of coachbuilt bodies.

### SPECIFICATIONS

| | |
|---|---|
| **Years produced:** | 1951-1953 (106 in total) |
| **Performance:** | 0-60mph: 8.1sec<br>Top speed: 120mph |
| **Power & torque:** | 140bhp/162lb ft |
| **Engine:** | Normally aspirated 2562cc V12, petrol, carburettor, 24 valves |
| **Drivetrain:** | Front-engine RWD |
| **Structure:** | Tubular frame |
| **Transmission:** | Four-speed manual |
| **Weight:** | 923kg |

### PRICE GUIDE (road cars)

| | |
|---|---|
| **Launch price:** | N/A |
| **Excellent:** | £2,750,000+ |
| **Good:** | £1,750,000 |
| **Average:** | £1,250,000 |
| **Project:** | £950,000 |

## FERRARI 340/342/375 America

The 340 was the final flowering of the 166 chassis. As for the V12, a long-block version had been designed by Aurelio Lampredi, and also used in Ferrari's Formula 1 cars. The combination was exciting, and a fitting finale for the 166, expecially as the ultimate Mexico developed 280bhp, almost three times the original car's power. 340 and 342 shared the 4.1-litre engine; the 375 had no less than 4.5-litres, and was available in road and competition car form. Values are often double those of the 166, although they vary hugely due to provenance.

### SPECIFICATIONS (340 Mexico)

| | |
|---|---|
| **Years produced:** | 1950-1955 (41 in total) |
| **Performance:** | 0-60mph: 6.0sec<br>Top speed: 142mph |
| **Power & torque:** | 280bhp/228lb ft |
| **Engine:** | Normally aspirated 4102cc V12, petrol, carburettor, 24 valves |
| **Drivetrain:** | Front-engine RWD |
| **Structure:** | Tubular frame |
| **Transmission:** | Four-speed manual |
| **Weight:** | 1000kg |

### PRICE GUIDE (375 Spider in brackets)

| | |
|---|---|
| **Launch price:** | N/A |
| **Excellent:** | £5,500,000 (£11,500,000) |
| **Good:** | £4,500,000 (£8,500,000) |
| **Average:** | £3,500,000 (£6,500,000) |
| **Project:** | £2,000,000 (£5,500,000) |

## FERRARI
## 250GT Boano/Ellena

The strange names come from the coachbuilding firm that bodied the cars for Ferrari. Although designed by Pininfarina, it was erecting a new plant and didn't have capacity to build them. The work was given to former employee Mario Boano, then, after around 80 were built, the contract was passed to his son-in-law Ezio Ellena, who assembled another 50. Early cars put out 220bhp from their 3.0-litre V12 engines, but this rose to 240bhp. Despite independent double wishbone front suspension, the chassis is fairly crude.

**SPECIFICATIONS**

| | |
|---|---|
| **Years produced:** | 1956-1959 (130 in total) |
| **Performance:** | 0-60mph: 7.1sec<br>Top speed: 126mph |
| **Power & torque:** | 260bhp/232lb ft |
| **Engine:** | Normally aspirated 2953cc V12, petrol, carburettor, 24 valves |
| **Drivetrain:** | Front-engine RWD |
| **Structure:** | Tubular frame |
| **Transmission:** | Four-speed manual |
| **Weight:** | 1315kg |

**PRICE GUIDE (add c40% for alloy cars)**

| | |
|---|---|
| **Launch price:** | N/A |
| **Excellent:** | £1,200,000 |
| **Good:** | £750,000 |
| **Average:** | £550,000 |
| **Project:** | £450,000 |

## FERRARI
## 250 California Spyder

Largely built for the American market, California Spiders were that bit more sporting than the 250 GT Cabriolets they were based on. By 1960, just under 50 long-wheelbase versions were built with 240bhp engines. The wheelbase was then chopped by 8in to create the short wheelbase (SWB) version. Power went up to 280bhp and another 50 of these were sold over the next three years. They can be worth as much as 40% more than the LWB cars. Note: covered headlights also add value: a SWB, covered-headlamp car might now fetch £13 million or more.

**SPECIFICATIONS**

| | |
|---|---|
| **Years produced:** | 1958-1962 (100 approx in total) |
| **Performance:** | 0-60mph: 7.2sec<br>Top speed: 137mph |
| **Power & torque:** | 240bhp/181lb ft |
| **Engine:** | Normally aspirated 2953cc V12, petrol, carburettor, 24 valves |
| **Drivetrain:** | Front-engine RWD |
| **Structure:** | Tubular frame |
| **Transmission:** | Four-speed manual |
| **Weight:** | 1277kg |

**PRICE GUIDE (LWB/SWB)**

| | |
|---|---|
| **Launch price:** | N/A |
| **Excellent:** | £9,000,000+ (£12,000,000+) |
| **Good:** | £6,000,000 (£9,000,000) |
| **Average:** | N/A |
| **Project:** | N/A |

## FERRARI
## 250GT SWB

Seriously collectable Ferraris, not least due to the fact that only just over 150 were built and almost half were competition cars. The racers reigned supreme in the GT classes and one was driven in period by Stirling Moss; such exploits rub off on the desirability and value of road cars. History and provenance can have just as much effect on an individual SWB's value as condition, say specialists like DK Engineering. All came with 3.0-litre V12s and power can range from 220/ 240bhp in road cars to 280bhp from competition-spec engines.

**SPECIFICATIONS**

| | |
|---|---|
| **Years produced:** | 1959-1962 (167 in total) |
| **Performance:** | 0-60mph: 6.4sec<br>Top speed: 167mph |
| **Power & torque:** | 280bhp/203lb ft |
| **Engine:** | Normally aspirated 2953cc V12, petrol, carburettor, 24 valves |
| **Drivetrain:** | Front-engine RWD |
| **Structure:** | Tubular frame |
| **Transmission:** | Four-speed manual |
| **Weight:** | 1180kg |

**PRICE GUIDE (add c40% for alloy cars)**

| | |
|---|---|
| **Launch price:** | N/A |
| **Excellent:** | £7,000,000 |
| **Good:** | £6,000,000 |
| **Average:** | £5,000,000 |
| **Project:** | N/A |

## FERRARI
## 250GT Cabriolet S2

Well-appointed and suitably expensive in its day, the GT Cabriolet was very much an open version of the 250 Coupé – less sporting and more sober-looking than the Spyders they were sold alongside. The giveaway is that Cabriolets had small quarterlights in the doors; you'd have to see the cars side-by-side to see they also had a taller windscreen. Under the bonnet, however, you'll find the same engine as in the LWB Spyder so, with little performance difference between them, the Cabriolet looks quite a bargain in comparison.

**SPECIFICATIONS**

| | |
|---|---|
| **Years produced:** | 1960-1962 (200 in total) |
| **Performance:** | 0-60mph: 7.1sec<br>Top speed: 161mph |
| **Power & torque:** | 240bhp/N/A |
| **Engine:** | Normally aspirated 2953cc V12, petrol, carburettor, 24 valves |
| **Drivetrain:** | Front-engine RWD |
| **Structure:** | Tubular frame |
| **Transmission:** | Four-speed manual |
| **Weight:** | 1200kg |

**PRICE GUIDE**

| | |
|---|---|
| **Launch price:** | N/A |
| **Excellent:** | £1,400,000 |
| **Good:** | £1,200,000 |
| **Average:** | £1,000,000 |
| **Project:** | £750,000 |

## FERRARI
## 250GTE 2+2

Built with the clear intention of taking a slice of the premium four-seater market, this was Ferrari's first production 2+2. It was powered by the same 3.0-litre V12 used in the 250 Coupés, but moved forward eight inches in the chassis to help create interior space without making the car look too long. The GTE's success is evident in the 955 examples sold over three years. The collectors' market, of course, tends not to appreciate big numbers like that – or Ferraris with extra seats – but values of the best examples have climbed steadily in recent years.

**SPECIFICATIONS**

| | |
|---|---|
| **Years produced:** | 1960-1963 (955 in total) |
| **Performance:** | 0-60mph: 8.0sec<br>Top speed: 136mph |
| **Power & torque:** | 240bhp/181lb ft |
| **Engine:** | Normally aspirated 2953cc V12, petrol, carburettor, 24 valves |
| **Drivetrain:** | Front-engine RWD |
| **Structure:** | Tubular frame |
| **Transmission:** | Four-speed manual with overdrive |
| **Weight:** | 1406kg |

**PRICE GUIDE**

| | |
|---|---|
| **Launch price:** | £6326 |
| **Excellent:** | £400,000 |
| **Good:** | £300,000 |
| **Average:** | £250,000 |
| **Project:** | £150,000 |

# FERRARI
## 400 Superamerica

The Ferrari tradition of naming its cars after the displacement of a single cylinder should have seen this called the 330, but it chose 400 instead, referring to the 4.0-litre capacity, perhaps as the model was very much headed for the land where more is better. Aimed at the super-rich, numbers were low with just 47 built over four years. Most were 'Aerodynamica' coupés, but Pininfarina also built 11 cabriolets that fetch roughly 50% more than the coupé. Covered headlights and SWB also add value, but all are hugely desirable and collectable.

**SPECIFICATIONS**

**Years produced:** 1960-1964 (58 in total)
**Performance:** 0-60mph: 9.2sec
Top speed: 160mph
**Power & torque:** 340bhp/235lb ft
**Engine:** Normally aspirated 3967cc V12, petrol, carburettor, 24 valves
**Drivetrain:** Front-engine RWD
**Structure:** Tubular frame
**Transmission:** Five-speed manual
**Weight:** 1363kg

**PRICE GUIDE (Cabrio in brackets)**

**Launch price:** N/A
**Excellent:** £2,500,000 (£4,000,000)
**Good:** £2,250,000 (£3,500,000)
**Average:** £1,750,000
**Project:** N/A

# FERRARI
## 250 GTO

In truth a pure racing car – though some are road-registered – the GTO was the ultimate evolution of the 250-series of front-engined berlinettas. Based on the chassis of the 250SWB but with much more aerodynamic bodywork (developed partly in a wind tunnel) and with a 300bhp version of the V12 from the Testa Rossa, the GTO was brilliantly successful in GT racing in the early 1960s. It has since become the most valuable of all Ferraris – indeed of all cars, with chassis no. 3413 fetching a world record auction price of $48.4m (c£36m) in 2018.

**SPECIFICATIONS**

**Years produced:** 1962-1964 (39 in total)
**Performance:** 0-60mph: 6.0sec
Top speed: 175mph
**Power & torque:** 300bhp/220lb ft
**Engine:** Normally aspirated 2953cc V12, petrol, carburettor, 24 valves
**Drivetrain:** Front-engine RWD
**Structure:** Tubular frame
**Transmission:** Five-speed manual
**Weight:** c1000kg

**PRICE GUIDE**

**Launch price:** N/A
**Excellent:** £40,000,000+
**Good:** N/A
**Average:** N/A
**Project:** N/A

# FERRARI
## 250GT Berlinetta Lusso

Last of the 250 GT line, the Lusso is also on many an aficionado's list of all-time best-looking Ferraris. On a chassis derived from the 250GTO, but with the engine moved forward to improve cabin space, the Lusso has a steel shell with all the opening panels, floor and firewall in aluminium – a fact that can add to the cost and complication of restoration. The engine is the familiar 3.0-litre V12 with three twin-choke Webers and 250bhp. Bucket seats add to the sporting feel, though still manage to be comfortable. Add c£100k+ for a RHD car.

**SPECIFICATIONS**

**Years produced:** 1962-1964 (350 in total)
**Performance:** 0-60mph: 8.0sec
Top speed: 149mph
**Power & torque:** 250bhp/217lb ft
**Engine:** Normally aspirated 2953cc V12, petrol, carburettor, 24 valves
**Drivetrain:** Front-engine RWD
**Structure:** Tubular frame
**Transmission:** Four-speed manual
**Weight:** 1020kg

**PRICE GUIDE**

**Launch price:** £5607
**Excellent:** £1,500,000+
**Good:** £1,350,000
**Average:** £1,200,000
**Project:** N/A

# FERRARI
## 275GTS

The GTS shared the new 3.3-litre V12 and all the advances of its GTB coupé brother (see next page), but you'd never have guessed from their looks. Their bodies – though both styled by Pininfarina – were totally different, with the softer, less aggressive-looking GTS staying much closer to the lines of previous 250GTs. Perhaps partly as a consequence of that, the GTS has always been worth less than the GTB, even though it is considerably rarer and – with a top speed in excess of 140mph – is hardly a slouch.

**SPECIFICATIONS**

**Years produced:** 1964-1966 (200 in total)
**Performance:** 0-60mph: 7.2sec
Top speed: 140mph+
**Power & torque:** 275bhp/188lb ft
**Engine:** Normally aspirated 3286cc V12, petrol, carburettor, 24 valves
**Drivetrain:** Front-engine RWD
**Structure:** Tubular frame
**Transmission:** Five-speed manual
**Weight:** 1152kg

**PRICE GUIDE**

**Launch price:** £5973
**Excellent:** £1,600,000
**Good:** £1,400,000
**Average:** £1,200,000
**Project:** N/A

# FERRARI
## 500 Superfast

Evolved from the 400 Superamerica, the 500 Superfast had a slightly longer wheelbase and only came in aerodynamic coupé form, with the 400's styling tidied up and improved upon. Surprisingly, the market long though they were worth less than those 400s, despite only 36 Superfasts being built. Some of that may be down to fear of the mighty, 5.0-litre V12 engine. Despite the low build numbers, much of the construction was unique to this model, so you wouldn't want to break one. Eight were built with right-hand drive. Best can now be up to £2.5m.

**SPECIFICATIONS**

**Years produced:** 1964-1966 (36 in total)
**Performance:** 0-60mph: 7.8sec
Top speed: 174mph
**Power & torque:** 400bhp/350lb ft
**Engine:** Normally aspirated 4963cc V12, petrol, carburettor, 24 valves
**Drivetrain:** Front-engine RWD
**Structure:** Tubular frame
**Transmission:** Five-speed manual
**Weight:** 1400kg

**PRICE GUIDE**

**Launch price:** £11,519
**Excellent:** £2,000,000+
**Good:** £1,750,000
**Average:** £1,500,000
**Project:** N/A

## FERRARI
### 330GT 2+2

Taking over from the commercially very successful 250GTE as Ferrari's four-seater option, the 330GT came with a litre more engine capacity for vastly improved performance figures – top speed was raised by 10mph over the older car. Unfortunately the 330GT also came with an awkward twin-headlamp arrangement that, in polite terms, received mixed reviews. Thankfully the Series II, introduced halfway through production, reverted to a prettier single-headlamp arrangement, and it's these cars the market prefers.

**SPECIFICATIONS**

**Years produced:** 1964-1967 (1075 in total)
**Performance:** 0-60mph: 6.3sec
Top speed: 152mph
**Power & torque:** 300bhp/288lb ft
**Engine:** Normally aspirated 3967cc V12, petrol, carburettor, 24 valves
**Drivetrain:** Front-engine RWD
**Structure:** Tubular frame
**Transmission:** Five-speed manual
**Weight:** 1442kg

**PRICE GUIDE**

**Launch price:** £6522
**Excellent:** £230,000
**Good:** £175,000
**Average:** £130,000
**Project:** £80,000

## FERRARI
### 275GTB/GTB4

Though the body was a gentle evolution from what had gone before, underneath the 275 is special and significant, as Ferrari finally introduced long-overdue advances in chassis technology. All-independent suspension, a disc brake at every corner, and a five-speed transaxle brought it into the modern era. Bodies were built in steel or alloy – with the latter being worth up to 50% more today. Power from the 3.3-litre V12 could be 250bhp, or 275bhp with the optional six-carb set-up. This was raised to 300bhp for the four-cam GTB/4.

**SPECIFICATIONS**

**Years produced:** 1964-1968 (730 in total)
**Performance:** 0-60mph: 6.0sec
Top speed: 162mph
**Power & torque:** 275bhp/188lb ft
**Engine:** Normally aspirated 3286cc V12, petrol, carburettor, 24 valves
**Drivetrain:** Front-engine RWD
**Structure:** Tubular frame
**Transmission:** Five-speed manual
**Weight:** 1098kg

**PRICE GUIDE (GTB4 in brackets)**

**Launch price:** £5973
**Excellent:** £2,000,000 (£2,300,000)
**Good:** £1,750,000 (£2,000,000)
**Average:** N/A
**Project:** N/A

## FERRARI
### 330GTC

Looking like a coupé version of the 275GTS with the nose of a 500 Superfast, the 330GTC lacks the styling purity of the coupés either side of it in the Ferrari family tree. It's a lot better from some angles than others and that is reflected in their values, though they are by no means cheap – even by Ferrari collectors' standards. They certainly suffer no shortfall in the performance department, the 4.0-litre V12's 300bhp offering up genuine 150mph capability. Continued use of a five-speed rear transaxle ensures good handling and cruising.

**SPECIFICATIONS**

**Years produced:** 1966-1968 (600 in total)
**Performance:** 0-60mph: 6.8sec
Top speed: 152mph
**Power & torque:** 300bhp/288lb ft
**Engine:** Normally aspirated 3967cc V12, petrol, carburettor, 24 valves
**Drivetrain:** Front-engine RWD
**Structure:** Tubular frame
**Transmission:** Five-speed manual
**Weight:** 1433kg

**PRICE GUIDE**

**Launch price:** £6515
**Excellent:** £650,000
**Good:** £600,000
**Average:** £500,000
**Project:** £400,000

## FERRARI
### 330GTS

In something of a break with Ferrari tradition, the 330 Spyder was simply the coupé 330GTC with the roof lopped off. Then again, given how much better the topless car looks, it's very likely that the Spyder was designed first and had the roof added. Buyers certainly value the Spyder significantly higher than the coupé, and that difference isn't all to do with the lack of a roof and only 100 being built compared with six times as many GTCs. The GTS really is that far ahead in style and bragging rights. Remarkably friendly to drive despite its 300bhp.

**SPECIFICATIONS**

**Years produced:** 1966-1968 (100 in total)
**Performance:** 0-60mph: 6.9sec
Top speed: 146mph
**Power & torque:** 300bhp/288lb ft
**Engine:** Normally aspirated 3967cc V12, petrol, carburettor, 24 valves
**Drivetrain:** Front-engine RWD
**Structure:** Tubular frame
**Transmission:** Five-speed manual
**Weight:** 1297kg

**PRICE GUIDE**

**Launch price:** £6515
**Excellent:** £2,000,000
**Good:** £1,600,000
**Average:** £1,400,000
**Project:** N/A

## FERRARI
### 365GTC/GTS

These were stop-gap models, little more than the 330GTC and GTS with the V12 bored out by 400cc to 4.4 litres. Visually the only way to tell them apart is that the row of three outlet vents on each front wing has vanished, to be replaced by a pair of flush-fit grilles to the rear of the bonnet. Mechanically the cars were identical to their predecessors with the exception of the braking system, which was switched from Dunlop/Girling to ATE. The GTS was dropped after just a year with just 20 built, which is why it's so highly prized today.

**SPECIFICATIONS**

**Years produced:** 1968-1970 (150/20 in total)
**Performance:** 0-60mph: 6.3sec
Top speed: 152mph
**Power & torque:** 320bhp/268lb ft
**Engine:** Normally aspirated 4390cc V12, petrol, carburettor, 24 valves
**Drivetrain:** Front-engine RWD
**Structure:** Tubular frame
**Transmission:** Five-speed manual
**Weight:** 1451kg

**PRICE GUIDE (GTS in brackets)**

**Launch price:** £7909
**Excellent:** £850,000 (£2,500,000+)
**Good:** £675,000 (£2,250,000)
**Average:** £550,000 (N/A)
**Project:** £450,000 (N/A)

## FERRARI
## 365GT 2+2

Replacement for the 330GT, the 365 was Ferrari's first 2+2 to have independent rear suspension – a Koni self-levelling system to boot. It's a big car, once dubbed 'the Queen Mary of Ferraris' by *Road & Track*, but the sleek lines are more successful than the 330's, especially at the front. With the V12 bored out to 4.4 litres it's not short of performance, grip is good and the standard power steering helps make it feel smaller from the driver's seat. 800 of them were built and it's never really caught on with collectors, so comparitively good value.

**SPECIFICATIONS**

**Years produced:** 1968-1970 (800 in total)
**Performance:** 0-60mph: 7.1sec
Top speed: 151mph
**Power & torque:** 320bhp/268lb ft
**Engine:** Normally aspirated 4390cc V12, petrol, carburettor, 24 valves
**Drivetrain:** Front-engine RWD
**Structure:** Tubular frame
**Transmission:** Five-speed manual
**Weight:** 1462kg

**PRICE GUIDE**

**Launch price:** £7500
**Excellent:** £230,000
**Good:** £150,000
**Average:** £130,000
**Project:** £70,000

## FERRARI
## 365GTB/4 Daytona

One of the legendary Ferraris, not least because it held the title of World's Fastest Production Car for some time at 174mph. That was all made possible by the quad-cam 4.4-litre V12 with its bank of six twin-choke Weber carbs – good for 352bhp in street trim. And though it was built as a road car, privateers were racing them as late as 1979. Headlamps were initially fixed behind a Perspex nose (add up to 20% for these), switching to pop-up lights in 1970. Nearly 1300 were built – a lot for a top-end Ferrari – which is why values have stalled.

**SPECIFICATIONS**

**Years produced:** 1968-1973 (1284 in total)
**Performance:** 0-60mph: 5.9sec
Top speed: 174mph
**Power & torque:** 352bhp/318lb ft
**Engine:** Normally aspirated 4390cc V12, petrol, carburettor, 24 valves
**Drivetrain:** Front-engine RWD
**Structure:** Tubular frame
**Transmission:** Five-speed manual
**Weight:** 1197kg

**PRICE GUIDE**

**Launch price:** £8750
**Excellent:** £700,000
**Good:** £600,000
**Average:** £550,000
**Project:** £400,000

## DINO
## 206/246GT

The 206 was undeniably pretty, with a mid-mounted V6 in an alloy body, a 2.0-litre wasn't quite enough for Ferrari's move into a volume market and only around 150 206GTs were built before it was replaced by the 246GT. OK, these were built in steel, with an iron (rather than alloy) engine block, but the 2.4-litre V6 gave it more zip. The public snapped them up and they continue to feature on many an enthusiast's wish list. Though only tiny numbers of 206s were built, all LHD, almost 2500 246 GTs were built, values of which are now on the up once again.

**SPECIFICATIONS**

**Years produced:** 1969-1974 (152/2487 produced)
**Performance:** 0-60mph: 7.1sec (246)
Top speed: 145mph
**Power & torque:** 195bhp/166lb ft
**Engine:** Normally aspirated 2418cc V6, petrol, carburettor, 12 valves
**Drivetrain:** Mid-engine RWD
**Structure:** Spaceframe
**Transmission:** Five-speed manual
**Weight:** 1077kg

**PRICE GUIDE (246GT in brackets)**

**Launch price:** £5486
**Excellent:** £500,000 (£400,000)
**Good:** £400,000 (£325,000)
**Average:** £350,000 (£275,000)
**Project:** £250,000 (£175,000)

## FERRARI
## 365GTC/4

Sharing its four-cam V12, though in a slightly lower state of tune and with six sidedraft (rather than downdraft) Webers, the GTC/4 was sold alongside the Daytona – notching up 500 sales in 18 short months. It sports a similar profile to the Daytona too, though there's just about room to squeeze two kids into the back of the GTC/4. It compares favourably to the Daytona in two ways: with its power steering, softer suspension and hydraulic clutch, the GTC/4 is nice to drive. It also happens to cost about a third of what you need for a Daytona.

**SPECIFICATIONS**

**Years produced:** 1971-1972 (500 in total)
**Performance:** 0-60mph: 6.2sec
Top speed: 163mph
**Power & torque:** 340bhp/312lb ft
**Engine:** Normally aspirated 4390cc V12, petrol, carburettor, 24 valves
**Drivetrain:** Front-engine RWD
**Structure:** Tubular frame
**Transmission:** Five-speed manual
**Weight:** 1450kg

**PRICE GUIDE**

**Launch price:** £10,251
**Excellent:** £275,000
**Good:** £225,000
**Average:** £175,000
**Project:** £100,000

## FERRARI
## 365GT4 2+2/400/412i

Aimed at the family man of style and substance. In all its different designations, this is the longest-running Ferrari of all time at 17 years. The 365s started with a 4.4-litre V12, but this grew to 4.8 litres (400) and finally five litres (412i) by 1986. Quick and fine-handling despite their size, the penalty comes at the pumps, where you can expect 10-12mpg. Prices quoted are for the 412i; 365s are a little more and 400s cost a little less but there's not much in it. Most came with a General Motors-sourced auto gearbox; rare manual quite a bit more sought-after.

**SPECIFICATIONS**

**Years produced:** 1972-1989 (525/1810/576 in total)
**Performance:** 0-60mph: 6.7sec
Top speed: 147mph
**Power & torque:** 340bhp/333lb ft
**Engine:** Normally aspirated 4390cc V12, petrol, carburettor, 24 valves
**Drivetrain:** Front-engine RWD
**Structure:** Monocoque
**Transmission:** Five-speed manual/three-speed auto
**Weight:** 1884kg

**PRICE GUIDE (manual in brackets)**

**Launch price:** £12,783
**Excellent:** £45,000 (£60,000)
**Good:** £33,000 (£45,000)
**Average:** £22,000 (£30,000)
**Project:** £12,000 (£15,000)

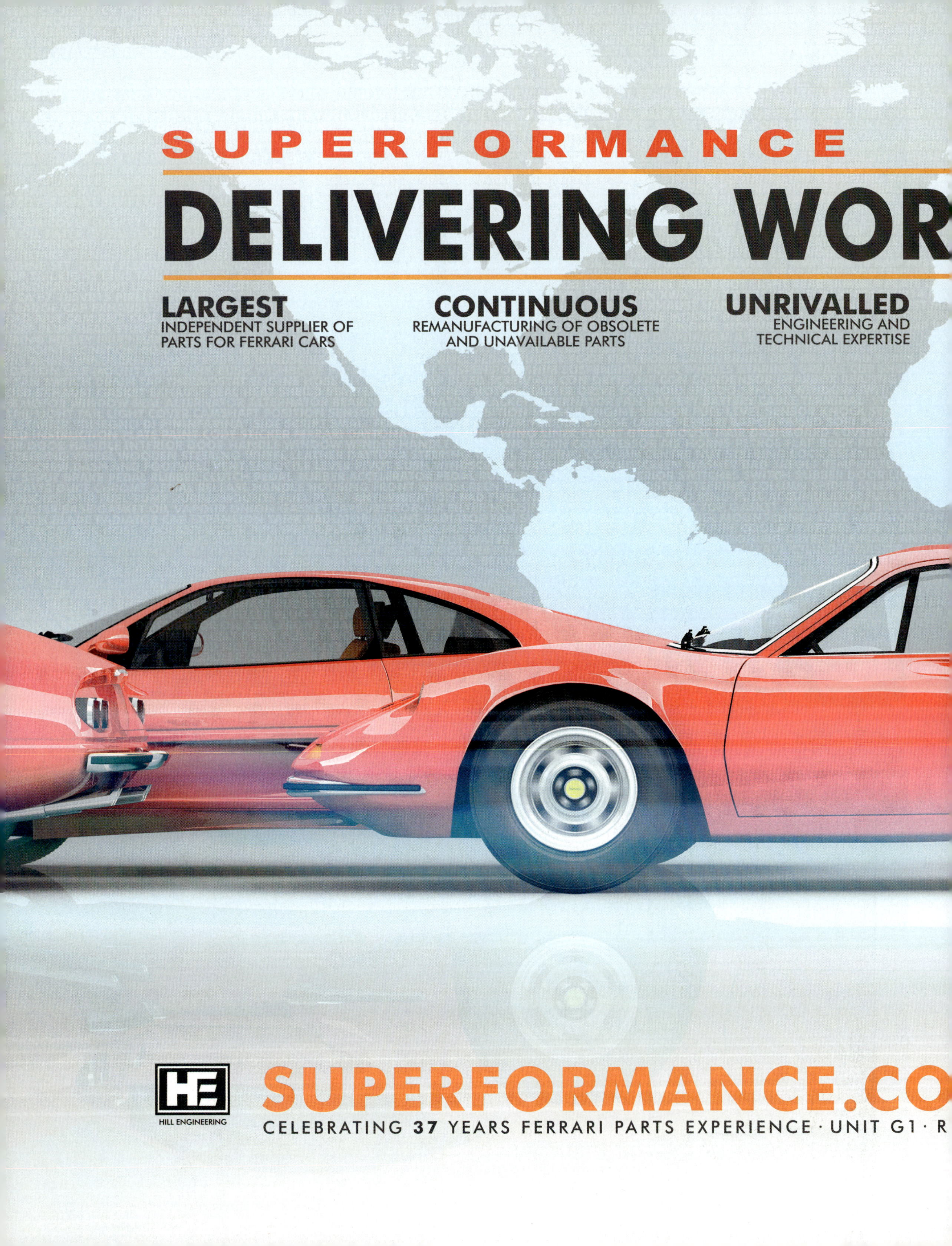

FERRARI PARTS SPECIALIST
DWIDE EVERY DAY
DEPENDABLE
BIG ENOUGH TO COPE
SMALL ENOUGH TO CARE
OFFICIAL
DISTRIBUTOR FOR
HILL ENGINEERING
FAST EXPRESS
WORLDWIDE SHIPPING DAILY
K +44 (0)1992 445 300
· STEPHENSON CLOSE · HODDESDON · HERTFORDSHIRE · EN11 0BW
CONTACT OUR OFFICE AT ADMIN@SUPERFORMANCE.CO.UK

## DINO
### 246GTS

The Targa-roofed spin on the Dino theme arrived in 1972, setting a trend for the fresh air option in mid-engined Ferraris that soon became the norm. As well as the lift-out roof panels, the other big change was deletion of the rear side windows. Not a big deal to many, but it is felt by some to detract ever so slightly from the fine balance of the original design. It's still one of the most beautiful cars ever built and would surely be worth even more if Ferrari hadn't managed to sell so many. Values have started to take off again in recent months.

**SPECIFICATIONS**

**Years produced:** 1972-1974 (1274 in total)
**Performance:** 0-60mph: 7.1sec
Top speed: 146mph
**Power & torque:** 195bhp/166lb ft
**Engine:** Normally aspirated 2418cc V6, petrol, carburettor, 12 valves
**Drivetrain:** Mid-engine RWD
**Structure:** Tubular frame
**Transmission:** Five-speed manual
**Weight:** 1100kg

**PRICE GUIDE**

**Launch price:** £5486
**Excellent:** £500,000
**Good:** £400,000
**Average:** £350,000
**Project:** £225,000

## FERRARI
### 365 Berlinetta Boxer

Having experimented with a small, mid-engined road car in the shape of the Dino, Ferrari went the whole hog with the Daytona's replacement – the Berlinetta Boxer. The Boxer bit refers to the new engine's flat-12 layout; all it shared with the outgoing V12 was its 4.4-litre capacity. Keeping with its race car image, the whole tail section lifts to reveal the bare bones of the chassis and the engine which, thanks to its low profile, sits above the transmission. Prices started to soar a few years ago, but the heat has gone out of them recently.

**SPECIFICATIONS**

**Years produced:** 1973-1976 (387 in total)
**Performance:** 0-60mph: 6.5sec
Top speed: 176mph
**Power & torque:** 380bhp/302lb ft
**Engine:** Normally aspirated 4390cc V12, petrol, carburettor, 24 valves
**Drivetrain:** Mid-engine RWD
**Structure:** Semi-monocoque
**Transmission:** Five-speed manual
**Weight:** 1235kg

**PRICE GUIDE**

**Launch price:** £15,492
**Excellent:** £350,000
**Good:** £300,000
**Average:** £275,000
**Project:** £200,000

## FERRARI
### Dino 308GT4

The 308 GT4 has the rare distinction of being designed by Bertone, making it the first Ferrari for nearly 20 years that wasn't styled by Pininfarina. It also contained the company's first production V8 engine – effectively two-thirds of a 365's V12 – and was its first mid-engined 2+2. None of these facts have helped endear it to latter-day Ferrari buyers, though it stayed in production for seven years and racked up almost 3000 sales. A competent and quick car, though of course they rust; find a good one and it makes a fine first Ferrari.

**SPECIFICATIONS**

**Years produced:** 1974-1980 (2826 in total)
**Performance:** 0-60mph: 6.7sec
Top speed: 147mph
**Power & torque:** 255bhp/209lb ft
**Engine:** Normally aspirated 2927cc V8, petrol, carburettor, 16 valves
**Drivetrain:** Mid-engine RWD
**Structure:** Monocoque
**Transmission:** Five-speed manual
**Weight:** 1265kg

**PRICE GUIDE**

**Launch price:** £7699
**Excellent:** £70,000
**Good:** £50,000
**Average:** £40,000
**Project:** £20,000

## FERRARI
### 308GTB 'Vetroresina'

Sharing the V8 engine from the recently-launched 308GT4, the pretty GTB was Ferrari's first ever glassfibre car, though that bold move fizzled out after less than two years and 712 examples. Quite simply it was cheaper and quicker to build in steel, and demand for the 308 was high. The steel cars were also heavier, and of course more prone to rust on the outer panels, and when you add that lot together, it makes the original GRP cars much more collectible than their successors, though prices have dropped back recently.

**SPECIFICATIONS**

**Years produced:** 1975-1977 (712 in total)
**Performance:** 0-60mph: 6.7sec
Top speed: 152mph
**Power & torque:** 255bhp/209lb ft
**Engine:** Normally aspirated 2927cc V8, petrol, carburettors, 16 valves
**Drivetrain:** Mid-engine RWD
**Structure:** Spaceframe
**Transmission:** Five-speed manual
**Weight:** 1265kg

**PRICE GUIDE**

**Launch price:** £11,992
**Excellent:** £155,000
**Good:** £130,000
**Average:** £110,000
**Project:** £65,000

## FERRARI
### 512BB/BBi

Took over from the 365BB as Ferrari's 12-cylinder range-topper and stayed there for over a decade. Similar to its predecessor, little was changed apart from the lower nose with integrated spoiler to reduce front-end lift. The 5.0-litre flat-12 was treated to Bosch fuel injection from 1981, which added a little more power and a little assistance to economy. Probably a better bet than a 365BB, but the fact that four times as many 512 Berlinetta Boxers were built makes them a little cheaper to put in your garage. It's all relative, of course...

**SPECIFICATIONS**

**Years produced:** 1976-1985 (1936 in total)
**Performance:** 0-60mph: 5.5sec (BB)
Top speed: 188mph
**Power & torque:** 360bhp/332lb ft
**Engine:** Normally aspirated 4942cc V12, petrol, carburettors, 24 valves
**Drivetrain:** Mid-engine RWD
**Structure:** Monocoque
**Transmission:** Five-speed manual
**Weight:** 1515kg

**PRICE GUIDE**

**Launch price:** £26,000
**Excellent:** £300,000
**Good:** £250,000
**Average:** £225,000
**Project:** £150,000

# FERRARI 308GTB/GTS (steel)

One of the company's great success stories and still regarded as one of the best ways to introduce yourself to Ferrari ownership. Early cars are the most powerful, with the 1980-on Bosch fuel-injection models (signified by an 'i' suffix) losing 40bhp to emission controls. Much of this was restored two years later with the four-valves-per-cylinder qv models, identified by cooling slats in the front bonnet. Note that cars built after January 1984 have corrosion-reducing Zincrox coating on the steel panels. Values currently holding steady.

**SPECIFICATIONS**

| | |
|---|---|
| **Years produced:** | 1977-1985 |
| **Performance:** | 0-60mph: 7.3sec<br>Top speed: 145mph |
| **Power & torque:** | 240bhp/209lb ft |
| **Engine:** | Normally aspirated 2926cc V8, petrol, carburettor, 16 valves |
| **Drivetrain:** | Mid-engine RWD |
| **Structure:** | Spaceframe |
| **Transmission:** | Five-speed manual |
| **Weight:** | 1265kg |

**PRICE GUIDE**

| | |
|---|---|
| **Launch price:** | £16,499 |
| **Excellent:** | £120,000 |
| **Good:** | £100,000 |
| **Average:** | £75,000 |
| **Project:** | £50,000 |

# FERRARI Mondial/QV

A cheaper four-seater alternative to Ferrari's 400i, the Mondial was built around 308GTB running gear. As such, it shared that car's mechanical upgrades: four valves per cylinder from 1982, 3.2 litres from 1985, then 3.4 litres from a longitudinal engine and transverse gearbox for the Mondial t from 1989. Those four seats, along with less than striking looks (for a Ferrari, at any rate), combine to make this the cheapest ticket to the Prancing Horse ball, though not all have been well cared for. A cabriolet version joined the coupé in 1984.

**SPECIFICATIONS**

| | |
|---|---|
| **Years produced:** | 1980-1994 (4274 in total) |
| **Performance:** | 0-60mph: 7.1sec<br>Top speed: 145mph |
| **Power & torque:** | 240bhp/213lb ft |
| **Engine:** | Normally aspirated 2927cc V8, petrol, electronic fuel injection, 16 valves |
| **Drivetrain:** | Mid-engine RWD |
| **Structure:** | Spaceframe |
| **Transmission:** | Five-speed manual |
| **Weight:** | 1446kg |

**PRICE GUIDE**

| | |
|---|---|
| **Launch price:** | £24,488 |
| **Excellent:** | £60,000 |
| **Good:** | £45,000 |
| **Average:** | £30,000 |
| **Project:** | £15,000 |

# FERRARI 288GTO

The revival of that legendary GTO badge on a car whose looks obviously derive from the ageing 308GTB could easily have been a travesty. It wasn't. Let's start with the lightweight glassfibre and Kevlar bodyshell, on a revised chassis with a 4in wheelbase stretch over the 308's. That was done to accommodate longitudinal mounting of the twin-turbocharged 2.9-litre engine. The result is electrifying performance that helped make the GTO an almost-instant collector's item. The low build number ensures superstar status and prices.

**SPECIFICATIONS**

| | |
|---|---|
| **Years produced:** | 1984-1987 (272 in total) |
| **Performance:** | 0-60mph: 4.8sec<br>Top speed: 190mph |
| **Power & torque:** | 400bhp/366lb ft |
| **Engine:** | Twin-turbocharged 2855cc V8, petrol, electronic fuel injection, 32 valves |
| **Drivetrain:** | Mid-engine RWD |
| **Structure:** | Spaceframe |
| **Transmission:** | Five-speed manual |
| **Weight:** | 1160kg |

**PRICE GUIDE**

| | |
|---|---|
| **Launch price:** | Special order only |
| **Excellent:** | £3,000,000 |
| **Good:** | £2,500,000 |
| **Average:** | £2,000,000 |
| **Project:** | N/A |

# FERRARI Testarossa

Perhaps the ultimate automotive status symbol to emerge from the 'greed is good' decade. The Testarossa's imposing size and in-your-face attitude tend to hide the fact that here we have a remarkably user-friendly supercar; mighty performance delivered in a smooth manner by a sweet and free-revving flat-12. It also has windows you can actually see out of. That the Testarossa is comparatively cheap to buy is partly because of the stigma of '80s excess, but mostly thanks to the huge numbers built. Add c15% for early, single-mirror cars.

**SPECIFICATIONS**

| | |
|---|---|
| **Years produced:** | 1984-1992 (7177 in total) |
| **Performance:** | 0-60mph: 5.2sec<br>Top speed: 180mph |
| **Power & torque:** | 390bhp/361lb ft |
| **Engine:** | Normally aspirated 4942cc flat 12, petrol, electronic fuel injection, 48 valves |
| **Drivetrain:** | Mid-engine RWD |
| **Structure:** | Monocoque |
| **Transmission:** | Five-speed manual |
| **Weight:** | 1506kg |

**PRICE GUIDE**

| | |
|---|---|
| **Launch price:** | £62,666 |
| **Excellent:** | £165,000 |
| **Good:** | £120,000 |
| **Average:** | £80,000 |
| **Project:** | £50,000 |

# FERRARI 328GTB/GTS

Not wanting to risk its golden goose, changes from the 308 were kept to a minimum and even then justified as improvements to aerodynamics and stability. Front and rear panels below bumper level were deepened, a larger grille fitted, and some lights changed. There's the same glorious howl from the mid-mounted quad-cam V8 but, in the 328, it uses an extra 200cc to provide 30bhp more than its predecessor along with a lot more torque. The only downside is the interior, which employs Fiat-issue switchgear. Values have levelled off.

**SPECIFICATIONS**

| | |
|---|---|
| **Years produced:** | 1985-1988 (1344/6068 in total) |
| **Performance:** | 0-60mph: 6.0sec<br>Top speed: 163mph |
| **Power & torque:** | 270bhp/224lb ft |
| **Engine:** | Normally aspirated 3186cc V8, petrol, electronic fuel injection, 32 valves |
| **Drivetrain:** | Mid-engine RWD |
| **Structure:** | Spaceframe |
| **Transmission:** | Five-speed manual |
| **Weight:** | 1263kg |

**PRICE GUIDE**

| | |
|---|---|
| **Launch price:** | £32,220 |
| **Excellent:** | £130,000 |
| **Good:** | £100,000 |
| **Average:** | £80,000 |
| **Project:** | £50,000 |

# FERRARI
## F40

Built to celebrate Ferrari's 40th birthday, the F40 is just the car for anyone who finds the 288GTO a bit on the tame side. The spec of the two cars carries a similarity too: twin-turbocharged V8 engine and a composite body mounted on a spaceframe chassis. The difference is that the F40 has an extra 78bhp from its slightly larger engine, and in the search for lightness it offers even less in the way of content – not even carpets or door panels. But buyers loved it and Ferrari built almost three times as many as originally intended. Values currently holding steady.

**SPECIFICATIONS**

**Years produced:** 1987-1992 (1315 in total)
**Performance:** 0-60mph: 3.9sec
Top speed: 201mph
**Power & torque:** 478bhp/426lb ft
**Engine:** Twin-turbocharged 2936cc V8, petrol, electronic fuel injection, 32 valves
**Drivetrain:** Mid-engine RWD
**Structure:** Spaceframe
**Transmission:** Five-speed manual
**Weight:** 1100kg

**PRICE GUIDE**

**Launch price:** £193,000
**Excellent:** £1,500,000
**Good:** £1,250,000
**Average:** £800,000
**Project:** N/A

# FERRARI
## 348tb/ts

Quite a departure from the 328 it replaced. The V8 engine is still there, but it's been much revised, upped to 3.4 litres with an extra 30bhp, and turned 90 degrees to be mounted longitudinally and set lower in the chassis. Great strides were made with aerodynamics too, and the side strakes and black grille over the tail-lights are straight out of the Testarossa design book, as is the relatively spacious cockpit. A reputation for edgy handling and unfavourable comparisons with the prettier 355 have kept values relatively low.

**SPECIFICATIONS**

**Years produced:** 1989-1995 (8844 in total)
**Performance:** 0-60mph: 5.6sec
Top speed: 170mph
**Power & torque:** 300bhp/237lb ft
**Engine:** Normally aspirated 3405cc V8, petrol, electronic fuel injection, 32 valves
**Drivetrain:** Mid-engine RWD
**Structure:** Monocoque
**Transmission:** Five-speed manual
**Weight:** 1393kg

**PRICE GUIDE**

**Launch price:** £67,499
**Excellent:** £75,000
**Good:** £55,000
**Average:** £40,000
**Project:** £25,000

# FERRARI
## 456

This was Ferrari resurrecting the front-engined GT for the 1990s, with shades of Daytona at the rear. At the time the V12-engined 456 was the most sophisticated car yet to emerge from Maranello and also one of the quickest – faster around Ferrari's test track than the mid-engined flat-12 512 TR. With two extra seats in the back and a decent boot, it's a true GT (or GTA if you get the auto). Expensive to maintain and lacking the visceral appeal of some, the 456 fell out of favour in the following years, but it's a lot of GT for your money. Add 10% for manual.

**SPECIFICATIONS**

**Years produced:** 1992-2004 (3289 in total)
**Performance:** 0-60mph: 5.2sec
Top speed: 186mph
**Power & torque:** 442bhp/405lb ft
**Engine:** Normally aspirated 5474cc V12, petrol, electronic fuel injection, 48 valves
**Drivetrain:** Front-engine RWD
**Structure:** Monocoque
**Transmission:** Six-speed manual
**Weight:** 1690kg

**PRICE GUIDE**

**Launch price:** £145,999
**Excellent:** £100,000
**Good:** £70,000
**Average:** £50,000
**Project:** £25,000

# FERRARI
## F355

After the slightly disappointing 348, the 355 signalled a return to form for Ferrari. It had to – Porsche had upped its game with the 911, and Honda's NSX was challenging the established order. The response moved the junior Ferrari into the supercar league. The much-revised engine had five-valve heads and a 75bhp power increase. It was mated to a slick-shifting six-speed gearbox (later with the option of an automated clutch), and there were electronic dampers and power steering. It was also gorgeous, as strong values continue to reflect.

**SPECIFICATIONS**

**Years produced:** 1994-1999 (5349 in total)
**Performance:** 0-60mph: 4.7sec
Top speed: 183mph
**Power & torque:** 375bhp/268lb ft
**Engine:** Normally aspirated 3496cc V8, petrol, electronic fuel injection, 40 valves
**Drivetrain:** Mid-engine RWD
**Structure:** Monocoque
**Transmission:** Six-speed manual or semi-auto
**Weight:** 1350kg

**PRICE GUIDE**

**Launch price:** £83,031
**Excellent:** £125,000
**Good:** £100,000
**Average:** £75,000
**Project:** £35,000

# FERRARI
## F50

Based heavily on F1 technology, the F50 was built to mark Ferrari's 50th birthday – a little prematurely as it went on sale just seven years after the F40. This time the celebrations involved what to Ferrari cognoscenti was a proper engine – a 4.7-litre V12 – with an old-school manual. That engine pumped out enough power to make this the first open-top production car to top 200mph. The construction was composite panels around a carbonfibre central tub. The results were raw, intoxicating, and much rarer than an F40, which is why values are rocketing.

**SPECIFICATIONS**

**Years produced:** 1995-1997 (349 in total)
**Performance:** 0-60mph: 3.7sec
Top speed: 202mph
**Power & torque:** 513bhp/347lb ft
**Engine:** Normally aspirated 4698cc V12, petrol, electronic fuel injection, 60 valves
**Drivetrain:** Mid-engine RWD
**Structure:** Carbon/composite tub/bodywork
**Transmission:** Six-speed manual
**Weight:** 1230kg

**PRICE GUIDE**

**Launch price:** £329,000
**Excellent:** £2,350,000
**Good:** £1,850,000
**Average:** £1,600,000
**Project:** N/A

# FERRARI
## 550 Maranello

Every time Ferrari launches a front-engined, V12 Grand Tourer, it is inevitably compared with the 365 GTB/4 Daytona. Few have quite justified that comparison like the 550 Maranello however. With its classic proportions, balanced handling and high-quality cabin, the 550 was an instant hit and immediately hailed as a modern classic. Even the styling, which initially seemed a little fussy, has aged gracefully, and that 5474cc engine still delivers knockout performance – it's effectively a 200mph car. Values have slipped back recently.

### SPECIFICATIONS

**Years produced:** 1996-2001
**Performance:** 0-60mph: 4.4sec
Top speed: 199mph
**Power & torque:** 478bhp/419lb ft
**Engine:** Normally aspirated 5474cc V12, petrol, electronic fuel injection, 48 valves
**Drivetrain:** Front-engine RWD
**Structure:** Monocoque
**Transmission:** Six-speed manual
**Weight:** 1690kg

### PRICE GUIDE

**Launch price:** £149,701
**Excellent:** £125,000
**Good:** £90,000
**Average:** £70,000
**Project:** N/A

# FERRARI
## 360 Modena

The 355 was a tough act to follow, but the 360 had all-aluminium construction, greater power than its predecessor, and considerably more torque. Higher levels of quality too, meaning the 360 became one of the first truly modern Ferraris – a car you could realistically use every day. That doesn't detract from the excitement factor, with strong performance, a searing engine note and a very capable chassis (the Challenge Stradale turned that feeling – and the noise – up to 11). Spiders usually fetch slightly more than coupés.

### SPECIFICATIONS

**Years produced:** 1998-2003 (20,482 in total)
**Performance:** 0-60mph: 4.5sec
Top speed: 180mph+
**Power & torque:** 394bhp/369lb ft
**Engine:** Normally aspirated 3596cc V8, petrol, electronic fuel injection, 40 valves
**Drivetrain:** Mid-engine RWD
**Structure:** Monocoque
**Transmission:** Six-speed manual or semi-auto
**Weight:** 1390kg

### PRICE GUIDE (Stradale in brackets)

**Launch price:** £101,243
**Excellent:** £80,000 (£200,000)
**Good:** £65,000 (£180,000)
**Average:** £50,000 (£160,000)
**Project:** N/A

# FERRARI
## 575M Maranello

Evolving from the 550 Maranello, the 575 brought a much-improved interior, larger 5.7-litre V12 engine and semi-automatic F1 transmission. Early cars were a little too soft, but things improved massively with the optional Fiorano suspension pack, which could also be retrofitted. For 2004, the Handling GTC pack sharpened the 575 up even more, with stiffer springs, revised dampers, bigger carbon-ceramic brakes, 19in split rims and more. Just 246 were built with manual 'boxes, and these command a large premium, say DK Engineering.

### SPECIFICATIONS

**Years produced:** 2002-2006 (2056 in total)
**Performance:** 0-60mph: 4.2sec
Top speed: 118mph
**Power & torque:** 508bhp/434lb ft
**Engine:** Normally aspirated 5748cc V12, petrol, electronic fuel injection, 48 valves
**Drivetrain:** Front-engine RWD
**Structure:** Monocoque
**Transmission:** Six-speed semi-auto or manual
**Weight:** 1730kg

### PRICE GUIDE (manual in brackets)

**Launch price:** £154,340
**Excellent:** £80,000 (£150,000)
**Good:** £70,000 (£140,000)
**Average:** £65,000 (£120,000)
**Project:** N/A

# FERRARI
## Enzo

Naming a car after the company founder signified that Ferrari had something very special in store for its latest halo model. It featured full carbonfibre construction, a 650bhp 6.0-litre naturally-aspirated V12 and driver-adjustable pushrod-actuated dampers. The six-speed F1 gearbox was a massive step on from previous iterations, and the Enzo also made huge strides with its electronic driver aids, while clever aero meant that aggressive fixed wings were not necessary. Most are painted Rosso Corsa, meaning rare and unusual colours add value.

### SPECIFICATIONS

**Years produced:** 2002-2004 (400 in total)
**Performance:** 0-60mph: 3.1sec
Top speed: 217mph
**Power & torque:** 650bhp/485lb ft
**Engine:** Normally aspirated 5998cc V12, petrol, electronic fuel injection, 48 valves
**Drivetrain:** Mid-engine RWD
**Structure:** Carbon fibre tub/bodywork
**Transmission:** Six-speed semi-auto
**Weight:** 1480kg

### PRICE GUIDE

**Launch price:** £450,000
**Excellent:** £2,500,000
**Good:** £1,800,000
**Average:** £1,500,000
**Project:** N/A

# FERRARI
## F430

Drawing on experience with the Enzo, the F430 signalled a continued shift towards ever-smarter technology in Ferrari's series production cars. Powered by the new, high-revving 'F136' 4.3-litre flat-plane-crank V8, it pushed 483bhp to the rear wheels via a new, lightning-fast F1 transmission and clever E-diff. Performance blew the 360, and most competitors, out of the water. Spider version was launched in 2005, with hardcore Scuderia arriving in 2008. The last V8 Ferrari to be offered with that glorious open-gated manual shifter.

### SPECIFICATIONS

**Years produced:** 2004-2009
**Performance:** 0-60mph: 4.0sec
Top speed: 196+mph
**Power & torque:** 483bhp/343lb ft
**Engine:** Normally aspirated 4308cc V8, petrol, electronic fuel injection, 32 valves
**Drivetrain:** Mid-engine RWD
**Structure:** Monocoque
**Transmission:** Six-speed manual/semi-auto
**Weight:** 1449kg

### PRICE GUIDE

**Launch price:** £117,000
**Excellent:** £90,000
**Good:** £70,000
**Average:** £50,000
**Project:** N/A

# FIAT

ONE OF the few car-makers to have survived through over 120 years of production, Fabbrica Italiana Automobili Torino debuted with a rear-engined two-cylinder machine in 1899. This was the same layout used for the iconic Fiat 500 (launched 58 years later) that the company will always be best remembered for. Even today no Italian cityscape is complete without them, though they have largely been replaced by the 'new' 500. Various licensing deals mean Fiat's products are built worldwide. Along the way, the company swallowed up Ferrari, Lancia, Alfa Romeo and the tuning firm Abarth, whose name still graces its more sporting models. Today part of the giant Fiat Chrysler Automobiles.

## FIAT 500/500B

The tiny Topolino two-seater was launched in 1936 but after the war it came back in restyled 500B and 500C form; the only post-war version that came to the UK, and even then imports didn't begin until 1954. Earlier cars like the one pictured have found their way here since. Nearly all of the post-war series were roll-back cabriolets, but there is the odd estate version around and even a woody – expect to pay a premium for either. The little four-cylinder engines are quite perky but still very economical.

**SPECIFICATIONS**

| | |
|---|---|
| **Years produced:** | 1948-1955 (143,836 in total) |
| **Performance:** | Top speed: 55mph<br>0-60mph: N/A |
| **Power & torque:** | 13bhp/N/A |
| **Engine:** | Normally aspirated 569cc four cylinder, petrol, carburettor, 8 valves |
| **Drivetrain:** | Front-engine RWD |
| **Structure:** | Separate chassis |
| **Transmission:** | Four-speed manual |
| **Weight:** | 740kg |

**PRICE GUIDE**

| | |
|---|---|
| **Launch price:** | £582 |
| **Excellent:** | £12,000 |
| **Good:** | £8000 |
| **Average:** | £5000 |
| **Project:** | £2000 |

## FIAT 8V

Developed by Dante Giacosa with a bespoke V8 engine and tubular spaceframe chassis, the 8V owed nothing to the rest of the Fiat range. It packed advanced features such as all-round independent suspension and an all-synchro gearbox, and proved to be a very effective sports car. 34 were bodied by Carozzeria Speciale FIAT, with the rest being split between Zagato, Ghia and Vignale. A mixture of coupés and spiders, all are exceptionally desirable. The more spectacular coupes – and convertibles – can easily fetch over £1 million today.

**SPECIFICATIONS**

| | |
|---|---|
| **Years produced:** | 1952-1954 (114 in total) |
| **Performance:** | Top speed: 118mph<br>0-60mph: 9.5sec |
| **Power & torque:** | 105bhp/110lb ft |
| **Engine:** | Normally aspirated 1996cc V8, petrol, carburettor, 8 valves |
| **Drivetrain:** | Front-engine RWD |
| **Structure:** | Spaceframe |
| **Transmission:** | Four-speed manual |
| **Weight:** | 930kg |

**PRICE GUIDE (depending on coachwork)**

| | |
|---|---|
| **Launch price:** | N/A |
| **Excellent:** | £1,500,000+ |
| **Good:** | £1,000,000+ |
| **Average:** | N/A |
| **Project:** | N/A |

## FIAT 600/600D

No, this wasn't merely a big-engined version of the Fiat 500. Though they share a strong family resemblance, the 600 was launched first and has the benefit of a water-cooled four-cylinder engine. That started out at 633cc, but grew to 767cc for 1960's revamped Fiat 600D. Being a direct competitor to the Mini spoiled things for the 600 in the UK, but there's a school of thought that says it's a better bet than the smaller, less practical 500. Fiat specialist Tony Castle-Miller, of Middle Barton Garage, says prices have levelled off recently.

**SPECIFICATIONS**

| | |
|---|---|
| **Years produced:** | 1955-1970 (891,107 in total) |
| **Performance:** | Top speed: 66mph |
| **Power & torque:** | 29bhp/40lb ft |
| **Engine:** | Normally aspirated 767cc four cylinder, petrol, carburettor, 8 valves |
| **Drivetrain:** | Rear-engine RWD |
| **Structure:** | Monocoque |
| **Transmission:** | Four-speed manual |
| **Weight:** | 585kg |

**PRICE GUIDE**

| | |
|---|---|
| **Launch price:** | £585 |
| **Excellent:** | £11,000 |
| **Good:** | £8500 |
| **Average:** | £3500 |
| **Project:** | £1750 |

## FIAT 600 Multipla

This is the version of the 600 that most classic car enthusiasts are more familiar with. It's also probably the world's smallest minibus, with six-seat capacity despite being under 12ft long. A rare and highly sought-after collectable in its own right, recent price rises have made their restoration a more sensible proposition. They share the same engines as the 600, but their progress has never been more than sedate. However, if originality is not at issue, these engines were developed into the 903cc unit and used in the Uno and Cinquecento.

**SPECIFICATIONS**

| | |
|---|---|
| **Years produced:** | 1955-1960 (130,000 in total) |
| **Performance:** | Top speed: 59mph |
| **Power & torque:** | 29bhp/40lb ft |
| **Engine:** | Normally aspirated 767cc four cylinder, petrol, carburettor, 8 valves |
| **Drivetrain:** | Rear-engine RWD |
| **Structure:** | Monocoque |
| **Transmission:** | Four-speed manual |
| **Weight:** | 700kg |

**PRICE GUIDE**

| | |
|---|---|
| **Launch price:** | £799 |
| **Excellent:** | £35,000 |
| **Good:** | £25,000 |
| **Average:** | £15,000 |
| **Project:** | £7500 |

## FIAT 500

Cheap to run and, with excellent spares support, the 500 makes the ideal classic for city dwellers. Pre-1965 cars had suicide doors and never more than 18bhp, except in the rare 500 Sport. The later 500F and 500L are a better bet, especially if you want to drive any distance, and have conventional front-hinged doors. Last model, the 500R has a detuned 594cc Fiat 126 engine; a point not lost on many Fiat 500 owners, who commonly fit the full-strength 126 engine. Lots of poor cars around £6000-£7000, warns Tony Castle-Miller of Middle Barton Garage.

### SPECIFICATIONS

**Years produced:** 1957-1975 (3,427,648 in total)
**Performance:** Top speed: 59mph
**Power & torque:** 18bhp/N/A
**Engine:** Normally aspirated 499cc twin, petrol, carburettor, 4 valves
**Drivetrain:** Rear-engine RWD
**Structure:** Separate chassis
**Transmission:** Four-speed manual
**Weight:** 500kg

### PRICE GUIDE

**Launch price:** £556
**Excellent:** £20,000
**Good:** £13,000
**Average:** £6000
**Project:** £2500

## FIAT 1800/2100/2300

Fiat's tidy and elegant middle-class saloon employed Pininfarina's generic styling scheme of the day, looking almost identical to the Peugeot 404 and Austin Cambridge. The centrepiece of the 1800 series was Lampredi's impressive new six-cylinder engine, which was powerful and smooth. Improved through its life, with the leaf-suspended rear end being replaced by coils and the drum brakes replaced by discs. An excellent and understated saloon that enjoys a low-profile, but faithful, following in the UK. Good value at current prices.

### SPECIFICATIONS (1800)

**Years produced:** 1959-1968 (c185,000 in total)
**Performance:** 0-60mph: 15.0sec
Top speed: 95mph
**Power & torque:** 76bhp/93lb ft
**Engine:** Normally aspirated 1796cc six cylinder, petrol, carburettor, 8 valves
**Drivetrain:** Front-engine RWD
**Structure:** Monocoque
**Transmission:** Four-speed manual
**Weight:** 1215kg

### PRICE GUIDE

**Launch price:** N/A
**Excellent:** £7000
**Good:** £5500
**Average:** £3500
**Project:** £2000

## FIAT 1500 Cabriolet

Predecessor to the better-known Fiat Spider, the 1500 cabriolet was also only available in left-hand drive. That and prices that were grossly inflated by import duty meant that few reached UK shores. No reason why you couldn't import from Europe though, where their numbers are much greater. Styling was by Pininfarina, which explains their passing resemblance to the Ferrari 275GTS, only smaller, and much cheaper. Advanced for its time with a five-speed gearbox and disc brakes. Engines are tough and reliable. Values currently static.

### SPECIFICATIONS

**Years produced:** 1960-1967 (c34,000 inc 1500S in total)
**Performance:** 0-60mph: 14.8sec
Top speed: 100mph
**Power & torque:** 72bhp/82lb ft
**Engine:** Normally aspirated 1481cc four cylinder, petrol, carburettor, 8 valves
**Drivetrain:** Front-engine RWD
**Structure:** Monocoque
**Transmission:** Five-speed manual
**Weight:** 970kg

### PRICE GUIDE

**Launch price:** £1197
**Excellent:** £12,000
**Good:** £7500
**Average:** £4250
**Project:** £2000

## FIAT 2300S Coupé

Fiat's large-car efforts have tended to lack commercial success, and sometimes it's difficult to understand why. While the Dino and 130 had obvious failings, the 2300S Coupé looked like the right product for its time. Styled by Ghia, the 2300S Coupé was very much a grand tourer, even featuring electric windows. Its 2.3-litre six-cylinder engine delivered plenty of power and was further boosted by twin carburettors. However, true to form, the 2300S wasn't a big seller, and remains one of the lost cousins of Fiat history. Quite desirable today.

### SPECIFICATIONS

**Years produced:** 1961-1968 (N/A total)
**Performance:** 0-60mph: 11.6sec
Top speed: 121mph
**Power & torque:** 136bhp/145lb ft
**Engine:** Normally aspirated 2279cc six cylinder, petrol, carburettor, 12 valves
**Drivetrain:** Front-engine RWD
**Structure:** Monocoque
**Transmission:** Four-speed manual
**Weight:** 1266kg

### PRICE GUIDE

**Launch price:** £2610
**Excellent:** £25,000
**Good:** £15,000
**Average:** £10,000
**Project:** £5000

## FIAT 850 Coupé

Based on the slightly dull and dumpy 850 saloon, the Coupé thankfully bore no resemblance to it, being more in the fashion of a scaled-down Dino. It had a perkier version of the saloon's 843cc engine too, which was upgraded to 903cc from 1968. Rear-mounted and water-cooled, it gives the baby coupé a decent turn of speed and its light weight contributes to the car's excellent handling abilities. It sold well in the UK, but our climate has wiped out most of them now. Survivors have become prized, or you could sniff out a left-hooker to import.

### SPECIFICATIONS

**Years produced:** 1965-1973 (342,873 in total)
**Performance:** 0-60mph: 15.6sec
Top speed: 84mph
**Power & torque:** 47bhp/45lb ft
**Engine:** Normally aspirated 843cc four cylinder, petrol, carburettor, 8 valves
**Drivetrain:** Rear-engine RWD
**Structure:** Monocoque
**Transmission:** Four-speed manual
**Weight:** 690kg

### PRICE GUIDE

**Launch price:** £850
**Excellent:** £15,000
**Good:** £9000
**Average:** £6500
**Project:** £2500

## FIAT
### 850 Spider

A small, pretty and nippy but rust-prone roadster. We could be talking about a Midget, but this is an Italian job with styling beautifully executed by Bertone. It includes a hood that neatly stows away beneath the rear deck. As with all the 850 range it's rear-engined, initially with 843cc, but receiving the more powerful and just as rev-happy 903cc unit in 1968. At the same time the original sloping headlamps were replaced by more efficient upright units. Most 850s went to America and, once again, none were built with right-hand-drive.

**SPECIFICATIONS**

**Years produced:** 1965-1973 (124,660 in total)
**Performance:** 0-60mph: 18.2sec
Top speed: 87mph
**Power & torque:** 47bhp/45lb ft
**Engine:** Normally aspirated 843cc four cylinder, petrol, carburettor, 8 valves
**Drivetrain:** Rear-engine RWD
**Structure:** Monocoque
**Transmission:** Four-speed manual
**Weight:** 735kg

**PRICE GUIDE**

**Launch price:** £1000
**Excellent:** £15,000
**Good:** £10,000
**Average:** £7500
**Project:** £3000

## FIAT
### 124

Advanced saloon that outshone and outsold the Ford Escort MkI. With disc brakes all round and a well-located rear axle on coil springs, it's a capable driver. Has suffered in classic terms from the usual Fiat rust problems, but mostly by growing up to become the long-running heart of the Lada range. Revvy overhead-valve engines are even impressive in base 1200 form, but the Special T is the one to have. Available in the UK from 1971 with a 1438cc twin-cam engine, which was upgraded to 1592cc from 1973. The best now have quite a following.

**SPECIFICATIONS**

**Years produced:** 1966-1974 (1,543,000 in total)
**Performance:** 0-60mph: 11.8sec
Top speed: 102mph
**Power & torque:** 80bhp/80lb ft
**Engine:** Normally aspirated 1438cc four cylinder, petrol, carburettor, 8 valves
**Drivetrain:** Front-engine RWD
**Structure:** Monocoque
**Transmission:** Four-speed manual
**Weight:** 950kg

**PRICE GUIDE**

**Launch price:** £774
**Excellent:** £12,000
**Good:** £7500
**Average:** £3000
**Project:** £1200

## FIAT
### 124 Coupé

A thin-pillared beauty from Fiat's own design team, blessed with real ability thanks to twin-cam engines and all-wheel disc brakes. Favoured models include the 1967-69 'AC', which is prettier with its single headlamps and lower bonnet line, and lighter so it handles better. The 1974-75 final 'CC'models also get snapped up as their 1800cc engine is the most powerful offered. A small thumbs-down for the BC-series cars that arrived in 1970 with softer suspension and twin headlamps. Sadly all suffered corrosion. Add £2k for the twin-cam Special T.

**SPECIFICATIONS**

**Years produced:** 1966-1975 (279,672 in total)
**Performance:** 0-60mph: 10.5sec
Top speed: 115mph
**Power & torque:** 118bhp/113lb ft
**Engine:** Normally aspirated 1438cc four cylinder, petrol, carburettor, 8 valves
**Drivetrain:** Front-engine RWD
**Structure:** Monocoque
**Transmission:** Four-speed manual
**Weight:** 980kg

**PRICE GUIDE**

**Launch price:** £1298
**Excellent:** £17,500
**Good:** £12,000
**Average:** £8000
**Project:** £3000

## FIAT
### 124 Spider

Pininfarina designed and built the bodies for these pretty sports cars, using any number of Ferrari styling cues and Fiat's excellent twin-cam engines. All are left-hand drive and around 85% were sold in America, although upwards of 1500 have since been imported into the UK. As with the 124 Coupé, the first and last cars are most popular with collectors: pre-1975 cars had lower suspension and prettier slimline bumpers, 1979-on have 2.0-litre Bosch fuel-injection engines. From 1982-85 all production passed to Pininfarina. Very best are now £25k-plus.

**SPECIFICATIONS**

**Years produced:** 1966-1985 (178,439 in total)
**Performance:** 0-60mph: 10.9sec
Top speed: 109mph
**Power & torque:** 102bhp/110lb ft
**Engine:** Normally aspirated 1438cc four cylinder, petrol, carburettor, 8 valves
**Drivetrain:** Front-engine RWD
**Structure:** Separate chassis
**Transmission:** Five-speed manual
**Weight:** 945kg

**PRICE GUIDE**

**Launch price:** Special order
**Excellent:** £25,000
**Good:** £17,500
**Average:** £12,000
**Project:** £6000

## FIAT
### Dino Spider

Fancy a convertible Ferrari? This is about as close as you'll get without having the actual Prancing Horse on the nose. Styled by Pininfarina and using the same engines that powered the Dino GT, they have rarity on their side as far as collectibility goes. Early models had an all-alloy 2.0-litre engine and a live axle on leaf springs. In 1969 it was all change to an iron-block 2.4-litre V6 with another 15bhp, and the rear suspension was changed to independent coil springs. Mechanical and body parts are still in good supply. Concours cars might fetch £150k-plus.

**SPECIFICATIONS**

**Years produced:** 1967-1973 (1583 in total)
**Performance:** 0-60mph: 8.0sec
Top speed: 124mph
**Power & torque:** 160bhp/127lb ft
**Engine:** Normally aspirated 1987cc V6, petrol, carburettor, 12 valves
**Drivetrain:** Front-engine RWD
**Structure:** Monocoque
**Transmission:** Five-speed manual
**Weight:** 1222kg

**PRICE GUIDE**

**Launch price:** Special order
**Excellent:** £135,000
**Good:** £100,000
**Average:** £75,000
**Project:** £50,000

## FIAT
### Dino Coupé 2000/2400

Though mechanically identical to the Dino Spiders, the Coupé has a completely different body, designed by Bertone. The same changes were made in 1969, from 2.0 to a 2.4-litre quad-cam V6, along with a tougher ZF five-speed gearbox and the independent rear suspension swiped from underneath Fiat's 130 saloon. The 2000 and 2400 bodies look identical at first sight, but changes in grille, badge and vents mean that only the bootlid is a straight swap between cars. The 2400 was assembled at the Ferrari factory – and looks good value right now.

**SPECIFICATIONS**

| | |
|---|---|
| **Years produced:** | 1967-1973 (6068 in total) |
| **Performance:** | 0-60mph: 8.1sec<br>Top speed: 124mph |
| **Power & torque:** | 160bhp/127lb ft |
| **Engine:** | Normally aspirated 1987cc V6, petrol, carburettor, 12 valves |
| **Drivetrain:** | Front-engine RWD |
| **Structure:** | Monocoque |
| **Transmission:** | Five-speed manual |
| **Weight:** | 1220kg |

**PRICE GUIDE**

| | |
|---|---|
| **Launch price:** | £3493 |
| **Excellent:** | £45,000 |
| **Good:** | £35,000 |
| **Average:** | £25,000 |
| **Project:** | £10,000 |

## FIAT
### 130

Fiat had no history of building big saloon cars before it surprised everyone with the technologically advanced, Mercedes-baiting, 130 – the world was bound to treat it with caution. But what a car. The styling may lack flair, but underneath we find all-independent suspension, passive rear steering and four disc brakes. Not bad for 1969. Capacity of the quad-cam V6 went up from 2.8 litres to 3.2 in 1971, and UK imports started in '72. Worth seeking out. Enzo Ferrari drove one every day: do you need any greater recommendation than that?

**SPECIFICATIONS**

| | |
|---|---|
| **Years produced:** | 1969-1976 (15,000 in total) |
| **Performance:** | 0-60mph: 11.4sec<br>Top speed: 118mph |
| **Power & torque:** | 165bhp/184lb ft |
| **Engine:** | 3235cc V6, petrol, carburettor, 12 valves |
| **Drivetrain:** | Front-engine RWD |
| **Structure:** | Monocoque |
| **Transmission:** | Five-speed manual |
| **Weight:** | 1615kg |

**PRICE GUIDE**

| | |
|---|---|
| **Launch price:** | £3818 |
| **Excellent:** | £6000 |
| **Good:** | £4000 |
| **Average:** | £2000 |
| **Project:** | £1500 |

## FIAT
### 128

Although its simple styling hinted at an update of the 124, what nestled under the skin makes this one of the most important cars of the 1960s. The 128 remains a Dante Giacosa masterpiece – powered by a transverse OHC engine and driven by the front wheels via an end-on gearbox. It's the recipe for a technical orthodoxy that has since been adopted by the entire industry. Despite that, and being a great car to drive, shoddy build and horrendous rust mean few survive. But its sheer rarity in the UK guarantees interest from Fiat fans. Two-door Rallye version can fetch up to £5k.

**SPECIFICATIONS**

| | |
|---|---|
| **Years produced:** | 1969-1984 (2,776,000 in total) |
| **Performance:** | 0-60mph: 14.8sec<br>Top speed: 87mph |
| **Power & torque:** | 55bhp/57lb ft |
| **Engine:** | Normally aspirated 1116cc four cylinder, petrol, carburettor, 8 valves |
| **Drivetrain:** | Front-engine FWD |
| **Structure:** | Monocoque |
| **Transmission:** | Four-speed manual |
| **Weight:** | 815kg |

**PRICE GUIDE**

| | |
|---|---|
| **Launch price:** | £871 |
| **Excellent:** | £3250 |
| **Good:** | £1750 |
| **Average:** | £1250 |
| **Project:** | £500 |

## FIAT
### 127

The 128 might have been the car that created Fiat's template for modern motoring, but it was the 127 that truly exploited it in 1971. The 127 used the 850's engine installed 128-style, and packaged in a stylish two-door 'shell. A hatchback was added a couple of years later, and the true Italian supermini was born. The 127 was a huge success, and over four million were built before the Uno replaced it – but it carried on in Brazil and Argentina. To find one today isn't the work of a moment, especially an early car, but if you do, you'll find Mini-stye fun and a little extra space.

**SPECIFICATIONS (127 Sport)**

| | |
|---|---|
| **Years produced:** | 1971-1983 (3,730,000 in total) |
| **Performance:** | 0-60mph: 14.0sec<br>Top speed: 100mph |
| **Power & torque:** | 70bhp/61lb ft |
| **Engine:** | Normally aspirated 1049cc four cylinder, petrol, carburettor, 8 valves |
| **Drivetrain:** | Front-engine FWD |
| **Structure:** | Monocoque |
| **Transmission:** | Four-speed manual |
| **Weight:** | 775kg |

**PRICE GUIDE**

| | |
|---|---|
| **Launch price:** | £799 |
| **Excellent:** | £3250 |
| **Good:** | £2000 |
| **Average:** | £950 |
| **Project:** | £500 |

## FIAT
### 130 Coupé

With straight-edged styling from Pininfarina's Rolls-Camargue/Lancia Gamma Coupé school, the 130 Coupé has a vast and elegant but almost intimidating presence. Arriving a couple of years later than the 130 saloon, the Coupés only ever came with the larger 3.2-litre four-cam V6, so there's plenty of performance to go with the tidy handling and, thankfully, this isn't spoilt by the light power steering. Many came with a three-speed automatic, but enough were specified with the ZF five-speed manual. Rather cool, and decent value.

**SPECIFICATIONS**

| | |
|---|---|
| **Years produced:** | 1972-1976 (4491 in total) |
| **Performance:** | 0-60mph: 10.6sec<br>Top speed: 123mph |
| **Power & torque:** | 165bhp/184lb ft |
| **Engine:** | 3235cc V6, petrol, carburettor, 12 valves |
| **Drivetrain:** | Front-engine RWD |
| **Structure:** | Monocoque |
| **Transmission:** | Five-speed manual/three-speed auto |
| **Weight:** | 1559kg |

**PRICE GUIDE**

| | |
|---|---|
| **Launch price:** | £6165 |
| **Excellent:** | £15,000 |
| **Good:** | £10,000 |
| **Average:** | £5000 |
| **Project:** | £2000 |

## FIAT X1/9

There's a lot to be said for a compact mid-engined two-seater with a targa top, not least in the handling department. So it seems unfair that, although the X1/9 was launched in Europe in 1972, the UK had to wait five years before right-hand-drive examples became available. Those early cars had 1.3-litre engines and four-speed gearboxes and were considered somewhat underpowered. Happily in 1978 the X1/9 received an uprated 1.5-litre engine and five-speed box. Sadly, it also gained US-spec impact absorbing bumpers.

### SPECIFICATIONS

**Years produced:** 1972-1989 (141,108 in total)
**Performance:** 0-60mph: 12.7sec (1300)
Top speed: 99mph
**Power & torque:** 75bhp/72lb ft
**Engine:** Normally aspirated 1290cc four cylinder, petrol, carburettor, 8 valves
**Drivetrain:** Mid-engine RWD
**Structure:** Monocoque
**Transmission:** Four/five-speed manual
**Weight:** 912kg

### PRICE GUIDE (1500 in brackets)

**Launch price:** £2997
**Excellent:** £9000 (£11,000)
**Good:** £6000 (£7500)
**Average:** £3500 (£5000)
**Project:** £1750 (£2250)

## FIAT 126

Continuing the appealing boxy styling established by the 127, Fiat's baby replacement for the 500 looked just the ticket to motorise a generation of trendy young Italians. The air-cooled two-cylinder engine stubbornly remained slung out to the rear, despite Fiat's move to FWD elsewhere in the range, and performance was leisurely at best. But it's cheap as chips to run and, thanks to a long production run in Italy and then Poland, there's still a plentiful supply of cars and parts. Prices have slipped a little after climbing steadily for a year or two.

### SPECIFICATIONS

**Years produced:** 1975-1978 (1,970,000)
**Performance:** 0-60mph: 42.3sec
Top speed: 63mph
**Power & torque:** 23bhp/29lb ft
**Engine:** Normally aspirated 594cc twin, petrol, carburettor, 4 valves
**Drivetrain:** Rear-engine RWD
**Structure:** Monocoque
**Transmission:** Four-speed manual
**Weight:** 580kg

### PRICE GUIDE

**Launch price:** £698
**Excellent:** £6000
**Good:** £4500
**Average:** £2750
**Project:** £1200

## FIAT 128 Coupé/3P

A car that lurks somewhere in that grey area between coupé and hatchback that was popularised by the VW Scirocco a year earlier. In fact '3P' stands for *tre porte* – Italian for three-door. With that cleared up, it's time to point out just how under-rated these cars are. Though they have long had a cult following, most in the UK lost the battle against corrosion years ago, though you can still find fair numbers in Italy and Greece. There's decent performance from the overhead-cam 1300, and entertaining handling too. Becoming collectable.

### SPECIFICATIONS

**Years produced:** 1975-1978 (330,897 in total)
**Performance:** 0-60mph: 11.7sec
Top speed: 93mph
**Power & torque:** 64bhp/61lb ft
**Engine:** Normally aspirated, 1116cc four cylinder, petrol, carburettor, 8 valves
**Drivetrain:** Front-engine RWD
**Structure:** Monocoque
**Transmission:** Four-speed manual
**Weight:** 820kg

### PRICE GUIDE

**Launch price:** £1398
**Excellent:** £9000
**Good:** £6000
**Average:** £4000
**Project:** £2000

## FIAT 131/Mirafiori

Well-engineered replacement for the 124 was built at Fiat's Mirafiori factory, hence the name it adopted in export markets. Conventionally engineered with rear-wheel drive and a range of single- and twin-cam engines, the 131 was perfectly conceived for the Cortina/Cavalier market. As ever, a huge seller in Italy and mainly overlooked elsewhere. The most memorable version is the twin-cam Supermirafiori model that hit the market in 1978 – although it was not the caged tiger the adverts hinted at – but most have succumbed to rust and as engine donors.

### SPECIFICATIONS (1300 L)

**Years produced:** 1974-1984 (1,850,000 in total)
**Performance:** 0-60mph: 16.1sec
Top speed: 91mph
**Power & torque:** 64bhp/75lb ft
**Engine:** Normally aspirated 1297cc four cylinder, petrol, carburettor, 8 valves
**Drivetrain:** Front-engine RWD
**Structure:** Monocoque
**Transmission:** Four-speed manual
**Weight:** 965kg

### PRICE GUIDE

**Launch price:** £1619
**Excellent:** £3000
**Good:** £2000
**Average:** £1250
**Project:** £600

## FIAT 131TC/Sport

Based on a two-door Mirafiori shell, the 131 Sport was, in effect, an Italian equivalent to the Escort RS2000 that was launched at the same time. Both have 2.0-litre engines with the Fiat's twin-cam efficiency compensating for the 131 Sport's extra weight. Both were pure road cars being sold on the back of rally successes. These days, however, the Fiat is substantially cheaper to buy than the Ford, though prices are rising. They were only sold in black, orange, silver or grey and the sporty trim included plastic wheelarch lips and a front spoiler.

### SPECIFICATIONS

**Years produced:** 1978-1984 (N/A total)
**Performance:** 0-60mph: 10.1sec
Top speed: 112mph
**Power & torque:** 115bhp/123lb ft
**Engine:** Normally aspirated, 1995cc four cylinder, petrol, carburettor, 8 valves
**Drivetrain:** Front-engine RWD
**Structure:** Monocoque
**Transmission:** Five-speed manual
**Weight:** 1020kg

### PRICE GUIDE

**Launch price:** £4636
**Excellent:** £10,000
**Good:** £7000
**Average:** £5000
**Project:** £2000

## FIAT
# Strada/Abarth 130TC

Fiat's entrant in the Golf sector, and eventual replacement for the 128, was the Strada. Its major appeal now lies in its oddball styling and vivacious driving experience, but when new it was trumpeted in a memorable advertising campaign for being 'handbuilt by Robots'. Alas, build quality was lax at best. 1982's Super Strada was an improvement, while the facelift models of '83 were better still. Prices are still low despite utter rarity. The one exception is the fast – and especially rare – Abarth 130TC with its 128bhp twin-cam engine, good for 0-60 in 7.9sec.

### SPECIFICATIONS (75 L)

| | |
|---|---|
| **Years produced:** | 1978-1988 (1,790,000 in total) |
| **Performance:** | 0-60mph: 13.3sec<br>Top speed: 95mph |
| **Power & torque:** | 75bhp/87lb ft |
| **Engine:** | Normally aspirated 1498cc four cylinder, petrol, carburettor, 8 valves |
| **Drivetrain:** | Front-engine FWD |
| **Structure:** | Monocoque |
| **Transmission:** | Five-speed manual |
| **Weight:** | 850kg |

### PRICE GUIDE (Abarth in brackets)

| | |
|---|---|
| **Launch price:** | £3990 |
| **Excellent:** | £1700 (£10,000) |
| **Good:** | £900 (£7000) |
| **Average:** | £650 (£4500) |
| **Project:** | £300 (£2000) |

## FIAT
# Panda

Fiat's attempt at a new entry-level people's car that harked back to the Renault 4 or Citroën 2CV made quite a first impression, almost winning the 1981 Car of the Year award. The plastic-clad exterior and flat glass smacked of minimalism, and the interior, with its deckchair seats and functional dashboard, was utterly utilitarian. The Panda worked because Italdesign made it look appealing. Panda II of 1986 ws slightly plusher, and remained a top-ten seller in Italy until 2003. Interesting Steyr-Puch 4x4 version still popular in mountainous Europe. Tough to find now.

### SPECIFICATIONS

| | |
|---|---|
| **Years produced:** | 1980-2003 (4,500,000 in total) |
| **Performance:** | 0-60mph: 17.9sec<br>Top speed: 85mph |
| **Power & torque:** | 45bhp/49lb ft |
| **Engine:** | Normally aspirated 903cc four cylinder, petrol, carburettor, 8 valves |
| **Drivetrain:** | Front-engine FWD |
| **Structure:** | Monocoque |
| **Transmission:** | Four-speed manual |
| **Weight:** | 680kg |

### PRICE GUIDE (4x4 in brackets)

| | |
|---|---|
| **Launch price:** | £2995 |
| **Excellent:** | £1350 (£5000) |
| **Good:** | £900 (£3500) |
| **Average:** | £650 (£1500) |
| **Project:** | £300 (£750) |

## FIAT
# Uno Turbo ie

In the mid-1980s the hot hatch ruled, and without one Fiat would have missed a great opportunity. Like Renault with the 5, the company went down the route of forced induction and the Uno Turbo i.e. was born. Fiat cleverly decided to price the Turbo to directly compete with the 205 GTi, but straight-line speed alone was not enough to take sales from the mighty lion, and the Uno lacked handling finesse. The car received a mild facelift in 1989, when power was increased from 105 to 118bhp. Has gained quite a following. Rare now, very best fetch £12k-plus.

### SPECIFICATIONS

| | |
|---|---|
| **Years produced:** | 1985-1994 (N/A in total) |
| **Performance:** | 0-60mph: 8.3sec<br>Top speed: 122mph |
| **Power & torque:** | 105bhp/108lb ft |
| **Engine:** | Turbocharged 1299cc four cylinder, petrol, fuel injection, 8 valves |
| **Drivetrain:** | Front-engine FWD |
| **Structure:** | Monocoque |
| **Transmission:** | Five-speed manual |
| **Weight:** | 845kg |

### PRICE GUIDE

| | |
|---|---|
| **Launch price:** | £6889 |
| **Excellent:** | £10,000 |
| **Good:** | £7500 |
| **Average:** | £4500 |
| **Project:** | £1900 |

## FIAT
# Coupé

When Fiat launched the Coupé in 1993, Chris Bangle's mix of curves and slashes sent a small shock-wave through the automotive world. This striking design along with the firepower of Fiat's 2.0 16v turbo engine (there was a non-turbo model too) created quite a stir, and there was more to come. In 1996, Fiat unveiled the Coupé 20-valve Turbo (0-60 in 6.5sec). Its 217bhp five-pot pushed the front-wheel-drive chassis to the limit, though a clever limited-slip diff helped point you in the right direction. A lot have been neglected, but a good one is an interesting entry-level classic. On the up.

### SPECIFICATIONS

| | |
|---|---|
| **Years produced:** | 1993-2000 (72,762 in total) |
| **Performance:** | 0-60mph: 7.5sec<br>Top speed: 140mph |
| **Power & torque:** | 195bhp/218lb ft |
| **Engine:** | Turbocharged 1995cc four cylinder, petrol, fuel injection, 16 valves |
| **Drivetrain:** | Front-engine FWD |
| **Structure:** | Monocoque |
| **Transmission:** | Five-speed manual |
| **Weight:** | 1244kg |

### PRICE GUIDE

| | |
|---|---|
| **Launch price:** | £19,249 |
| **Excellent:** | £8000 |
| **Good:** | £4000 |
| **Average:** | £2000 |
| **Project:** | £750 |

## FIAT
# Barchetta

The fact it's left-hand-drive almost adds to the appeal of the Barchetta, which despite being front-drive and Punto-based, is still a hoot to drive. The 1.7-litre four-pot with variable valve timing delivers a healthy 130bhp, enough to get you to 60mph in a smidge under 8sec, and it handles agreeably. Production stopped in 2002 when coachbuilder Maggiora – who assembled the Barchetta – went bankrupt. Fiat moved production to its Mirafiori plant in Turin and thoroughly updated the car for a 2004 relaunch. If an MX-5 is too obvious, try a Barchetta. Watch out for structural rust, though.

### SPECIFICATIONS

| | |
|---|---|
| **Years produced:** | 1995-2005 |
| **Performance:** | 0-60mph: 7.9sec<br>Top speed: 120mph |
| **Power & torque:** | 130bhp/121lb ft |
| **Engine:** | Normally aspirated 1747cc four cylinder, petrol, fuel injection, 16 valves |
| **Drivetrain:** | Front-engine FWD |
| **Structure:** | Monocoque |
| **Transmission:** | Five-speed manual |
| **Weight:** | 1059kg |

### PRICE GUIDE

| | |
|---|---|
| **Launch price:** | £13,000 |
| **Excellent:** | £6500 |
| **Good:** | £4500 |
| **Average:** | £2500 |
| **Project:** | £1200 |

# FORD (UK)

It was in Manchester, England, in 1911 that the first Ford factory outside the US opened, assembling Model Ts. Fords designed specifically for the British market started in 1932 with the Model Y, and a European-minded range evolved with the subsequent Zephyr, Zodiac, Anglia and best-selling Cortina. In the late-'60s, the UK arm merged with its German counterpart to produce cars intended to be sold all over the continent; models such as the Mustang-like Capri and the Escort were phenomenally successful. Later products such as the Sierra and Focus helped cement Ford's position as one of Europe's biggest players, while its RS models became prized by enthusiasts.

## FORD Pilot V8

The V8 Pilot was the British Ford flagship immediately post-war. In essence it was an amalgam of the pre-war V8-62 body with a new 2.5-litre engine. This proved not quite up to the task of propelling such a large lump of metal around, so the old and lazy 3622cc V8 that Ford used in so many wartime military vehicles came out of retirement. Despite the size of its engine, its power was just 85bhp, giving this lumbering but bulletproof beast a top speed of 83mph. Despite this, it proved popular as a police car.

### SPECIFICATIONS

**Years produced:** 1947-1951 (21,487 in total)
**Performance:** 0-60mph: 20.5sec
Top speed: 83mph
**Power & torque:** 85bhp/140lb ft
**Engine:** Normally aspirated 3622cc V8, petrol, carburettor, 16 valves
**Drivetrain:** Front-engine RWD
**Structure:** Separate chassis
**Transmission:** Three-speed manual
**Weight:** 1473kg

### PRICE GUIDE

**Launch price:** £585
**Excellent:** £13,500
**Good:** £9500
**Average:** £6250
**Project:** £3000

## FORD Consul MkI/Convertible

Ford UK adopted unitary construction for its all-new Consul of 1950, the entry-level model in the new EOTA range (the internal code) that also included the Zephyr and Zephyr Zodiac. The Consul 'made do' with a 1508cc four-cylinder overhead valve engine of 48hp plus a three-speed transmission, although its MacPherson strut front suspension and fully hydraulic brakes meant that what performance there was could be made the most of. The slab-sided styling was very American in appearance, but suited the convertibles very well (as values atest).

### SPECIFICATIONS

**Years produced:** 1950-1956 (231,481 in total)
**Performance:** 0-60mph: 27.7sec
Top speed: 75mph
**Power & torque:** 47bhp/72lb ft
**Engine:** Normally aspirated 1508cc four cylinder, petrol, carburettor, 8 valves
**Drivetrain:** Front-engine RWD
**Structure:** Monocoque
**Transmission:** Three-speed manual
**Weight:** 1041kg

### PRICE GUIDE (Convertible in brackets)

**Launch price:** £544
**Excellent:** £7250 (£15,500)
**Good:** £5000 (£10,250)
**Average:** £2200 (£7000)
**Project:** £1200 (£3250)

## FORD Zephyr/Zodiac Mk I

The next step up from the Mk I Consul was the Zephyr, distinguished by its different grille, longer wheelbase and 2262cc six-cylinder engine of 68bhp giving better, smoother performance. Unveiled in 1951, the range was further complemented by the Zephyr Zodiac of 1953, with a high compression (71bhp) engine, leather, fog lamps and, just so everybody knew it was special, two-tone paint and gold-coloured badges. As well as the coachbuilt estates, there was the convertible with its power-operated hood. Values holding firm.

### SPECIFICATIONS

**Years produced:** 1950-1956 (152,677 in total)
**Performance:** 0-60mph: 20.1sec
Top speed: 84mph
**Power & torque:** 68bhp/112lb ft
**Engine:** Normally aspirated, 2262cc six cylinder, petrol, carburettor, 12 valves
**Drivetrain:** Front-engine RWD
**Structure:** Monocoque
**Transmission:** Three-speed manual
**Weight:** 1181kg

### PRICE GUIDE (Add 20% for Zodiac)

**Launch price:** £684
**Excellent:** £12,000
**Good:** £7750
**Average:** £4300
**Project:** £1800

## FORD Pop/Anglia/Prefect 100E

Unitary construction reached small Fords in 1953 with the 100E models. Looking like scaled-down Consuls and Zephyrs, 100Es came in basic two-door Anglia form or as the higher-spec Prefect, with four doors. Sidevalve engine technology persisted – the all-new 1172cc engine just happened to be exactly the same capacity as that in the old Anglias and Prefects. When the 105E Anglia was launched in 1959 the 100E became the Popular, a no-nonsense, low-budget machine intended to lure customers away from the Mini.

### SPECIFICATIONS

**Years produced:** 1953-1962 (572,510 in total)
**Performance:** 0-60mph: 33.2sec
Top speed: 68mph
**Power & torque:** 36bhp/52lb ft
**Engine:** Normally aspirated 1172cc four cylinder, petrol, carburettor, 8 valves
**Drivetrain:** Front-engine RWD
**Structure:** Monocoque
**Transmission:** Three-speed manual
**Weight:** 749kg

### PRICE GUIDE

**Launch price:** £348
**Excellent:** £4500
**Good:** £2750
**Average:** £1200
**Project:** £500

## FORD
# Consul MkII

The first of the 'Three Graces' – the advertising slogan Ford used for this MkII family – was the Consul. It was the cheapest of the bunch, with four cylinders rather than the six found in the Zephyr and Zodiac, and a lesser level of trim. Convertibles had manually operated hoods and estates were only available as special coachbuilt orders. Ford also introduced a future industry standard by having a combined key-operated ignition and starter. The Consul Deluxe of 1957 was equipped almost to Zodiac level and had two-tone paintwork.

**SPECIFICATIONS**

**Years produced:** 1956-1962 (290,951 in total)
**Performance:** 0-60mph: 23.2sec
Top speed: 79mph
**Power & torque:** 59bhp/91lb ft
**Engine:** Normally aspirated 1702cc four cylinder, petrol, carburettor, 8 valves
**Drivetrain:** Front-engine RWD
**Structure:** Monocoque
**Transmission:** Three-speed manual
**Weight:** 1143kg

**PRICE GUIDE** (Add 50% for convertible)

**Launch price:** £520
**Excellent:** £7750
**Good:** £5500
**Average:** £2500
**Project:** £1200

## FORD
# Prefect 107E

The exciting new Anglia 105E of 1959 brought a revolution to small Fords... but not, unfortunately, four doors. So, for those who wanted the practicality of a four-door car and the innovation of an overhead valve engine but weren't that bothered about fashion-conscious looks, there was the Prefect 107E. In effect, this was the four-door 100E shape fitted with the 105E's overhead-valve engine and four-speed transmission, plus some plusher touches than had been the case on previous 100Es. Two-tone paintwork was standard.

**SPECIFICATIONS**

**Years produced:** 1959-1961 (38,154 in total)
**Performance:** 0-60mph: 27.2sec
Top speed: 73mph
**Power & torque:** 39bhp/52.5lb ft
**Engine:** Normally aspirated 996cc four cylinder, petrol, carburettor, 8 valves
**Drivetrain:** Front-engine RWD
**Structure:** Monocoque
**Transmission:** Four-speed manual
**Weight:** 800kg

**PRICE GUIDE**

**Launch price:** £622
**Excellent:** £5500
**Good:** £2800
**Average:** £1650
**Project:** £750

## FORD
# Anglia 105E/123E

One of the most significant Fords ever, the Anglia 105E brought new levels of sophistication to the company's British arm. At last, here was an eager overhead-valve engine and nifty handling. These alone might have made the Anglia a family favourite, but allied to this was the eye-catching mini-Ford Thunderbird fins 'n' chrome styling and that infamous reverse-rake rear window, which was like nothing seen in Britain before. Estate versions arrived in 1961, closely followed by the 123E Super the following year. Values holding steady.

**SPECIFICATIONS**

**Years produced:** 1959-1967 (1,083,960 in total)
**Performance:** 0-60mph: 26.9sec
Top speed: 77mph
**Power & torque:** 39bhp/52lb ft
**Engine:** Normally aspirated 997cc four cylinder, petrol, carburettor, 8 valves
**Drivetrain:** Front-engine RWD
**Structure:** Monocoque
**Transmission:** Four-speed manual
**Weight:** 786kg

**PRICE GUIDE**

**Launch price:** £610
**Excellent:** £7000
**Good:** £5500
**Average:** £1750
**Project:** £700

## FORD
# Consul Capri/GT

The Consul Classic was one of the prettiest cars ever built by Ford in the UK. While the saloon just looked clumsy and fussy, the coupé was svelte and elegant. Unfortunately, performance didn't live up to the looks, although the Capri GT of 1963 managed to squeeze 78bhp from its twin-carburettor 1498cc engine, meaning 95mph flat-out. Out of the total production run of 18,716, a mere 2002 were GTs. Ford would revive the Capri name in 1969, with much more successful results, but these original Capris are now highly sought-after.

**SPECIFICATIONS**

**Years produced:** 1961-1963 (18,716 in total)
**Performance:** 0-60mph: 14.1sec
Top speed: 93.3mph
**Power & torque:** 70bhp/91lb ft
**Engine:** Normally aspirated 1498cc four cylinder, petrol, carburettor, 8 valves
**Drivetrain:** Front-engine RWD
**Structure:** Monocoque
**Transmission:** Four-speed manual
**Weight:** 950kg

**PRICE GUIDE** (Add 15% for GT)

**Launch price:** £916
**Excellent:** £13,500
**Good:** £7500
**Average:** £3500
**Project:** £1700

## FORD
# Consul Classic

Seeking to repeat the success of the Anglia, Ford launched the similarly-styled Consul Classic in 1961. The reverse-rake window was back but the larger canvas gave Ford the opportunity to really go to town with the Transatlantic touches. But it proved a little too much for conservative British tastes, especially once the Cortina arrived to occupy a similar niche. The original 1340cc engine was replaced by a 1498cc unit in 1962. After only two years the car was dropped. The looks make it an interesting classic today though.

**SPECIFICATIONS**

**Years produced:** 1961-1963 (109,045 in total)
**Performance:** 0-60mph: 20.1sec
Top speed: 80mph
**Power & torque:** 59bhp/79lb ft
**Engine:** Normally aspirated 1340cc four cylinder, petrol, carburettor 8 valves
**Drivetrain:** Front-engine RWD
**Structure:** Monocoque
**Transmission:** Four-speed manual
**Weight:** 930kg

**PRICE GUIDE**

**Launch price:** £767
**Excellent:** £8700
**Good:** £5500
**Average:** £2200
**Project:** £1200

## FORD
# Zephyr/Zodiac MkIII

For their 1962 MkIII incarnation Ford's Zephyrs put on considerable weight and adopted a razor-sharp style with prominent fins framing the wide, capacious boot and huge bonnet. As the Consul name was now being used elsewhere, the four-cylinder version – using the same 1703cc engine as on the MkII, albeit giving an extra 5bhp to give 65bhp – became known as the Zephyr 4; those blessed with an additional two cylinders were dubbed Zephyr 6. Externally the 6s had a different split grille and other dashes of affluence. Values edging up.

**SPECIFICATIONS**

**Years produced:** 1962-1966 (79,285/229,450 in total)
**Performance:** 0-60mph: 17.5sec
Top speed: 87mph
**Power & torque:** 98bhp/134lb ft
**Engine:** Normally aspirated 2553cc six cylinder, petrol, carburettor, 12 valves
**Drivetrain:** Front-engine RWD
**Structure:** Monocoque
**Transmission:** Four-speed manual
**Weight:** 1242kg

**PRICE GUIDE** (Add 10% for Zodiac)

**Launch price:** £772
**Excellent:** £8500
**Good:** £5200
**Average:** £2600
**Project:** £1200

## FORD
# Lotus Cortina MkI

Dropping the 105bhp twin-cam into Ford's lightweight Cortina bodyshell created a saloon car legend. Almost all came in white with the green side flashes, and their minimalist quarter-bumpers became de riguer for several generations of Ford tuners. The first year's production came with aluminium doors, bonnet and bootlid, along with an A-frame for the rear axle location. This is prone to cracking its mounts and was changed for leaf springs, but those earlier cars still command a big premium. Competitive racers can be £80k-plus.

**SPECIFICATIONS**

**Years produced:** 1963-1966 (3301 in total)
**Performance:** 0-60mph: 13.8sec
Top speed: 108mph
**Power & torque:** 115bhp/108lb ft
**Engine:** Normally aspirated 1558cc four cylinder, petrol, carburettor, 8 valves
**Drivetrain:** Front-engine RWD
**Structure:** Monocoque
**Transmission:** Four-speed manual
**Weight:** 842kg

**PRICE GUIDE (A-frame cars in brackets)**

**Launch price:** £1100
**Excellent:** £47,500 (£60,000)
**Good:** £36,000 (£43,000)
**Average:** £24,000 (£31,000)
**Project:** £15,000 (£20,000)

## FORD
# Corsair

In the 1960s the Corsair was introduced to plug the void between Cortina and Zephyr. The handsome looks suggested Ford's Thunderbird reduced in size to British proportions. After two years the original 1498cc engine was replaced by a 1662cc V4 which, while it may have given more oomph, wasn't noted for its smoothness or sophistication. In 1967, capacity went up again, this time to 1996cc. This led to one of Ford's 'E' offshoots, the 2000E, which justified its Executive status with a different grille, wooden dash and a black vinyl roof.

**SPECIFICATIONS**

**Years produced:** 1963-1970 (294,591 in total)
**Performance:** 0-60mph: 13.5sec
Top speed: 97mph
**Power & torque:** 88bhp/116lb ft
**Engine:** Normally aspirated 1663cc V4, petrol, carburettor, 8 valves
**Drivetrain:** Front-engine RWD
**Structure:** Monocoque
**Transmission:** Four-speed manual
**Weight:** 995kg

**PRICE GUIDE** (Add 25% for GT and 2000E)

**Launch price:** £650
**Excellent:** £5500
**Good:** £3750
**Average:** £1800
**Project:** £800

## FORD
# Cortina MkII/1600E

While the MkII Cortina used much of the old MkI for its underpinnings, its well-proportioned and boxy body was all new, helping to spearhead the move in the UK towards less curvaceous looks for cars during the tail end of the 1960s. Appreciative customers were given a multitude of different trim and engine options from 1297cc to 1599cc and quite austere saloons and estates through to sporty and posh Executive versions. The legendary 1600E had Lotus suspension, Rostyle wheels, a plush interior and black grille and is still the one everyone wants.

**SPECIFICATIONS**

**Years produced:** 1966-1970 (963,750 in total)
**Performance:** 0-60mph: 11.8sec (1600E)
Top speed: 96mph
**Power & torque:** 88bhp/96lb ft
**Engine:** Normally aspirated 1599cc four cylinder, petrol, carburettor, 8 valves
**Drivetrain:** Front-engine RWD
**Structure:** Monocoque
**Transmission:** Four-speed manual
**Weight:** 924kg

**PRICE GUIDE (1600E in brackets)**

**Launch price:** £799
**Excellent:** £6500 (£10,000)
**Good:** £4850 (£7500)
**Average:** £2300 (£3750)
**Project:** £750 (£1500)

## FORD
# Cortina-Lotus

Comes with slightly more power than the MkI, but to some extent the moment had passed and it was quickly overshadowed by the Escort Twin Cam that was launched the following year. Less successful in competition than the Lotus Cortina MkI too, and built in higher numbers, so values fall well shy of their predecessors', and will remain that way. Still a handy tool, even if 109.5bhp doesn't feel as fast as it used to. Beware of fakes as rust and the unscrupulous mean more than a few have been created from Cortina GT bodyshells over the years. Best are prized now.

**SPECIFICATIONS**

**Years produced:** 1966-1970 (4032 in total)
**Performance:** 0-60mph: 9.9sec
Top speed: 102mph
**Power & torque:** 110bhp/107lb ft
**Engine:** Normally aspirated 1558cc four cylinder, petrol, carburettor, 8 valves
**Drivetrain:** Front-engine RWD
**Structure:** Monocoque
**Transmission:** Four-speed manual
**Weight:** 905kg

**PRICE GUIDE**

**Launch price:** £1068
**Excellent:** £26,000
**Good:** £17,500
**Average:** £9500
**Project:** £6000

## FORD
# Zephyr/Zodiac MkIV

The Zephyr and Zodiac range had grown consistently with every new reincarnation but, for the MkIV, things just went over the top. With their enormously long bonnets and short, stubby ends, the 1966-72 range looked like aircraft carriers on wheels... and handled in a similar way. V-configuration engines featured throughout; the Zephyr 4 had a 1996cc V4, the Zephyr 6 had a 2495cc V6, and the meaty Zodiac weighed in with a 2994cc V6. Top of the range was the Jaguar wannabe Executive model, loaded with occupant-pampering goodies and gadgets. Values levelling off.

**SPECIFICATIONS**

| | |
|---|---|
| **Years produced:** | 1966-1972 (149,263 in total) |
| **Performance:** | 0-60mph: 17.1sec<br>Top speed: 95mph |
| **Power & torque:** | 88bhp/123lb ft |
| **Engine:** | Normally aspirated 1996cc V4, petrol, carburettor, 8 valves |
| **Drivetrain:** | Front-engine RWD |
| **Structure:** | Monocoque |
| **Transmission:** | Four-speed manual |
| **Weight:** | 1250kg |

**PRICE GUIDE (add c20% for Zodiac)**

| | |
|---|---|
| **Launch price:** | £933 |
| **Excellent:** | £6250 |
| **Good:** | £3750 |
| **Average:** | £1500 |
| **Project:** | £800 |

## FORD
# Escort MkI

Originally intended to be the new Anglia, the Escort name was adopted instead for the fresh small Ford after the formation of Ford of Europe in 1967. With less distinctive styling than the Anglia, it proved to be a huge hit, for its simplicity, neat appearance and good performance endeared it to millions. Even the basic 1098cc version proved surprisingly sporty, thanks to rack-and-pinion steering and effective MacPherson strut front suspension, while some of the higher-powered 'specialist' models were effectively rally machines for the road.

**SPECIFICATIONS**

| | |
|---|---|
| **Years produced:** | 1968-1975 (895,873 in total) |
| **Performance:** | 0-60mph: 20.6sec<br>Top speed: 83mph |
| **Power & torque:** | 58bhp/72lb ft |
| **Engine:** | Normally aspirated 1098cc four cylinder, petrol, carburettor, 8 valves |
| **Drivetrain:** | Front-engine RWD |
| **Structure:** | Monocoque |
| **Transmission:** | Four-speed manual |
| **Weight:** | 745kg |

**PRICE GUIDE**

| | |
|---|---|
| **Launch price:** | £635 |
| **Excellent:** | £7000 |
| **Good:** | £4250 |
| **Average:** | £1800 |
| **Project:** | £1000 |

## FORD
# Escort Twin Cam

The word 'Lotus' was silently attached to the Escort Twin Cam, for this model was basically the Lotus Cortina engine and running gear clothed in the lighter two-door Escort bodyshell; something which made it even more of a wolf in sheepish clothing. Available from the start of MkI production in 1968, this 1558cc-engined machine had a very usable 106bhp – more than double that of the standard Escort 1100 – and a top speed of around 113mph. Constructed in limited numbers for homologation purposes and now highly prized. Values rocketing.

**SPECIFICATIONS**

| | |
|---|---|
| **Years produced:** | 1968-1971 (1263 in total) |
| **Performance:** | 0-60mph: 8.7sec<br>Top speed: 113mph |
| **Power & torque:** | 109bhp/106lb ft |
| **Engine:** | Normally aspirated 1558cc four cylinder, petrol, carburettor, 8 valves |
| **Drivetrain:** | Front-engine RWD |
| **Structure:** | Monocoque |
| **Transmission:** | Four-speed manual |
| **Weight:** | 785kg |

**PRICE GUIDE**

| | |
|---|---|
| **Launch price:** | £1263 |
| **Excellent:** | £50,000 |
| **Good:** | £35,000 |
| **Average:** | £22,500 |
| **Project:** | N/A |

## FORD
# Capri MkI

According to Ford, this was 'The car you always promised yourself'. And, for 1.2 million customers, they were telling the truth, such was the sales success of this Mustang wannabe. The Capri was inspired by its American cousin and nobody cared that much that it was simply a Cortina in a party frock. The long bonnet swallowed up the four-cylinder 1300s and 1600s and even the V4 1996cc and V6 2994cc engines fitted with space to spare. GT badging was used to distinguish between 1300, 1600 and 2000 models. Values edging upwards.

**SPECIFICATIONS**

| | |
|---|---|
| **Years produced:** | 1968-1973 (1,172,900 in total) |
| **Performance:** | 0-60mph: 13sec<br>Top speed: 100mph |
| **Power & torque:** | 72bhp/70lb ft |
| **Engine:** | Normally aspirated 1598cc four cylinder, petrol, carburettor, 8 valves |
| **Drivetrain:** | Front-engine RWD |
| **Structure:** | Monocoque |
| **Transmission:** | Four-speed manual |
| **Weight:** | 920kg |

**PRICE GUIDE** (Add 50% for GT)

| | |
|---|---|
| **Launch price:** | £1041 |
| **Excellent:** | £9500 |
| **Good:** | £5000 |
| **Average:** | £2500 |
| **Project:** | £1300 |

## FORD
# Capri MkI 3000

The big daddies of the mainstream MkI Capri range were the 3000 models, available as the performance-orientated 3000GT, the more luxury-focused 3000E and (from 1972) the flagship 3000GXL. Trumpeted as Ford's fastest ever production line cars, with a maximum velocity around the 120mph mark, these big bruisers of the Capri world could be distinguished by their bonnet bulges... at least until the smaller-engined models also adopted the same posing pouches in 1972: shame they had nothing to fill them! Values flying.

**SPECIFICATIONS**

| | |
|---|---|
| **Years produced:** | 1968-1973 (347,700 in total) |
| **Performance:** | 0-60mph: 9.2sec<br>Top speed: 114mph |
| **Power & torque:** | 128bhp/173lb ft |
| **Engine:** | Normally aspirated 2994cc V6, petrol, carburettor, 12 valves |
| **Drivetrain:** | Front-engine RWD |
| **Structure:** | Monocoque |
| **Transmission:** | Four-speed manual |
| **Weight:** | 1057kg |

**PRICE GUIDE** (Add 25% for GXL)

| | |
|---|---|
| **Launch price:** | £1087 |
| **Excellent:** | £18,500 |
| **Good:** | £13,000 |
| **Average:** | £4500 |
| **Project:** | £2500 |

# FORD
## Escort RS1600

Ford set up its Advanced Vehicle Operations in Essex in 1970 and first-born was the RS1600. This was an extension of the Escort Twin Cam, fitted with the new 16-valve Cosworth BDA twin-cam. The engine was developed from a Formula 2 racing unit and, even in detuned state, it made the Escort a furious machine, with the potential to hit almost 120mph. Most buyers ended up tuning them back up again and using them for competition. The RS1600 demanded a lot of care and attention beyond the means of most 'ordinary' owners. Values holding.

**SPECIFICATIONS**

**Years produced:** 1970-1973 (1200 in total)
**Performance:** 0-60mph: 8.3sec
Top speed: 114mph
**Power & torque:** 120bhp/112lb ft
**Engine:** Normally aspirated, 1599cc four cylinder, petrol, carburettor, 8 valves
**Drivetrain:** Front-engine RWD
**Structure:** Monocoque
**Transmission:** Four-speed manual
**Weight:** 785kg

**PRICE GUIDE**

**Launch price:** £1447
**Excellent:** £57,000
**Good:** £40,000
**Average:** £32,000
**Project:** £19,000

# FORD
## Escort Mexico/RS2000

Ford's victory in the tough and demanding 1970 World Cup Rally to Mexico gave the perfect excuse to unleash another 'hotted up' Escort upon an unsuspecting public. Based on the RS1600, the Mexico forwent the specialist twin-cam engine of that car and opted for a simpler – and therefore more reliable – 1598cc Kent overhead valve engine instead. 2.0-litre Pinto power (first seen in the MkIII Cortina) arrived in 1973 to create the RS2000 out of essentially the same platform. All look the part with lairy colours, decals and stripes. Values firm.

**SPECIFICATIONS**

**Years produced:** 1970-1975 (9382/4324 in total)
**Performance:** 0-60mph: 9.0sec
Top speed: 108mph
**Power & torque:** 100bhp/108lb ft
**Engine:** Normally aspirated, 1993cc four cylinder, petrol, carburettor, 8 valves
**Drivetrain:** Front-engine RWD
**Structure:** Monocoque
**Transmission:** Four-speed manual
**Weight:** 915kg

**PRICE GUIDE**

**Launch price:** £1150/1586
**Excellent:** £35,000
**Good:** £26,000
**Average:** £18,000
**Project:** £10,000

# FORD
## Cortina MkIII

A new Cortina for a new decade, the MkIII was ideal for the more flamboyant and funky era that was the '70s. The 'Coke bottle' styling had overtones of American Fords and there was a mass of different options: X, XL, GT or GXL anyone? And would Sir like that with a 1300, 1600 or 2000 engine in his two-door or four-door saloon or estate? In all, there were 35 variants of Cortina at its launch. While its predecessor had been a MkI makeover, the MkIII was completely fresh, with new coil-and-wishbone suspension. Now with quite a following.

**SPECIFICATIONS**

**Years produced:** 1970-1976 (1,126,559 in total)
**Performance:** 0-60mph: 12.9sec
Top speed: 104mph
**Power & torque:** 98bhp/111lb ft
**Engine:** Normally aspirated, 1993cc four cylinder, petrol, carburettor, 8 valves
**Drivetrain:** Front-engine RWD
**Structure:** Monocoque
**Transmission:** Four-speed manual
**Weight:** 1000kg

**PRICE GUIDE** (Add 25% for 2000E)

**Launch price:** £700
**Excellent:** £7000
**Good:** £4000
**Average:** £1850
**Project:** £1000

# FORD
## Consul/Granada

Forever immortalised by *The Sweeney*, the 1972-77 Consul and Granada series was Ford's return to reality after the excesses of the previous Zephyr/Zodiac range. The Consuls served as the entry level models – with 1996cc V4 and 2495cc of 2994cc V6 engines – while the Granadas were the better-equipped and more expensive choice. Ford's recent purchase of Italian coachbuilder Ghia resulted in the luxurious Granada Ghia in 1974, soon joined by the Ghia Coupé. Consuls were discontinued in 1975, after which more basic Granadas filled the void.

**SPECIFICATIONS**

**Years produced:** 1972-1977 (50,747 in total)
**Performance:** 0-60mph: 10.4sec
Top speed: 109mph
**Power & torque:** 120bhp/132lb ft
**Engine:** Normally aspirated, 2495cc V6, petrol, carburettor, 12 valves
**Drivetrain:** Front-engine RWD
**Structure:** Monocoque
**Transmission:** Four-speed manual
**Weight:** 1270kg

**PRICE GUIDE** (Add 30% for Coupé)

**Launch price:** £1416
**Excellent:** £9000
**Good:** £5000
**Average:** £2250
**Project:** £1000

# FORD
## Capri MkII

Falling sales caused Ford to have a rethink for the MkII Capri, launched in 1974. Some of the primitive raucousness of the original was taken away and replaced with more sophisticated practicality, and a hatchback instead of a boot. The body was also smoothed out, although not enough to make the car particularly aerodynamic. Still, it was better to drive than the original Capri, with a more civilised interior too. Currently less valuable than the MkI and MkIII, making this the thinking man's Capri – 3000S and Midnight Special are the ones to have.

**SPECIFICATIONS (1600S)**

**Years produced:** 1974-1977 (727,657 in total)
**Performance:** 0-60mph: 11.4sec
Top speed: 104mph
**Power & torque:** 88bhp/93lb ft
**Engine:** Normally aspirated 1593cc four cylinder, petrol, carburettor, 8 valves
**Drivetrain:** Front-engine RWD
**Structure:** Monocoque
**Transmission:** Four-speed manual
**Weight:** 1023kg

**PRICE GUIDE** (Pay almost double for 3000)

**Launch price:** £1336
**Excellent:** £8500
**Good:** £3850
**Average:** £1600
**Project:** £800

# FORD
## Escort MkII

In 1975, the MkII Escort came along and, like the Cortina before it, lost many of the curves of the original in favour of a square-cut look that many considered bland. However, bland often sells well if the rest of the package is good, and the MkII proved this, with around two million sold during its five-year life. Underneath the boxy body, everything was much the same as on the MkI model, albeit with the addition of a 1599cc engine to complement the existing 1098cc and 1298cc ones. Trim levels were just as varied as before. Interest continues to grow.

### SPECIFICATIONS

**Years produced:** 1975-1980 (960,000 in total)
**Performance:** 0-60mph: 20.8sec
Top speed: 79mph
**Power & torque:** 41bhp/52lb ft
**Engine:** Normally aspirated 1097cc four cylinder, petrol, carburettor, 8 valves
**Drivetrain:** Front-engine RWD
**Structure:** Monocoque
**Transmission:** Four-speed manual
**Weight:** 875kg

### PRICE GUIDE

**Launch price:** £1299
**Excellent:** £7000
**Good:** £5000
**Average:** £2600
**Project:** £1300

# FORD
## Escort MkII Sport/RS Mexico

Ford continued to offer sporty Escorts for both the masses and more focused drivers. Intended for more general consumption were the Sport and Mexico. The Sport used a 1599cc engine with 84bhp extracted from it, just enough to make it capable of the ton. However, to give the impression that it was capable of more, it had special wheels, spotlamps perched above its split front bumpers and pinstriping with '1600 Sport' branding. The Mexico, sold from 1976-78, did similar with its looks, but added touches from the RS2000. Both on the up.

### SPECIFICATIONS (Mexico)

**Years produced:** 1975-1980
**Performance:** 0-60mph: 10.5sec
Top speed: 107mph
**Power & torque:** 95bhp/92lb ft
**Engine:** Normally aspirated, 1593cc four cylinder, petrol, carburettor, 8 valves
**Drivetrain:** Front-engine RWD
**Structure:** Monocoque
**Transmission:** Four-speed manual
**Weight:** 903kg

### PRICE GUIDE (RS Mexico in brackets)

**Launch price:** £2978
**Excellent:** £10,500 (£22,000)
**Good:** £7500 (£14,000)
**Average:** £4000 (£8000)
**Project:** £2000 (£5000)

# FORD
## Escort MkII RS2000

When the Escort MkII was launched, the RS name continued with the Cosworth-engined RS1800, produced in tiny numbers. More widespread Rallye Sport production was initiated with the RS2000 of 1976, which substituted the diva-ish Cosworth unit for a sturdier 2.0-litre Pinto engine. However, the real talking point about the RS2000 was its polyurethane 'droop snoot' front end and air dam, a modification that clearly distinguished it from any other Escort. Even so, poor sales led to a revamped version in 1978. Values have been flying of late.

### SPECIFICATIONS

**Years produced:** 1976-1980 (10,039 in total)
**Performance:** 0-60mph: 8.5sec
Top speed: 108mph
**Power & torque:** 110bhp/119lb ft
**Engine:** Normally aspirated, 1993cc four cylinder, petrol, carburettor, 8 valves
**Drivetrain:** Front-engine RWD
**Structure:** Monocoque
**Transmission:** Four-speed manual
**Weight:** 925kg

### PRICE GUIDE

**Launch price:** £2857
**Excellent:** £22,000
**Good:** £14,000
**Average:** £8000
**Project:** £5000

# FORD
## Cortina MkIV

The 1976 MkIV marked the convergence of Germany's Taunus and the UK's Cortina and, from that point on, a pan-European model strategy. Under the skin it was similar to the MkIII, but the range now included a Cologne V6 for the top-of-the-line Ghia models. The MkIV was a UK best-seller every month it was on sale, and that success was all about being able to offer its demanding customer base everything it wanted. Today, it lacks the '70s retro appeal of the MkIII despite being longer lived and more successful. German-made cars have lasted far better. On the up.

### SPECIFICATIONS (2.3 Ghia)

**Years produced:** 1976-1979
**Performance:** 0-60mph: 12.2sec
Top speed: 99mph
**Power & torque:** 108bhp/130lb ft
**Engine:** Normally aspirated 2293cc V6, petrol, carburettor, 12 valves
**Drivetrain:** Front-engine RWD
**Structure:** Monocoque
**Transmission:** Three-speed automatic
**Weight:** 1128kg

### PRICE GUIDE

**Launch price:** £1950
**Excellent:** £5500
**Good:** £2700
**Average:** £1200
**Project:** £850

# FORD
## Granada MkII

Granada MkIIs adopted Ford's new family appearance of squared-off lines. The angular appearance worked especially well with the larger proportions, cunningly disguising that what was underneath was mainly MkI. Fresh V6s were added in 2293cc and 2792cc capacities plus, for those who prized economy over performance, a 2112cc diesel. Trim levels of L, GL, S and Ghia covered all bases and there were limited editions such as the Sapphire and Chasseur. The 1981 facelift cars were a big improvement. Values have been edging up.

### SPECIFICATIONS

**Years produced:** 1977-1985 (918,969 in total)
**Performance:** 0-60mph: 8.9sec
Top speed: 117mph
**Power & torque:** 160bhp/163lb ft
**Engine:** Normally aspirated 2792cc V6, petrol, mechanical fuel injection, 12 valves
**Drivetrain:** Front-engine RWD
**Structure:** Monocoque
**Transmission:** Five-speed manual
**Weight:** 1455kg

### PRICE GUIDE

**Launch price:** £5913
**Excellent:** £6000
**Good:** £3000
**Average:** £1300
**Project:** £850

# FORD Capri MkIII

As exciting as the MkII was rational, the Capri MkIII was one of the industry's most effective facelifts. Quad headlights, wrap-around bumpers and a plethora of TV appearances restored the Capri's mojo. The Essex-powered 3000S and Ghia were replaced by the 2792cc Cologne V6-powered 2.8 Injection in 1981 and gave the flagship a 127mph maximum speed – Porsche 944 performance for two-thirds the price. Best of all was the Brooklands Green 280, the last Capri of them all – a mere 1038 were made. Values of the best are rising fast.

### SPECIFICATIONS (2.8 Injection)

**Years produced:** 1978-1987
**Performance:** 0-60mph: 7.7sec
Top speed: 127mph
**Power & torque:** 160bhp/163lb ft
**Engine:** Normally aspirated 2994cc V6, petrol, mechanical fuel injection, 12 valves
**Drivetrain:** Front-engine RWD
**Structure:** Monocoque
**Transmission:** Five-speed manual
**Weight:** 1230kg

### PRICE GUIDE (3000/2.8i in brackets)

**Launch price:** £7995
**Excellent:** £8200 (£18,000)
**Good:** £5500 (£12,000)
**Average:** £3500 (£6000)
**Project:** £1500 (£3000)

# FORD Escort XR3/XR3i

With cars such as the Volkswagen Golf stealing sales, 1980's Escort MkIII moved to a front-wheel-drive hatchback configuration to compete. The XR3 had the Golf GTI firmly as its target. A tuned 1597cc CVH engine produced 96bhp thanks to a twin-choke carburettor, while front and rear spoilers and blacked-out trim made it visually appealing to '80s eyes. Better was to come though with the fuel-injection XR3i of 1983. Boy racers soon fell in love with the XRs, in the same way their fathers had with the old rear-wheel-drive Escorts. Prices moving up.

### SPECIFICATIONS

**Years produced:** 1981-1986
**Performance:** 0-60mph: 9.7sec
Top speed: 113mph
**Power & torque:** 94bhp/97lb ft
**Engine:** Normally aspirated 1598cc four cylinder, petrol, carburettor, 8 valves
**Drivetrain:** Front-engine FWD
**Structure:** Monocoque
**Transmission:** Five-speed manual
**Weight:** 970kg

### PRICE GUIDE

**Launch price:** £6250
**Excellent:** £6000
**Good:** £4250
**Average:** £2000
**Project:** £800

# FORD Fiesta XR2

Ford finally entered the mini-car market in 1976 with the Fiesta; an unqualified success right from the word go. Surprisingly, it took nearly six years before a genuine performance version was added to the range, in the neat and tidy form of the XR2, with a larger, more powerful engine than any other Fiesta. Black plastic trim decorated the interior and exterior, there were alloy wheels, and large circular driving lamps were added. Ford's 'Cooper clone continued through the MkII and MkIII versions of the Fiesta, until dropped in 1994. Values on the up.

### SPECIFICATIONS

**Years produced:** 1981-1989
**Performance:** 0-60mph: 9.4sec
Top speed: 106mph
**Power & torque:** 94bhp/97lb ft
**Engine:** Normally aspirated 1597cc four cylinder, petrol, carburettor, 8 valves
**Drivetrain:** Front-engine FWD
**Structure:** Monocoque
**Transmission:** Five-speed manual
**Weight:** 840kg

### PRICE GUIDE (Add 25% for Mk1)

**Launch price:** £5713
**Excellent:** £8500
**Good:** £4850
**Average:** £2850
**Project:** £1350

# FORD Sierra

The Sierra was a brave replacement for the Cortina, and slightly surprising. The aerodynamic body, penned by Patrick Le Quément, clothed conventional engineering – Pinto engines, RWD, and Granada-style rear suspension. Sales were slow as buyers baulked at buying a 'jellymould', but Ford stuck with the concept. In 1987, it was facelifted, a Sapphire saloon version was added, and success soon followed. It isn't long ago that every street was littered with Sierras, but most have now disappeared. XR4i and XR4x4 brought a welcome dash of driver appeal.

### SPECIFICATIONS

**Years produced:** 1982-1992 (3,444,229 in total)
**Performance:** 0-60mph: 10.5sec
Top speed: 118mph
**Power & torque:** 114bhp/130lb ft
**Engine:** Normally aspirated 2294cc V6, petrol, carburettor, 12 valves
**Drivetrain:** Front-engine RWD
**Structure:** Monocoque
**Transmission:** Four-speed manual
**Weight:** 1115kg

### PRICE GUIDE (XR4i/XR4x4 in brackets)

**Launch price:** £4783
**Excellent:** £3000 (£5500)
**Good:** £1700 (£2500)
**Average:** £850 (£1500)
**Project:** £350 (£700)

# FORD Escort RS Turbo

With the XR3i and homologation-special RS1600i very close in both looks and performance, Ford decided to make the volume-production Escort RS line a little more enticing with 1985's RS Turbo. Mechanically, the car took the best features from the XR3i and RS1600i then bolted a Garrett T3 turbocharger onto the 1597cc CVH engine to increase power to a laggy 132bhp for a 125mph top speed. Seven-spoke alloys, a bodykit and aerodynamic aids marked out the RS Turbo as the '80s boy racer's favourite. Values soaring.

### SPECIFICATIONS

**Years produced:** 1984-1990 (8604 in total)
**Performance:** 0-60mph: 8.2sec
Top speed: 125mph
**Power & torque:** 132bhp/133lb ft
**Engine:** Turbocharged 1597cc four cylinder, petrol, fuel injection, 8 valves
**Drivetrain:** Front-engine FWD
**Structure:** Monocoque
**Transmission:** Five-speed manual
**Weight:** 940kg

### PRICE GUIDE (Series 1)

**Launch price:** £9951
**Excellent:** £17,500
**Good:** £10,500
**Average:** £5750
**Project:** £2200

## FORD
# Granada/Scorpio

Even though the Sierra had proved slow-selling, Ford pressed-on with the similarly styled Granada Mk3. In Europe, the all-new car received an all-new name – Scorpio – but in the UK Ford didn't want to risk further alienating existing customers with its new hatchback. The Granada was memorable not only for its radical styling, but also for its standardisation of anti-lock brakes, a European first. Four-pot versions were underpowered, but V6s were capable. Later Cosworth models are genuine future classics, while the 1990s saloon and estate are mini-cabbers' favourites.

**SPECIFICATIONS (2.4i Ghia)**

| | |
|---|---|
| **Years produced:** | 1985-1994 (755,037 in total) |
| **Performance:** | 0-60mph: 9.5sec<br>Top speed: 120mph |
| **Power & torque:** | 128bhp/150lb ft |
| **Engine:** | Normally aspirated 2395cc V6, petrol, electronic fuel injection, 12 valves |
| **Drivetrain:** | Front-engine RWD |
| **Structure:** | Monocoque |
| **Transmission:** | Five-speed manual |
| **Weight:** | 1306kg |

**PRICE GUIDE** (Add 50% for Cosworth)

| | |
|---|---|
| **Launch price:** | £8514 |
| **Excellent:** | £2200 |
| **Good:** | £1350 |
| **Average:** | £700 |
| **Project:** | £400 |

## FORD
# Sierra RS Cosworth

As if the grandiosity of the bespoilered Sierra XR4i wasn't enough, Ford went even more extreme with the Sierra RS Cosworth. Launched in 1986, it used a 1993cc double-overhead camshaft engine, with the now requisite turbocharger attached, to give an output of 204bhp. Just 5545 were built. Even rarer and even more highly prized is the RS500 version, just 500 of which were built for homologation purposes. With power boosted to 224bhp, uprated brakes, modified bodywork and hand assembly by Tickford, this is the ultimate 1980s fast Ford.

**SPECIFICATIONS**

| | |
|---|---|
| **Years produced:** | 1985-1987 (5545 in total) |
| **Performance:** | 0-60mph: 6.2sec<br>Top speed: 142mph |
| **Power & torque:** | 204bhp/203lb ft |
| **Engine:** | Turbocharged 1993cc four cylinder, petrol, electronic fuel injection, 16 valves |
| **Drivetrain:** | Front-engine RWD |
| **Structure:** | Monocoque |
| **Transmission:** | Five-speed manual |
| **Weight:** | 1240kg |

**PRICE GUIDE (RS500 in brackets)**

| | |
|---|---|
| **Launch price:** | £15,950 (£19,995) |
| **Excellent:** | £30,000 (£50,000) |
| **Good:** | £20,000 (£37,500) |
| **Average:** | £12,000 (£25,000) |
| **Project:** | £7000 (£15,000) |

## FORD
# Sapphire RS Cosworth

Things calmed down with the launch of the Sapphire Cosworth in 1988, which was much more discreet and down-to-earth than previous Sierra Cosworths. As its name suggests, it was based on the Sapphire saloon version of the Sierra and used the existing 1993cc Cosworth twin-cam turbo. Perhaps wisely, now missing were the flashy spoilers, replaced by just a small and subtle one on the bootlid. Even the two available colours were sensible too; white or grey. 11,000 were made before the Sapphire RS Cosworth 4x4 replaced it in 1990.

**SPECIFICATIONS**

| | |
|---|---|
| **Years produced:** | 1987-1992 (20,250 in total) |
| **Performance:** | 0-60mph: 6.5sec<br>Top speed: 151mph |
| **Power & torque:** | 204bhp/203lb ft |
| **Engine:** | Turbocharged 1993cc four cylinder, petrol, electronic fuel injection, 16 valves |
| **Drivetrain:** | Front-engine RWD |
| **Structure:** | Monocoque |
| **Transmission:** | Five-speed manual |
| **Weight:** | 1250kg |

**PRICE GUIDE**

| | |
|---|---|
| **Launch price:** | £19,500 |
| **Excellent:** | £15,000 |
| **Good:** | £8500 |
| **Average:** | £5000 |
| **Project:** | £3500 |

## FORD
# Escort RS Cosworth

Just like the pumped-up Sierra that preceded it, the Escort RS Cosworth was a supercar for the people: brash, confident and up for anything. Backed up by a successful rallying career, over 7000 were sold, despite the crippling insurance premiums they attracted. The turbocharged two-litre twin-cam in original cars kicked out 227bhp. This dropped to 217bhp from 1994 when the turbo was changed to a smaller Garrett T25 unit. In compensation, this made the car much nicer to drive, with better throttle response. Values holding.

**SPECIFICATIONS**

| | |
|---|---|
| **Years produced:** | 1992-1996 (7000 in total) |
| **Performance:** | 0-60mph: 5.7sec<br>Top speed: 140mph |
| **Power & torque:** | 227bhp/223lb ft |
| **Engine:** | Turbocharged 1993cc four cylinder, petrol, electronic fuel injection, 16v |
| **Drivetrain:** | Front-engine AWD |
| **Structure:** | Monocoque |
| **Transmission:** | Five-speed manual |
| **Weight:** | 1275kg |

**PRICE GUIDE**

| | |
|---|---|
| **Launch price:** | £23,495 |
| **Excellent:** | £30,000 |
| **Good:** | £22,500 |
| **Average:** | £16,000 |
| **Project:** | £10,000 |

## FORD
# Puma/Racing Puma

The highlight of Ford's strong late-'90s line-up, the cutesy Puma coupe was based on the Mk4 Fiesta platform, further fettled to create the best-handling car in the range. Engine choices were 1.4- and 1.7-litre four-cylinders with 89 and 123bhp respectively, the latter being the one to have. In 2000 came the Racing Puma with an extra 30bhp. Developed by Ford's motorsport division, but never intended for competition, it had much wider tracks covered by widened arches in aluminium. Just 500 were built, boosting values.

**SPECIFICATIONS**

| | |
|---|---|
| **Years produced:** | 1997-2001 (Racing Puma 2000-01) |
| **Performance:** | 0-60mph: 7.0sec (Racing Puma)<br>Top speed: 137mph |
| **Power & torque:** | 153bhp/119lb ft |
| **Engine:** | Normally aspirated 1679cc four cylinder, petrol, electronic injection, 16 valves |
| **Drivetrain:** | Front-engine FWD |
| **Structure:** | Monocoque |
| **Transmission:** | Five-speed manual |
| **Weight:** | 1174kg |

**PRICE GUIDE (Racing Puma in brackets)**

| | |
|---|---|
| **Launch price:** | £14,725 (£22,750) |
| **Excellent:** | £1700 (£11,000) |
| **Good:** | £900 (£8000) |
| **Average:** | £500 (£5500) |
| **Project:** | £150 (£3200) |

## FORD
### Focus RS Mk1

The mk1 Focus made a perfect candidate for the RS treatment. While 212bhp might not sound a huge amount today, it was enough for a 5.9sec 0-60mph sprint. Unlike its Cosworth predecessor, power was sent to the front wheels only, but an aggressive Quaife limited-slip differential made this feel like a very serious bit of kit. Big Brembo calipers are barely contained by huge five-spoke 18in OZ Racing wheels. Black, blue and silver theme inside, with high-back Sparco seats. Many are squirrelled away as investments, and values are static for now.

**SPECIFICATIONS**

| | |
|---|---|
| **Years produced:** | 2002-2003 (4501 in total) |
| **Performance:** | 0-60mph: 5.9sec<br>Top speed: 143mph |
| **Power & torque:** | 212bhp/229lb ft |
| **Engine:** | Turbocharged 1988cc four cylinder, petrol, electronic fuel injection, 16 valves |
| **Drivetrain:** | Front-engine FWD |
| **Structure:** | Monocoque |
| **Transmission:** | Five-speed manual |
| **Weight:** | 1275kg |

**PRICE GUIDE**

| | |
|---|---|
| **Launch price:** | £19,995 |
| **Excellent:** | £15,000 |
| **Good:** | £11,000 |
| **Average:** | £9000 |
| **Project:** | £7000 |

## FORD
### GT

While replicas of the original Le Mans-winning GT40 are rife, Ford's 2004 re-imagining was a genuine supercar for the 21st century. It took the iconic shape, but that's where the similarities end, being longer, wider and taller. Built almost entirely from aluminium around a stiff spaceframe chassis, it was powered by a quad-cam 5.4-litre supercharged V8. It was fast – a genuine 200mph supercar – but also brilliant to drive with a big V8 and manual 'box, but a modern chassis that really lets you exploit it. Just like its 1960s inspiration, a genuine Ferrari-beater.

**SPECIFICATIONS**

| | |
|---|---|
| **Years produced:** | 2004-2006 (4038 in total) |
| **Performance:** | 0-60mph: 3.7sec<br>Top speed: 205mph |
| **Power & torque:** | 550bhp/500lb ft |
| **Engine:** | Supercharged 5409cc V8, petrol, electronic fuel injection, 32 valves |
| **Drivetrain:** | Mid-engine RWD |
| **Structure:** | Aluminium spaceframe |
| **Transmission:** | Six-speed manual |
| **Weight:** | 1538kg |

**PRICE GUIDE**

| | |
|---|---|
| **Launch price:** | £120,900 |
| **Excellent:** | £275,000 |
| **Good:** | £200,000 |
| **Average:** | £150,000 |
| **Project:** | N/A |

# FORD (USA)

THE FORD Motor Company was founded by Henry Ford in Dearborn near Detroit in June 1903. The company made its fortune by introducing methods for large-scale manufacturing of cars and large-scale management of an industrial workforce using elaborately engineered manufacturing sequences typified by moving assembly lines. Henry Ford's methods came to be known around the world as Fordism by 1914. The first mass-produced Ford was the Model T, which motorised the USA before going on to sell 15 million copies worldwide. The company remains a huge player, and is currently the USA's second-largest car manufacturer behind General Motors.

## FORD
### Mustang

The original Mustang was exactly the right car at the right time and thus this sports car for the masses sold a million in less than two years. Available as a notchback coupé, convertible or, from 1965, a fastback coupé, the array of trim and engine options meant that there was a 'Stang to satisfy anyone... although it was in powerful V8 form that this fast Ford was most fulfilling. While handling was soft compared with Europe's best, rival manufacturers were soon rushing to offer their own 'Pony Car' pretenders. Add 40% for fastback, 50% for roadster.

**SPECIFICATIONS**

| | |
|---|---|
| **Years produced:** | 1964-1968 (2,204,038 in total) |
| **Performance:** | 0-60mph: 10sec<br>Top speed: 115mph |
| **Power & torque:** | 225bhp/305lb ft |
| **Engine:** | Normally aspirated 4728cc V8, petrol, carburettor, 16 valves |
| **Drivetrain:** | Front-engine RWD |
| **Structure:** | Monocoque |
| **Transmission:** | Four-speed manual |
| **Weight:** | 1450kg |

**PRICE GUIDE** (Coupe version)

| | |
|---|---|
| **Launch price:** | £1925 |
| **Excellent:** | £22,500 |
| **Good:** | £16,000 |
| **Average:** | £10,000 |
| **Project:** | £4000 |

## FORD
### Mustang (1969-1973)

After four massive years of sales success, the Mustang received its first major facelift. The new car grew in all directions and gained bulging flanks at the expense of the earlier car's sculpted look, and sales began to fall off a cliff. It was wasn't only the mid-life changes that blunted the Mustang's appeal; that was just as much down to changing times. The ultimates were the Mach 1 and Boss, which Ford produced to fight the Shelby cars in the showrooms. These cars had up to 375bhp and could sprint to 60mph in under six seconds. They are valued accordingy.

**SPECIFICATIONS**

| | |
|---|---|
| **Years produced:** | 1969-1973 (900,909 in total) |
| **Performance:** | 0-60mph: N/A<br>Top speed: 115mph |
| **Power & torque:** | 177bhp/284lb ft |
| **Engine:** | Normally aspirated 5753cc V8, petrol, carburettor, 16 valves |
| **Drivetrain:** | Front-engine RWD |
| **Structure:** | Monocoque |
| **Transmission:** | 3/4-speed manual/three-speed auto |
| **Weight:** | 1527kg |

**PRICE GUIDE**

| | |
|---|---|
| **Launch price:** | Not sold in UK |
| **Excellent:** | £25,000 |
| **Good:** | £15,000 |
| **Average:** | £12,000 |
| **Project:** | £8000 |

# FRAZER NASH

FRAZER NASH STARTED out in 1924 building idiosyncratic chain-driven sports cars, but was taken over in 1929 and began importing BMWs instead, thus allowing it to use BMW mechanicals – such as the 2.0-litre 328 engine – in its competition-orientated machines. Spartan bodywork gradually expanded into more elegant lines and more power came along courtesy of BMW's 3.2-litre V6 engine. Frazer Nash named several of its models after events and venues in which it had achieved sporting success, such as Le Mans, Sebring, Mille Miglia and Targa Florio. In 1960, the company decided to retreat from car production and concentrate on other engineering disciplines.

## FRAZER NASH
### Le Mans Replica

Following the privateer success for Frazer Nash in the 1949 Le Mans 24 Hour race, the company produced its own version following on from the tradition first started with the 1932 TT Replica. The Le Mans was powered by a 1971cc BMW straight six delivering a healthy 120bhp and, with the lightweight 'High Speed' body, proved prodigiously quick. Like all Nashes the Le Mans Replica was completely handbuilt, the customer getting the final say on engine configuration and suspension set-up. Cars with history are now worth up to £1m.

**SPECIFICATIONS**

**Years produced:** 1948-1953 (34 in total)
**Performance:** 0-60mph: 8.8sec
Top speed: 110mph
**Power & torque:** 125bhp/N/A
**Engine:** Normally aspirated 1971cc straight six, petrol, carburettor, 12 valves
**Drivetrain:** Front-engine RWD
**Structure:** Separate chassis
**Transmission:** Four-speed
**Weight:** 635kg

**PRICE GUIDE**

**Launch price:** £3074
**Excellent:** £700,000
**Good:** £500,000
**Average:** £350,000
**Project:** N/A

## FRAZER NASH
### Fast Roadster/Mille Miglia

A roadgoing sports car with direct competition heritage – the Fast Roadster, Cabriolet and Mille Miglia were Frazer Nash's attempts to widen the appeal of its product line. But under the skin, it was almost pure Le Mans Replica. The full-width body certainly looked the part, even if housing the spare wheel Bristol-style caused an odd-looking bulge in the front wing. The Cabriolet runs on a lengthened wheelbase. Rare and fabulously valuable, and also a wonderful driver's tool especially in 125bhp Mille Miglia specification. Hardly ever come up for sale.

**SPECIFICATIONS**

**Years produced:** 1949-1953 (12 in total)
**Performance:** 0-60mph: 9.3sec
Top speed: 110mph
**Power & torque:** 125bhp/N/A
**Engine:** Normally aspirated 1971cc straight six, petrol, carburettor, 12 valves
**Drivetrain:** Front-engine RWD
**Structure:** Separate chassis
**Transmission:** Four-speed
**Weight:** 735kg

**PRICE GUIDE**

**Launch price:** N/A
**Excellent:** £400,000
**Good:** £300,000
**Average:** £200,000
**Project:** N/A

# GILBERN

THE ONLY TRULY Welsh car manufacturer, Gilbern is also one of the few firms to graduate from kit-cars to completed production vehicles, though all used the same production method of a glassfibre body over a steel tube chassis. The Gilbern name is a combination of its two founders, Giles Smith and Bernard Friese. Early GTs were based on BMC mechanical parts, but over the years the company used more and more parts from the cheaper source of Ford, starting with its V6 engines for the Genie and Invader models. By the Invader III all mechanical parts were stamped with the Ford logo. The energy crisis and VAT changes (which upped the prices of kit cars) killed the company off in 1974.

## GILBERN
### GT

Good looking little 2+2 from Wales, with a glassfibre body over a tube frame. To some degree or other the 277 built were sold as kit-cars to avoid purchase tax, so parts and spec can vary a little between cars. They were initially offered with A-series or MGA engines, but most survivors you'll find will have MGB power, along with front suspension from the same source. Thanks to an enthusiastic club parts sourcing is much better than you might expect, right down to reproduction bodies and chassis if necessary.

**SPECIFICATIONS**

**Years produced:** 1959-1967 (277 in total)
**Performance:** 0-60mph: 12.0sec
Top speed: 111mph
**Power & torque:** 95bhp/110lb ft
**Engine:** Normally aspirated 1798cc four cylinder, petrol, carburettor, 8 valves
**Drivetrain:** Front-engine RWD
**Structure:** Glassfibre body/tubular chassis
**Transmission:** Four-speed manual
**Weight:** 813kg

**PRICE GUIDE**

**Launch price:** £748
**Excellent:** £15,000
**Good:** £9000
**Average:** £5000
**Project:** £3000

## GILBERN Genie

Gilbern's move upmarket to full GT status. Larger, more angular body now contains a Ford Zephyr V6, mostly in 3.0 capacity, though some were sold with 2.5s. Another big change was that you could buy a Genie factory-built as well as in component form. The first 30 or so came with MGB front suspension and rear axle, then these were upgraded to MGC spec. Somewhere close to 200 were built. Overdrive was an option worth finding now, and some even came with electric windows. Twin fuel tanks add to their kudos. Values currently holding firm.

**SPECIFICATIONS**

**Years produced:** 1966-1970 (197 in total)
**Performance:** 0-60mph: 10.7sec
Top speed: 115mph
**Power & torque:** 141bhp/181lb ft
**Engine:** Normally aspirated 2994cc V6, petrol, carburettor, 12 valves
**Drivetrain:** Front-engine RWD
**Structure:** Glassfibre body/tubular chassis
**Transmission:** Four-speed manual
**Weight:** 965kg

**PRICE GUIDE**

**Launch price:** £1752
**Excellent:** £11,000
**Good:** £6500
**Average:** £3250
**Project:** £1750

## GILBERN Invader

The MkI and II Invaders differed visually only in detail from the Genie they replaced. Flush-fitting doorhandles and rear pillar vents are the biggest giveaways. Underneath, the front suspension is still MGC-based, but with double wishbones and coil-overs replacing the MG's lever-arm dampers. For 1971-72 there was also an estate version, of which 105 were built. MkIII uses the same 3.0-litre engine, but a switch to Cortina MkIII axles and suspension brings the need for flared wheelarches. A full-width grille adds further distinction. Values steady.

**SPECIFICATIONS**

**Years produced:** 1969-1974 (603 in total)
**Performance:** 0-60mph: 10.7sec
Top speed: 115mph
**Power & torque:** 141bhp/181lb ft
**Engine:** Normally aspirated 2994cc V6, petrol, carburettor, 12 valves
**Drivetrain:** Front-engine RWD
**Structure:** Glassfibre body/tubular chassis
**Transmission:** Four-speed manual
**Weight:** 903kg

**PRICE GUIDE**

**Launch price:** N/A
**Excellent:** £12,500
**Good:** £7500
**Average:** £4500
**Project:** £2500

# GINETTA

The four car-mad Walklett brothers – Bob, Ivor, Trevers and Douglas – founded Ginetta and built their first car in Woodbridge, Suffolk, in 1958. The company built both competition and road cars, all using glassfibre bodies and steel frames, until the going got tough in the mid-1970s, after which they kept going by refurbishing existing Ginettas, and eventually reintroducing the popular G4. After the Walkletts retired in 1989, Ginetta was sold to a Sheffield consortium and production moved north, where the G20 and G33 were launched. In 2005 the company was acquired by LNT Automotive and production moved to Leeds, with the focus now primarily on racing cars.

## GINETTA G15

As the more obviously road-focused model it's clear why the G15 became Ginetta's best-selling model. Powered by the excellent Coventry Climax based Hillman Imp engine, mid-mounted in the lightweight glassfibre 'shell, weight distribution was near-perfect and handling predictably good as a result. The suspension set-up was a mixture of Triumph and Hillman and used to great effect. A more powerful G15S was launched and pushed the top speed up to 115mph – but sadly the G15 was taken out of production in 1973.

**SPECIFICATIONS**

**Years produced:** 1968-1974 (800 in total)
**Performance:** 0-60mph: 12.9sec
Top speed: 94mph
**Power & torque:** 50bhp/49lb ft
**Engine:** Normally aspirated 875cc four cylinder, petrol, carburettor, 8 valves
**Drivetrain:** Rear engine RWD
**Structure:** Glassfibre body/tubular chassis
**Transmission:** Four-speed manual
**Weight:** 501kg

**PRICE GUIDE**

**Launch price:** £1024
**Excellent:** £9000
**Good:** £7500
**Average:** £3500
**Project:** £1500

## GINETTA G21

The more upmarket G21 reflected Ginetta's ambitions in the wake of the collapse of the kit-car market. Its sleek glassfibre body was fitted over a new tubular steel chassis and a choice of Sunbeam Rapier H120 or Ford V6 engines meant that there was real power on tap. The two-seater coupé wasn't offered with an opening rear hatch and, in the wake of the MGB GT and the Mk2 Ford Capri, this seemed like an oversight – but despite this some 180 were sold, the vast majority of them purchased not as kits but as complete factory-built cars.

**SPECIFICATIONS**

**Years produced:** 1973-1978 (180 in total)
**Performance:** 0-60mph: 9.7sec
Top speed: 112mph
**Power & torque:** 85bhp/91lb ft
**Engine:** Normally aspirated 1725cc four cylinder, petrol, carburettor, 8 valves
**Drivetrain:** Front-engine RWD
**Structure:** Glassfibre body/tubular chassis
**Transmission:** Four-speed manual
**Weight:** 737kg

**PRICE GUIDE**

**Launch price:** £1875
**Excellent:** £9500
**Good:** £6250
**Average:** £3500
**Project:** £1500

## GINETTA G32

A new look for the 1980s saw Ginetta going for the Toyota MR2 with its Ford-based mid-engined G32. Again, suspension was an off-the-shelf set-up taken from Ford, while the XR2 engine in the middle gave plenty of performance. After being in the business for so long, Ginetta had perfected getting a high quality finish from its glassfibre bodies, although the cunning use of the Fiesta's doors no doubt added to the feeling of solidity. Rare and unusual now, but satisfying if you can find the right one – and easy to keep on the road. Good value, too.

### SPECIFICATIONS

| | |
|---|---|
| **Years produced:** | 1989-1992 |
| **Performance:** | 0-60mph: N/A<br>Top speed: N/A |
| **Power & torque:** | 90bhp/98lb ft |
| **Engine:** | Normally aspirated 1597cc four cylinder, petrol, carburettor, 8 valves |
| **Drivetrain:** | Mid-engine RWD |
| **Structure:** | Glassfibre body/tubular chassis |
| **Transmission:** | Five-speed manual |
| **Weight:** | 753kg |

### PRICE GUIDE

| | |
|---|---|
| **Launch price:** | £10,490 |
| **Excellent:** | £5500 |
| **Good:** | £3750 |
| **Average:** | £2800 |
| **Project:** | £1750 |

## GINETTA G33 V8

The G33 saw the return of 'back to basics' at Ginetta. Its body was a development of the curvaceous G27's (which harked back to the G4), and a Rover V8 engine shoehorned into the front provided TVR-rivalling thrills and soundtrack. But, being a Ginetta it was more track-focused than its Blackpool rival, making it a harder-edged alternative. The chassis was galvanised and holding it up was a fully independent suspension set-up featuring double wishbones all-round. Good old-fashioned fun, and a cheap TVR Griffith alternative.

### SPECIFICATIONS

| | |
|---|---|
| **Years produced:** | 1990-1996 |
| **Performance:** | 0-60mph: 5.3sec<br>Top speed: 137mph |
| **Power & torque:** | 198bhp/220lb ft |
| **Engine:** | Normally aspirated 3946cc V8, petrol, electronic fuel injection, 16 valves |
| **Drivetrain:** | Front-engine RWD |
| **Structure:** | Glassfibre body/tubular chassis |
| **Transmission:** | Five-speed manual |
| **Weight:** | 874kg |

### PRICE GUIDE

| | |
|---|---|
| **Launch price:** | £18,187 |
| **Excellent:** | £13,500 |
| **Good:** | £10,000 |
| **Average:** | £7500 |
| **Project:** | £5000 |

# GORDON-KEEBLE

THE COMPANY may have been shortlived, but the car it produced was a stunner. John Gordon (previously behind the Peerless GT) and Jim Keeble used a beautiful glassfibre Giugiaro-styled 2+2 body and the Corvette V8 engine to produce a 135mph super-coupé that was as good to drive as look at. But a price 40% higher than a Jaguar E-type's meant buyers were hard to find and the money ran out in 1965 after just 90 had been built. The company was bought by Geoffrey West and Harold Smith, who built another nine before giving up the following year. An amazing 90% of the cars produced have survived thanks to enthusiasts, and they remain utterly desirable.

## GORDON-KEEBLE GK1

With achingly pretty Giugiaro styling and the vocal accompaniment of a Corvette V8, you'd never know these were lovingly assembled in a large shed near Southampton. Just 99 were built before the company folded for the second and last time, but enthusiastic support and a glassfibre body over a square tube chassis means that almost all of the cars survive. Commonly found (and much better to drive) with a power-assisted rack-and-pinion steering conversion. Easy to drive quickly and simple to look after. Values have levelled off.

### SPECIFICATIONS

| | |
|---|---|
| **Years produced:** | 1964-1966 (99 in total) |
| **Performance:** | 0-60mph: 7.5sec<br>Top speed: 136mph |
| **Power & torque:** | 300bhp/360lb ft |
| **Engine:** | Normally aspirated 5354cc V8, petrol, carburettor, 16 valves |
| **Drivetrain:** | Front-engine RWD |
| **Structure:** | Glassfibre body/tubular chassis |
| **Transmission:** | Four-speed manual |
| **Weight:** | 1436kg |

### PRICE GUIDE

| | |
|---|---|
| **Launch price:** | £2798 |
| **Excellent:** | £80,000 |
| **Good:** | £55,000 |
| **Average:** | £40,000 |
| **Project:** | £20,000 |

# HEALEY

ENGINEER AND racer Donald Healey made a name for himself at Triumph before the war; after it, he formed his own motor company to build curvaceous roadsters and coupés using Riley parts. No British four-seater was faster than his Westland and Elliot models when launched. In 1949 came the Silverstone, a sleek and light sports car with stripped-down styling, aimed at weekend racers. An alliance with American firm Nash resulted in an attempt to sell cars in the USA, but little came of this endeavour. Healey then designed his iconic 100 sports car which so bewitched the British Motor Corporation that it agreed to build in under the Austin-Healey name from 1954.

## HEALEY Elliott

Former Triumph technical director Donald Healey started building his own cars in 1946, and the Elliott saloon was an important step in the development of his company. Considered the fastest closed four-seater available, these were thinly disguised racing cars, lightened with almost obsessive ruthlessness. At the Mille Miglia in 1948, Johnny Lurani and Giuglelmo Sandri won the production touring class in an Elliott, while Healey and son,Geoffrey finished ninth overall in a Westland Roadster. Values for the best have climbed steadily but are now stabilising.

**SPECIFICATIONS**

**Years produced:** 1948-1950 (64 in total)
**Performance:** 0-60mph: 12.3sec
Top speed: 102mph
**Power & torque:** 104bhp/132lb ft
**Engine:** Normally aspirated 2443cc four cylinder, petrol, carburettor, 8 valves
**Drivetrain:** Front-engine RWD
**Structure:** Separate chassis
**Transmission:** Four-speed manual
**Weight:** 1143kg

**PRICE GUIDE**

**Launch price:** £1566
**Excellent:** £38,000
**Good:** £22,000
**Average:** £15,000
**Project:** £7000

## HEALEY Silverstone

The Silverstone showed just how far Healey had come in such a short time – it was an excellent road- or competition-car, and proved itself more than capable of living with much more expensive machinery. The short-framed car had an anti-roll bar and tenacious handling on the circuit. It was stylish too, and Healey easily sold every car built. However, this promising roadster was prematurely taken out of production when the deal between Nash and Healey to produce the Nash-Healey was concluded. Highly prized today.

**SPECIFICATIONS**

**Years produced:** 1949-1950 (105 in total)
**Performance:** 0-60mph: 11.0sec
Top speed: 105mph
**Power & torque:** 104bhp/132lb ft
**Engine:** Normally aspirated 2443cc four cylinder, petrol, carburettor, 8 valves
**Drivetrain:** Front-engine RWD
**Structure:** Separate chassis
**Transmission:** Four-speed manual
**Weight:** 940kg

**PRICE GUIDE**

**Launch price:** £1246
**Excellent:** £160,000
**Good:** £82,500
**Average:** £60,000
**Project:** N/A

## HEALEY Abbott

The Westland Roadster was Healey's first production car, and although it was capable of great things in competition it wasn't ideal as a road car. It might have enjoyed the benefits of a stiff box section chassis, all-round coil springs and the Riley engine helped it to a 105mph top speed but it lacked creature comforts. The Abbott drophead coupé was introduced to put that right with sharper style, a more compliant ride and lower gearing to improve tractability. It may have been slower but it was a more accomplished all-rounder.

**SPECIFICATIONS**

**Years produced:** 1950-1954 (77 in total)
**Performance:** 0-60mph: 14.6sec
Top speed: 104mph
**Power & torque:** 106bhp/136lb ft
**Engine:** Normally aspirated 2443cc four cylinder, petrol, carburettor, 8 valves
**Drivetrain:** Front-engine RWD
**Structure:** Separate chassis
**Transmission:** Four-speed manual
**Weight:** 1143kg

**PRICE GUIDE**

**Launch price:** £1854
**Excellent:** £40,000
**Good:** £28,000
**Average:** £18,000
**Project:** £8000

## HEALEY Tickford

Based on the Elliott, but more stylishly executed, the Healey Tickford is far cleaner-looking and more appealing than the original, perhaps taking the car away from its competition roots and into more exalted territory. Dynamically, it lost out to the Elliott, thanks to additional weight and a loss of agility. In dynamism's place it received a proper boot and glass (instead of Perspex) side windows. In the end, it outsold the original by two-to-one, proving that Healey's designs were good enough to warrant the premium they carried. Values holding firm.

**SPECIFICATIONS**

**Years produced:** 1950-1954 (224 in total)
**Performance:** 0-60mph: 14.6sec
Top speed: 104mph
**Power & torque:** 104bhp/132lb ft
**Engine:** Normally aspirated 2443cc four cylinder, petrol, carburettor, 8 valves
**Drivetrain:** Front-engine RWD
**Structure:** Separate chassis
**Transmission:** Four-speed manual
**Weight:** 1546kg

**PRICE GUIDE**

**Launch price:** £1854
**Excellent:** £32,000
**Good:** £17,000
**Average:** £12,500
**Project:** £6000

# HEINKEL

DURING THE WAR, Heinkel had made military aircraft but, banned from doing this, it turned to bicycles and scooters instead. In 1956, it expanded into building bubblecars (following the path of BMW with its Isetta), both in three- and four-wheeled form. The quirky Heinkels were somewhat more sophisticated and spacious, however, than the closely-related Isetta. German production stopped in 1958, but continued under licence in Ireland and the UK (under the Trojan name) as well as in Argentina. Unfortunately for Hainkel, the impact of compact cars such as the Mini decimated bubblecar sales during the early 1960s and, by 1965, production had ceased worldwide.

## HEINKEL/TROJAN
### Cabin Cruiser/200

The archetypal bubblecar, the Heinkel was also produced in the UK by Trojan from 1961 as the Cabin Cruiser. Given its 197cc engine, cruiser was hardly an apt title for this economy special. As bubblecars go, the Heinkel was certainly an improvement over the BMW it was based on – it had space (just) for four people, was lighter, and could cruise happily at up to 50mph. Survival rate of these cars is exceptionally high, and that is down simply to their great build quality – as well as excellent club and specialist support. Prices have softened recently.

**SPECIFICATIONS**

| | |
|---|---|
| **Years produced:** | 1956-1965 (23,000 in total) |
| **Performance:** | 0-60mph: N/A<br>Top speed: 53mph |
| **Power & torque:** | 9.2bhp/N/A |
| **Engine:** | Normally aspirated 174cc single cylinder, petrol, carburettor, 2 valves |
| **Drivetrain:** | Rear-engine RWD |
| **Structure:** | Monocoque |
| **Transmission:** | Four-speed manual |
| **Weight:** | 279kg |

**PRICE GUIDE**

| | |
|---|---|
| **Launch price:** | N/A |
| **Excellent:** | £21,500 |
| **Good:** | £13,500 |
| **Average:** | £6300 |
| **Project:** | £3500 |

# HILLMAN

FOUNDED IN 1907 by bicycle manufacturer William Hillman, the Hillman brand became successful despite – or perhaps because of – its range of frankly quite dull cars. After Hillman's death in 1921 the company passed to his son-in-laws John Black and Spencer Wilks, who respectively would later run Standard and Rover. Their moves were precipitated by a takeover from Humber in 1928, soon after which both companies were sucked into the Rootes Group. Hillman became the badge applied to Rootes' entry-level vehicles, with a succession of friendly-family cars such as the mainstay Minxes and later the Hunter, continuing until Chrysler killed off the name in 1976.

## HILLMAN
### Minx Phase III-VIIIA

The pre-war looks of the Minx Phase I and II were revamped with the Phase III cars of 1948, which switched to 'full-width' styling, completely unitary construction and coil-and-wishbone independent front suspension. After that, Hillman continued with its process of annual improvements, enlarging engines to give more power, upgrading the suspension, and tweaking the bodywork to keep it fresh. The alterations were subtle, but ensured that the breed kept up with its rivals until it was replaced by the Series Minxes of 1956.

**SPECIFICATIONS**

| | |
|---|---|
| **Years produced:** | 1948-1957 (378,785 in total) |
| **Performance:** | 0-60mph: 29.7sec<br>Top speed: 73mph |
| **Power & torque:** | 35bhp/N/A |
| **Engine:** | Normally aspirated 1185cc four cylinder, petrol, carburettor, 8 valves |
| **Drivetrain:** | Front-engine RWD |
| **Structure:** | Monocoque |
| **Transmission:** | Four-speed manual |
| **Weight:** | 933kg |

**PRICE GUIDE (double for convertible)**

| | |
|---|---|
| **Launch price:** | £505 |
| **Excellent:** | £4000 |
| **Good:** | £2600 |
| **Average:** | £1350 |
| **Project:** | £600 |

## HILLMAN
### Minx Californian

The USA was always a big target for British car firms, and Hillman had a head start on its competitors thanks to Studebaker-inspired styling by American Raymond Loewy. As its name suggested the Californian coupé was blatantly aimed across the Atlantic, where style was often much more important than substance. In essence, it was a 1953 Minx drophead coupé with a permanent hardtop attached, but the three-piece rear screen was very eye-catching and the roof's contrasting paint made the car stand out. Prices holding.

**SPECIFICATIONS**

| | |
|---|---|
| **Years produced:** | 1953-1956 |
| **Performance:** | 0-60mph: 34.7sec<br>Top speed: 69mph |
| **Power & torque:** | 37bhp/58lb ft |
| **Engine:** | Normally aspirated 875cc four cylinder, petrol, carburettor, 8 valves |
| **Drivetrain:** | Front-engine RWD |
| **Structure:** | Monocoque |
| **Transmission:** | Four-speed manual |
| **Weight:** | 990kg |

**PRICE GUIDE**

| | |
|---|---|
| **Launch price:** | £681 |
| **Excellent:** | £6500 |
| **Good:** | £3600 |
| **Average:** | £2000 |
| **Project:** | £1200 |

## HILLMAN
### Minx Series I-IIIc

Hillman's new generation of family cars had smart and nicely-rounded styling, inspired by contemporary American trends. Sunbeam Rapiers and Singer Gazelles also used the same basic shell and body, but it was the Minx for the masses that was the big seller of course. With better performance and handling, plus more space inside, the Series cars were a significant step forward. Rootes fiddled with the formula almost every year; major changes included the 1390cc overhead valve engine rising to 1494cc with the Series III of 1958.

**SPECIFICATIONS**

| | |
|---|---|
| **Years produced:** | 1956-1963 (341,681 in total) |
| **Performance:** | 0-60mph: 27.7sec<br>Top speed: 77mph |
| **Power & torque:** | 48bhp/N/A |
| **Engine:** | Normally aspirated 1390cc four cylinder, petrol, carburettor, 8 valves |
| **Drivetrain:** | Front-engine RWD |
| **Structure:** | Monocoque |
| **Transmission:** | Four-speed manual |
| **Weight:** | 965kg |

**PRICE GUIDE**

| | |
|---|---|
| **Launch price:** | £748 |
| **Excellent:** | £3700 |
| **Good:** | £2250 |
| **Average:** | £1000 |
| **Project:** | £500 |

## HILLMAN
### Super Minx

What had been planned as the new Minx eventually appeared in 1961 as the Hillman Super Minx. As it was bigger, heavier and (therefore) more expensive, Rootes had decided to release it as a separate model, with 'Super' added to highlight its improvements over the standard Minx. The bodyshell kept the family resemblance; underneath the mechanicals were mainly Minx. As well as the saloon and estate (left), there was a rather becoming four-seater convertible from 1962 (now worth twice saloon prices).

**SPECIFICATIONS**

| | |
|---|---|
| **Years produced:** | 1961-1967 |
| **Performance:** | 0-60mph: 22.5sec<br>Top speed: 83mph |
| **Power & torque:** | 58bhp/86lb ft |
| **Engine:** | Normally aspirated 1592cc four cylinder, petrol, carburettor, 8 valves |
| **Drivetrain:** | Front-engine RWD |
| **Structure:** | Monocoque |
| **Transmission:** | Four-speed manual |
| **Weight:** | 1069kg |

**PRICE GUIDE (double for convertible)**

| | |
|---|---|
| **Launch price:** | £856 |
| **Excellent:** | £3750 |
| **Good:** | £2000 |
| **Average:** | £1000 |
| **Project:** | £400 |

## HILLMAN
### Imp

A heroic failure for Rootes, the 1963 Imp was the company's attempt to tackle the Mini. And it was a great little machine, with a 37bhp alloy 875cc Coventry Climax engine mounted in the back. The all-independent suspension made it nimble on bends and the opening rear screen added practicality. Had it come along before the Mini, it might have been the big little star instead of BMC's baby. However, reliability issues and suspicion about its unusual nature robbed it of sales and it never recovered, despite being available until 1976.

**SPECIFICATIONS**

| | |
|---|---|
| **Years produced:** | 1963-1976 (440,032 in total) |
| **Performance:** | 0-60mph: 18.5sec<br>Top speed: 81mph |
| **Power & torque:** | 39bhp/52lb ft |
| **Engine:** | Normally aspirated 875cc four cylinder, petrol, carburettor, 8 valves |
| **Drivetrain:** | Rear-engine RWD |
| **Structure:** | Monocoque |
| **Transmission:** | Four-speed manual |
| **Weight:** | 694kg |

**PRICE GUIDE**

| | |
|---|---|
| **Launch price:** | £508 |
| **Excellent:** | £4250 |
| **Good:** | £3000 |
| **Average:** | £1300 |
| **Project:** | £600 |

## HILLMAN
### Avenger/Avenger Tiger

The regular Avenger seemed to go out of fashion really quickly. So much so that it has almost zero classic appeal. Except that in 1973, Hillman produced the Avenger Tiger, intended for club level competition. Its twin-carb engine was easily tuned, with upgrades available off the shelf. Tiger I and Tiger II models were produced, and it was the latter that lasted longer. All models were available in lairy colours with aerodynamic upgrades. Fun, but no Escort RS – and, although few were made, the car lived on in the form of the Chrysler Sunbeam Ti.

**SPECIFICATIONS**

| | |
|---|---|
| **Years produced:** | 1972-1973 (648 in total) |
| **Performance:** | 0-60mph: 11.8sec<br>Top speed: 100mph |
| **Power & torque:** | 78bhp/86lb ft |
| **Engine:** | Normally aspirated 1598cc four cylinder, petrol, carburettor, 8 valves |
| **Drivetrain:** | Front-engine RWD |
| **Structure:** | Monocoque |
| **Transmission:** | Four-speed manual |
| **Weight:** | 880kg |

**PRICE GUIDE (Tiger)**

| | |
|---|---|
| **Launch price:** | £1302 |
| **Excellent:** | £12,500 |
| **Good:** | £7500 |
| **Average:** | £4700 |
| **Project:** | £2250 |

# HONDA

As a successful maker of bicycles and motorbikes, it was almost inevitable that Honda would branch out as the Japanese automobile industry expanded. It unveiled its first car in 1962 and for the first few years concentrated on building small models. As the range grew, so did the cars, with the long-running Civic becoming a common model worldwide. The Accord and Prelude also helped to establish Honda's global reputation, while its sophisticated, mid-engined NSX was a would-be Ferrari. Honda was one of the first mainstream manufacturers to market a hybrid electric vehicle, with its Insight, and remains probably the most respected and prestigious of Japanese auto manufacturers.

## HONDA
### S800

In true Honda tradition the S800's party piece was under the bonnet. Only Honda would create a 791cc engine capable of producing 70bhp at 8000rpm, giving the car an impressive top speed of over 100mph. This impressive performance was not at the cost of fuel economy, which came in at 35mpg. Available as a coupé or a roadster, the car was loved by many but, with a shade over 10,000 sales worldwide, it was not massively successful. The S800 was the last Honda to wear the S badge until the S2000 in 1999. All values currently holding.

**SPECIFICATIONS**

| | |
|---|---|
| **Years produced:** | 1966-1971 (25,853 in total) |
| **Performance:** | 0-60mph: 13.4sec<br>Top speed: 101mph |
| **Power & torque:** | 70bhp/49lb ft |
| **Engine:** | Normally aspirated 791cc four cylinder, petrol, carburettor, 8 valves |
| **Drivetrain:** | Front-engine RWD |
| **Structure:** | Monocoque |
| **Transmission:** | Four-speed manual |
| **Weight:** | 771kg |

**PRICE GUIDE (Convertible in brackets)**

| | |
|---|---|
| **Launch price:** | £779 |
| **Excellent:** | £20,000 (£25,000) |
| **Good:** | £13,000 (£17,000) |
| **Average:** | £8000 (£12,000) |
| **Project:** | £2750 (£4500) |

## HONDA
## N360/N600

Honda's first car designed to compete in Japan's Kei-Class was a fair attempt at bettering Issigonis's Mini. It was launched in 360cc form in 1966 and featured an advanced specification that allowed it to punch well above its weight – its 354cc air-cooled OHC two-cylinder engine pushed out 31bhp, and it handled tidily thanks to a well-engineered FWD layout. In 1968, N360 was upgraded to N600 and blessed with an impressive 85mph top speed. Despite being a technical miracle, it failed to sell in big numbers in Europe – but it's prized today by collectors.

### SPECIFICATIONS (N360)

| | |
|---|---|
| **Years produced:** | 1967-1972 (1,165,441 in total) |
| **Performance:** | 0-60mph: 29.3sec<br>Top speed: 72mph |
| **Power & torque:** | 27bhp/24lb ft |
| **Engine:** | Normally aspirated 354cc twin, petrol, carburettor, 4 valves |
| **Drivetrain:** | Front-engine FWD |
| **Structure:** | Monocoque |
| **Transmission:** | Four-speed manual |
| **Weight:** | 508kg |

### PRICE GUIDE

| | |
|---|---|
| **Launch price:** | £536 |
| **Excellent:** | £5500 |
| **Good:** | £3000 |
| **Average:** | £1750 |
| **Project:** | £450 |

## HONDA
## Z600 Coupé

In Japan, the most important sector of the market is the Kei-class category. If your car falls within its stringent size, engine capacity and weight restrictions, you pay drastically reduced tax and insurance rates. Many Japanese car manufacturers embraced the Kei car and Honda was one of them. The Z600 pushed the limits of the Kei car regulations but, despite its limitations, the Z600 had no problem keeping up with traffic. All UK Z600s were painted orange with a black stripe running along the flanks. Has gained quite a following.

### SPECIFICATIONS

| | |
|---|---|
| **Years produced:** | 1973-1974 (40,586 in total) |
| **Performance:** | 0-60mph: 32.6sec<br>Top speed: 78mph |
| **Power & torque:** | 32bhp/32lb ft |
| **Engine:** | Normally aspirated 599cc twin, petrol, carburettor, 4 valves |
| **Drivetrain:** | Front-engine FWD |
| **Structure:** | Monocoque |
| **Transmission:** | Four-speed manual |
| **Weight:** | 580kg |

### PRICE GUIDE

| | |
|---|---|
| **Launch price:** | £755 |
| **Excellent:** | £8500 |
| **Good:** | £3500 |
| **Average:** | £2200 |
| **Project:** | £750 |

## HONDA
## Civic I/II

Honda stuck to the N600's technical package when it came to creating the Civic, but scaled it up usefully to add global appeal. It arrived on the scene in 1972, making the Civic one of the first superminis to hit the market. Sales in the USA came just in time for Honda to capitalise on the demand for Japanese imports and more economical cars, and became a huge hit Stateside as a result. Sweet engines and a stylish interior stood the Civic apart from the opposition, and paved the way for Honda's huge success. The second generation was the basis of the Triumph Acclaim.

### SPECIFICATIONS (1300 De Luxe)

| | |
|---|---|
| **Years produced:** | 1972-1983 |
| **Performance:** | 0-60mph: 13.5sec<br>Top speed: 90mph |
| **Power & torque:** | 68bhp/72lb ft |
| **Engine:** | Normally aspirated 1335cc four cylinder, petrol, carburettor, 12 valves |
| **Drivetrain:** | Front-engine FWD |
| **Structure:** | Monocoque |
| **Transmission:** | Four-speed manual |
| **Weight:** | 735kg |

### PRICE GUIDE

| | |
|---|---|
| **Launch price:** | £999 |
| **Excellent:** | £3250 |
| **Good:** | £2300 |
| **Average:** | £800 |
| **Project:** | £500 |

## HONDA
## Prelude I

Based on the second-generation Civic but powered by the Accord's free-spinning 1.6-litre engine, the Prelude was a sweet little coupé that sold steadily and paved the way for the company's gradual move upmarket. It was cramped and had an interior that could charitably be described as eccentric, and in the UK it was also rather expensive, all of which limited the Prelude's appeal in comparison with talented players such as the VW Scirocco and Alfasud Sprint. Well-kept examples fetch decent money today, and are even being imported from Japan.

### SPECIFICATIONS

| | |
|---|---|
| **Years produced:** | 1979-1982 (264,842 in total) |
| **Performance:** | 0-60mph: 11.3sec<br>Top speed: 98mph |
| **Power & torque:** | 80bhp/93lb ft |
| **Engine:** | Normally aspirated 1602cc four cylinder, petrol, carburettor, 8 valves |
| **Drivetrain:** | Front-engine FWD |
| **Structure:** | Monocoque |
| **Transmission:** | Five-speed manual |
| **Weight:** | 920kg |

### PRICE GUIDE

| | |
|---|---|
| **Launch price:** | £4950 |
| **Excellent:** | £4000 |
| **Good:** | £2500 |
| **Average:** | £1000 |
| **Project:** | £600 |

## HONDA
## CRX 1.6i/VTEC

One of the important lessons learned from the early CRX was that cars destined for Europe need a lot more rust protection than they do in Japan. Barely any Series 1 CRXs survive today, as many of them lost their battle with rust many years ago. Honda took this on board with the second incarnation of the CRX and, with a line-up of more powerful engines, it became a big hit in Europe. The 1.6 VTEC engine was a real firecracker that, like most Honda engines, delivered all of its power near to its 7600rpm rev-limit. Has developed a real following.

### SPECIFICATIONS

| | |
|---|---|
| **Years produced:** | 1984-1991 |
| **Performance:** | 0-60mph: 8.0sec<br>Top speed: 132mph |
| **Power & torque:** | 158bhp/111lb ft |
| **Engine:** | Normally aspirated 1595cc four cylinder, petrol, electronic fuel injection, 16 valves |
| **Drivetrain:** | Front-engine FWD |
| **Structure:** | Monocoque |
| **Transmission:** | Five-speed manual |
| **Weight:** | 1105kg |

### PRICE GUIDE

| | |
|---|---|
| **Launch price:** | £6950 |
| **Excellent:** | £7500 |
| **Good:** | £5000 |
| **Average:** | £2250 |
| **Project:** | £1000 |

## HONDA NSX

The world's first everyday-useable supercar. When it was launched in 1990 it left the Italian competition for dead in terms of reliability, practicality and build quality, causing Ferrari to up its game. And those same qualities make it a joy today. The chassis – all aluminium like the bodywork – was perfected at Suzuka with input from Ayrton Senna. Bigger 3.2-litre engine arrived in 1997; facelift came in 2002. Despite its brilliance, the NSX never sold in great numbers and today the best examples are highly prized, although targas and autos less so.

**SPECIFICATIONS (3.0)**

| | |
|---|---|
| **Years produced:** | 1990-2005 |
| **Performance:** | 0-60mph: 5.3sec<br>Top speed: 157mph |
| **Power & torque:** | 274bhp/209lb ft |
| **Engine:** | Normally aspirated 2977cc V6, petrol, electronic fuel injection, 24v |
| **Drivetrain:** | Mid-engine RWD |
| **Structure:** | Monocoque |
| **Transmission:** | Five-speed manual |
| **Weight:** | 1350kg |

**PRICE GUIDE**

| | |
|---|---|
| **Launch price:** | £58,000 |
| **Excellent:** | £65,000 |
| **Good:** | £45,000 |
| **Average:** | £35,000 |
| **Project:** | £20,000 |

## HONDA Integra Type-R

The 'DC2' Integra Type-R ranks among the very best front-wheel-drive cars ever made. The naturally aspirated 1.8-litre VTEC four-cylinder was hand assembled, produced 104bhp per litre, reached peak power at a heady 8000rpm, and its limiter didn't cut in until 9000rpm. This was backed up by a stiff chassis, a limited-slip diff and a bare-essentials cabin (with super-snug Recaros). Colour choice limited to white, red and black. Round headlights indicate a UK car; rectangular ones a Japanese import.

**SPECIFICATIONS**

| | |
|---|---|
| **Years produced:** | 1996-2000 |
| **Performance:** | 0-60mph: 6.2sec<br>Top speed: 145mph |
| **Power & torque:** | 187bhp/131lb ft |
| **Engine:** | Normally aspirated 1797cc four cylinder, petrol, electronic injection, 16 valves |
| **Drivetrain:** | Front-engine FWD |
| **Structure:** | Monocoque |
| **Transmission:** | Five-speed manual |
| **Weight:** | 1101kg |

**PRICE GUIDE**

| | |
|---|---|
| **Launch price:** | £19,500 |
| **Excellent:** | £12,000 |
| **Good:** | £7000 |
| **Average:** | £5000 |
| **Project:** | £3000 |

## HONDA S2000

Honda's 50th birthday present to itself, the S2000 had an enviable combination of ingredients. With 237bhp, its VTEC engine was the most powerful naturally aspirated 2-litre four-cylinder ever fitted to a production car. This was mated to a six-speed close-ratio gearbox, backed up by a stiff 'X-beam' steel shell, all-wishbone suspension and limited-slip diff. The slightly soft chassis didn't quite gel with the screaming engine, but the S2000 still makes an intriguing alternative to a Boxster. Late run-out cars can command £20k-plus.

**SPECIFICATIONS**

| | |
|---|---|
| **Years produced:** | 1999-2009 (110,000 built) |
| **Performance:** | 0-60mph: 6.1sec<br>Top speed: 150mph |
| **Power & torque:** | 237bhp/153lb ft |
| **Engine:** | Normally aspirated 1997cc four cylinder, petrol, electronic injection, 16 valves |
| **Drivetrain:** | Front-engine RWD |
| **Structure:** | Monocoque |
| **Transmission:** | Six-speed manual |
| **Weight:** | 1260kg |

**PRICE GUIDE**

| | |
|---|---|
| **Launch price:** | £25,995 |
| **Excellent:** | £15,000 |
| **Good:** | £9500 |
| **Average:** | £5000 |
| **Project:** | £3000 |

## HONDA Accord Type-R

The '90s Accord seemed an unlikely candidate for a Type-R makeover, but what a transformation. Sound-proofing was reduced, the sunroof ditched, Recaro seats and a titanium gearknob installed. The 2.2-litre four had 209bhp, a 7500rpm red line and that all-important VTEC kick above 5500rpm – a signature of hotter Hondas. A high-rise rear wing (optional, but most have it), larger wheels, firmer suspension and a limited-slip differential completed the package. Rare too: fewer than 2000 were sold in the UK. Values slowly edging up.

**SPECIFICATIONS**

| | |
|---|---|
| **Years produced:** | 1999-2003 |
| **Performance:** | 0-60mph: 7.2sec<br>Top speed: 142mph |
| **Power & torque:** | 209bhp/158lb ft |
| **Engine:** | Normally aspirated 2157cc four cylinder, petrol, electronic injection, 16 valves |
| **Drivetrain:** | Front-engine FWD |
| **Structure:** | Monocoque |
| **Transmission:** | Five-speed manual |
| **Weight:** | 1306kg |

**PRICE GUIDE**

| | |
|---|---|
| **Launch price:** | £22,995 |
| **Excellent:** | £4000 |
| **Good:** | £2850 |
| **Average:** | £1700 |
| **Project:** | £1000 |

# HUMBER

ESTABLISHED IN Coventry in 1868 as a bicycle business, Thomas Humber's company had moved on to cars by 1898. Between the wars, its products became known for being well-engineered and rugged. When the Rootes Group took over in 1930, it set up Humber as the luxury arm of its operation; the Royal family, Winston Churchill and Field Marshall Montgomery were all customers. Big Humbers continued after the war but, not long after Chrysler took over the struggling Rootes concern in 1964, these larger cars were dropped and the smaller-proportioned Sceptre flew the flag for Humber until the demise of the marque in 1976, when the Anglo-French Chrysler 180 took over as flagship.

## HUMBER
# Super Snipe/Pullman II-IV

A curious blend of the old-style Super Snipes/ Pullmans and the freshly-redesigned Hawks. The cabin and rear end weren't touched, but the front was given a Raymond Loewy makeover, with headlamps now incorporated into the wings. And running boards, which had been dropped in 1940, enjoyed a surprise revival. Dropheads were offered until 1950, and these can fetch up to double the quoted prices. Subtle improvements continued until 1952 and the MkIV model, which finally adopted the complete Hawk body style.

**SPECIFICATIONS**

| | |
|---|---|
| **Years produced:** | 1948-1957 (56,935 in total) |
| **Performance:** | 0-60mph: 20.6sec<br>Top speed: 81mph |
| **Power & torque:** | 100bhp/N/A |
| **Engine:** | Normally aspirated 4086cc straight six, petrol, carburettor, 12 valves |
| **Drivetrain:** | Front-engine RWD |
| **Structure:** | Separate chassis |
| **Transmission:** | Four-speed manual |
| **Weight:** | 1247kg |

**PRICE GUIDE**

| | |
|---|---|
| **Launch price:** | £1144 |
| **Excellent:** | £9500 |
| **Good:** | £6200 |
| **Average:** | £2500 |
| **Project:** | £800 |

## HUMBER
# Hawk MkIII-VIA

For the new Humber Hawk, the Rootes Group turned to legendary American stylist Raymond Loewy, who created an American-flavoured and modern design with a very imposing and elongated front end. The look endured to include the MkVIA version until this was dropped in 1957. Although the first MkIII cars used the same 1944cc four-cylinder sidevalve engine and gearbox as previous Hawks, independent front suspension was introduced. Further changes included a bigger engine for the 1950s MkIV.

**SPECIFICATIONS**

| | |
|---|---|
| **Years produced:** | 1949-1957 (59,282 in total) |
| **Performance:** | 0-60mph: 30.7sec<br>Top speed: 71mph |
| **Power & torque:** | 56bhp/N/A |
| **Engine:** | Normally aspirated 1944cc four cylinder, petrol, carburettor, 8 valves |
| **Drivetrain:** | Front-engine RWD |
| **Structure:** | Separate chassis |
| **Transmission:** | Four-speed manual |
| **Weight:** | 1247kg |

**PRICE GUIDE**

| | |
|---|---|
| **Launch price:** | £799 |
| **Excellent:** | £6500 |
| **Good:** | £4250 |
| **Average:** | £2000 |
| **Project:** | £800 |

## HUMBER
# Hawk Series I-IVA

Unitary construction reached Humber with the Hawk Series 1 of 1957. Trumpeted as the largest bodyshell being built in the UK at the time, its size was due to Transatlantic styling: a big dollop of Detroit converted to Coventry dimensions. The 2267cc overhead valve engine from the previous generation of Hawk, giving 83mph from its 73bhp, was retained until the final Series IVA model. Series II cars had disc brakes, but the biggest change to the family came with the MkIV of 1964, when the cabin changed to a sleeker profile with more glass.

**SPECIFICATIONS**

| | |
|---|---|
| **Years produced:** | 1957-1967 (41,191 in total) |
| **Performance:** | 0-60mph: 20.6sec<br>Top speed: 83mph |
| **Power & torque:** | 73bhp/N/A |
| **Engine:** | Normally aspirated 2267cc four cylinder, petrol, carburettor, 8 valves |
| **Drivetrain:** | Front-engine RWD |
| **Structure:** | Monocoque |
| **Transmission:** | Four-speed manual |
| **Weight:** | 1433kg |

**PRICE GUIDE**

| | |
|---|---|
| **Launch price:** | £1261 |
| **Excellent:** | £6000 |
| **Good:** | £4250 |
| **Average:** | £1850 |
| **Project:** | £800 |

## HUMBER
# Super Snipe I-VA

As was Rootes' way, the final generation of Humber Super Snipe continued with the practice of using the less powerful, less luxurious Hawk as its basis, but giving it more power (and two more cylinders) plus some extra class-conscious touches. The original 1958 Series Super Snipes had a 2651cc six-cylinder engine, which rose to 2965cc the following year. For 1960 the nose was smartly restyled with quad-headlamps, one of the first British cars to have this arrangement and something never bestowed upon the Hawk. Add 20% for Series I models.

**SPECIFICATIONS**

| | |
|---|---|
| **Years produced:** | 1958-1967 (30,031 in total) |
| **Performance:** | 0-60mph: 19.0sec<br>Top speed: 92mph |
| **Power & torque:** | 105bhp/N/A |
| **Engine:** | Normally aspirated 2651cc straight six, petrol, carburettor, 12 valves |
| **Drivetrain:** | Front-engine RWD |
| **Structure:** | Monocoque |
| **Transmission:** | Three-speed manual with overdrive |
| **Weight:** | 1492kg |

**PRICE GUIDE**

| | |
|---|---|
| **Launch price:** | £1494 |
| **Excellent:** | £8000 |
| **Good:** | £5750 |
| **Average:** | £2200 |
| **Project:** | £1000 |

## HUMBER
# Sceptre SI-II

Rootes introduced a new range of mid-sized cars in the early 1960s. At the top of this badge engineering tree, which also comprised the Hillman Super Minx and Singer Vogue, was the Humber Sceptre. More sporty than usual for a Humber – originally, the Sceptre was to be the new Sunbeam Rapier – the bodyshell was considerably altered from the other offshoots with a wraparound screen, quad-headlamps and a lowered roofline. The Series II of 1965 saw Rootes' well-liked 1725cc engine adopted, albeit with a cheaper Hillman-influenced nose.

**SPECIFICATIONS**

| | |
|---|---|
| **Years produced:** | 1963-1967 (28,996 in total) |
| **Performance:** | 0-60mph: 17.1sec<br>Top speed: 90mph |
| **Power & torque:** | 80bhp/91lb ft |
| **Engine:** | Normally aspirated 1592cc four cylinder, petrol, carburettor, 8 valves |
| **Drivetrain:** | Front-engine RWD |
| **Structure:** | Monocoque |
| **Transmission:** | Four-speed manual |
| **Weight:** | 1124kg |

**PRICE GUIDE**

| | |
|---|---|
| **Launch price:** | £977 |
| **Excellent:** | £4750 |
| **Good:** | £3250 |
| **Average:** | £1800 |
| **Project:** | £750 |

# INNOCENTI

INNOCENTI MADE ITS name making Lambretta scooters during the 1950s, and made the logical move into car manufacture in 1961, initially building Italian versions of the Austin A40 (but with a proper hatchback) and Austin-Healey Sprite. It became a successful business during the 1960s building Minis and BMC 1100s, before being purchased by an acquisitive British Leyland in 1972. That wasn't a happy marriage, and although the rebodied hatchback Mini of 1973 was a success, the local version of the Allegro (called Regent) was not. The partnership dissolved in 1975 as BL disintegrated, and Innocenti was picked up by Alejandro de Tomaso the following year. The marque died in 1997.

## INNOCENTI Spider/C

Italian company Innocenti established itself as a car manufacturer by taking BMC products and making them a whole lot more appealing. The Tom Tjaada-styled Spider (pictured) and its coupé sister (known simply as the Innocenti C) were based on the Austin-Healey Sprite – itself a good-looking car – but somehow the Innocenti versions managed to look even more appealing and Euro-chic. Few were exported, and even fewer made it to the UK, where the high price compared with BMC's car made it a non-starter. Exclusive and fun if you can find one.

**SPECIFICATIONS**

| | |
|---|---|
| **Years produced:** | 1961-1970 (7658 in total) |
| **Performance:** | 0-60mph: 20.5sec<br>Top speed: 86mph |
| **Power & torque:** | 43bhp/52lb ft |
| **Engine:** | Normally aspirated 948cc four cylinder, petrol, carburettor, 8 valves |
| **Drivetrain:** | Front-engine RWD |
| **Structure:** | Monocoque |
| **Transmission:** | Four-speed manual |
| **Weight:** | 602kg |

**PRICE GUIDE (Spider)**

| | |
|---|---|
| **Launch price:** | N/A in UK |
| **Excellent:** | £17,000 |
| **Good:** | £10,000 |
| **Average:** | £5750 |
| **Project:** | £2750 |

## INNOCENTI Mini 90/120

By the 1970s, everyone knew that the Mini needed a hatchback. But with BL firefighting elsewhere, it was a project that was prioritised behind more profitable models. However, Innocenti couldn't wait and commissioned Bertone to style a new hatchback body for its Mini, which was losing out against the Fiat 127 on the Italian market. The resulting car was stylish and had many people asking why BL couldn't do the same. A few made it to the UK, but rust was a major problem. The sporting De Tomaso version was a striking and apt replacement for the Mini-Cooper.

**SPECIFICATIONS**

| | |
|---|---|
| **Years produced:** | 1974-1983 |
| **Performance:** | 0-60mph: 11.9sec<br>Top speed: 90mph |
| **Power & torque:** | 65bhp/72lb ft |
| **Engine:** | Normally aspirated 1275cc four cylinder, petrol, carburettor, 8 valves |
| **Drivetrain:** | Front-engine FWD |
| **Structure:** | Monocoque |
| **Transmission:** | Four-speed manual |
| **Weight:** | 715kg |

**PRICE GUIDE**

| | |
|---|---|
| **Launch price:** | N/A in UK |
| **Excellent:** | £6500 |
| **Good:** | £3000 |
| **Average:** | £1500 |
| **Project:** | £1000 |

# ISO

AFTER TRYING its hand at producing fridges, scooters, air-conditioning and the Isetta bubblecar, Iso turned its attention to the luxury car market in 1962 with the Rivolta, a steel-bodied car with more than a passing resemblance to the Gordon-Keeble GK1. Like all subsequent Isos it was powered by an American V8 engine. The car Iso is best remembered for, the Grifo, created by Giotto Bizzarrini, was launched the following year and stayed in production until Iso closed its doors in 1974. With a range of cars that had reached their sell-by date, the final nail was driven into the company's coffin by the oil crisis and huge downward pressure on speed limits.

## ISO Rivolta

The Rivolta was an example of the Italo-American breed that proved popular during the 1960s and '70s and which allowed drivers to sample Ferrari-style glamour and performance without the price. The Rivolta had all the credentials to deliver the goods: Giugiaro styling; Bizzarini chassis and a 140mph top speed from its General Motors-sourced V8. Under the skin its box-section frame with de Dion rear suspension was a recipe for success and, indeed, the Rivolta sold nearly 800 examples during its eight-year production run. Values currently holding.

**SPECIFICATIONS**

| | |
|---|---|
| **Years produced:** | 1962-1970 (797 in total) |
| **Performance:** | 0-60mph: 7.8sec<br>Top speed: 135mph |
| **Power & torque:** | 300bhp/360lb ft |
| **Engine:** | Normally aspirated 5354cc V8, petrol, carburettor, 16 valves |
| **Drivetrain:** | Front-engine RWD |
| **Structure:** | Spaceframe |
| **Transmission:** | Four-speed manual |
| **Weight:** | 1549kg |

**PRICE GUIDE**

| | |
|---|---|
| **Launch price:** | £3999 |
| **Excellent:** | £75,000 |
| **Good:** | £50,000 |
| **Average:** | £35,000 |
| **Project:** | £20,000 |

# ISO
## Grifo

Continuing the Iso formula, the Grifo was another appealing 'bitza' that transcended the sum of its parts to become something of a supercar pacesetter. The Corvette power unit was good for 300bhp and gave the sleek Bertone-bodied grand tourer a 150mph-plus top speed with acceleration to match. Considered very much a rich playboy's supercar, the Grifo had the handling and poise to cut it against Ferrari, Maserati and Lamborghini's finest. Survival rate is reasonably good, although you'll struggle to find an unrestored car. Values up.

### SPECIFICATIONS

| | |
|---|---|
| **Years produced:** | 1963-1974 (322 in total) |
| **Performance:** | 0-60mph: 7.0sec<br>Top speed: 143mph |
| **Power & torque:** | 300bhp/360lb ft |
| **Engine:** | Normally aspirated 5354cc V8, petrol, carburettor, 16 valves |
| **Drivetrain:** | Front-engine RWD |
| **Structure:** | Spaceframe |
| **Transmission:** | Four-speed manual |
| **Weight:** | 1450kg |

### PRICE GUIDE

| | |
|---|---|
| **Launch price:** | £5950 |
| **Excellent:** | £235,000 |
| **Good:** | £190,000 |
| **Average:** | £150,000 |
| **Project:** | £90,000 |

# ISO
## Fidia

The gorgeous Giugiaro-styled Fidia started out as the Rivolta S4 when it was launched at the 1967 Frankfurt motor show, but with such an arresting style it seemed only right to have its own name in 1969. Initially promoted as '*le quattro poltrone piu veloci del mondo*' ('the world's fastest four-seater'), the Fidia picked up a degree of celebrity kudos (John Lennon had one), but sales were never strong enough to sustain the company as the crises of the 1970s deepened. Few come up for sale these days; despite mixed pedigree, they command good prices.

### SPECIFICATIONS

| | |
|---|---|
| **Years produced:** | 1967-1975 (192 in total) |
| **Performance:** | 0-60mph: 8.0sec<br>Top speed: 137mph |
| **Power & torque:** | 300bhp/360lb ft |
| **Engine:** | Normally aspirated 5354cc V8, petrol, carburettor, 16 valves |
| **Drivetrain:** | Front-engine RWD |
| **Structure:** | Spaceframe |
| **Transmission:** | Four-speed manual |
| **Weight:** | 1500kg |

### PRICE GUIDE

| | |
|---|---|
| **Launch price:** | £7225 |
| **Excellent:** | £80,000 |
| **Good:** | £60,000 |
| **Average:** | £45,000 |
| **Project:** | £25,000 |

# ISO
## Grifo 7-Litre

Although it was no slouch, Iso decided that the standard Grifo needed a shot of additional power to get on terms with the Ferrari Daytona and Maserati Ghibli. This was duly delivered thanks to a 7.0-litre (427ci) engine delivering no less than 390bhp. By 1968 supercar standards this was serious stuff and pushed Iso to the head of the pack. Top speed was a claimed 170mph and 0-60mph was around six seconds – quick even by today's standards. The Grifo disappeared from new car price lists when Iso went out of business in 1974. Values flying.

### SPECIFICATIONS

| | |
|---|---|
| **Years produced:** | 1969-1974 (90 in total) |
| **Performance:** | 0-60mph: 6.1sec<br>Top speed: 171mph |
| **Power & torque:** | 390bhp/460lb ft |
| **Engine:** | Normally aspirated 6999cc V8, petrol, carburettor, 16 valves |
| **Drivetrain:** | Front-engine RWD |
| **Structure:** | Spaceframe |
| **Transmission:** | Four-speed manual |
| **Weight:** | 1410kg |

### PRICE GUIDE

| | |
|---|---|
| **Launch price:** | £8700 |
| **Excellent:** | £350,000 |
| **Good:** | £275,000 |
| **Average:** | £175,000 |
| **Project:** | £110,000 |

# ISO
## Lele

Iso believed in platform sharing so it's understandable that the underpinnings used for the Grifo and Fidia were also put to good use when concocting a replacement for the Rivolta. Unlike the original car, the Lele failed to impress buyers who were turned off by the clumsy Gandini-styled coupé. Given that the 1973 oil crisis killed supercar sales stone dead, struggling Iso didn't have enough in the cupboard to ride the storm, and disappeared in 1974. The last few Leles were powered by a Ford V8 and offered with automatic transmission.

### SPECIFICATIONS

| | |
|---|---|
| **Years produced:** | 1969-1974 (317 in total) |
| **Performance:** | 0-60mph: 7.3sec<br>Top speed: 155mph |
| **Power & torque:** | 350bhp/361lb ft |
| **Engine:** | Normally aspirated 5358cc V8, petrol, carburettor, 16 valves |
| **Drivetrain:** | Front-engine RWD |
| **Structure:** | Spaceframe |
| **Transmission:** | Four-speed manual |
| **Weight:** | 1640kg |

### PRICE GUIDE

| | |
|---|---|
| **Launch price:** | £7725 |
| **Excellent:** | £35,000 |
| **Good:** | £23,000 |
| **Average:** | £15,000 |
| **Project:** | £8000 |

# ISUZU

THE TOKYO Ishikawajima Shipuilding and Engineering Co started out by making licence-built Wolseleys between 1918 and 1927. With valuable experience gained, the company turned its attention to making its own, US-inspired cars until the onset of World War Two. Various mergers and acquisitions later, Isuzu Motors was born in 1949. Its first self-designed production car, the Bellel, arrived in 1961, and was built alongside Isuzu's own version of the Hillman Minx. In 1971, General Motors took a stake in the company, and all subsequent Isuzus were based upon its platforms, including the Gemini – a version of the GM T-Car that lent itself to becoming the basis of the Piazza.

## ISUZU
### 117 Coupé

During its formative years, the Japanese car industry leaned on European designers to inject a sense of style into its cars. For the sporting version of Isuzu's forgettable Florian saloon, Giorgetto Giugiaro (while at Ghia) was commissioned to come up with a suitably export-friendly design. The Isuzu 117 Coupé was the result and, for the class of '68, it was very impressive indeed and remaining in production until 1981. Engines were mostly twin-cams with the exception of the original 1.6 and – unusually – a 2.2-litre diesel. Double these prices for early hand-built cars.

**SPECIFICATIONS (1800)**

| | |
|---|---|
| **Years produced:** | 1968-1981 |
| **Performance:** | 0-60mph: 9.5sec<br>Top speed: 112mph |
| **Power & torque:** | 115bhp/112lb ft |
| **Engine:** | Normally aspirated 1818cc four cylinder, petrol, carburettor, 8 valves |
| **Drivetrain:** | Front-engine RWD |
| **Structure:** | Monocoque |
| **Transmission:** | Four-speed manual |
| **Weight:** | 1070kg |

**PRICE GUIDE (round headlight car in brackets)**

| | |
|---|---|
| **Launch price:** | N/A in UK |
| **Excellent:** | £10,000 (£15,000) |
| **Good:** | £6000 (£8500) |
| **Average:** | £3500 (£4200) |
| **Project:** | £1250 (£1800) |

## ISUZU
### Piazza

When it came to replacing the 117, Isuzu once again turned to Giugiaro (now running Italdesign) – this time adopting his Ace of Clubs design. Humble saloon mechanicals again formed the basis for a coupé, this time from the Gemini (closely related to the Vauxhall Chevette). The rudimentary suspension layout struggled to harness the power of its 2.0-litre turbo engine, so the company turned to Lotus. The Norfolk engineers did a good job, but not enough to save the Piazza in the UK. It's now a popular retro classic, thanks to its exploitable RWD chassis.

**SPECIFICATIONS (Turbo)**

| | |
|---|---|
| **Years produced:** | 1980-1990 (114,000 in total) |
| **Performance:** | 0-60mph: 8.4sec<br>Top speed: 130mph |
| **Power & torque:** | 150bhp/166lb ft |
| **Engine:** | Turbocharged 1994cc four cylinder, petrol, electronic fuel injection, 8 valves |
| **Drivetrain:** | Front-engine RWD |
| **Structure:** | Monocoque |
| **Transmission:** | Five-speed manual |
| **Weight:** | 1247kg |

**PRICE GUIDE**

| | |
|---|---|
| **Launch price:** | £11,950 |
| **Excellent:** | £3500 |
| **Good:** | £1850 |
| **Average:** | £1200 |
| **Project:** | £650 |

# JAGUAR

FOUNDED BY William Lyons in 1922 as Swallow Sidecars (soon abbreviated to SS), 'Jaguar' was only originally used as one of the firm's model designations. Following the Second World War – when SS had very unfortunate connotations – the whole business simply became Jaguar instead. The newly christened company became a world leader with cars like the XK and E-type, while the XJ saloon was the mainstay of the British Leyland years from 1968 to 1984. After a period in the private sector, Jaguar was sold to Ford and thence to Indian industrial giant Tata, with whose financial might it has enjoyed a renaissance, culminating in the F-type, a true successor to the legendary 'E'.

## JAGUAR
### 1.5 Litre Saloon

This is the entry-level model in a threesome of elegant saloons that went a very long way towards cementing Jaguar's position as the pre-eminent producer of sporting four-doors. Despite its modest engine capacity, the 1.5 Litre was quick enough to justify its styling. Introduced on the eve of World War Two, and brought back shortly afterwards, its technical specification didn't look that advanced (a rigid axle was no great shakes by 1945), but the whole exceeded the sum of the parts. Values are modest considering its place in Jaguar's history.

**SPECIFICATIONS**

| | |
|---|---|
| **Years produced:** | 1938-1949 (13,046 in total) |
| **Performance:** | 0-60mph: 25.1sec<br>Top speed: 72mph |
| **Power & torque:** | 65bhp/97lb ft |
| **Engine:** | Normally aspirated 1776cc four cylinder, petrol, carburettor, 8 valves |
| **Drivetrain:** | Front-engine RWD |
| **Structure:** | Separate chassis |
| **Transmission:** | Four-speed manual |
| **Weight:** | 1346kg |

**PRICE GUIDE**

| | |
|---|---|
| **Launch price:** | £684 |
| **Excellent:** | £35,000 |
| **Good:** | £25,000 |
| **Average:** | £17,000 |
| **Project:** | £7000 |

## JAGUAR
### 3.5 Litre Saloon/DHC

Rather like the 1.5 Litre Jaguar, but with rather a lot more power on tap, the 3.5 really was the first of the new-generation Jaguar saloons with the pace to back up its looks. The performance was impressive for a saloon car, especially for a pre-war car, thanks in no small part to the 125bhp it pushed out. Most of them ended up being exported and, as a result, are now scarce in the UK. Despite this, values lag behind the more illustrious sports cars – although the beautiful drophead version in particular has been steadily rising in recent years.

**SPECIFICATIONS**

| | |
|---|---|
| **Years produced:** | 1938-1951 (14,215 in total) |
| **Performance:** | 0-60mph: 14.7sec<br>Top speed: 92mph |
| **Power & torque:** | 125bhp/136lb ft |
| **Engine:** | Normally aspirated 3485cc straight six, petrol, carburettor, 12 valves |
| **Drivetrain:** | Front-engine RWD |
| **Structure:** | Separate chassis |
| **Transmission:** | Four-speed manual |
| **Weight:** | 1626kg |

**PRICE GUIDE (Drophead in brackets)**

| | |
|---|---|
| **Launch price:** | £889 |
| **Excellent:** | £70,000 (£90,000) |
| **Good:** | £45,000 (£65,000) |
| **Average:** | £25,000 (£40,000) |
| **Project:** | £11,000 (£15,000) |

## JAGUAR
## 2.5 Litre/MkV

The first properly post-war Jaguar saloon was actually a bit of a stop-gap between the pre-war cars and the all-new metal on the horizon. The sweeping bodywork was all-new, but quite similar to what had come before, while the chassis would go on to underpin all of Jaguar's '50s saloons. Independent front suspension finally made an appearance, bringing the MkV into line with its rivals, and improving road manners. The limited production run – especially of the drophead – means finding the right one takes time.

### SPECIFICATIONS

| | |
|---|---|
| **Years produced:** | 1946-1951 (8905 in total) |
| **Performance:** | 0-60mph: 17sec<br>Top speed: 87mph |
| **Power & torque:** | 125bhp/N/A |
| **Engine:** | Normally aspirated 2663cc straight six, petrol, carburettor, 12 valves |
| **Drivetrain:** | Front-engine RWD |
| **Structure:** | Separate chassis |
| **Transmission:** | Four-speed manual |
| **Weight:** | 1676kg |

### PRICE GUIDE (Drophead in brackets)

| | |
|---|---|
| **Launch price:** | £1189 |
| **Excellent:** | £40,000 (£75,000) |
| **Good:** | £30,000 (£50,000) |
| **Average:** | £20,000 (£35,000) |
| **Project:** | £9000 (£12,000) |

## JAGUAR
## XK120

Quite simply, the XK120 was the sports car that elevated Jaguar into the big time. Introduced at the 1948 Earls Court Motor Show, it featured an all-new twin-overhead camshaft straight six that lived well into the 1980s. And it was fast: the 120mph maximum speed was the reason for its name. Yet the XK120's real forté was its sheer all-round driving pleasure for such a low price. The earliest aluminium roadsters are easily the most valuable, with SEs commanding a premium, and the later Drophead Coupés not far behind.

### SPECIFICATIONS

| | |
|---|---|
| **Years produced:** | 1948-1954 (7612 in total) |
| **Performance:** | 0-60mph: 10.1sec<br>Top speed: 120mph |
| **Power & torque:** | 190bhp/200lb ft |
| **Engine:** | Normally aspirated 3442cc straight six, petrol, carburettor, 12 valves |
| **Drivetrain:** | Front-engine RWD |
| **Structure:** | Separate chassis |
| **Transmission:** | Four-speed manual |
| **Weight:** | 1346kg |

### PRICE GUIDE (Alloy car in brackets)

| | |
|---|---|
| **Launch price:** | £1263 |
| **Excellent:** | £135,000 (£375,000) |
| **Good:** | £90,000 (£300,000) |
| **Average:** | £70,000 (£225,000) |
| **Project:** | £40,000 (£135,000) |

## JAGUAR
## XK120 Coupé

Once Jaguar had caught up with XK120 Roadster demand and production of steel-bodied examples was running smoothly, it developed the coupé to widen appeal. Aside from the obvious addition of a roof, the biggest difference between this and the Roadster is the use of a mostly steel floorpan, in place of plywood. As with all XK120s there was an SE option, which added 20bhp through the use of high-lift cams, uprated valve springs and a lightened flywheel. Wire wheels were fitted to SEs, and were a popular retro-fit on non-SE models.

### SPECIFICATIONS

| | |
|---|---|
| **Years produced:** | 1951-1954 (2678 in total) |
| **Performance:** | 0-60mph: 9.9sec<br>Top speed: 120mph |
| **Power & torque:** | 160bhp/195lb ft |
| **Engine:** | Normally aspirated 3442cc straight six, petrol, carburettor, 12 valves |
| **Drivetrain:** | Front-engine RWD |
| **Structure:** | Separate chassis |
| **Transmission:** | Four-speed manual |
| **Weight:** | 1143kg |

### PRICE GUIDE

| | |
|---|---|
| **Launch price:** | £1389 |
| **Excellent:** | £110,000 |
| **Good:** | £70,000 |
| **Average:** | £50,000 |
| **Project:** | £25,000 |

## JAGUAR
## MkVII-IX

Jaguar's post-war run of desirable and capable large saloons was truly kickstarted with the arrival of the MkVII in 1950. Although similar under the skin to the outgoing MkV, the newer car's forward-looking styling and use of the XK engine (first seen in the XK120) made it a genuine 100mph proposition. Subsequent revisions refined the big saloon and added even more power into the mix. Surprisingly good to drive for their size, for many years the MkVII-IX saloons lacked the cult following of later cars, but values have been climbing steadily.

### SPECIFICATIONS

| | |
|---|---|
| **Years produced:** | 1951-1961 (47,190 in total) |
| **Performance:** | 0-60mph: 13.6sec<br>Top speed: 104mph |
| **Power & torque:** | 160bhp/195lb ft |
| **Engine:** | Normally aspirated 3442cc straight six, petrol, carburettor, 12 valves |
| **Drivetrain:** | Front engine RWD |
| **Structure:** | Separate chassis |
| **Transmission:** | Four-speed manual/three-speed auto |
| **Weight:** | 1753kg |

### PRICE GUIDE

| | |
|---|---|
| **Launch price:** | £1276 |
| **Excellent:** | £50,000 |
| **Good:** | £30,000 |
| **Average:** | £20,000 |
| **Project:** | £10,000 |

## JAGUAR
## XK140

Introduced as a replacement to the XK120, the XK140 was slightly bigger and heavier, but more powerful. These characteristics changed the whole driving experience and, rather than being an uncompromised sports car, it was a much more comfortable and relaxed long distance cruiser – unless you were in the coupé's tight rear seats. Upgrades included the standard fitment of rack and pinion steering (from the C-type) as well as optional power-assisted steering. Coupés are worth less than roadsters, but are still very satisfying to drive.

### SPECIFICATIONS

| | |
|---|---|
| **Years produced:** | 1954-57 (2808 in total) |
| **Performance:** | 0-60mph: 8.4sec<br>Top speed: 121mph |
| **Power & torque:** | 210bhp/213lb ft |
| **Engine:** | Normally aspirated 3442cc straight six, petrol, carburettor, 12 valves |
| **Drivetrain:** | Front-engine RWD |
| **Structure:** | Separate chassis |
| **Transmission:** | Four-speed manual with overdrive |
| **Weight:** | 1422kg |

### PRICE GUIDE (Roadster/DHC in brackets)

| | |
|---|---|
| **Launch price:** | £1616 |
| **Excellent:** | £90,000 (£135,000) |
| **Good:** | £60,000 (£110,000) |
| **Average:** | £35,000 (£80,000) |
| **Project:** | £20,000 (£35,000) |

## JAGUAR
### MkI 2.4/3.4

The starting point in Jaguar's move into the compact sporting saloon market. Just like the D-type, the 2.4 featured unitary construction – it was the first roadgoing Jaguar to do so. The detuned, short-stroke 2.4-litre XK engine didn't tax the independent suspension set-up much, but was a restful cruiser. Much better was the 3.4, which had the XK140 engine. In recent times, the Mk1 has emerged from the Mk2's shadow to become a star in its own right. Comparitive rarity helps values. Concours examples might even command as much as £100k.

**SPECIFICATIONS**

**Years produced:** 1955-1959 (c37,000 in total)
**Performance:** 0-60mph: 9.1sec (3.4)
Top speed: 120mph
**Power & torque:** 210bhp/216lb ft
**Engine:** Normally aspirated 3442cc straight six, petrol, carburettor, 12 valves
**Drivetrain:** Front-engine RWD
**Structure:** Monocoque
**Transmission:** Four-speed manual/three-speed auto
**Weight:** 1448kg

**PRICE GUIDE (3.4 in brackets)**

**Launch price:** £1344 (£1672)
**Excellent:** £30,000 (£50,000)
**Good:** £20,000 (£35,000)
**Average:** £15,000 (£25,000)
**Project:** £10,000 (£15,000)

## JAGUAR
### XK150

At 1364kg, the XK150 was not the lightweight sports car the XK120 had once been. Certain aluminium panels were added to try to reduce the overall weight, but it still tipped the scales at 50kg more than the XK140. It was, though, the first Jaguar available with all-round disc brakes. In 1958, the XK150S was launched with an impressive 250bhp at first, then 265bhp a year later when the capacity increased to 3.8 litres. An S is worth an extra 15%, but the big money is paid for the Roadster and especially the 3.8S version (add 25% for these).

**SPECIFICATIONS**

**Years produced:** 1957-1961 (4450 in total)
**Performance:** 0-60mph: 8.5sec (3.4S)
Top speed: 124mph
**Power & torque:** 250bhp/240lb ft
**Engine:** Normally aspirated 3442cc straight six, petrol, carburettor, 12 valves
**Drivetrain:** Front-engine RWD
**Structure:** Monocoque
**Transmission:** Four-speed manual with overdrive
**Weight:** 1447kg

**PRICE GUIDE (Roadster/DHC in brackets)**

**Launch price:** £1764
**Excellent:** £90,000 (£135,000)
**Good:** £70,000 (£110,000)
**Average:** £45,000 (£70,000)
**Project:** £25,000 (£35,000)

## JAGUAR
### Mk2 2.4/3.4/3.8

Generally speaking, facelifted cars don't look as good as those they replace. But Jaguar tore up the form book with its compact saloon, which was transformed by the fitment of revised upper door pressings, a deeper windscreen and wider rear track. The effect was to brighten the interior and update the overall style and, in doing so, to create the most iconic '60s saloon of them all. The 2.4 was still a modest performer, but the 3.4 and 3.8 were the super-saloons of their day. Today, a concours 3.8 manual could fetch as much as £100,000.

**SPECIFICATIONS**

**Years produced:** 1959-1967 (83,976 of all Mk2s)
**Performance:** 0-60mph: 8.5sec (3.8)
Top speed: 125mph
**Power & torque:** 220bhp/240lb ft
**Engine:** Normally aspirated 3781cc straight six, petrol, carburettor, 12 valves
**Drivetrain:** Front-engine RWD
**Structure:** Monocoque
**Transmission:** Four-speed manual
**Weight:** 1499kg

**PRICE GUIDE (2.4/3.4/3.8)**

**Launch price:** £1534
**Excellent:** £27,000/£45,000/£55,000
**Good:** £18,000/£27,000/£33,000
**Average:** £12,000/£15,000/£18,000
**Project:** £5000/£8000/£8000

## JAGUAR
### MkX/420G

Jaguar really went for it when devising a flagship to replace its MkIX saloon. Physically huge and easily capable of seating six, the MkX was far more agile than its corpulent footprint implied, especially in 3.8-litre manual form. All cars had power-assisted steering as standard and disc brakes all-round with servo assistance. The torquier 4.2-litre engine arrived in 1964 and made the MkX even more effortless; then it became the 420G in 1966. The car lived on to form the basis of the DS420 limousine, favoured by mayors all over Britain. Values have climbed in recent years.

**SPECIFICATIONS (3.8)**

**Years produced:** 1961-1970 (18,519/5763 in total)
**Performance:** 0-60mph: 12.1sec
Top speed: 120mph
**Power & torque:** 265bhp/260lb ft
**Engine:** Normally aspirated 3781cc straight six, petrol, carburettor, 12 valves
**Drivetrain:** Front-engine RWD
**Structure:** Monocoque
**Transmission:** Four-speed manual
**Weight:** 1791kg

**PRICE GUIDE**

**Launch price:** £2393
**Excellent:** £40,000
**Good:** £20,000
**Average:** £10,000
**Project:** £5000

## JAGUAR
### E-type 3.8

When it launched in 1961, the E-type redefined the way in which we all viewed sports cars, and how much you could expect for your money. Although the famous 150mph runs in pre-production models were never replicated by owners, the E-type was still fast enough to send sports car manufacturers back to their drawing boards. The recipe was simple enough: a 3.8-litre XK engine married to a beautiful and aerodynamic body designed by Malcolm Sayer, underpinned by all-independent suspension. All E-type values have softened in last 12-18 months.

**SPECIFICATIONS**

**Years produced:** 1961-1964 (46,300 in total)
**Performance:** 0-60mph: 7.1sec
Top speed: 149mph
**Power & torque:** 265bhp/260lb ft
**Engine:** Normally aspirated 3781cc straight six, petrol, carburettor, 12 valves
**Drivetrain:** Front-engine RWD
**Structure:** Monocoque
**Transmission:** Four-speed manual
**Weight:** 1219kg

**PRICE GUIDE (Roadster in brackets)**

**Launch price:** £2098
**Excellent:** £160,000 (£225,000)
**Good:** £125,000 (£195,000)
**Average:** £75,000 (£110,000)
**Project:** £40,000 (£60,000)

## JAGUAR
### S-type

Because the XJ6 was still years away from production, Jaguar decided that it needed an intermediate model to plug the gap between the Mk2 and the enormous MkX. Using the Mk2 as a starting point, the company created the S-type by adding the MkX's independent rear suspension and extended rear end, as well as improving its interior. The end result was a luxury sports saloon that actually drives better than the car it was based upon, usefully extending the life (and profitability) of the Mk2 platform. Still slightly undervalued.

**SPECIFICATIONS**

**Years produced:** 1963-1968 (24,900 in total)
**Performance:** 0-60mph: 14.2sec
Top speed: 114mph
**Power & torque:** 210bhp/216lb ft
**Engine:** Normally aspirated 3442cc straight six, petrol, carburettor, 12 valves
**Drivetrain:** Front-engine RWD
**Structure:** Monocoque
**Transmission:** Four-speed manual/three-speed auto
**Weight:** 1626kg

**PRICE GUIDE**

**Launch price:** £1669
**Excellent:** £30,000
**Good:** £20,000
**Average:** £12,000
**Project:** £5000

## JAGUAR
### E-type 4.2 S1

Jaguar continued to develop the E-type throughout its life. The first results of this programme of improvements came in 1964, when the newly enlarged XK engine was installed under the E-type's bonnet. Although the maximum power output remained unchanged at 265bhp, torque was usefully increased, improving driveability. Other improvements included the arrival of a fully-synchronised Moss gearbox. Coupés aren't as highly prized as Roadsters; 2+2s remain relatively unloved (top money for a 2+2 is c£65,000).

**SPECIFICATIONS**

**Years produced:** 1964-1968 (c63,000 in total)
**Performance:** 0-60mph: 7.4sec
Top speed: 139mph
**Power & torque:** 265bhp/283lb ft
**Engine:** Normally aspirated 4235cc straight six, petrol, carburettor, 12 valves
**Drivetrain:** Front-engine RWD
**Structure:** Monocoque
**Transmission:** Four-speed manual
**Weight:** 1295kg

**PRICE GUIDE (Coupé/Roadster)**

**Launch price:** £1896
**Excellent:** £130,000/£220,000
**Good:** £110,000/£180,000
**Average:** £65,000/£110,000
**Project:** £35,000/£50,000

## JAGUAR
### 420

The Jaguar 420 was basically an S-type fitted with the 4.2-litre version of the XK engine. The front end was completely restyled, previewing the upcoming XJ6 (as well as aping the 420G) and, although it looked slightly unbalanced, there was no question over the way the 420 went. By the time of its launch in 1968, the MkI/Mk2 platform had been stretched as far as possible in an attempt to maintain sales. The interior was further improved with the arrival of a padded facia top, the first move towards the safety-led designs that followed.

**SPECIFICATIONS**

**Years produced:** 1966-1968 (9600 in total)
**Performance:** 0-60mph: 9.9sec
Top speed: 123mph
**Power & torque:** 245bhp/283lb ft
**Engine:** Normally aspirated 4235cc straight six, petrol, carburettor, 12 valves
**Drivetrain:** Front-engine RWD
**Structure:** Monocoque
**Transmission:** Four-speed manual/three-speed auto
**Weight:** 1676kg

**PRICE GUIDE**

**Launch price:** £1930
**Excellent:** £25,000
**Good:** £15,000
**Average:** £8000
**Project:** £5000

## JAGUAR
### 240/340

After a good innings, the Mk2 was finally facelifted in 1967 to become the 240/340. These models were priced below the outgoing cars, and evidence of cost-cutting was most notable inside where leather gave way to man-made Ambla. Despite its popularity in the Mk2, power-assisted steering wasn't even offered as an option on the 240, making the car feel a lot more ponderous than it might. The engine was upgraded with a 4.2-style cylinder head, and that finally gave it enough power to break the 100mph barrier. The 340 in particular is good value.

**SPECIFICATIONS**

**Years produced:** 1967-1969 (6840 in total)
**Performance:** 0-60mph: 8.8sec (340)
Top speed: 115mph
**Power & torque:** 133bhp/146lb ft
**Engine:** Normally aspirated 3442cc straight six, petrol, carburettor, 12 valves
**Drivetrain:** Front-engine RWD
**Structure:** Monocoque
**Transmission:** Four-speed manual/three-speed auto
**Weight:** 1524kg

**PRICE GUIDE (240/340)**

**Launch price:** £1365
**Excellent:** £25,000/£30,000
**Good:** £18,000/£22,000
**Average:** £10,000/£15,000
**Project:** £4000/£6000

## JAGUAR
### E-type S1½/2

The Series 1½ was, as the name suggests, a bridge between the SI and S2. Only current for a year, its main role seems to have been to introduce new-style headlamps with no covers but more chrome trim. They may not have looked so good but they worked better. The S2 brought a larger grille opening, heavier front bumpers and bigger lamps. Mechanical changes were limited to an improved cooling system and (thank goodness!) better brakes, changed from Lockheed to Girling. Again, 2+2s are unloved, hence a tidy one can be as little as £50k.

**SPECIFICATIONS**

**Years produced:** 1967-1970 (c19,000 in total)
**Performance:** 0-60mph: 7.4sec
Top speed: 149mph
**Power & torque:** 265bhp/283lb ft
**Engine:** Normally aspirated 4235cc straight six, petrol, carburettor, 12 valves
**Drivetrain:** Front-engine RWD
**Structure:** Monocoque
**Transmission:** Four-speed manual
**Weight:** 1295kg

**PRICE GUIDE (Coupe/Roadster)**

**Launch price:** £2117
**Excellent:** £90,000/£140,000
**Good:** £65,000/£110,000
**Average:** £45,000/£80,000
**Project:** £20,000/£40,000

TURRINO WHEELS
TURRINO
Jaguar E-Type
6.5 x 15 wide lip Turrino alloy rims, stainless centres & spokes
Thanks to Morten Kjeldgaard for the use of the photo and his car
info@turrinowheels.com
+44 (0) 1780 470460
www.turrinowheels.com

Martin Robey GROUP
Classic Parts Specialist for Jaguar and Jensen Cars
JAGUAR & DAIMLER
JENSEN
JENSEN HEALEY
JAGUAR - E-TYPE - MKII - 420 - S-TYPE - XJ - XJS - XK JENSEN - INTERCEPTOR - HEALEY - GT - CV8
FUEL TANKS FOR CLASSIC JAGUARS
MKII
E-TYPE SI, SII, SIII
S-TYPE / 420
XJ SERIES
COMPLETE E-TYPE SERIES I & II BODYSHELLS & SUB ASSEMBLIES
PRIVILEGE ACCOUNT
UP TO 10% DISCOUNT*
*EXCLUDING E-TYPE BONNETS AND SOFT TRIM
FOR 12 MONTHS
VISIT WWW.MARTINROBEY.COM FOR MORE INFO
E-TYPE SERIES I & II FLOOR ASSEMBLIES FROM £1648.50+VAT
ENGINE - BODY - BRAKING - COOLING - FUEL SYSTEM - SUSPENSION - STEERING - EXHAUST - CLUTCH - GEARBOX - ELECTRICAL - MORE...
Tel: +44(0)2476 386 903
E-mail: info@martinrobey.co.uk
Web: www.martinrobey.com

## JAGUAR XJ6 S1 2.8/4.2

This was the first generation of the very successful XJ model range, and introduced a new platform strategy that saw a single range replace the mixed bag of previous models. It wasn't an entirely new car under the skin, but the whole package set new standards for grace, space and pace. The fully independent suspension gave world-beating ride/handling, and though the 2.8-litre version of the XK engine lacked urge and reliability, the 4.2 was still a strong performer. According to some specialists, truly exceptional S1 4.2s can command c£50k.

### SPECIFICATIONS

**Years produced:** 1968-1973 (59,077 in total)
**Performance:** 0-60mph: 8.8sec (4.2)
Top speed: 124mph
**Power & torque:** 245bhp/280lb ft
**Engine:** Normally aspirated 4235cc straight six, petrol, carburettor, 12 valves
**Drivetrain:** Front-engine RWD
**Structure:** Monocoque
**Transmission:** Four-speed manual/three-speed auto
**Weight:** 1537kg

**PRICE GUIDE (2.8/4.2)**
**Launch price:** £1797
**Excellent:** £18,000/£30,000
**Good:** £12,000/£20,000
**Average:** £6000/£10,000
**Project:** £1500/£2500

## JAGUAR E-type S3 V12

Walter Hassan, one of Britain's pre-eminent post-war engineers and mastermind behind the Coventry Climax Formula 1 engines, worked with Harry Mundy to produce an all-new V12. It was Jaguar's first production V12, designed for maximum smoothness with single overhead camshafts. When fitted in the E-type, the turbine-smooth V12 was hailed an immediate success, especially in the USA – which market it was aimed at. Maximum speed was still shy of 150mph though, and fuel consumption was atrocious. Roadster prices strong.

### SPECIFICATIONS

**Years produced:** 1971-1975 (c26,000 in total)
**Performance:** 0-60mph: 6.4sec
Top speed: 146mph
**Power & torque:** 276bhp/304lb ft
**Engine:** Normally aspirated 5343cc V12, petrol, carburettor, 24 valves
**Drivetrain:** Front-engine RWD
**Structure:** Monocoque
**Transmission:** Four-speed manual/three-speed auto
**Weight:** 1410kg

**PRICE GUIDE (2+2 Coupé/Roadster)**
**Launch price:** £2245
**Excellent:** £70,000/£140,000
**Good:** £55,000/£110,000
**Average:** £28,000/£70,000
**Project:** £15,000/£25,000

## JAGUAR XJ12 S1-3

Although the Hassan-designed V12 impressed in the E-type Series 3, it found its true home in the larger XJ bodyshell. With up to 300bhp in the later versions, it offered dominant performance and up to 150mph in the right circumstances. The XJ12's mechanical smoothness could be its undoing as age and unreliability took hold – engines would drop a cylinder or two without being too noticeable, while the complex suspension set-up could break the odd bush here or there without the driver feeling a thing. Engine and body restorations are expensive.

### SPECIFICATIONS

**Years produced:** 1972-1993 (42,461 in total)
**Performance:** 0-60mph: 7.4sec
Top speed: 146mph
**Power & torque:** 265bhp/304lb ft
**Engine:** Normally aspirated 5343cc V12, petrol, carburettor, 24 valves
**Drivetrain:** Front-engine RWD
**Structure:** Monocoque
**Transmission:** Automatic
**Weight:** 1760kg

**PRICE GUIDE (Series 1/2/3)**
**Launch price:** £3726
**Excellent:** £32,000/£26,000/£20,000
**Good:** £22,000/£15,000/£12,000
**Average:** £12,000/£8000/£5000
**Project:** £3500/£2500/£2000

## JAGUAR XJ 5.3C

Prematurely announced in the summer of 1973, it would be a further two years before the two-door XJ finally went on sale. The timing wasn't exactly great, though, as the world had been pushed into the midst of a fuel crisis and then recession, all of which took the best part of a decade to be overcome. A vinyl roof was fitted as standard to all models, and the frameless windows (which caused much trouble during development) were noisy at speed and often leaked. Fuel injection was added later, and caused further problems. Values have been climbing fast.

### SPECIFICATIONS

**Years produced:** 1973-1977
**Performance:** 0-60mph: 7.6sec
Top speed: 148mph
**Power & torque:** 285bhp/294lb ft
**Engine:** Normally aspirated 5343cc V12, petrol, carburettor, 24 valves
**Drivetrain:** Front-engine RWD
**Structure:** Monocoque
**Transmission:** Three-speed automatic
**Weight:** 1762kg

**PRICE GUIDE**
**Launch price:** £6850
**Excellent:** £45,000
**Good:** £35,000
**Average:** £20,000
**Project:** £7000

## JAGUAR XJ6 Coupé

The V12-powered XJ 5.3C might have stolen all of the glamour at the launch of the two-door XJ, but the 4.2-litre version comfortably sold the most. With a 20kg weight advantage over the four-door XJ, acceleration was slightly improved, but cruising really was this car's forté. Sales never met management's expectations, mainly because of the recession, but also because of a rapidly deteriorating reputation on the back of poor build quality during the 1970s. Never made it into Series III form, which hints at unfulfilled potential.

### SPECIFICATIONS

**Years produced:** 1973-1977 (8378 in total)
**Performance:** 0-60mph: 8.8sec
Top speed: 124mph
**Power & torque:** 173bhp/227lb ft
**Engine:** Normally aspirated 4235cc straight six, petrol, carburettor, 12 valves
**Drivetrain:** Front-engine RWD
**Structure:** Monocoque
**Transmission:** Four-speed manual/three-speed auto
**Weight:** 1689kg

**PRICE GUIDE**
**Launch price:** £5480
**Excellent:** £37,500
**Good:** £25,000
**Average:** £15,000
**Project:** £5000

# JAGUAR
## XJ6 S2/S3

Jaguar made many detail improvements to the XJ to create the S2. The new heating and ventilation system was welcome, as was the improved fuel economy. The interior received a substantial update, but the only visual differences externally were the smaller grille and raised bumpers, to help the XJ meet US safety regulations. Unfortunately, the Series II was plagued with poor build quality and reliability issues. Many of those were addressed with the rubber-bumpered S3 introduced in 1979. Add up to 25% for rare S3 Vanden Plas.

### SPECIFICATIONS

**Years produced:** 1973-1986
**Performance:** 0-60mph: 8.8sec
Top speed: 124mph
**Power & torque:** 167bhp/230lb ft
**Engine:** Normally aspirated 4235cc straight six, petrol, carburettor, 12 valves
**Drivetrain:** Front-engine RWD
**Structure:** Monocoque
**Transmission:** Four-speed manual/three-speed auto
**Weight:** 1680kg

### PRICE GUIDE

**Launch price:** £2253
**Excellent:** £25,000
**Good:** £15,000
**Average:** £8000
**Project:** £2000

# JAGUAR
## XJ-S

Based on a shortened XJ6 chassis, the XJ-S was the long awaited E-type replacement and ended up missing the mark by several miles, even if it successfully continued in the spirit of the Series 3. The new car was not a sporting drive in the way the earlier E-types were, but a grand tourer, with over-light power-assisted steering. In fact the XJ-S remained in production for more than 20 years – the longest run of any Jaguar – and went on to become a financial success for the company. Early manuals are sought-after and can fetch up to 40% more.

### SPECIFICATIONS

**Years produced:** 1975-1981
**Performance:** 0-60mph: 6.9sec
Top speed: 153mph
**Power & torque:** 285bhp/294lb ft
**Engine:** Normally aspirated 5343cc V12, petrol, electronic fuel injection, 12 valves
**Drivetrain:** Front-engine RWD
**Structure:** Monocoque
**Transmission:** Four-speed manual/three-speed auto
**Weight:** 1770kg

### PRICE GUIDE

**Launch price:** £8900
**Excellent:** £30,000
**Good:** £17,000
**Average:** £10,000
**Project:** £3000

# JAGUAR
## XJ-S Cabriolet

The launch of a new Jaguar engine isn't exactly a common event, and is usually executed in stages. As when the first V12s were fitted to the E-type, when Jaguar finished its slant-six AJ6 engine in 1983, it installed it in the XJ-S before making it available to saloon buyers three years later. The Cabrio XJ-S was a halfway house to full open-top motoring, as it retained a heavy (and ugly) roll-over structure and the coupé's passenger doors. It paved the way for a full convertible in later years. V12 version came in 1985 and makes a great tourer.

### SPECIFICATIONS

**Years produced:** 1983-1987
**Performance:** 0-60mph: 8.7sec (3.6)
Top speed: 136mph
**Power & torque:** 223bhp/277lb ft
**Engine:** Normally aspirated 3690cc straight six, petrol, electronic fuel injection, 24 valves
**Drivetrain:** Front-engine RWD
**Structure:** Monocoque
**Transmission:** Five-speed manual/three-speed auto
**Weight:** 1611kg

### PRICE GUIDE (3.6/5.3)

**Launch price:** £33,400
**Excellent:** £25,000/£30,000
**Good:** £15,000/£18,000
**Average:** £10,000/£12,000
**Project:** £4000/£5000

# JAGUAR
## XJ-S 3.6

As well as ushering in the Cabriolet bodyshell, the arrival of the AJ6 engine gave Jaguar the chance to refocus the car's marketing. Although it lacked the ultimate grunt of the V12, the new engine and manual transmission package added sporting appeal into the mix and, although it shouldn't have worked, the six-cylinder XJ-S actually went on to sell rather well. High performance 'TWR' versions were introduced to reflect the tastes of the 1980s, as well as a range of questionable body kits and trim options, which diluted the original car's appeal.

### SPECIFICATIONS

**Years produced:** 1983-1991 (92,750 in total)
**Performance:** 0-60mph: 7.4sec
Top speed: 142mph
**Power & torque:** 225bhp/240lb ft
**Engine:** Normally aspirated 3690cc straight six, petrol, electronic fuel injection, 24 valves
**Drivetrain:** Front-engine RWD
**Structure:** Monocoque
**Transmission:** Five-speed manual/three-speed auto
**Weight:** 1660kg

### PRICE GUIDE

**Launch price:** £19,249
**Excellent:** £20,000
**Good:** £12,000
**Average:** £6000
**Project:** £2000

# JAGUAR
## XJ6 (XJ40)

Development work on the XJ40 had begun in the early 70s, and eventually took more than 15 years. The long wait was down to the 1973 fuel crisis, then a lack of funding and management direction from BL. The new XJ6 finally made its debut in 1986, by which time its styling looked rather dated. Despite this, the XJ40 was great to drive, although early cars had various niggles. Later 3.2 and 4.0 versions from 1990 onwards are the best sorted. Also desirable is the 6-litre V12 version that appeared in 1993. Many have rusted away, but the very best are now prized.

### SPECIFICATIONS

**Years produced:** 1986-1994 (204,474 in total)
**Performance:** 0-60mph: 8.2sec (4.0)
Top speed: 141mph
**Power & torque:** 223bhp/278lb ft
**Engine:** Normally aspirated 3980cc straight six, petrol, electronic fuel injection, 24v
**Drivetrain:** Front-engine RWD
**Structure:** Monocoque
**Transmission:** Five-speed manual/four-speed auto
**Weight:** 1810kg

### PRICE GUIDE

**Launch price:** £25,200
**Excellent:** £12,000
**Good:** £8000
**Average:** £3000
**Project:** £1000

## JAGUAR XJ-S V12 Convertible

This is the best of the XJ-S range, a full convertible this time, with an electrically operated hood that incorporates a heated glass rear window. And as if to confirm its status, the XJ-S Convertible was only available with the V12 engine and an auto gearbox. To make up for the loss of the Cabriolet's roof supports, there's a new subframe at the front to brace the body, though they are still not completely free of scuttle shake. The V12 Convertible made a comeback from 1993-95 with a 6.0-litre engine and 2+2 seating. These cars are worth c25% more.

**SPECIFICATIONS**

| | |
|---|---|
| Years produced: | 1988-1991, 1993-1995 |
| Performance: | 0-60mph: 8.0sec<br>Top speed: 150mph |
| Power & torque: | 285bhp/309lb ft |
| Engine: | Normally aspirated 5343cc V12, petrol, electronic fuel injection, 24 valves |
| Drivetrain: | Front-engine RWD |
| Structure: | Monocoque |
| Transmission: | Three-speed automatic |
| Weight: | 1900kg |

**PRICE GUIDE**

| | |
|---|---|
| Launch price: | £36,000 |
| Excellent: | £35,000 |
| Good: | £25,000 |
| Average: | £15,000 |
| Project: | £5000 |

## JAGUAR XJS/XJR-S

1991's restyle of the XJS (note the lack of hyphen now) brought longer rear side windows and a much smoother tail, along with a redesigned interior that features even more wood trim. There were many changes under the skin too, including the increase in engine capacity for the six-cylinder to create the 4.0 version. The V12 continued as the flagship, particularly well-regarded in high-performance XJR-S guise. There was also a Convertible model, with extra bracing to improve the body's rigidity. Add up to 50% to the prices for these cars.

**SPECIFICATIONS**

| | |
|---|---|
| Years produced: | 1991-1996 (27,406 of all variants) |
| Performance: | 0-60mph: 7.3sec (4.0)<br>Top speed: 143mph |
| Power & torque: | 235bhp/285lb ft |
| Engine: | Normally aspirated 3980cc straight six, petrol, electronic fuel injection, 24v |
| Drivetrain: | Front-engine RWD |
| Structure: | Monocoque |
| Transmission: | Five-speed manual |
| Weight: | 1730kg |

**PRICE GUIDE (XJR-S in brackets)**

| | |
|---|---|
| Launch price: | £33,400 |
| Excellent: | £20,000 (£30,000) |
| Good: | £15,000 (£20,000) |
| Average: | £7000 (£12,000) |
| Project: | £3000 (£5000) |

## JAGUAR XJ/XJR (X300)

Mechanically similar to the XJ40, the styling of Jaguar's mid-1990s saloon recalled earlier XJ models, with the trademark curvaceous bonnet and quad round headlamps making a return. The X300 also made huge steps forward in terms of build quality and reliability, and buyers lapped it up. The 6-litre V12 continued, but the pride of the fleet was the XJR, which thanks to the addition of a supercharger to Jaguar's 4.0 straight-six developed BMW M5 rivalling power. Manual versions are rare and desirable and well worth seeking out.

**SPECIFICATIONS**

| | |
|---|---|
| Years produced: | 1994-1997 (92,038 in total) |
| Performance: | 0-60mph: 5.9sec (XJR)<br>Top speed: 155mph |
| Power & torque: | 321bhp/378lb ft |
| Engine: | Supercharged 3980cc straight six, petrol, electronic fuel injection, 24v |
| Drivetrain: | Front-engine RWD |
| Structure: | Monocoque |
| Transmission: | Five-speed manual/four-speed auto |
| Weight: | 1875kg |

**PRICE GUIDE (XJR in brackets)**

| | |
|---|---|
| Launch price: | £45,450 (XJR) |
| Excellent: | £8000 (£12,000) |
| Good: | £5000 (£7500) |
| Average: | £3000 (£5000) |
| Project: | £1000 (£2000) |

## JAGUAR XJ220

When the XJ220 was unveiled at the 1988 British Motor Show, the crowds were awe-struck. The V12-powered 200mph+ four-wheel-drive supercar had been developed by engineers in their own time and promised to beat the Italians at their own game. Deposits were taken and production was promised for 1990. Two years later, the production version emerged with rear-wheel drive and a twin-turbo V6. Many demanded their deposits back. Today however the XJ220 is being reappraised and revalued as a genuine jaw-dropping supercar and landmark Jag.

**SPECIFICATIONS**

| | |
|---|---|
| Years produced: | 1992-1994 (281 in total) |
| Performance: | 0-60mph: 3.7sec<br>Top speed: 213mph |
| Power & torque: | 542bhp/475lb ft |
| Engine: | Twin-turbocharged 3498cc V6, petrol, electronic fuel injection, 24 valves |
| Drivetrain: | Mid-engine RWD |
| Structure: | Monocoque |
| Transmission: | Five-speed manual |
| Weight: | 1470kg |

**PRICE GUIDE**

| | |
|---|---|
| Launch price: | £415,554 |
| Excellent: | £400,000 |
| Good: | £375,000 |
| Average: | £325,000 |
| Project: | N/A |

## JAGUAR XK8/XKR

The ageing XJS was finally pensioned off in 1996 and replaced by the curvaceous new XK, available as coupé or convertible. Though the chassis was carried over, the 290bhp 4-litre AJ-V8 engine was brand new and gave the XK8 coupé a 0-60mph time of 6.6sec, while top speed was limited to 155mph. Early cars had engine problems, so do your homework. Later 4.2s can fetch up to 50% more than prices here. In 1998, the supercharged XKR was added to the range, peak power rising to 370bhp, 0-60 dropping to just 5.1sec.

**SPECIFICATIONS**

| | |
|---|---|
| Years produced: | 1996-2006 (c90,000 in total) |
| Performance: | 0-60mph: 5.1sec (XKR)<br>Top speed: 155mph (limited) |
| Power & torque: | 370bhp/387lb ft |
| Engine: | Supercharged 3996cc V8, petrol, electronic injection, 32 valves |
| Drivetrain: | Front-engine RWD |
| Structure: | Monocoque |
| Transmission: | Five-speed automatic |
| Weight: | 1641kg |

**PRICE GUIDE (XKR in brackets)**

| | |
|---|---|
| Launch price: | £48,700 (£56,700) |
| Excellent: | £10,000 (£15,000) |
| Good: | £8000 (£12,000) |
| Average: | £4000 (£8000) |
| Project: | £2000 (£4000) |

## JAGUAR XJ8/XJR (X308)

A year after the new AJ-V8 engine appeared in the XK, it also found its way into the XJ saloon, in 237bhp 3.2 and 286bhp 4-litre forms, replacing both the in-line six and V12. Again, early cars had engine problems, so do your homework. This updated 'X308' XJ looked similar to the outgoing model: one change was a sweeping one-piece dash. The manual gearbox was finally dropped, so all V8 XJs have a five-speed auto. As with the XK there was a supercharged option, the 370bhp XJR an appealing Brit alternative to BMW's M5.

**SPECIFICATIONS**

| | |
|---|---|
| **Years produced:** | 1997-2003 (c120,000 in total) |
| **Performance:** | 0-60mph: 5.6sec (XJR) |
| | Top speed: 155mph (limited) |
| **Power & torque:** | 370bhp/387lb ft |
| **Engine:** | Supercharged 3996cc V8, petrol, electronic injection, 32 valves |
| **Drivetrain:** | Front-engine RWD |
| **Structure:** | Monocoque |
| **Transmission:** | Five-speed automatic |
| **Weight:** | 1775kg |

**PRICE GUIDE (XJR in brackets)**

| | |
|---|---|
| **Launch price:** | £40,950 (£51,950) |
| **Excellent:** | £6000 (£10,000) |
| **Good:** | £3000 (£5000) |
| **Average:** | £2000 (£3000) |
| **Project:** | £750 (£1000) |

## JAGUAR S-type/ S-type R

A car that was styled to evoke the classic Mk2 and S-type Jags of the 1960s is now of an age where it is starting to gain classic appeal all of its own. The earliest 'New S-types' are now more than 20 years old, and with a choice of lusty 240bhp V6 or 281bhp V8 petrol engines and lashings of wood and leather, the best are excellent value right now, while the 390bhp supercharged R (0-60mph in 5.6sec) launched in 2002 is a real Q-car (left). Early Ss suffered engine bore wear and patchy build quality, so buy the newest you can afford.

**SPECIFICATIONS**

| | |
|---|---|
| **Years produced:** | 1998-2008 |
| **Performance:** | 0-60mph: 7.8sec (3.0 V6) |
| | Top speed: 146mph |
| **Power & torque:** | 240bhp/221lb ft |
| **Engine:** | Normally aspirated 2976cc V6, petrol, electronic injection, 24 valves |
| **Drivetrain:** | Front-engine RWD |
| **Structure:** | Monocoque |
| **Transmission:** | Five-speed manual/four-speed auto |
| **Weight:** | 1637kg |

**PRICE GUIDE (S-type R in brackets)**

| | |
|---|---|
| **Launch price:** | £27,613 3.0 V6 (£47,400 R) |
| **Excellent:** | £4000 (£10,000) |
| **Good:** | £2000 (£8000) |
| **Average:** | £1000 (£6000) |
| **Project:** | £500 (£2000) |

# JENSEN

BROTHERS RICHARD and Alan Jensen started the family firm as a coachbuilder in 1934, but had built their own car by 1936, using Ford V8 engines. Post-war Jensens were large and impressive machines with the emphasis on grand touring. After experimenting with glassfibre-bodied cars (the 541 and individualistic CV8), Jensen suddenly leapt to fame and some fortune with the handsome and powerful Interceptor, powered by a Chrysler V8. It also built a less-successful but revolutionary four-wheel-drive and ABS-braked version, dubbed FF, but it couldn't repeat the success of the Interceptor, despite a 1970s tie-up with Healey to build sports cars, and bankruptcy struck in 1976.

## JENSEN 541

Although the aerodynamically-styled 541 was launched in 1953, Jensen didn't manage to get it into production until 1955, by which time the decision had been taken to use glassfibre for its body. Most of the running gear came courtesy of Austin, including the hefty 3993cc six-cylinder engine. In the 541's lighter body, it gave a much better account of itself than in BMC's big limos. 1957's 541R had more power and commands a premium, while 1960's 541S was longer and wider for greater space inside. Unusual, characterful and likable.

**SPECIFICATIONS**

| | |
|---|---|
| **Years produced:** | 1954-1962 (549 in total) |
| **Performance:** | 0-60mph: 9.2sec |
| | Top speed: 116mph |
| **Power & torque:** | 130bhp |
| **Engine:** | Normally aspirated 3990cc straight six, petrol, carburettor, 12 valves |
| **Drivetrain:** | Front-engine RWD |
| **Structure:** | Glassfibre body/separate chassis |
| **Transmission:** | Four-speed manual |
| **Weight:** | 1422kg |

**PRICE GUIDE**

| | |
|---|---|
| **Launch price:** | £2147 |
| **Excellent:** | £75,000 |
| **Good:** | £50,000 |
| **Average:** | £32,000 |
| **Project:** | £20,000 |

## JENSEN C-V8

Jensen furthered its knowledge of glassfibre construction with 1962's CV-8, a striking-looking machine characterised by slanting quad headlamps. This time round an enormous 5916cc Chrysler V8 replaced the Austin engine. Mated to an automatic transmission it was capable of pushing the C-V8 to 130mph, but this wasn't enough for Jensen so, in 1964, in went a 335bhp 6276cc. This raised potential speed to 140mph but also meant horrendous fuel consumption. 1965's MkIII saw further tweaks to those front lights. All are surprisingly good to drive.

**SPECIFICATIONS**

| | |
|---|---|
| **Years produced:** | 1962-1965 (500 in total) |
| **Performance:** | 0-60mph: 8.4sec |
| | Top speed: 129mph |
| **Power & torque:** | 305bhp/N/A |
| **Engine:** | Normally aspirated 5916cc V8, petrol, carburettor, 16 valves |
| **Drivetrain:** | Front-engine RWD |
| **Structure:** | Glassfibre body/separate chassis |
| **Transmission:** | Three-speed manual |
| **Weight:** | 1517kg |

**PRICE GUIDE**

| | |
|---|---|
| **Launch price:** | £3861 |
| **Excellent:** | £80,000 |
| **Good:** | £55,000 |
| **Average:** | £30,000 |
| **Project:** | £20,000 |

## JENSEN
### Interceptor/Convertible

One of the biggest and best British bruisers of the luxury GT world, 1966's Interceptor propelled Jensen into the limelight. The handsome lines were by Touring of Milan and, initially, the bodies (steel instead of glassfibre) were built by Vignale in Italy before Jensen switched production to the UK. Power came from a range of big and thirsty Chrysler V8s. The most powerful version – and the most highly prized today – is the SP (for Six-Pack) with its three twin-barrel Holley carburettors. Very best fetch £110k+, say specialists Cropredy Bridge.

**SPECIFICATIONS**

| | |
|---|---|
| **Years produced:** | 1966-1976 (6175/508) |
| **Performance:** | 0-60mph: 7.3sec<br>Top speed: 133mph |
| **Power & torque:** | 325bhp/425lb ft |
| **Engine:** | Normally aspirated 6286cc V8, petrol, carburettor, 16 valves |
| **Drivetrain:** | Front-engine RWD |
| **Structure:** | Monocoque |
| **Transmission:** | Three-speed automatic |
| **Weight:** | 1768kg |

**PRICE GUIDE (Convertible in brackets)**

| | | |
|---|---|---|
| **Launch price:** | £2394 | (£6774) |
| **Excellent:** | £90,000 | (£110,000) |
| **Good:** | £65,000 | (£80,000) |
| **Average:** | £45,000 | (£50,000) |
| **Project:** | £15,000 | (£20,000) |

## JENSEN
### FF

The advanced and forward-thinking Jensen FF was the world's first performance car with permanent four-wheel drive and anti-lock brakes. Introduced in 1966, alongside the Interceptor, it was closely related to that car but had a longer wheelbase, twin vents in the front wings and a bonnet scoop. Mechanically it was very different of course, although the same Chrysler 6276cc V8 did the business under the bonnet. FF stood for Ferguson Formula, the tractor company behind the all-wheel drive system. Concours cars now fetch over £160k.

**SPECIFICATIONS**

| | |
|---|---|
| **Years produced:** | 1968-1971 (320 in total) |
| **Performance:** | 0-60mph: 8.4sec<br>Top speed: 130mph |
| **Power & torque:** | 325bhp/425lb ft |
| **Engine:** | Normally aspirated 6276cc V8, petrol, carburettor, 16 valves |
| **Drivetrain:** | Front-engine AWD |
| **Structure:** | Monocoque |
| **Transmission:** | Three-speed automatic |
| **Weight:** | 1828kg |

**PRICE GUIDE**

| | |
|---|---|
| **Launch price:** | £5340 |
| **Excellent:** | £155,000 |
| **Good:** | £115,000 |
| **Average:** | £85,000 |
| **Project:** | £40,000 |

## JENSEN
### Jensen-Healey

After British Leyland dropped its range of Austin-Healey sports cars, Donald and Geoffrey Healey joined Jensen to develop a successor. The result was the 1972 convertible sports car simply known as the Jensen-Healey, using a mix of different parts from other manufacturers. The 1973cc twin-cam 16-valve engine was from Lotus, the suspension and steering from the Vauxhall Viva and the gearbox was a Sunbeam item. The mix never quite gelled, so this 'Healey remains far more affordable than its Austin predecessors and today something of a bargain.

**SPECIFICATIONS**

| | |
|---|---|
| **Years produced:** | 1972-1976 (10,504 in total) |
| **Performance:** | 0-60mph: 7.8sec<br>Top speed: 119mph |
| **Power & torque:** | 144bhp/134lb ft |
| **Engine:** | Normally aspirated 1973cc four cylinder, petrol, carburettor, 8 valves |
| **Drivetrain:** | Front-engine RWD |
| **Structure:** | Monocoque |
| **Transmission:** | Four-speed manual |
| **Weight:** | 1061kg |

**PRICE GUIDE**

| | |
|---|---|
| **Launch price:** | £1810 |
| **Excellent:** | £14,000 |
| **Good:** | £9000 |
| **Average:** | £6000 |
| **Project:** | £3000 |

## JENSEN
### GT

With Healey's connection with Jensen now ended, the 1975 sporting estate that grew out of the Jensen-Healey convertible in 1975 was simply known as the Jensen GT. It used the same mechanicals – a 1973cc Lotus twin-cam engine mated to a Getrag five-speed gearbox – that, by then, was reliable. But grafting a fixed roof onto what was basically a convertible body still failed to produce a great car, despite the extra practicality and luxurious touches such as a walnut dashboard and electric windows. Rarity boosts values.

**SPECIFICATIONS**

| | |
|---|---|
| **Years produced:** | 1975-1976 (473 in total) |
| **Performance:** | 0-60mph: 8.7sec<br>Top speed: 119mph |
| **Power & torque:** | 144bhp/134lb ft |
| **Engine:** | Normally aspirated 1973cc four cylinder, petrol, carburettor, 8 valves |
| **Drivetrain:** | Front-engine RWD |
| **Structure:** | Monocoque |
| **Transmission:** | Five-speed manual |
| **Weight:** | 1096kg |

**PRICE GUIDE**

| | |
|---|---|
| **Launch price:** | £4178 |
| **Excellent:** | £15,000 |
| **Good:** | £10,000 |
| **Average:** | £6000 |
| **Project:** | £3000 |

# JOWETT

AFTER YEARS of experimentation, brothers William and Benjamin Jowett produced their first cars in Bradford in 1910, powered by the lightweight flat-twin engine that would still be used in their Bradford van after WW2. The cars gained a steady reputation for humble durability, and a four-cylinder version was finally added to the range in 1937. Post war, the company moved upmarket with the Javelin 'executive' saloon and Jupiter sports car, which raced with surprising success at Le Mans. The unreliability of early versions hurt Jowett, but this highly innovative company was ultimately killed off when its body supplier, Briggs, was taken over by Ford in 1953.

## JOWETT
### Javelin

A brave attempt by this small British manufacturer, and technologically advanced for the immediate post-war period. The Javelin was designed by Gerald Palmer to give sporting performance and handling, good aerodynamics and comfortable seating for five. It succeeded on all fronts and they were snapped up by professionals. Innovative and well-built, with torsion bar suspension and lightweight flat-four engine, they still feel surprisingly good to drive today and cruise happily at 65-70mph. Good value today.

**SPECIFICATIONS**

| | |
|---|---|
| **Years produced:** | 1947-1953 (23,307 in total) |
| **Performance:** | 0-60mph: 22.2sec<br>Top speed: 78mph |
| **Power & torque:** | 50bhp/N/A |
| **Engine:** | Normally aspirated 1486cc flat four, petrol, carburettor, 8 valves |
| **Drivetrain:** | Front-engine RWD |
| **Structure:** | Separate chassis |
| **Transmission:** | Four-speed manual |
| **Weight:** | 1003kg |

**PRICE GUIDE**

| | |
|---|---|
| **Launch price:** | £819 |
| **Excellent:** | £8500 |
| **Good:** | £6150 |
| **Average:** | £3350 |
| **Project:** | £1600 |

## JOWETT
### Jupiter

This was Jowett's only sports car and was created by using Javelin mechanical bits in a tubular spaceframe. Though no beauty in the conventional sense, with its high nose and low tail, the body is at least distinctive and was created from a mixture of steel and aluminium panels. The whole front hinges upwards to give superb engine access. The MkIA from 1952 has a larger boot, with a bootlid this time. Three class wins at Le Mans and one in the Monte Carlo Rally proved the Jupiter's worth and attracted enthusiast buyers. Fun to drive, and well regarded.

**SPECIFICATIONS**

| | |
|---|---|
| **Years produced:** | 1950-1953 (825 in total) |
| **Performance:** | 0-60mph: 16.8sec<br>Top speed: 84mph |
| **Power & torque:** | 60bhp/N/A |
| **Engine:** | Normally aspirated 1486cc flat four, petrol, carburettor, 8 valves |
| **Drivetrain:** | Front-engine RWD |
| **Structure:** | Spaceframe |
| **Transmission:** | Four-speed manual |
| **Weight:** | 1003kg |

**PRICE GUIDE**

| | |
|---|---|
| **Launch price:** | £1017 |
| **Excellent:** | £26,000 |
| **Good:** | £17,500 |
| **Average:** | £12,000 |
| **Project:** | £8000 |

# KOENIGSEGG

Koenigsegg

FOUNDED by young Swedish car enthusiast and entrepreneur Christian von Koenigsegg in 1994, Koenigsegg produced its first full production car, the CC8S, in 2002 when Christian was just 30. The car, the initial design of which was penned by Christian himself, was remarkably well-developed and ferociously fast, setting the template for a whole series of increasingly exotic and prodigiously powerful road-going hypercars, all built at the company's base in Ängelholm, Sweden. A number of the cars have featured various green technologies, and in 2019 Koenigsegg sold a 20 per cent stake in the company to National Electric Vehicle Sweden (NEVS) for a reported US$171 million.

## KOENIGSEGG
### CC8S/CCR

Rather as Pagani had done when it launched the Zonda, Koenigsegg shot straight into the upper echelons of the supercar world when it unleashed the CC8S in 2002. Powered by a supercharged V8 originally based on a Ford unit but extensively developed in-house, the CC8S featured full carbonfibe construction and exotic detailing that could stand comparison with the world's best. A more powerful CCR version came next, which briefly held the title of world's fastest car at 241mph before it was eclipsed by Bugatti's Veyron.

**SPECIFICATIONS**

| | |
|---|---|
| **Years produced:** | 2002-2006 (20 in total) |
| **Performance:** | 0-60mph: 3.3sec (CC8S)<br>Top speed: 240mph (claimed) |
| **Power & torque:** | 655bhp/553lb ft |
| **Engine:** | Supercharged 4700cc V8, petrol, electronic injection, 32 valves |
| **Drivetrain:** | Mid-engine RWD |
| **Structure:** | Carbonfibre tub and body |
| **Transmission:** | Six-speed manual |
| **Weight:** | 1175kg |

**PRICE GUIDE**

| | |
|---|---|
| **Launch price:** | £330,000 |
| **Excellent:** | £1,000,000 |
| **Good:** | £800,000 |
| **Average:** | N/A |
| **Project:** | N/A |

# LAGONDA

FROM TINY ACORNS... American Wilbur Gunn built his first twin-cylinder tri-car in his greenhouse in Staines, England in 1906. In the 1920s, his Lagonda marque moved into sports car production and by 1935 it had won at Le Mans. Before the war, WO Bentley was brought in as technical director and designed a V12 engine for use in the firm's products. In 1947, Lagonda was sold to David Brown and paired up with Aston Martin. Lagonda stole all the headlines in 1976 with its astonishing (and astonishingly complicated) saloon with ultra-sharp wedge-shaped styling. The badge lay dormant for many years but Aston Martin plans to use it for a new range of all-electric luxury saloons and SUVs.

## LAGONDA 2.6/3.0

Lagonda's 2.6 was introduced in 1946, just before David Brown took the company over to combine it with Aston Martin. It was a smaller car than pre-war Lagondas, and WO Bentley oversaw the design of its engine and chassis. The latter was advanced for the time, with all-independent suspension. Bodies were saloon or drophead coupé, the open car being worth considerably more today. The Lagonda was relaunched as the 3.0-litre in 1953, with the same chassis, a larger-bore engine and revised bodywork created by Tickford.

**SPECIFICATIONS**

| | |
|---|---|
| Years produced: | 1948-1957 (780 in total) |
| Performance: | 0-60mph: 18.8sec<br>Top speed: 100mph |
| Power & torque: | 105bhp/133lb ft |
| Engine: | Normally aspirated 2580cc straight six, petrol, carburettor, 12 valves |
| Drivetrain: | Front-engine RWD |
| Structure: | Separate chassis |
| Transmission: | Four-speed manual |
| Weight: | 1471kg |

**PRICE GUIDE (DHC in brackets)**

| | |
|---|---|
| Launch price: | £3110 |
| Excellent: | £60,000 (£100,000) |
| Good: | £40,000 (£70,000) |
| Average: | £30,000 (£50,000) |
| Project: | £15,000 (£20,000) |

## LAGONDA Rapide

From the front wheels back, Lagonda's 1961 to 1964 Rapide was a handsome and dignified machine. Ahead of that it was rather more challenging thanks to a sloped quad-headlamp nose and outlandish grilles. Given that it was designed by Touring this look was a big disappointment and no doubt contributed to the fact that only 54 were built. The car used an elongated DB4 chassis with suspension tweaks, and a 236bhp 4-litre six-cylinder engine that wouldn't graduate to Aston Martin until the DB5 three years later. Values are holding steady.

**SPECIFICATIONS**

| | |
|---|---|
| Years produced: | 1961-1964 (55 in total) |
| Performance: | 0-60mph: N/A<br>Top speed: 130mph |
| Power & torque: | 236bhp/265lb ft |
| Engine: | Normally aspirated 3995cc straight six, petrol, carburettor, 12 valves |
| Drivetrain: | Front-engine RWD |
| Structure: | Superleggera |
| Transmission: | Three-speed auto/four-speed manual |
| Weight: | 1715kg |

**PRICE GUIDE**

| | |
|---|---|
| Launch price: | £4950 |
| Excellent: | £225,000 |
| Good: | £175,000 |
| Average: | £120,000 |
| Project: | £50,000 |

## LAGONDA Series 1 V8

Based on the contemporary Aston Martin V8 but with a stretched wheelbase, the 1974 Lagonda four-door saloon was the first car since the 1961 Rapide to wear the Lagonda badge, and it was not a success. Most of the blame can be attached to the 1974 oil crisis, which seriously limited the appeal of any V8-powered supersaloon, let alone one that would rarely see MPG in double figures. In fact the Lagonda was an impressive and capable machine, and is today highly valued by collectors, but during the two years of production just seven were sold.

**SPECIFICATIONS**

| | |
|---|---|
| Years produced: | 1974-1976 (7 in total) |
| Performance: | 0-60mph: 6.2sec<br>Top speed: 149mph |
| Power & torque: | 280bhp/301lb ft |
| Engine: | Normally aspirated 5340cc V8, petrol, fuel injection, 12 valves |
| Drivetrain: | Front-engine RWD |
| Structure: | Superleggera |
| Transmission: | Three-speed auto/five-speed manual |
| Weight: | 2000kg |

**PRICE GUIDE**

| | |
|---|---|
| Launch price: | £14,040 |
| Excellent: | £400,000+ |
| Good: | £350,000 |
| Average: | N/A |
| Project: | N/A |

## LAGONDA Series 2-4

Even Aston Martin wasn't immune to the craziness of the 1970s: behold the strangely glorious Lagonda, launched in 1977, officially the Series 2 but known to everyone as 'the wedge'. If the William Towns lines weren't enough, inside it was a technological tour de force of touch-sensitive switches, digital displays and futuristic gizmos. These proved its Achilles' heel, for the Lagonda soon became best-known for its unreliability. Simplification followed, and then a facelift to soften the lines for the series 4 of 1987. Exceptional late cars can fetch as much as £130k.

**SPECIFICATIONS**

| | |
|---|---|
| Years produced: | 1977-1990 (645 in total) |
| Performance: | 0-60mph: 8.8sec<br>Top speed: 143mph |
| Power & torque: | 280bhp/302lb ft |
| Engine: | Normally aspirated 5340cc V8, petrol, fuel injection, 16 valves |
| Drivetrain: | Front-engine RWD |
| Structure: | Monocoque |
| Transmission: | Three-speed automatic |
| Weight: | 2023kg |

**PRICE GUIDE**

| | |
|---|---|
| Launch price: | £24,570 |
| Excellent: | £115,000 |
| Good: | £85,000 |
| Average: | £50,000 |
| Project: | £30,000 |

# LAMBORGHINI

WEALTHY TRACTOR magnate Ferruccio Lamborghini started building cars after falling out with Enzo Ferrari over how a supercar should be built. Aiming to outdo the Prancing Horse, Lamborghini adopted a rampant bull logo and launched the V12 350GT in 1963. But what really made its name was the mid-engined Miura three years later. Its subsequent run of over-the-top supercars continues to this day, though it's been a rocky road as the company passed first to a Swiss syndicate in 1972, was declared bankrupt in 1977 (but continued production), then went to Chrysler in 1987, and to Audi (via two other owners) in 1998. Thankfully the cars remain as blissfully outrageous as ever.

## LAMBORGHINI
## 350GT

Here's where it all began, allegedly because Ferruccio Lamborghini was unhappy with the level of service he received from Enzo Ferrari when a car he bought from the Scuderia went wrong. When Lamborghini started his sports car company, he poached a number of Ferrari engineers to help create his first car – most notably Giotto Bizzarrini, who created the V12 engine, and Giampaolo Dallara, who sorted out the chassis. When the Touring-bodied 350GT arrived on the scene, Enzo had to take Ferruccio seriously. Values had been soaring in recent years, but have now levelled off.

### SPECIFICATIONS

**Years produced:** 1964-1966 (120 in total)
**Performance:** 0-60mph: 6.8sec
Top speed: 155mph
**Power & torque:** 320bhp/241lb ft
**Engine:** Normally aspirated 3464cc V12, petrol, carburettor, 24 valves
**Drivetrain:** Front-engine RWD
**Structure:** Spaceframe
**Transmission:** Five-speed manual
**Weight:** 1200kg

### PRICE GUIDE

**Launch price:** £6950
**Excellent:** £500,000
**Good:** £400,000
**Average:** £350,000
**Project:** £225,000

## LAMBORGHINI
## 400GT 2+2

Lamborghini commissioned Touring to extend the 350GT. The coachbuilder came up with an all-new body based on a lengthened wheelbase that managed to incorporate a pair of occasional rear seats – it may have looked almost identical to the smaller car, but every panel was changed. To keep keen drivers happy, the newly developed 4.0-litre version of Bizzarni's V12 was installed, maintaining supercar-style performance. Specialist Mike Pullen at Carrera Sport points out that although the 400 is more accomplished, values favour the 350GT.

### SPECIFICATIONS

**Years produced:** 1966-1968 (242 in total)
**Performance:** 0-60mph: 7.5sec
Top speed: 155mph
**Power & torque:** 320bhp/276lb ft
**Engine:** Normally aspirated 3929cc V12, petrol, carburettor, 24 valves
**Drivetrain:** Front-engine RWD
**Structure:** Spaceframe
**Transmission:** Five-speed manual
**Weight:** 1380kg

### PRICE GUIDE

**Launch price:** £7995
**Excellent:** £425,000
**Good:** £375,000
**Average:** £325,000
**Project:** £175,000

## LAMBORGHINI
## Miura P400/P400S

The Miura made its first appearance in chassis form at the 1965 Turin show, attracting orders and deposits before the body itself was even designed. That box chassis (full of holes for lightness) housed an engine and transmission placed transversely just ahead of the rear wheels. The V12 engine sat on top of the gearbox with the two sharing the same oil. Nothing like it had been seen before. Every coachbuilder in Italy clamoured for the opportunity to clothe the chassis. Bertone was chosen, and a legend was born. After years of soaring prices, they've levelled-off recently.

### SPECIFICATIONS (P400S)

**Years produced:** 1966-1968 (475 in total)
**Performance:** 0-60mph: 5.5sec
Top speed: 177mph
**Power & torque:** 370bhp/286lb ft
**Engine:** Normally aspirated 3939cc V12, petrol, carburettor, 24 valves
**Drivetrain:** Mid-engine RWD
**Structure:** Spaceframe
**Transmission:** Five-speed manual
**Weight:** 1040kg

### PRICE GUIDE (S in brackets)

**Launch price:** £10,860
**Excellent:** £900,000 (£1,100,000)
**Good:** £700,000 (£900,000)
**Average:** £600,000 (£750,000)
**Project:** £350,000 (£450,000)

## LAMBORGHINI
## Islero

The Islero was introduced to the public at the 1968 Geneva Motor Show. It was not as aggressive as the Espada or Miura, catering more for the grand touring crowd. However, it offered luxurious benefits such as air conditioning and a more spacious interior, and was designed with one eye on the American market. An S version followed in 1969 which was shortlived, with only 100 being produced. The Islero is named after a fighting bull that killed the famous matador Manuel Rodriguez in August 1947. Values slowly creeping up.

### SPECIFICATIONS

**Years produced:** 1968-1970 (125 in total)
**Performance:** 0-60mph: 6.2sec
Top speed: 165mph
**Power & torque:** 350bhp/290lb ft
**Engine:** Normally aspirated 3929cc V12, petrol, carburettor, 24 valves
**Drivetrain:** Front-engine RWD
**Structure:** Spaceframe
**Transmission:** Five-speed manual
**Weight:** 1460kg

### PRICE GUIDE

**Launch price:** £7950
**Excellent:** £200,000
**Good:** £175,000
**Average:** £150,000
**Project:** £75,000

## LAMBORGHINI
## Miura P400 SV

If the 350/400GTs paved the way for Lamborghini to become a major player in the supercar scene, the trendsetting Miura left Ferrari floundering in its wake. At a time when a mid-engined layout was very much for competition and niche cars, Lamborghini embraced the format for its range-topping sports car. The ultimate series-production Miura was the SV, which had its power boosted to a claimed 385bhp (the SVJ and Jota were specials), and a top speed of around 180mph if you were brave. According to market analysts, a concours-condition SV should now fetch over £2 million.

### SPECIFICATIONS

**Years produced:** 1968-1971 (140 in total)
**Performance:** 0-60mph: 5.0sec
Top speed: 180mph
**Power & torque:** 385bhp/286lb ft
**Engine:** Normally aspirated 3939cc V12, petrol, carburettor, 24 valves
**Drivetrain:** Mid-engine RWD
**Structure:** Spaceframe
**Transmission:** Five-speed manual
**Weight:** 1040kg

### PRICE GUIDE

**Launch price:** £10,860
**Excellent:** £1,900,000
**Good:** £1,450,000
**Average:** £1,200,000
**Project:** N/A

## LAMBORGHINI Espada

In 1968, Lamborghini presented a four-seater GT. Called the Espada 400GT, its styling was inspired by that of the memorable mid-engined Marzal concept car of 1966, and maintained the Marzal's expansive proportions despite being front-engined. The first Espada prototype retained the Marzal's gullwing door design too, which was abandoned for the production model. Despite its four-seater layout, the Espada was almost as agile as its two-seater sisters and every bit as exotic. After several years of soaring prices, they've been pegged back recently.

**SPECIFICATIONS**

| | |
|---|---|
| **Years produced:** | 1968-1978 (186 in total) |
| **Performance:** | 0-60mph: 6.5sec<br>Top speed: 155mph |
| **Power & torque:** | 325bhp/276lb ft |
| **Engine:** | Normally aspirated 3939cc V12, petrol, carburettor, 24 valves |
| **Drivetrain:** | Front-engine RWD |
| **Structure:** | Spaceframe |
| **Transmission:** | Five-speed manual/three-speed auto |
| **Weight:** | 1480kg |

**PRICE GUIDE**

| | |
|---|---|
| **Launch price:** | £10,295 |
| **Excellent:** | £180,000 (more for Series 1 cars) |
| **Good:** | £130,000 |
| **Average:** | £75,000 |
| **Project:** | £35,000 |

## LAMBORGHINI Jarama 400 GT

Never a popular Lamborghini, the Jarama ended up being the company's final front-engined sports car, as after that it ended up concentrating on the mid-engined Countach and Urraco. In a market in which styling counts above all else, the clumsy-looking Jarama struggled against some very elegant rivals, not least the more commodious Lamborghini Espada. As a way of getting onto the Lamborghini ownership ladder, the Jarama always made sense, being relatively cheap for a front-engined V12 and seriously quick. Not cheap any longer though, as the market has slowly warmed to it.

**SPECIFICATIONS**

| | |
|---|---|
| **Years produced:** | 1970-1973 (177 in total) |
| **Performance:** | 0-60mph: 7.2sec<br>Top speed: 162mph |
| **Power & torque:** | 350bhp/290lb ft |
| **Engine:** | Normally aspirated 3939cc V12, petrol, carburettor, 24 valves |
| **Drivetrain:** | Front-engine RWD |
| **Structure:** | Separate chassis |
| **Transmission:** | Five-speed manual |
| **Weight:** | 1540kg |

**PRICE GUIDE**

| | |
|---|---|
| **Launch price:** | £9800 |
| **Excellent:** | £165,000 |
| **Good:** | £130,000 |
| **Average:** | £95,000 |
| **Project:** | £30,000 |

## LAMBORGHINI Urraco P250/P300

The P300 was a direct answer to Ferrari's new 308 GT4, the successor to the famous Dino. The original P250 needed changing; the price was too high and the workmanship wasn't up to the desired level. The Urraco should have been a big success, but with poor build quality and limp-wristed performance in P250 form it failed to take off. The 265bhp P300 put right the latter problem, pushing the Urraco to over 160mph, but the former was a more deep-seated issue that failed to be resolved. Still, as Countach values have shot up, these baby Lambos have been dragged up with them.

**SPECIFICATIONS**

| | |
|---|---|
| **Years produced:** | 1972-1979 (710 in total) |
| **Performance:** | 0-60mph: 7.4sec (P300)<br>Top speed: 161mph |
| **Power & torque:** | 265bhp/195lb ft |
| **Engine:** | Normally aspirated 2996cc V8, petrol, carburettor, 16 valves |
| **Drivetrain:** | Mid-engine RWD |
| **Structure:** | Spaceframe |
| **Transmission:** | Five-speed manual |
| **Weight:** | 1300kg |

**PRICE GUIDE (P300 in brackets)**

| | |
|---|---|
| **Launch price:** | £9975 |
| **Excellent:** | £95,000 (£115,000) |
| **Good:** | £70,000 (£90,000) |
| **Average:** | £50,000 (£70,000) |
| **Project:** | £25,000 (£35,000) |

## LAMBORGHINI Countach LP400

Although the Miura was a tough act to follow, Lamborghini did it in style with the Countach, perhaps the most iconic bedroom poster car of all. With a dramatic wedge style, scissor doors and a *claimed* maximum speed approaching 200mph from its 375bhp V12, the Countach was a concept car for the road. It also put right many of the Miura's most serious problems, most notably its shocking aerodynamics. Cramped, noisy and impossible to see out of, the Countach is a true great – and values are now reflecting this. Super-rare 'Periscopica' version is particularly prized.

**SPECIFICATIONS**

| | |
|---|---|
| **Years produced:** | 1974-1978 (150 in total) |
| **Performance:** | 0-60mph: 6.8sec<br>Top speed: 180mph |
| **Power & torque:** | 375bhp/268lb ft |
| **Engine:** | Normally aspirated 3929cc V12, petrol, carburettor, 24 valves |
| **Drivetrain:** | Mid-engine RWD |
| **Structure:** | Spaceframe |
| **Transmission:** | Five-speed manual |
| **Weight:** | 1065kg |

**PRICE GUIDE ('Periscopica' in brackets)**

| | |
|---|---|
| **Launch price:** | £17,285 |
| **Excellent:** | £600,000 (£1,150,000) |
| **Good:** | £500,000 (£900,000) |
| **Average:** | £450,000 (£800,000) |
| **Project:** | £300,000 (£500,000) |

## LAMBORGHINI Silhouette P300

Based on the Urraco P300, the Silhouette was an ultimately unsuccessful attempt to take on the Ferrari 308GTS. An appealing-looking car with phone-dial alloys and ultra-low profile tyres – just like a Countach – it wasn't strong enough to make the grade. It fell by the wayside when Lamborghini went through horrendous financial problems during the late 1970s, a time when Sant'Agata's model range was reduced to the Countach only. With a mere 54 built, the Silhouette will always have rarity on its side – and steady values reflect that.

**SPECIFICATIONS**

| | |
|---|---|
| **Years produced:** | 1976-1979 (54 in total) |
| **Performance:** | 0-60mph: 6.8sec<br>Top speed: 150mph |
| **Power & torque:** | 255bhp/210lb ft |
| **Engine:** | Normally aspirated 2996cc V8, petrol, carburettor, 16 valves |
| **Drivetrain:** | Mid-engine RWD |
| **Structure:** | Spaceframe |
| **Transmission:** | Five-speed manual |
| **Weight:** | 1240kg |

**PRICE GUIDE**

| | |
|---|---|
| **Launch price:** | £13,684 |
| **Excellent:** | £150,000 |
| **Good:** | £100,000 |
| **Average:** | £80,000 |
| **Project:** | £50,000 |

## LAMBORGHINI Jalpa

The Jalpa was Lamborghini's last throw of the Urraco dice. The Silhouette had been out of production for two years, so it was an odd decision to revamp it for another attack on the 308. The Jalpa was usefully quicker thanks to its enlarged (by Alfieri) 3.5-litre V8 engine, but the '70s throwback styling and Airfix interior should have been a barrier to sales. However, during its nine-year production run, the Jalpa bucked the trend and sold 200 in its most successful year – making it Lamborghini's biggest-selling V8. Values have slipped slightly.

**SPECIFICATIONS**

| | |
|---|---|
| **Years produced:** | 1981-1988 (410 in total) |
| **Performance:** | 0-60mph: 6.0sec<br>Top speed: 150mph |
| **Power & torque:** | 255bhp/231lb ft |
| **Engine:** | Normally aspirated 3485cc V8, petrol, carburettor, 16 valves |
| **Drivetrain:** | Mid-engine RWD |
| **Structure:** | Spaceframe |
| **Transmission:** | Five-speed manual |
| **Weight:** | 1510kg |

**PRICE GUIDE**

| | |
|---|---|
| **Launch price:** | £26,001 |
| **Excellent:** | £90,000 |
| **Good:** | £80,000 |
| **Average:** | £70,000 |
| **Project:** | £30,000 |

## LAMBORGHINI Countach LP400S/500S

Adding the bodykit and wider tyres (and often that outrageous rear wing, which wasn't an official factory option by the way) had the effect of actually making the 1978 LP400S slower than the original LP400. The obvious answer was a more powerful engine, but that would have to wait until 1982, when Lambo's finances improved following the arrival of the Mimram family. Additional torque and lower gearing added considerable punch and, once again, placed the Countach ahead of its arch rival, the Ferrari BB. Values lag behind LP400 – the nearest thing to a bargain Countach?

**SPECIFICATIONS**

| | |
|---|---|
| **Years produced:** | 1978-1985 |
| **Performance:** | 0-60mph: 5.6sec (LP500S)<br>Top speed: 170mph |
| **Power & torque:** | 385bhp/303lb ft |
| **Engine:** | Normally aspirated 4754cc V12, petrol, carburettor, 24 valves |
| **Drivetrain:** | Mid-engine RWD |
| **Structure:** | Spaceframe |
| **Transmission:** | Five-speed manual |
| **Weight:** | 1485kg |

**PRICE GUIDE**

| | |
|---|---|
| **Launch price:** | N/A |
| **Excellent:** | £425,000 |
| **Good:** | £350,000 |
| **Average:** | £275,000 |
| **Project:** | £100,000 |

## LAMBORGHINI Countach 5000QV

The Countach Quattrovalvole was built for a single purpose: to go faster than the Ferrari Testarossa. Engineering genius Giulio Alfieri created twin-cam four-valve cylinder heads, re-engineered the carburettor set-up, and allied the ensemble to a larger 5167cc block, upping maximum power by 70bhp – and making this the best Countach yet. Sales picked up and, when the 1988 Anniversary model was rolled out, they went into overdrive. By the time Countach production ended, it had become the company's longest-lived car.

**SPECIFICATIONS**

| | |
|---|---|
| **Years produced:** | 1985-1990 (610 in total) |
| **Performance:** | 0-60mph: 4.8sec<br>Top speed: 182mph |
| **Power & torque:** | 455bhp/369lb ft |
| **Engine:** | Normally aspirated 5167cc V12, petrol, carburettor, 48 valves |
| **Drivetrain:** | Mid-engine RWD |
| **Structure:** | Spaceframe |
| **Transmission:** | Five-speed manual |
| **Weight:** | 1490kg |

**PRICE GUIDE (Anniversary in brackets)**

| | |
|---|---|
| **Launch price:** | N/A |
| **Excellent:** | £375,000 (£300,000) |
| **Good:** | £300,000 (£250,000) |
| **Average:** | £280,000 (£225,000) |
| **Project:** | £120,000 (£100,000) |

## LAMBORGHINI Diablo

The replacement for the Countach, brought up to date, and suitably scaled up. The original design had been penned by Marcello Gandini (who already had Miura and Countach on his CV), but following Chrysler's takeover in 1987 the shape was softened, causing problems between stylist and employer. More significantly, at its launch in 1990 the Diablo became the company's first 200mph car. Early ones were heavy to drive; the 4wd VT that introduced power steering from 1993 was much better; the SV better yet. SV, Roadster and 6.0 all attract premiums.

**SPECIFICATIONS (VT)**

| | |
|---|---|
| **Years produced:** | 1990-2001 (2884 all variants) |
| **Performance:** | 0-60mph: 4.2sec<br>Top speed: 202mph |
| **Power & torque:** | 492bhp/428lb ft |
| **Engine:** | Normally aspirated 5709cc V12, petrol, fuel injection, 48 valves |
| **Drivetrain:** | Mid-engine AWD |
| **Structure:** | Spaceframe |
| **Transmission:** | Five-speed manual |
| **Weight:** | 1490kg |

**PRICE GUIDE**

| | |
|---|---|
| **Launch price:** | £160,000 |
| **Excellent:** | £180,000 |
| **Good:** | £140,000 |
| **Average:** | £110,000 |
| **Project:** | £75,000 |

## LAMBORGHINI Murciélago

Audi bought Lamborghini in 1998, and the Luc Donckerwolke-styled Murciélago was the first all-new model launched on its watch. As wild as any predecessor, thanks to a new 6.2 variant of the howling Bizzarrini V12, the iconic scissor doors and a new semi-automatic 'E-gear' transmission. Prices here are for the standard coupé (2001-2006); roadsters attract a premium, as does the later LP640. Most sought-after is the hardcore SV – you'll struggle to find one for less than £350k, says Geoff Armstrong of the Lamborghini Club.

**SPECIFICATIONS**

| | |
|---|---|
| **Years produced:** | 2001-2010 (4099 in total) |
| **Performance:** | 0-60mph: 4.0sec<br>Top speed: 206mph |
| **Power & torque:** | 572bhp/479lb ft |
| **Engine:** | Normally aspirated 6192cc V12, petrol, electronic fuel injection, 48 valves |
| **Drivetrain:** | Mid-engine RWD |
| **Structure:** | Spaceframe |
| **Transmission:** | Six-speed manual/semi-auto |
| **Weight:** | 1650kg |

**PRICE GUIDE (6.2)**

| | |
|---|---|
| **Launch price:** | £170,248 |
| **Excellent:** | £140,000 |
| **Good:** | £120,000 |
| **Average:** | £110,000 |
| **Project:** | N/A |

# VAS VEHICLE SOLUTIONS

The UK's Premier Lamborghini Specialist

**Lamborghini Murcielago LP670-4 SV**
Ceramic brakes, High level rear wing small decal option, 600 miles, 2009, **£POA**

**Lamborghini Murcielago LP670-4 SV**
Ceramic brakes, high level rear wing, large decal option, 8,000 miles, 2010, **£379,990**

**Lamborghini Aventador LP 770-4 SVJ**
Branding pack, Carbon fibre interior package, Carbon fibre mirror casings, Lifting system, Style package, Transparent engine cover, Yellow brake callipers, 2,000 miles, 2019, **£369,890**

**Lamborghini Aventador LP 770-4 SVJ**
20/21 inch Leirion gloss black alloy wheels, Carbon driving zone, Lifting system, Magneto-rheological suspension, Multi-function steering wheel, Satellite Navigation, 30 miles, 2019, **£368,990**

**Lamborghini Aventador LP 750-4 SV Roadster**
Carbon exterior upgrade, carbon interior, carbon fixed air intake sensonum sound system, 250 miles, 2017, **£349,990**

**Lamborghini Aventador LP 750-4 SV**
Nero alcantara interior and contrast Grigio stitching, Transparent engine cover, Carbon fibre exterior pack, Lifting system. 4000 miles, 2017, **£299,990**

**Lamborghini Aventador LP 750-4 SV Roadster**
20/21" Dianthus forged high gloss black alloy wheels, LIS with navigation system and DAB radio, magneto-rheological suspension with lifting system, branding package with alcantara, 5500 miles, 2016, **£299,990**

**Lamborghini Aventador S LP 740-4 S**
5th Year warranty, Carbon exterior pack, Carbon fibre engine bay trim, Sensonum premium sound system, Transparent engine cover, 3,000 miles, 2018, **£239,990**

**Lamborghini Murcielago LP640 Roadster**
Q-citura stitching, Hemera alloy wheels, Ceramic brakes, Lifting system, 5,000 miles, 2009, **£199,990**

**Lamborghini Murcielago LP640 Coupe**
Q-citura stitching, Hemera alloy wheels, Ceramic brakes, Lifting system, Branding pack 5,000 miles, 2009, **£199,990**

**Lamborghini Huracan LP 640-4 Performante Spyder**
20" Loge alloy wheels, Sensonum sound system, electric heated comfort seats, Branding package, 6000 miles 2018, **£192,990**

**Lamborghini Aventador LP 700-4 Roadster**
Branding pack, Dione forged alloy wheels, Reverse camera, Satellite Navigation, Transparent engine cover, 12,000 miles, 2015, **£182,990**

**Lamborghini Aventador LP 700-4 Roadster**
Branding pack, Clear engine bay cover, Dione forged alloy wheels, Lifting system, Multi-function steering wheel, 11,000 miles, 2014, **£179,990**

**Lamborghini Aventador LP 700-4**
Dione forged alloy wheels, Q-citura stitching, Carbon fibre engine bay, Lamborghini race exhaust, Sensonam sound, 7,000 miles 2015 **£178,990**

**Lamborghini Aventador LP 700-4**
Carbon fibre engine bay trim, Carbon fibre exterior pack, Carbon fibre interior package, Lifting system, Style package, 13,000 miles, 2013, **£169,990**

**BUYING OR SELLING LAMBORGHINI MOTORCARS**

**+44 01580 714 597 sales@vvsuk.co.uk www.vvsuk.co.uk**

(Viewing by appointment only) **Address: VVS UK LTD PARK FARM, GOUDHURST ROAD, CRANBROOK KENT TN172LJ**

**www.lamborghinibuyer.com Additional Websites: www.justlamborghini.com**

## LAMBORGHINI Gallardo

Quickly going on to become Lamborghini's best-seller, the early Gallardo was powered by an epic-sounding V10, and could be had with a manual or semi-automatic paddleshift 'E-gear' option. Thanks to Audi (again) this was the 'affordable' Lamborghini many had always wanted. Later 552bhp 5.2-litre engine introduced with the 2008 facelift had a different firing order and much improved E-gear. Four-wheel-drive-only, until the Balboni Edition in 2009. Prices here are early 5.0 coupé; pay £5k+ more for equivalent Spyder.

**SPECIFICATIONS**

**Years produced:** 2003-2013 (14,022 in total)
**Performance:** 0-60mph: 4.2sec
Top speed: 192mph
**Power & torque:** 493bhp/376lb ft
**Engine:** Normally aspirated 4961cc V10, petrol, fuel injection, 40 valves
**Drivetrain:** Mid-engine RWD
**Structure:** Spaceframe
**Transmission:** Six-speed manual/semi-auto
**Weight:** 1520kg

**PRICE GUIDE**

**Launch price:** £120,000
**Excellent:** £70,000
**Good:** £60,000
**Average:** £50,000
**Project:** N/A

# LANCIA

THE SON OF a food processing and canning magnate, Vincenzo Lancia cut his teeth at Fiat before starting his own factory in Turin in 1906. The company quickly gained a reputation for styling flair and use of advanced technology, with vee-engines, five-speed gearboxes and independent suspension long before others were brave enough to try. Sadly, its approach proved less than cost-effective and, with deepening financial trouble, Fiat stepped in during 1969. Despite a fine series of cars with motorsport pedigree, from Fulvia to Integrale, the legacy of a reputation damaged by rusty Betas saw Lancia leave the UK market in 1994, but the badge continues elsewhere on cars with largely Fiat underpinnings.

## LANCIA Aprilia

Looking at the Aprilia's specification sheet, it's easy to see that it was lightyears ahead of its time. The features list included monocoque construction, independent suspension all-round, pillarless styling honed in the wind tunnel, and a jewel-like 1354cc V4 engine that produced enough power to ensure the Aprilia outpaced much more glamorous rivals. Three wheelbases were offered, and you could also buy coachbuilt versions. Post-war examples were upgraded with 1.5-litre engines and remained in production until 1949. All values holding firm.

**SPECIFICATIONS**

**Years produced:** 1937-1949 (27,635 in total)
**Performance:** 0-60mph: N/A
Top speed: 80mph
**Power & torque:** 46bhp/N/A
**Engine:** Normally aspirated 1352cc V4, petrol, carburettor, 8 valves
**Drivetrain:** Front-engine RWD
**Structure:** Monocoque
**Transmission:** Four-speed manual
**Weight:** 850kg

**PRICE GUIDE**

**Launch price:** N/A
**Excellent:** £60,000
**Good:** £35,000
**Average:** £30,000
**Project:** £15,000

## LANCIA Aurelia Saloon

Considering the Aprilia blazed such a trail, it's scarcely believable that Lancia went and did the same with the Aurelia. The main advance was the engine – the world's first production V6; a 60-degree design developed during World War Two. It was smooth and lusty, and proved the perfect power unit for long-distance touring. In the B10 saloon it was initially available in 1754cc and 1991cc forms. The wind-cheating styling was developed with assistance from Pininfarina and still looks strikingly understated, modern and elegant today.

**SPECIFICATIONS**

**Years produced:** 1950-1958 (12,705 in total)
**Performance:** 0-60mph: 17.9sec
Top speed: 91mph
**Power & torque:** 87bhp/118lb ft
**Engine:** Normally aspirated 226cc V6, petrol, carburettor, 12 valves
**Drivetrain:** Front-engine RWD
**Structure:** Monocoque
**Transmission:** Four-speed manual
**Weight:** 1232kg

**PRICE GUIDE**

**Launch price:** £2863
**Excellent:** £40,000
**Good:** £30,000
**Average:** £20,000
**Project:** £10,000

## LANCIA Appia

The Appia, introduced in 1953, featured a narrow-angle V4 engine designed by Vittorio Jano and was the last Lancia with sliding pillar suspension. The 1st series car had a number of teething problems that were addressed by the pretty 2nd series car (pictured) introduced in 1956. The 2nd series had a 30mm longer wheelbase, a more useable boot and a redesigned interior. Over 100,000 Appias were eventually produced across three series and ten years, including a platform chassis model, around which various Italian coachbuilders created gems such as the Appia Zagato.

**SPECIFICATIONS (2nd series)**

**Years produced:** 1956-1959 (22,433 total)
**Performance:** 0-60mph: 23sec
Top speed: 82mph
**Power & torque:** 43bhp/52lb ft
**Engine:** Normally aspirated 1080cc V4, petrol, carburettor, 8 valves
**Drivetrain:** Front-engine RWD
**Structure:** Monocoque
**Transmission:** Four-speed manual
**Weight:** 900kg

**PRICE GUIDE**

**Launch price:** N/A
**Excellent:** £22,000
**Good:** £16,000
**Average:** £13,000
**Project:** £5000

## LANCIA
# Aurelia B20 GT

Pininfarina was responsible for building the B20 GT coupé, even though Ghia styled the bodies, which are elegantly proportioned and exquisitely detailed. Now considered to be the cars that coined the Gran Turismo epithet, the 2.0- and 2.5-litre versions were quick, smooth and effortless. Fewer than 4000 B20 GTs were built, and those that remain have risen steeply in value in recent years as demand continues to outstrip supply. In all, six series of Aurelias were built, with trim and performance upgrades being drafted in on an almost annual basis.

**SPECIFICATIONS (4th series)**

| | |
|---|---|
| **Years produced:** | 1953-1958 (3424 in total) |
| **Performance:** | 0-60mph: 12.3sec<br>Top speed: 103mph |
| **Power & torque:** | 75bhp/89lb ft |
| **Engine:** | Normally aspirated 1991cc V6, petrol, carburettor, 12 valves |
| **Drivetrain:** | Front-engine RWD |
| **Structure:** | Monocoque |
| **Transmission:** | Four-speed manual |
| **Weight:** | 1194kg |

**PRICE GUIDE**

| | |
|---|---|
| **Launch price:** | £3472 |
| **Excellent:** | £210,000 |
| **Good:** | £160,000 |
| **Average:** | £130,000 |
| **Project:** | £80,000 |

## LANCIA
# Aurelia B24 Spider

In 1954, to coincide with the arrival of the fourth series cars, the B24 Spider was unveiled – easily the most desirable of all the Aurelias unless you carry passengers. Although its front-end styling was similar to the B10 and B20 GT's, from the front wheels back it was radically different. The wheelbase was shortened by 203mm and Pininfarina produced the sensational coachwork. Production was limited, although many cars have survived – but with higher market values to match their elevated styling and engineering. The Spider name was rather shortlived.

**SPECIFICATIONS**

| | |
|---|---|
| **Years produced:** | 1955-1956 (240 in total) |
| **Performance:** | 0-60mph: N/A<br>Top speed: 115mph |
| **Power & torque:** | 118bhp/127lb ft |
| **Engine:** | Normally aspirated 2451cc V6, petrol, carburettor, 12 valves |
| **Drivetrain:** | Front-engine RWD |
| **Structure:** | Monocoque |
| **Transmission:** | Four-speed manual |
| **Weight:** | 1070kg |

**PRICE GUIDE**

| | |
|---|---|
| **Launch price:** | £N/A |
| **Excellent:** | £1,300,000 |
| **Good:** | £950,000 |
| **Average:** | £750,000 |
| **Project:** | £450,000 |

## LANCIA
# Aurelia B24 Convertible

For the penultimate round of changes to the Aurelia, and just over a year after it first appeared, the B24 was revised. In the process it lost the Spider name, becoming the B24 Convertible. Alongside the fifth series B20 GTs, which received a sturdier transaxle, the B24 gained wind-up windows, improved seating, and a new, more conventional windscreen with opening quarter lights that proved more useful when motoring with the hood up. Because there were more Convertibles than Spiders, values are correspondingly lower but still remain strong.

**SPECIFICATIONS**

| | |
|---|---|
| **Years produced:** | 1957-1958 (510 in total) |
| **Performance:** | 0-60mph: 12.7sec<br>Top speed: 107mph |
| **Power & torque:** | 110bhp/125lb ft |
| **Engine:** | Normally aspirated 2451cc V6, petrol, carburettor, 12 valves |
| **Drivetrain:** | Front-engine RWD |
| **Structure:** | Monocoque |
| **Transmission:** | Four-speed manual |
| **Weight:** | 1215kg |

**PRICE GUIDE**

| | |
|---|---|
| **Launch price:** | £N/A |
| **Excellent:** | £500,000 |
| **Good:** | £350,000 |
| **Average:** | £280,000 |
| **Project:** | £120,000 |

## LANCIA
# Flaminia Coupé/GT

The Flaminia range replaced the Aurelia, with saloon, coupé and cabriolet versions. The latter two were both coachbuilt, with bodies by a number of styling houses. The best-selling Coupé (left) was penned by Pininfarina and had a 2+2 layout. The original 2.5-litre V6 was replaced by a 2.8 in 1962. Rarer and more desirable today is the two-seater Carrozzeria Touring-designed GT, which had a shortened wheelbase and aluminium body. The Flaminia was the last Lancia to be offered in so many coachbuilt variations. Values are high as a consequence, although not in the Aurelia league. Yet.

**SPECIFICATIONS (Coupé, 2.5)**

| | |
|---|---|
| **Years produced:** | 1959-1967 (5294 in total) |
| **Performance:** | 0-60mph: 13.0sec (2.5)<br>Top speed: 113mph |
| **Power & torque:** | [illegible]/137lb ft |
| **Engine:** | Normally aspirated 2458cc V6, petrol, carburettor, 12 valves |
| **Drivetrain:** | Front-engine RWD |
| **Structure:** | Monocoque |
| **Transmission:** | Four-speed manual |
| **Weight:** | 1520kg |

**PRICE GUIDE (GT 3C in brackets)**

| | |
|---|---|
| **Launch price:** | £3388 (£3869) |
| **Excellent:** | £60,000 (£90,000) |
| **Good:** | £45,000 (£60,000) |
| **Average:** | £23,000 (£34,000) |
| **Project:** | £6000 (£8000) |

## LANCIA
# Flaminia Sport Zagato

The Flaminia Sport was coachbuilt by Zagato, and was almost incomparably handsome. The Sport sat on the same wheelbase as the GT and, unlike the Pininfarina and Touring cars, which were angular, the aluminium-bodied Sport was more rounded, harking back to the more timeless style of the B20 GT. It became the Super Sport in 1964, the new name reflecting the additional performance from its 2.8-litre V6. Zagato styling signatures, such as the pop-out doorhandles, were retained, although the Sport and Super Sport's styling differed significantly.

**SPECIFICATIONS (Sport)**

| | |
|---|---|
| **Years produced:** | 1960-1967 (593 in total) |
| **Performance:** | 0-60mph: 12.7sec<br>Top speed: 112mph |
| **Power & torque:** | 119bhp/127lb ft |
| **Engine:** | Normally aspirated 2458cc V6, petrol, carburettor, 12 valves |
| **Drivetrain:** | Front-engine RWD |
| **Structure:** | Monocoque |
| **Transmission:** | Four-speed manual |
| **Weight:** | 1520kg |

**PRICE GUIDE**

| | |
|---|---|
| **Launch price:** | £3888 |
| **Excellent:** | £400,000 |
| **Good:** | £260,000 |
| **Average:** | £180,000 |
| **Project:** | £80,000 |

## LANCIA
### Flavia Sport Zagato

Once again, Zagato was drafted in to create an individual-looking Sport, although for the Flavia it was more outlandish than usual. The curvaceous bodywork was a long way away from the square-rigged conventionality of the Berlina, and even the Coupé looked restrained in comparison. In lightweight form and with twin carburettors, the Sport lived up to its name, proving quick and agile on the road. Sales weren't good though, and in the wake of the Fiat takeover of Lancia in 1969, bespoke models such as this were very much off the menu.

**SPECIFICATIONS**

**Years produced:** 1962-1969
**Performance:** 0-60mph: 11.9sec
Top speed: 117mph
**Power & torque:** 101bhp/103lb ft
**Engine:** Normally aspirated 1800cc V4, petrol, carburettor, 8 valves
**Drivetrain:** Front-engine FWD
**Structure:** Superleggera
**Transmission:** Four-speed manual
**Weight:** 1800kg

**PRICE GUIDE**

**Launch price:** £2736
**Excellent:** £40,000
**Good:** £30,000
**Average:** £25,000
**Project:** £15,000

## LANCIA
### Flavia Coupé

A year after the arrival of the Flavia saloon, the eye-catching Coupé model arrived. Continuing a long tradition of co-operation with Pininfarina, its pretty two-door body style moved Lancia styling away from the classicism of the earlier models. The Coupé initially came with a 90bhp twin-carburettor version of the 1.5-litre flat-four, but this was uprated to 100bhp and 1.8 litres in 1963, before going to the full 126bhp and 2.0 litres in 1971. Rust has been the main enemy of these cars, although many have now been restored – and values are sure to continue rising in time.

**SPECIFICATIONS**

**Years produced:** 1962-1973 (26,084 in total)
**Performance:** 0-60mph: 13.2sec
Top speed: 103mph
**Power & torque:** 91bhp/108lb ft
**Engine:** Normally aspirated 1800cc flat-4, petrol, carburettor, 8 valves
**Drivetrain:** Front-engine FWD
**Structure:** Monocoque
**Transmission:** Four-speed manual
**Weight:** 1160kg

**PRICE GUIDE**

**Launch price:** £2275
**Excellent:** £25,000
**Good:** £20,000
**Average:** £14,000
**Project:** £5000

## LANCIA
### Fulvia Coupé

After a couple of years of saloon production, the special variations of the Fulvia started to be released. The major news was the two-door Coupé that, like the Flavia, was distinguishable by its handsome bodywork on a shortened floorpan. It shared no external panels with the saloon. Performance was improved with a 1.2-litre 80bhp version of the engine being installed at launch, but upgraded to a 90bhp 1298cc power unit later in its life. Handling was known for its precision and neutrality, a point devastatingly proved in motor sport with the more potent HF. Values holding steady.

**SPECIFICATIONS**

**Years produced:** 1965-1976 (139,817 in total)
**Performance:** 0-60mph: 15.8sec
Top speed: 100mph
**Power & torque:** 80bhp/77lb ft
**Engine:** Normally aspirated 1216cc V4, petrol, carburettor, 8 valves
**Drivetrain:** Front-engine FWD
**Structure:** Monocoque
**Transmission:** Four-speed manual
**Weight:** 940kg

**PRICE GUIDE**

**Launch price:** £1490
**Excellent:** £21,000
**Good:** £15,000
**Average:** £12,000
**Project:** £6000

## LANCIA
### Fulvia Coupé HF

The Fulvia's crowning achievement was to win the 1972 International Rally Championship with the HF Rallye, the competition version of the Fulvia Coupé. Powered by a tuned version of the 1298cc engine producing 87bhp, the HF was lighter than the standard Coupé, thanks to the aluminium bonnet, doors and bootlid, and Plexiglass windows. Considered too raw for the road, the HF was further developed into the Rallye 1.6 HF, a fire-breathing 1584cc version developing 115bhp. Today HFs are highly sought-after, with values to match – the Rallye HF *Fanalone* ('big lights') can fetch £100k+.

**SPECIFICATIONS**

**Years produced:** 1965-1976 (139,817 in total)
**Performance:** 0-60mph: 11.9sec
Top speed: 103mph
**Power & torque:** 87bhp/83lb ft
**Engine:** Normally aspirated 1298cc V4, petrol, carburettor, 8 valves
**Drivetrain:** Front-engine FWD
**Structure:** Monocoque
**Transmission:** Four-speed manual
**Weight:** 894kg

**PRICE GUIDE**

**Launch price:** £1548
**Excellent:** £80,000
**Good:** £30,000
**Average:** £20,000
**Project:** £8000

## LANCIA
### Fulvia Sport Zagato

Slightly more palatable-looking than the Zagato-bodied Flavia, the aluminium Fulvia was still a challenging looker. But those concept car lines promised a great driving experience and, thankfully, the Sport Zagato lived up to its off-the-wall styling. Like the HF, the Zagato was lighter than the standard Coupé, and the power-to-weight ratio delivered by the lively V4 power units was enhanced usefully. Upgraded during its life, the Sport Zagato even picked up luxury fitments such as electric windows, a sure sign that buyers were demanding more fripperies in the 1970s.

**SPECIFICATIONS**

**Years produced:** 1968-1972
**Performance:** 0-60mph: 13.0sec
Top speed: 109mph
**Power & torque:** 87bhp/84lb ft
**Engine:** Normally aspirated 1298cc V4, petrol, carburettor, 8 valves
**Drivetrain:** Front-engine FWD
**Structure:** Monocoque
**Transmission:** Five-speed manual
**Weight:** 960kg

**PRICE GUIDE**

**Launch price:** N/A
**Excellent:** £50,000
**Good:** £27,000
**Average:** £17,000
**Project:** £7000

## LANCIA
## Beta Berlina

A gem of a saloon that was streets ahead of other family offerings when it appeared in 1972 with four-wheel disc brakes, twin-cam engine, independent suspension and a five-speed gearbox. Rust in front subframes and wings, with ferocious media hype to match, saw to the car's UK demise, despite the '76 S2 being vastly better and Lancia's introduction of a six-year anti-corrosion warranty before the troubles came to light. Most of the afflicted S1 Betas have gone to the crusher, but there are still cared-for S2s to be found and enjoyed.

**SPECIFICATIONS**

**Years produced:** 1972-1981 (194,914 in total)
**Performance:** 0-60mph: 10.5sec
Top speed: 109mph
**Power & torque:** 110bhp/106lb ft
**Engine:** Normally aspirated 1756cc four cylinder, petrol, carburettor, 8 valves
**Drivetrain:** Front-engine FWD
**Structure:** Monocoque
**Transmission:** Five-speed manual
**Weight:** 1095kg

**PRICE GUIDE**

**Launch price:** £1594
**Excellent:** £6000
**Good:** £4000
**Average:** £2000
**Project:** £500

## LANCIA
## Stratos

It started life as a Bertone concept car in 1970, but the Lancia competition director Cesare Fiorio saw something in the squat little wedge that no one else did: a potential rally car. Fiorio knew that the Dino V6 engine from Ferrari was now within his grasp. A plan was hatched and, within three years, a production version was released (and 500 built), while the rally car was developed from it. From this inspired idea Lancia's domination of world rallying ensued. Road cars were hard to sell, and some languished in showrooms for five years. Highly prized today, and beware imitations.

**SPECIFICATIONS**

**Years produced:** 1973-1975 (500 in total)
**Performance:** 0-60mph: 6.0sec
Top speed: 143mph
**Power & torque:** 187bhp/166lb ft
**Engine:** Normally aspirated 2419cc V6, petrol, carburettor, 12 valves
**Drivetrain:** Mid-engine RWD
**Structure:** Glassfibre body/tubular chassis
**Transmission:** Five-speed manual
**Weight:** 980kg

**PRICE GUIDE (road cars)**

**Launch price:** £7000
**Excellent:** £500,000
**Good:** £400,000
**Average:** N/A
**Project:** N/A

## LANCIA
## Beta Coupé

Launched a year after the saloon it was based on, the Coupé used a 19cm shorter floorpan but still found room for adults in the rear seats. That shorter wheelbase combines well with a reduction of 90kg from the saloon's weight, creating a car that is even sharper to drive and suffers less from its lack of power-assisted steering. Engine options are the same rev-happy 1300-2000cc twin-cams as the saloon's, with Bosch fuel injection from 1981 and the addition of a supercharged version, badged Volumex, for 1983-84. Add 30% for the latter.

**SPECIFICATIONS**

**Years produced:** 1973-1984 (111,801 in total)
**Performance:** 0-60mph: 9.8sec
Top speed: 114mph
**Power & torque:** 108bhp/114lb ft
**Engine:** Normally aspirated 1585cc four cylinder, petrol, carburettor, 8 valves
**Drivetrain:** Front-engine FWD
**Structure:** Monocoque
**Transmission:** Five-speed manual
**Weight:** 1000kg

**PRICE GUIDE**

**Launch price:** £2153
**Excellent:** £10,000
**Good:** £5000
**Average:** £3000
**Project:** £1000

## LANCIA
## Beta Spider

In theory this is just a Beta Coupé with a clever roof, but this is Lancia so it's more complicated than that. The targa-top with folding rear window section and different window frames was designed by Pininfarina and built by Zagato, which was enough for the car to be badged Lancia Zagato in America. They also changed the tail-lights for units shared with the Bristol Beaufighter. Unusually it's a four-seater convertible. Only sold with 1600 or 2000 engines, though there's not much difference between them in performance.

**SPECIFICATIONS**

**Years produced:** 1975-1982 (9390 in total)
**Performance:** 0-60mph: 9.5sec
Top speed: 115mph
**Power & torque:** 119bhp/129lb ft
**Engine:** Normally aspirated 1995cc four cylinder, petrol, carburettor, 8 valves
**Drivetrain:** Front-engine FWD
**Structure:** Monocoque
**Transmission:** Five-speed manual
**Weight:** 1048kg

**PRICE GUIDE**

**Launch price:** £3128
**Excellent:** £12,000
**Good:** £6000
**Average:** £3750
**Project:** £1500

## LANCIA
## Montecarlo

This is actually a Beta in name only, parts shared with the rest of the range being limited to the engine block and internal door lock buttons. It's a mid-engined two-seater, originally envisaged as the Fiat X1/20 – then someone realised it could be priced higher with a Lancia badge. Only sold with a 2.0-litre engine in Europe, S1 versions had problems with locking front brakes, cured simply by removing the servo. 1980-on S2s were better in other ways too. With fine handling balance and expressive steering, they're underrated driver's cars.

**SPECIFICATIONS**

**Years produced:** 1975-1984 (7595 in total)
**Performance:** 0-60mph: 8.6sec
Top speed: 120mph
**Power & torque:** 118bhp/122lb ft
**Engine:** Normally aspirated 1995cc four cylinder, petrol, carburettor, 8 valves
**Drivetrain:** Mid-engine RWD
**Structure:** Monocoque
**Transmission:** Five-speed manual
**Weight:** 970kg

**PRICE GUIDE (add £500 for Spider)**

**Launch price:** £5927
**Excellent:** £20,000
**Good:** £15,000
**Average:** £9000
**Project:** £3000

# LANCIA
## Gamma Berlina

If one car summed up the bitter-sweet nature of large Italian cars of the 1970s, it had to be the Gamma. Originally conceived as part of a joint venture with Citroën that never bore fruit, the Gamma ended up being developed by Lancia alone. The Gamma drove well, but its undoing was its new flat four – it leaked oil, overheated and snapped its cambelt for good measure. And then it rusted away. If you can see past the faults, there's a great car trying to escape, but there are so few survivors now that hardly any people will ever find out.

**SPECIFICATIONS**

| | |
|---|---|
| **Years produced:** | 1975-1984 (15,296 in total) |
| **Performance:** | 0-60mph: 9.4sec<br>Top speed: 120mph |
| **Power & torque:** | 140bhp/154lb ft |
| **Engine:** | Normally aspirated 2844cc flat four, petrol, carburettor, 8 valves |
| **Drivetrain:** | Front-engine FWD |
| **Structure:** | Monocoque |
| **Transmission:** | Five-speed manual |
| **Weight:** | 1320kg |

**PRICE GUIDE**

| | |
|---|---|
| **Launch price:** | £7136 |
| **Excellent:** | £9000 |
| **Good:** | £4500 |
| **Average:** | £1750 |
| **Project:** | £950 |

# LANCIA
## Beta HPE

The initials stand for High Performance Estate, created by fitting a Coupé front end and doors (with different window frames) to a saloon floorpan and finishing off with a hatchback rear section that pays homage to the Reliant Scimitar GTE. The result is a lot more stylish than it sounds, and you get the softer ride of the saloon with the lower seating position of the Coupé. In keeping with its superior intentions, only 1600 and 2000 engines were offered, with an optional 135bhp supercharged version of the 2.0-litre (add 25%) for the last year of production.

**SPECIFICATIONS**

| | |
|---|---|
| **Years produced:** | 1975-1985 (71,258 in total) |
| **Performance:** | 0-60mph: 10.6sec<br>Top speed: 116mph |
| **Power & torque:** | 115bhp/130lb ft |
| **Engine:** | Normally aspirated 1995cc four cylinder, petrol, carburettor, 8 valves |
| **Drivetrain:** | Front-engine FWD |
| **Structure:** | Monocoque |
| **Transmission:** | Five-speed manual |
| **Weight:** | 1060kg |

**PRICE GUIDE**

| | |
|---|---|
| **Launch price:** | £3688 |
| **Excellent:** | £8000 |
| **Good:** | £5000 |
| **Average:** | £3000 |
| **Project:** | £1500 |

# LANCIA
## Gamma Coupé

The Gamma Berlina was perhaps the ultimate evolution of Pininfarina's BMC 1800 Aerodynamica concept car, first shown in 1966. The fastback saloon echoed the times perfectly yet failed to capture buyers' imaginations. However the Coupé – also styled by Pininfarina – emerged as one of the finest-looking cars of the 1970s. It might have been saddled with the same problems as the Berlina but owners have been more prepared to restore and repair than to throw away, and that's down purely to the way the Coupé looks. Buy by all means, but treat like a China doll.

**SPECIFICATIONS**

| | |
|---|---|
| **Years produced:** | 1976-1984 (6789 in total) |
| **Performance:** | 0-60mph: 9.4sec<br>Top speed: 120mph |
| **Power & torque:** | 140bhp/154lb ft |
| **Engine:** | Normally aspirated 2484cc flat four, petrol, electronic fuel injection, 8 valves |
| **Drivetrain:** | Front-engine FWD |
| **Structure:** | Monocoque |
| **Transmission:** | Five-speed manual |
| **Weight:** | 1290kg |

**PRICE GUIDE**

| | |
|---|---|
| **Launch price:** | £9186 |
| **Excellent:** | £12,000 |
| **Good:** | £7000 |
| **Average:** | £4000 |
| **Project:** | £1500 |

# LANCIA
## Delta HF Turbo

In an attempt to join the 1980s hot hatch club, Lancia uprated its stylish Delta with a turbocharged version of the classic Fiat twin-cam (originally 1.6, later 2.0 litres). Performance was strong and, thanks to Martini stripes on all-white paintwork (for the special edition), it stood out from the crowd, too. The Delta HF Turbo earned itself a reputation for being fast and fun. Not the last word in finesse or refinement, but a hoot to drive. The 4wd version that appeared in 1985 to homologate the Delta for rallying was a taste of even greater things to come.

**SPECIFICATIONS**

| | |
|---|---|
| **Years produced:** | 1984-1986 |
| **Performance:** | 0-60mph: 8.5sec (1.6)<br>Top speed: 126mph |
| **Power & torque:** | 140bhp/141lb ft |
| **Engine:** | Turbocharged 1585cc four cylinder, petrol, electronic fuel injection, 8 valves |
| **Drivetrain:** | Front-engine FWD |
| **Structure:** | Monocoque |
| **Transmission:** | Five-speed manual |
| **Weight:** | 1000kg |

**PRICE GUIDE**

| | |
|---|---|
| **Launch price:** | £8790 |
| **Excellent:** | £6750 |
| **Good:** | £4250 |
| **Average:** | £2500 |
| **Project:** | £1200 |

# LANCIA
## Delta HF Integrale

To keep the Delta on the pace for rallying, the HF's 2-litre twin-cam got a bigger turbo to deliver 185bhp. With enhanced 4wd, wider tyres and bigger brakes, the Integrale was fast, agile and charismatic. Although part of the UK Lancia range, the Integrale was never converted to right-hand drive, so if you come across a right-hooker check to see which company carried out the conversion. Expect to pay 25% more for the 197bhp 16v model, introduced in 1989 and distinguished chiefly by a bigger bonnet bulge and wider wheels.

**SPECIFICATIONS**

| | |
|---|---|
| **Years produced:** | 1987-1991 (c22,500 in total) |
| **Performance:** | 0-60mph: 6.5sec (8v)<br>Top speed: 133mph |
| **Power & torque:** | 185bhp/224lb ft |
| **Engine:** | Turbocharged 1995cc four cylinder, petrol, electronic fuel injection, 8 valves |
| **Drivetrain:** | Front-engine AWD |
| **Structure:** | Monocoque |
| **Transmission:** | Five-speed manual |
| **Weight:** | 1267kg |

**PRICE GUIDE**

| | |
|---|---|
| **Launch price:** | £13,980 |
| **Excellent:** | £25,000 |
| **Good:** | £20,000 |
| **Average:** | £12,000 |
| **Project:** | £5000 |

evo
THE THRILL OF DRIVING
S GO 9961
subscribe.evo.co.uk
@evomagazine
@evomagazine
@officialevomagazine
evo

## LANCIA
### Delta HF Integrale Evo

The Integrale Evoluzione was introduced at the end of 1991 – its purpose to keep Lancia competitive on the international rallying scene (the Integrale scored six consecutive world titles in all). There was a wider track front and rear, covered by even more swollen wheelarches, and more sophisticated suspension, while the engine was remapped to give 210bhp, dropping the 0-60 time to just 5.7sec. The Evo II arrived in mid-1993 with power up to 215bhp from the now catalysed engine and a raft of further improvements. The best Evo IIs now fetch £55k+.

**SPECIFICATIONS**

| | |
|---|---|
| **Years produced:** | 1991-1994 (c15,000 in total) |
| **Performance:** | 0-60mph: 5.7sec (Evo I)<br>Top speed: 137mph |
| **Power & torque:** | 210bhp/215lb ft |
| **Engine:** | Turbocharged 1995cc four cylinder, petrol, fuel injection, 16 valves |
| **Drivetrain:** | Front-engine AWD |
| **Structure:** | Monocoque |
| **Transmission:** | Five-speed manual |
| **Weight:** | 1291kg |

**PRICE GUIDE**

| | |
|---|---|
| **Launch price:** | £25,000 |
| **Excellent:** | £52,000 |
| **Good:** | £38,000 |
| **Average:** | £26,000 |
| **Project:** | £14,000 |

## LANCIA
### Thema/Thema Turbo

The Thema was the first of the joint Fiat/Alfa/Saab 'Type 4' cars to hit the market. The body was Giugiaro-generic, but the plush Alcantara-trimmed interior was very inviting. Pick of the range from launch was the 2.0-litre turbo, initially offered in 8-valve form. The combination of speed and serenity was an appealing one, even if 165bhp going through the front wheels could be a recipe for torque steer. Later 16-valve cars had 185bhp (dropping the 0-60 time to just 6.8sec), while facelifts improved the car little by little. Prices are creeping up, but still good value.

**SPECIFICATIONS (ie Turbo)**

| | |
|---|---|
| **Years produced:** | 1984-1994 |
| **Performance:** | 0-60mph: 7.2sec<br>Top speed: 135mph |
| **Power & torque:** | 165bhp/210lb ft |
| **Engine:** | Turbocharged 1995cc four cylinder, petrol, electronic fuel injection, 8 valves |
| **Drivetrain:** | Front-engine FWD |
| **Structure:** | Monocoque |
| **Transmission:** | Five-speed manual |
| **Weight:** | 1285kg |

**PRICE GUIDE**

| | |
|---|---|
| **Launch price:** | £11,000 |
| **Excellent:** | £6000 |
| **Good:** | £4000 |
| **Average:** | £2000 |
| **Project:** | £1000 |

## LANCIA
### Thema 8.32

The Ferrari V8 that was shoehorned into Lancia's flagship saloon was not actually assembled by Ferrari. The job of screwing it together was outsourced to Ducati engineers, and it featured a 90° crank in place of the 308's flat-planer. The epic soundtrack and moderate performance were not enough to sell it, and UK sales were dire, with just nine 8.32s officially sold. It did slightly better in Europe, but the killer for it was the Thema 16V Turbo, which was about as quick and much cheaper. Didn't have the 8.32's hand-stitched hide trim, mind.

**SPECIFICATIONS**

| | |
|---|---|
| **Years produced:** | 1988-1990 (3971 in total) |
| **Performance:** | 0-60mph: 6.8sec<br>Top speed: 149mph |
| **Power & torque:** | 215bhp/210lb ft |
| **Engine:** | Normally aspirated 2927cc V8, petrol, electronic fuel injection, 32 valves |
| **Drivetrain:** | Front-engine FWD |
| **Structure:** | Monocoque |
| **Transmission:** | Five-speed manual |
| **Weight:** | 1400kg |

**PRICE GUIDE**

| | |
|---|---|
| **Launch price:** | £40,095 |
| **Excellent:** | £25,000 |
| **Good:** | £15,000 |
| **Average:** | £10,000 |
| **Project:** | £4000 |

# LAND ROVER

INITIALLY, LAND ROVER referred just to a vehicle; the original Rover off-roader launched in 1948. As the range expanded, so Land Rover became a marque in its own right, with vehicles such as the Range Rover, Defender, Freelander and Discovery sheltering under the auspices of its badge. Historically an inseparable part of Rover, the marque was sold to Ford in 2000 when owner BMW broke up the company, and it became closely connected with Jaguar during its Blue Oval days. Ford's financial troubles forced it to sell Jaguar Land Rover to Indian conglomerate Tata; with the acquisition of Land Rover came the rights to the parent Rover name as well. A revival is unlikely...

## LAND ROVER
### Series I

In the aftermath of World War Two, Rover chief engineer Maurice Wilks owned a 'demobbed' Jeep and was impressed with its abilities. It wore out and, as there was no British replacement on the market, he decided to build his own. The Land Rover appeared in 1948 and proved so popular that demand massively outstripped supply. It went on to become an enduring success that helped keep the rest of Rover afloat during the 1950s. Now known as the S1, these early cars are enduring classics. Pre-1953 models are particularly prized, though values have levelled off.

**SPECIFICATIONS**

| | |
|---|---|
| **Years produced:** | 1948-1957 |
| **Performance:** | 0-60mph: N/A<br>Top speed: 55mph |
| **Power & torque:** | 50bhp/N/A |
| **Engine:** | Normally aspirated 1595cc four cylinder, petrol, carburettor, 8 valves |
| **Drivetrain:** | Front-engine AWD |
| **Structure:** | Separate chassis |
| **Transmission:** | Four-speed manual/high & low ratios |
| **Weight:** | 1177kg |

**PRICE GUIDE (Pre-'53 in brackets)**

| | |
|---|---|
| **Launch price:** | £450 |
| **Excellent:** | £25,000 (£40,000) |
| **Good:** | £15,000 (£30,000) |
| **Average:** | £6000 (£17,000) |
| **Project:** | £2250 (£6000) |

## LAND ROVER SII/SIIA

A decade after the Land Rover's launch, when it was still hugely popular, the Series II appeared with revised styling and powered by a new 2.25-litre petrol engine. The Series IIA that followed 18 months later was improved to include a 2.6-litre petrol engine in the LWB version, and a new 2.25-litre diesel, significantly expanding the car's appeal in export markets. Considered the ultimate DIY car, Land Rovers are revered for the ease with which you can work on them, and the SII remains good value, though prices have been rising steadily.

### SPECIFICATIONS

| | |
|---|---|
| **Years produced:** | 1958-1971 |
| **Performance:** | 0-60mph: 36.1sec<br>Top speed: 65mph |
| **Power & torque:** | 77bhp/N/A |
| **Engine:** | Normally aspirated 2286cc four cylinder, petrol, carburettor, 8 valves |
| **Drivetrain:** | Front-engine AWD |
| **Structure:** | Separate chassis |
| **Transmission:** | Four-speed manual/high & low ratios |
| **Weight:** | 1092kg |

### PRICE GUIDE

| | |
|---|---|
| **Launch price:** | £640 |
| **Excellent:** | £17,500 |
| **Good:** | £9500 |
| **Average:** | £4250 |
| **Project:** | £1500 |

## LAND ROVER SIII

Series III models are easy to spot thanks to the repositioned headlights (late SIIAs had them, too) and plastic radiator grille. The updated – more safety-conscious – interior and all-synchromesh gearbox acknowledged that the opposition was catching up, and the option of overdrive catered for those who needed their Land Rovers for serious on-road work. It was during SIII production that the Rover V8 was added to the range, initially in low-compression form to allow it to run whatever grade of fuel its owner threw at it.

### SPECIFICATIONS

| | |
|---|---|
| **Years produced:** | 1971-1985 |
| **Performance:** | 0-60mph: 29.1sec<br>Top speed: 68mph |
| **Power & torque:** | 70bhp/119lb ft |
| **Engine:** | Normally aspirated 2286cc four cylinder, petrol, carburettor, 8 valves |
| **Drivetrain:** | Front-engine AWD |
| **Structure:** | Separate chassis |
| **Transmission:** | Four-speed manual/high & low ratios |
| **Weight:** | 1380kg |

### PRICE GUIDE

| | |
|---|---|
| **Launch price:** | £1002 |
| **Excellent:** | £12,000 |
| **Good:** | £6000 |
| **Average:** | £3200 |
| **Project:** | £1300 |

## RANGE ROVER Classic

Instigator of the SUV and a classless conveyance, the Range Rover introduced the joys of off-roading to a whole new clientele. Powered by Rover's ex-Buick V8 and using chassis technology similar to the Land Rover's, its off-road ability was beyond reproach, while the hose-clean interior proved just the ticket for those with an active lifestyle. Styling was so lean that the Range Rover was at home in the politest places. It became ever-more luxurious and its appeal remained undimmed over a 25-year run. Exceptional cars fetch considerably more.

### SPECIFICATIONS

| | |
|---|---|
| **Years produced:** | 1970-1995 |
| **Performance:** | 0-60mph: 14.2sec<br>Top speed: 99mph |
| **Power & torque:** | 135bhp/185lb ft |
| **Engine:** | Normally aspirated 3528cc V8, petrol, carburettor, 16 valves |
| **Drivetrain:** | Front-engine AWD |
| **Structure:** | Separate chassis |
| **Transmission:** | Four-speed manual/three-speed auto |
| **Weight:** | 1760kg |

### PRICE GUIDE (early 2-door in brackets)

| | |
|---|---|
| **Launch price:** | £1998 |
| **Excellent:** | £30,000 (£47,500) |
| **Good:** | £18,500 (£33,500) |
| **Average:** | £8000 (£22,000) |
| **Project:** | £3500 (£13,500) |

## LAND ROVER Defender

Launched in 1983 as the 'Ninety' and 'One Ten', this new coil-sprung Land Rover was a revelation, adding higher levels of refinement and improved off-road ability. With new 4wd hardware derived from the Range Rover, a nicer interior and range of reliable petrol and diesel engines, it revitalised the beloved Land Rover. Renamed Defender in 1991, it continued to endear itself to enthusiasts until 2016. Td5s (1998-2007) a firm favourite. Last-of-the-line Heritage models already proving collectible and fetch serious money.

### SPECIFICATIONS

| | |
|---|---|
| **Years produced:** | 1983-2016 |
| **Performance:** | 0-60mph: 17.5sec (Td5)<br>Top speed: 81mph |
| **Power & torque:** | 120bhp/221lb ft |
| **Engine:** | Turbocharged 2495cc five cylinder, diesel, 10 valves |
| **Drivetrain:** | Front-engine AWD |
| **Structure:** | Separate chassis |
| **Transmission:** | Five-speed manual |
| **Weight:** | 1770kg |

### PRICE GUIDE (Td5 in brackets)

| | |
|---|---|
| **Launch price:** | £9212 |
| **Excellent:** | £15,000 (£18,000) |
| **Good:** | £9500 (12,000) |
| **Average:** | £6500 (£8500) |
| **Project:** | £4000 (£6000) |

## LAND ROVER Discovery 1

Developed to fill the gap between the Defender and upmarket Range Rover, the Discovery was available in three-door from launch, with either twin-carb V8 or 200 TDi engines. 1990 saw the introduction of the five-door and fuel-injected V8, with the much-improved 300 TDi and 3.9 V8 coming in 1994. For many years diesels were more desirable as dependable workhorses, but now in classic territory the V8s are growing in popularity. Launch-spec 'G-WAC' cars are worth slightly more. Cheap to run, but look out for rust.

### SPECIFICATIONS

| | |
|---|---|
| **Years produced:** | 1989-1998 |
| **Performance:** | 0-60mph: 17.1sec (200 TDi)<br>Top speed: 92mph |
| **Power & torque:** | 111bhp/195lb ft |
| **Engine:** | Turbocharged 2495cc four cylinder, diesel, 8 valves |
| **Drivetrain:** | Front-engine AWD |
| **Structure:** | Separate chassis |
| **Transmission:** | Five-speed manual |
| **Weight:** | 2012kg |

### PRICE GUIDE

| | |
|---|---|
| **Launch price:** | £16,885 |
| **Excellent:** | £7500 |
| **Good:** | £4200 |
| **Average:** | £2700 |
| **Project:** | £750 |

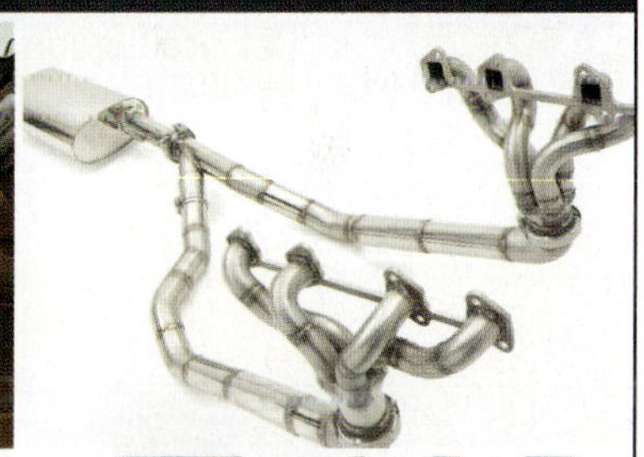

## RANGE ROVER
### P38

Replacing the original Range Rover was not easy. Many of the core ingredients – separate chassis, Rover V8 engine and plush interior – remained but the new model was bigger and more refined, with a lot more 1990s tech. Despite a reputation for unreliability, the P38 can make a great modern classic if you get one that has been maintained properly. Later cars suffered far fewer electrical issues, and none rusts particularly badly. BMW diesel engine strong and reliable, but the 4.6-litre Rover V8 is the one to have. Values rising slowly.

**SPECIFICATIONS**

| | |
|---|---|
| **Years produced:** | 1994-2002 |
| **Performance:** | 0-60mph: 9.3sec (V8)<br>Top speed: 125mph |
| **Power & torque:** | 225bhp/277lb ft |
| **Engine:** | Normally aspirated 4552cc V8, petrol, fuel injection, 16 valves |
| **Drivetrain:** | Front-engine AWD |
| **Structure:** | Separate chassis |
| **Transmission:** | Five-speed manual/four-speed auto |
| **Weight:** | 2220kg |

**PRICE GUIDE**

| | |
|---|---|
| **Launch price:** | £36,995 |
| **Excellent:** | £6000 |
| **Good:** | £3500 |
| **Average:** | £1800 |
| **Project:** | £700 |

## RANGE ROVER
### L322

Finally switching to a unitary body brought many benefits, not least improved ride and handling. Much of the L322 development was undertaken with BMW money, but it was actually launched two years after Land Rover's sale to Ford. That means early cars get BMW V8 petrol and straight-six diesel, with in-house Ford and Jaguar engines and technology post-2006. Wonderful things to be in and temptingly cheap, but potential for scarily high running costs. A good one might be expensive to run, a bad one potentially ruinous.

**SPECIFICATIONS**

| | |
|---|---|
| **Years produced:** | 2002-2012 |
| **Performance:** | 0-60mph: 8.7sec (4.4 V8)<br>Top speed: 129mph |
| **Power & torque:** | 282bhp/325lb ft |
| **Engine:** | Naturally aspirated 4398cc V8, petrol, fuel injection, 32 valves |
| **Drivetrain:** | Front-engine AWD |
| **Structure:** | Monocoque |
| **Transmission:** | Five/six/eight-speed auto |
| **Weight:** | 2440kg |

**PRICE GUIDE**

| | |
|---|---|
| **Launch price:** | £55,100 |
| **Excellent:** | £10,000 |
| **Good:** | £9500 |
| **Average:** | £6000 |
| **Project:** | £1200 |

# LEA-FRANCIS

THIS BRITISH company has had a chequered existence. Its first incarnation as a car firm was in 1904 but, after a few years, it reverted to making motorcycles. Car production restarted in 1920, focusing on sports models, but the company folded in 1937. A reborn entity bounded back but its products were never built in great numbers and, by 1954, it was all over once more for Lea-Francis. There was an attempted comeback in 1960 with the controversially-styled Lynx, but with no takers. The marque and its assets were subsequently bought by arch-enthusiast Barrie Price, and a retro-look prototype, the 30/230, appeared in 1998, but again no orders were forthcoming.

## LEA-FRANCIS
### 14 Saloon

As one of the original British motor industry players, the pre-war years had been good for Lea-Francis. Its competition cars had proved themselves and earned an enviable reputation with enthusiasts. After the war, the firm concentrated on saloon car production, initially with its 14hp saloon. The 14 sat very much at the upper end of the market and found fewer buyers than anticipated, but the addition of a 2.5-litre engine in 1949 widened appeal. Lea-Francis continued with this line until 1953, then abandoned car production to concentrate on other activities.

**SPECIFICATIONS**

| | |
|---|---|
| **Years produced:** | 1946-1954 (3137 in total) |
| **Performance:** | 0-60mph: N/A<br>Top speed: 70mph |
| **Power & torque:** | 55bhp/N/A |
| **Engine:** | Normally aspirated 1469cc four cylinder, petrol, carburettor, 8 valves |
| **Drivetrain:** | Front-engine RWD |
| **Structure:** | Separate chassis |
| **Transmission:** | Four-speed manual |
| **Weight:** | 1270kg |

**PRICE GUIDE**

| | |
|---|---|
| **Launch price:** | £951 |
| **Excellent:** | £12,000 |
| **Good:** | £9000 |
| **Average:** | £5000 |
| **Project:** | £3000 |

## LEA-FRANCIS
### 14hp/2.5-litre Sports

A classic English sports car powered by the saloon's 1.8-litre engine, following the established template that proved so popular in export markets. The twin-cam engine was intriguing because it aped Riley's pre-war design, and delivered enough power for a top speed of 85mph. Later models gained independent front suspension and proved to be excellent-handling cars, while the 2.5-litre Sports that followed in 1950 added extra power into the mix, becoming a genuine 100mph four-seater. Values are strong: best now worth over £50k.

**SPECIFICATIONS**

| | |
|---|---|
| **Years produced:** | 1947-1953 (186 in total) |
| **Performance:** | 0-60mph: 19.2sec<br>Top speed: 87mph |
| **Power & torque:** | 87bhp/N/A |
| **Engine:** | Normally aspirated 1767cc four cylinder, petrol, carburettor, 8 valves |
| **Drivetrain:** | Front-engine RWD |
| **Structure:** | Separate chassis |
| **Transmission:** | Four-speed manual |
| **Weight:** | 1016kg |

**PRICE GUIDE**

| | |
|---|---|
| **Launch price:** | £1266 |
| **Excellent:** | £50,000 |
| **Good:** | £35,000 |
| **Average:** | £27,000 |
| **Project:** | £15,000 |

# LOTUS

COLIN CHAPMAN began building competition specials in 1948 and eventually expanded into selling kits to the public, forming Lotus Engineering in 1952. But it was the Seven of 1957 that really brought the small-scale manufacturer to the attention of the masses, along with the good-looking glassfibre Elite. The Elan (1962-1973) became a benchmark for how a sports car should handle and the Esprit (1976-2004) had supercar looks and (eventually) performance.

Following Chapman's death in 1982, Lotus passed through a number of hands, including GM and the Korean firm Proton. Since 2017 the biggest stakeholder has been Chinese carmaker Geely, which also owns Volvo among others.

## LOTUS Six

Intended as a street-legal weekend racer, the predecessor to the legendary Seven uses a lightweight spaceframe clothed in alloy panels and fitted with Ford brakes and rear axle. All were sold in kit form, so specification can vary widely. Most commonly used engines were Ford, either in sidevalve 1172cc or OHV 1500 form, though some had 1250cc MG units. In all cases the lack of weight means a lot more fun and performance than you might expect. Highly prized today and cars with race history can fetch £80k+, says specialist Paul Matty.

**SPECIFICATIONS**

| | |
|---|---|
| Years produced: | 1953-1956 (100 in total) |
| Performance: | 0-60mph: N/A<br>Top speed: 93mph |
| Power & torque: | 36bhp/N/A |
| Engine: | Normally aspirated 1172cc four cylinder, petrol, carburettor, 8 valves |
| Drivetrain: | Front-engine RWD |
| Structure: | Tub and spaceframe |
| Transmission: | Three-speed manual |
| Weight: | N/A (very light) |

**PRICE GUIDE**

| | |
|---|---|
| Launch price: | £185 |
| Excellent: | £65,000 |
| Good: | £50,000 |
| Average: | £35,000 |
| Project: | £20,000 |

## LOTUS Seven S1/S2

A legend that lives on today. Refinements over the Six include wishbone front suspension and hydraulic brakes. S1s initially sold with Ford's sidevalve engine, with later S1s and S2s offered with the 948cc BMC A-series and its four-speed 'box; from 1961 there was also the option of the 997cc Anglia engines. Don't be surprised by later upgrades though. S2s are distinguished by their glassfibre nosecones, but they also have a less complex spaceframe and revised rear axle location. Early cars can feel quite crude, even by general Seven standards, but undeniably engaging!

**SPECIFICATIONS**

| | |
|---|---|
| Years produced: | 1957-1968 (242/1350 in total) |
| Performance: | 0-60mph: 17.8sec<br>Top speed: 76mph |
| Power & torque: | 40bhp/58lb ft |
| Engine: | Normally aspirated 1172cc four cylinder, petrol, carburettor, 8 valves |
| Drivetrain: | Front-engine RWD |
| Structure: | Tub and spaceframe |
| Transmission: | Three-speed manual |
| Weight: | 457kg |

**PRICE GUIDE**

| | |
|---|---|
| Launch price: | £1036 |
| Excellent: | £35,000 |
| Good: | £25,000 |
| Average: | £20,000 |
| Project: | £10,000 |

## LOTUS Super Seven

Really pushing the 'race car for the road' theme, the Super Sevens came with longer glassfibre front wings and Cosworth-tuned Ford engines of 1340, 1500 or 1600cc capacity and phenomenal performance. To rein this back, those with the larger engines came with the welcome addition of disc brakes. Many were still sold as kits, and they've always appealed to those of a tinkering nature, so expect the unexpected as far as specification goes. A dozen or so 'Super Sevens' were fitted with Lotus twin-cam engines, but only genuine ones are worth the extra these command.

**SPECIFICATIONS**

| | |
|---|---|
| Years produced: | 1957-1968 (500+ in total) |
| Performance: | 0-60mph: 9.0sec<br>Top speed: 102mph |
| Power & torque: | 95bhp/103lb ft |
| Engine: | Normally aspirated 1498cc four cylinder, petrol, carburettor, 8 valves |
| Drivetrain: | Front-engine RWD |
| Structure: | Tub and spaceframe |
| Transmission: | Four-speed manual |
| Weight: | 435kg |

**PRICE GUIDE**

| | |
|---|---|
| Launch price: | £1250 |
| Excellent: | £35,000 |
| Good: | £25,000 |
| Average: | £20,000 |
| Project: | £10,000 |

## LOTUS Elite

The undoubted star of the 1957 Earl's Court Motor Show, but Lotus kept buyers waiting until the summer of 1959 to enjoy this technical marvel. Use of a chassis-less glassfibre monocoque and aluminium Coventry-Climax 1200cc 71bhp engine resulted in the incredibly light weight that made this car perform and handle so well. 1960 brought a Series II model with improved rear suspension and trim, plus the SE with its close-ratio ZF gearbox and optional breathing package for an extra 10bhp. Utterly fabulous, but noisy inside, and quite a squeeze for six-footers. Values have softened recently.

**SPECIFICATIONS**

| | |
|---|---|
| Years produced: | 1958-1963 (998 in total) |
| Performance: | 0-60mph: 11.4sec<br>Top speed: 112mph |
| Power & torque: | 71bhp/77lb ft |
| Engine: | Normally aspirated 1216cc four cylinder, petrol, carburettor, 8 valves |
| Drivetrain: | Front-engine RWD |
| Structure: | Glassfibre monocoque |
| Transmission: | Four-speed manual |
| Weight: | 660kg |

**PRICE GUIDE**

| | |
|---|---|
| Launch price: | £1951 |
| Excellent: | £85,000 |
| Good: | £65,000 |
| Average: | £55,000 |
| Project: | £25,000 |

# LOTUS
## Elan DHC

The lightweight sports car against whose handling all others would be measured for decades. Independent suspension on a backbone chassis was the stuff of genius, and makes the indifferent fit and finish of the glassfibre bodies almost irrelevant. Gradually improved through four series, each of which outsold the last: S2 gained larger front brake calipers; S3 (from 1966) has frames for the windows, centre-lock alloy wheels and a higher final drive ratio; S4 got a bonnet bulge to cover its twin Stromberg carbs, but reverted to Webers in late 1969. SE means 115bhp and close-ratio gearbox.

### SPECIFICATIONS

**Years produced:** 1962-1971 (c10,500 in total)
**Performance:** 0-60mph: 8.0sec
Top speed: 110mph
**Power & torque:** 100bhp/102lb ft
**Engine:** Normally aspirated 1499cc four cylinder, petrol, carburettor, 8 valves
**Drivetrain:** Front-engine RWD
**Structure:** Glassfibre body/backbone chassis
**Transmission:** Four-speed manual
**Weight:** 585kg

### PRICE GUIDE

**Launch price:** £1499
**Excellent:** £50,000
**Good:** £35,000
**Average:** £25,000
**Project:** £12,000

# LOTUS
## Elan S3/S4 Coupé

Hardtop version of the Elan was used to introduce the S3, and arrived the year before its soft-top brother. In line with Lotus's intention to move upmarket and justify its 'quality' prices, fit and finish was improved over the earlier Elans, and the Coupé came with a smarter dashboard and frames for the door windows to reduce wind noise. The windows themselves were now electrically operated. SE model was offered from July 1966 with 115bhp engine, standard servo brakes, a close-ratio gearbox, plus a slightly taller rear axle ratio to make things a little quieter at high speeds.

### SPECIFICATIONS

**Years produced:** 1965-1971 (c4500 in total)
**Performance:** 0-60mph: 8.7sec
Top speed: 114mph
**Power & torque:** 105bhp/108lb ft
**Engine:** Normally aspirated 1558cc four cylinder, petrol, carburettor, 8 valves
**Drivetrain:** Front-engine RWD
**Structure:** Glassfibre body/backbone chassis
**Transmission:** Four-speed manual
**Weight:** 688kg

### PRICE GUIDE

**Launch price:** £1312
**Excellent:** £50,000
**Good:** £35,000
**Average:** £22,000
**Project:** £10,000

# LOTUS
## Europa S1/S2

Colin Chapman's first mid-engined road car was aimed squarely at the glamorous European market, where Italians were making inroads with the layout. Based around Renault 16 running gear, all S1s went for export. They also had their glassfibre body bonded to the steel chassis, making repairs a nightmare. Europa S2s were sold in the UK from 1969, with bodies bolted to the chassis and electric windows. All but US exports came with 1470cc Renault engines, though many 1565cc units have since been transplanted from dead Renaults. Twin Cam is really the one everyone wants.

### SPECIFICATIONS

**Years produced:** 1967-1971
**Performance:** 0-60mph: 9.3sec
Top speed: 117mph
**Power & torque:** 78bhp/76lb ft
**Engine:** Normally aspirated 1470cc four cylinder, petrol, carburettor, 8 valves
**Drivetrain:** Mid-engine RWD
**Structure:** Glassfibre body/backbone chassis
**Transmission:** Four-speed manual
**Weight:** 706kg

### PRICE GUIDE

**Launch price:** £1996
**Excellent:** £30,000
**Good:** £18,000
**Average:** £10,000
**Project:** £6000

# LOTUS
## Seven S3

Sold alongside the Super Seven, the S3 came with Ford engines in a saner state of tune, though all sizes from 1300-1600cc were available. Tuning options came from Holbay, not Cosworth for these. This is the car that was revived officially by Caterham (and unofficially by everyone else), but the 350 or so originals command a decent premium for all that heritage. Still largely sold as kits originally, which means fit and finish has always been variable, and many examples are likely to have been rebuilt several times during their life. Values have slipped recently, but the fun factor is as high as ever.

### SPECIFICATIONS

**Years produced:** 1968-1970 (1413 in total)
**Performance:** 0-60mph: 7.7sec
Top speed: 99mph
**Power & torque:** 84bhp/96lb ft
**Engine:** Normally aspirated 1598cc four cylinder, petrol, carburettor, 8 valves
**Drivetrain:** Front-engine RWD
**Structure:** Tub and spaceframe
**Transmission:** Four-speed manual
**Weight:** 549kg

### PRICE GUIDE

**Launch price:** £775
**Excellent:** £32,500
**Good:** £27,000
**Average:** £20,000
**Project:** £12,000

# LOTUS
## Elan Plus 2

Taking one step further away from the racetrack, Lotus widened its range to include something for buyers with young families. By stretching the Elan's chassis by a foot and widening the track, child-sized rear seats could be accommodated. This was also the first Lotus not to be sold in kit form. The 118bhp engine tune helps with the extra weight, and power was raised to 126bhp from 1970 for the Plus 2S/130. Better quality trim is a feature, and from 1972 the 130-5 comes with a five-speed gearbox. The market has finally woken up to this fun, useable classic, says specialist Paul Matty.

### SPECIFICATIONS

**Years produced:** 1967-1974 (3300 in total)
**Performance:** 0-60mph: 8.2sec
Top speed: 123mph
**Power & torque:** 118bhp/112lb ft
**Engine:** Normally aspirated 1558cc four cylinder, petrol, carburettor, 8 valves
**Drivetrain:** Front-engine RWD
**Structure:** Glassfibre body/backbone chassis
**Transmission:** Four-speed manual
**Weight:** 854kg

### PRICE GUIDE

**Launch price:** £1923
**Excellent:** £45,000
**Good:** £35,000
**Average:** £18,000
**Project:** £10,000

## LOTUS
# Seven S4

Stylistically, Lotus lost the plot with the S4. In some ways it's a better car, with decent legroom at last, improved front and rear suspension and all-glassfibre bodywork over a new steel chassis. Unfortunately that all added an extra couple of hundred pounds to the weight, slightly blunting the scorching performance and handling that Sevens are all about. And that new bodywork falls somewhere between archaic special and racing beach buggy. You can see why Caterham went back to the S3 when it took over manufacture. That said, values have been edging up in the last year.

### SPECIFICATIONS

| | |
|---|---|
| **Years produced:** | 1970-1973 (887 in total) |
| **Performance:** | 0-60mph: 8.7sec<br>Top speed: 116mph |
| **Power & torque:** | 115bhp/108lb ft |
| **Engine:** | Normally aspirated 1598cc four cylinder, petrol, carburettor, 8 valves |
| **Drivetrain:** | Front-engine RWD |
| **Structure:** | Tub and spaceframe |
| **Transmission:** | Four-speed manual |
| **Weight:** | 579kg |

### PRICE GUIDE

| | |
|---|---|
| **Launch price:** | £1245 |
| **Excellent:** | £18,750 |
| **Good:** | £13,500 |
| **Average:** | £9000 |
| **Project:** | £5000 |

## LOTUS
# Elan Sprint

Introduced to boost flagging sales, the Sprint justified its name thanks to a substantial boost in the engine department. A big-valve head with high-lift cams and a raised compression ratio lifted output to 126bhp and the drivetrain was suitably toughened to cope. Both coupé and roadster versions were built, with gold-painted bumpers and two-tone paint to set them apart from other Elans – single-tone paint was an extra-cost option. With prices approaching those of E-type Jags, only around 1000 were sold, some of the last with five-speed gearboxes. Concours cars fetch £60k+.

### SPECIFICATIONS

| | |
|---|---|
| **Years produced:** | 1971-1973 |
| **Performance:** | 0-60mph: 6.7sec<br>Top speed: 121mph |
| **Power & torque:** | 126bhp/113lb ft |
| **Engine:** | Normally aspirated 1558cc four cylinder, petrol, carburettor, 8 valves |
| **Drivetrain:** | Front-engine RWD |
| **Structure:** | Glassfibre body/backbone chassis |
| **Transmission:** | Four-speed manual |
| **Weight:** | 721kg |

### PRICE GUIDE

| | |
|---|---|
| **Launch price:** | £1706 |
| **Excellent:** | £55,000 |
| **Good:** | £40,000 |
| **Average:** | £30,000 |
| **Project:** | £20,000 |

## LOTUS
# Europa Twin Cam/Special

Accusations that the Europa was underpowered were dealt with by the simple expedient of fitting the Lotus twin-cam unit, initially in 105bhp form, but with 126bhp in the Special in 1972. Most of these celebrated Lotus's grand prix success by being painted John Player Special colours. Both of these Europas still used the Renault 16 gearbox (with an improved gear linkage), though the Specials could also be had with a five-speed version from the 17TS. Visually, these twin-cam models differed from the S1/S2 by having cut-down rear 'buttresses' to improve visibility.

### SPECIFICATIONS

| | |
|---|---|
| **Years produced:** | 1971-1975 (1580 in total) |
| **Performance:** | 0-60mph: 7.7sec<br>Top speed: 109mph |
| **Power & torque:** | 105bhp/108lb ft |
| **Engine:** | Normally aspirated 1558cc four cylinder, petrol, carburettor, 8 valves |
| **Drivetrain:** | Front-engine RWD |
| **Structure:** | Glassfibre body/backbone chassis |
| **Transmission:** | Four-speed manual |
| **Weight:** | 737kg |

### PRICE GUIDE

| | |
|---|---|
| **Launch price:** | £1996 |
| **Excellent:** | £36,000 |
| **Good:** | £24,000 |
| **Average:** | £15,000 |
| **Project:** | £6000 |

## LOTUS
# Elite

In an effort to shed its kit-car image, Lotus took a giant leap upmarket in 1974 with the Elite – a four-seater coupé with an opening glass tailgate. In concept the Elite owed much to the Reliant Scimitar GTE, even if it was less obviously a shooting brake. The all-new 2.0-litre Lotus twin-cam Type 921 first appeared in the Jensen-Healey but, by the time Lotus started selling it in its own cars, most of the teething problems had been sorted. Expanded to a torquier 2.2 litres from 1980, when a Getrag five-speed gearbox was also fitted. Increasing interest in the best examples.

### SPECIFICATIONS

| | |
|---|---|
| **Years produced:** | 1974-1983 (2398 in total) |
| **Performance:** | 0-60mph: 7.8sec<br>Top speed: 124mph |
| **Power & torque:** | 160bhp/140lb ft |
| **Engine:** | Normally aspirated 1973cc four cylinder, petrol, carburettor, 16 valves |
| **Drivetrain:** | Front-engine RWD |
| **Structure:** | Glassfibre body/backbone chassis |
| **Transmission:** | Five-speed manual |
| **Weight:** | 1107kg |

### PRICE GUIDE

| | |
|---|---|
| **Launch price:** | £5445 |
| **Excellent:** | £18,000 |
| **Good:** | £10,000 |
| **Average:** | £4000 |
| **Project:** | £950 |

## LOTUS
# Éclat

As the American market didn't take to the Elite's styling, it was joined the following year by the Type 76 Éclat, pretty much the same car but with the rear panels reshaped into a more familiar fastback form, also losing about 45kg in weight in the process. The Oliver Winterbottom-penned and exceptionally wedgy Éclat had more mainstream appeal even if it was less practical than the Esprit, although that could have been as much about the lower list price. Model range numbered 521, 522 and 523, with the higher the number, the higher the equipment level.

### SPECIFICATIONS

| | |
|---|---|
| **Years produced:** | 1974-1983 (1299 in total) |
| **Performance:** | 0-60mph: 7.8sec<br>Top speed: 124mph |
| **Power & torque:** | 160bhp/140lb ft |
| **Engine:** | Normally aspirated 1973cc four cylinder, petrol, carburettor, 16 valves |
| **Drivetrain:** | Front-engine RWD |
| **Structure:** | Glassfibre body/backbone chassis |
| **Transmission:** | Five-speed manual |
| **Weight:** | 1107kg |

### PRICE GUIDE

| | |
|---|---|
| **Launch price:** | £4995 |
| **Excellent:** | £15,000 |
| **Good:** | £9000 |
| **Average:** | £4000 |
| **Project:** | £950 |

## LOTUS
## Esprit S1

Lotus turned to Giugiaro to design a flagship that gained instant pin-up status, and an appearance as a Bond car in *The Spy Who Loved Me*. Still using the established Elan system of a glassfibre body over a backbone chassis, the Esprit had its 2.0-litre twin-cam engine mid-mounted. With modest output but relatively low weight, 160bhp placed the Esprit's performance on the coat-tails of the junior supercar league. Handling was flat and grippy, setting new standards for the opposition to aim for. Reliability not the best. Values currently firm, with concours cars now £80k-plus.

**SPECIFICATIONS**

| | |
|---|---|
| **Years produced:** | 1976-1977 (718 in total) |
| **Performance:** | 0-60mph: 8.4sec<br>Top speed: 135mph |
| **Power & torque:** | 160bhp/140lb ft |
| **Engine:** | Normally aspirated 1973cc four cylinder, petrol, carburettor, 16 valves |
| **Drivetrain:** | Mid-engine RWD |
| **Structure:** | Glassfibre body/backbone chassis |
| **Transmission:** | Five-speed manual |
| **Weight:** | 1006kg |

**PRICE GUIDE**

| | |
|---|---|
| **Launch price:** | £7883 |
| **Excellent:** | £80,000 |
| **Good:** | £45,000 |
| **Average:** | £35,000 |
| **Project:** | £15,000 |

## LOTUS
## Esprit S2/S2.2

The original Esprit was a standard-bearer, but it wasn't without flaws. Cooling was marginal and the interior design lacked cohesion. In an attempt to put those faults right, Lotus quickly lauched the S2. It was marked out by minor modifications that included 'ears' behind the rear side windows to improve engine airflow, Speedline alloys and Rover SD1 taillights (to replace the Fiat X1/9 originals). For the final year of production, a 2.2-litre engine increased performance and driveability at no cost in fuel consumption. Excellent cars now fetching strong money.

**SPECIFICATIONS**

| | |
|---|---|
| **Years produced:** | 1977-1981 (1060 in total) |
| **Performance:** | 0-60mph: 8.4sec<br>Top speed: 135mph |
| **Power & torque:** | 160bhp/140lb ft |
| **Engine:** | Normally aspirated 1973cc four cylinder, petrol, carburettor, 16 valves |
| **Drivetrain:** | Mid-engine RWD |
| **Structure:** | Separate chassis |
| **Transmission:** | Five-speed manual |
| **Weight:** | 1026kg |

**PRICE GUIDE**

| | |
|---|---|
| **Launch price:** | £8500 |
| **Excellent:** | £40,000 |
| **Good:** | £20,000 |
| **Average:** | £15,000 |
| **Project:** | £6000 |

## LOTUS
## Turbo Esprit

Lotus was now touching supercar territory, with 0-60mph in under six seconds, and with almost peerless handling the Esprit could now be compared with Porsches and Ferraris. The extra 50bhp over the normal 2.2-litre Esprit comes from a Garrett T3 turbocharger, though the whole of the engine was re-engineered to cope. The first 104 were in Essex Petroleum livery (today, the best of these fetch c£75k+). In 1985 the suspension was revised to use more Toyota and fewer Triumph parts. Shortlived HC version had a little extra power. All prices holding steady.

**SPECIFICATIONS**

| | |
|---|---|
| **Years produced:** | 1980-1987 (1658 in total) |
| **Performance:** | 0-60mph: 5.6sec<br>Top speed: 141mph |
| **Power & torque:** | 215bhp/220lb ft |
| **Engine:** | Turbocharged 2174cc four cylinder, petrol, carburettor, 16 valves |
| **Drivetrain:** | Mid-engine RWD |
| **Structure:** | Glassfibre body/backbone chassis |
| **Transmission:** | Five-speed manual |
| **Weight:** | 1148kg |

**PRICE GUIDE**

| | |
|---|---|
| **Launch price:** | £25,980 |
| **Excellent:** | £65,000 (add £10,000+ for Essex) |
| **Good:** | £40,000 |
| **Average:** | £25,000 |
| **Project:** | £15,000 |

## LOTUS
## Esprit S3

Wearing most of the body, chassis and interior revisions introduced for the Turbo model the year before, the Esprit S3 also signalled a major leap forward in quality and reliability. There's a lot more sound insulation too, allegedly reducing noise levels inside by 50%. Despite the larger bumpers and air scoops, the design stays true to Giugiaro's concept. The rear wheels and tyres are larger, and lower-profile rubber is used to further sharpen the Esprit's superb handling and grip. Experts say these are a much better bet to live with than the S1 and S2 and good value.

**SPECIFICATIONS**

| | |
|---|---|
| **Years produced:** | 1981-1987 (767 in total) |
| **Performance:** | 0-60mph: 6.5sec<br>Top speed: 135mph |
| **Power & torque:** | 160bhp/160lb ft |
| **Engine:** | Normally aspirated 2174cc four cylinder, petrol, carburettor, 16 valves |
| **Drivetrain:** | Mid-engine RWD |
| **Structure:** | Glassfibre body/backbone chassis |
| **Transmission:** | Five-speed manual |
| **Weight:** | 1020kg |

**PRICE GUIDE**

| | |
|---|---|
| **Launch price:** | £13,461 |
| **Excellent:** | £35,000 |
| **Good:** | £25,000 |
| **Average:** | £15,000 |
| **Project:** | £6000 |

## LOTUS
## Excel

Thoroughly revised version of the Éclat, sold at first as the Éclat Excel to avoid the expense of putting the new car through Type Approval. Most body changes are on the rear half of the car, but the big stuff is underneath the skin with Toyota Supra five-speed transmission and brakes, plus broader, lower rear wishbones. The chassis was galvanised, too. The body was revised again in 1984 with Audi Quattro-style blisters, and from 1986 the SE version offered 180bhp, up 20bhp from the standard car. The same year the SA was launched with a ZF four-speed auto. Undervalued.

**SPECIFICATIONS**

| | |
|---|---|
| **Years produced:** | 1982-1992 (2074 in total) |
| **Performance:** | 0-60mph: 7.4sec<br>Top speed: 128mph |
| **Power & torque:** | 160bhp/160lb ft |
| **Engine:** | Normally aspirated 2174cc four cylinder, petrol, carburettor, 16 valves |
| **Drivetrain:** | Front-engine RWD |
| **Structure:** | Glassfibre body/backbone chassis |
| **Transmission:** | Five-speed manual |
| **Weight:** | 1135kg |

**PRICE GUIDE**

| | |
|---|---|
| **Launch price:** | £13,787 |
| **Excellent:** | £15,000 |
| **Good:** | £10,000 |
| **Average:** | £4000 |
| **Project:** | £2000 |

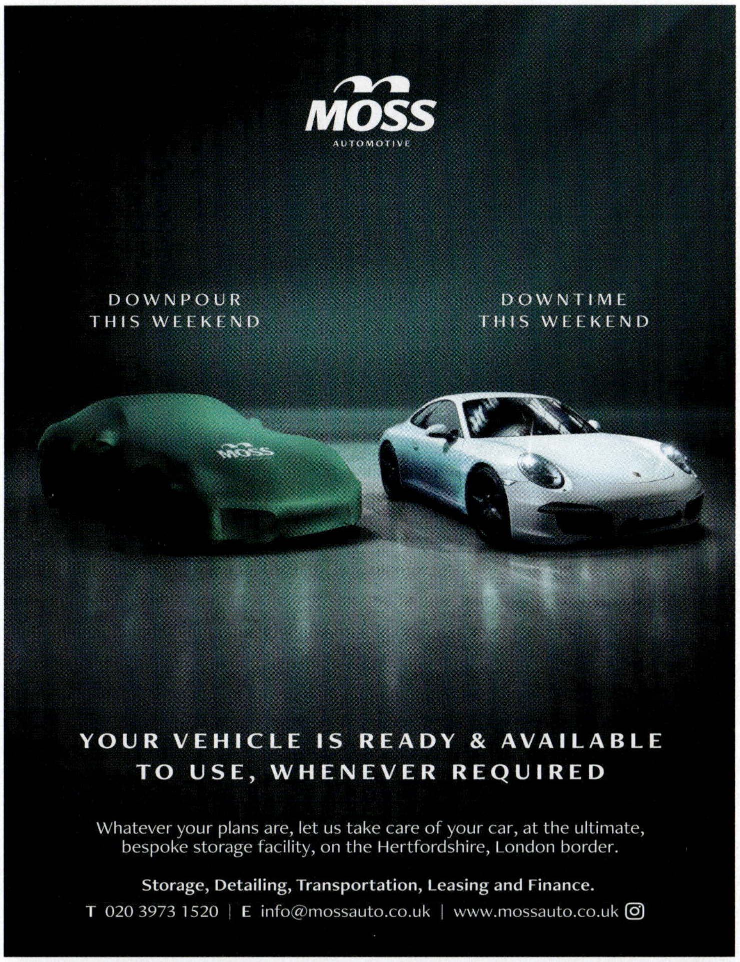
MOSS
AUTOMOTIVE
DOWNPOUR THIS WEEKEND
DOWNTIME THIS WEEKEND
YOUR VEHICLE IS READY & AVAILABLE TO USE, WHENEVER REQUIRED
Whatever your plans are, let us take care of your car, at the ultimate, bespoke storage facility, on the Hertfordshire, London border.
Storage, Detailing, Transportation, Leasing and Finance.
T 020 3973 1520 | E info@mossauto.co.uk | www.mossauto.co.uk

# LOTUS
## Esprit Turbo (X180) & SE

A subtle redesign by Peter Stevens knocked some of the sharp edges off Giugiaro's original styling, and there was also more interior space. Mechanically, both normally aspirated and Turbo versions carried on as before, with the exception of a little extra power in the lesser car to pull more weight. The Citroën SM transmission was replaced with Renault GTA units, along with outboard rear brakes. The SE, introduced in 1989 with a water-to-air intercooler, saw power climb to 264bhp and was the first Lotus to crack 0-60mph in under 5sec. Good value right now, says Paul Matty.

### SPECIFICATIONS

**Years produced:** 1987-1992 (3120 in total)
**Performance:** 0-60mph: 4.7sec (SE)
Top speed: 167mph
**Power & torque:** 264bhp/260lb ft
**Engine:** Turbocharged 2174cc four cylinder, petrol, fuel injection, 16 valves
**Drivetrain:** Mid-engine RWD
**Structure:** Glassfibre body/backbone chassis
**Transmission:** Five-speed manual
**Weight:** 1329kg

**PRICE GUIDE (SE in brackets)**

**Launch price:** £28,900 (£33,500)
**Excellent:** £20,000 (£25,000)
**Good:** £15,000 (£20,000)
**Average:** £10,000 (£15,000)
**Project:** £6500 (£9000)

# LOTUS
## Elan M100

Proof that sports cars can be front-wheel drive, as Lotus once again led the pack in handling technology. Almost all the first batch were turbocharged SE versions, though some 130bhp non-turbo models were sold; all use a long-lived Isuzu 1600 engine that Lotus helped design. Sadly, Lotus was losing money on every one of the 3855 Elans sold, so the plug was pulled after two years. When Bugatti bought Lotus in 1994, another 800 was made, subtly improved and using up engine stock. Badged S2, these are more sought-after today, but all versions are slowly developing a following.

### SPECIFICATIONS

**Years produced:** 1989-1994 (4655 in total)
**Performance:** 0-60mph: 6.5sec (SE)
Top speed: 136mph
**Power & torque:** 165bhp/148lb ft
**Engine:** Turbocharged 1588cc four cylinder, petrol, fuel injection, 16 valves
**Drivetrain:** Front-engine FWD
**Structure:** Monocoque with plastic panels
**Transmission:** Five-speed manual
**Weight:** 1085kg

**PRICE GUIDE**

**Launch price:** £19,850
**Excellent:** £15,000
**Good:** £11,000
**Average:** £7500
**Project:** £3000

# LOTUS
## Esprit Sport 300

Developed from Lotus's endurance racer, the Sport 300 is the rarest and most highly prized of all Esprit variants. A lighter composite body helped to shave around 80kg off the weight compared with a standard car and it was stiffer too, as was the backbone chassis. Brakes and suspension were uprated and thanks to a hybrid T3/T4 turbo and more efficient chargecooler, power was raised to a truly impressive 300bhp – hence the name. Fittings for a rollcage and race seats make it a cool trackday car. Just 64 examples are believed to have been built, which helps sustain values.

### SPECIFICATIONS

**Years produced:** 1992-1995 (64 produced)
**Performance:** 0-60mph: 4.5sec
Top speed: 162mph
**Power & torque:** 300bhp/287lb ft
**Engine:** Turbocharged 2174cc four cylinder, petrol, fuel injection, 16 valves
**Drivetrain:** Mid-engine RWD
**Structure:** Glassfibre body/backbone chassis
**Transmission:** Five-speed manual
**Weight:** 1243kg

**PRICE GUIDE**

**Launch price:** £64,995
**Excellent:** £70,000
**Good:** £50,000
**Average:** £35,000
**Project:** £17,000

# LOTUS
## Esprit S4

With a restyle by Julian Thomson that brought all manner of scoops, ducts, spoilers and bulges, the Esprit was given a dramatic makeover for the mid-1990s. It had the muscle to back it up too, early models having 264bhp on tap, while the S4S from 1994 had a full 300bhp. There was a new high-torque five-speed transmission, plus further advances in suspension dynamics to keep Lotus ahead in the game it plays best, while power steering was fitted as standard to an Esprit for the first time. Also look out for the excellent, stripped-down GT3 version that arrived in 1996.

### SPECIFICATIONS

**Years produced:** 1993-1997 (367 built)
**Performance:** 0-60mph: 4.7sec
Top speed: 165mph
**Power & torque:** 264bhp/261lb ft
**Engine:** Turbocharged 2174cc four cylinder, petrol, fuel injection, 16 valves
**Drivetrain:** Mid-engine RWD
**Structure:** Glassfibre body/backbone chassis
**Transmission:** Five-speed manual
**Weight:** 1320kg

**PRICE GUIDE**

**Launch price:** £46,995
**Excellent:** £40,000
**Good:** £27,000
**Average:** £21,000
**Project:** £12,000

# LOTUS
## Elise S1

After the FWD Elan experiment, the RWD Elise was a return to Lotus basics. It tipped the scales at just 731kg thanks to its bonded aluminium tub, and that lightness showed: direction changes felt instantaneous, power assistance for the steering wasn't required, and 118bhp from the 1.8 K-series engine was plenty. Not that there weren't more powerful models, of course. The VVC version of the K-series made possible the 111S (143bhp) and Sport 160 (158bhp for the first 50 built, 148bhp thereafter). Limited editions attract premiums.

### SPECIFICATIONS

**Years produced:** 1996-2001 (10,619 built)
**Performance:** 0-60mph: 6.1sec
Top speed: 126mph
**Power & torque:** 118bhp/122lb ft
**Engine:** Normally aspirated 1796cc four cylinder, petrol, electronic injection, 16 valves
**Drivetrain:** Mid-engine RWD
**Structure:** Aluminium tub with plastic panels
**Transmission:** Five-speed manual
**Weight:** 731kg

**PRICE GUIDE**

**Launch price:** £18,990
**Excellent:** £22,000
**Good:** £16,500
**Average:** £13,000
**Project:** £6000

# LOTUS
## Esprit V8/Sport 350

After 20 years with four-cylinder power, in 1996 the Esprit was finally offered with a V8. The Lotus-developed 3.5-litre was twin turbocharged and produced 350bhp, enabling the Esprit V8 to go from 0-60mph in 4.8sec and on to 175mph. In 1998 the V8-GT arrived – essentially a stripped-out V8 with a £10k price cut. A year later came the most extreme V8 Esprit of all: the Sport 350, with stiffer suspension, AP Racing brakes, revised ECU, race-style rear wing, and a 0-60 time of 4.3sec. Just 48 were built. Values currently on the up.

**SPECIFICATIONS**

| | |
|---|---|
| **Years produced:** | 1996-2001 (Sport 350 1999-2001) |
| **Performance:** | 0-60mph: 4.3sec (Sport 350)<br>Top speed: 175mph |
| **Power & torque:** | 350bhp/295lb ft |
| **Engine:** | Turbocharged 3506cc V8, petrol, electronic fuel injection, 32 valves |
| **Drivetrain:** | Mid-engine RWD |
| **Structure:** | Glassfibre body/backbone chassis |
| **Transmission:** | Five-speed manual |
| **Weight:** | 1299kg |

**PRICE GUIDE (Sport 350 in brackets)**

| | |
|---|---|
| **Launch price:** | £60,000 (£64,950) |
| **Excellent:** | £50,000 (£65,000) |
| **Good:** | £35,000 (£50,000) |
| **Average:** | £25,000 (£40,000) |
| **Project:** | £17,000 (£25,000) |

# LOTUS
## 340R

Legend has it the 340R was originally named because it was supposed to have 340bhp per ton. It didn't quite achieve that figure – 293bhp/ton was as good as it got – but no matter, this Elise derivative was still incredibly light, tipping the scales at just 658kg. Offered as standard with a 177bhp version of the VHPD K-series engine, all were ordered with the optional 190bhp upgrade. Despite its extreme looks, the 340R was surprisingly useable on the road: think Elise turned up to 12. Values have taken a hit recently.

**SPECIFICATIONS**

| | |
|---|---|
| **Years produced:** | 2000 (340 built) |
| **Performance:** | 0-60mph: 4.5sec<br>Top speed: 126mph |
| **Power & torque:** | 190bhp/122lb ft |
| **Engine:** | Normally aspirated 1796cc four cylinder, petrol, electronic injection, 16 valves |
| **Drivetrain:** | Mid-engine RWD |
| **Structure:** | Aluminium tub with plastic panels |
| **Transmission:** | Five-speed manual |
| **Weight:** | 658kg |

**PRICE GUIDE**

| | |
|---|---|
| **Launch price:** | £35,000 |
| **Excellent:** | £50,000 |
| **Good:** | £40,000 |
| **Average:** | £30,000 |
| **Project:** | N/A |

# LOTUS
## Exige S1

So much more than an Elise with a roof, the S1 Exige felt more like a race-car that just happened to be legal for the road – and trackdays. The reworked body, with its Kamm tail and functional-looking front spoiler (with exposed fixings) and rear wing, gave a real Group C racer vibe and generated 100kg of downforce at 100mph. The VHPD 1.8-litre K-series (177bhp as standard, 192bhp as an option) sounded like it belonged in a racer, too. A delight to drive, and a true mini-supercar. Values have softened in last 12 months.

**SPECIFICATIONS**

| | |
|---|---|
| **Years produced:** | 2000-2001 (583 built) |
| **Performance:** | 0-60mph: 4.6sec<br>Top speed: 136mph |
| **Power & torque:** | 177bhp/127lb ft |
| **Engine:** | Normally aspirated 1796cc four cylinder, petrol, electronic injection, 16 valves |
| **Drivetrain:** | Mid-engine RWD |
| **Structure:** | Aluminium tub with plastic panels |
| **Transmission:** | Five-speed manual |
| **Weight:** | 780kg |

**PRICE GUIDE**

| | |
|---|---|
| **Launch price:** | £31,471 |
| **Excellent:** | £50,000 |
| **Good:** | £40,000 |
| **Average:** | £30,000 |
| **Project:** | N/A |

# LOTUS
## Elise S2

New crash regs required Lotus to re-engineer the Elise for 2001 and the car got a neat restyle at the same time. Power came initially from the familiar 1.8-litre K-series in a number of different tunes, from standard 120bhp all the way up to 190bhp in the track-focused 190 Sport. From 2004 there was a switch to Toyota engines and transmissions, the new 111R boasting a high-revving 189bhp from its 1.8-litre VVTL-i unit, a six-speed gearbox and ABS. Again, lots of variants: 134bhp 'S' with five-speed 'box is a nice entry-point to the S2.

**SPECIFICATIONS**

| | |
|---|---|
| **Years produced:** | 2001-2011 |
| **Performance:** | 0-60mph: 5.6sec (K-series)<br>Top speed: 125mph |
| **Power & torque:** | 120bhp/124lb ft |
| **Engine:** | Normally aspirated 1796cc four cylinder, petrol, electronic injection, 16 valves |
| **Drivetrain:** | Mid-engine RWD |
| **Structure:** | Aluminium tub with plastic panels |
| **Transmission:** | Five-speed manual |
| **Weight:** | 726kg |

**PRICE GUIDE (111R in brackets)**

| | |
|---|---|
| **Launch price:** | £22,995 (£27,995) |
| **Excellent:** | £19,000 (£23,000) |
| **Good:** | £16,000 (£18,000) |
| **Average:** | £13,000 (£14,000) |
| **Project:** | £6000 (£8000) |

# LOTUS
## Exige S2

The launch of the second-generation Exige coincided with the arrival of Toyota powertrains at Lotus for 2004, so the Exige S2 had the same 189bhp 1.8-litre VVTL-i unit and six-speed gearbox as the reworked S2 Elise. Supercharged Exige S introduced in 2006 saw power boosted to 220bhp and the 0-60mph time drop from 4.9 to 4.1sec with a top speed of 148mph. Even more powerful Exige S 240 and 260 models followed. S2 Exiges seem to lack the collectability of the S1 model, but all are cracking driver's cars.

**SPECIFICATIONS**

| | |
|---|---|
| **Years produced:** | 2004-2011 |
| **Performance:** | 0-60mph: 4.9sec<br>Top speed: 147mph |
| **Power & torque:** | 189bhp/133lb ft |
| **Engine:** | Normally aspirated 1796cc four cylinder, petrol, electronic injection, 16 valves |
| **Drivetrain:** | Mid-engine RWD |
| **Structure:** | Aluminium tub with plastic panels |
| **Transmission:** | Six-speed manual |
| **Weight:** | 875kg |

**PRICE GUIDE (S 220 in brackets)**

| | |
|---|---|
| **Launch price:** | £29,995 |
| **Excellent:** | £25,000 (£30,000) |
| **Good:** | £20,000 (£25,000) |
| **Average:** | £15,000 (£20,000) |
| **Project:** | £10,000 (£12,000) |

# MARCOS

THE MARCOS NAME is a contraction of the surnames of founders Jem Marsh and Frank Costin, who in 1959 built a sports car around a plywood chassis. Aesthetically it was a disaster, but it proved very capable in racing. In 1964 came a new and much more attractive shape, the 1800, ultimately fitted with a variety of Ford, Volvo and Triumph engines. Other models included the diminutive Mini-Marcos, using Mini components. Marcos went bust in 1972, but returned in 1981 to build limited numbers of cars based on its classic coupé. There was an attempt to relaunch the marque in the early Noughties with the Chevrolet-engined TSO, but Marcos finally closed its doors in 2007.

## MARCOS 1800 GT/1500/1600

The 1800 GT was introduced to move Marcos into the MGB market, despite being available in kit form. Powered by a Volvo engine (an unusual step for a British specialist at the time) and featuring an advanced suspension layout, it was a quick and fine-handling alternative. In an attempt to widen the appeal of the GT, Ford engines replaced the expensive Volvo one, while the sophisticated semi-trailing arm/de Dion rear suspension layout of the 1800 was thrown out in favour of a simpler live axle. Good specialist back-up make it a sensible and charismatic sports-GT.

**SPECIFICATIONS (1800GT)**

| | |
|---|---|
| **Years produced:** | 1964-1969 (99/82/192 in total) |
| **Performance:** | 0-60mph: 9.1sec<br>Top speed: 115mph |
| **Power & torque:** | 114bhp/110lb ft |
| **Engine:** | Normally aspirated 1798cc four cylinder, petrol, carburettor, 8 valves |
| **Drivetrain:** | Front-engine RWD |
| **Structure:** | Glassfibre body/separate chassis |
| **Transmission:** | Four-speed manual with overdrive |
| **Weight:** | 767kg |

| | PRICE GUIDE (GT) | 1500/1600 |
|---|---|---|
| **Launch price:** | £1645 | £1606 |
| **Excellent:** | £38,000 | £25,000 |
| **Good:** | £27,000 | £20,000 |
| **Average:** | £20,000 | £15,000 |
| **Project:** | £10,000 | £9000 |

## MARCOS Mini-Marcos

A cottage industry of specialists had emerged making the humble BMC Mini do things Alec Issignonis had never imagined. The Mini-Marcos was one such car, combining a lightweight low-drag body with the front-wheel-drive car's drivetrain and suspension. It proved a successful combination, not only dynamically but commercially too – and when Marcos folded in 1971, the Mini-Marcos continued in various guises, and arguably inspired the Midas of the 1980s. The original has plenty of appeal, and prices are currently on the up, according to specialists Redline Sportscars.

**SPECIFICATIONS**

| | |
|---|---|
| **Years produced:** | 1965-1974 (700 in total) |
| **Performance:** | 0-60mph: N/A<br>Top speed: 75mph |
| **Power & torque:** | 34bhp/44lb ft |
| **Engine:** | Normally aspirated 848cc four cylinder, petrol, carburettor, 8 valves |
| **Drivetrain:** | Front-engine FWD |
| **Structure:** | Glassfibre monocoque |
| **Transmission:** | Four-speed manual |
| **Weight:** | 483kg |

| | PRICE GUIDE |
|---|---|
| **Launch price:** | £199 |
| **Excellent:** | £20,000 |
| **Good:** | £15,000 |
| **Average:** | £12,000 |
| **Project:** | £8000 |

## MARCOS 3-litre

Marcos finally abandoned its plywood underpinnings with the 3-litre and went for a square tube chassis that cost less to build, was easier to maintain, and ultimately made it easier to sell. The 3-litre was a clear indicator that Marcos was moving upmarket and, although the Ford V6-powered car looked near-identical to its four-cylinder cousins, it offered much more performance – and therefore sales appeal. It wasn't cheap and, in moving away from its competition roots, Marcos struggled to find new buyers – especially in the wake of the cheap and plentiful Ford Capri 3000.

**SPECIFICATIONS**

| | |
|---|---|
| **Years produced:** | 1968-1972 (561 in total) |
| **Performance:** | 0-60mph: 7.8sec<br>Top speed: 125mph |
| **Power & torque:** | 136bhp/193lb ft |
| **Engine:** | Normally aspirated 2994cc V6, petrol, carburettor, 12 valves |
| **Drivetrain:** | Front-engine RWD |
| **Structure:** | Glassfibre body/separate chassis |
| **Transmission:** | Four-speed manual with overdrive |
| **Weight:** | 884kg |

| | PRICE GUIDE |
|---|---|
| **Launch price:** | £2350 |
| **Excellent:** | £25,000 |
| **Good:** | £18,000 |
| **Average:** | £10,000 |
| **Project:** | £8000 |

## MARCOS Mantis M70

Marcos never made a car called the Marmite, but the effect was much the same with the early '70s Mantis. Hoping to expand the appeal of the brand, Jem Marsh introduced the marque's first four-seater in 1970, powered by a TR6 engine. The brochure talked of 'high all-round visibility' and described the Mantis as 'ideal for the man who is going places and wants to travel in style'. Most found the Mantis's looks just plain weird. Only 32 were sold before the company went bust in 1972, and only a dozen are thought to survive.

**SPECIFICATIONS**

| | |
|---|---|
| **Years produced:** | 1970-1972 (32 built) |
| **Performance:** | 0-60mph: 9sec<br>Top speed: 120mph |
| **Power & torque:** | 150bhp/164lb ft |
| **Engine:** | Normally aspirated 2498cc straight six, petrol, carburettor, 12 valves |
| **Drivetrain:** | Front-engine RWD |
| **Structure:** | Glassfibre body/separate chassis |
| **Transmission:** | Four-speed manual |
| **Weight:** | 1043kg |

| | PRICE GUIDE |
|---|---|
| **Launch price:** | £N/A |
| **Excellent:** | £25,000 |
| **Good:** | £18,000 |
| **Average:** | £10,000 |
| **Project:** | £6000 |

## MARCOS
# Mantula

The launch of the Mantula capped a welcome return for the reborn Marcos of the 1980s. Powered by the Rover V8 and featuring a body that was a subtle development of the Dennis Adams original but with more effective aerodynamics, the Mantula offered big-engined thrills for a modest outlay. In 1986, a Spyder version was introduced for the first time, and updated independent suspension helped keep all of that power on the road. Later Mantulas had the 3.9 V8; more modest four-cylinder Cortina-engined versions were also available. Factory-built convertibles tend to fetch best prices.

**SPECIFICATIONS**

| | |
|---|---|
| **Years produced:** | 1984-1992 (380 of all variants) |
| **Performance:** | 0-60mph: 5.7sec<br>Top speed: 155mph |
| **Power & torque:** | 190bhp/220lb ft |
| **Engine:** | Normally aspirated 3532cc V8, petrol, fuel injection, 16 valves |
| **Drivetrain:** | Front-engine RWD |
| **Structure:** | Glassfibre body/steel backbone chassis |
| **Transmission:** | Five-speed manual |
| **Weight:** | 900kg |

**PRICE GUIDE**

| | |
|---|---|
| **Launch price:** | £16,694 |
| **Excellent:** | £23,000 |
| **Good:** | £16,000 |
| **Average:** | £10,000 |
| **Project:** | £5000 |

## MARCOS
# Mantara/Mantaray

In the early 1990s Marcos dropped all its kit cars and introduced the Mantara – a step on from the Mantula, available as coupé or Spyder, with flared wheelarches, wider tracks and MacPherson strut front suspension. Once again, the Rover V8 (now in 3.9- and 4.6-litre forms) provided the power, and Marcos found itself going head to head with TVR's Griffith and Chimaera. In 1998 it evolved into the mildly restyled Mantaray. It was also campaigned in GT racing, spawning a series of ever-wilder 'LM' road cars, with the ultimate version – the LM600 – being powered by a 6-litre Chevrolet V8.

**SPECIFICATIONS**

| | |
|---|---|
| **Years produced:** | 1993-2001 (26 built) |
| **Performance:** | 0-60mph: 5.4sec<br>Top speed: 140mph |
| **Power & torque:** | 190bhp/227lb ft |
| **Engine:** | Normally aspirated 3946cc V6, petrol, mechanical fuel injection, 16 valves |
| **Drivetrain:** | Front-engine RWD |
| **Structure:** | Glassfibre body/steel backbone chassis |
| **Transmission:** | Five-speed manual |
| **Weight:** | 930kg |

**PRICE GUIDE (LM in brackets)**

| | |
|---|---|
| **Launch price:** | £24,000 |
| **Excellent:** | £24,000 (£35,000) |
| **Good:** | £18,000 (£27,000) |
| **Average:** | £15,000 (£20,000) |
| **Project:** | £8000 (£12,000) |

## MARCOS
# Mantis

In 1997 Marcos resurrected the Mantis name for a new series of coupés and convertibles based on the Mantara LM (see above) but now powered by an all-aluminium 4.6-litre 350bhp Ford V8. With a remodelled bonnet, bulging arches and jutting spoilers, it was a far cry from the original mid-'60s Marcos. For the GT, a Vortech supercharger boosted power to over 500bhp. It sounded thunderous, went like stink, and it even handled! Just 16 supercharged cars were built. Prices are on the rise, say specialists Redline Sportscars.

**SPECIFICATIONS**

| | |
|---|---|
| **Years produced:** | 1997-2001 (51 in total) |
| **Performance:** | 0-60mph: 4.0sec (GT)<br>Top speed: 170mph+ |
| **Power & torque:** | 506bhp/452lb ft |
| **Engine:** | Supercharged 4600cc V8, petrol, electronic fuel injection, 32 valves |
| **Drivetrain:** | Front-engine RWD |
| **Structure:** | Carbonfibre body/steel backbone |
| **Transmission:** | Five-speed manual |
| **Weight:** | 1197kg |

**PRICE GUIDE**

| | |
|---|---|
| **Launch price:** | £64,331 (GT) |
| **Excellent:** | £43,000 |
| **Good:** | £35,000 |
| **Average:** | £30,000 |
| **Project:** | N/A |

# MASERATI

INITIALLY BUILDING cars just for racing, Italian firm Maserati began to focus on road cars from 1946 with the A6/1500 model. But it was with the 3500GT of 1957 that it got serious, building a true Ferrari challenger. It continued in that vein over the next few decades with models such as the Ghibli and Bora being stand-out offerings. The latter was built while Citroën owned the firm, from 1969 to 1975. De Tomaso then took over and Maserati was downgraded to the equivalent of an Italian BMW or Mercedes. To the delight of enthusiasts, under the umbrella of the Fiat-Chrysler group, it is today once again building exotic and stylish sports and GT cars, as well as the inevitable luxury SUVs.

## MASERATI
# 3500GT

Maserati made its name in motor racing, having produced the legendary 250F, which took Juan Manuel Fangio to championship glory in 1957. That same year the company turned its full attention to the business of building road cars, unveiling the 3500GT. With this car, Maserati evolved into a serious producer of road cars (the A6 models were always low volume semi-racers), competing strongly with Ferrari. The Touring-bodied coupé certainly looked the part and, with an Alfieri designed engine and racer-derived chassis, it was as good to drive as it was to look at.

**SPECIFICATIONS**

| | |
|---|---|
| **Years produced:** | 1957-1964 (2000 in total) |
| **Performance:** | 0-60mph: 7.6sec<br>Top speed: 145mph |
| **Power & torque:** | 220bhp/253lb ft |
| **Engine:** | Normally aspirated 3485cc straight six, petrol, carburettor, 12 valves |
| **Drivetrain:** | Front-engine RWD |
| **Structure:** | Monocoque |
| **Transmission:** | Four-speed manual |
| **Weight:** | 1270kg |

**PRICE GUIDE**

| | |
|---|---|
| **Launch price:** | £5800 |
| **Excellent:** | £250,000 |
| **Good:** | £180,000 |
| **Average:** | £125,000 |
| **Project:** | £40,000 |

# MASERATI 3500GT Spyder

During its seven-year production run, the 3500GT became an established member of the sporting elite, with the coupé taking the lion's share of sales. But the lighter Vignale-bodied Spyder, sitting on a shortened wheelbase, was every bit as capable. It gained Borrani wire wheels in 1959 and a five-speed gearbox the following year, and Lucas fuel injection in 1961. A handful of one-offs were also produced, and are fabulously valuable, though all 3500GT values have remained static over the last 12 months, according to Andy Heywood at specialists McGrath Maserati.

**SPECIFICATIONS**

**Years produced:** 1959-1964 (242 in total)
**Performance:** 0-60mph: 7.6sec
Top speed: 136mph
**Power & torque:** 235bhp/232lb ft
**Engine:** Normally aspirated 3485cc straight six, petrol, carburettor, 12 valves
**Drivetrain:** Front-engine RWD
**Structure:** Separate chassis
**Transmission:** Four-speed manual
**Weight:** 1406kg

**PRICE GUIDE**

**Launch price:** N/A
**Excellent:** £750,000
**Good:** £550,000
**Average:** £400,000
**Project:** £300,000

# MASERATI Sebring

In essence, the Sebring was a shortened 3500GT that wore a beautiful Vignale body, styled by Giovanni Michelotti. In terms of looks, the Sebring was a perfect car for its time, although the straight-six engine was beginning to look a little outclassed compared with the latest opposition from Ferrari. But this car was designed for America, and it was style and equipment that were the prime motivators in its creation – so air-conditioning and an automatic gearbox were on the options list. For the Sebring II, a 4.0-litre version of the straight six was fitted. Values of the best holding firm.

**SPECIFICATIONS**

**Years produced:** 1963-1969 (600 in total)
**Performance:** 0-60mph: 8.4sec
Top speed: 137mph
**Power & torque:** 235bhp/232lb ft
**Engine:** Normally aspirated 3485cc straight six, petrol, fuel injection, 12 valves
**Drivetrain:** Front-engine RWD
**Structure:** Separate chassis
**Transmission:** Five-speed manual
**Weight:** 1510kg

**PRICE GUIDE**

**Launch price:** £4801
**Excellent:** £250,000
**Good:** £180,000
**Average:** £85,000
**Project:** £40,000

# MASERATI Mistral

The Frua-bodied Mistral was the last of the six-cylinder line of Maseratis that started with the 3500GT. Its name comes from the wind that blows across the south of France – the first Maserati with a wind-inspired name. The engine was a direct descendent of the 350S's, lusty and long-lasting. The engine line-up included 3.5, 3.7 and 4.0-litre versions of the six, though the 3.5 went into the Spyder only. Performance was usefully improved, as the short-wheelbase Mistral weighed 200kg less than the Sebring. Values have slipped a little in the last 12-18 months.

**SPECIFICATIONS**

**Years produced:** 1963-1970 (948 in total)
**Performance:** 0-60mph: 6.9sec
Top speed: 145mph
**Power & torque:** 255bhp/267lb ft
**Engine:** Normally aspirated 4012cc straight six, petrol, fuel injection, 12 valves
**Drivetrain:** Front-engine RWD
**Structure:** Tubular chassis
**Transmission:** Five-speed manual
**Weight:** 1270kg

**PRICE GUIDE**

**Launch price:** £5980
**Excellent:** £220,000
**Good:** £180,000
**Average:** £125,000
**Project:** £40,000

# MASERATI Mistral Spyder

Slightly happier-looking than the coupé, the Mistral Spyder bears an uncanny resemblance to the later AC 428 – both were styled by Pietro Frua. It was so close that there's some parts interchangeability between the two, a side benefit of being built in the same factory. Unusually, the Mistral was offered with either aluminium or steel bodywork, with no discernible difference in weight, though the survival rate of the former is much higher than for the latter. The final 4.0-litre Mistral was a genuinely quick car, with a top speed of over 140mph. Values have peaked for now.

**SPECIFICATIONS**

**Years produced:** 1963-1970 (120 in total)
**Performance:** 0-60mph: 6.8sec
Top speed: 145mph
**Power & torque:** 255bhp/267lb ft
**Engine:** Normally aspirated 4012cc straight six, petrol, fuel injection, 12 valves
**Drivetrain:** Front-engine RWD
**Structure:** Tubular chassis
**Transmission:** Five-speed manual
**Weight:** 1300kg

**PRICE GUIDE**

**Launch price:** £5980
**Excellent:** £700,000
**Good:** £500,000
**Average:** £350,000
**Project:** £180,000

# MASERATI Quattroporte

The Quattroporte was significant for Maserati because it was the first of its cars to be powered by the new V8 engine, initially in 4.1-litre form, later 4.7. The family resemblance with the Mistral was strong, as it was also a Frua design, while underneath it was built on a sports car-like tubular frame. The platform went on to underpin a generation of Maserati sports cars, and rightly so, considering how good the Quattroporte was – and still is – to drive. There's something peculiarly Italian about being the fastest saloon in the world with an exotic-sounding name that means 'four door'.

**SPECIFICATIONS**

**Years produced:** 1963-1971 (776 in total)
**Performance:** 0-60mph: 8.3sec
Top speed: 130mph
**Power & torque:** 260bhp/267lb ft
**Engine:** Normally aspirated 4136cc V8, petrol, carburettor, 16 valves
**Drivetrain:** Front-engine RWD
**Structure:** Monocoque
**Transmission:** Five-speed manual
**Weight:** 1728kg

**PRICE GUIDE**

**Launch price:** £5986
**Excellent:** £100,000
**Good:** £75,000
**Average:** £50,000
**Project:** £25,000

# MASERATI
## Mexico

Following on from the Quattroporte in 1965, the Mexico was the next Maserati to be fitted with the new V8 engine. The four-seater coupé was styled by Vignale and, after the exuberance of the previous Frua-bodied cars, it lacked the visual drama to go with its high price. However, with the later 4.7-litre V8 fitted, it was seriously quick, with more than enough muscle to replace the Sebring. Sadly the new car failed to emulate its predecessor's sales success in the USA – a situation that hurt Maserati's finances significantly. Subtle but desirable – and values reflect this.

**SPECIFICATIONS**

| | |
|---|---|
| **Years produced:** | 1966-1972 (485 in total) |
| **Performance:** | 0-60mph: N/A<br>Top speed: 143mph |
| **Power & torque:** | 260bhp/268lb ft |
| **Engine:** | Normally aspirated 4136cc V8, petrol, carburettor, 16 valves |
| **Drivetrain:** | Front-engine RWD |
| **Structure:** | Tubular chassis |
| **Transmission:** | Five-speed manual |
| **Weight:** | 1651kg |

**PRICE GUIDE**

| | |
|---|---|
| **Launch price:** | £7216 |
| **Excellent:** | £180,000 |
| **Good:** | £140,000 |
| **Average:** | £90,000 |
| **Project:** | £40,000 |

# MASERATI
## Ghibli

Sitting at the top of the Maserati range, and vying with the very best from Ferrari for the title 'fastest car in the world', the Ghibli is one of the finest GT cars to emerge from the 1960s. Subsequently overshadowed by the Daytona and Miura, the Ghibli combined Giorgetto Giugiaro's styling (while he was still at Ghia) with Maserati's muscle to create a genuine 150mph+ roadburner. The chassis engineering was beginning to look a little old hat, as it was a further variation of the Quattroporte's tubular frame – but it was effective nevertheless. Spyder values have been pegged back.

**SPECIFICATIONS**

| | |
|---|---|
| **Years produced:** | 1969-1974 (1274 in total) |
| **Performance:** | 0-60mph: 7.0sec<br>Top speed: 155mph |
| **Power & torque:** | 330bhp/290lb ft |
| **Engine:** | Normally aspirated 4719cc V8, petrol, carburettor, 16 valves |
| **Drivetrain:** | Front-engine RWD |
| **Structure:** | Tubular chassis |
| **Transmission:** | Five-speed manual |
| **Weight:** | 1352kg |

| | COUPE | SPYDER |
|---|---|---|
| **Launch price:** | £10,180 | n/a |
| **Excellent:** | £275,000 | £850,000 |
| **Good:** | £200,000 | £700,000 |
| **Average:** | £130,000 | £500,000 |
| **Project:** | £50,000 | £300,000 |

# MASERATI
## Indy

Compared with the Mexico it replaced, the Indy was a huge success. Based on a shortened version of the QP's chassis, but with a wider track, the Vignale-styled Indy looked terrific. The 2+2 coupé also saw a change in Maserati construction technique, as the chassis and body were now welded (instead of bolted) together. None of that mattered on the road where, in 4.7-litre form, the Indy could exceed 160mph in the right conditions, making it one of the world's fastest four-seater cars. Best of the lot is the 4.9, but it's left-hand drive only. Values have softened in past year.

**SPECIFICATIONS**

| | |
|---|---|
| **Years produced:** | 1969-1974 (1136 in total) |
| **Performance:** | 0-60mph: 7.2sec (4.2)<br>Top speed: 154mph |
| **Power & torque:** | 260bhp/268lb ft |
| **Engine:** | Normally aspirated 4136cc V8, petrol, carburettor, 16 valves |
| **Drivetrain:** | Front-engine RWD |
| **Structure:** | Monocoque |
| **Transmission:** | Five-speed manual |
| **Weight:** | 1651kg |

**PRICE GUIDE**

| | |
|---|---|
| **Launch price:** | £8320 |
| **Excellent:** | £100,000 |
| **Good:** | £80,000 |
| **Average:** | £50,000 |
| **Project:** | £25,000 |

# MASERATI
## Bora

Considering it was a relative latecomer to the mid-engined supercar club (although it beat the Ferrari BB to the market by two years), the Maserati Bora established itself as a front-runner. Like the Ghibli, the Bora was styled by Giugiaro, who had by now gone it alone to form Ital Design, but the design studio had also devised the all-new steel unitary construction underneath it. The Bora was fitted with the Indy V8 in 4.7- or 4.9-litre form. Thanks to Maserati's association with Citroën at the time, high pressure hydraulics powered the brakes and steering.

**SPECIFICATIONS**

| | |
|---|---|
| **Years produced:** | 1971-1978 (524 in total) |
| **Performance:** | 0-60mph: 6.5sec<br>Top speed: 165mph |
| **Power & torque:** | 310bhp/339lb ft |
| **Engine:** | Normally aspirated 4719cc V8, petrol, carburettor, 16 valves |
| **Drivetrain:** | Mid-engine RWD |
| **Structure:** | Monocoque |
| **Transmission:** | Five-speed manual |
| **Weight:** | 1550kg |

**PRICE GUIDE**

| | |
|---|---|
| **Launch price:** | £22,911 |
| **Excellent:** | £170,000 |
| **Good:** | £130,000 |
| **Average:** | £100,000 |
| **Project:** | £55,000 |

# MASERATI
## Khamsin

To show its commitment to the front-engined cause, Maserati introduced the Khamsin to sell alongside the Bora/Merak twins. Styling and body engineering was by Marcello Gandini at Bertone. The suspension and brakes were closely related to the mid-engined cars' but the high-geared power-assisted steering was lifted from the Citroën SM, and proved remarkably successful once owners had acclimatised to it. Poor interior layout and visibility were forgiven for the 160mph-plus potential. Specialists McGrath Maserati say values have fallen back over the last 12-18 months.

**SPECIFICATIONS**

| | |
|---|---|
| **Years produced:** | 1973-1982 (421 in total) |
| **Performance:** | 0-60mph: 7.1sec<br>Top speed: 171mph |
| **Power & torque:** | 320bhp/354lb ft |
| **Engine:** | Normally aspirated 4930cc V8, petrol, carburettor, 16 valves |
| **Drivetrain:** | Front-engine RWD |
| **Structure:** | Tubular chassis |
| **Transmission:** | Five-speed manual |
| **Weight:** | 1530kg |

**PRICE GUIDE**

| | |
|---|---|
| **Launch price:** | £13,999 |
| **Excellent:** | £170,000 |
| **Good:** | £130,000 |
| **Average:** | £75,000 |
| **Project:** | £40,000 |

# MASERATI
## Merak

Created to fight the Ferrari 308 and Lamborghini Urraco, the Maserati Merak was a super-stylish parts-bin special that proved rather effective. The body was a lightly revised version of the Bora's (losing its flush rear window in the process), and the engine was a lightly tuned version of the Citroën SM's Maserati-designed 3.0-litre V6, boasting 190bhp. Never a light car, the Merak struggled to keep up with rivals, but the 220bhp SS version did much to make amends. Values have slipped back, says Andy Heywood at McGrath Maserati, but it's still essential to buy a good one.

### SPECIFICATIONS

| | |
|---|---|
| **Years produced:** | 1974-1982 (1820 in total) |
| **Performance:** | 0-60mph: 8.2sec<br>Top speed: 135mph |
| **Power & torque:** | 190bhp/188lb ft |
| **Engine:** | Normally aspirated 2965cc V6, petrol, carburettor, 12 valves |
| **Drivetrain:** | Mid-engine RWD |
| **Structure:** | Monocoque |
| **Transmission:** | Five-speed manual |
| **Weight:** | 1339kg |

### PRICE GUIDE

| | |
|---|---|
| **Launch price:** | £7996 |
| **Excellent:** | £85,000 |
| **Good:** | £60,000 |
| **Average:** | £30,000 |
| **Project:** | £15,000 |

# MASERATI
## Kyalami

After De Tomaso's takeover of Maserati, badge engineering was introduced. The De Tomaso Longchamp was slightly facelifted, fitted with the Indy V8 (initially in 4.1-litre form), and re-marketed as the Maserati Kyalami. Although this version of the Ghia-styled car looked better than the original, it was not appealing enough to bring in a significant number of new buyers. Perhaps it was the price – which had taken a significant hike over the Ford-engined car it was based upon – but, more likely, there was simply no market for it in the late 70s. Decent value right now.

### SPECIFICATIONS

| | |
|---|---|
| **Years produced:** | 1976-1983 (187 in total) |
| **Performance:** | 0-60mph: 7.6sec<br>Top speed: 147mph |
| **Power & torque:** | 270bhp/289lb ft |
| **Engine:** | Normally aspirated 4136cc V8, petrol, carburettor, 16 valves |
| **Drivetrain:** | Front-engine RWD |
| **Structure:** | Monocoque |
| **Transmission:** | Five-speed manual |
| **Weight:** | 1740kg |

### PRICE GUIDE

| | |
|---|---|
| **Launch price:** | £21,996 |
| **Excellent:** | £60,000 |
| **Good:** | £40,000 |
| **Average:** | £25,000 |
| **Project:** | £15,000 |

# MASERATI
## Quattroporte III

Another back-to-basics offering, and none the worse for it. Where the Quattroporte II had flopped on its unconventional engineering and anodyne styling, its replacement returned to the formula that made the original car so successful – a big V8, discreet styling, and a supercar driving experience combined with additional accommodation. Sales were not as strong as they could have been, although in 4.9-litre form the Quattroporte III remained in production throughout the 1980s to be sold alongside the new Biturbo. Its merits have been reflected in strengthening values.

### SPECIFICATIONS

| | |
|---|---|
| **Years produced:** | 1979-1990 (1876 in total) |
| **Performance:** | 0-60mph: N/A<br>Top speed: 143mph |
| **Power & torque:** | 280bhp/289lb ft |
| **Engine:** | Normally aspirated 4930cc V8, petrol, carburettor, 16 valves |
| **Drivetrain:** | Front-engine RWD |
| **Structure:** | Monocoque |
| **Transmission:** | Three-speed automatic |
| **Weight:** | 1900kg |

### PRICE GUIDE

| | |
|---|---|
| **Launch price:** | £56,912 |
| **Excellent:** | £50,000 |
| **Good:** | £30,000 |
| **Average:** | £20,000 |
| **Project:** | £10,000 |

# MASERATI
## Biturbo-222-425

Maserati model development took a new direction in 1981. The supercar market was surrendered to Ferrari and Lamborghini as the company chased volume with its new BMW 3-Series-rivalling Biturbo. At the heart of the new car was an elegant new four-cam V6 of either 2.0 or 2.5 litres, its output boosted by a brace of turbos. The interior was plush – and its centrepiece clock was a real novelty. The Biturbo made for a left-field alternative to a BMW 323i, although big sales were never forthcoming. The four-door 425 was introduced in 1983. Prices for the best are edging slowly upwards.

### SPECIFICATIONS

| | |
|---|---|
| **Years produced:** | 1981-1994 |
| **Performance:** | 0-60mph: 7.2sec<br>Top speed: 126mph |
| **Power & torque:** | 192bhp/220lb ft |
| **Engine:** | Twin turbocharged 2491cc V6, petrol, carburettor, 18 valves |
| **Drivetrain:** | Front-engine RWD |
| **Structure:** | Monocoque |
| **Transmission:** | Five-speed manual |
| **Weight:** | 1242kg |

### PRICE GUIDE

| | |
|---|---|
| **Launch price:** | £28,795 |
| **Excellent:** | £17,000 |
| **Good:** | £10,000 |
| **Average:** | £5000 |
| **Project:** | £2000 |

# MASERATI
## Biturbo Spyder

Maserati chopped the roof off the Biturbo coupé to create this stylish four-seater convertible. Like the tin-topped versions, it wasn't without issues and, as well as suffering from niggling build and quality shortcomings, premature corrosion was a very real problem. Image and prices dropped massively in a short time, and they've never really recovered. Despite low classic values, there's a real sense of the exotic when it comes to keeping a Biturbo on the road, and restoration costs can be horrifying – especially if the engine needs major work.

### SPECIFICATIONS

| | |
|---|---|
| **Years produced:** | 1984-1991 |
| **Performance:** | 0-60mph: 6.1sec<br>Top speed: 140mph |
| **Power & torque:** | 241bhp/246lb ft |
| **Engine:** | Twin-turbocharged 1996cc V6, petrol, electronic fuel injection, 18 valves |
| **Drivetrain:** | Front-engine RWD |
| **Structure:** | Monocoque |
| **Transmission:** | Five-speed manual |
| **Weight:** | 1251kg |

### PRICE GUIDE

| | |
|---|---|
| **Launch price:** | N/A |
| **Excellent:** | £20,000 |
| **Good:** | £13,000 |
| **Average:** | £8000 |
| **Project:** | £3000 |

## MASERATI Karif

Basically a 'notchback' coupé version of the Spyder, the Karif (named after a desert wind) was another variation on the Biturbo theme, fitted with the largest of the V6 variants, a 2.8-litre unit with peak power quoted as 280bhp, providing very decent performance (and lairy handling) in an understated package with a typically sybaritic interior. De Tomaso planned it as a limited edition of 250, though in the event only 222 were sold. Of those, a mere 25 were right-hand drive, making the Karif one of the rarest of all Maseratis.

### SPECIFICATIONS

**Years produced:** 1988-1993 (222 in total)
**Performance:** 0-60mph: 4.8sec
Top speed: 158mph
**Power & torque:** 280bhp/284lb ft
**Engine:** Twin-turbocharged 2790cc V6, petrol, electronic fuel injection, 18 valves
**Drivetrain:** Front-engine RWD
**Structure:** Monocoque
**Transmission:** Five-speed manual
**Weight:** 1281kg

### PRICE GUIDE

**Launch price:** N/A
**Excellent:** £23,000
**Good:** £15,000
**Average:** £10,000
**Project:** £5000

## MASERATI Shamal

The Biturbo platform was certainly adaptable – in 1989 the exterior was heavily revised (by Marcello Gandini), and a quad-cam 32-valve 3.2-litre V8 was shoehorned under the bonnet. Inside, it was just as luxurious as the Biturbo, and made extensive use of wood and leather – while retaining that clock. It certainly looked different, but the main draw for the Shamal was its performance – with 325bhp on tap, it topped out at nearly 170mph, making it one of the fastest Maseratis ever. Handling was excellent, helped by the electronic active control suspension – when it was working.

### SPECIFICATIONS

**Years produced:** 1989-1995 (369 produced)
**Performance:** 0-60mph: 5.1sec
Top speed: 169mph
**Power & torque:** 326bhp/315lb ft
**Engine:** Twin-turbocharged 3217cc V8, petrol, electronic fuel injection, 32 valves
**Drivetrain:** Front-engine RWD
**Structure:** Monocoque
**Transmission:** Six-speed manual
**Weight:** 1290kg

### PRICE GUIDE

**Launch price:** £63,450
**Excellent:** £85,000
**Good:** £70,000
**Average:** £50,000
**Project:** £20,000

## MASERATI Ghibli II

A great name returned in 1992 with the arrival of the Ghibli II, the final variation on the biturbo theme. Clearly taking its lead from the Shamal but slightly toned down – and around £20k more affordable too – the Ghibli was powered by twin-turbo V6s of either 2.0 or 2.8 litres, the former producing a remarkable 306bhp. The Ghibli II went on to form the basis of a GT racer and spawned a number of special editions, including the Ghibli Cup, which is particularly sought-after today and commands £50k+. In 1998, Maserati's biturbo range was replaced by the Fiat-funded 3200GT and curves were back.

### SPECIFICATIONS

**Years produced:** 1992-1997 (2337 in total)
**Performance:** 0-60mph: 5.6sec
Top speed: 160mph
**Power & torque:** 306bhp/275lb ft
**Engine:** Twin-turbocharged 1996cc V6, petrol, electronic fuel injection, 24 valves
**Drivetrain:** Front-engine RWD
**Structure:** Monocoque
**Transmission:** Five- or six-speed manual
**Weight:** 1242kg

### PRICE GUIDE

**Launch price:** £42,813
**Excellent:** £50,000
**Good:** £35,000
**Average:** £15,000
**Project:** £5000

## MASERATI Quattroporte IV

The mid-'90s QP was basically a lengthened, four-door version of the Ghibli II, initially with that car's 2.8-litre biturbo V6 in 280bhp tune, though from 1995 it had the 3.2-litre biturbo V8 from the Shamal. Thus equipped and with 330bhp on tap, it was a seriously rapid machine, and with neat styling by Gandini (including his trademark rear wheelarch) and the usual sumptuous Maserati interior, it makes a characterful alternative to big Mercs and BMWs of the same era. If you can find one, that is: only 28 RHD examples were sold.

### SPECIFICATIONS

**Years produced:** 1994-2001 (2400 in total)
**Performance:** 0-60mph: 5.8sec (V8)
Top speed: 167mph
**Power & torque:** 330bhp/331lb ft
**Engine:** Twin-turbocharged 3217cc V8, petrol, electronic fuel injection, 32 valves
**Drivetrain:** Front-engine RWD
**Structure:** Monocoque
**Transmission:** Six-speed manual/four-speed auto
**Weight:** 1535kg

### PRICE GUIDE

**Launch price:** £58,825
**Excellent:** £15,000
**Good:** £10,000
**Average:** £8000
**Project:** £3000

## MASERATI 3200GT

In the late-'90s, Fiat placed Maserati under Ferrari's wing, and the latter invested £35m in its erstwhile rival. First fruit was the 3200GT in late 1998. With a name that harked back to the classic 3500GT, striking styling by Giugiaro's Italdesign, a twin-turbo 370bhp V8 (a revised version of the unit from the Shamal and QP IV) offering 170mph+, and four proper seats plus a decent boot, the 3200GT was warmly welcomed. Looks decent value at the moment, but buy carefully via specialists, as big bills await the unwary.

### SPECIFICATIONS

**Years produced:** 1998-2002 (4795 in total)
**Performance:** 0-60mph: 5.0sec
Top speed: 174mph
**Power & torque:** 370bhp/362lb ft
**Engine:** Twin-turbocharged 3217cc V8, petrol, electronic fuel injection, 32 valves
**Drivetrain:** Front-engine RWD
**Structure:** Monocoque
**Transmission:** Six-speed manual/four-speed auto
**Weight:** 1586kg

### PRICE GUIDE

**Launch price:** £60,575
**Excellent:** £22,000
**Good:** £18,000
**Average:** £10,000
**Project:** £5000

## MASERATI
### 4200GT/Spyder

Officially the Maserati Coupé/Spyder, but usually referred to as the 4200GT to distinguish it from the 3200GT, this was another good-looking car from the pen of Giorgetto Giugiaro. Big news was an all-new, Ferrari-developed V8 engine, which is considerably cheaper to maintain than the Maserati unit in the 3200. All-round the 4200 is a better car, though many lamented the loss of the 3200's 'boomerang' rear lights. GranSport version introduced in 2005 is particularly well-regarded; add around 15% to these prices for one of those.

**SPECIFICATIONS**

| | |
|---|---|
| **Years produced:** | 2001-2007 (13,423 in total) |
| **Performance:** | 0-60mph: 4.9sec<br>Top speed: 176mph |
| **Power & torque:** | 385bhp/332lb ft |
| **Engine:** | 4244cc naturally aspirated V8, petrol, fuel injection, 32 valves |
| **Drivetrain:** | Front-engine RWD |
| **Structure:** | Monocoque |
| **Transmission:** | Six-speed manual/clutchless manual |
| **Weight:** | c1700kg |

**PRICE GUIDE Coupé/Spyder**

| | |
|---|---|
| **Launch price:** | £74,950 (Spyder) |
| **Excellent:** | £22,000/£30,000 |
| **Good:** | £15,000/£22,000 |
| **Average:** | £12,000/£18,000 |
| **Project:** | £8000/£12,000 |

## MASERATI
### Quattroporte V

Another great-looking Noughties Maserati, again with that Ferrari-developed V8. For the early years of production, the QP was available only with a robotised manual gearbox called DuoSelect; buyers had to wait three years for a proper auto. Today, the auto is the one to have if you do a lot of city driving, say McGrath Maserati, but the DuoSelect is the driver's car, not least because its rear-mounted gearbox gives a better balance. Facelifted cars post-2008 are worth a lot more; early cars are where the bargains are.

**SPECIFICATIONS**

| | |
|---|---|
| **Years produced:** | 2003-2012 (25,256 in total) |
| **Performance:** | 0-60mph: 5.1sec<br>Top speed: 171mph |
| **Power & torque:** | 394bhp/333lb ft |
| **Engine:** | 4244cc naturally aspirated V8, petrol, fuel injection, 32 valves |
| **Drivetrain:** | Front-engine RWD |
| **Structure:** | Monocoque |
| **Transmission:** | Six-speed clutchless manual |
| **Weight:** | 1930kg |

**PRICE GUIDE (pre/post facelift)**

| | |
|---|---|
| **Launch price:** | £69,995 |
| **Excellent:** | £22,000/£40,000 |
| **Good:** | £15,000/£30,000 |
| **Average:** | £12,000/£25,000 |
| **Project:** | £6000/£10,000 |

# MATRA

MATRA – Mécanique-Aviation-Traction – was a French aerospace group that took over René Bonnet and continued making its sports car. It penned its own glassfibre design – the 530 – in 1967 as a V4 mid-engined coupé and targa model. It then jumped into bed with Simca to build the exciting Bagheera. Ironically the marque is better known for the 'lifestyle' Rancho that effectively invented the idea of rugged-looking faux off-roaders. The Renault Espace and Avantime were also built by the company, although they never carried the Matra name. The former was a runaway success, the latter a brave but total failure, which caused Matra to retreat from car-building in 2003.

## MATRA
### Djet V

Aerospace company Matra wasn't the first company to build the Djet, but it would go on to build a business around it. René Bonnet created the innovative car but couldn't make it pay, so Matra – which was already building the bodies – took it on to create the Matra-Bonnet Djet V. The body was light, it was powered by a tweaked Renault 8 Gordini engine, and it performed admirably thanks to a great power-to-weight ratio. The Djet proved useful in motor sport too, giving Matra the impetus it needed to front-line competition, both at Le Mans and in Formula 1.

**SPECIFICATIONS**

| | |
|---|---|
| **Years produced:** | 1965-1967 (1681 in total) |
| **Performance:** | 0-60mph: 13.5sec<br>Top speed: 99mph |
| **Power & torque:** | 72bhp/56lb ft |
| **Engine:** | Normally aspirated 1108cc four cylinder, petrol, carburettor, 8 valves |
| **Drivetrain:** | Mid-engine RWD |
| **Structure:** | Glassfibre body/separate chassis |
| **Transmission:** | Four-speed manual |
| **Weight:** | 615kg |

**PRICE GUIDE**

| | |
|---|---|
| **Launch price:** | N/A in UK |
| **Excellent:** | £35,000 |
| **Good:** | £20,000 |
| **Average:** | £8000 |
| **Project:** | N/A |

## MATRA
### 530

By the time it came to introducing a replacement for the Djet V, Matra's confidence had soared, and it decided on a car that was more unconventional. Still mid-engined and strangely styled, the 530 proved to be rather good on the road, despite using the unpromising Ford V4 engine. Construction was a steel unibody clothed in a glassfibre shell, and suspension was independent all-round. Handling was more than a match for its feeble 75bhp engine, and that would be a running theme for Matra sports cars for the coming decade. Rare and collectable for francophiles.

**SPECIFICATIONS**

| | |
|---|---|
| **Years produced:** | 1967-1973 (9609 in total) |
| **Performance:** | 0-60mph: 15.6sec<br>Top speed: 95mph |
| **Power & torque:** | 73bhp/98lb ft |
| **Engine:** | Normally aspirated 1699cc V4, petrol, carburettor, 8 valves |
| **Drivetrain:** | Mid-engine RWD |
| **Structure:** | Steel unibody with glassfibre shell |
| **Transmission:** | Four-speed manual |
| **Weight:** | 875kg |

**PRICE GUIDE**

| | |
|---|---|
| **Launch price:** | £2160 |
| **Excellent:** | £20,000 |
| **Good:** | £15,000 |
| **Average:** | £8000 |
| **Project:** | £2500 |

## MATRA Bagheera

The Matra-Simca Bagheera was one of the most innovative sports cars produced in over a decade. Featuring three-abreast seating, composite panels draped over a steel spaceframe, and mid-engined power-pack, the Bagheera was cheap, stylish and interesting. Performance never matched its looks, but the Simca-derived power units were willing enough, if unrefined, and the Bagheera could run rings around far more expensive cars. Structural corrosion has been the Bagheera's enemy, but plenty survive and back-up from the enthusiast clubs is excellent.

**SPECIFICATIONS**

| | |
|---|---|
| **Years produced:** | 1973-1980 |
| **Performance:** | 0-60mph: 12.3sec<br>Top speed: 101mph |
| **Power & torque:** | 82bhp/78lb ft |
| **Engine:** | Normally aspirated 1294cc four cylinder, petrol, carburettor, 8 valves |
| **Drivetrain:** | Mid-engine RWD |
| **Structure:** | Composite body/spaceframe |
| **Transmission:** | Four-speed manual |
| **Weight:** | 885kg |

**PRICE GUIDE**

| | |
|---|---|
| **Launch price:** | £5370 (UK, 1977) |
| **Excellent:** | £8500 |
| **Good:** | £4750 |
| **Average:** | £2500 |
| **Project:** | £1000 |

## MATRA Murena

The Murena was a logical development of the Bagheera. It was clothed in a new aerodynamic body and, importantly, underpinned by a galvanised steel spaceframe that would prove resistant to rust. The top engine option was a 2.2-litre Talbot Tagora engine, which provided the go to match its excellent handling – something that the Bagheera had lacked. Sadly, politics between Peugeot-Talbot and Matra saw the Murena prematurely halted in 1985, by which time the innovative French company was gearing up to produce the Espace.

**SPECIFICATIONS**

| | |
|---|---|
| **Years produced:** | 1980-1983 |
| **Performance:** | 0-60mph: 9.2sec<br>Top speed: 124mph |
| **Power & torque:** | 118bhp/139lb ft |
| **Engine:** | Normally aspirated 2155cc four cylinder, petrol, carburettor, 8 valves |
| **Drivetrain:** | Mid-engine RWD |
| **Structure:** | Composite body/spaceframe |
| **Transmission:** | Five-speed manual |
| **Weight:** | 1050kg |

**PRICE GUIDE**

| | |
|---|---|
| **Launch price:** | N/A in UK |
| **Excellent:** | £9500 |
| **Good:** | £5000 |
| **Average:** | £2700 |
| **Project:** | £1000 |

## MATRA Rancho

Simca's 1100 VF3 van proved the unlikely starting point for Matra-Simca's pioneering Rancho. The faux off-roader was sneered at by the press, but customers loved it, and the Rancho proved to be an unlikely hit of the late '70s. Rough and tough, with big plastic bumpers, it was perfect for mean city streets, but the 1.4-litre Simca engine struggled to haul the large body on the motorway. Engines became rattly almost the moment it left the factory, and rust set in soon after – the rear section was glassfibre, so at least some of it would survive unscathed.

**SPECIFICATIONS**

| | |
|---|---|
| **Years produced:** | 1977-1984 (56,700 in total) |
| **Performance:** | 0-60mph: 14.9sec<br>Top speed: 89mph |
| **Power & torque:** | 80bhp/89lb ft |
| **Engine:** | Normally aspirated 1442cc four cylinder, petrol, carburettor, 8 valves |
| **Drivetrain:** | Front-engine FWD |
| **Structure:** | Monocoque |
| **Transmission:** | Four-speed manual |
| **Weight:** | 1130kg |

**PRICE GUIDE**

| | |
|---|---|
| **Launch price:** | £5133 (UK, 1978) |
| **Excellent:** | £4000 |
| **Good:** | £2000 |
| **Average:** | £1500 |
| **Project:** | £1000 |

# MAZDA

ALTHOUGH FOUNDED in 1920, Hiroshima's Toyo Kogyo Cork company didn't build its first car – under the Mazda name, in tribute to founder Jujiro Matsuda as well as the Zoroastrian god – until 1960. The company soon became known for its experiments in rotary engine technology, with the RX-7 its best-known and biggest-selling exponent of the type, and one of the few cars to ever make the Wankel work well. Mazda was also applauded for the MX-5 roadster, launched in 1989, which pioneered a renaissance for small sports cars. After operating in a partnership since 1979, Ford acquired a controlling stake in 1997, leading to several joint projects and shared resources.

## MAZDA Cosmo 110S

The early years of the Japanese motor industry were exciting ones, so when Mazda decided to build a sports car in the mid-60s, it really went for broke. The Cosmo was powered by a Wankel engine, making it the world's first twin-rotor production car, beating the NSU Ro80 into production by months. It suffered from the usual problems associated with the rotary, such as rotor tip wear, but when it was running, the Cosmo was smooth and exciting to drive. Few made, and you'll pay handsomely for one now, with prices still rising. Series 1 cars tend to carry a 50% premium.

**SPECIFICATIONS**

| | |
|---|---|
| **Years produced:** | 1967-1972 (1519 in total) |
| **Performance:** | 0-60mph: 9.3sec<br>Top speed: 120mph |
| **Power & torque:** | 108bhp/96lb ft |
| **Engine:** | Normally aspirated 1964cc twin-rotor Wankel, petrol, carburettor |
| **Drivetrain:** | Front-engine RWD |
| **Structure:** | Monocoque |
| **Transmission:** | Four-speed manual |
| **Weight:** | 930kg |

**PRICE GUIDE**

| | |
|---|---|
| **Launch price:** | £2607 |
| **Excellent:** | £80,000 |
| **Good:** | £40,000 |
| **Average:** | £25,000 |
| **Project:** | N/A |

## MAZDA
## RX4/929

Mazda persisted with the Wankel more than any other manufacturer, and through diligent development managed to make it work reasonably successfully. But the 929 was the last in the line of large saloons, killed in the end by a voracious for petrol – not good in the midst of a fuel-led recession. The RX4 coupé boasts '70s Transatlantic Japanese styling that just gets better with age, but predictably there aren't many left now thanks to a proclivity for rusting. There's an active following, and rebuilds using modern components give acceptable engine life.

**SPECIFICATIONS (929 Coupé)**

| | |
|---|---|
| **Years produced:** | 1972-1979 (213,998 in total) |
| **Performance:** | 0-60mph: 14.0sec<br>Top speed: 92mph |
| **Power & torque:** | 83bhp/99lb ft |
| **Engine:** | Normally aspirated 1769cc twin-rotor Wankel, petrol, carburettor |
| **Drivetrain:** | Front-engine RWD |
| **Structure:** | Monocoque |
| **Transmission:** | Four-speed manual |
| **Weight:** | 1095kg |

**PRICE GUIDE (Coupe)**

| | |
|---|---|
| **Launch price:** | £1649 |
| **Excellent:** | £7500 |
| **Good:** | £4250 |
| **Average:** | £2000 |
| **Project:** | £1200 |

## MAZDA
## RX-7 Series 1

This was Mazda's attempt to make the world take the rotary engine seriously. With over half-a-million sales of this first series RX-7, it clearly worked. However, the seemingly unassailable problem of the Wankel's poor economy means it could never go mainstream. The RX-7 makes the most of the engine's light weight, with perfect 50:50 weight distribution. The early version is best left to enthusiasts; from 1981 it was a better car, with an extra 10bhp, rear disc brakes, a spoiler on the back and more comprehensive equipment. On the up.

**SPECIFICATIONS**

| | |
|---|---|
| **Years produced:** | 1979-1985 (471,018 in total) |
| **Performance:** | 0-60mph: 9.5sec<br>Top speed: 115mph |
| **Power & torque:** | 105bhp/106lb ft |
| **Engine:** | Normally aspirated 2292cc twin-rotor Wankel, petrol, carburettor |
| **Drivetrain:** | Front-engine RWD |
| **Structure:** | Monocoque |
| **Transmission:** | Five-speed manual |
| **Weight:** | 980kg |

**PRICE GUIDE**

| | |
|---|---|
| **Launch price:** | £8549 |
| **Excellent:** | £7000 |
| **Good:** | £4500 |
| **Average:** | £1850 |
| **Project:** | £800 |

## MAZDA
## RX-7 Series 2

The second-generation RX-7's all-new styling stole a lot of cues from the Porsche 928 and 944 and managed to look more substantial without growing in size, and only adding 80lb in weight. It gave safer handling thanks to new rear suspension, and sharper steering with rack-and-pinion instead of recirculating ball. The revised 13A engine kicks out more power – especially in the Turbo version that became available in the UK from 1988 with up to 200bhp. The following year a convertible was added, though these are harder to find. Edging up slowly.

**SPECIFICATIONS**

| | |
|---|---|
| **Years produced:** | 1986-1992 (272,027 in total) |
| **Performance:** | 0-60mph: 8.5sec<br>Top speed: 134mph |
| **Power & torque:** | 149bhp/135lb ft |
| **Engine:** | Turbocharged 2254cc twin-rotor, petrol, electronic fuel injection |
| **Drivetrain:** | Front-engine RWD |
| **Structure:** | Monocoque |
| **Transmission:** | Five-speed manual |
| **Weight:** | 1221kg |

**PRICE GUIDE**

| | |
|---|---|
| **Launch price:** | £13,995 |
| **Excellent:** | £6250 |
| **Good:** | £3700 |
| **Average:** | £1750 |
| **Project:** | £700 |

## MAZDA
## 323 4WD Turbo

Look beyond the forgettable styling, and you'll find an engaging and capable '80s hot hatch masquerading as your grandmother's shopping trolley. The 323 4WD Turbo was conceived for rallying and was given its go-faster stripes by the application of an IHI turbo and prodigious boost. Handling was also incredibly well resolved, as you'd expect for a competition-bred machine. Think of it as a bargain-basement Delta Integrale and you'd be doing it a disservice, though you wouldn't be too far off the mark. Few left in original condition now.

**SPECIFICATIONS**

| | |
|---|---|
| **Years produced:** | 1985-1989 |
| **Performance:** | 0-60mph: 7.9sec<br>Top speed: 125mph |
| **Power & torque:** | 150bhp/144lb ft |
| **Engine:** | Turbocharged 1597cc four cylinder, petrol, fuel injection, 16 valves |
| **Drivetrain:** | Front-engine AWD |
| **Structure:** | Monocoque |
| **Transmission:** | Five-speed manual |
| **Weight:** | 1110kg |

**PRICE GUIDE**

| | |
|---|---|
| **Launch price:** | £11,750 |
| **Excellent:** | £6500 |
| **Good:** | £3750 |
| **Average:** | £2000 |
| **Project:** | £1500 |

## MAZDA
## MX-5 MkI

The perfect car for those who want the trad British sports car experience without the oil leaks, poor reliability and fiddly roofs. With a gutsy twin-cam engine, the MX-5 offers sufficient performance, though not enough to upset the terrific handling. Totally dependable even at high mileages, though rust can be an issue, most obviously where the sills join the rear wings. The lighter early 1.6s are favoured by some, but avoid the cheapo post-1994 1.6s as they're down on power. Japanese 'Eunos' versions are often better specced. Values for the best are holding firm.

**SPECIFICATIONS**

| | |
|---|---|
| **Years produced:** | 1990-1997 (421,107 in total) |
| **Performance:** | 0-60mph: 8.6sec<br>Top speed: 116mph |
| **Power & torque:** | 114bhp/100lb ft |
| **Engine:** | Normally aspirated 1597cc in-line four, petrol, electronic fuel injection, 16v |
| **Drivetrain:** | Front-engine RWD |
| **Structure:** | Monocoque |
| **Transmission:** | Five-speed manual |
| **Weight:** | 970kg |

**PRICE GUIDE**

| | |
|---|---|
| **Launch price:** | £14,249 |
| **Excellent:** | £4500 |
| **Good:** | £3000 |
| **Average:** | £1400 |
| **Project:** | £800 |

## MAZDA
## RX-7 Series 3

For the third generation of its coupé, Mazda got serious. There was more power from a twin-turbo '13B' rotary engine – a Porsche-worrying 252bhp. With a low centre of gravity and perfect weight distribution, the handling was also highly praised. Perhaps best of all, the lines were the most attractive yet – though few completely unmolested examples remain. Not many were sold in the UK by Mazda, but their numbers have since been more than doubled by 'grey' imports, so make sure you know what you're looking at. Spirit R version can fetch over £25k.

### SPECIFICATIONS

| | |
|---|---|
| **Years produced:** | 1992-2002 (68,589 in total) |
| **Performance:** | 0-60mph: 5.4sec<br>Top speed: 153mph |
| **Power & torque:** | 252bhp/218lb ft |
| **Engine:** | Twin-turbocharged 2616c twin-rotor, petrol, electronic fuel injection |
| **Drivetrain:** | Front-engine RWD |
| **Structure:** | Monocoque |
| **Transmission:** | Five-speed manual |
| **Weight:** | 1310kg |

### PRICE GUIDE

| | |
|---|---|
| **Launch price:** | £32,536 |
| **Excellent:** | £8500 |
| **Good:** | £5500 |
| **Average:** | £4000 |
| **Project:** | £1500 |

## MAZDA
## MX-5 Mk2

If it ain't broke... After the runaway success of the Mk1 MX-5, Mazda sensibly stuck to the same formula for the Mk2 (or 'NB') model. So it came with rugged 1.6 and 1.8-litre four-pot engines, five and six-speed manual gearboxes, the same all-wishbone suspension, and the same fine balance between ride and handling, sportiness and usability. It was another huge hit. As before, there were numerous special editions, most of them purely cosmetic makeovers. Pick of the range is the 1.8iS, but all are fun. Check carefully for rust.

### SPECIFICATIONS

| | |
|---|---|
| **Years produced:** | 1998-2005 (c350,000 in total) |
| **Performance:** | 0-60mph: 7.4sec (1.8i)<br>Top speed: 123mph |
| **Power & torque:** | 138bhp/120lb ft |
| **Engine:** | Normally aspirated 1839cc in-line four, petrol, electronic fuel injection, 16v |
| **Drivetrain:** | Front-engine RWD |
| **Structure:** | Monocoque |
| **Transmission:** | Five- or six-speed manual |
| **Weight:** | 1025kg |

### PRICE GUIDE

| | |
|---|---|
| **Launch price:** | £15,995 (1.8i) |
| **Excellent:** | £3500 |
| **Good:** | £2000 |
| **Average:** | £1200 |
| **Project:** | £750 |

## MAZDA
## RX-8

With a buzzy Wankel engine and love-or-hate-them rear 'suicide' doors, the RX-8 is no ordinary sports coupé. Based on an extended MX-5 platform, the rotary engine helped to give the RX-8 50/50 weight distribution. It makes for an excellent drivers' car, but it's infamous reputation for poor fuel economy is justified. The Renesis rotary engine produces either 237bhp or 189bhp, and it absolutely loves to rev. Many will need an engine rebuild, if they haven't aready had one, but specialists offer this for sensible money.

### SPECIFICATIONS

| | |
|---|---|
| **Years produced:** | 2003-2012 |
| **Performance:** | 0-60mph: 6.0sec<br>Top speed: 150mph |
| **Power & torque:** | 237bhp/156lb ft |
| **Engine:** | Normally aspirated 1308cc twin rotor, petrol, electronic fuel injection |
| **Drivetrain:** | Front-engine RWD |
| **Structure:** | Monocoque |
| **Transmission:** | Six-speed manual |
| **Weight:** | 1350kg |

### PRICE GUIDE

| | |
|---|---|
| **Launch price:** | £21,995 |
| **Excellent:** | £6000 |
| **Good:** | £3000 |
| **Average:** | £1000 |
| **Project:** | £500 |

# McLAREN

NEW ZEALANDER Bruce McLaren founded his eponymous race team in 1963. It won its first F1 GP in 1968, but its greatest early success was in the Can-Am sportscar series. After Bruce's tragic death while testing at Goodwood in 1970, the team continued and went on to win a huge number of constructors' and drivers' championships, from 1981 onwards under the direction of team principal Ron Dennis. It was Dennis, too, who in 1989 formed McLaren Automotive to venture into road car production. Its first model was the F1 (below), launched in 1992. It subsequently collaborated with Mercedes on the SLR, and in 2011 launched the first of a new series of mid-engined sports cars, the MP4-12C.

## McLAREN
## F1

McLaren gave the task of engineering its roadgoing supercar to racecar designer Gordon Murray, and it was Murray's twin obsessions with lightness and driving purity that made the F1 what it was. Its 240mph top speed was almost a by-product, enabled by the fabulous 6-litre V12 engine designed by BMW's Paul Roche. The Peter Stevens-styled three-seater was a masterpiece, but sales were slow and the planned production run was eventually cut short. Values continue to soar; an upgraded LM-spec car set a new auction benchmark at $19.8m in 2019.

### SPECIFICATIONS

| | |
|---|---|
| **Years produced:** | 1993-1998 (106 including track cars) |
| **Performance:** | 0-60mph: 3.2sec<br>Top speed: 240mph |
| **Power & torque:** | 627bhp/479lb ft |
| **Engine:** | Normally aspirated 6064cc V12, petrol, electronic injection, 48 valves |
| **Drivetrain:** | Mid-engine RWD |
| **Structure:** | Carbonfibre tub and bodywork |
| **Transmission:** | Six-speed manual |
| **Weight:** | 1137kg |

### PRICE GUIDE

| | |
|---|---|
| **Launch price:** | £540,000 |
| **Excellent:** | £13,000,000+ |
| **Good:** | £10,000,000+ |
| **Average:** | N/A |
| **Project:** | N/A |

# MERCEDES-BENZ

MERCEDES WAS FOUNDED in 1901, named after founder Emile Jellinek's daughter, but merged with Karl Benz's 1885 firm in 1926. The combination of expertise resulted in some magnificent and stately machines prior to World War Two. After the conflict, Mercedes-Benz continued with upmarket and sporty models. The 300SL Gullwing fittingly became world-renowned and widely regarded as the first true supercar. The company forged a reputation as a maker of high quality and enduring vehicles with a touch of luxury; its 600 and S-class saloons were Rolls-Royce rivals, while its long-running SL sports cars have always been successful and sought-after.

## MERCEDES-BENZ 300 Cabriolet D

This convertible version of the 300 saloon was built in limited numbers and was most commonly seen with the leaders of any number of nations waving from the rear seats. Side windows and frames lower fully to make it a full convertible. A car with enormous presence, it also requires an enormous wallet should you need to undertake restoration work, though the ever-increasing value of a good one goes some way towards reflecting this. Very rare and not often seen for sale. Top examples almost priceless and projects unheard of. Rarely come up for sale.

### SPECIFICATIONS

**Years produced:** 1951-1956 (707 in total)
**Performance:** 0-60mph: 17.0sec
Top speed: 99mph
**Power & torque:** 123bhp/163lb ft
**Engine:** Normally aspirated 2996cc straight six, petrol, carburettor, 12 valves
**Drivetrain:** Front-engine RWD
**Structure:** Separate chassis
**Transmission:** Four-speed manual
**Weight:** 1940kg

### PRICE GUIDE

**Launch price:** N/A in UK
**Excellent:** £425,000
**Good:** £245,000
**Average:** £125,000
**Project:** £60,000

## MERCEDES-BENZ 300A/B/C/D

Mercedes' return to the production of prestige automobiles six years after the end of WW2 resulted in this 4000lb giant. The range has since been dubbed 'Adenauer' as the car became closely associated with the German chancellor of the time, Dr Konrad Adenauer. It was built on the X-frame chassis of its pre-war counterparts, with an alloy-head straight six. Sold in the UK from 1953, and better from 1954 when a servo was added to the brakes. Good examples are sought-after and rising in value, but there are still projects out there.

### SPECIFICATIONS

**Years produced:** 1951-1962 (11,430 in total)
**Performance:** 0-60mph: 15.0sec
Top speed: 109mph
**Power & torque:** 148bhp/178lb ft
**Engine:** Normally aspirated 2996cc four cylinder, petrol, carburettor, 12 valves
**Drivetrain:** Front-engine RWD
**Structure:** Separate chassis
**Transmission:** Four-speed manual/three-speed auto
**Weight:** 1740kg

### PRICE GUIDE

**Launch price:** £3500
**Excellent:** £65,000
**Good:** £40,000
**Average:** £25,000
**Project:** £10,000

## MERCEDES-BENZ 300S/Sc Cabriolet/Roadster

Built on a 6in shorter 300 saloon chassis, this still-giant two-seater harked back to the 540K of Mercedes' pre-war glory days. The S was more expensive than the 300SL Gullwing in 1954. The quick way to tell the Cabriolet and Roadster apart is that the former has 'pram irons' on the side of the folding top. The Sc was introduced in 1955, the small 'c' denoting Bosch fuel injection. Prices have stabilised for these seldom-seen luxury cars.

### SPECIFICATIONS

**Years produced:** 1952-1958 (760 in total)
**Performance:** 0-60mph: 15.0sec
Top speed: 109mph
**Power & torque:** 140bhp/178lb ft
**Engine:** Normally aspirated 2996cc straight six, petrol, carburettor, 12 valves
**Drivetrain:** Front-engine RWD
**Structure:** Separate chassis
**Transmission:** Four-speed manual
**Weight:** N/A

### PRICE GUIDE

**Launch price:** £5529
**Excellent:** £575,000
**Good:** £295,000
**Average:** £150,000
**Project:** N/A

## MERCEDES-BENZ 180-220S 'Ponton'

These are generally referred to by their 'Ponton' nickname, which is German for pontoon and refers to the bridge-like suspension subframe. The 180 and 190 have four-cylinder engines and were much better after 1957, when they received an overhead-cam engine in place of the old sidevalve unit. There was also a popular though underpowered 180D diesel option. 220s sit on a longer wheelbase and have six-cylinder engines, so they are worth more. Some lovely cars around for reasonable money, but plenty of cheap cars still available.

### SPECIFICATIONS

**Years produced:** 1953-1962 (280,807 in total)
**Performance:** 0-60mph: 15.2sec
Top speed: N/A
**Power & torque:** 58bhp/82lb ft
**Engine:** Normally aspirated 1767cc four cylinder, petrol, carburettor, 8 valves
**Drivetrain:** Front-engine RWD
**Structure:** Monocoque
**Transmission:** Four-speed manual
**Weight:** 1070kg

### PRICE GUIDE

**Launch price:** £1694
**Excellent:** £20,000
**Good:** £10,000
**Average:** £3500
**Project:** £2000

SLSHOP | OWNER SERVICES

# SLSHOP HEALTH CHECKS

Developed exclusively for the R107, W113 and R129 SL, our comprehensive Health Check and consultancy is an industry leading service that cannot be found anywhere else. This Health Check is a comprehensive review of your car, which takes place on the ramps, in our service bay and out on the road. A Health Check is more than just a status report, it's a chance for you to really examine your car and your future plans. It gives reassurance for you and the car, an opportunity to discuss your intended direction with an impartial expert. For customers who have recently acquired an SL, whether as part of an inheritance, from an auction or from any other source it's a great opportunity to really understand exactly what is sitting in your garage. Our consultancy platform provides a structured approach for the next steps in your SL journey. Many fine restorations have started with a Health Check, but we've also saved customers from investing money in the wrong areas or in the wrong car entirely.

## COMPLETE HEALTH CHECK

Our industry leading Health Check is specific to the SL, designed to give you a full and complete report on the wellbeing of your classic car. A great place to start if you have recently purchased a car or are about to embark on a programme of restoration.

## BULKHEAD CHECK

The bulkhead is arguably the one area on your car that has the potential to produce the largest bills. This Bulkhead Health Check aims to reveal the true extent of any bulkhead corrosion hidden within your SL, and form a road map to rectify the issue.

## STRUCTURIAL CHECK

Our Complete Structural Check combines the Under Body Check with the Bulkhead Check giving a comprehensive picture of the condition of all metalwork beneath and inside your SL.

## ENGINE CHECK

Chasing misfires, leaks, wobbles and squeaks results in frustration and confusion. By performing a complete Engine Health Check, you will be provided with the best possible information on the health of your engine, from top to bottom.

## BRAKE CHECK

A complete report on your entire braking system, putting you in the best possible position to make a decision on what to do next to improve your SL. We work through each area of the system, from the sole of your shoe to the disc itself.

## UNDERBODY CHECK

Our Underbody Check is designed to give a full report on the integrity of a car, covering the all-important metalwork and mounting points from front to back.

Perfect for getting an understanding of your SL

**RUSSELL OWENS**
Customer Liaison Manager

01789 337 070 (Option 3)
theSLSHOP.com/ownerservices
russell@theSLSHOP.com

## MERCEDES-BENZ 300SL Gullwing

Rarely seen but instantly recognised, this is not just a car but a true icon, generally known simply by the name Gullwing. Behind the legend is a high quality sports coupé with a racing heritage, built over a spaceframe chassis, and with the world's first production fuel-injection engine. The rest of the spec seems a little less impressive today: drum brakes, a four-speed gearbox, and swing-axle rear suspension. Most had steel bodies, but 29 were built in aluminium, for which you might well have to multiply the prices here by five!

**SPECIFICATIONS**

**Years produced:** 1954-1957 (1400 in total)
**Performance:** 0-60mph: 8.8sec
Top speed: 135mph
**Power & torque:** 215bhp/203lb ft
**Engine:** Normally aspirated 2996cc straight six, petrol, mechanical injection, 12 valves
**Drivetrain:** Front-engine RWD
**Structure:** Spaceframe
**Transmission:** Four-speed manual
**Weight:** 1293kg

**PRICE GUIDE**

**Launch price:** £4393
**Excellent:** £1,125,000
**Good:** £875,000
**Average:** £575,000
**Project:** N/A

## MERCEDES-BENZ 190SL Roadster

The SL tag is supposed to translate as 'sports light', but despite aluminium doors, bonnet and bootlid, the 190SL is still too heavy to do anything properly sporting with its 1.9-litre four-cylinder engine. Settle for the fact that it is a good, if not exhilarating drive, with bags of style. In fact it's just the thing for those who can't afford the 300SL. Build quality is superb, and they've survived in good enough numbers to make finding one simple enough. Values are currently stable, and some projects are still appearing. Very best command up to £200k.

**SPECIFICATIONS**

**Years produced:** 1955-1963 (25,881 in total)
**Performance:** 0-60mph: 13.3sec
Top speed: 109mph
**Power & torque:** 104bhp/114lb ft
**Engine:** Normally aspirated 1897cc four cylinder, petrol, carburettor, 8 valves
**Drivetrain:** Front-engine RWD
**Structure:** Steel monocoque
**Transmission:** Four-speed manual
**Weight:** 1140kg

**PRICE GUIDE**

**Launch price:** £2693
**Excellent:** £145,000
**Good:** £80,000
**Average:** £45,000
**Project:** £25,000

## MERCEDES-BENZ 220S/SE Cabriolet

Based on the 220 Ponton saloon but on a five-inch shorter floorpan, with much prettier bodywork distinguished by really long doors. Priced roughly 75% higher than a saloon when new, they sold in small numbers. The 220S had a 100bhp six-cylinder engine with twin Solex carburettors, and was joined in 1958 by the 220SE, with the 'E' standing for fuel injection, a Bosch unit that added 15bhp – and even more to the car's already high price. Prices have recently dipped quite a bit, though the very best concours-condition cars might fetch up to £150k.

**SPECIFICATIONS**

**Years produced:** 1956-1960
**Performance:** 0-60mph: 15.2sec
Top speed: 101mph
**Power & torque:** 98bhp/119lb ft
**Engine:** Normally aspirated 2195cc straight six, petrol, carburettor, 12 valves
**Drivetrain:** Front-engine RWD
**Structure:** Moncoque
**Transmission:** Four-speed manual
**Weight:** N/A

**PRICE GUIDE**

**Launch price:** £3715
**Excellent:** £85,000
**Good:** £60,000
**Average:** £45,000
**Project:** £30,000

## MERCEDES-BENZ 220S/SE Coupé

Launched a year later than the Cabriolet, the Coupé version is identical apart from the fixed roof and upright rather than slanted frames for the rear of the side window. Being based on a saloon floorpan means it's a full four-seater, and that US-influenced hardtop styling ensures plenty of headroom, even for those in the back. Built from the best materials, but before the era of rust protection so many will have suffered. Fuel-injection SE is preferred, so you may find the carburettor S version for less. Both are rare in right-hand drive. Prices holding steady.

**SPECIFICATIONS**

**Years produced:** 1957-1960
**Performance:** 0-60mph: 17.1sec
Top speed: 100mph
**Power & torque:** 98bhp/119lb ft
**Engine:** Normally aspirated 2195cc straight six, petrol, carburettor, 12 valves
**Drivetrain:** Front-engine RWD
**Structure:** Monocoque
**Transmission:** Four-speed manual
**Weight:** 1350kg

**PRICE GUIDE**

**Launch price:** N/A
**Excellent:** £55,000
**Good:** £32,000
**Average:** £24,000
**Project:** £16,000

## MERCEDES-BENZ 300SL Roadster (W198)

The replacement for the Gullwing, the Roadster has a revised spaceframe chassis to make room for normal doors, which added 200lb to the weight. It's a softer, more relaxing car to drive than the competition-bred Gullwing. The more extensive use of chrome inside and out isn't to all tastes, but the Roadster at least enjoyed disc brakes from 1961, then got a much lighter aluminium engine block the following year, for which you'll now pay a premium. Rare, highly desirable – and excellent examples sometimes sell for more than SL Gullwings.

**SPECIFICATIONS**

**Years produced:** 1957-1963 (1856 in total)
**Performance:** 0-60mph: 8.1sec
Top speed: 130mph
**Power & torque:** 215bhp/228lb ft
**Engine:** Normally aspirated 2996cc straight six, petrol, mechanical injection, 12 valves
**Drivetrain:** Front-engine RWD
**Structure:** Spaceframe
**Transmission:** Four-speed manual
**Weight:** 1383kg

**PRICE GUIDE**

**Launch price:** £4393
**Excellent:** £925,000
**Good:** £700,000
**Average:** £495,000
**Project:** N/A

## MERCEDES-BENZ 190-230 Fintail Saloon

Those tailfins that gave these cars their nickname were shamelessly tacked on to attract American buyers, and it worked: the Fintail Mercs sold extremely well, but without looking like some Pontiac pastiche. They proved handy for rallying too, with a 220SE winning the Monte Carlo rally. Low-rent models have single round headlights, with the more desirable versions treated to stacked headlamps and double-decked bumpers. Four- and six-cylinder engine are available, with diesel options for the former. Values currently holding steady.

**SPECIFICATIONS**

**Years produced:** 1959-1968 (966,085 in total)
**Performance:** 0-60mph: 12.8sec
Top speed: 90mph
**Power & torque:** 90bhp/113lb ft
**Engine:** Normally aspirated 1897cc four cylinder, petrol, carburettor, 8 valves
**Drivetrain:** Front-engine RWD
**Structure:** Monocoque
**Transmission:** Four-speed manual
**Weight:** 1224kg

**PRICE GUIDE**

**Launch price:** £1987
**Excellent:** £17,000
**Good:** £8000
**Average:** £3000
**Project:** £2000

## MERCEDES-BENZ 300SE Fintail Saloon

The range-topping 300SE gets a mention of its own as there's so much more to it. Extra chrome helps it stand out, but underneath there are real changes. Riding on self-levelling air suspension, the car also benefits from all-wheel disc brakes and has power steering as standard. That 3.0-litre straight-six is a detuned version of the engine used in the 300SL, and there was a choice of four-speed manual or automatic transmission. From 1963 there was also a 300SEL, providing more room thanks to a 4in longer wheelbase. Cheap examples still plentiful.

**SPECIFICATIONS**

**Years produced:** 1961-1965 (6748 in total)
**Performance:** 0-60mph: 10.9sec
Top speed: 115mph
**Power & torque:** 157bhp/185lb ft
**Engine:** Normally aspirated 2996cc straight six, petrol, fuel injection, 12 valves
**Drivetrain:** Front-engine RWD
**Structure:** Monocoque
**Transmission:** Four-speed manual
**Weight:** N/A

**PRICE GUIDE**

**Launch price:** £3814
**Excellent:** £18,500
**Good:** £8500
**Average:** £4000
**Project:** £2500

## MERCEDES-BENZ 220SEb Coupé/Cabriolet

The first incarnations of Paul Bracq's elegant coupé and convertible body designs, which lasted over a decade and are regarded by some as Mercedes-Benz's best-looking cars of the classic era. Interior trimmings are also of the highest quality. It may not have had anything like the same performance, but you can see why these cost similar money to an Aston DB4 back in 1962. Four-speed automatics were standard fitment, and you won't find many with the optional four-speed manual. Note: cabriolets fetch almost double the prices here.

**SPECIFICATIONS**

**Years produced:** 1961-1965 (16,902 in total)
**Performance:** 0-60mph: 12.8sec
Top speed: 106mph
**Power & torque:** 120bhp/139lb ft
**Engine:** Normally aspirated, 2195cc straight six, petrol, carburettor, 12 valves
**Drivetrain:** Front-engine RWD
**Structure:** Monocoque
**Transmission:** Four-speed automatic
**Weight:** 1410kg

**PRICE GUIDE (Coupés)**

**Launch price:** £4288
**Excellent:** £38,000
**Good:** £27,000
**Average:** £14,000
**Project:** £10,000

## MERCEDES-BENZ 300SE Coupé/Cabriolet

Delivered some of the performance lacking in the 220SEb models thanks to 160bhp and then 170bhp versions of the big fuel-injection six-cylinder engine. The 300SEs also employed the self-levelling air suspension of the 300 saloons, giving them the sort of ride you would comment favourably on in a modern luxury car, though the system can also be troublesome if neglected. With a propensity for rust, there aren't a lot about, hence good ones are sought-after. Cabrios fetch almost twice as much, but values of both versions are currently stable.

**SPECIFICATIONS**

**Years produced:** 1962-1967 (3127 in total)
**Performance:** 0-60mph: 10.7sec
Top speed: 115mph
**Power & torque:** 167bhp/184lb ft
**Engine:** Normally aspirated 2996cc straight six, petrol, fuel injection, 12 valves
**Drivetrain:** Front-engine RWD
**Structure:** Monocoque
**Transmission:** Four-speed automatic
**Weight:** 1600kg

**PRICE GUIDE (Coupés)**

**Launch price:** £4931
**Excellent:** £47,000
**Good:** £28,500
**Average:** £18,000
**Project:** £10,000

## MERCEDES-BENZ 230/250/280SL

In keeping with the fashion to apply generic names to Mercedes-Benz ranges to help cut through the maze of numbers, you'll find 'Pagoda' commonly attached to these sports cars, thanks to the kicked-up edges to the roofline of the optional hardtop. Offering more power and performance than the 190SL it replaced, the 230SL proved its worth by winning the Spa-Sofia-Liège rally. The torquier 250SL replaced it, but was only around for 1967. The 280 offered the most power but also a chassis tuned more to comfort. Prices currently taking a breather.

**SPECIFICATIONS**

**Years produced:** 1963-1971 (c49,000 in total)
**Performance:** 0-60mph: 9.0sec (280)
Top speed: 124mph
**Power & torque:** 168bhp/177lb ft
**Engine:** Normally aspirated 2778cc straight six, petrol, fuel injection, 12 valves
**Drivetrain:** Front-engine RWD
**Structure:** Monocoque
**Transmission:** Four-speed manual/four-speed auto
**Weight:** 1360kg

**PRICE GUIDE (280SL in brackets)**

**Launch price:** £3595
**Excellent:** £95,000 (£135,000+)
**Good:** £65,000 (£85,000)
**Average:** £32,000 (£47,500)
**Project:** £23,500 (£28,000)

AN INDEPENDENT ASTON MARTIN MAGAZINE
VANTAGE
If you have a passion for Aston Martins, you'll love Vantage.
astonmagazine.co.uk
GB

## MERCEDES-BENZ
### 600

Mercedes-Benz threw everything at this technical tour de force, designed to be bought by governments rather than mere business magnates. They weighed 2.5 tonnes (more for the long-wheelbase Pullman seven-seater), and that was before bulletproof glass was added. There's air suspension, vacuum central locking, two heating and ventilation systems, and to haul it around a 6.3-litre V8 with Bosch injection. Stayed in production for 18 years and notched up remarkable sales. Prices higher for Pullmans, while very rare Landaulet is in the millions.

**SPECIFICATIONS**

| | |
|---|---|
| **Years produced:** | 1964-1981 (2677 in total) |
| **Performance:** | 0-60mph: 9.7sec<br>Top speed: 127mph |
| **Power & torque:** | 247bhp/369lb ft |
| **Engine:** | Normally aspirated 6332cc V8, petrol, fuel injection, 16 valves |
| **Drivetrain:** | Front-engine RWD |
| **Structure:** | Monocoque |
| **Transmission:** | Four-speed automatic |
| **Weight:** | 2475kg |

**PRICE GUIDE**

| | |
|---|---|
| **Launch price:** | £8752 |
| **Excellent:** | £85,000 |
| **Good:** | £55,000 |
| **Average:** | £35,000 |
| **Project:** | £25,000 |

## MERCEDES-BENZ
### S-Class (W108/W109)

The dawn of the S-Class, styled in a timeless if unexciting manner by Paul Bracq. Entry level was the 250S with a 130bhp 2.5-litre straight-six, with the Bosch fuel-injection 250SE offering another 20bhp. At the top of the range, packed with luxuries and safety items, was the 300 (3.0 litres, 168bhp), with the SEL – 4in longer than the standard cars – roughly twice the price of the entry-level 250S. In late 1968 the 300SE was dropped and the 300SEL – confusingly – got the 280SE's 2.8-litre engine. Best cars now hard to find and all are gaining value.

**SPECIFICATIONS**

| | |
|---|---|
| **Years produced:** | 1965-1969 (7625 in total) |
| **Performance:** | 0-60mph: 11.2sec (300SE)<br>Top speed: 115mph |
| **Power & torque:** | 168bhp/184lb ft |
| **Engine:** | Normally aspirated 2996cc straight six, petrol, fuel injection, 12 valves |
| **Drivetrain:** | Front-engine RWD |
| **Structure:** | Monocoque |
| **Transmission:** | Four-speed automatic |
| **Weight:** | 1575kg |

**PRICE GUIDE 250/280 (300SE in brackets)**

| | |
|---|---|
| **Launch price:** | £2575 (£5669) |
| **Excellent:** | £24,000 (£28,500) |
| **Good:** | £14,000 (£17,500) |
| **Average:** | £8500 (£9500) |
| **Project:** | £3250 (£4250) |

## MERCEDES-BENZ
### 250/280SE Coupé/Cabrio

With the 1965 launch of the S-class saloon, the smaller-engined versions of the Coupé and Cabriolet were improved and rationalised by being given the 2.5-litre engine from the new cars. That added 30bhp, and rear disc brakes were fitted at the same time. Two years later, when the 300SE was dropped, the 280SE replaced both that and the 250SE with its 2.8-litre 160bhp straight six, with revised fuel injection for better economy. A five-speed manual gearbox was an option from 1969. Cabriolets are worth almost double Coupé values.

**SPECIFICATIONS**

| | |
|---|---|
| **Years produced:** | 1965-1972 (6213 in total) |
| **Performance:** | 0-60mph: 11.8sec<br>Top speed: 118mph |
| **Power & torque:** | 148bhp/159lb ft |
| **Engine:** | Normally aspirated 2497cc straight six, petrol, fuel injection, 12 valves |
| **Drivetrain:** | Front-engine RWD |
| **Structure:** | Monocoque |
| **Transmission:** | Four-speed manual |
| **Weight:** | 1480kg |

**PIRCE GUIDE (Coupés)**

| | |
|---|---|
| **Launch price:** | £4275 |
| **Excellent:** | £49,000 |
| **Good:** | £32,000 |
| **Average:** | £22,500 |
| **Project:** | £12,000 |

## MERCEDES-BENZ
### 300SEL 6.3 (W109)

In 1968, Mercedes-Benz engineers went slightly bonkers and dropped the 6.3-litre V8 from the 600 into the long-wheelbase 300's bodyshell, keeping luxuries such as air suspension. With the engine's massive torque, the result was a muscle car in disguise, and unlike most American muscle cars it came with dual-circuit four-wheel disc brakes. This was a luxury saloon that could outpace most sports cars at the time, though you had to cough up more than the price of a Ferrari Daytona for the pleasure. Cult status today; very best might hit £100k.

**SPECIFICATIONS**

| | |
|---|---|
| **Years produced:** | 1967-1972 (6526 in total) |
| **Performance:** | 0-60mph: 5.7sec<br>Top speed: 141mph |
| **Power & torque:** | 247bhp/369lb ft |
| **Engine:** | Normally aspirated 6332cc V8, petrol, carburettor, 16 valves |
| **Drivetrain:** | Front-engine RWD |
| **Structure:** | Monocoque |
| **Transmission:** | Four-speed automatic |
| **Weight:** | 1780kg |

**PRICE GUIDE**

| | |
|---|---|
| **Launch price:** | £7743 |
| **Excellent:** | £75,000 |
| **Good:** | £42,500 |
| **Average:** | £28,000 |
| **Project:** | £18,000 |

## MERCEDES-BENZ
### 230.6/250/280E Saloon

These saloons use the same bodyshell as the W115 cars but have six-cylinder engines, giving them the Mercedes-Benz range designation W114. At entry level is the 230.6 with 120bhp, joined at first by the 130bhp 250. The confusion begins in 1970 when the 250 is given a single-cam 2.8-litre engine, though the regular 250 continued for two years. Then a 280 joined the range, using a twin-cam 2.8-litre engine, in carburettor form, or as the 280E, with fuel injection. Functional, strong, elegant, and gaining a following. Top, low-mile cars could be up to £25k.

**SPECIFICATIONS**

| | |
|---|---|
| **Years produced:** | 1967-1976 |
| **Performance:** | 0-60mph: 12.8sec<br>Top speed: 112mph |
| **Power & torque:** | 128bhp/147lb ft |
| **Engine:** | Normally aspirated 2496cc straight six, petrol, carburettor, 12 valves |
| **Drivetrain:** | Front-engine RWD |
| **Structure:** | Monocoque |
| **Transmission:** | Four-speed manual |
| **Weight:** | 1375kg |

**PRICE GUIDE**

| | |
|---|---|
| **Launch price:** | £4753 |
| **Excellent:** | £16,500 |
| **Good:** | £7000 |
| **Average:** | £3750 |
| **Project:** | £1500 |

## MERCEDES-BENZ
### 250/280CE Coupé (W114)

Only the fuel-injection versions of these pillarless coupés came to the UK market, though carburettor versions were sold elsewhere, without the 'E' on the end of their name. They were based on the W114 saloons, retaining their length and wheelbase but with a shortened passenger compartment and a roof that was two inches lower. The 150bhp 250CE gave way to the 280CE in 1972. This later car came with the 185bhp twin-cam 2.8-litre engine. Really top examples are now rare and fetch strong money; fewer cheap examples around these days.

**SPECIFICATIONS**

**Years produced:** 1968-1976 (21,787/11,518 in total)
**Performance:** 0-60mph: 8.9sec
Top speed: 118mph
**Power & torque:** 150bhp/174lb ft
**Engine:** Normally aspirated 2497cc straight six, petrol, fuel injection, 12 valves
**Drivetrain:** Front-engine RWD
**Structure:** Monocoque
**Transmission:** Three-speed automatic
**Weight:** 1360kg

**PRICE GUIDE**

**Launch price:** £3475
**Excellent:** £28,000
**Good:** £15,000
**Average:** £5500
**Project:** £2750

## MERCEDES-BENZ
### 280SE 3.5 Coupé/ Cabriolet (W111)

These are the ones that everyone wants but few can afford. From late 1969 Mercedes-Benz dropped its 3.5-litre V8s into the Coupés and Cabrios to create a reassuringly expensive range-topper with 25% more power than the six-cylinder cars. Today, the SE 3.5s have become cooler than a penguin's fridge. Of course the much rarer Cabriolets take the top honours, with prices more than double those given here for Coupés – in excess of £250k for very best.

**SPECIFICATIONS**

**Years produced:** 1969-1971 (4502 in total)
**Performance:** 0-60mph: 9.0sec
Top speed: 130mph
**Power & torque:** 197bhp/211lb ft
**Engine:** Normally aspirated 3499cc V8, petrol, mechanical fuel injection, 16 valves
**Drivetrain:** Front-engine RWD
**Structure:** Monocoque
**Transmission:** Four-speed automatic
**Weight:** 1570kg

**PRICE GUIDE (Coupés)**

**Launch price:** £5158
**Excellent:** £85,000
**Good:** £65,000
**Average:** £35,000
**Project:** £27,500

## MERCEDES-BENZ
### 280SE 3.5/300SEL 3.5 (W108/W109)

For anyone enjoying the puzzle of a 2.8-litre 300SEL, here we have the same S-class bodies fitted with a 3.5-litre V8 to bridge the gap between the six-cylinder cars and the crazy 300SEL 6.3. So the best versions of the W108/109 S-class remain something of an enigma. The 300 still has air suspension, so mechanically shy buyers might prefer a 280. There was also a 280SEL 3.5, but only 951 were built. Really top examples now rare, with values soaring.

**SPECIFICATIONS**

**Years produced:** 1969-1972 (11,309/9483 in total)
**Performance:** 0-60mph: 8.4sec
Top speed: 115mph
**Power & torque:** 157bhp/185lb ft
**Engine:** Normally aspirated 2996cc straight six, petrol, fuel injection, 12 valves
**Drivetrain:** Front-engine RWD
**Structure:** Monocoque
**Transmission:** Four-speed automatic
**Weight:** 1673kg

**PRICE GUIDE**

**Launch price:** £5158
**Excellent:** £28,000
**Good:** £14,000
**Average:** £8000
**Project:** £3000

## MERCEDES-BENZ
### 350/450SLC (C107)

Mercedes-Benz took a bit of a shortcut to creating these 2+2 coupés. In effect, what you have is an R107 roadster with 14 inches added to the wheelbase, a fixed roof and some rear seats. Of course there's a bit more to it that that, as the job was achieved while only adding 110lb to the car's weight. Launched with a 3.5-litre V8, it was joined the following year by a 4.5-litre version that outsold the smaller engine by more than two to one. SLC gaining quite a following, and ultra-low-mileage examples may be as much as £50k.

**SPECIFICATIONS**

**Years produced:** 1971-1980 (13,925/31,739 in total)
**Performance:** 0-60mph: 9.3sec
Top speed: 130mph
**Power & torque:** 217bhp/265lb ft
**Engine:** Normally aspirated 4520cc V8, petrol, mechanical fuel injection, 16 valves
**Drivetrain:** Front-engine RWD
**Structure:** Monocoque
**Transmission:** Four-speed automatic
**Weight:** 1630kg

**PRICE GUIDE**

**Launch price:** £7875
**Excellent:** £22,500
**Good:** £14,000
**Average:** £6000
**Project:** £3000

## MERCEDES-BENZ
### SL (R107)

The 350SL was introduced as a replacement for the Pagoda 280SL, and once again both soft and hard tops were offered. There's more than a passing resemblance between the two cars, but the 350SL's body is three inches longer and 300lb heavier. The 450's extra litre of engine capacity didn't add much power, but torque took a big leap and allowed it to be fitted with a much taller rear axle ratio. In 1980 the range was facelifted, and new 280/300 straight-six models and 380/420 V8-engined variants were introduced. Values currently holding steady.

**SPECIFICATIONS**

**Years produced:** 1971-1989
**Performance:** 0-60mph: 9.3sec (350SL)
Top speed: 126mph
**Power & torque:** 200bhp/211lb ft
**Engine:** Normally aspirated 3499cc V8, petrol, electronic fuel injection, 16 valves
**Drivetrain:** Front-engine RWD
**Structure:** Monocoque
**Transmission:** Four-speed manual/three-speed auto
**Weight:** 1545kg

**PRICE GUIDE 350/450 (280/300/380/420)**

**Launch price:** £7395 (350)
**Excellent:** £32,500 (£45,000)
**Good:** £22,000 (£25,000)
**Average:** £9000 (£11,000)
**Project:** £5000 (£5000)

## MERCEDES-BENZ S-class (W116)

This is the second generation of S-class cars, and the one that cemented Mercedes' reputation at the top of the saloon-car pecking order. The 280s were the basic models, though not that basic, and came with a twin-cam straight-six that produced either 160bhp with carbs (S) or 185bhp using injection (SE). They had a fair turn of speed and excellent handling thanks to new semi-trailing arm rear suspension. Still cheaper than they deserve to be. The V8-engined 350s and 450s were billed as 'the best car in the world' at the time – and probably were.

**SPECIFICATIONS**

**Years produced:** 1972-1980 (430,200 in total)
**Performance:** 0-60mph: 9.3sec (450SE)
Top speed: 130mph
**Power & torque:** 221bhp/279lb ft
**Engine:** Normally aspirated 4520cc V8, petrol, mechanical fuel injection, 16 valves
**Drivetrain:** Front-engine RWD
**Structure:** Monocoque
**Transmission:** Three-speed automatic
**Weight:** 1765kg

**PRICE GUIDE**

**Launch price:** £5597 (280S)
**Excellent:** £18,000
**Good:** £10,000
**Average:** £5000
**Project:** £2500

## MERCEDES-BENZ 450SEL 6.9 (W116)

With its all-dominating S-class cars selling so well, the range was losing the cachet of exclusivity, and Mercedes-Benz needed something extra for the image-conscious plutocrat. A 6.9-litre V8 engine did the trick, along with self-levelling oleopneumatic suspension. Reassuringly expensive, the same money would buy you two XJ-S V12s and a Lancia Beta HPE, but the 450SEL 6.9 still sold in surprising numbers. Ferociously expensive to run, but, as with the 300SEL 6.3, now has cult status and very much on the up. Concours cars could be £100k very soon.

**SPECIFICATIONS**

**Years produced:** 1975-1980 (7380 in total)
**Performance:** 0-60mph: 7.5sec
Top speed: 140mph
**Power & torque:** 286bhp/405lb ft
**Engine:** Normally aspirated 6834cc V8, petrol, injection, 16 valves
**Drivetrain:** Front-engine RWD
**Structure:** Monocoque
**Transmission:** Three-speed automatic
**Weight:** 1935kg

**PRICE GUIDE**

**Launch price:** £21,995
**Excellent:** £55,000
**Good:** £35,000
**Average:** £22,000
**Project:** £11,000

## MERCEDES-BENZ 200/230E/280E (W123)

It was a case of more of the same when Mercedes-Benz came to replacing the popular stack-headlight W115 saloon. The W123 was possibly the company's high watermark when it came to build quality and longevity although, in the UK, you paid for the privilege of owning one. Base-model 200 and 200D were both flaccid, with the 230E a much better all-rounder. Twin-cam 280E is an all-purpose sporting saloon, but without the exciting dynamics associated with the rival BMW 528i. Good examples sought-after, and T-series estates can be double.

**SPECIFICATIONS (230E)**

**Years produced:** 1975-1985 (2,696,915 in total)
**Performance:** 0-60mph: 11.5sec
Top speed: 112mph
**Power & torque:** 134bhp/151lb ft
**Engine:** Normally aspirated 2299cc four cylinder, petrol, injection, 8 valves
**Drivetrain:** Front-engine RWD
**Structure:** Monocoque
**Transmission:** Four-speed manual
**Weight:** 1380kg

**PRICE GUIDE (Saloons)**

**Launch price:** £6235
**Excellent:** £7000
**Good:** £5000
**Average:** £2700
**Project:** £1000

## MERCEDES-BENZ 230/280CE (C123)

Based on the W123 saloons, but with 10cm nipped out of the wheelbase, these pillarless coupés shared the same hard-wearing interior. Top of the range was the 177bhp fuel-injection 280CE, while entry level was covered by the 230C, which put out 109bhp on carbs. Some markets got the in-between 280C with 156bhp, again on carbs. Both of those were dropped in 1980 to make way for the 230CE, with fuel injection and a new 2.3-litre engine. Output was now 136bhp, while the 280CE crept up to 185bhp. The very best now fetch around £20k.

**SPECIFICATIONS (230CE)**

**Years produced:** 1977-1985 (99,147 in total)
**Performance:** 0-60mph: 11.5sec
Top speed: 112mph
**Power & torque:** 134bhp/151lb ft
**Engine:** Normally aspirated 2299cc four cylinder, petrol, injection, 8 valves
**Drivetrain:** Front-engine RWD
**Structure:** Monocoque
**Transmission:** Four-speed manual
**Weight:** 1380kg

**PRICE GUIDE**

**Launch price:** £8951
**Excellent:** £18,000
**Good:** £8500
**Average:** £5500
**Project:** £2000

## MERCEDES-BENZ G-Wagen

More Land Rover than Range Rover, the Mercedes-Benz G-Wagen was a real beast of burden with incredible off-road ability to match. Engineered by Steyr-Daimler Puch in Austria, it was designed with military use in mind, so hardly a recipe for luxury and comfort. A high price, lack of equipment and that utilitarian style hampered sales in the UK, especially in the wake of the Mitsubishi Shogun and Isuzu Trooper. But as a classic off-roader the G-Wagen has bags of appeal, thanks to its timeless design and rugged build. Prices currently stable.

**SPECIFICATIONS (230GE)**

**Years produced:** 1979-date
**Performance:** 0-60mph: 15.5sec
Top speed: 88mph
**Power & torque:** 125bhp/142lb ft
**Engine:** Normally aspirated 2299cc four cylinder, petrol, fuel injection, 8 valves
**Drivetrain:** Front-engine AWD
**Structure:** Separate chassis
**Transmission:** Four-speed manual
**Weight:** 1830kg

**PRICE GUIDE**

**Launch price:** £14,195 (UK launch, 1981)
**Excellent:** £25,000
**Good:** £18,500
**Average:** £5000
**Project:** £2500

## MERCEDES-BENZ
### S-class (W126)

Third-generation S-class consolidated the success of the W116, adding extra safety features and even more sophistication. It soon became the limo of choice for celebrities, business leaders and heads of state, and in a 12-year lifespan more than 800,000 were built. There was a massive range of engines, including straight-six and V8 petrol, and diesels, too. Top-of-the-range 560SEL had 296bhp V8, which made it for a while the world's fastest saloon with a top speed of 155mph. Starting to attract interest, with condition rather than spec dictating values.

**SPECIFICATIONS**

**Years produced:** 1980-1991 (818,036 in total)
**Performance:** 0-60mph: 7.1sec (560SEL)
Top speed: 155mph
**Power & torque:** 296bhp/335lb ft
**Engine:** Normally aspirated 5547cc V8, petrol, injection, 16 valves
**Drivetrain:** Front-engine RWD
**Structure:** Monocoque
**Transmission:** Four-speed auto/five-speed manual
**Weight:** 1830kg

**PRICE GUIDE**

**Launch price:** £46,144 (560SEL)
**Excellent:** £25,000
**Good:** £18,000
**Average:** £8500
**Project:** £2000

## MERCEDES-BENZ
### 380/420/500/560SEC

If the S-class saloon was the best car in the world during the '80s then this – built on a 4in shorter S-class floorpan – must have been the best coupé. The 380 came with 204bhp and steel wheels, with ABS only an optional extra until 1985. The 420 replaced it at the 1986 facelift, good for 218bhp. The range-topper for five years, the 500SEC came with 245bhp, electric seats, ABS and a walnut dash. The ultimate, though, is the 295bhp, 156mph 560, with its flared arches and limited-slip diff. Very best 560SECs now £40k+, but cheap cars still around.

**SPECIFICATIONS**

**Years produced:** 1981-1991 (74,060 in total)
**Performance:** 0-60mph: 6.8sec (560)
Top speed: 156mph
**Power & torque:** 296bhp/335lb ft
**Engine:** Normally aspirated 5547cc V8, petrol, injection, 16 valves
**Drivetrain:** Front-engine RWD
**Structure:** Monocoque
**Transmission:** Four-speed automatic
**Weight:** 1748kg

**PRICE GUIDE (560SEC in brackets)**

**Launch price:** £25,700 (£52,185)
**Excellent:** £15,000 (£30,000+)
**Good:** £9500 (£16,500)
**Average:** £4500 (£8500)
**Project:** £1500 (£2500)

## MERCEDES-BENZ
### 500/560SL (R107)

Expensive flagships of the SL range, though it turned out to be the best-selling model. 500SL was there from the start, standing out from lesser SLs by the addition of a fairly subtle bootlid lip spoiler. It lost a little power when retuned for economy in September 1981, gaining a taller diff' ratio at the same time, so those early cars are more sought after. The 560SL joined the 500 in 1985 but didn't displace it, merely adding power, badge one-upmanship, and a thirst for fuel. Values steady, but the very best 560s can command £60k and more.

**SPECIFICATIONS**

**Years produced:** 1982-1989
**Performance:** 0-60mph: 7.7sec
Top speed: 134mph
**Power & torque:** 245bhp/294lb ft
**Engine:** Normally aspirated 4973cc V8, petrol, injection, 16 valves
**Drivetrain:** Front-engine RWD
**Structure:** Monocoque
**Transmission:** Four-speed automatic
**Weight:** 1605kg

**PRICE GUIDE**

**Launch price:** £20,300
**Excellent:** £45,000
**Good:** £25,000
**Average:** £11,500
**Project:** £5000

## MERCEDES-BENZ
### 190 (W201)

Darlings of the '80s upwardly mobile, almost two million 190s rolled out of the factory. Mercedes-Benz did an excellent job of scaling its big-car looks down into a BMW 3-series rivalling package. Largely ignored by the classic car market until recently, good examples are starting to be snapped up for what look like bargain prices. Only the Cosworth-tweaked and spoiler-clad 16V models in 2.3 and 2.5-litre form have attracted much collector attention, but basic models are slowly on the up and good examples make a great starter classic.

**SPECIFICATIONS (190)**

**Years produced:** 1982-1993 (1,874,668 in total)
**Performance:** 0-60mph: 13.4sec
Top speed: 109mph
**Power & torque:** 00bhp/122lb ft
**Engine:** Normally aspirated 1997cc four cylinder, petrol, carburettor, 8 valves
**Drivetrain:** Front-engine RWD
**Structure:** Monocoque
**Transmission:** Five-speed manual
**Weight:** 1080kg

**PRICE GUIDE**

**Launch price:** £9685
**Excellent:** £8250
**Good:** £5000
**Average:** £2200
**Project:** £800

## MERCEDES-BENZ
### 190E 2.3/2.5-16

The '80s were an exciting time for Mercedes-Benz, as it went downmarket to chase BMW buyers. The 190E had done a great job of stealing 3-series sales, but lacked a little of that car's glamour. The 190E 2.3-16 was conceived for Touring Car racing and, thanks to a clever cylinder head from Cosworth, delivered ample power and torque to turn this staid-looking car into a flying machine. The 1988 2.5-litre version with 200bhp was even more exciting. Best may fetch up to £25k. Evo I and II are a lot more – an Evo II anything from £100k to £300k depending on condition and mileage.

**SPECIFICATIONS (2.3-16)**

**Years produced:** 1985-1993 (see above)
**Performance:** 0-60mph: 7.3sec
Top speed: 144mph
**Power & torque:** 182bhp/173lb ft
**Engine:** Normally aspirated 2299cc four cylinder, petrol, fuel injection, 16 valves
**Drivetrain:** Front-engine RWD
**Structure:** Monocoque
**Transmission:** Five-speed manual
**Weight:** 1230kg

**PRICE GUIDE**

**Launch price:** £21,045
**Excellent:** £18,000
**Good:** £11,000
**Average:** £7500
**Project:** £3600

## MERCEDES-BENZ 200E/300E (W124)

Replacing the W123 was a case of more of the same for Mercedes-Benz. Although the style was very much rooted in the '80s, closely mirroring the 190E, the engines and running gear were carried over from the older car. Considered by many aficionados as the final 'hewn-from-granite' Mercedes-Benzes, the W124 is a satisfying ownership proposition. There aren't many weaknesses – the engines go on forever, and the interior would survive a nuclear attack. Rust nibbles at the edges, and people are finding profit in breaking rather than repair. Still a good introductory classic.

**SPECIFICATIONS (300E Auto)**

| | |
|---|---|
| **Years produced:** | 1985-1995 (3800 in total) |
| **Performance:** | 0-60mph: 8.4sec<br>Top speed: 136mph |
| **Power & torque:** | 188bhp/192lb ft |
| **Engine:** | Normally aspirated 2962cc straight six, petrol, fuel injection, 12 valves |
| **Drivetrain:** | Front-engine RWD |
| **Structure:** | Monocoque |
| **Transmission:** | Five-speed manual/four-speed auto |
| **Weight:** | 1470kg |

**PRICE GUIDE**

| | |
|---|---|
| **Launch price:** | £12,500 |
| **Excellent:** | £4500 |
| **Good:** | £2000 |
| **Average:** | £1000 |
| **Project:** | £500 |

## MERCEDES-BENZ 300CE (W124)

This sleek coupé was based on a shortened saloon floorpan, in this case that of the surprisingly entertaining and almost indestructible E-class. The 300CE drives even better than it looks, and started out with a 188bhp 12-valve engine. This was joined for the 1990 model year by a 24-valve version with 231bhp. You may have to pay a little more than suggested for one of those, especially if it comes with manual transmission. Most were sold with Mercedes' tough four-speed auto, but the manual cars are the more coveted now. Values stable.

**SPECIFICATIONS**

| | |
|---|---|
| **Years produced:** | 1987-1993 (19,320 in total) |
| **Performance:** | 0-60mph: 8.1sec<br>Top speed: 140mph |
| **Power & torque:** | 177bhp/188lb ft |
| **Engine:** | Normally aspirated 2962cc straight six, petrol, injection, 12 valves |
| **Drivetrain:** | Front-engine RWD |
| **Structure:** | Monocoque |
| **Transmission:** | Five-speed manual/four-speed auto |
| **Weight:** | 1390kg |

**PRICE GUIDE**

| | |
|---|---|
| **Launch price:** | £30,100 |
| **Excellent:** | £14,000 |
| **Good:** | £7500 |
| **Average:** | £3750 |
| **Project:** | £1000 |

## MERCEDES-BENZ 300/500SL (R129)

Finally ditching the classic looks of the SL roadsters, Mercedes-Benz came up with this more aggressive and almost chrome-free offering. Filled with toys like a power-operated roof, pop-up roll-over bar and dual-range four-speed automatic gearbox, some even came with suspension that lowers itself at speed. Six-cylinder 300 has either 190bhp or 231bhp in 24v twin-cam form; the 500 packs a 326bhp V8 and later ones could be had with a five-speed auto. Unlike most earlier SLs, the 500 matches GT style with proper sports car go. Still one to watch.

**SPECIFICATIONS**

| | |
|---|---|
| **Years produced:** | 1989-1993 |
| **Performance:** | 0-60mph: 5.9sec (500SL)<br>Top speed: 155mph (limited) |
| **Power & torque:** | 326bhp/332lb ft |
| **Engine:** | Normally aspirated 4973cc V8, petrol, electronic fuel injection, 32 valves |
| **Drivetrain:** | Front-engine RWD |
| **Structure:** | Monocoque |
| **Transmission:** | Four/five-speed automatic |
| **Weight:** | 1889kg |

**PRICE GUIDE (500SL in brackets)**

| | |
|---|---|
| **Launch price:** | £63,460 |
| **Excellent:** | £11,000 (£14,000) |
| **Good:** | £8500 (£9500) |
| **Average:** | £6000 (£7000) |
| **Project:** | £2500 (£2500) |

## MERCEDES-BENZ 500E (W124)

With the 326bhp 5-litre V8 from the latest 500SL roadster shoehorned into the W124 saloon body, wider wheels and tyres and massive disc brakes with four-piston cailpers, the 500E of the early 1990s was a real wolf in sheep's clothing and highly rated by road testers of the time. Developed largely by Porsche, and partly hand-assembled at the company's Zuffenhausen factory, the 500E was both sports saloon and continent-eating limo. Left-hand-drive-only limited UK sales but many are now coming in from Japan. Low-mileage cars desirable.

**SPECIFICATIONS**

| | |
|---|---|
| **Years produced:** | 1990-1994 (10,479 in total) |
| **Performance:** | 0-60mph: 5.5sec<br>Top speed: 155mph (limited) |
| **Power & torque:** | 326bhp/354lb ft |
| **Engine:** | Normally aspirated 4973cc V8, petrol, electronic injection, 32 valves |
| **Drivetrain:** | Front-engine RWD |
| **Structure:** | Monocoque |
| **Transmission:** | Four-speed automatic |
| **Weight:** | 1700kg |

**PRICE GUIDE**

| | |
|---|---|
| **Launch price:** | £57,220 |
| **Excellent:** | £22,000 |
| **Good:** | £16,000 |
| **Average:** | £9000 |
| **Project:** | £6000 |

## MERCEDES-BENZ SLK (R170)

Noting the success of Mazda's MX-5 in the early '90s, Mercedes developed its own affordable, compact roadster and in 1996 unveiled the SLK, slotting in below the SL. Power came from a supercharged 2.3-litre four, the SLK 230 Kompressor offering decent performance combined with Mercedes levels of refinement and the novelty of a folding steel hard top. From 2000 a naturally aspirated V6, the SLK320, offered 218bhp, 0-60 in 7sec and a top speed of 152mph. New, much improved SLK range arrived in 2004.

**SPECIFICATIONS**

| | |
|---|---|
| **Years produced:** | 1996-2004 (c311,000 in total) |
| **Performance:** | 0-60mph: 7.4sec (SLK230)<br>Top speed: 140mph |
| **Power & torque:** | 326bhp/354lb ft |
| **Engine:** | Supercharged 2295cc four cylinder, petrol, electronic injection, 16 valves |
| **Drivetrain:** | Front-engine RWD |
| **Structure:** | Monocoque |
| **Transmission:** | Five/six-speed manual/four-speed auto |
| **Weight:** | 1377kg |

**PRICE GUIDE (SLK230)**

| | |
|---|---|
| **Launch price:** | £30,140 |
| **Excellent:** | £8500 |
| **Good:** | £5000 |
| **Average:** | £2000 |
| **Project:** | £1250 |

## MERCEDES-BENZ SL55/65 AMG (R230)

The R230-generation SL first appeared in 2001, but it was two years later that the real excitement began with the arrival of the SL55 AMG with its powerful and wonderfully vocal 470bhp supercharged V8. In 2004 it was joined in the SL range by the even more powerful SL65 with a stupendous 612bhp bi-turbo 6-litre V12 and an eye-watering £145,970 price tag. The SL55 is comparitively common, which keeps prices at a reasonable level; the SL65 is the one the collectors want, but it comes at a price. Running costs for either are not for the faint-hearted.

**SPECIFICATIONS**

| | |
|---|---|
| **Years produced:** | 2003-2006 |
| **Performance:** | 0-60mph: 4.6sec (SL55)<br>Top speed: 155mph (limited) |
| **Power & torque:** | 470bhp/516lb ft |
| **Engine:** | Supercharged 5439cc V8, petrol, electronic fuel injection, 24 valves |
| **Drivetrain:** | Front-engine RWD |
| **Structure:** | Monocoque |
| **Transmission:** | Five-speed automatic |
| **Weight:** | 1955kg |

**PRICE GUIDE (SL65 in brackets)**

| | |
|---|---|
| **Launch price:** | £93,535 (£145,970) |
| **Excellent:** | £35,000 (£70,000) |
| **Good:** | £24,000 (£49,000) |
| **Average:** | £16,000 (£34,000) |
| **Project:** | £9500 (£20,000) |

## MERCEDES-BENZ SLR McLaren

The extraordinary SLR came about because at the time Mercedes owned 40 per cent of the McLaren group and the two companies decided on a joint venture to produce a world-beating super-GT. With Gordon Murray, creator of the McLaren F1, leading the engineering, the SLR should have been brilliant, but in reality it was overweight, had a cramped cabin and suffered odd-feeling brakes and tricky handling. Still, it looked spectacular and went like stink. Convertible and limited-edition speedster followed, the latter commanding a substantial premium today.

**SPECIFICATIONS**

| | |
|---|---|
| **Years produced:** | 2003-2010 (2157 in total) |
| **Performance:** | 0-60mph: 3.4sec<br>Top speed: 208mph |
| **Power & torque:** | 626bhp/575lb ft |
| **Engine:** | Supercharged 5439cc V8, petrol, electronic fuel injection, 24 valves |
| **Drivetrain:** | Front-engine RWD |
| **Structure:** | Carbonfibre tub and body |
| **Transmission:** | Five-speed automatic |
| **Weight:** | 1618kg |

**PRICE GUIDE (coupé)**

| | |
|---|---|
| **Launch price:** | £313,465 |
| **Excellent:** | £295,000 |
| **Good:** | £250,000 |
| **Average:** | £200,000 |
| **Project:** | N/A |

# MESSERSCHMITT

IT'S A POPULAR myth that the Messerschmitt bubblecars used cockpits from unfinished fighters for their bodywork, although aviation experience did influence Willy Messerschmitt's globular three-wheelers. They were produced from 1953, as the company was banned from building aircraft after the war. Designed by Fritz Frend, Messerschmitts became known for their terrier-like turns of speed, especially the four-wheeled Tg500 which was fittingly known as the Tiger. The drop-off in the microcar market in the 1960s caused by the boom in small 'real' cars resulted in Messerschmitt production ending in 1964. It subsequently returned to building aircraft.

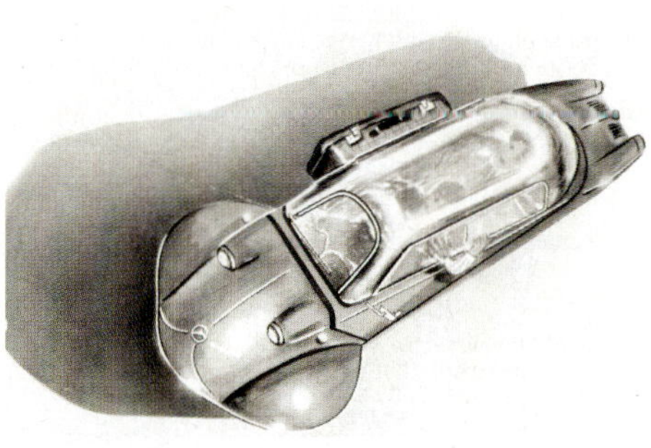

## MESSERSCHMITT KR175

The Messerschmitt KR175 (for Kabinenroller) was introduced for up-and-coming German families who needed inexpensive transport during tough times. Aircraft engineer Fritz Fend was behind the bubblecar and based it on the cockpit of a Messerschmitt plane. Initially powered by a single-cylinder engine, the lightweight machine was capable of 60mph – quite a feat considering the top speeds of standard family cars at the time. High levels of build quality and simple construction means that the survival rate is high, reflecting the cult status these cars now enjoy.

**SPECIFICATIONS**

| | |
|---|---|
| **Years produced:** | 1953-1964 (19,668 in total) |
| **Performance:** | 0-60mph: N/A<br>Top speed: 50 mph |
| **Power & torque:** | 9bhp/N/A |
| **Engine:** | Normally aspirated 173cc two-stroke single cylinder, petrol, carburettor |
| **Drivetrain:** | Rear-engine RWD |
| **Structure:** | Tubular chassis |
| **Transmission:** | Four-speed manual |
| **Weight:** | 220kg |

**PRICE GUIDE**

| | |
|---|---|
| **Launch price:** | DM 2100 |
| **Excellent:** | £26,000 |
| **Good:** | £22,000 |
| **Average:** | £12,500 |
| **Project:** | £6000 |

## MESSERSCHMITT Tg500 Tiger

The main difference between the Tg500 and its lower-powered predecessors was the extra wheel. Now with the full complement of four, the uprated 500cc 20bhp Sachs twin-cylinder was housed in a more suitable chassis. Performance of the ultimate go-faster bubblecar was verging on the silly, with a top speed of over 75mph and a 0-60mph time of 18.7 seconds – enough to see off full-sized cars such as the Austin A30 and Morris Minor with ease. Sales were slow though, with fewer than 500 built, and that makes the Tiger highly collectable today.

**SPECIFICATIONS**

| | |
|---|---|
| **Years produced:** | 1958-1961 (320 in total) |
| **Performance:** | 0-60mph: 28.1sec<br>Top speed: 78 mph |
| **Power & torque:** | 19.5bhp/24lb ft |
| **Engine:** | Normally aspirated 460cc two-stroke twin, petrol, carburettor, |
| **Drivetrain:** | Rear-engine RWD |
| **Structure:** | Tubular chassis, steel body |
| **Transmission:** | Four-speed manual |
| **Weight:** | 370kg |

**PRICE GUIDE**

| | |
|---|---|
| **Launch price:** | DM 3650 |
| **Excellent:** | £80,000 |
| **Good:** | £62,500 |
| **Average:** | £42,500 |
| **Project:** | £30,000 |

# MG

CECIL KIMBER WAS manager of Morris Garages in Oxford when he commissioned some sports cars to be built on a Morris chassis in 1923. Their appeal prompted more models and MG soon became one of the favourite pre-war British sporting marques. In 1952, it joined BMC and introduced the much-loved MGA, then the MGB, which was produced from 1962 to 1980. After the Abingdon factory was closed, MG existed only as a badge on BL products until the RV8 of 1992 announced a rebirth. The mid-engined MGF was a return to form, but it wasn't to last, MG going into administration in 2005. Since then the badge has been Chinese-owned and has appeared on a range of mildly sporty hatchbacks.

## MG TC

The first post-war MG, almost identical to the pre-war TB, but with a 4in wider body and much-needed additional interior space. Easy to distinguish from the earlier car by its new instrumentation. Underneath it featured shackles instead of sliding trunnions for the front and rear springs, which had a positive effect on ride quality. Powered by the 1250cc OHV four-cylinder engine with twin SU carburettors to improve breathing (54.4bhp at 5200rpm), it had a top speed of nearly 80mph. Values have been holding steady.

### SPECIFICATIONS

**Years produced:** 1945-1949 (10,001 in total)
**Performance:** 0-60mph: 27.25sec
Top speed: 78mph
**Power & torque:** 54.4bhp/64lb ft
**Engine:** Normally aspirated 1250cc four cylinder, petrol, carburettor, 8 valves
**Drivetrain:** Front-engine RWD
**Structure:** Separate chassis
**Transmission:** Four-speed manual
**Weight:** 838kg

### PRICE GUIDE

**Launch price:** £526
**Excellent:** £32,000
**Good:** £25,000
**Average:** £15,000
**Project:** £9000

## MG Y-type 1.25-litre

MG's first post-war saloon car had plenty of pre-war style and panache, although it lacked genuine performance. But the good value four-seat saloon proved a mainstay in the range while the T-types continued to evolve. Its engine – the single-carburettor version of the XPAG TC's (46bhp at 4800rpm) – was shared with its open-toppped cousins. New to the saloons was independent front suspension, rack-and-pinion steering and bolt-on disc wheels. Rare YT Tourer model could command a £10k premium – if you can find one.

### SPECIFICATIONS

**Years produced:** 1947-1953 (8336 in total)
**Performance:** 0-60mph: 27.3sec
Top speed: 71mph
**Power & torque:** 46bhp/58lb ft
**Engine:** Normally aspirated 1250cc four cylinder, petrol, carburettor, 8 valves
**Drivetrain:** Front-engine RWD
**Structure:** Separate chassis
**Transmission:** Four-speed manual
**Weight:** 1060kg

### PRICE GUIDE (saloon)

**Launch price:** £565
**Excellent:** £15,000
**Good:** £10,000
**Average:** £7500
**Project:** £2500

## MG TD

Follow-up to the much-loved TC, with most finding their way overseas during the austere years of the post-war era. The new rack-and-pinion steering and Y-Type chassis sharpened the Midget's game considerably, and increased rigidity improved durability. These cars were offered with left-hand drive, which obviously helped with the export drive. Engine-wise, it was the same story as before, with the 1250cc XPAG engine in 54bhp form putting in a fine performance, and an upgrade to 57bhp for 1950's MkII livened things up.

### SPECIFICATIONS

**Years produced:** 1949-1953 (29,664 in total)
**Performance:** 0-60mph: 18.2sec
Top speed: 78mph
**Power & torque:** 54bhp/64lb ft
**Engine:** Normally aspirated 1250cc four cylinder, petrol, carburettor, 8 valves
**Drivetrain:** Front-engine RWD
**Structure:** Separate chassis
**Transmission:** Four-speed manual
**Weight:** 876kg

### PRICE GUIDE

**Launch price:** £751
**Excellent:** £28,000
**Good:** £22,000
**Average:** £15,000
**Project:** £7000

## MG TF

The final flowering of the pre-war Midget concept was the TF that, like its predecessors, proved massively popular in the US. It was a straight-forward development of the TD MkII, and the TF's most obvious changes from the older car are its raked radiator grille, lowered bonnet line and faired headlamps. Despite this, it was looking rather old by 1953, and sales in the UK were slowing. Originally powered by the TD's engine, but later 1500 had XPAG engine of 1466cc and a top speed of c90mph. Add c£4k for these. Wire wheels also add value.

### SPECIFICATIONS

**Years produced:** 1953-1955 (9600 in total)
**Performance:** 0-60mph: 18.9sec
Top speed: 81mph
**Power & torque:** 57bhp/65lb ft
**Engine:** Normally aspirated 1250cc four cylinder, petrol, carburettor, 8 valves
**Drivetrain:** Front-engine RWD
**Structure:** Separate chassis
**Transmission:** Four-speed manual
**Weight:** 916kg

### PRICE GUIDE

**Launch price:** £780
**Excellent:** £32,000
**Good:** £27,000
**Average:** £18,000
**Project:** £9000

## MG
# Magnette ZA/ZB

This post-BMC MG was elegant, affordable and made a leap into the mainstream for MG. The chassisless saloon, based on the Wolseley 4/44, with independent front suspension, rack-and-pinion steering and BMC B-series power, sold well and established MG as part of BMC's badge-engineering portfolio. The 60bhp B-series engine lacked sparkle, even with twin SU carbs, but was helped in ZB form when power was uprated to 68bhp. MG specialists Brown & Gammons say prices have been holding steady, but check carefully for rot.

### SPECIFICATIONS

| | |
|---|---|
| **Years produced:** | 1953-1958 (36,650 in total) |
| **Performance:** | 0-60mph: 22.6sec<br>Top speed: 82mph |
| **Power & torque:** | 60bhp/71lb ft |
| **Engine:** | Normally aspirated 1489cc four cylinder, petrol, carburettor, 8 valves |
| **Drivetrain:** | Front-engine RWD |
| **Structure:** | Monocoque |
| **Transmission:** | Four-speed manual |
| **Weight:** | 1118kg |

#### PRICE GUIDE

| | |
|---|---|
| **Launch price:** | £713 |
| **Excellent:** | £20,000 |
| **Good:** | £12,000 |
| **Average:** | £8000 |
| **Project:** | £3000 |

## MG
# MGA Roadster

This aerodynamic and beautiful two-seat roadster was a huge leap forward from the T-type Midgets. With twin-carburettor B-series engine, independent front suspension and rack-and-pinion steering, the differences were like night and day. Initially offered with the 1489cc four-cylinder B-series OHV engine with 68bhp, it was uprated to a 1600 model in May 1959. Lockheed front discs made their first appearance with this larger 80bhp engine. The final version, the 1622cc MkII, ran from 1961-62. Later cars command a premium, as does De Luxe model.

### SPECIFICATIONS

| | |
|---|---|
| **Years produced:** | 1955-1962 (101,000 in total) |
| **Performance:** | 0-60mph: 15.6sec<br>Top speed: 98mph |
| **Power & torque:** | 68bhp/77lb ft |
| **Engine:** | Normally aspirated 1489cc four cylinder, petrol, carburettor, 8 valves |
| **Drivetrain:** | Front-engine RWD |
| **Structure:** | Separate chassis |
| **Transmission:** | Four-speed manual |
| **Weight:** | 890kg |

#### PRICE GUIDE (1500, add c£3k for 1600)

| | |
|---|---|
| **Launch price:** | £595 |
| **Excellent:** | £35,000 |
| **Good:** | £28,000 |
| **Average:** | £18,000 |
| **Project:** | £10,000 |

## MG
# MGA Coupé

The MGA made liberal use of the BMC parts bin, with its B-series power unit coming straight from the Morris Oxford. Performance from the original 1500 was hardly sparkling, but quick enough to impress the Americans, who bought MGAs by the container-load. Coupé sold in smaller numbers than Roadster in period, and is valued slightly lower today. As with Roadster, later 1600 and 1622 models fetch £2-3k more. 'Barn finds' have gone for serious sums in recent times, but keep in mind that a full restoration could cost £50k+, say experts Brown & Gammons.

### SPECIFICATIONS

| | |
|---|---|
| **Years produced:** | 1956-1962 |
| **Performance:** | 0-60mph: 15.0sec<br>Top speed: 100mph |
| **Power & torque:** | 72bhp/N/A |
| **Engine:** | Normally aspirated 1489cc four cylinder, petrol, carburettor, 8 valves |
| **Drivetrain:** | Front-engine RWD |
| **Structure:** | Separate chassis |
| **Transmission:** | Four-speed manual |
| **Weight:** | 927kg |

#### PRICE GUIDE

| | |
|---|---|
| **Launch price:** | £595 |
| **Excellent:** | £30,000 |
| **Good:** | £25,000 |
| **Average:** | £15,000 |
| **Project:** | £8000 |

## MG
# MGA Twin Cam

The trouble with the MGA was its lack of power. Although most owners were happy with the standard 1500 and 1600cc cars, there was demand from a hardcore of buyers who wanted more. MG was happy to oblige and came up with the Twin Cam. Engine guru Harry Weslake designed a new twin-cam head for the B-series engine, which improved breathing and top-end power. The 108bhp upgrade was enough to satisfy owners with a need for speed, although it gained a reputation for unreliability. Highly prized today, with concours cars now c£50k+.

### SPECIFICATIONS

| | |
|---|---|
| **Years produced:** | 1958-1960 (2111 inc Coupé in total) |
| **Performance:** | 0-60mph: 9.1sec<br>Top speed: 113mph |
| **Power & torque:** | 108bhp/N/A |
| **Engine:** | Normally aspirated 1588cc four cylinder, petrol, carburettor, 8 valves |
| **Drivetrain:** | Front-engine RWD |
| **Structure:** | Separate chassis |
| **Transmission:** | Four-speed manual |
| **Weight:** | 952kg |

#### PRICE GUIDE

| | |
|---|---|
| **Launch price:** | £1266 |
| **Excellent:** | £45,000 |
| **Good:** | £35,000 |
| **Average:** | £20,000 |
| **Project:** | £10,000 |

## MG
# Magnette MkIII/IV

With a stable full of marques, BMC used its quota to the maximum with the Farina saloons. Few would have thought the staid and podgy B-series-powered car was a suitable basis for a new-age MG Magnette, but with twin carburettors and a wood-and-leather interior, it just about managed to pass it off. Later MkIVs are the ones to have with their 1622cc 68bhp engines providing just enough performance to keep up with the flow. Today, these cars are still readily available for relatively little money, and provide plenty of enjoyment.

### SPECIFICATIONS

| | |
|---|---|
| **Years produced:** | 1959-1968 (31,104 in total) |
| **Performance:** | 0-60mph: 20.6sec<br>Top speed: 84mph |
| **Power & torque:** | 64bhp/N/A |
| **Engine:** | Normally aspirated 1489cc four cylinder, petrol, carburettor, 8 valves |
| **Drivetrain:** | Front-engine RWD |
| **Structure:** | Monocoque |
| **Transmission:** | Four-speed manual |
| **Weight:** | 1118kg |

#### PRICE GUIDE

| | |
|---|---|
| **Launch price:** | £1013 |
| **Excellent:** | £7000 |
| **Good:** | £4000 |
| **Average:** | £2000 |
| **Project:** | £500 |

## MG Midget

This unit-construction two-seater, initially a twin of the mk2 Austin-Healey Sprite, was hugely popular through four generations. Early cars had the BMC A-series 948cc four-cylinder OHV engine, and were a hoot to drive despite the low 46bhp power output, although the arrival of the 1098cc 56bhp version in October 1962 helped. MkIII (pictured) upgunned to 1275cc and 65bhp from 1966. Final 'Midget 1500' model had plastic bumpers and 1493cc Triumph Spitfire engine (still 65bbhp but with more torque). All are fun to drive with excellent specialist support.

**SPECIFICATIONS**

| | |
|---|---|
| **Years produced:** | 1961-1979 (226,427 in total) |
| **Performance:** | 0-60mph: 10.8sec<br>Top speed: 95mph |
| **Power & torque:** | 65bhp/72lb ft |
| **Engine:** | Normally aspirated 1275cc four cylinder, petrol, carburettor, 8 valves (MkIII) |
| **Drivetrain:** | Front-engine RWD |
| **Structure:** | Monocoque |
| **Transmission:** | Four-speed manual |
| **Weight:** | 685kg |

**PRICE GUIDE**

| | |
|---|---|
| **Launch price:** | £670 |
| **Excellent:** | £10,000 |
| **Good:** | £7500 |
| **Average:** | £4000 |
| **Project:** | £2000 |

## MG MGB Roadster MkI

Although MG found sucess with its T-type Midgets and MGA, the B took sales to a new level, for many years being the world's best-selling sports car. Four-speed gearbox (overdrive available), rack-and-pinion steering, independent front suspension and disc brakes were standard right from the start and meant it was a delight to drive compared with its rivals, while there was plenty of power on tap, thanks to its recently upgraded 1.8-litre B-series engine. These early Bs have quite a following, and concours-condition cars can fetch £25k-plus.

**SPECIFICATIONS**

| | |
|---|---|
| **Years produced:** | 1962-1967 (513,276 in total) |
| **Performance:** | 0-60mph: 12.2sec<br>Top speed: 103mph |
| **Power & torque:** | 95bhp/110lb ft |
| **Engine:** | Normally aspirated 1798cc four cylinder, petrol, carburettor, 8 valves |
| **Drivetrain:** | Front-engine RWD |
| **Structure:** | Monocoque |
| **Transmission:** | Four-speed manual |
| **Weight:** | 920kg |

**PRICE GUIDE**

| | |
|---|---|
| **Launch price:** | £690 |
| **Excellent:** | £20,000 |
| **Good:** | £15,000 |
| **Average:** | £10,000 |
| **Project:** | £4000 |

## MG 1100/1300

The humble Austin 1100 initially seemed like an unsuitable starting point for an MG version, but as it happens, the small saloon acquitted itself very well indeed. Tenacious front-wheel-drive handling and a well-appointed interior made the MG 1100 a genuinely sporting saloon. It wasn't perfect, though – it proved difficult for mechanics to work on, and had a terrible reputation for rust, which was rightly deserved. Survival rate is low considering the huge number produced, but those that are left are not expensive to buy, and cost peanuts to run.

**SPECIFICATIONS**

| | |
|---|---|
| **Years produced:** | 1962-1971 (124,860/32,549 in total) |
| **Performance:** | 0-60mph: 15.6sec<br>Top speed: 78mph |
| **Power & torque:** | 48bhp/60lb ft |
| **Engine:** | Normally aspirated 1098cc four cylinder, petrol, carburettor, 8 valves |
| **Drivetrain:** | Front-engine FWD |
| **Structure:** | Monocoque |
| **Transmission:** | Four-speed manual |
| **Weight:** | 832kg |

**PRICE GUIDE**

| | |
|---|---|
| **Launch price:** | £949 |
| **Excellent:** | £5000 |
| **Good:** | £4000 |
| **Average:** | £2000 |
| **Project:** | £600 |

## MG MGB GT

It's sometimes easy to forget just how much of an impact the MGB GT made on the marketplace. That fastback roof, designed by Pininfarina, followed conventional GT styling cues but for a fraction of the price. The raised windscreen height and side windows meant that there was a realistic amount of headroom for those in the front, although rear-seat passengers didn't get such an easy ride. Underneath the glamorous new skin, the GT was pure Roadster, and that meant tidy handling and decent performance. Very best can be up to £20k.

**SPECIFICATIONS**

| | |
|---|---|
| **Years produced:** | 1965-1967 (21,835 in total) |
| **Performance:** | 0-60mph: 13.0sec<br>Top speed: 104mph |
| **Power & torque:** | 97bhp/105lb ft |
| **Engine:** | Normally aspirated 1798cc four cylinder, petrol, carburettor, 8 valves |
| **Drivetrain:** | Front-engine RWD |
| **Structure:** | Monocoque |
| **Transmission:** | Four-speed manual |
| **Weight:** | 1108kg |

**PRICE GUIDE**

| | |
|---|---|
| **Launch price:** | £834 |
| **Excellent:** | £15,000 |
| **Good:** | £10,000 |
| **Average:** | £6000 |
| **Project:** | £2500 |

## MG MGC/ C GT

In an attempt to extend the appeal of the MGB and also plug the gap in BMC's range with the demise of the big Healeys, Abingdon's engineers came up with the bright idea of fitting a C-series engine. The power and torque was adequate for this GT's potential upmarket ambitions, but those looking for sporting handling would be disapppointed with the understeery balance. Later development (and better tyres) have improved things and, with proper tuning, the C-series can really deliver. Values very much on the up, say specialists Brown & Gammons.

**SPECIFICATIONS**

| | |
|---|---|
| **Years produced:** | 1967-1969 (9002 in total) |
| **Performance:** | 0-60mph: 10.2sec<br>Top speed: 120mph |
| **Power & torque:** | 145bhp/170lb ft |
| **Engine:** | Normally aspirated 2912cc straight six, petrol, carburettor, 12 valves |
| **Drivetrain:** | Front-engine RWD |
| **Structure:** | Monocoque |
| **Transmission:** | Four-speed manual with overdrive |
| **Weight:** | 1116kg |

**PRICE GUIDE (GT in brackets)**

| | |
|---|---|
| **Launch price:** | £1102 |
| **Excellent:** | £35,000 (£25,000) |
| **Good:** | £28,000 (£20,000) |
| **Average:** | £17,500 (£12,000) |
| **Project:** | £10,000 (£7000) |

## MG
# MGB/ B GT MkII/III

Upgrading the evergreen MGB to MkII spec was enough to keep sales on a high. The four-speed gearbox finally received synchromesh on all forward ratios, and an optional Borg-Warner auto became available. In 1970 the MkII was treated to a BL-style front end, which did away with the chrome grille and slats. MG fans hated the cost-constrained new style, and it was soon canned. The return to chrome ushered in the MkIII, which received a number of improvements to keep the MGB looking fresh. Soft-tops can be up to 50% more than GTs.

### SPECIFICATIONS

| | |
|---|---|
| **Years produced:** | 1967-1974 (310,077 in total) |
| **Performance:** | 0-60mph: 13sec<br>Top speed: 104mph |
| **Power & torque:** | 84bhp/105lb ft |
| **Engine:** | Normally aspirated 1798cc four cylinder, petrol, carburettor, 8 valves |
| **Drivetrain:** | Front-engine RWD |
| **Structure:** | Monocoque |
| **Transmission:** | Four-speed manual |
| **Weight:** | 920kg |

**PRICE GUIDE (GT in brackets)**

| | |
|---|---|
| **Launch price:** | Not known |
| **Excellent:** | £18,000 (£12,000) |
| **Good:** | £12,000 (£8,000) |
| **Average:** | £8,000 (£5000) |
| **Project:** | £3000 (£2500) |

## MG
# MGB GT V8

The concept of a V8-engined MGB GT wasn't new; Ken Costello had been converting MGBs to Rover V8 engines for some time. And when production of the C-series engine was cut, MG introduced its own Rover V8-engined B GT – just as the effects of the 1973 energy crisis were hitting hard. Although a fine car, the GT V8 sold poorly, a victim of circumstance and poor marketing. Today it's becoming increasingly sought-after, though watch out for home conversions. Rubber-bumper cars generally around 20% less than prices here.

### SPECIFICATIONS

| | |
|---|---|
| **Years produced:** | 1973-1976 (2591 in total) |
| **Performance:** | 0-60mph: 9sec<br>Top speed: 125mph |
| **Power & torque:** | 137bhp/192lb ft |
| **Engine:** | Normally aspirated 3528cc V8, petrol, carburettor, 16 valves |
| **Drivetrain:** | Front-engine RWD |
| **Structure:** | Monocoque |
| **Transmission:** | Four-speed manual |
| **Weight:** | 1158kg |

**PRICE GUIDE (chrome bumper cars)**

| | |
|---|---|
| **Launch price:** | £2294 |
| **Excellent:** | £35,000 |
| **Good:** | £27,000 |
| **Average:** | £15,000 |
| **Project:** | £10,000 |

## MG
# MGB (rubber bumper)

North American regulations forced a raised ride height and polyurethane-covered bumpers required to withstand 5mph impacts without sustaining damage. Although condemned at the time by fans, the federalised MGB was actually a successful styling job compared with its Italian rivals. Later B-series engines in North America were reduced to a single Zenith Stromberg carb, emissions equipment and a catalyst. Now these black-bumper cars offer the best everyday-useability and value of all the Bs, and their values have been climbing.

### SPECIFICATIONS

| | |
|---|---|
| **Years produced:** | 1974-1980 (128,653 in total) |
| **Performance:** | 0-60mph: 13.0sec<br>Top speed: 104mph |
| **Power & torque:** | 82bhp/104lb ft |
| **Engine:** | Normally aspirated 1798cc four cylinder, petrol, carburettor, 8 valves |
| **Drivetrain:** | Front-engine RWD |
| **Structure:** | Monocoque |
| **Transmission:** | Four-speed manual |
| **Weight:** | 971kg |

**PRICE GUIDE (GT in brackets)**

| | |
|---|---|
| **Launch price:** | Not known |
| **Excellent:** | £15,000 (£12,000) |
| **Good:** | £10,000 (£8000) |
| **Average:** | £6000 (£4000) |
| **Project:** | £2000 (£1000) |

## MG
# Metro/Metro Turbo

The first MG to appear after the closure of Abingdon in 1980 was a return to the badge-engineering ways of old. In becoming an MG in 1981, the Austin Metro received a trim upgrade and an uprated A-series engine delivering an additional 12bhp. Just over a year later, the Metro Turbo was added to the MG line-up and became a big seller. Featuring a Garrett T3 turbo, the engine was worked on by Lotus to develop 93bhp. It could have been more, but power was capped to prolong gearbox life. Most have now succumbed to rust, but survivors have a following.

### SPECIFICATIONS

| | |
|---|---|
| **Years produced:** | 1982-1990 (37,500/21,968 in total) |
| **Performance:** | 0-60mph: 9.9sec (Turbo)<br>Top speed: 112mph |
| **Power & torque:** | 93bhp/87lb ft |
| **Engine:** | Turbocharged 1275cc four cylinder, petrol, carburettor, 8 valves |
| **Drivetrain:** | Front-engine FWD |
| **Structure:** | Monocoque |
| **Transmission:** | Four-speed manual |
| **Weight:** | 840kg |

**PRICE GUIDE (Turbo in brackets)**

| | |
|---|---|
| **Launch price:** | £4799 |
| **Excellent:** | £4000 (£8000) |
| **Good:** | £2000 (£4000) |
| **Average:** | £1000 (£2500) |
| **Project:** | £500 (£1000) |

## MG
# Maestro/Montego/Turbo

More badge engineering based on Austin-Rover's Maestro hatch and Montego saloon. Early cars had a 1.6-litre R-series engine derived from the Austin Maxi's, and proved troublesome in use thanks to a hastily conceived twin-Weber carburettor set-up. 1984's shortlived 1600's S-series engine was replaced by a 2.0-litre O-series fuel-injection engine. Capable and good to drive (if specified with PAS). Turbo versions were real rocketships, with 0-60mph in 6.7sec claimed for the Maestro Turbo, which has developed quite a cult following.

### SPECIFICATIONS

| | |
|---|---|
| **Years produced:** | 1983-1991 |
| **Performance:** | 0-60mph: 6.7sec (Turbo)<br>Top speed: 128mph |
| **Power & torque:** | 150bhp/169lb ft |
| **Engine:** | Turbocharged 1994cc four cylinder, petrol, electronic fuel injection, 8 valves |
| **Drivetrain:** | Front-engine FWD |
| **Structure:** | Monocoque |
| **Transmission:** | Five-speed manual |
| **Weight:** | 1094kg |

**PRICE GUIDE (Turbo in brackets)**

| | |
|---|---|
| **Launch price:** | £7279 (£11,300) |
| **Excellent:** | £2000 (£7000) |
| **Good:** | £1200 (£4500) |
| **Average:** | £900 (£3000) |
| **Project:** | £300 (£750) |

## MG RV8

The early-'90s success of Mazda's MX-5 and various TVRs prompted Rover to resurrect the MGB for one final fling. The engine was a 3.9-litre Range Rover EFi V8 with 185bhp. A five-speed gearbox, derived from the Rover SD1, was used along with a new Salisbury axle. Significant modifications were made to the suspension and brakes to bring the car up to date. The interior featured magnolia leather and burr elm. Most RV8s made were sold in Japan, but many have since made their way back to the UK. Exceptional, low-mileage cars can be up to £50k.

### SPECIFICATIONS

| | |
|---|---|
| **Years produced:** | 1993-1995 (1983 in total) |
| **Performance:** | 0-60mph: 6.0sec<br>Top speed: 135mph |
| **Power & torque:** | 185bhp/235lb ft |
| **Engine:** | Normally aspirated 3947cc V8, petrol, electronic fuel injection, 16 valves |
| **Drivetrain:** | Front-engine RWD |
| **Structure:** | Monocoque |
| **Transmission:** | Five-speed manual |
| **Weight:** | 1280kg |

### PRICE GUIDE

| | |
|---|---|
| **Launch price:** | £26,500 |
| **Excellent:** | £25,000 |
| **Good:** | £20,000 |
| **Average:** | £15,000 |
| **Project:** | £7500 |

## MG MGF/TF

The F was the first all-new MG since the demise of the B and its mid-engined layout showed Rover Group was serious about building a world-class sports car. Basic 1.8-litre K-series offered 118bhp, the more sophisticated VVC (Variable Valve Control) unit giving 143bhp and 0-60mph in a handy 7sec, while Hydragas suspension gave a comfortable ride to go with the agile handling. Revised TF from 2002 had slightly more power and conventional suspension. Low prices make them tempting, but running costs aren't so cheap, so buy carefully.

### SPECIFICATIONS (VVC)

| | |
|---|---|
| **Years produced:** | 1995-2011 (77,269 in total) |
| **Performance:** | 0-60mph: 7.0sec<br>Top speed: 126mph |
| **Power & torque:** | 143bhp/128lb ft |
| **Engine:** | Normally aspirated 1796cc in-line four, petrol, electronic fuel injection, 16v |
| **Drivetrain:** | Mid-engine RWD |
| **Structure:** | Monocoque |
| **Transmission:** | Five-speed manual |
| **Weight:** | 1070kg |

### PRICE GUIDE

| | |
|---|---|
| **Launch price:** | £11,300 |
| **Excellent:** | £4000 |
| **Good:** | £2000 |
| **Average:** | £1000 |
| **Project:** | £400 |

## MG ZT190/260

Taking the Rover 75 as a basis for a gentleman's sporting saloon resulted in something surprisingly fun and extremely capable. Top-spec was initially the 188bhp ZT190, powered by Rover's characterful KV6 engine. Something unexpected came in 2003 though, with the launch of the 4.6-litre Mustang V8-powered ZT260. This saw the car re-engineered from front- to rear-wheel-drive. It was done on a shoestring, but the result was brilliant, a properly brawny British performance saloon. Not that quick in today's world, but supercharger conversions are very popular...

### SPECIFICATIONS

| | |
|---|---|
| **Years produced:** | 2001-2005 |
| **Performance:** | 0-60mph: 6.7sec (260)<br>Top speed: 155mph |
| **Power & torque:** | 255bhp/302lb ft |
| **Engine:** | Normally aspirated 4601cc V8, petrol, electronic fuel injection, 16 valves |
| **Drivetrain:** | Front-engine RWD |
| **Structure:** | Monocoque |
| **Transmission:** | Five-speed manual |
| **Weight:** | 1770kg |

### PRICE GUIDE

| | |
|---|---|
| **Launch price:** | £33,490 (260) |
| **Excellent:** | £12,000 |
| **Good:** | £9000 |
| **Average:** | £6000 |
| **Project:** | £3000 |

## MG XPower SV/SV-R

Through some business opportunism, MG acquired the carbonfibre chassis of the late-90s DeTomaso Mangusta, which it decided to repurpose as a new flagship, powered by a 4.6-litre Ford V8, with styling by Peter Stevens. Sadly, money shortages meant it was rather underdeveloped. SV-R added more visual aggression and a Roush-tuned 32-valve 5.0-litre V8. It was even offered with a factory-approved nitrous oxide kit, which reportedly took power to 1000bhp. Collectible, say Brown & Gammons, but body parts are tricky to find, which makes insurance pricey.

### SPECIFICATIONS

| | |
|---|---|
| **Years produced:** | 2003-2005 (82 in total) |
| **Performance:** | 0-60mph: 4.9sec (SV-R)<br>Top speed: 176mph |
| **Power & torque:** | 400bhp/376lb ft |
| **Engine:** | Normally aspirated 4996cc V8, petrol, electronic fuel injection, 32 valves |
| **Drivetrain:** | Front-engine RWD |
| **Structure:** | Carbonfibre body with steel box chassis |
| **Transmission:** | Five-speed manual |
| **Weight:** | 1495kg |

### PRICE GUIDE (SV-R in brackets)

| | |
|---|---|
| **Launch price:** | £83,000 (SV-R) |
| **Excellent:** | £35,000 (£50,000) |
| **Good:** | £30,000 (£40,000) |
| **Average:** | £25,000 (£35,000) |
| **Project:** | N/A |

# MINI

THE FIRST BMC Minis were badged as Austins and Morrises, but, from the MkIII variant in 1969, Mini was launched as a marque in its own right, albeit solely responsible for the cars after which it was named; the original Alec Issigonis invention as well as the Clubman and Cooper variants. Largely unappreciated during the 1970s, this once most-basic of machines moved upmarket in the 1980s when it became cemented in the British national psyche. The last classic Mini was built in 2000 – after 41 years of continuous manufacture – and BMW now uses MINI as a badge for its maxi-sized look-alikes. The popularity of these should ensure the name continues well into the future.

## MINI
# MkI

Alec Issigonis's cheap small car for BMC was innovative with its front-wheel drive and space-saving transverse engine layout but, more than that, it was incredibly entertaining to drive. It soon became a best-seller. The Austin version was initially called the Se7en, but became the Mini in 1961. The 848cc A-series engine was used throughout the life of the MkI; one significant change was the adoption of Hydrolastic suspension in place of the original rubber-cone type in 1964. Very early (1959) cars in exceptional condition can now command up to £30k.

**SPECIFICATIONS**

| | |
|---|---|
| **Years produced:** | 1959-1967 (1,572,756 in total) |
| **Performance:** | 0-60mph: 27.1sec<br>Top speed: 72mph |
| **Power & torque:** | 34bhp/33lb ft |
| **Engine:** | Normally aspirated 848cc four cylinder, petrol, carburettor, 8 valves |
| **Drivetrain:** | Front-engine RWD |
| **Structure:** | Monocoque |
| **Transmission:** | Four-speed manual |
| **Weight:** | 626kg |

**PRICE GUIDE**

| | |
|---|---|
| **Launch price:** | £496 |
| **Excellent:** | £12,000 |
| **Good:** | £8000 |
| **Average:** | £5250 |
| **Project:** | £2200 |

## MINI
# Cooper 997/998

Mini creator Alec Issigonis was against the idea of a performance version. Fortunately, his wishes didn't prevail, and a legend was born in the 1961 Mini-Cooper, as tweaked by F1 guru John Cooper. The first cars used a 997cc twin-carb A-series, changed for a 998cc unit from 1964. Front disc brakes were standard and Coopers stood out thanks to their two-tone paint schemes and special grilles. Speeds of around 90mph may not have been all-out fast, but the Cooper's handling brilliance turned it into a potent rally machine. Concours cars now £25k+.

**SPECIFICATIONS**

| | |
|---|---|
| **Years produced:** | 1961-1969 (64,224 in total) |
| **Performance:** | 0-60mph: 17.2sec<br>Top speed: 85mph |
| **Power & torque:** | 55bhp/54lb ft |
| **Engine:** | Normally aspirated 997cc four cylinder, petrol, carburettor, 8 valves |
| **Drivetrain:** | Front-engine FWD |
| **Structure:** | Monocoque |
| **Transmission:** | Four-speed manual |
| **Weight:** | 626kg |

**PRICE GUIDE**

| | |
|---|---|
| **Launch price:** | £679 |
| **Excellent:** | £22,000 |
| **Good:** | £16,000 |
| **Average:** | £9000 |
| **Project:** | £5000 |

## MINI
# Cooper 1071S

Cooper had more experience with A-series engines in the 1100cc racing class and put that knowledge to good use with the first Mini-Cooper S. Its enlarged 1071cc engine managed 70bhp and there were larger disc brakes to cope with its extra performance. The S looked the same as the Cooper save for 'S' badges on the bonnet and boot, and ventilated steel wheels. Inside, the upholstery was finished to more luxurious Mini Super De Luxe specification. A petite but potent rocket but even better was soon to follow. Values have been levelled off recently.

**SPECIFICATIONS**

| | |
|---|---|
| **Years produced:** | 1963-1964 (4031 in total) |
| **Performance:** | 0-60mph: 13.5sec<br>Top speed: 90mph |
| **Power & torque:** | 70bhp/62lb ft |
| **Engine:** | Normally aspirated 1071cc four cylinder, petrol, carburettor, 8 valves |
| **Drivetrain:** | Front-engine FWD |
| **Structure:** | Monocoque |
| **Transmission:** | Four-speed manual |
| **Weight:** | 630kg |

**PRICE GUIDE**

| | |
|---|---|
| **Launch price:** | £695 |
| **Excellent:** | £36,000 |
| **Good:** | £27,000 |
| **Average:** | £17,500 |
| **Project:** | £12,000 |

## MINI
# Cooper 970S

The reduction in engine size and power for 1964's 970S Cooper might have seemed a strange move but it was built simply as a homologation special with a short-stroke 970cc engine developing 65bhp. The specialist engine was pricey to manufacture, so BMC made it a special-order model; thus very few were sold. Aside from the engine, the mechanical specification was the same as for the 1071S. Hydrolastic suspension made an appearance three months after launch but the car itself then only lasted a further seven months. Holding firm.

**SPECIFICATIONS**

| | |
|---|---|
| **Years produced:** | 1964-1965 (963 in total) |
| **Performance:** | 0-60mph: N/A<br>Top speed: 92mph |
| **Power & torque:** | 65bhp/N/A |
| **Engine:** | Normally aspirated 970cc four cylinder, petrol, carburettor, 8 valves |
| **Drivetrain:** | Front-engine FWD |
| **Structure:** | Monocoque |
| **Transmission:** | Four-speed manual |
| **Weight:** | 630kg |

**PRICE GUIDE**

| | |
|---|---|
| **Launch price:** | £671 |
| **Excellent:** | £33,000 |
| **Good:** | £24,500 |
| **Average:** | £15,000 |
| **Project:** | £11,000 |

## MINI
# Cooper 1275S MkI

Cooper's crowning glory was the 1275S, the MkI version of which lasted from 1964 to 1967 and won the Monte Carlo rallies in 1965 and '67. The long-stroke 1275cc A-series gave 76bhp, enough to launch the car to almost 100mph. Single-colour paint schemes were available alongside the usual two-tone ones, making these Coopers great little Q-cars, as there wasn't too much else to distinguish one from a standard Mini. Hydrolastic suspension came along in 1964, then an oil cooler and twin fuel tanks from 1966. The very best can fetch up to £40k

**SPECIFICATIONS**

| | |
|---|---|
| **Years produced:** | 1964-1967 (21,141 in total) |
| **Performance:** | 0-60mph: 11.2sec<br>Top speed: 96mph |
| **Power & torque:** | 76bhp/79lb ft |
| **Engine:** | Normally aspirated 1275cc four cylinder, petrol, carburettor, 8 valves |
| **Drivetrain:** | Front-engine FWD |
| **Structure:** | Monocoque |
| **Transmission:** | Four-speed manual |
| **Weight:** | 635kg |

**PRICE GUIDE**

| | |
|---|---|
| **Launch price:** | £756 |
| **Excellent:** | £35,000 |
| **Good:** | £26,500 |
| **Average:** | £17,000 |
| **Project:** | £11,000 |

## MINI
# Moke

The Moke was developed as a military vehicle but the forces, er, failed to appreciate it. So, instead, BMC sold it as a fun fashion accessory. You weren't one of the in-crowd if you hadn't driven one down Carnaby Street – unless, of course, you were Patrick McGoohan in *The Prisoner*. Production switched to Australia in 1968, with a rise in engine size from 848cc to 998cc, and then 1098cc with the MkII of 1969. The Moke Californian of 1971 had a 1275cc unit. Portuguese manufacture began in 1980 and ended in 1993. Values holding firm.

**SPECIFICATIONS**

**Years produced:** 1964-1993 (14,518 to 1968)
**Performance:** 0-60mph: 21.8sec
Top speed: 65mph
**Power & torque:** 34bhp/N/A
**Engine:** Normally aspirated 848cc four cylinder, petrol, carburettor, 8 valves
**Drivetrain:** Front-engine FWD
**Structure:** Monocoque
**Transmission:** Four-speed manual
**Weight:** 406kg

**PRICE GUIDE**

**Launch price:** £405
**Excellent:** £17,500
**Good:** £10,000
**Average:** £5500
**Project:** £3000

## MINI
# Cooper S MkII/III

The 1275cc Cooper S continued into MkII guise, with the same changes as the humbler Minis such as a reshaped grille, bigger rear window and enlarged back lights. Other Minis had dispensed with their marque names but the S continued to be available in Austin and Morris forms. The 998cc variant was dropped in 1969 but the 1275 Cooper S made it through to MkIII form with concealed door hinges and wind-up windows. It kept Hydrolastic suspension until British Leyland's agreement with Cooper was cancelled in 1971 and the model disappeared.

**SPECIFICATIONS**

**Years produced:** 1967-1971 (16,396 in total)
**Performance:** 0-60mph: 10.9sec
Top speed: 96mph
**Power & torque:** 76bhp/79lb ft
**Engine:** Normally aspirated 1275cc four cylinder, petrol, carburettor, 8 valves
**Drivetrain:** Front-engine FWD
**Structure:** Monocoque
**Transmission:** Four-speed manual
**Weight:** 630kg

**PRICE GUIDE**

**Launch price:** £631
**Excellent:** £26,000
**Good:** £20,000
**Average:** £13,500
**Project:** £7500

## MINI
# MkII-V

The short-lived MkII (1967-69) had a new grille and the option of a 998cc engine, while the MkIII (1969-76) hid the door hinges and replaced the sliding windows with wind-up ones. The old Austin and Morris badges were dropped, with the Mini now a marque in its own right. Hydrolastic suspension – more expensive to fit – was dropped in favour of the original rubber-cone type. Changes for the MkIV (1976-84) were more subtle, with alterations to the interior and subframe. The MkV took over from 1985-92, with 12in wheels and front disc brakes.

**SPECIFICATIONS**

**Years produced:** 1967-1992
**Performance:** 0-60mph: 27.1sec
Top speed: 72mph
**Power & torque:** 39bhp/51lb ft
**Engine:** Normally aspirated 998cc four cylinder, petrol, carburettor, 8 valves
**Drivetrain:** Front-engine RWD
**Structure:** Monocoque
**Transmission:** Four-speed manual
**Weight:** 616kg

**PRICE GUIDE**

**Launch price:** £509
**Excellent:** £5700
**Good:** £3200
**Average:** £1650
**Project:** £500

## MINI
# 1275GT

Seeking to save money, British Leyland replaced the Mini-Cooper with an uprated version of the Mini Clubman. However, just as the blunt-fronted Clubman lacked the character of the original Mini, so the 1275GT was a disappointment compared with the Cooper, with only a single-carburettor 1275cc engine of 59bhp. It wasn't that bad a car, with front disc brakes and more sophisticated equipment inside, and at least it stood out more than other Minis with its Rostyle wheels and decals. But it tried to supersede a legend, and that was a big ask.

**SPECIFICATIONS**

**Years produced:** 1969-1980 (110,673 in total)
**Performance:** 0-60mph: 13.3sec
Top speed: 90mph
**Power & torque:** 59bhp/67lb ft
**Engine:** Normally aspirated 1275cc four cylinder, petrol, carburettor, 8 valves
**Drivetrain:** Front-engine FWD
**Structure:** Monocoque
**Transmission:** Four-speed manual
**Weight:** 675kg

**PRICE GUIDE**

**Launch price:** £834
**Excellent:** £9500
**Good:** £5750
**Average:** £2250
**Project:** £1200

## MINI
# Clubman

Despite its sales success, the original Mini had never made any money for BMC. So successor British Leyland launched what it regarded as an enhanced version in 1969, which was accordingly more expensive. The Clubman had a longer, squared-off nose. The interior was revamped, with instruments now in front of the driver instead of in the centre, and Hydrolastic suspension was retained until 1971. An estate was available from launch, complete with fake plastic wood trim down the sides. A cheap way into Mini ownership these days.

**SPECIFICATIONS**

**Years produced:** 1969-1982 (473,189 in total)
**Performance:** 0-60mph: 21.0sec
Top speed: 75mph
**Power & torque:** 45bhp/55lb ft
**Engine:** Normally aspirated 1098cc four cylinder, petrol, carburettor, 8 valves
**Drivetrain:** Front-engine FWD
**Structure:** Monocoque
**Transmission:** Four-speed manual
**Weight:** 670kg

**PRICE GUIDE**

**Launch price:** £720
**Excellent:** £4000
**Good:** £2250
**Average:** £1250
**Project:** £500

## MINI
### Cooper RSP

Responding to enthusiast demand, Rover Group brought back the Mini-Cooper in 1990 as a limited edition of just 1000 (known as RSP for Rover Special Projects). Such was the interest that the decision was taken to reintroduce it as a mainstream model, with a 61bhp 1275cc Rover Metro engine plus alloy wheels, white roof and more sporting interior. An 'S' package from John Cooper boosted power to 78bhp, while the 40th birthday celebration Cooper S Works of 1999 was the most powerful of them all, with 90bhp. All are great fun and eminently useable.

**SPECIFICATIONS (S)**

| | |
|---|---|
| Years produced: | 1991-2000 (1650 in total) |
| Performance: | 0-60mph: 10.7sec<br>Top speed: 96mph |
| Power & torque: | 78bhp/78lb ft |
| Engine: | Normally aspirated 1275cc four cylinder, petrol, fuel injection, 8 valves |
| Drivetrain: | Front-engine FWD |
| Structure: | Monocoque |
| Transmission: | Four-speed manual |
| Weight: | 706kg |

**PRICE GUIDE**

| | |
|---|---|
| Launch price: | £9004 |
| Excellent: | £8000 |
| Good: | £6500 |
| Average: | £4750 |
| Project: | £2200 |

## NEW MINI
### Cooper/Cooper S

BMW's reborn Mini was no relation whatsoever to the early cars – except that it managed to capture all of the style and all of the fun of the original, but in a thoroughly modern package. And proof that the formula was absolutely right can be found on every street in the land. Don't let this ubiquity put you off – even in basic One trim, the 2001-2006 first-gen New Minis are great fun to drive; Cooper brings a bit more zip, the supercharged Cooper S substantially more (with extra running costs). Convertible adds a neat electric hood but also a few wobbles over bumps.

**SPECIFICATIONS**

| | |
|---|---|
| Years produced: | 2001-2006 |
| Performance: | 0-60mph: 9.0sec (Cooper)<br>Top speed: 124mph |
| Power & torque: | 113bhp/110lb ft |
| Engine: | Normally aspirated 1598cc four-cylinder, petrol, fuel injection, 16 valves |
| Drivetrain: | Front-engine FWD |
| Structure: | Monocoque |
| Transmission: | Five-speed manual |
| Weight: | 1050kg |

**PRICE GUIDE (Cooper)**

| | |
|---|---|
| Launch price: | £11,600 |
| Excellent: | £3000 |
| Good: | £2000 |
| Average: | £1000 |
| Project: | £500 |

# MITSUBISHI

MITSUBISHI MOTORS

MITSUBISHI BEGAN building cars in 1917, when the Mitsubishi Shipbuilding Company introduced the Model A – Japan's first series-production car. It wasn't entirely a success, as it was handbuilt and fearsomely expensive. A mere 22 were built, before the car-building idea was chalked up to experience. Mitsubishi as we know it was created in 1934 when the company's shipbuilding and aircraft manufacturing operations were merged. The new Mitsubishi Heavy Industry company's car operation began with the Colt 1000 and Minica *kei car* in 1963 and really hit its stride in the 1980s and 90s when success in world rallying bred a line of high-performance competition-inspired road cars.

## MITSUBISHI
### Lancer 2000 Turbo

1980's second-generation Lancer was given a boost following the addition of a turbocharger. Initially the 1.8-litre EX Turbo pushed out 135bhp but, when it came to the UK in 1982, the Lancer Turbo had been bored out to 2.0 litres and a full 168bhp. The 4G63 engine that powered it would go on to power the legendary Evo models, and score heavily in world rallying. The chiselled '80s styling was improved drastically by the full-depth chin spoiler with reverse '2000 Turbo' badging, BMW 2002-style. Now a performance icon for lovers of Oriental classics.

**SPECIFICATIONS**

| | |
|---|---|
| Years produced: | 1982-1988 |
| Performance: | 0-60mph: 7.1sec<br>Top speed: 124mph |
| Power & torque: | 168bhp/181lb ft |
| Engine: | Turbocharged 1997cc four cylinder, petrol, fuel injection, 8 valves |
| Drivetrain: | Front-engine RWD |
| Structure: | Monocoque |
| Transmission: | Five-speed manual |
| Weight: | 1052kg |

**PRICE GUIDE**

| | |
|---|---|
| Launch price: | £8499 |
| Excellent: | £7500 |
| Good: | £5000 |
| Average: | £2750 |
| Project: | £1750 |

## MITSUBISHI
### Starion

Considering it was Mitsubishi's first foray into the high-performance coupé market, the Starion proved incredibly popular. The turbocharged Mitsubishi not only looked good but went exceedingly well thanks to its turbocharged power unit shared with the Lancer Turbo. It was constantly developed during its eight-year life, and eventually appeared in wide-body form as well as being powered by one of the modern-era's largest four-cylinder engines - a 2.6-litre. And in case you were wondering, the name is actually a shortened form of 'Star of Orion'.

**SPECIFICATIONS (2.0)**

| | |
|---|---|
| Years produced: | 1982-1989 |
| Performance: | 0-60mph: 8.3sec<br>Top speed: 132mph |
| Power & torque: | 168bhp/181lb ft |
| Engine: | Turbocharged 1997cc four cylinder, petrol, fuel injection, 8 valves |
| Drivetrain: | Front-engine RWD |
| Structure: | Monocoque |
| Transmission: | Four-speed manual |
| Weight: | 1220kg |

**PRICE GUIDE**

| | |
|---|---|
| Launch price: | £11,734 |
| Excellent: | £7000 |
| Good: | £3750 |
| Average: | £1800 |
| Project: | £800 |

## MITSUBISHI 3000GT

A technological tour de force when it was launched in 1990, the 3000GT (also known as GTO in Japan and the Dodge Stealth in the US) boasted four-wheel drive, four-wheel steering, electonic suspension control and even active aerodynamics on the early versions. Power came from a quad-cam 3-litre V6 with twin turbochargers. But while its performance was never in doubt, the GT's super-sophisticated chassis felt rather woolly when driven hard. Still, as a technological statement and an attention-grabbing GT, it has sustained an enthusiastic following.

### SPECIFICATIONS

| | |
|---|---|
| **Years produced:** | 1990-2001 |
| **Performance:** | 0-60mph: 6.2sec<br>Top speed: 155mph (limited) |
| **Power & torque:** | 300bhp/300lb ft |
| **Engine:** | Twin-turbocharged 2972cc V6, petrol, fuel injection, 24 valves |
| **Drivetrain:** | Front-engine AWD |
| **Structure:** | Monocoque |
| **Transmission:** | Five-speed manual |
| **Weight:** | 1740kg |

### PRICE GUIDE

| | |
|---|---|
| **Launch price:** | £35,500 |
| **Excellent:** | £5500 |
| **Good:** | £4000 |
| **Average:** | £2750 |
| **Project:** | £1200 |

## MITSUBISHI Lancer Evo I, II & III

The now-legendary Evo was a series of road cars built to homologate the Lancer for international rallying, and the earliest versions are perhaps the ultimate wolves in sheep's clothing. Nowhere near as outlandish as later evolutions, their understated appearance is part of the appeal and even today few other cars are quicker across the ground. The Evo I and II were never sold through the official dealer channels in the UK, so any cars you look at will be 'grey' imports, but this is no cause for concern if they've been serviced by recognised specialists.

### SPECIFICATIONS

| | |
|---|---|
| **Years produced:** | 1992-1995 |
| **Performance:** | 0-60mph: 5.1sec (Evo I)<br>Top speed: 112mph (limited) |
| **Power & torque:** | 247bhp/228lb ft |
| **Engine:** | Turbocharged 1997cc four cylinder, petrol, fuel injection, 16 valves |
| **Drivetrain:** | Front-engine AWD |
| **Structure:** | Monocoque |
| **Transmission:** | Five-speed manual |
| **Weight:** | 1240kg |

### PRICE GUIDE

| | |
|---|---|
| **Launch price:** | £n/a |
| **Excellent:** | £5000 |
| **Good:** | £3000 |
| **Average:** | £2000 |
| **Project:** | £1250 |

## MITSUBISHI Lancer Evo IV, V & VI

For the Evo IV introduced in 1997, Mitsubishi's homologation special took its biggest leap yet. Engine and transmission were turned through 180deg to improve handling, peak power was now 276bhp, there were new front and rear diffs and electronic 'Active Yaw Control', and it was all wrapped in much more aggressive-looking bodywork. The Evo was now a huge cult hit. The Evo V and VI brought more torque, better braking and even more visual clout. Most highly prized of the lot is the Evo VI Makinen Edition (left).

### SPECIFICATIONS

| | |
|---|---|
| **Years produced:** | 1997-2001 (c25,000 in total) |
| **Performance:** | 0-60mph: 4.8sec (Evo VI)<br>Top speed: 140mph |
| **Power & torque:** | 276bhp/274lb ft |
| **Engine:** | Turbocharged 1997cc four cylinder, petrol, fuel injection, 16 valves |
| **Drivetrain:** | Front-engine AWD |
| **Structure:** | Monocoque |
| **Transmission:** | Five-speed manual |
| **Weight:** | 1345kg |

### PRICE GUIDE (Makinen in brackets)

| | |
|---|---|
| **Launch price:** | c£30,000 |
| **Excellent:** | £10,000 (£30,000) |
| **Good:** | £7500 (£22,000) |
| **Average:** | £6000 (£15,000) |
| **Project:** | £3000 (N/A) |

# MONTEVERDI

SWITZERLAND isn't best-known for car production, but Monteverdi stands out. This performance marque was formed in 1967 by Basel garage owner Peter Monteverdi to put his Chrysler V8-engined GT cars into production. Encouraging sales made the company ambitious and it launched the mid-engined Hai as a Ferrari and Lamborghini pretender in 1970. Brave, but only two were built. Monteverdi moved to restyling existing cars, such as the Sierra (a Plymouth Volare) and the 4x4 Safari (based on, of all things, an International Harvester Scout). The company called it a day in 1984 and ceased production, converting its factory into a car museum the following year.

## MONTEVERDI High Speed 375L/375C

Peter Monteverdi was a Swiss BMW dealer and racing driver who wanted to make an indelible mark on the luxury car market, by offering one of his own. The Frua-styled 375 was the result, and went on to sell surprisingly well despite its huge price tag. Beneath that Italianate body beat the heart of a hefty Chrysler V8, which developed up to 390bhp, all held together by a tubular chassis. The later Berlinetta model was even more potent, thanks to the fitment of a Hemi engine from the mid-engined Hai (below). Its 450bhp was the recipe for thrills aplenty. Values holding firm.

### SPECIFICATIONS (375S)

| | |
|---|---|
| **Years produced:** | 1967-1977 |
| **Performance:** | 0-60mph: 6.5sec<br>Top speed: 162mph |
| **Power & torque:** | 390bhp/481lb ft |
| **Engine:** | Normally aspirated 7206cc V8, petrol, carburettor, 16 valves |
| **Drivetrain:** | Front-engine RWD |
| **Structure:** | Tubular chassis |
| **Transmission:** | Three-speed automatic |
| **Weight:** | 1600kg |

### PRICE GUIDE

| | |
|---|---|
| **Launch price:** | £9250 |
| **Excellent:** | £135,000 |
| **Good:** | £100,000 |
| **Average:** | £50,000 |
| **Project:** | N/A |

## MONTEVERDI
### High Speed 375/4

The Fissore-built, Frua-styled Monteverdi High Speed limousine was nothing if not extravagent. The coupé upon which it was based was hardly a compact machine, measuring 4.80m and packing 7.2 litres of Chrysler V8 power. To make a limousine, a further 50cm was added, most of which was within the wheelbase, creating a surprisingly handsome low-line saloon. During its seven-year production run, 30 were built before Monteverdi gave up bespoke vehicle manufacture in favour of modified versions of existing saloons, such as the Tiara and Sierra.

**SPECIFICATIONS**

| | |
|---|---|
| **Years produced:** | 1970-1977 (30 in total) |
| **Performance:** | 0-60mph: 7.5sec<br>Top speed: 145mph |
| **Power & torque:** | 390bhp/481lb ft |
| **Engine:** | Normally aspirated 7206cc V8, petrol, carburettor, 16 valves |
| **Drivetrain:** | Front-engine RWD |
| **Structure:** | Tubular chassis |
| **Transmission:** | Three-speed automatic |
| **Weight:** | 1755kg |

**PRICE GUIDE**

| | |
|---|---|
| **Launch price:** | N/A in UK |
| **Excellent:** | £85,000 |
| **Good:** | £60,000 |
| **Average:** | £35,000 |
| **Project:** | N/A |

## MONTEVERDI
### Hai 450SS/GTS

With the Lamborghini Miura and De Tomaso Mangusta setting the supercar pace with their mid-mounted engines, it was inevitable that the ambitious Peter Monteverdi would have a go at building his own version. The Fiore-styled Hai was the result. It certainly looked the part and had Miura-matching pace. Sadly, the project didn't progress beyond the second prototype car (the GTS), despite plans to build 49, leaving the Hai a fascinating might-have-been. Despite its obscurity, the original Geneva Motor Show car sold in 2010 for €398,000.

**SPECIFICATIONS**

| | |
|---|---|
| **Years produced:** | 1970-1973 (2 in total) |
| **Performance:** | 0-60mph: 5.5sec<br>Top speed: 175mph (est) |
| **Power & torque:** | 450bhp/481lb ft |
| **Engine:** | Normally aspirated 7206cc V8, petrol, carburettor, 16 valves |
| **Drivetrain:** | Mid-engine RWD |
| **Structure:** | Tubular chassis |
| **Transmission:** | Three-speed automatic |
| **Weight:** | 1455kg |

**PRICE GUIDE**

| | |
|---|---|
| **Launch price:** | N/A |
| **Excellent:** | c£500,000 |
| **Good:** | N/A |
| **Average:** | N/A |
| **Project:** | N/A |

## MONTEVERDI
### Safari

The Safari was a clear demonstration of what made Monteverdi's products so clever. Under the clean and handsome Euro-suit lurked an International Harvester Scout, an American off-roader rarely seen in Europe. That car was a US SUV pioneer and, along with the Range Rover, the Monteverdi did the same for Europe. The combination of luxurious equipment levels and automatic transmission were features that you couldn't get in the Range Rover until the early '80s. Rare outside Switzerland and, when they come up for sale, expect to pay a premium price.

**SPECIFICATIONS**

| | |
|---|---|
| **Years produced:** | 1977-1982 |
| **Performance:** | 0-60mph: 13.5sec<br>Top speed: 105mph |
| **Power & torque:** | 150bhp/210lb ft |
| **Engine:** | Normally aspirated 5210cc V8, petrol, carburettor, 16 valves |
| **Drivetrain:** | Front-engine 4WD |
| **Structure:** | Separate body and chassis |
| **Transmission:** | Three-speed automatic |
| **Weight:** | 2120kg |

**PRICE GUIDE**

| | |
|---|---|
| **Launch price:** | £N/A |
| **Excellent:** | £38,000 |
| **Good:** | £27,500 |
| **Average:** | £20,000 |
| **Project:** | N/A |

# MORGAN

THE PROTOTYPE MORGAN, a three-wheeler, was constructed in 1909 in Malvern and remained in production until 1952. From 1936, Morgan moved into four-wheeled cars and showed a stubborn resistance to depart from its formula. Its handbuilt creations have very traditional pre-war-style wood-framed bodywork featuring a variety of modern engines. Its most famous model is the Plus 8, built from 1968 to 2004 with Rover's V8 engine giving stirring performance. Today, Morgan is still an eccentric British institution, but with more modern high-tech engineering under its new models' individual styling. Still seemingly immune to the whims of mere fashion, its cars remain ever-popular.

## MORGAN
### 4/4 Series 1

The first post-war Morgan was similar to its pre-war cousin in styling, and almost identical underneath. The chassis was tubular, featuring Z-section side members, while the sliding pillar suspension and coil springs were just as before. For the first 4/4, a special overhead-cam Standard engine was used, mated to a Moss gearbox. It was a recipe that worked, and would continue to do so for a very long time indeed. Some of the features, such as cable brakes, remained in place but, over time, they were replaced by contemporary set-ups. On the up.

**SPECIFICATIONS**

| | |
|---|---|
| **Years produced:** | 1945-1950 (249 in total) |
| **Performance:** | 0-60mph: N/A<br>Top speed: 77mph |
| **Power & torque:** | 40bhp/N/A |
| **Engine:** | Normally aspirated 1267cc four cylinder, petrol, carburettor, 8 valves |
| **Drivetrain:** | Front-engine RWD |
| **Structure:** | Separate chassis |
| **Transmission:** | Four-speed manual |
| **Weight:** | 721kg |

**PRICE GUIDE**

| | |
|---|---|
| **Launch price:** | £455 |
| **Excellent:** | £32,500 |
| **Good:** | £25,000 |
| **Average:** | £15,500 |
| **Project:** | £8000 |

# MORGAN
## Plus 4

Adding 4in to the wheelbase of the 4/4 to make room for a second row of seats was a wise move, as it opened up the appeal of these vintage sports cars to those with small families. A move to hydraulically assisted brakes was a welcome move, as was the lightly restyled front end. During its 19-year run, it went through a 2.1-litre Standard Vanguard engine before moving to the Triumph TR2's. Front discs were finally fitted as standard in 1961, which was a good thing, as the final TR4-engined models were 100mph cars. Double these prices for Super Sports.

**SPECIFICATIONS**

**Years produced:** 1950-1969 (3737 in total)
**Performance:** 0-60mph: 14.1sec
Top speed: 85mph
**Power & torque:** 68bhp/113lb ft
**Engine:** Normally aspirated 1991cc four cylinder, petrol, carburettor, 8 valves
**Drivetrain:** Front-engine RWD
**Structure:** Separate chassis
**Transmission:** Four-speed manual
**Weight:** 838kg

**PRICE GUIDE**

**Launch price:** £652
**Excellent:** £35,000
**Good:** £27,000
**Average:** £16,000
**Project:** £7000

# MORGAN
## 4/4 Series II-V

After a hiatus of four years, the 4/4 was put back into production. The number of TR2 engines used in the Plus 4 models was being restricted by Triumph so Morgan turned to Ford for its cheap and readily available 1172cc sidevalve engine, to create a new entry-level model. The wheelbase of the 4/4 was standardised with the Plus 4, thus streamlining production. The Series IV received a wider, better-looking body, disc brakes and a larger 1340cc Ford engine. Despite hardly changing in style, the 4/4 remained consistently popular though the years.

**SPECIFICATIONS**

**Years produced:** 1955-1968 (1197 in total)
**Performance:** 0-60mph: 29.4sec
Top speed: 71mph
**Power & torque:** 36bhp/N/A
**Engine:** Normally aspirated 1172cc four cylinder, petrol, carburettor, 8 valves
**Drivetrain:** Front-engine RWD
**Structure:** Separate chassis
**Transmission:** Four-speed manual
**Weight:** 660kg

**PRICE GUIDE**

**Launch price:** £639
**Excellent:** £28,000
**Good:** £22,000
**Average:** £13,000
**Project:** £6500

# MORGAN
## Plus 8

The Rover V8 engine found its way under the bonnet of a bewildering array of cars. However, Morgan's decision to buy up a stockpile of the ex-GM engines was most surprising but satisfying once it became clear just how much fun the Plus 8 actually was. It was a pragmatic move by Morgan, though, as supplies of suitable four-cylinder engines were beginning to dry up. The earliest examples made 161bhp – identical to the Rover P5 V8 – and endowed the lightweight 4/4-derived sports car with explosive acceleration and exciting handling. Values rising.

**SPECIFICATIONS**

**Years produced:** 1968-1972 (482 in total)
**Performance:** 0-60mph: 6.7sec
Top speed: 124mph
**Power & torque:** 161bhp/210lb ft
**Engine:** Normally aspirated 3528cc V8, petrol, carburettor, 16 valves
**Drivetrain:** Front-engine RWD
**Structure:** Separate chassis
**Transmission:** Four-speed manual
**Weight:** 839kg

**PRICE GUIDE**

**Launch price:** £1478
**Excellent:** £42,000
**Good:** £34,000
**Average:** £22,500
**Project:** £11,000

# MORGAN
## 4/4 1600

For increasingly affluent car buyers, the rather austere and underpowered 4/4 was looking a little out of its depth. There was nothing wrong with the way it looked, but rather the way it went. Morgan rectified this in 1968 by fitting the Ford Kent engine, boosting power to a more palatable 74bhp. The Plus 4 model was dropped, with the option of 2+2 seating being passed to the 4/4 line. It remained available in this form until 1982, when the Ford CVH used in the front-wheel-drive Escort was dropped in, improving power and economy if not refinement.

**SPECIFICATIONS**

**Years produced:** 1968-1981 (3708 in total)
**Performance:** 0-60mph: 9.8sec
Top speed: 100mph
**Power & torque:** 74bhp/85lb ft
**Engine:** Normally aspirated 1599cc four cylinder, petrol, carburettor, 8 valves
**Drivetrain:** Front-engine RWD
**Structure:** Separate chassis
**Transmission:** Four-speed manual
**Weight:** 688kg

**PRICE GUIDE**

**Launch price:** £858
**Excellent:** £23,000
**Good:** £17,000
**Average:** £12500
**Project:** £5500

# MORGAN
## Plus 8 (1973-86)

Morgan continued to develop the Plus 8 and, by 1973, the aluminium-engined vintage-style hot rod had the worst of its handling foibles sorted out. An all-synchromesh Rover 2000 gearbox was installed to replace the old Moss unit, a higher-output SD1-tune V8 came later and, in 1977, along with the much-needed five-speed gearbox, the option of aluminium body panels was introduced. Sales continued steadily throughout the worst of the 1970s recession, and supply was carefully managed by keeping the waiting list long, at around eight years. Edging up.

**SPECIFICATIONS**

**Years produced:** 1973-1986
**Performance:** 0-60mph: 6.7sec
Top speed: 124mph
**Power & torque:** 161bhp/210lb ft
**Engine:** Normally aspirated 3528cc V8, petrol, carburettor, 16 valves
**Drivetrain:** Front-engine RWD
**Structure:** Separate chassis
**Transmission:** Five-speed manual
**Weight:** 898kg

**PRICE GUIDE**

**Launch price:** £1478
**Excellent:** £32,000
**Good:** £24,000
**Average:** £17,000
**Project:** £9500

## MORGAN
### Plus 8 Injection

Following the arrival of the Rover SD1 Vitesse in 1982, Morgan kept pace with developments by introducing its Lucas fuel-injection 190bhp engine into the Plus 8. Given the Morgan's interesting handling, it seemed that the last thing it needed was additional grunt, but the power hikes continued long into the 21st century, first with the 3.9-litre Range Rover V8 (still 190bhp but more torque) and then a 4.6-litre pushing out 240bhp. It was a recipe that worked, and sales remained strong through to the launch of the current generation of cars.

**SPECIFICATIONS**

| | |
|---|---|
| **Years produced:** | 1984-2004 |
| **Performance:** | 0-60mph: 5.6sec<br>Top speed: 120mph |
| **Power & torque:** | 190bhp/220lb ft |
| **Engine:** | Normally aspirated 3528cc V8, petrol, electronic fuel injection, 16 valves |
| **Drivetrain:** | Front-engine RWD |
| **Structure:** | Separate chassis |
| **Transmission:** | Five-speed manual |
| **Weight:** | 839kg |

**PRICE GUIDE**

| | |
|---|---|
| **Launch price:** | £12,999 |
| **Excellent:** | £32,000 |
| **Good:** | £25,000 |
| **Average:** | £18,000 |
| **Project:** | £10,000 |

## MORGAN
### Plus 4

The Plus Four made a return in 1985, initially powered by the Ford CVH, then by an optional Fiat twin-cam. Typically, these Fiat-engined cars proved lively to drive and much faster than their Ford-engined counterparts. The Plus Four name continued after the end of these 1.6-litre cars, thanks to the arrival of the 2.0-litre twin-cam Rover M16 engine, which offered 122bhp and a top speed of over 110mph. However, these four-seat Morgans never achieved the popularity of their two-seat counterparts.

**SPECIFICATIONS**

| | |
|---|---|
| **Years produced:** | 1985-2000 |
| **Performance:** | 0-60mph: 9.0sec<br>Top speed: 112mph |
| **Power & torque:** | 122bhp/127lb ft |
| **Engine:** | Normally aspirated 1995cc four cylinder, petrol, electronic fuel injection, 8 valves |
| **Drivetrain:** | Front-engine RWD |
| **Structure:** | Separate chassis |
| **Transmission:** | Five-speed manual |
| **Weight:** | 848kg |

**PRICE GUIDE**

| | |
|---|---|
| **Launch price:** | £10,901 |
| **Excellent:** | £20,000 |
| **Good:** | £14,500 |
| **Average:** | £10,000 |
| **Project:** | £8000 |

## MORGAN
### Aero 8/AeroMax

As the first all-new Morgan in a generation, the Aero 8 was defined not by its 4.4-litre BMW V8 engine, nor its incredibly stiff and light aluminium chassis. No, it was the cross-eyed but characterful face that really made an impression, thanks to the slightly peculiar-looking pair of VW Beetle headlights. It was actually a thoroughly modern Morgan under the skin and great to drive, while a switch to Mini lights in 2007 improved the looks. A run of 100 AeroMax coupés, with stunning fastback bodywork, were built from 2008. It's these that most attract collector interest.

**SPECIFICATIONS**

| | |
|---|---|
| **Years produced:** | 2001-2010 |
| **Performance:** | 0-60mph: 4.8sec<br>Top speed: 160mph |
| **Power & torque:** | 286bhp/317lb ft |
| **Engine:** | Normally aspirated 4398cc V8, petrol, electronic fuel injection, 32 valves |
| **Drivetrain:** | Front-engine RWD |
| **Structure:** | Aluminium chassis |
| **Transmission:** | Six-speed manual |
| **Weight:** | 1240kg |

**PRICE GUIDE (AeroMax in brackets)**

| | |
|---|---|
| **Launch price:** | £49,950 |
| **Excellent:** | £50,000 (£150,000) |
| **Good:** | £35,000 (£130,000) |
| **Average:** | £25,000 (£95,000) |
| **Project:** | N/A |

# MORRIS

BICYCLE MANUFACTURER William Morris took the oft-trod path into building cars in 1913, with his Oxford and Cowley becoming the best-selling cars of the 1920s, and the Eight repeating the same trick the next decade. In 1948 Morris launched one of the enduring British greats, the Minor, which would continue until 1971. As part of the Nuffield Group, Morris became a major part of BMC in 1952, although many vehicles that carried its badging also shared bodies and mechanics with other BMC members. Under British Leyland from 1968, Morris's main model was the Marina, which evolved into the Ital in 1981, three years before Morris was discontinued as a marque.

## MORRIS
### Minor Series MM

The original Minor, complete with sidevalve engine, is a sedate performer, but delightful handling aids its progress. At first sold only as a two-door saloon or Tourer, with grille-mounted headlamps, until the four-door saloon was introduced in September 1950. These had their headlamps mounted in restyled front wings, and the change was adopted by two-doors and Tourers from January 1951. It's the early 'low lamp' Minors that attract collectors. Prices here are for low lamp saloons. Add 40% for Tourers; deduct 20% for high-headlamp MMs.

**SPECIFICATIONS**

| | |
|---|---|
| **Years produced:** | 1948-1953 (176,002 in total) |
| **Performance:** | 0-60mph: 36.5sec<br>Top speed: 62mph |
| **Power & torque:** | 27bhp/N/A |
| **Engine:** | Normally aspirated 918cc four cylinder, petrol, carburettor, 8 valves |
| **Drivetrain:** | Front-engine RWD |
| **Structure:** | Monocoque |
| **Transmission:** | Four-speed manual |
| **Weight:** | 787kg |

**PRICE GUIDE**

| | |
|---|---|
| **Launch price:** | £359 |
| **Excellent:** | £8500 |
| **Good:** | £5750 |
| **Average:** | £2600 |
| **Project:** | £1400 |

## MORRIS Six

Morris's top-of-the-range early post-war offering combines the rounded body styling of the Minor/Oxford MO with the long bonnet and upright grille of pre-war offerings. It's not the most comfortable mix, but salvation lies in the straight-six engine that gives the car a decent turn of speed. The Six uses the MO's body from the screen back, but with different front door pressings and a 13in longer wheelbase. It uses cam steering, which isn't as good as the Oxford's rack-and-pinion. Not made in great numbers and survivors are rare.

**SPECIFICATIONS**

**Years produced:** 1948-1953 (12,400 in total)
**Performance:** 0-60mph: 22.4sec
Top speed: 83mph
**Power & torque:** 70bhp/100lb ft
**Engine:** Normally aspirated 2215cc straight six, petrol, carburettor, 12 valves
**Drivetrain:** Front-engine RWD
**Structure:** Monocoque
**Transmission:** Four-speed manual
**Weight:** 1276kg

**PRICE GUIDE**

**Launch price:** £608
**Excellent:** £6200
**Good:** £3700
**Average:** £1800
**Project:** £800

## MORRIS Oxford MO

In effect a big brother to the Minor, the Oxford promises more of everything, but the extra bulk it carries means that none of it works quite as well. The 1500cc sidevalve engine, though ploddingly reliable, is rather gutless with just 41bhp, and the column-change for the four-speed gearbox borders on bearable. A wood-framed Traveller estate was introduced in 1952, pre-dating the similar Minor by a year. These have collector appeal, are now very rare and should be worth significantly more than the saloon values quoted here.

**SPECIFICATIONS**

**Years produced:** 1948-1954 (159,960 in total)
**Performance:** 0-60mph: 31.1sec
Top speed: 71mph
**Power & torque:** 41bhp/67lb ft
**Engine:** Normally aspirated 1476cc four cylinder, petrol, carburettor, 8 valves
**Drivetrain:** Front-engine RWD
**Structure:** Monocoque
**Transmission:** Four-speed manual
**Weight:** 1092kg

**PRICE GUIDE (saloon)**

**Launch price:** £505
**Excellent:** £5000
**Good:** £3250
**Average:** £1350
**Project:** £700

## MORRIS Minor Series II

Still with the charm of a split windscreen, but now powered by the A-series engine from Austin's A30. This engine appeared only in four-door models during 1952, but all models received it from February '53. Later that year the wood-framed Traveller was added to the range. From late '54 there was a new face with five horizontal grille slats, plus a new dashboard. Many of these cars have been fitted with the stronger 948cc engine from a later Minor, with no detrimental effect to value. Convertible and Traveller particularly prized.

**SPECIFICATIONS**

**Years produced:** 1952-1956 (269,838 in total)
**Performance:** 0-60mph: N/A
Top speed: 62mph
**Power & torque:** 30bhp/40lb ft
**Engine:** Normally aspirated 803cc four cylinder, petrol, carburettor, 8 valves
**Drivetrain:** Front-engine RWD
**Structure:** Monocoque
**Transmission:** Four-speed manual
**Weight:** 787kg

**PRICE GUIDE (Tourer/Traveller in brackets)**

**Launch price:** £582
**Excellent:** £5750 (£12,000)
**Good:** £2800 (£8000)
**Average:** £1300 (£6000)
**Project:** £500 (£2000)

## MORRIS Oxford II/III/IV

A big step forward from the Oxford MO, with an all-new body and 1500cc B-series engine. Became the Series III in October 1956 with a facelift that included a more stylish, fluted bonnet and finned rear wings. Drives better than it looks thanks to torsion bar front suspension and rack-and-pinion steering. Wood-framed two-door Traveller estate version of the SII/III is worth double the price of a saloon. It was replaced in 1957 by the estate-only Series IV Oxford, with an all-steel four-door body. These command about 25% more than saloons.

**SPECIFICATIONS**

**Years produced:** 1954-1960 (145,458 in total)
**Performance:** 0-60mph: 29.0sec
Top speed: 73mph
**Power & torque:** 52bhp/78lb ft
**Engine:** Normally aspirated 1489cc four cylinder, petrol, carburettor, 8 valves
**Drivetrain:** Front-engine RWD
**Structure:** Monocoque
**Transmission:** Four-speed manual
**Weight:** 1067kg

**PRICE GUIDE**

**Launch price:** £745
**Excellent:** £4500
**Good:** £2800
**Average:** £1450
**Project:** £800

## MORRIS Isis

Much like the Six it replaced, the Isis is based closely on the Oxford, but this time the front end is stretched by eight inches to make room for a single-carb version of the six-cylinder C-series engine. Mesh rather than painted slats in the grille set apart later versions, though occupants will notice the right-hand floor-change for the gearbox, to allow three-abreast seating. Updates for rarer Series II in 1956 include fluted bonnet, rear fins, and an extra 4bhp. Highly prized and hard-to-find estates worth about a third more than saloons.

**SPECIFICATIONS**

**Years produced:** 1955-1958 (12,155 in total)
**Performance:** 0-60mph: 17.8sec
Top speed: 86mph
**Power & torque:** 86bhp/N/A
**Engine:** Normally aspirated 2639cc straight six, petrol, carburettor, 12 valves
**Drivetrain:** Front-engine RWD
**Structure:** Monocoque
**Transmission:** Four-speed manual
**Weight:** 1397kg

**PRICE GUIDE**

**Launch price:** £802
**Excellent:** £6000
**Good:** £3750
**Average:** £1900
**Project:** £850

## MORRIS
### Minor 1000

These are the best Minors for those who want one to drive as well as to show. The larger A-series engines finally provided power to match the handling, more so after September 1962 when a 1098cc engine replaced the 948. Larger front brakes were added at the same time. The 1000s are easily distinguished by their curved one-piece windscreen and larger rear window. Convertibles were dropped in June 1969, saloon production ended in November 1970, but Travellers soldiered on until April 1971. Add at least 50% for Convertible/Traveller prices.

**SPECIFICATIONS**

| | |
|---|---|
| **Years produced:** | 1956-1971 (847,491 in total) |
| **Performance:** | 0-60mph: 22.2sec<br>Top speed: 77mph |
| **Power & torque:** | 48bhp/60lb ft |
| **Engine:** | Normally aspirated 1098cc four cylinder, petrol, carburettor, 8 valves |
| **Drivetrain:** | Front-engine RWD |
| **Structure:** | Monocoque |
| **Transmission:** | Four-speed manual |
| **Weight:** | 787kg |

**PRICE GUIDE (saloon)**

| | |
|---|---|
| **Launch price:** | £603 |
| **Excellent:** | £6000 |
| **Good:** | £3650 |
| **Average:** | £1650 |
| **Project:** | £500 |

## MORRIS
### Marina/Ital

Replacing the much-loved Minor was never going to be easy, even if it had been with a great car. The Marina was a strictly conventional machine, with much of its running gear Minor-based and therefore elderly for the era. Saloon, coupé and estate were available, with engines in 1275cc or 1798cc sizes, the latter unit from the MGB. That should have made the cars quite sporty, but handling was seriously suspect. Gradually improved until it was replaced by the Ital (really just a comprehensive facelift) in 1980. Values have risen, albeit slowly.

**SPECIFICATIONS (1.8TC)**

| | |
|---|---|
| **Years produced:** | 1971-1980 (809,612 in total) |
| **Performance:** | 0-60mph: 12.1sec<br>Top speed: 100mph |
| **Power & torque:** | 95bhp/106lb ft |
| **Engine:** | Normally aspirated 1798cc four cylinder, petrol, carburettor, 8 valves |
| **Drivetrain:** | Front-engine RWD |
| **Structure:** | Monocoque |
| **Transmission:** | Four-speed manual |
| **Weight:** | 965kg |

**PRICE GUIDE**

| | |
|---|---|
| **Launch price:** | £923 |
| **Excellent:** | £3200 |
| **Good:** | £1800 |
| **Average:** | £1000 |
| **Project:** | £500 |

# NOBLE

LIKE SO MANY Great British sports car makers, Noble Automotive had the humblest of beginnings. Lee Noble built his first mid-engined sports car, the M10, in his garage at home in 1999. He got the idea after years as an engineer for Ultima, as well as a spell with Ascari in the late 1990s. The M10 showed promise, but the M12 was the real deal. With production outsourced to South Africa and the cars finished in Leicestershire, Noble's plan was to offer supercar performance at an affordable price, and that's exactly why it worked so well. Lee Noble left in 2009, but Noble continued, with development and production of the M600 supercar. A new model, the M500, is currently in the pipeline.

## NOBLE
### M12 GTO/M400

It might have a Ford Mondeo engine (and rear lights) but with a pair of turbochargers it's good for 310bhp in standard form. While it looks extreme, the key to the M12's magic was its low weight and supple chassis, tuned to make light work of UK roads. Revised GTO-3 introduced the 3.0-litre 352bhp V6 engine. Track-focused M400 was much more aggressive, featuring a 425bhp tuned engine and a raft of updates to address the regular car's shortcomings, along with quicker steering and stiffer suspension. The one to have, and valued accordingly.

**SPECIFICATIONS**

| | |
|---|---|
| **Years produced:** | 2000-2007 |
| **Performance:** | 0-60mph: 3.5sec<br>Top speed: 185mph |
| **Power & torque:** | 425bhp/390lb ft |
| **Engine:** | Twin-turbo 2968cc V6, petrol, electronic fuel injection, 24 valves |
| **Drivetrain:** | Mid-engine RWD |
| **Structure:** | Spaceframe with composite panels |
| **Transmission:** | Six-speed manual |
| **Weight:** | 1060kg |

**PRICE GUIDE (M400 in brackets)**

| | |
|---|---|
| **Launch price:** | £61,995 (M400) |
| **Excellent:** | £50,000 (£65,000) |
| **Good:** | £35,000 (£50,000) |
| **Average:** | £25,000 (£35,000) |
| **Project:** | N/A |

# NSU

IT WAS WITH Belgian vehicles that the Neckarsulm motorcycle and bicycle manufacturer got its start building cars in 1905 but, after some popularity, NSU ceased construction in 1929 when its factory was sold to Fiat. That was until 1957, when it re-entered the market with the compact rear-engined NSU Prinz. In 1964, it launched the world's first rotary-engined production car, the Wankel Spider, and followed it up in 1967 with the Ro80, a technological tour-de-force that was voted Car of the Year for 1968. Massice warranty claims forced NSU into the arms of Volkswagen and, after the final Ro80 was sold in April 1977, VW dropped the name so it could concentrate on Audis.

## NSU
# Sport Prinz Coupé

Rare and unusual today, the Sport Prinz Coupé was a good-looking marriage of Italian style and German engineering that should have done better than it did. The bodywork was styled by Scaglione and built in Italy by Bertone. Powered by the Prinz's air-cooled flat twin, the lightweight coupé was capable of 76mph, and seldom felt underpowered on the road despite its tiny engine capacity. It delighted dynamically, thanks to its quick steering and agile handling. More than 20,000 built but few left to choose from today. Prices have been on the rise.

**SPECIFICATIONS**

| | |
|---|---|
| **Years produced:** | 1958-1967 (20,831 in total) |
| **Performance:** | 0-60mph: 27.8sec<br>Top speed: 78mph |
| **Power & torque:** | 30bhp/33lb ft |
| **Engine:** | Normally aspirated 598cc twin, petrol, carburettor, 4 valves |
| **Drivetrain:** | Rear-engine RWD |
| **Structure:** | Monocoque |
| **Transmission:** | Four-speed manual |
| **Weight:** | 556kg |

**PRICE GUIDE**

| | |
|---|---|
| **Launch price:** | £976 |
| **Excellent:** | £7750 |
| **Good:** | £4600 |
| **Average:** | £2400 |
| **Project:** | £100 |

## NSU
# Prinz 4

When the NSU Prinz 4 arrived in 1961, it was the height of small-car fashion. Aside from the Mini, all of the important European baby cars had their engines slung out back, and many were still air-cooled. The Prinz 4 was well-built and packed with nice features – disc brakes and a slick all-synchromesh gearbox made it a pleasure to drive. However, time passed it by, and as the opposition went front-wheel drive, NSU didn't have the resources to develop a suitable replacement. The company ran out of money, and was taken over by the Volkswagen group. Values currently on the up.

**SPECIFICATIONS**

| | |
|---|---|
| **Years produced:** | 1961-1973 (576,023 in total) |
| **Performance:** | 0-60mph: 27.7sec<br>Top speed: 73mph |
| **Power & torque:** | 30bhp/33lb ft |
| **Engine:** | Normally aspirated 598cc twin, petrol, carburettor, 4 valves |
| **Drivetrain:** | Rear-engine RWD |
| **Structure:** | Monocoque |
| **Transmission:** | Four-speed manual |
| **Weight:** | 565kg |

**PRICE GUIDE**

| | |
|---|---|
| **Launch price:** | £729 |
| **Excellent:** | £6000 |
| **Good:** | £3200 |
| **Average:** | £1350 |
| **Project:** | £500 |

## NSU
# Wankel Spider

For much of the 1960s, the future of the internal combustion engine remained up in the air. Felix Wankel's rotary design emerged as a credible alternative, being both smooth and compact, and it's no surprise that manufacturers were clamouring to build their own versions. The first production rotary was the NSU Wankel Spider, an open-topped variation on the Sport Prinz theme. It was a potent little car – the 497cc rotary put out 50bhp and pushed the Spider to over 100mph – but proved too expensive and unreliable for serious sales success.

**SPECIFICATIONS**

| | |
|---|---|
| **Years produced:** | 1964-1967 (2375 in total) |
| **Performance:** | 0-60mph: 17.6sec<br>Top speed: 92mph |
| **Power & torque:** | 50bhp/70lb ft |
| **Engine:** | Normally aspirated 497cc single-rotor Wankel, petrol, carburettor |
| **Drivetrain:** | Rear-engine RWD |
| **Structure:** | Monocoque |
| **Transmission:** | Four-speed manual |
| **Weight:** | 770kg |

**PRICE GUIDE**

| | |
|---|---|
| **Launch price:** | £1391 |
| **Excellent:** | £17,000 |
| **Good:** | £8200 |
| **Average:** | £4600 |
| **Project:** | £1700 |

## NSU
# 1000

A larger, more civilised version of the Prinz 4. Powered by a new 1.0-litre four-cylinder air-cooled engine, the 1000 failed to make a sales impact, probably because it too closely resembled the cheaper car it was based upon. The main differences were a longer wheelbase, restyled front end and plastic cooling vents – and just like its smaller brother, it was a great little car to drive. The 1000 survived the Volkswagen takeover, making it to 1973, but its replacement – the Audi 50 – shared no parts with it. Values have been edging upwards.

**SPECIFICATIONS**

| | |
|---|---|
| **Years produced:** | 1964-1972 (196,000 in total) |
| **Performance:** | 0-60mph: 20.5sec<br>Top speed: 80mph |
| **Power & torque:** | 43bhp/52lb ft |
| **Engine:** | Normally aspirated 996cc four cylinder, petrol, carburettor, 8 valves |
| **Drivetrain:** | Rear-engine RWD |
| **Structure:** | Monocoque |
| **Transmission:** | Four-speed manual |
| **Weight:** | 620kg |

**PRICE GUIDE**

| | |
|---|---|
| **Launch price:** | £673 |
| **Excellent:** | £6000 |
| **Good:** | £3500 |
| **Average:** | £1400 |
| **Project:** | £750 |

## NSU
# Ro80

The NSU Ro80 redefined levels of expectation for buyers in the executive class. It handled beautifully, was huge inside, looked amazing and rode as well as any luxury saloon. It was crowned Car of the Year and, for a while, the Ro80 had the world at its feet. Then the problems started... Its rotary engine was silken but prone to failure, and warranty costs crippled NSU. Modern technology has conquered the rotor-tip problem, and with the correct support a Ro80 is a brilliant classic car to own and good value, too. A constant reminder of what might have been.

**SPECIFICATIONS**

| | |
|---|---|
| **Years produced:** | 1966-1977 (37,204 in total) |
| **Performance:** | 0-60mph: 14.2sec<br>Top speed: 117mph |
| **Power & torque:** | 114bhp/139lb ft |
| **Engine:** | Normally aspirated 1990cc twin-rotor Wankel, petrol, carburettor |
| **Drivetrain:** | Front-engine FWD |
| **Structure:** | Monocoque |
| **Transmission:** | Three-speed semi-automatic |
| **Weight:** | 1190kg |

**PRICE GUIDE**

| | |
|---|---|
| **Launch price:** | £2249 |
| **Excellent:** | £8250 |
| **Good:** | £6000 |
| **Average:** | £2750 |
| **Project:** | £1250 |

## NSU 1200 TT/TTS

The NSU 1200TT proved popular with competitive drivers, and was successful in motor sport. Making the most of the basic car's lightness, the TT version was created when the engine was expanded to 1.2-litres. The excellent handling and roadholding of the 1000 it was based on were complemented by the 1200's additional power, and the TT/TTS ended up becoming Germany's answer to the Mini-Cooper and Simca 1000 Rallye. Due to their high-quality construction, a large number have survived in Germany; fewer in the UK. Add 20% for TTS.

### SPECIFICATIONS

| | |
|---|---|
| **Years produced:** | 1967-1972 (63,289/2404 in total) |
| **Performance:** | 0-60mph: 14.8sec<br>Top speed: 96mph |
| **Power & torque:** | 64bhp/65lb ft |
| **Engine:** | Normally aspirated 1172cc four cylinder, petrol, carburettor, 8 valves |
| **Drivetrain:** | Rear-engine RWD |
| **Structure:** | Monocoque |
| **Transmission:** | Four-speed manual |
| **Weight:** | 650kg |

### PRICE GUIDE (TT)

| | |
|---|---|
| **Launch price:** | £824 |
| **Excellent:** | £16,000 |
| **Good:** | £12,000 |
| **Average:** | £6000 |
| **Project:** | £2000 |

# OGLE

DAVID OGLE founded Ogle Associates at his home in Stevenage in England in 1954, expanding in 1959 to employ noted designer Tom Karen. First products to emerge from the company were special-bodied Minis and Daimlers, but the company diversified into production with the impressive SX1000. Ogle himself was killed driving one of his prototypes in 1962, but the company continued, with Tom Karen taking over as managing director. At this point, SX1000 production ceased, and Karen focused the company's activity as a design house. It styled a number of impressive designs, notably the Triplex GTS – which evolved into the Reliant Scimitar GTE.

## OGLE SX1000

David Ogle ventured into specialist car production in 1960, but truly came into his own when he applied his styling and engineering skills to the Mini. The SX1000 was at the vanguard of the Mini-boom that also included the Marcos and the Deep-Sanderson, and was created by mating a stumpy glassfibre body to a Mini van floorpan and kitting it out with a leather-clad interior. It was quick, too, thanks to improved aerodynamics, a kerbweight 130kg less than the donor car's, and 76bhp from the Cooper S engine. Now eligible for Goodwood.

### SPECIFICATIONS

| | |
|---|---|
| **Years produced:** | 1961-1967 (70 in total) |
| **Performance:** | 0-60mph: 9.0sec<br>Top speed: 110mph |
| **Power & torque:** | 76bhp/79lb ft |
| **Engine:** | Normally aspirated 1275cc four cylinder, petrol, carburettor, 8 valves |
| **Drivetrain:** | Front-engine FWD |
| **Structure:** | Monocoque |
| **Transmission:** | Four-speed manual |
| **Weight:** | 500kg |

### PRICE GUIDE

| | |
|---|---|
| **Launch price:** | N/A |
| **Excellent:** | £15,000 |
| **Good:** | £11,500 |
| **Average:** | £8000 |
| **Project:** | £5000 |

# OPEL

OPEL, FOUNDED in 1898, built Lutzmann and Darracq cars before coming out with its own in 1906. Impressed by its modern factory, General Motors took over in 1928 to gain a foothold in the European market and, under GM leadership, Opel became the European market leader by the end of the 1930s. After the war, the Kapitan and Rekord ranges were the mainstay of Opel's catalogues, joined by the smaller Kadett in 1962. During the 1970s and 80s, Opel's range was combined with that of GM's British arm, Vauxhall, the two marques separated by little more than their badging, with Opel carrying out the engineering. In 2017, both Opel and Vauxhall were acquired from GM by the French PSA group.

## OPEL Kadett A/B

Opel waited until 1962 before launching its small car of the post-war era. This was the Kadett A and very successful it was too, though it was never sold in the UK. What came afterwards was even better. The Kadett B had restyled looks mated to the same chassis, but with a bigger selection of engines, ranging from 1078cc to 1897cc. As well as the saloons and estates, there was a pretty coupé that, in Rallye form, made use of the 1897cc engine with twin carburettors to give 90bhp. These are the ones that excite Opel collectors.

### SPECIFICATIONS

| | |
|---|---|
| **Years produced:** | 1962-1973 (2,311,389 in total) |
| **Performance:** | 0-60mph: 13.8sec<br>Top speed: 89mph |
| **Power & torque:** | 60bhp/65lb ft |
| **Engine:** | Normally aspirated 1196cc four cylinder, petrol, carburettor, 8 valves |
| **Drivetrain:** | Front-engine RWD |
| **Structure:** | Monocoque |
| **Transmission:** | Four-speed manual |
| **Weight:** | 800kg |

### PRICE GUIDE

| | |
|---|---|
| **Launch price:** | £708 |
| **Excellent:** | £4750 |
| **Good:** | £3200 |
| **Average:** | £1600 |
| **Project:** | £650 |

# OPEL
## Rekord/Commodore D

The Commodore, launched in 1967, was an upmarket version of the Opel Rekord. Sold as a saloon or coupé, it was only available with six-cylinder engines, initially 2239cc and 2490cc units, although a 2784cc followed in 1970 and was used in the most desirable GS2800 variant, boasting 143bhp. The second-generation Commodore came on the scene in 1972, sharing its floorpan with the Vauxhall Victor FE. It upped the luxury inside, with the fuel-injection GS/E model as the flagship from 1974 up until the end of the line in 1977.

### SPECIFICATIONS

| | |
|---|---|
| **Years produced:** | 1967-1977 (156,330 in total) |
| **Performance:** | 12.1sec<br>Top speed: 108mph |
| **Power & torque:** | 130bhp/137lb ft |
| **Engine:** | Normally aspirated 2490cc straight six, petrol, fuel injection, 12 valves |
| **Drivetrain:** | Front-engine RWD |
| **Structure:** | Monocoque |
| **Transmission:** | Four-speed manual/three-speed auto |
| **Weight:** | 1234kg |

### PRICE GUIDE

| | |
|---|---|
| **Launch price:** | £1380 |
| **Excellent:** | £6500 |
| **Good:** | £4200 |
| **Average:** | £2000 |
| **Project:** | £800 |

# OPEL
## GT

Given Opel's General Motors heritage, nobody should have been too surprised when the GT popped up in 1968 looking like a shrunken Corvette (although it had been previously seen as a concept car at the 1965 Frankfurt Motor Show). The Kadett provided most of the underpinnings, while the body was built by Brissoneau & Lotz in France. The rotating headlamps were manually operated. Most GTs ended up in the US, presumably with owners who couldn't afford to run the full-sized Corvette. Very nimble, fun, and distinctive.

### SPECIFICATIONS

| | |
|---|---|
| **Years produced:** | 1968-1973 (103,463 in total) |
| **Performance:** | 11.0sec<br>Top speed: 116mph |
| **Power & torque:** | 88bhp/110lb ft |
| **Engine:** | Normally aspirated 1897cc four cylinder, petrol, carburettor, 8 valves |
| **Drivetrain:** | Front-engine RWD |
| **Structure:** | Monocoque |
| **Transmission:** | Four-speed manual |
| **Weight:** | 970kg |

### PRICE GUIDE

| | |
|---|---|
| **Launch price:** | £1882 |
| **Excellent:** | £13,000 |
| **Good:** | £8750 |
| **Average:** | £4000 |
| **Project:** | £1200 |

# OPEL
## Manta A

'We want a Capri!' That was the cry of most European manufacturers after Ford launched its coupé in 1969, and the Manta was Opel's attempt to get in on the act. It used the Ascona as its basis, with a new nose up front and well-proportioned coupé bodywork behind. 1584cc and 1897cc overhead-camshaft engines did service under the bonnet although mainland Europe also had the option of a 1196cc engine. A small number of turbocharged models, based on the plusher Berlinetta, were built and sold in Britain.

### SPECIFICATIONS

| | |
|---|---|
| **Years produced:** | 1970-1975 (498,553 in total) |
| **Performance:** | 0-60mph: 12.2sec<br>Top speed: 105mph |
| **Power & torque:** | 90bhp/108lb ft |
| **Engine:** | Normally aspirated 1897cc four cylinder, petrol, carburettor, 8 valves |
| **Drivetrain:** | Front-engine RWD |
| **Structure:** | Monocoque |
| **Transmission:** | Four-speed manual |
| **Weight:** | 955kg |

### PRICE GUIDE

| | |
|---|---|
| **Launch price:** | £1475 |
| **Excellent:** | £7250 |
| **Good:** | £4500 |
| **Average:** | £2200 |
| **Project:** | £1100 |

# OPEL
## Kadett GT/E

The most appealing of all Kadetts was the Coupé, which is something of a cult car in Germany, and at the very top of the tree was the GT/E version. The fastest Kadett was distinguished by its two-tone paint and earned its stripes by using the Manta's 1.9-litre cam-in-head engine with fuel injection. Clearly it was influenced by the Group 2 rally car, right down to the Opel Team paint scheme. With 105bhp on tap, it was a genuinely quick car, and the well-damped, sharp-steering chassis was more than capable of harnessing the additional power.

### SPECIFICATIONS

| | |
|---|---|
| **Years produced:** | 1973-1979 |
| **Performance:** | 0-60mph: 9.0sec<br>Top speed: 110mph |
| **Power & torque:** | 105bhp/110lb ft |
| **Engine:** | Normally aspirated 1897cc four cylinder, petrol, fuel injected, 8 valves |
| **Drivetrain:** | Front-engine RWD |
| **Structure:** | Monocoque |
| **Transmission:** | Four-speed manual |
| **Weight:** | 915kg |

### PRICE GUIDE

| | |
|---|---|
| **Launch price:** | £3166 |
| **Excellent:** | £5700 |
| **Good:** | £3750 |
| **Average:** | £1700 |
| **Project:** | £800 |

# OPEL
## Manta B

In 1975, the Opel Manta and its sister the Ascona were given a full make-over. Out went the Corvette-inspired curves to be replaced by a sharp new '70s suit. The Manta's handling was taut and faithful, and performance more than acceptable in fuel-injection GT/E form. The range expanded in 1978 to include a hatchback. In 1981, Opel freshened the existing car's styling with glassfibre bumpers, and introduced a new 1.8-litre engine for the cooking models. The GT/E version continued with the same 110bhp fuel-injection 2.0-litre. Has built up quite a following.

### SPECIFICATIONS (GT/E)

| | |
|---|---|
| **Years produced:** | 1978-1988 (603,000 in total) |
| **Performance:** | 0-60mph: 8.5sec<br>Top speed: 120mph |
| **Power & torque:** | 110bhp/119lb ft |
| **Engine:** | Normally aspirated 1979cc four cylinder, petrol, electronic fuel injection, 8 valves |
| **Drivetrain:** | Front-engine RWD |
| **Structure:** | Monocoque |
| **Transmission:** | Five-speed manual |
| **Weight:** | 1065kg |

### PRICE GUIDE

| | |
|---|---|
| **Launch price:** | £6444 (1984) |
| **Excellent:** | £6000 |
| **Good:** | £3900 |
| **Average:** | £2000 |
| **Project:** | £1000 |

## OPEL
### Senator/Monza

Opel's 1978 entrant in the executive car market was its most convincing effort yet. Based on the Senator saloon, the Monza was a good-looking and well-equipped three-door coupé that proved agile despite its bulk. Its dramatic straight-line ability – 0-60mph in 8.5 seconds, top speed of 133mph – was made possible by its six-cylinder fuel-injection engine. Variations on the theme included the ES, with a limited-slip differential to cope with all that power, and the GSE with Recaro seats, digital instrumentation and a prominent rear spoiler. Add 25% for late GSE.

**SPECIFICATIONS (Monza GS/E)**

| | |
|---|---|
| **Years produced:** | 1978-1986 (129,644/43,500 in total) |
| **Performance:** | 0-60mph: 9.3sec<br>Top speed: 123mph |
| **Power & torque:** | 180bhp/183lb ft |
| **Engine:** | Normally aspirated 2969cc straight six, petrol, electronic fuel injection, 12 valves |
| **Drivetrain:** | Front-engine RWD |
| **Structure:** | Monocoque |
| **Transmission:** | Four/five-speed manual |
| **Weight:** | 1375kg |

**PRICE GUIDE**

| | |
|---|---|
| **Launch price:** | £9762 |
| **Excellent:** | £4500 |
| **Good:** | £3000 |
| **Average:** | £1350 |
| **Project:** | £500 |

# PAGANI

JUST AS LAMBORGHINI had done in the early 1960s when it suddenly burst onto the scene, so it was at the 1999 Geneva motor show that a hitherto unknown Italian company called Pagani unveiled a dramatic new supercar, the Zonda.

The brainchild of Argentinian Horacio Pagani, an ex-Lamborghini engineer, the carbonfibre-bodied C12 featured a Mercedes V12 and a quality of design and construction that put most established supercar players to shame. What's more, when road testers had a chance to sample the Zonda, they found that dynamically it had them licked, too. Pagani is now firmly a member of the supercar establishment and the values of its earliest cars have soared in recent times.

## PAGANI
### Zonda C12/S

At its launch in 1999, the stunning, carbonfibre-bodied Zonda featured a 6-litre 389bhp Mercedes V12, which, combined with a kerbweight of just 1250kg, guaranteed dazzling performance, with a brilliant chassis to match. But that was just the start. Only a handful of C12s were made before it was usurped in 2001 by the 'S' version, its 7-litre 547bhp V12 specially built by Mercedes' AMG division, giving near-200mph performance. A new star was born, and values of these early Zondas have been rising ever since.

**SPECIFICATIONS**

| | |
|---|---|
| **Years produced:** | 1999-2002 (21 in total) |
| **Performance:** | 0-60mph: 3.7sec (S)<br>Top speed: 197mph |
| **Power & torque:** | 547bhp/553lb ft |
| **Engine:** | Normally aspirated 7010cc V12, petrol, electronic injection, 48 valves |
| **Drivetrain:** | Mid-engine RWD |
| **Structure:** | Carbonfibre tub and body |
| **Transmission:** | Six-speed manual |
| **Weight:** | 1250kg |

**PRICE GUIDE**

| | |
|---|---|
| **Launch price:** | £350,000 |
| **Excellent:** | £1,000,000+ |
| **Good:** | £800,000+ |
| **Average:** | N/A |
| **Project:** | N/A |

# PANHARD

ONE OF THE earliest French car companies, Panhard et Levassor's first vehicle was a Daimler-engined machine in 1891. Panhard then grew to become one of the most prominent manufacturers of motoring's pioneering years, marketing a wide range of models, eventually specialising in very large, very expensive and very exclusive products. One of the more notable was the Art Deco-influenced Dynamic of 1937. Post-war, Panhard altered direction completely and became known for quirky streamlined styling and air-cooled two-cylinder engines. Citroën took over in 1967 and devoted Panhard to building light military vehicles, something it still does to this day.

## PANHARD
### 24 Series

'Amazing' isn't a word that troubles the French car industry as often as it might, but that superlative perfectly fits the Panhard 24. It might have been powered by a weedy two-cylinder engine but, such was its aerodynamic efficiency, the French coupé could push 100mph and deliver excellent fuel consumption. Sadly, there wasn't a market for this prescient (and expensive) car, and it contributed to Panhard's financial collapse and Citroën's takeover. A few remain in the UK, and have a keen following, even if keeping one roadworthy is challenging.

**SPECIFICATIONS**

| | |
|---|---|
| **Years produced:** | 1963-1967 (22,245 in total) |
| **Performance:** | 0-60mph: 22.3sec<br>Top speed: 89mph |
| **Power & torque:** | 50bhp/56lb ft |
| **Engine:** | Normally aspirated 848cc two-cylinder, petrol, carburettor, 4 valves |
| **Drivetrain:** | Front-engine FWD |
| **Structure:** | Monocoque |
| **Transmission:** | Four-speed manual |
| **Weight:** | 840kg |

**PRICE GUIDE**

| | |
|---|---|
| **Launch price:** | N/A in UK |
| **Excellent:** | £9500 |
| **Good:** | £4500 |
| **Average:** | £2750 |
| **Project:** | £1250 |

# PANTHER

THE NICHE manufacturers' niche manufacturer, Panther Westwinds was founded by Robert Jankel in 1972 to build retro cars with styling inspired by 1930s greats. It even had its factory at Brooklands. Panther then branched out into such diversities as the Rio – a Triumph Dolomite repanelled and trimmed to look like a small Rolls – and the six-wheeled two-seater Panther 6 supercar. Young C Kim took over in 1980 and switched body manufacture to South Korea. Much money was spent developing the ill-fated (thought striking and advanced) mid-engined, four-wheel-drive, Cosworth-powered Solo sports coupé. Despite a SsangYong buyout in 1988, production folded in 1990.

## PANTHER J72

The J72 owed its looks to Jaguar's SS100, although it was more parody than replica. This being the 1970s, there was a ready market for such brash expressions of style (or lack of it), and a number of celebrities bought into British businessman Robert Jankel's dream machine. There was little sophistication to the J72, but it was very fast thanks to its Jaguar six-cylinder engines; even more so when the V12 was added in 1974. The J72 stayed in production until 1981, during which time 426 examples of this expensive vintage wannabe were constructed.

### SPECIFICATIONS

**Years produced:** 1972-1981 (426 in total)
**Performance:** 0-60mph: 6.4sec
Top speed: 114mph
**Power & torque:** 190bhp/200lb ft
**Engine:** Normally aspirated 4235cc straight six, petrol, carburettor, 12 valves
**Drivetrain:** Front-engine RWD
**Structure:** Separate chassis
**Transmission:** Four-speed manual with overdrive
**Weight:** 1136kg

### PRICE GUIDE

**Launch price:** £4380
**Excellent:** £47,000
**Good:** £33,500
**Average:** £22,500
**Project:** £12,000

## PANTHER De Ville

Clearly inspired by the Bugatti Royale, the Panther De Ville was a Jaguar V12-powered pastiche with Austin 1800 doors. It was also the most expensive car on UK price lists in its day. Much of the underpinnings came from Jaguar, as with Panther's previous efforts, making it refined and swift. It was beautifully built too, and attracted a limited and wealthy following. Available as a four- or six-door saloon and as a two-door open-top, the De Ville was the ultimate in ostentatious motoring in a dark decade. Most have survived, and are loved by doting owners.

### SPECIFICATIONS

**Years produced:** 1974-1985 (60 in total)
**Performance:** 0-60mph: 12.4sec
Top speed: 109mph
**Power & torque:** 190bhp/200lb ft
**Engine:** Normally aspirated 4235cc straight six, petrol, carburettor, 12 valves
**Drivetrain:** Front-engine RWD
**Structure:** Separate chassis
**Transmission:** Four-speed manual with overdrive
**Weight:** 1882kg

### PRICE GUIDE

**Launch price:** £27,000
**Excellent:** £50,000
**Good:** £35,500
**Average:** £23,500
**Project:** £13,000

## PANTHER Rio

The Rio was always destined to fail. It was a good idea by Robert Jankel to launch a car that offered top-drawer luxury in a more manageable package, but the execution was spoiled by the fact that the Rio too closely resembled the car it was based on – the Triumph Dolomite. The body was re-skinned in hand-beaten aluminium, and that pushed the price up to such a degree that for the cost of a Rio Especiale you could buy a Jaguar XJ12 and still have money left over. A surprising number of the original 35 still survive, and good ones are quite sought-after.

### SPECIFICATIONS

**Years produced:** 1975-1977 (35 in total)
**Performance:** 0-60mph: 9.6sec
Top speed: 115mph
**Power & torque:** 127bhp/124lb ft
**Engine:** Normally aspirated 1998cc four cylinder, petrol, carburettor, 16 valves
**Drivetrain:** Front-engine RWD
**Structure:** Monocoque
**Transmission:** Four-speed manual with overdrive
**Weight:** 1100kg

### PRICE GUIDE

**Launch price:** £5377
**Excellent:** £7500
**Good:** £5000
**Average:** £3000
**Project:** £1500

## PANTHER Lima/Kallista

With its Morganesque looks and Vauxhall mechanicals (Magnum 2279cc slant-four engine), the Lima was significantly cheaper than its stablemates. The glassfibre body surrounding MG Midget doors and windscreen made it lightweight and well-behaved, while 108bhp meant decent performance, more so with 1978's turbo version. After financial problems forced Robert Jankel to sell up, Panther ended up in the hands of a Korean conglomerate and the Lima was relaunched as the Kallista, with an aluminium body and Ford engines, including a V6.

### SPECIFICATIONS

**Years produced:** 1976-1990 (897 in total)
**Performance:** 0-60mph: 7.5sec (Kallista)
Top speed: 120mph
**Power & torque:** 150bhp/159lb ft
**Engine:** Normally aspirated 2792cc V6, petrol, fuel injection, 12 valves
**Drivetrain:** Front-engine RWD
**Structure:** Separate chassis
**Transmission:** Five-speed manual
**Weight:** 965kg

### PRICE GUIDE (Kallista in brackets)

**Launch price:** £8997
**Excellent:** £9000 (£12,000)
**Good:** £7500 (£9000)
**Average:** £4850 (£6500)
**Project:** £1600 (£1900)

# PEERLESS/WARWICK

NOT TO BE confused with the top-class pre-war US manufacturer, Peerless came about in 1957 when the Slough-based garage bearing the name was bought by Warwickshire hotelier James Byrnes in order to build a Triumph TR3-based GT car. The car was originally being built in London by John Gordon to an attractive design by Bernie Rodger – and Peerless's premises were perfect for assembling it. Sadly, the project failed to gain much momentum and the company failed in 1960. Rodger resurrected production in Berkshire – and it was here that an additional 20-50 cars, with minor changes, were assembled under the Warwick name. Production finally ended in 1962.

## PEERLESS/WARWICK GT

As an affordable GT the Peerless certainly met all of its targets. The mixture of spaceframe structure with de Dion rear axle and Triumph TR3 running gear was a wonderful set of ingredients with which to build a new sporting car. But like all such ventures, finance was always the issue, and no matter how promising the car looks and drives, if the company can't afford to develop it properly then it's likely to fail. This was the case with the Peerless GT and, although it deserved to do well, it lasted a mere three years and only 325 were made. Values rising.

**SPECIFICATIONS**

| | |
|---|---|
| **Years produced:** | 1958-1962 (325 in total) |
| **Performance:** | 0-60mph: 12.8sec<br>Top speed: 103mph |
| **Power & torque:** | 100bhp/N/A |
| **Engine:** | Normally aspirated 1991cc four cylinder, petrol, carburettor, 8 valves |
| **Drivetrain:** | Front-engine RWD |
| **Structure:** | Spaceframe/glassfibre body |
| **Transmission:** | Four-speed manual with overdrive |
| **Weight:** | 953kg |

**PRICE GUIDE**

| | |
|---|---|
| **Launch price:** | £1498 |
| **Excellent:** | £20,000 |
| **Good:** | £15,000 |
| **Average:** | £9500 |
| **Project:** | £4000 |

# PEUGEOT

ONE OF THE world's oldest motor manufacturers: Armand Peugeot started with a steam car in 1889 and began dropping Daimler petrol engines into his chassis two years later. Racers grew Peugeot's pre-war reputation, along with some adventurous styling, but after World War Two the company's success was largely built on not being Citroën. By sticking to tried and trusted engineering, its more conservative cars were less troublesome, gaining loyal owners. Ironically, this led to Peugeot taking over Citroën in the 1970s, along with Chrysler Europe. The result was some financial strains, from which the group was rescued by the runaway success of the Peugeot 205.

## PEUGEOT 203

The 203 was Peugeot's first all-new post-war design and, although it lacked the 202's idiosyncratic styling, it was a groundbreaking technical package. The alloy-headed engine and hydraulic brakes were novelties, while the independent front suspension and rack-and-pinion steering set the company's products on their way towards a reputation for dynamic pleasure. Like all Peugeots for the next 30 years, the 203 enjoyed a long production run – 12 years – and ended up donating much of its platform to its replacement. Values holding firm.

**SPECIFICATIONS**

| | |
|---|---|
| **Years produced:** | 1948-1963 (686,628 in total) |
| **Performance:** | 0-60mph: N/A<br>Top speed: 71mph |
| **Power & torque:** | 45bhp/59lb ft |
| **Engine:** | Normally aspirated 1290cc four cylinder, petrol, carburettor, 8 valves |
| **Drivetrain:** | Front-engine RWD |
| **Structure:** | Monocoque |
| **Transmission:** | Four-speed manual |
| **Weight:** | 930kg |

**PRICE GUIDE**

| | |
|---|---|
| **Launch price:** | £986 |
| **Excellent:** | £8500 |
| **Good:** | £5250 |
| **Average:** | £2200 |
| **Project:** | £1400 |

## PEUGEOT 403 saloon

Peugeot's 1950s saloon was little more than a reskin of the 203. I was larger, more luxurious, and ended up being sold alongside the older car as an upgrade for an increasingly affluent market. Pinin Farina assisted with the styling – leading to an enduring partnership – but with full-width bodywork and neat detailing, it struck a chord with the French middle classes. The popular Familiale version was innovative for offering three rows of seats, while the diesel version sold well in its home country as a rugged and reliable workhorse.

**SPECIFICATIONS**

| | |
|---|---|
| **Years produced:** | 1955-1966 (1,214,121 in total) |
| **Performance:** | 0-60mph: 24.0sec<br>Top speed: 76mph |
| **Power & torque:** | 58bhp/74lb ft |
| **Engine:** | Normally aspirated 1468cc four cylinder, petrol, carburettor, 8 valves |
| **Drivetrain:** | Front-engine RWD |
| **Structure:** | Monocoque |
| **Transmission:** | Four-speed manual |
| **Weight:** | 1300kg |

**PRICE GUIDE**

| | |
|---|---|
| **Launch price:** | £1129 |
| **Excellent:** | £5500 |
| **Good:** | £3000 |
| **Average:** | £1750 |
| **Project:** | £800 |

## PEUGEOT
## 403 Décapotable

Pininfarina's reputation for producing stylish convertibles and coupés from family cars arguably started here. The 403 Décapotable, to give the car its correct title, shared its wheelbase and running gear with the saloon, but looked a lot more appealing. First shown at the 1956 Paris Salon, it instantly found favour with buyers. The high-compression 1.5-litre engine gave reasonable performance, but this car was always about touring. Values are firm, despite (or maybe due to) reruns of TV's *Columbo* – and the appearances of his unkempt example.

### SPECIFICATIONS

**Years produced:** 1957-1961 (2050 in total)
**Performance:** 0-60mph: 24.0sec
Top speed: 76mph
**Power & torque:** 58bhp/74lb ft
**Engine:** Normally aspirated 1468cc four cylinder, petrol, carburettor, 8 valves
**Drivetrain:** Front-engine RWD
**Structure:** Monocoque
**Transmission:** Four-speed manual
**Weight:** 1300kg

### PRICE GUIDE

**Launch price:** N/A in UK
**Excellent:** £16,000
**Good:** £12,000
**Average:** £7000
**Project:** £3000

## PEUGEOT
## 404 saloon

At first glance, the Farina-styled 404 looks like a copy of BMC's and Fiat's contemporary mid-sized saloons, with 403 underpinnings. In reality, the 404 was a nicer car to drive and offered a clever design as, although it looked like a grand saloon, it was actually smaller than the car it was supposed to replace. In the end – and in good Peugeot tradition – the 404 and 403 ran concurrently for three years, before the newer car went on to sell millions worldwide. You still see a few in north Africa, thanks to solid build and simple DIY maintenance.

### SPECIFICATIONS

**Years produced:** 1960-1978 (1,847,568 in total)
**Performance:** 0-60mph: 18.1sec
Top speed: 82mph
**Power & torque:** 68bhp/94lb ft
**Engine:** Normally aspirated 1618cc four cylinder, petrol, carburettor, 8 valves
**Drivetrain:** Front-engine RWD
**Structure:** Monocoque
**Transmission:** Four-speed manual
**Weight:** 1070kg

### PRICE GUIDE

**Launch price:** £1297
**Excellent:** £6500
**Good:** £4400
**Average:** £2600
**Project:** £1200

## PEUGEOT
## 404 Cabriolet

Unlike some Peugeot/Pininfarina collaborations, the 404 Cabriolet and its coupé brother were a full rebody of an existing platform, sharing no external panels. Given such a free rein, it's not surprising that the Italian styling house came up with such a stunning car – and one that, thanks to its scarcity, is in strong demand today. Its wheelbase is shared with the saloon, so the 404 Cabriolet is a full four-seater. Power came from Peugeot's well-regarded 1.6-litre engine, and delivered excellent performance, especially in fuel injection form.

### SPECIFICATIONS

**Years produced:** 1962-1968 (3728 in total)
**Performance:** 0-60mph: 12.2sec
Top speed: 92mph
**Power & torque:** 79bhp/100lb ft
**Engine:** Normally aspirated 1608cc four cylinder, petrol, carburettor, 8 valves
**Drivetrain:** Front-engine RWD
**Structure:** Monocoque
**Transmission:** Four-speed manual
**Weight:** 1030kg

### PRICE GUIDE

**Launch price:** £2367
**Excellent:** £27,000
**Good:** £22,500
**Average:** £15,000
**Project:** £8000

## PEUGEOT
## 204/304 Coupé

Whereas the Peugeot 204 and 304 have been unfairly consigned to the ranks to the automotive hall of mediocrity, the coupé versions were a further Pininfarina masterclass in product maximisation. The pretty three-door fastback used a hatchback rear door, and comfortable seating for two adults plus two children, despite a wheelbase shortened by 12 inches. Surviving examples are good to drive and are likely to have been well cared for, but take care when looking for corrosion – it can strike anywhere, and often does.

### SPECIFICATIONS

**Years produced:** 1965-1979 (42,756 in total)
**Performance:** 0-60mph: 18.2sec
Top speed: 91mph
**Power & torque:** 53bhp/82lb ft
**Engine:** Normally aspirated 1130cc four cylinder, petrol, carburettor, 8 valves
**Drivetrain:** Front-engine FWD
**Structure:** Monocoque
**Transmission:** Four-speed manual
**Weight:** 838kg

### PRICE GUIDE

**Launch price:** £983
**Excellent:** £6000
**Good:** £4250
**Average:** £2500
**Project:** £1200

## PEUGEOT
## 204/304 saloon

The 204 and 304 were a leap forward for Peugeot as they were the firm's first cars with transverse engines driving the front wheels. With independent rear suspension, servo-assisted brakes and anti-roll bars, the modern layout delivered surefooted handling and a comfortable ride, in true French style. The 304 was similar in concept, but with a longer front and rear, plusher interiors and a more powerful 1.3-litre engine, making it more satisfying to own. Downsides were few, but lack of glamour was one, corrosion another.

### SPECIFICATIONS

**Years produced:** 1965-1980 (1,387,473/1,334,309 in total)
**Performance:** 0-60mph: 16.2sec
Top speed: 90mph
**Power & torque:** 55bhp/66lb ft
**Engine:** Normally aspirated 1130cc four cylinder, petrol, carburettor, 8 valves
**Drivetrain:** Front-engine FWD
**Structure:** Monocoque
**Transmission:** Four-speed manual
**Weight:** 880kg

### PRICE GUIDE

**Launch price:** £992
**Excellent:** £3500
**Good:** £2200
**Average:** £1200
**Project:** £600

# PEUGEOT
## 204/304 Cabriolet

Unlike the Coupé, the 204 Cabriolet was never officially sold in the UK, making buying one a lengthy and involved process. But there are a few in the UK, which have quite a cult following thanks to head-turning looks and neat dynamics. The later 304, however, *did* make it here, and examples aren't too difficult to track down. The newer car's uprated engine delivered sprightly performance and excellent economy, and if you're looking for an easy-to-drive, appealing ragtop that's just a little bit different, this could be ideal for you.

**SPECIFICATIONS**

**Years produced:** 1967-1975 (18,181 in total)
**Performance:** 0-60mph: 14.5sec
Top speed: 96mph
**Power & torque:** 74bhp/80lb ft
**Engine:** Normally aspirated 1288cc four cylinder, petrol, carburettor, 8 valves
**Drivetrain:** Front-engine FWD
**Structure:** Monocoque
**Transmission:** Four-speed manual
**Weight:** 895kg

**PRICE GUIDE**

**Launch price:** £1496
**Excellent:** £8000
**Good:** £5250
**Average:** £3200
**Project:** £1200

# PEUGEOT
## 504 saloon

Launched at the Paris Motor Show in 1968, the 504 saloon was Peugeot's flagship until the full-sized 604 arrive seven years later. The engine was mounted longitudinally, driving the rear wheels, and the combination of soft spring and damper rates with massive suspension travel made the 504 an excellent performer on poor (or non-existent) road surfaces. European 504s are a rare sight today, but they are still one of the most common forms of transport throughout Africa, due to their simplicity and reliability.

**SPECIFICATIONS**

**Years produced:** 1968-1983 (3,073,185 in total)
**Performance:** 0-60mph: 12.7sec
Top speed: 106mph
**Power & torque:** 93bhp/124lb ft
**Engine:** Normally aspirated 1971cc four cylinder, petrol, carburettor, 8 valves
**Drivetrain:** Front-engine RWD
**Structure:** Monocoque
**Transmission:** Four-speed manual
**Weight:** 1175kg

**PRICE GUIDE**

**Launch price:** £1500
**Excellent:** £3250
**Good:** £2500
**Average:** £1300
**Project:** £600

# PEUGEOT
## 504 Cabriolet

With a production run of just over 8000, and with a reputation for rust, it's a surprise just how many 504 Cabriolets have survived. Yet with such graceful styling and superb road manners, it became a classic the moment it left the production line. With fuel injection as standard, the open 504 proved fast and effective, especially the final five-speed version. It was never directly replaced, Peugeot subsequently concentrating instead on smaller cabrios. V6 models are more sought-after than four-cylinder cars, but all are on the up.

**SPECIFICATIONS**

**Years produced:** 1968-1983
**Performance:** 0-60mph: 9.9sec
Top speed: 105mph
**Power & torque:** 110bhp/131lb ft
**Engine:** Normally aspirated 1971cc four cylinder, petrol, carburettor, 8 valves
**Drivetrain:** Front-engine RWD
**Structure:** Monocoque
**Transmission:** Four-speed manual
**Weight:** 1165kg

**PRICE GUIDE (V6 in brackets)**

**Launch price:** £1594
**Excellent:** £21,000 (£23,000)
**Good:** £15,000 (£17,500)
**Average:** £8500 (£9500)
**Project:** £3200 (£3650)

# PEUGEOT
## 504 Coupé

The same Peugeot/Pininfarina recipe used for the 404 Coupé was used once again for its replacement, which hit the road in 1969. With an all-new body on a slightly shortened 504 platform, the 504 Coupé combined the excellent road manners of this no-nonsense French saloon with a healthy dose of glamorous Italian style. The top-of-the-range version was treated to a Peugeot-Renault-Volvo V6 (which also saw service in the DeLorean DMC-12 and Alpine A310 V6) in 1974, creating easily the company's most desirable car of the period.

**SPECIFICATIONS**

**Years produced:** 1969-1983 (26,477 in total)
**Performance:** 0-60mph: 10.5sec
Top speed: 111mph
**Power & torque:** 110bhp/131lb ft
**Engine:** Normally aspirated 1971cc four cylinder, petrol, carburettor, 8 valves
**Drivetrain:** Front-engine RWD
**Structure:** Monocoque
**Transmission:** Four-speed manual
**Weight:** 1165kg

**PRICE GUIDE (V6 in brackets)**

**Launch price:** £2609
**Excellent:** £7000 (£13,000)
**Good:** £5500 (£10,500)
**Average:** £3000 (£6500)
**Project:** £1200 (£2750)

# PEUGEOT
## 604

To look at the 604 today, it's hard to believe that so few were sold in the UK. Its Pininfarina styling appeared to all intents and purposes like a four-door Fiat 130 coupé, while the ride quality was typically Gallic-soft. Yet fail it did – and that means they're almost impossible to find now. All petrol cars were powered by the PRV V6, either carb-fed or fuel injection, and were quick, if thirsty. The 604 was the first Peugeot to be powered by a turbodiesel (80bhp from 2.3 litres still resulted in lethargic performance), but the choice of the range is a five-speed fuel-injection Ti model.

**SPECIFICATIONS**

**Years produced:** 1975-1986 (240,100 in total)
**Performance:** 0-60mph: 9.9sec
Top speed: 120mph
**Power & torque:** 144bhp/159lb ft
**Engine:** Normally aspirated 2664cc V6, petrol, fuel injection, 12 valves
**Drivetrain:** Front-engine RWD
**Structure:** Monocoque
**Transmission:** Five-speed manual
**Weight:** 1475kg

**PRICE GUIDE**

**Launch price:** £4600
**Excellent:** £3500
**Good:** £2750
**Average:** £1500
**Project:** £750

## PEUGEOT 305

The 305 was another intelligent if understated Peugeot that was more accomplished to drive than its boring styling would have you believe. A long wheelbase and relaxed springing meant it was a cruiser, not a sprinter, but it could hustle along deceptively quickly. The 1.3- and 1.5-litre engines were lively and economical, too. Like fine wine, the 305 improved with age – the estate version was huge, and the facelifted models of 1983 were boosted by 205GTi power. All that held it back in the UK was the lack of a hatchback and definable image.

### SPECIFICATIONS (305 SR)

| | |
|---|---|
| **Years produced:** | 1977-1988 (1,740,300 in total) |
| **Performance:** | 0-60mph: 13.2sec<br>Top speed: 97mph |
| **Power & torque:** | 73bhp/86lb ft |
| **Engine:** | Normally aspirated 1472cc four cylinder, petrol, carburettor, 8 valves |
| **Drivetrain:** | Front-engine FWD |
| **Structure:** | Monocoque |
| **Transmission:** | Four-speed manual |
| **Weight:** | 940kg |

### PRICE GUIDE

| | |
|---|---|
| **Launch price:** | £2999 |
| **Excellent:** | £1250 |
| **Good:** | £800 |
| **Average:** | £500 |
| **Project:** | £300 |

## PEUGEOT 505

Like the 504 it replaced, the 505 was one of the most rugged saloons on the planet. The main reason for the car's success in developing countries was its ability to handle rutted and very poor road surfaces; the 505 was produced in Nigeria until 2006, although European production stopped in 1993 when it was made redundant by the smaller 405 and the larger 605. The diesels were always the biggest sellers, and if you opted for the estate it could be fitted with a third row of seats, giving room for eight. GTi version, with 130bhp, is developing a following.

### SPECIFICATIONS

| | |
|---|---|
| **Years produced:** | 1979-1993 |
| **Performance:** | 0-60mph: 10.0sec (GTi)<br>Top speed: 114mph |
| **Power & torque:** | 130bhp/136lb ft |
| **Engine:** | Normally aspirated 2165cc four cylinder, petrol, electronic fuel injection, 8 valves |
| **Drivetrain:** | Front-engine RWD |
| **Structure:** | Monocoque |
| **Transmission:** | Five-speed manual |
| **Weight:** | 1235kg |

### PRICE GUIDE (GTi in brackets)

| | |
|---|---|
| **Launch price:** | £9595 |
| **Excellent:** | £1750 (£3750) |
| **Good:** | £1400 (£2400) |
| **Average:** | £900 (£1500) |
| **Project:** | £300 (£800) |

## PEUGEOT 205/205 GTi

All 205s are good to drive and painless to own, but the GTi is in another league. In the eyes of many, it's simply the most fun 'hot hatch' ever. Initially available only with a 1.6-litre engine, in 1986 the 205 received the 130bhp 1905cc unit, instantly giving more rapid acceleration and a higher top speed – although it is still debated which is the better car. The 1.6 is slightly lighter and better balanced, yet the 1.9 is ultimately faster. Tendency for lift-off oversteer largely tamed by modern tyres. CTi cabrio is fun, too. Low-milers routinely fetch £15-20k.

### SPECIFICATIONS

| | |
|---|---|
| **Years produced:** | 1984-1994 |
| **Performance:** | 0-60mph: 8.6sec (GTi 1.6)<br>Top speed: 120mph |
| **Power & torque:** | 105bhp/99lb ft |
| **Engine:** | Normally aspirated 1580cc four cylinder, petrol, electronic fuel injection, 8 valves |
| **Drivetrain:** | Front-engine FWD |
| **Structure:** | Monocoque |
| **Transmission:** | Five-speed manual |
| **Weight:** | 850kg |

### PRICE GUIDE (GTi) (1.9 in brackets)

| | |
|---|---|
| **Launch price:** | £6295 |
| **Excellent:** | £9000 (£12,000) |
| **Good:** | £5000 (£6000) |
| **Average:** | £2250 (£2750) |
| **Project:** | £1250 (£1500) |

## PEUGEOT 205 T16

The Group B era is still regarded as the finest ever seen in rallying – and with the supercars built within a loose framework of rules, the manufacturers came up with some interesting packages. Peugeot's mid-engined 205 T16 was the most successful of all, winning two Group B championships, and proving convincingly that Audi's quattro was beatable. The road version was detuned to 200bhp (compared with 450bhp for the rally car), and wasn't much quicker than the GTi 1.9 in a straight line, but it was more than capable in the bends. Values have been levelling-off recently.

### SPECIFICATIONS

| | |
|---|---|
| **Years produced:** | 1985 (200 in total) |
| **Performance:** | 0-60mph: 7.7sec<br>Top speed: 135mph |
| **Power & torque:** | 200bhp/190lb ft |
| **Engine:** | Turbocharged 1775cc four cylinder, petrol, electronic fuel injection, 16v |
| **Drivetrain:** | Mid-engine AWD |
| **Structure:** | Spaceframe |
| **Transmission:** | Five-speed manual |
| **Weight:** | 1150kg |

### PRICE GUIDE

| | |
|---|---|
| **Launch price:** | N/A in UK |
| **Excellent:** | £140,000 |
| **Good:** | £100,000 |
| **Average:** | £75,000 |
| **Project:** | N/A |

## PEUGEOT 309 GTi

Big brother to the 205 GTi but, unlike the 205, it was available only as a 1.9. It featured uprated front and rear suspension, 15in Speedline alloy wheels and a subtle bodykit. Peugeot offered the car solely in three-door form to begin with, though it was later sold in five-door form. In France, the exciting XU9J4 – Mi16 – engine was also offered, packing 160bhp. Though always living in the shadow of its darling smaller brother, in fact the 309 GTi was arguably the better all-round car. 'Goodwood' special edition can be worth up to £6000.

### SPECIFICATIONS

| | |
|---|---|
| **Years produced:** | 1987-1993 |
| **Performance:** | 0-60mph: 8.7sec<br>Top speed: 119mph |
| **Power & torque:** | 130bhp/119lb ft |
| **Engine:** | Normally aspirated 1905cc four cylinder, petrol, electronic fuel injection, 8 valves |
| **Drivetrain:** | Front-engine FWD |
| **Structure:** | Monocoque |
| **Transmission:** | Five-speed manual |
| **Weight:** | 930kg |

### PRICE GUIDE

| | |
|---|---|
| **Launch price:** | £9595 |
| **Excellent:** | £4700 |
| **Good:** | £2850 |
| **Average:** | £1900 |
| **Project:** | £1000 |

## PEUGEOT
## 405 Mi16

The Mi16 is one of the best performance saloons of the '80s. Its XU9J4 engine was a volume-produced, normally aspirated development of the T16 unit used in Peugeot's Group B 205 rally car. Sadly, due to cost, PSA switched to a cast-iron block in the post-1992 models. This heavier engine was also less powerful, but torque was up, giving the model a more useable powerband. The 405 possessed the best suspension and steering set-up in its class, and remains a legend to this day – although finding one in good condition is becoming a challenge. Values are rising.

**SPECIFICATIONS**

**Years produced:** 1987-1995
**Performance:** 0-60mph: 8.2sec
Top speed: 138mph
**Power & torque:** 160bhp/131lb ft
**Engine:** Normally aspirated 1905cc four cylinder, petrol, electronic fuel injection, 16v
**Drivetrain:** Front-engine FWD
**Structure:** Monocoque
**Transmission:** Five-speed manual
**Weight:** 1108kg

**PRICE GUIDE**

**Launch price:** £14,995
**Excellent:** £4500
**Good:** £2700
**Average:** £1750
**Project:** £1200

## PEUGEOT
## 106 Rallye

Despite its tiny dimensions, the Rallye is a proper homologation special. The original 1.3-litre version, launched in 1993, was designed for sub-1400cc international rallying. Around 1000 road versions came to the UK. The S2 version, launched in 1997, had a torquier 1.6-litre engine. Just 500 came to the UK between 1997 and 1998, although production continued in France until 2000. Later 16-valve versions weren't officially imported, but some early UK cars have been converted to 16v engines. Whichever you choose, it's an engaging and cherishable hatch with a sporting edge.

**SPECIFICATIONS (S1)**

**Years produced:** 1993-1996
**Performance:** 0-60mph: 9.3sec
Top speed: 118mph
**Power & torque:** 100bhp/80lb ft
**Engine:** Normally aspirated 1294cc four cylinder, petrol, electronic fuel injection, 8 valves
**Drivetrain:** Front-engine FWD
**Structure:** Monocoque
**Transmission:** Five-speed manual
**Weight:** 826kg

**PRICE GUIDE (add 50% for S1 cars)**

**Launch price:** £9585
**Excellent:** £4500
**Good:** £2750
**Average:** £1850
**Project:** £1200

## PEUGEOT
## 306 GTI 6/Rallye

Although many idolise the 205 GTI, in many ways the 306 GTI 6 perfected Peugeot's hot hatch formula. Passive rear-steer helped make it handle more progressively, while the high-revving engine and close-ratio six-speed 'box were a joy. Add 30% for phase 1 cars. Stripped-out Rallye (only available in phase 2 form) is mechanically identical and weighs marginally less, but low build numbers and cool stripes equal stronger prices. Numbers still thinning due to easy 205 GTI engine transplants but values are edging up.

**SPECIFICATIONS**

**Years produced:** 1996-2001
**Performance:** 0-60mph: 7.8sec
Top speed: 130mph
**Power & torque:** 167bhp/145lb ft
**Engine:** Normally aspirated 1998cc four cylinder, petrol, electronic fuel injection, 16v
**Drivetrain:** Front-engine FWD
**Structure:** Monocoque
**Transmission:** Six-speed manual
**Weight:** 1163kg (Rallye)

**PRICE GUIDE (Rallye in brackets)**

**Launch price:** £16,675
**Excellent:** £3250 (£5000)
**Good:** £1900 (£2700)
**Average:** £1250 (£1700)
**Project:** £500 (£1000)

# PIPER

PIPER WAS FOUNDED in 1966 by Kent-based garage owner George Henrotte, who had been running the Gemini F3 team. After finding that motor racing was a quick way of spending large amounts of cash you don't have, he returned to running the family garage – with ambitions to build his own sports car. He and designer Tony Hilder joined forces and produced the GTT (see overleaf). The Piper name came from the Scottish piper logo of Henrotte's Campbell's Garage. The company moved premises and underwent a number of management changes, ending up trading under the name of Emmbrook Engineering, based in Lincolnshire. After 150 GTT/P2s, the operation faded away.

## PIPER
## GTT/P2

The Piper GTT was designed by Tony Hilder for racer and garage owner George Henrotte. It caused a sensation when it was launched, and went into production initially in kit form, using Ford and Triumph suspension parts, with the engine choice being down to the owner – usually a 1.6-litre Ford crossflow with a modified head. The P2, introduced in 1971, was a more refined version. Initially the car sold well, and quite a few survive today, but Piper fell foul of tax changes and the 1973 oil crisis, and the company folded in 1975. Good ones are prized now.

**SPECIFICATIONS**

**Years produced:** 1968-1975 (150 in total)
**Performance:** 0-60mph: N/A
Top speed: 115mph
**Power & torque:** 84bhp/92lb ft
**Engine:** Normally aspirated 1599cc four cylinder, petrol, carburettor, 8 valves
**Drivetrain:** Front-engine RWD
**Structure:** Spaceframe/glassfibre body
**Transmission:** Four-speed manual
**Weight:** N/A

**PRICE GUIDE**

**Launch price:** £1435
**Excellent:** £25,000
**Good:** £16,000
**Average:** £11,500
**Project:** £7500

# PLYMOUTH

PLYMOUTH AUTOMOBILE was launched in 1928 as Chrysler's entry-level marque – and to take the fight to Chevrolet and Ford. Plymouths were originally sold within Chrysler dealerships, but, as the marque developed, it was increasingly marketed as a separate entity with its own showrooms. It would go through many changes and probably had its best years in the 1960s, with the Barracuda and Fury – which would lead to the legendary Road Runner. Its most prolific year was 1973, with 973,000 cars built, but, by the late-1970s, Plymouths were merely badge-engineered versions of Chrysler, Dodge or Mitsubishi models, and in 2001 the marque was dropped.

## PLYMOUTH Barracuda

Neatly-styled Valiant saloon-based fastback that gave Plymouth an effective Mustang rival in the pony car market. Pioneering features were the wraparound back window and folding rear seats, but it wasn't until 1967, and the arrival of the reskinned and higher-powered versions, that the model really started to forge a path in the marketplace. Fastback was more popular than the notchback, yet all proved to be effective players in the musclecar market once the 330bhp 383ci small-block V8 was installed. Ignore the six-cylinder if it's old-school fun you're after.

**SPECIFICATIONS**

**Years produced:** 1964-1969 (c267,000 in total)
**Performance:** 0-60mph: 7.5sec
Top speed: 120mph
**Power & torque:** 180bhp/260lb ft
**Engine:** Normally aspirated 4496cc V8, petrol, carburettor, 16 valves
**Drivetrain:** Front-engine RWD
**Structure:** Monocoque
**Transmission:** Four-speed manual
**Weight:** 1475kg

**PRICE GUIDE**

**Launch price:** N/A in UK
**Excellent:** £25,000
**Good:** £18,000
**Average:** £12,000
**Project:** £7500

## PLYMOUTH Road Runner/Superbird

Among the most famous of all the American musclecars, the Road Runner and Superbird earned their legendary status even as they rolled off the production line. The Road Runner was fully backed by Warner Bros and even boasted a 'beep beep' horn, while the astonishing-looking Superbird had genuine NASCAR heritage. The Superbird was as fast as it looked – its 440ci Hemi developed 425bhp and, if you were brave, a top speed that approached 150mph. However, less-than-inspiring brakes and soft suspension mean this is not a car for British B-roads.

**SPECIFICATIONS (RR 440)**

**Years produced:** 1968-1970 (125,904/1920 in total)
**Performance:** 0-60mph: 7.5sec
Top speed: 120mph
**Power & torque:** 330bhp/410lb ft
**Engine:** Normally aspirated 7206cc V8, petrol, carburettor, 16 valves
**Drivetrain:** Front-engine RWD
**Structure:** Monocoque
**Transmission:** Four-speed manual
**Weight:** 1700kg

**PRICE GUIDE (Superbird in brackets)**

| | | |
|---|---|---|
| **Launch price:** | N/A in UK | |
| **Excellent:** | £40,000 | (£150,000) |
| **Good:** | £27,500 | (£100,000) |
| **Average:** | £17,000 | (£70,000) |
| **Project:** | £9000 | (£40,000) |

# PONTIAC

PONTIAC

PONTIAC ACTUALLY started out as a sister marque for General Motors' Oakland in 1926. But the upstart soon overtook the original in terms of popularity and, by 1933, replaced it entirely. It then became Chevrolet's partner marque, proving especially popular in Central and South America. Pontiac ended up being marketed as the performance division of General Motors, and gained popularity with the Firebird and Trans-Am models. But from those heady years, it slowly began to fade. In April 2009, and as a result of the group's financial problems, GM announced that it was winding-up Pontiac. The last Pontiacs were built in late 2009, and the last of those sold in 2010.

## PONTIAC Firebird/Trans Am

The Firebird was sister car to the popular Chevrolet Camaro, and arrived in 1967 to pick up a healthy slice of the US market. The 1970 models sported the more familiar shape that became something of an icon internationally thanks to countless film appearances, such as in *Smokey and the Bandit*. V8 models were the ones to have, especially in Trans Am form, though as the '70s progressed, power outputs fell. However, by the turn of the 1980s, turbocharged versions restored some of the lost oomph. Early cars and more powerful special editions can be worth £40k-plus.

**SPECIFICATIONS (1976 Trans-Am)**

**Years produced:** 1970-1981 (1,061,719 in total)
**Performance:** 0-60mph: 8.4sec
Top speed: 120mph
**Power & torque:** 200bhp/330lb ft
**Engine:** Normally aspirated 7463cc V8, petrol, carburettor, 16 valves
**Drivetrain:** Front-engine RWD
**Structure:** Monocoque
**Transmission:** Four-speed manual
**Weight:** 1701kg

**PRICE GUIDE**

**Launch price:** £8014
**Excellent:** £20,000
**Good:** £13,500
**Average:** £6000
**Project:** £3000

## PONTIAC
### Fiero

Gutless Fiat X1/9 pastiche or advanced sports car? The Pontiac Fiero was certainly a brave experiment by General Motors that deserved to sell better than it did. It was the first American mid-engined car and the first two-seater Pontiac in over 50 years. But the sporty-looking car didn't go as well as it looked, and the 2.5-litre Iron Duke engine did its best impression of a boat anchor, although the later V6 was a massive improvement. The experiment failed – relatively speaking – and production lasted only five years and one facelift, with over 350,000 examples built.

**SPECIFICATIONS**

**Years produced:** 1984-1988 (355,000 in total)
**Performance:** 0-60mph: 12.0sec
Top speed: 97mph
**Power & torque:** 92bhp/134lb ft
**Engine:** Normally aspirated 2471cc four cylinder, petrol, fuel injection, 8 valves
**Drivetrain:** Mid-engine RWD
**Structure:** Plastic body panels over steel frame
**Transmission:** Five-speed manual
**Weight:** 1136kg

**PRICE GUIDE**

**Launch price:** N/A in UK
**Excellent:** £4000
**Good:** £2300
**Average:** £1200
**Project:** £350

# PORSCHE

FERDINAND PORSCHE would become famous for the inventing the VW Beetle but, after WW2, his son Ferry joined him in the motoring hall of fame as the man behind the first Porsche sports cars. As they were based on Volkswagens, they had air-cooled rear engines. The 356 was followed by the iconic 911 in 1964, a long-lived legend among performance cars. Later vehicles, such as the 924, 928 and 944, adopted water-cooled front-mounted engines. Porsche today is one of the most successful of all sports car manufacturers, thanks to endless 911 evolution and a willingness to innovate and diversify, with a range of saloons and SUVs as well as the mid-engined Boxster/Cayman.

## PORSCHE
### 356

The first 49 Porsches were built in Gmünd, Austria, and while historically important, these underpowered 1100cc cars are best left to collectors. Production proper started at Stuttgart in 1950, with steel bodies. The first year it was all coupés, then cabrios arrived in 1951. Two-piece screens were fitted until April 1952, after which they were one-piece with a bend in the centre. Engine options soon grew to 1100, 1300 and 1500. The 'S' version of the latter rated up to 72bhp, but was complex and short-lived. Exceptional cars can fetch £200k-plus, says specialist Paul Stephens.

**SPECIFICATIONS**

**Years produced:** 1949-1955 (7627 in total)
**Performance:** 0-60mph: 17sec
Top speed: 87mph
**Power & torque:** 55bhp/78lb ft
**Engine:** Normally aspirated 1488cc four cylinder, petrol, carburettor, 8 valves
**Drivetrain:** Rear-engine RWD
**Structure:** Monocoque
**Transmission:** Four-speed manual
**Weight:** 830kg

**PRICE GUIDE**

**Launch price:** £1971
**Excellent:** £170,000+
**Good:** £150,000
**Average:** £85,000
**Project:** £70,000

## PORSCHE
### 356 A/B/C

With updated looks, more civilised interiors and engines increased to 1600cc (although there were still 1300s for some markets), Porsche's 356 hit the big time and sales more than doubled. 'Super' means more power, along with higher prices. The 356B added twin-choke carbs and some styling revisions, the most obvious being larger bumpers and front bonnet chrome. The 356C brought disc brakes, while the lowest-powered engine was now 75bhp, up from the 60bhp of the 356B 'Normal'. Right-hand drive adds a significant premium. Soft-tops boost prices by c30%.

**SPECIFICATIONS**

**Years produced:** 1955-1965 (68,676 in total)
**Performance:** 0-60mph: 14.1sec
Top speed: 102mph
**Power & torque:** 60bhp/81lb ft
**Engine:** Normally aspirated 1582cc flat four, petrol, carburettor, 8 valves
**Drivetrain:** Rear-engine RWD
**Structure:** Monocoque
**Transmission:** Four-speed manual
**Weight:** 815kg

**PRICE GUIDE (A/B/C)**

**Launch price:** £1891
**Excellent:** £175,000/£135,000/£115,000
**Good:** £150,000/£95,000/£75,000
**Average:** £75,000/£65,000/£55,000
**Project:** £50,000/£25,000/£25,000

## PORSCHE
### 356 Carrera

With four gear-driven camshafts, dry-sump lubrication, twin sparkplugs and even roller-bearing crankshafts on early models, 356 Carreras are not for the faint of heart or wallet. Incredibly rare, built with competition in mind, and producing most of their power high up in the rev range, they don't even make good road cars. However, none of that detracts from their collectibility. Even the 1500 versions will hit 120mph. The ultimate is the 2.0-litre Carrera 2, 126 of which were built starting in 1962. Be aware that this was a year before the arrival of disc brakes for these cars.

**SPECIFICATIONS**

**Years produced:** 1955-1962
**Performance:** 0-60mph: N/A
Top speed: 125mph
**Power & torque:** 100bhp/88lb ft
**Engine:** Normally aspirated 1498cc flat four, petrol, carburettor, 8 valves
**Drivetrain:** Rear-engine RWD
**Structure:** Monocoque
**Transmission:** Four-speed manual
**Weight:** 850kg

**PRICE GUIDE**

**Launch price:** N/A
**Excellent:** £500,000+
**Good:** £330,000
**Average:** £195,000
**Project:** N/A

## PORSCHE
## 356 Speedster

Like their badges, Speedsters have become gold-plated cult classics. Much imitated by replica builders, the originals are high on many collectors' wanted lists and have been known to change hands for six-figure sums, despite nearly 3000 having been built. Most are in America, which is no surprise as that's the market they were built for. They were actually made at the suggestion of USA Porsche importer Max Hoffman, who wanted a stripped-down version of the 356 that could be driven during the week and raced at weekends, much like later Porsche Club Sports.

### SPECIFICATIONS

| | |
|---|---|
| **Years produced:** | 1956-1956 (2910 in total) |
| **Performance:** | 0-60mph: 14.5sec<br>Top speed: 108mph |
| **Power & torque:** | 75bhp/82lb ft |
| **Engine:** | Normally aspirated 1582cc flat four, petrol, carburettor, 8 valves |
| **Drivetrain:** | Rear-engine RWD |
| **Structure:** | Monocoque |
| **Transmission:** | Four-speed manual |
| **Weight:** | 760kg |

### PRICE GUIDE

| | |
|---|---|
| **Launch price:** | £1971 |
| **Excellent:** | £350,000+ |
| **Good:** | £250,000 |
| **Average:** | £175,000 |
| **Project:** | £120,000 |

## PORSCHE
## 911 2.0

As the 911 legend has grown, so desire for the pure, original, short-wheelbase version of Porsche's concept has increased with it. The flat-six engine is only a 2.0-litre, but it's a highly tuned one wearing overhead cams and two triple-choke carbs. Within months of production starting, a 911 came fifth in the Monte Carlo Rally, and these models are still successfully campaigned in historic events. Very early cars ('64) can attract a large premium. Semi-convertible targa version was launched in early 1967, but despite its relative rarity no price premium is attached.

### SPECIFICATIONS

| | |
|---|---|
| **Years produced:** | 1964-1967 (10,753 in total) |
| **Performance:** | 0-60mph: 8.3sec<br>Top speed: 131mph |
| **Power & torque:** | 130bhp/128lb ft |
| **Engine:** | Normally aspirated 1991cc flat six, petrol, carburettor, 12 valves |
| **Drivetrain:** | Rear-engine RWD |
| **Structure:** | Monocoque |
| **Transmission:** | Five-speed manual |
| **Weight:** | 1080kg |

### PRICE GUIDE (1966/65/64)

| | |
|---|---|
| **Launch price:** | £2996 |
| **Excellent:** | £125,000/£250,000/£400,000 |
| **Good:** | £100,000/£150,000/£200,000 |
| **Average:** | £50,000/£100,000/£150,000 |
| **Project:** | £30,000/£75,000/£100,000 |

## PORSCHE
## 912/912E

Keen to retain a slightly more affordable model in the range after production of the 356 ended, Porsche installed a 90bhp version of that car's four-cylinder engine in a 911 bodyshell, mostly featuring the optional five-speed gearbox. That sounds potentially disappointing, but with low weight and better handling than the 911, this is a fine sports car in its own right. It briefly reappeared in 1975 as the 912E, fitted with a 2.0-litre VW engine. Sold only in the US, this filled the gap between the outgoing 914-4 and Porsche's new 924. Prices are slightly lower for the VW version.

### SPECIFICATIONS

| | |
|---|---|
| **Years produced:** | 1965-1969 + 1975 (30,300/2092 in total) |
| **Performance:** | 0-60mph: 11.9sec<br>Top speed: 119mph |
| **Power & torque:** | 90bhp/90lb ft |
| **Engine:** | Normally aspirated 1599cc flat four, petrol, carburettor, 8 valves |
| **Drivetrain:** | Rear-engine RWD |
| **Structure:** | Monocoque |
| **Transmission:** | Four-speed manual |
| **Weight:** | 970kg |

### PRICE GUIDE (912E in brackets)

| | |
|---|---|
| **Launch price:** | £2467 |
| **Excellent:** | £50,000 (£35,000) |
| **Good:** | £35,000 (£25,000) |
| **Average:** | £25,000 (£20,000) |
| **Project:** | £12,000 (£10,000) |

## PORSCHE
## 911S

This is the hot one, ready for competition use thanks to forged alloy pistons and wheels, plus vented disc brakes. Output started at 160bhp, then grew to 170bhp with the 1969 introduction of fuel injection. The following year there was another 10bhp to go with the new 2.2-litre engine capacity, and then we finally arrived at 190bhp with the 2.4-litre 'S' for the 1972 model year. As with the slightly less sporty 911s, both coupé and targa versions were offered. Pre-1968 short-wheelbase cars are the most sought after by collectors, but the later ones are most fun.

### SPECIFICATIONS

| | |
|---|---|
| **Years produced:** | 1966-1973 (14,841 in total) |
| **Performance:** | 0-60mph: 8.0sec<br>Top speed: 137mph |
| **Power & torque:** | 170bhp/135lb ft |
| **Engine:** | Normally aspirated 1991cc flat six, petrol, carburettor, 12 valves |
| **Drivetrain:** | Rear-engine RWD |
| **Structure:** | Monocoque |
| **Transmission:** | Five-speed manual |
| **Weight:** | 995kg |

### PRICE GUIDE

| | |
|---|---|
| **Launch price:** | £3556 |
| **Excellent:** | £170,000+ |
| **Good:** | £135,000 |
| **Average:** | £80,000 |
| **Project:** | £35,000 |

## PORSCHE
## 911 L/T/E

From 1967 the regular 130bhp 911 was renamed 911L. And along with the sporty 'S' version, there was also an entry-level model with 110bhp called the 911T (for Touring). As standard it had a four- rather than five-speed 'box. From August 1968 the B-series body arrived with a longer wheelbase to improve handling. At this point the 911L gained fuel injection and wider wheels and became the 140bhp 911E. For 1970 there was 2.2 litres and 125/155bhp (T/E). Two years later, capacity grew to 2.4 litres and power to 130/165bhp. The E commands a premium, as does right-hand drive.

### SPECIFICATIONS (2.2 T)

| | |
|---|---|
| **Years produced:** | 1967-1973 (62,402 in total) |
| **Performance:** | 0-60mph: 7.9sec<br>Top speed: 140mph |
| **Power & torque:** | 125bhp/131lb ft |
| **Engine:** | Normally aspirated 2195cc six cylinder, petrol, carburettor, 12 valves |
| **Drivetrain:** | Rear-engine RWD |
| **Structure:** | Monocoque |
| **Transmission:** | Five-speed manual |
| **Weight:** | 1020kg |

### PRICE GUIDE

| | |
|---|---|
| **Launch price:** | £2745 |
| **Excellent:** | £85,000 (add up to £30k for the E) |
| **Good:** | £65,000 |
| **Average:** | £45,000 |
| **Project:** | £25,000 |

## VW-PORSCHE
### 914

This was developed in conjunction with Volkswagen to replace the four-cylinder 912. The engine was borrowed from the VW 411, and it being mid- rather than rear-mounted gave the 914 excellent handling, aided by the all-independent suspension. The targa roof clipped neatly out of the way to the underside of the bootlid when you wanted fresh air. From 1973 the 1.7 was joined by a 2.0, and the following year the smaller engine capacity was raised to 1.8 litres. Low power and that VW connection haven't helped popularity, and values seem to be stuck in a bit of a rut.

**SPECIFICATIONS**

**Years produced:** 1969-1975 (115,646 in total)
**Performance:** 0-60mph: 14.8sec
Top speed: 110mph
**Power & torque:** 80bhp/97lb ft
**Engine:** Normally aspirated 1679cc flat four, petrol, carburettor, 8 valves
**Drivetrain:** Mid-engine RWD
**Structure:** Monocoque
**Transmission:** Five-speed manual
**Weight:** 898kg

**PRICE GUIDE**

**Launch price:** £2261
**Excellent:** £20,000
**Good:** £15,000
**Average:** £8000
**Project:** £5000

## VW-PORSCHE
### 914-6

The main difference between this and the 914-4 was its six-cylinder engine. In fact, it was the 2.0-litre flat-six from the 911, although, to avoid too much in-house competition, the lowest-spec version from the 911T was used, with only 110bhp. With just 3360 sold compared to over 115,000 of the 914-4, these models are also rare, though the low numbers had something to do with the price hike over their kid brother that made them 50% more expensive than an E-type. Most went to America and none was built with right-hand drive. Values holding, according to Paul Stephens.

**SPECIFICATIONS**

**Years produced:** 1969-1972 (3360 in total)
**Performance:** 0-60mph: 8.3sec
Top speed: 125mph
**Power & torque:** 110bhp/115lb ft
**Engine:** Normally aspirated 1991cc flat six, petrol, carburettor, 12 valves
**Drivetrain:** Mid-engine RWD
**Structure:** Monocoque
**Transmission:** Five-speed manual
**Weight:** 1020kg

**PRICE GUIDE**

**Launch price:** £3475
**Excellent:** £60,000
**Good:** £25,000
**Average:** £15,000
**Project:** £10,000

## PORSCHE
### 911 Carrera 2.7 RSL/RST

To qualify Porsche for sub-3.0-litre GT racing, the firm had to build 500 of this homologation special – but it wound up selling three times that. The basis was the 2.4S, with a big-bore engine and every conceivable lightening method, from thinner steel panels to throwing away the rear seats. Really a race car you could drive on the road, it was the first 911 to have wider rear wheels than fronts; 200 RSLs were built and 1380 of the slightly softer RST (T for Touring). Again, right-hand drive commands a premium, and naturally the racer is much more valuable (add another 50% to our prices).

**SPECIFICATIONS**

**Years produced:** 1972-1973 (200/1380 in total)
**Performance:** 0-60mph: 6.1sec
Top speed: 149mph
**Power & torque:** 210bhp/188lb ft
**Engine:** Normally aspirated 2687cc flat six, petrol, carburettor, 12 valves
**Drivetrain:** Rear-engine RWD
**Structure:** Monocoque
**Transmission:** Five-speed manual
**Weight:** 975kg

**PRICE GUIDE (Lightweight in brackets)**

**Launch price:** £5825
**Excellent:** £500,000+ (£600,000+)
**Good:** £400,000
**Average:** £250,000
**Project:** £200,000

## PORSCHE
### 911 2.7/Carrera

The 1973 911 represented a change in 911 ethos, with less frantic engines producing lower power but more torque. K-Jetronic injection made it more economical, while the body and wheels were wider. It heralded the start of impact bumpers as well. From August 1975 bodies were galvanised, so subsequent cars were very resistant to rust. 'Carrera' was no longer just for racing specials but denoted the range-topper, so they came fully loaded. The 911S had an extra 25bhp and as much as 50% higher values in today's market. Right-hand drive again attracts a big premium.

**SPECIFICATIONS**

**Years produced:** 1973-1977
**Performance:** 0-60mph: 8.5sec
Top speed: 130mph
**Power & torque:** 148bhp/173lb ft
**Engine:** Normally aspirated 2687cc flat six, petrol, fuel injection, 12 valves
**Drivetrain:** Rear-engine RWD
**Structure:** Monocoque
**Transmission:** Five-speed manual
**Weight:** 1161kg

**PRICE GUIDE (Carrera in brackets)**

**Launch price:** £6249
**Excellent:** £60,000 (£150,000)
**Good:** £35,000 (£100,000)
**Average:** £20,000 (£75,000)
**Project:** £15,000 (£50,000)

## PORSCHE
### 911 Turbo

Not just a fast car but an instant pin-up beloved of teenage boys. Having experimented with 'chargers in racing, Porsche saw turbos as the way forward for performance road cars, and the 911 Turbo was the result. With fat arches to cover the 7in and 8in rims, plus that enormous rear spoiler, the model was a trend-setter. But what really mattered was how well it went; it boasted incredible acceleration, superb grip and handling, plus enormous brakes to match. The gearbox was only a four-speed, but such was the torque that this didn't hold it back. Values stable.

**SPECIFICATIONS**

**Years produced:** 1975-1977 (2873 in total)
**Performance:** 0-60mph: 6.1sec
Top speed: 153mph
**Power & torque:** 260bhp/253lb ft
**Engine:** Turbocharged 2994cc flat six, petrol, mechanical fuel injection, 12 valves
**Drivetrain:** Rear-engine RWD
**Structure:** Monocoque
**Transmission:** Four-speed manual
**Weight:** 1195kg

**PRICE GUIDE**

**Launch price:** £14,749
**Excellent:** £200,000+
**Good:** £100,000
**Average:** £75,000
**Project:** £50,000

# PORSCHE 924

The firm was commissioned by Volkswagen to develop the 924 project – originally conceived as a replacement for the VW-Porsche 914 – but bought the rights to the car when VW changed tack. The 924 used an Audi engine with Porsche cylinder head, and the gearbox was in unit with the rear axle to provide near-perfect 53/47 weight distribution. Build quality was to the usual superb Porsche standards, and the 924 was an instant sales success, quickly tripling the company's factory output. Best ones to buy are from 1981-on, as whole bodies were hot zinc dipped. Very best are now £20k-plus.

**SPECIFICATIONS**

**Years produced:** 1976-1988 (122,304 in total)
**Performance:** 0-60mph: 9.5sec
Top speed: 124mph
**Power & torque:** 125bhp/122lb ft
**Engine:** Normally aspirated 1984cc four cylinder, petrol, electronic fuel injection, 8 valves
**Drivetrain:** Front-engine RWD
**Structure:** Monocoque
**Transmission:** Five-speed manual
**Weight:** 1080kg

**PRICE GUIDE**

**Launch price:** £6999
**Excellent:** £20,000
**Good:** £9500
**Average:** £2500
**Project:** £1000

# PORSCHE 911 SC 3.0

Gaining the 3.0-litre block from the previous season's Turbo, the SC became Porsche's sole non-turbo 911, although a lengthy options list ensured enough variety. Cast alloy 15in wheels were standard, with forged 16in rims a cost extra, as was the Sport option of a Turbo rear spoiler. Power grew quickly from the original 180bhp to 188bhp for the 1980 model year, and 204bhp just 12 months later, although with improvements in economy. From 1982 the coupé and targa were joined by a cabriolet, Porsche's first full convertible since the 356. These command only a small premium.

**SPECIFICATIONS**

**Years produced:** 1978-1983
**Performance:** 0-60mph: 6.5sec
Top speed: 141mph
**Power & torque:** 180bhp/196lb ft
**Engine:** Normally aspirated 2994cc flat six, petrol, fuel injection, 12 valves
**Drivetrain:** Rear-engine RWD
**Structure:** Monocoque
**Transmission:** Five-speed manual
**Weight:** 1160kg

**PRICE GUIDE**

**Launch price:** £14,100
**Excellent:** £50,000+
**Good:** £35,000
**Average:** £25,000
**Project:** £15,000

# PORSCHE 928

Porsche's intended replacement for the 911 may not have achieved that goal, but it wasn't for lack of performance or technological wizardry. An alloy V8 was attached to a rear-mounted gearbox, and the galvanised body had aluminium doors and bonnet plus body-coloured plastic bumpers – pretty radical for its time. The original 4.5 litres was upped to 4.7 for the 300bhp 928S in 1982. Two years later, that was raised to 310bhp in the S2. Other models followed, all varying the basic recipe. By the run-out GTS model, capacity had grown to 5.4 litres and power to 345bhp.

**SPECIFICATIONS**

**Years produced:** 1978-1995 (61,056 in total)
**Performance:** 0-60mph: 6.2sec
Top speed: 158mph
**Power & torque:** 240bhp/257lb ft
**Engine:** Normally aspirated 4474cc V8, petrol, electronic fuel injection, 16 valves
**Drivetrain:** Front-engine RWD
**Structure:** Monocoque
**Transmission:** Five-speed manual/four-speed auto
**Weight:** 1468kg

**PRICE GUIDE (928/S)**

**Launch price:** £19,499
**Excellent:** £15,000/£30,000
**Good:** £10,000/£20,000
**Average:** £7000/£12,000
**Project:** £1500/£3000

# PORSCHE 911 Turbo 3.3

The short run of original Turbos was merely a warm up for the main act. With an extra 300cc and an intercooler built into the rear spoiler, the 911 Turbo's power jumped another 40bhp, putting it firmly in the supercar class. This also helped mask the previous model's turbo lag – to some extent. Further development to the suspension reduced the car's power-off tail-wagging tendencies. A five-speed gearbox finally arrived for the 1989 model year, these cars attracting as much as a £50k premium today. LE and other special variants are also worth more.

**SPECIFICATIONS**

**Years produced:** 1978-1989 (21,589 in total)
**Performance:** 0-60mph: 5.4sec
Top speed: 162mph
**Power & torque:** 300bhp/304lb ft
**Engine:** Turbocharged 2994cc flat six, petrol, electronic fuel injection, 12 valves
**Drivetrain:** Rear-engine RWD
**Structure:** Monocoque
**Transmission:** Four/five-speed manual
**Weight:** 1195kg

**PRICE GUIDE**

**Launch price:** £23,200
**Excellent:** £110,000+
**Good:** £75,000
**Average:** £45,000
**Project:** £30,000

# PORSCHE 924 Turbo

With Porsche at the forefront of turbo technology, and the 924 chassis ripe for exploitation with more power, this car's development was inevitable. Thanks to a 45bhp power boost that raised top speed by nearly 20mph, a five-speed gearbox and uprated suspension, the 924 Turbo was very well received and more than 12,000 were sold in five years. Easily identified by the row of four extra air intakes in the nose and NACA duct in the bonnet, they also got five- rather than four-bolt wheels and were the first 924s to use the discreet but effective rear lip spoiler. Best now fetch £30k.

**SPECIFICATIONS**

**Years produced:** 1979-1983 (12,385 in total)
**Performance:** 0-60mph: 7.7sec
Top speed: 142mph
**Power & torque:** 174bhp/184lb ft
**Engine:** Turbocharged 1984cc four cylinder, petrol, carburettor, 8 valves
**Drivetrain:** Front-engine RWD
**Structure:** Monocoque
**Transmission:** Five-speed manual
**Weight:** 1180kg

**PRICE GUIDE**

**Launch price:** £13,629
**Excellent:** £23,000
**Good:** £15,000
**Average:** £7000
**Project:** £3000

## PORSCHE
# 924 Carrera GT

This car took inspiration from prototype ideas for the forthcoming 944, which you can see in the distinctive bloated arches fabricated from flexible polyurethane. Porsche built 406 Carrera GTs to homologate the 924 for racing at Le Mans. Based on the 924 Turbo, its engine output was boosted by 40bhp thanks to an intercooler and internal modifications. The Carrera GT was sold only in red, silver or black, and just 75 right-hand-drive examples were built for the UK market. No surprise, then, that values have been flying in recent years as its rarity and abilities are recognised.

**SPECIFICATIONS**

**Years produced:** 1980-1981 (406 in total)
**Performance:** 0-60mph: 6.5sec
Top speed: 150mph
**Power & torque:** 207bhp/207lb ft
**Engine:** Turbocharged 1984cc four cylinder, petrol, electronic fuel injection, 8 valves
**Drivetrain:** Front-engine RWD
**Structure:** Monocoque
**Transmission:** Five-speed manual
**Weight:** 1179kg

**PRICE GUIDE**

**Launch price:** £19,210
**Excellent:** £100,000
**Good:** £75,000
**Average:** £55,000
**Project:** N/A

## PORSCHE
# 944/944S

It shared the 924's profile, but the flared arches, wider wheels and deeper front valance turned the older car's delicacy into aggression. A 2.5-litre engine that was effectively half a 928's V8 delivered on the promise. Handling and grip were assured, and the 944 went on to outsell even the 924. Interior revisions in 1985 gave it an oval dashboard. For 1988-'89 engine capacity rose to 2.7 litres, adding low-down pulling power. 'S' version had new 16v cylinder head that boosted power to 188bhp; pay slightly more for these but beware added expense if they go wrong.

**SPECIFICATIONS**

**Years produced:** 1982-1989 (117,790 in total)
**Performance:** 0-60mph: 8.3sec (944)
Top speed: 138mph
**Power & torque:** 163bhp/151lb ft
**Engine:** Normally aspirated 2479cc four cylinder, petrol, electronic fuel injection, 8 valves
**Drivetrain:** Front-engine RWD
**Structure:** Monocoque
**Transmission:** Five-speed manual
**Weight:** 1180kg

**PRICE GUIDE (Coupé)**

**Launch price:** £12,999
**Excellent:** £20,000
**Good:** £12,000
**Average:** £7000
**Project:** £1500

## PORSCHE
# 911 Carrera 3.2

Last of the second-generation 911s and still a viable daily driver. The choice of coupé, targa and cabriolet (today worth a substantial premium) continued from the SC, though all now had 150mph capability. Even better, fuel economy was further improved and beat virtually everything else in this class. Could be had with either the standard or wider Turbo-look body, complete with spoilers and wide wheels. Despite more drag and an extra 50kg blunting performance, this was the bigger seller. The 1987 model year got an improved five-speed gearbox. Exceptional cars can make £100k.

**SPECIFICATIONS**

**Years produced:** 1984-1989 (76,473 in total)
**Performance:** 0-60mph: 5.6sec
Top speed: 153mph
**Power & torque:** 231bhp/209lb ft
**Engine:** Normally aspirated 3164cc flat six, petrol, fuel injection, 12 valves
**Drivetrain:** Rear-engine RWD
**Structure:** Monocoque
**Transmission:** Five-speed manual
**Weight:** 1210kg

**PRICE GUIDE**

**Launch price:** £23,366
**Excellent:** £75,000
**Good:** £50,000
**Average:** £35,000
**Project:** £20,000

## PORSCHE
# 924S

A master of subtlety, the 924S appealed to those who were fond of the 'Q-car' concept – there was a lot more going on than the body led you to believe. Aside from the Teledial wheels and extra 'S' on the badge at the rear, nothing gave the game away that this was virtually a 944 wearing the 924's slimline body. However, it was all there, from the new 2.5-litre overhead-cam engine to the four-wheel vented disc brakes. Engine power was raised from 150bhp to 160bhp for the 1988 model year, at the same time as Le Mans editions in black or white were offered with lowered, uprated suspension.

**SPECIFICATIONS**

**Years produced:** 1985-1988 (16,282 in total)
**Performance:** 0-60mph: 7.9sec
Top speed: 136mph
**Power & torque:** 160bhp/155lb ft
**Engine:** Normally aspirated 2479cc four cylinder, petrol, electronic fuel injection, 8 valves
**Drivetrain:** Front-engine RWD
**Structure:** Monocoque
**Transmission:** Five-speed manual
**Weight:** 1164kg

**PRICE GUIDE**

**Launch price:** £21,031
**Excellent:** £20,000
**Good:** £12,000
**Average:** £6000
**Project:** £1500

## PORSCHE
# 944 Turbo

As with the 924, a turbo version was always on the cards. Here the 2.5-litre engine was boosted by nearly 60bhp, with clutch and gearbox uprated to suit. The chassis got thicker anti-roll bars and four-pot brake calipers, and a smoother nose and larger rear spoiler distinguished the model from the 944. For 1988 only, the SE was offered with 250bhp thanks to a larger turbo. The transmission was further beefed up, a limited-slip diff was standard, brakes were uprated and Koni dampers fitted. For 1989-91, SE spec was adopted for the normal 944 Turbo. Very best can fetch £35k.

**SPECIFICATIONS**

**Years produced:** 1985-1991 (25,245 in total)
**Performance:** 0-60mph: 5.9sec
Top speed: 152mph
**Power & torque:** 220bhp/243lb ft
**Engine:** Turbocharged 2479cc four cylinder, petrol, electronic fuel injection, 8 valves
**Drivetrain:** Front-engine RWD
**Structure:** Monocoque
**Transmission:** Five-speed manual
**Weight:** 1280kg

**PRICE GUIDE**

**Launch price:** £25,311
**Excellent:** £30,000
**Good:** £16,000
**Average:** £10,000
**Project:** £2500

## PORSCHE
### 911 Carrera Club Sport

Harking back to the 1973 Carrera 2.7s, this was a stripped-out version of the 3.2, made some 100kg lighter than most by stripping out non-essentials like the rear seats, sound deadening, electric windows and even the passenger's sun visor. The engine put out the same power but revved more freely, and 300rpm higher, thanks to lightweight inlet valves and a reprogrammed ECU. Just 340 examples were made, and only 53 of those were in right-hand-drive form for the UK market. Available here in any colour you liked – as long as that was Grand Prix White with red wheel centres.

**SPECIFICATIONS**

**Years produced:** 1987-1988 (340 in total)
**Performance:** 0-60mph: 5.6sec
Top speed: 149mph
**Power & torque:** 210bhp/188lb ft
**Engine:** Normally aspirated 3164cc flat six, petrol, fuel injection, 12 valves
**Drivetrain:** Rear-engine RWD
**Structure:** Monocoque
**Transmission:** Five-speed manual
**Weight:** 960kg

**PRICE GUIDE**

**Launch price:** £34,389
**Excellent:** £165,000
**Good:** £125,000
**Average:** £100,000
**Project:** £50,000

## PORSCHE
### 959

Conceived for the short-lived Group B motor sport formula, the 959 was Porsche's riposte to the Ferrari 288GTO. Unlike the boisterous but largely conventional Italian supercar, this was a technological tour de force with permanent four-wheel drive and twin sequential turbos. This set-up went some way to eliminating the dreaded lag which typified forced induction when the car was originally dreamed up in the early 1980s. It never really fulfilled its potential in motor sport, but established itself as a thoroughbred '80s supercar. All were left-hand drive. Values have levelled off.

**SPECIFICATIONS**

**Years produced:** 1987-1988 (345 in total)
**Performance:** 0-60mph: 3.6sec
Top speed: 197mph
**Power & torque:** 444bhp/369lb ft
**Engine:** Turbocharged 2849cc flat six, petrol, electronic fuel injection, 24 valves
**Drivetrain:** Rear-engine AWD
**Structure:** Monocoque
**Transmission:** Six-speed manual
**Weight:** 1350kg

**PRICE GUIDE**

**Launch price:** £155,266
**Excellent:** £900,000+
**Good:** £650,000
**Average:** £N/A
**Project:** £N/A

## PORSCHE
### 928 S4

For the S4, the 928's V8 grew to 5.0 litres and now had twin-cam heads with four valves per cylinder. Power went up to 316bhp, but the big difference was low-end pulling power. The popular auto gearbox option was now a Mercedes four-speeder. An 'intelligent' cooling system featured louvres in the air intake that were computer-controlled to change their angle in line with coolant temperature; when closed, they made the car more aerodynamic. Smoother front and rear bumpers lifted the looks. GT and GTS with 345bhp attract a premium. Exceptional examples can fetch up to £45k.

**SPECIFICATIONS**

**Years produced:** 1987-1991 (16,213 in total)
**Performance:** 0-60mph: 5.7sec
Top speed: 170mph
**Power & torque:** 316bhp/317lb ft
**Engine:** Normally aspirated 4957cc V8, petrol, electronic fuel injection, 32 valves
**Drivetrain:** Front-engine RWD
**Structure:** Monocoque
**Transmission:** Five-speed manual
**Weight:** 1538kg

**PRICE GUIDE**

**Launch price:** £30,679
**Excellent:** £30,000
**Good:** £15,000
**Average:** £8000
**Project:** £3000

## PORSCHE
### 911 Speedster

A retro-styled homage to the 1950s 356 Speedster. Strictly a two-seater, it was all 3.2 Carrera underneath, but above the waist there was a shorter windscreen and a hard tonneau that gave the back a bit of a hump. Weather protection was on the rudimentary side, but that didn't matter too much as the bulk of the 2000 or so built headed to America. As the car became an instant collectable, few Speedsters were pressed into daily service, so good ones aren't hard to find. Interestingly, the narrow-bodied variant attracts a premium today. Very best can be £200k.

**SPECIFICATIONS**

**Years produced:** 1988-1989 (2100 in total)
**Performance:** 0-60mph: 6.1sec
Top speed: 152mph
**Power & torque:** 228bhp/210lb ft
**Engine:** Normally aspirated 3164cc flat six, petrol, fuel injection, 12 valves
**Drivetrain:** Rear-engine RWD
**Structure:** Monocoque
**Transmission:** Five-speed manual
**Weight:** 1140kg

**PRICE GUIDE**

**Launch price:** £57,852
**Excellent:** £175,000
**Good:** £125,000
**Average:** £75,000
**Project:** £N/A

## PORSCHE
### 911 Carrera 2/4 (964)

Beneath that familiar body was an entirely new structure designed to meet ever-changing technical and safety requirements. With integrated bumpers and other tricks, the body was a great deal more aerodynamic, too. There was also the gadget man's dream of a rear spoiler that popped up automatically at 50mph. The 964 was launched first in 4wd Carrera 4 form, but the rear-drive C2 released a year later was by far the best-selling version (and is worth slightly more today). As with past 911s, the range featured coupé, targa and cabriolet. Turbo can be £175k-plus.

**SPECIFICATIONS**

**Years produced:** 1989-1993 (55,682 in total)
**Performance:** 0-60mph: 5.7sec
Top speed: 162mph
**Power & torque:** 246bhp/229lb ft
**Engine:** Normally aspirated 3600cc flat six, petrol, fuel injection, 12 valves
**Drivetrain:** Rear-engine, RWD
**Structure:** Monocoque
**Transmission:** Five-speed manual/automatic
**Weight:** 1385kg

**PRICE GUIDE (C4 in brackets)**

**Launch price:** £53,995
**Excellent:** £70,000 (£60,000)
**Good:** £45,000 (£40,000)
**Average:** £32,000 (£32,000)
**Project:** £20,000 (£20,000)

## PORSCHE
## 911 Carrera RS (964)

Harking back to the classic, motorsport-inspired RS models of the early 1970s, in 1992 Porsche produced a super-lightweight, rear-drive-only version of the 964. Power was up to 260bhp, there was a close-ratio gearbox, and the suspension was both lower and stiffer. The body was lighter and stiffer, the stripped-out interior featured race-style bucket seats and even the window glass was thinner, adding to an overall weight saving of around 150kg. Great to drive, and very collectable. Pay a premium for right-hand drive.

**SPECIFICATIONS**

**Years produced:** 1992-1994 (2282 built)
**Performance:** 0-60mph: 5.4sec
Top speed: 162mph
**Power & torque:** 260bhp/230lb ft
**Engine:** Normally aspirated 3600cc flat six, petrol, fuel injection, 12 valves
**Drivetrain:** Rear-engine, RWD
**Structure:** Monocoque
**Transmission:** Five-speed manual
**Weight:** 1230kg

**PRICE GUIDE**

**Launch price:** £69,000
**Excellent:** £195,000
**Good:** £150,000
**Average:** £125,000
**Project:** £80,000

## PORSCHE
## 944 S2

For the 1989 model year the S2 replaced both standard and 'S' spec 944s. A new aluminium cylinder block employing Formula One technology allowed a capacity increase to 3.0 litres. Power was up 21bhp on the 944S, and torque took an even bigger jump. Externally the S2 adopted the lower-drag nose and tail panels from the Turbo, which along with a taller final drive ratio helped the car to hit almost 150mph. The Turbo's braking system was also adopted. For the final two years of production a cabriolet version was offered as well – add 25% for those.

**SPECIFICATIONS**

**Years produced:** 1989-1992 (19,120 in total)
**Performance:** 0-60mph: 6.7sec
Top speed: 149mph
**Power & torque:** 208bhp/207lb ft
**Engine:** Normally aspirated 2990cc four cylinder, petrol, electronic fuel injection, 16 valves
**Drivetrain:** Front-engine RWD
**Structure:** Monocoque
**Transmission:** Five-speed manual
**Weight:** 1320kg

**PRICE GUIDE**

**Launch price:** £31,304
**Excellent:** £25,000
**Good:** £15,000
**Average:** £7500
**Project:** £3000

## PORSCHE
## 911 Carrera 2/4 (993)

The mid-90s 993 was the final generation of air-cooled 911s, and as such will always have a special place in the affections of Porsche enthusiasts. The bodywork had a number of new panels and the overall look was much smoother and more integrated. The biggest change under the skin was new multi-link rear suspension, which made the handling more secure while improving ride quality. Manuals are worth up to £7k more than Tiptronics, while wide-bodied cars are more sought-after. Turbo and particularly the Turbo S variants are stupidly fast and fetch £125k-£175k.

**SPECIFICATIONS (C2)**

**Years produced:** 1993-1998 (68,029 of all variants)
**Performance:** 0-60mph: 5.3sec
Top speed: 166mph
**Power & torque:** 268bhp/243lb ft
**Engine:** Normally aspirated 3600cc flat six, petrol, fuel injection, 12 valves
**Drivetrain:** Rear-engine, RWD
**Structure:** Monocoque
**Transmission:** Six-speed manual/four-speed automatic
**Weight:** 1370kg

**PRICE GUIDE (C4 in brackets)**

**Launch price:** £46,378
**Excellent:** £70,000 (£60,000)
**Good:** £50,000 (£50,000)
**Average:** £35,000 (£35,000)
**Project:** £20,000 (£20,000)

## PORSCHE
## 968/968 Club Sport

The 968 was an updated 944 with the styling flavour of big-brother 928 and peak power from the 3-litre four, now with variable valve timing, increased to 240bhp. It was quick and competent but just a little bit dull. The real excitment came with the Club Sport model launched in 1993. Lowered, lightened, and stripped of luxury equipment (as well as the rear seats), the CS was one of the finest driver's cars of its era. The very best now fetch £35k-plus. A 'Sport' model was also sold in the UK – a CS with the rear seats and some of the goodies refitted! Also pay a premium for cabrios.

**SPECIFICATIONS (CS)**

**Years produced:** 1992-1995 (12,831 of all variants)
**Performance:** 0-60mph: 6.1sec
Top speed: 149mph
**Power & torque:** 240bhp/225lb ft
**Engine:** Normally aspirated 2990cc four cylinder, petrol, electronic fuel injection, 16v
**Drivetrain:** Front-engine RWD
**Structure:** Monocoque
**Transmission:** Five-speed manual
**Weight:** 1320kg

**PRICE GUIDE (Club Sport in brackets)**

**Launch price:** £28,975
**Excellent:** £20,000 (£35,000)
**Good:** £15,000 (£25,000)
**Average:** £10,000 (£20,000)
**Project:** £6000 (£10,000)

## PORSCHE
## Boxster/Boxster S (986)

Its name a mash-up of 'boxer' (referring to the flat-six engine) and 'roadster', the Boxster was Porsche's first mid-engined car since the 914 of the early '70s. As then, the Boxster gave Porsche an 'entry level' model below the 911. In fact much of the hardware – and indeed the whole front of the car – was shared with the 996-gen 911. The basic model had a 204bhp 2.5-litre engine (2.7 from 2000); more exciting for enthusiasts was the S launched in late 1999, a capacity increase to 3.2 litres seeing peak power climb to 252bhp.

**SPECIFICATIONS**

**Years produced:** 1996-2004 (c160,000 in total)
**Performance:** 0-60mph: 5.9sec (S)
Top speed: 161mph
**Power & torque:** 252bhp/225lb ft
**Engine:** Normally aspirated 3179cc flat six, petrol, fuel injection, 24 valves
**Drivetrain:** Mid-engine, RWD
**Structure:** Monocoque
**Transmission:** Six-speed manual
**Weight:** 1295kg

**PRICE GUIDE**

**Launch price:** £42,161
**Excellent:** £10,000
**Good:** £6000
**Average:** £5000
**Project:** £2000

## PORSCHE
## 911 Carrera 2/4 (996)

The 996-gen 911 saw major departures from the classic 911 formula. For one, the bodyshell was completely new (even the 993 had parts of its structure that could be traced back to 1963). And two, the flat-six was now water-cooled. Diehards weren't keen – they also railed at the component-sharing with the Boxster – but today the 996 is a great budget route into Porsche ownership. The C4S is particularly well-regarded (and now £30k+) while the 420bhp, 190mph Turbo and even faster Turbo S models are supercar bargains.

**SPECIFICATIONS**

**Years produced:** 1998-2004 (c175,000 in total)
**Performance:** 0-60mph: 4.6sec (C2)
Top speed: 173mph
**Power & torque:** 300bhp/258lb ft
**Engine:** Normally aspirated 3397cc flat six, petrol, fuel injection, 24 valves
**Drivetrain:** Rear-engine, RWD
**Structure:** Monocoque
**Transmission:** Six-speed manual/five-speed automatic
**Weight:** 1320kg

**PRICE GUIDE (Turbo in brackets)**

**Launch price:** £55,950 (£86,000)
**Excellent:** £25,000 (£55,000)
**Good:** £17,000 (£40,000)
**Average:** £12,000 (£25,000)
**Project:** £6000 (N/A)

## PORSCHE
## 911 GT3 (996)

Not only one of the great Porsches, but simply one of the finest driver's cars of all time. The GT3 was very different to any other 996-gen 911, from its dry-sump 'Mezger' flat-six, derived from the unit used in the 962 race-car, to its lower, stiffer suspension, huge cross-drilled discs, extreme aero and stripped-out interior. A 'Clubsport' package included race-style buckets and a half roll-cage. Second-generation model from 2003 saw power go up to 376bhp. More extreme GT3 RS from late 2003 is currently £100k-plus.

**SPECIFICATIONS**

**Years produced:** 1999-2005 (1868 in total)
**Performance:** 0-60mph: 4.5sec
Top speed: 187mph
**Power & torque:** 355bhp/258lb ft
**Engine:** Normally aspirated 3600cc flat six, petrol, fuel injection, 24 valves
**Drivetrain:** Rear-engine, RWD
**Structure:** Monocoque
**Transmission:** Six-speed manual
**Weight:** 1350kg

**PRICE GUIDE (first-gen)**

**Launch price:** £76,500
**Excellent:** £70,000
**Good:** £60,000
**Average:** £50,000
**Project:** N/A

## PORSCHE
## Carrera GT

Porsche put everything it knew into the Carrera GT, its first out-and-out supercar since the 959. The chassis had its origins in a prototype Le Mans racer, while the 5.7-litre V10 engine was a development of a Porsche-designed F1 unit. The structure was a pure carbonfibre monocoque and there was race-style inboard suspension and carbon-ceramic brakes. The CGT gained a reputation for knife-edge handling at the limits of grip, though this has been largely tamed by fitting more modern tyres. Prized by collectors and only likely to appreciate in the long term.

**SPECIFICATIONS**

**Years produced:** 2004-2006 (1270 in total)
**Performance:** 0-60mph: 3.9sec
Top speed: 205mph
**Power & torque:** 604bhp/435lb ft
**Engine:** Normally aspirated 5733cc V10, petrol, electronic injection, 40 valves
**Drivetrain:** Mid-engine RWD
**Structure:** Carbonfibre tub and body
**Transmission:** Six-speed manual
**Weight:** 1380kg

**PRICE GUIDE**

**Launch price:** £323,000
**Excellent:** £600,000
**Good:** £500,000
**Average:** £400,000
**Project:** N/A

## PORSCHE
## 911 Carrera (997)

An evolution of the 996-generation 911, the 997 had a more classical Porsche look, ditching the 'fried egg' headlights of its predecessor. The basic 3.6 Carrera had slightly more power at 321bhp while the 3.8-litre 'S' had 350bhp, dropping the 0-60mph time to 4.8sec and lifting the top speed to 182mph. All-wheel-drive Carrera 4 and 4S models came in 2005, with the Turbo and GT3 following in late 2006. There was also a GT2 – essentially a Turbo but rear-drive only. 2009 saw a facelift, a revised engine with direct injection, and the option of PDK dual-clutch transmisison.

**SPECIFICATIONS**

**Years produced:** 2004-2012
**Performance:** 0-60mph: 5.0sec (Carrera 2)
Top speed: 177mph
**Power & torque:** 321bhp/273lb ft
**Engine:** Normally aspirated 3596cc flat six, petrol, electronic injection, 24 valves
**Drivetrain:** Rear-engine RWD
**Structure:** Monocoque
**Transmission:** Six-speed manual
**Weight:** 1420kg

**PRICE GUIDE (pre-09 Carrera/Turbo/GT3)**

**Launch price:** £58,380/£97,840/£79,540
**Excellent:** £40,000/£60,000/£110,000
**Good:** £30,000/£50,000/£90,000
**Average:** £20,000/£40,000/£70,000
**Project:** N/A

# RELIANT

STARTING OUT in 1935 with three-wheelers, Reliant progressed to the full picnic with its four-wheeled glassfibre Sabre sports car in 1961. However, it was the 1968 Scimitar GTE sports estate that made everybody started to take notice – mainly because the idea of a fast, luxurious coupé-cum-estate was a novel one. A convertible - the GTC – followed, too. But the GTE turned out to be the high point of Reliant's existence, as the firm was unable to come up with a suitable successor. In later years, it relied on its Robin three-wheeler (as well as the extra-wheel-endowed Kitten offshoot) for business, but this wasn't enough to sustain the company and its life as a car maker came to an end in 2002.

# RELIANT
## Sabre

The Reliant Sabre actually started out as a model designed as a Ford special from Ashley, to which Autocars of Israel then bought the rights. Reliant was called in to engineer the vehicle – originally called the Sabra – for production and introduction into the USA, using Ford Consul power and a ZF gearbox. Once ready, Reliant sold the car as the Sabre in the UK, where it failed to make much of an impression. The rest were sent to Israel in kit form. After a few years in production, only around 200 Sabras and Sabres were built. Values holding steady.

**SPECIFICATIONS**

| | |
|---|---|
| **Years produced:** | 1961-1964 (208 in total) |
| **Performance:** | 0-60mph: 14.4sec<br>Top speed: 93mph |
| **Power & torque:** | 90bhp/91lb ft |
| **Engine:** | Normally aspirated 1703cc four cylinder, petrol, carburettor, 8 valves |
| **Drivetrain:** | Front-engine RWD |
| **Structure:** | Steel chassis/glassfibre body |
| **Transmission:** | Four-speed manual |
| **Weight:** | 797kg |

**PRICE GUIDE**

| | |
|---|---|
| **Launch price:** | £1165 |
| **Excellent:** | £11,250 |
| **Good:** | £8000 |
| **Average:** | £3000 |
| **Project:** | £1500 |

# RELIANT
## Regal 3/25 and 3/30

Most famous for its central role in the BBC sitcom *Only Fools and Horses*, the Reliant Regal has become something of an icon in Supervan form. Until a few years ago, these hardy little three-wheelers were a common sight on British roads, which is testament to their long-lasting glassfibre bodies. The OHV 600cc (later 700cc) engine was directly related to the Austin Seven's, and was one of the first aluminium motors built in the UK. The Regal's sharp styling was a big improvement over its predecessor's, and possibly contributed to strong sales of up to 20,000 per year.

**SPECIFICATIONS (3/30)**

| | |
|---|---|
| **Years produced:** | 1962-1973 (c100,000 in total) |
| **Performance:** | 0-60mph: 25.0sec<br>Top speed: 75mph |
| **Power & torque:** | 30bhp/34lb ft |
| **Engine:** | Normally aspirated 701cc four cylinder, petrol, carburettor, 8 valves |
| **Drivetrain:** | Front-engine RWD |
| **Structure:** | Steel chassis/glassfibre body |
| **Transmission:** | Four-speed manual |
| **Weight:** | 455kg |

**PRICE GUIDE (add 20% for van)**

| | |
|---|---|
| **Launch price:** | £515 |
| **Excellent:** | £3000 |
| **Good:** | £1500 |
| **Average:** | £800 |
| **Project:** | £350 |

# RELIANT
## Scimitar SE4 coupé

Reliant's next attempt at a sports car was a lot more successful. The handsome coupé was originally designed by Ogle, and first shown on a Daimler SP250 chassis, but Reliant was so impressed with the design that it bought the rights and immediately set about putting the car into production using the Sabre Six's running gear and an all-new steel chassis. In 1964, the Scimitar went on sale and sold well. Subsequent Ford Essex V6-powered versions kept the factory busy until 1970, when it was phased out in favour of the Scimitar GTE. Values edging up.

**SPECIFICATIONS**

| | |
|---|---|
| **Years produced:** | 1964-1970 (1004 in total) |
| **Performance:** | 0-60mph: 11.4sec<br>Top speed: 117mph |
| **Power & torque:** | 120bhp/140lb ft |
| **Engine:** | Normally aspirated 2553cc straight six, petrol, carburettor, 12 valves |
| **Drivetrain:** | Front-engine RWD |
| **Structure:** | Steel chassis/glassfibre body |
| **Transmission:** | Four-speed manual |
| **Weight:** | 1003kg |

**PRICE GUIDE**

| | |
|---|---|
| **Launch price:** | £1292 |
| **Excellent:** | £10,250 |
| **Good:** | £6200 |
| **Average:** | £3700 |
| **Project:** | £1350 |

# RELIANT
## Scimitar GTE SE5

Reliant scored a major hit with the Scimitar GTE. It had been the firm's idea to ask Ogle's Tom Karen to redesign the SE4 into a sporting estate, and when the new car subsequently appeared it proved highly successful. As well as being good looking and usefully commodious, the 3.0-litre Ford V6 gave the GTE plenty of performance. The body style proved such a trendsetter that other manufacturers raced to produce their own versions, with Volvo's P1800ES and Lancia's Beta HPE being the most faithful homages. Despite that, values remain low.

**SPECIFICATIONS**

| | |
|---|---|
| **Years produced:** | 1968-1975 (5127 in total) |
| **Performance:** | 0-60mph: 8.9sec<br>Top speed: 121mph |
| **Power & torque:** | 138bhp/192lb ft |
| **Engine:** | Normally aspirated 2994cc V6, petrol, carburettor, 12 valves |
| **Drivetrain:** | Front-engine RWD |
| **Structure:** | Steel chassis/glassfibre body |
| **Transmission:** | Four-speed manual |
| **Weight:** | 991kg |

**PRICE GUIDE**

| | |
|---|---|
| **Launch price:** | £1759 |
| **Excellent:** | £7000 |
| **Good:** | £4000 |
| **Average:** | £1750 |
| **Project:** | £650 |

# RELIANT
## Robin

In 1973, the Regal was replaced by the smarter Ogle-styled Robin. Aside from the improved visuals, the new car received an upgunned 850cc engine and new twin-rail chassis. Despite the massive popularity of the emergent supermini generation, the Robin sold well on account of being able to be driven on a motorcycle licence in the UK – and that was possibly its only redeeming feature for keen motorists. The ex-bikers who bought the Robin were treated to excellent fuel consumption and cheap road tax – but it's a marginal car, and the butt of many jokes.

**SPECIFICATIONS**

| | |
|---|---|
| **Years produced:** | 1973-1982 |
| **Performance:** | 0-60mph: 16.9sec<br>Top speed: 81mph |
| **Power & torque:** | 40bhp/46lb ft |
| **Engine:** | Normally aspirated 848cc four cylinder, petrol, carburettor, 8 valves |
| **Drivetrain:** | Front-engine RWD |
| **Structure:** | Steel chassis/glassfibre body |
| **Transmission:** | Four-speed manual |
| **Weight:** | 495kg |

**PRICE GUIDE**

| | |
|---|---|
| **Launch price:** | £990 |
| **Excellent:** | £2500 |
| **Good:** | £1400 |
| **Average:** | £800 |
| **Project:** | £350 |

## RELIANT Kitten

Two years after the Robin's launch, Reliant replaced its Rebel with the Kitten. The visual similarity with the Robin was a side-effect of being closely based on the Tom Karen original – and in the Kitten's creation, Reliant produced arguably the first '70s UK supermini. In reality, the car was expensive compared with mainstream rivals, cramped and unrefined, but it was also the most economical four-wheeler money could buy. Interestingly, the Kitten is now finding favour with the engine-swap brigade, thanks to RWD. Estate version is exceptionally rare, but quite useful.

**SPECIFICATIONS**

| | |
|---|---|
| **Years produced:** | 1975-1982 |
| **Performance:** | 0-60mph: 18.0sec<br>Top speed: 81mph |
| **Power & torque:** | 40bhp/46lb ft |
| **Engine:** | Normally aspirated 848cc four cylinder, petrol, carburettor, 8 valves |
| **Drivetrain:** | Front-engine RWD |
| **Structure:** | Steel chassis/glassfibre body |
| **Transmission:** | Four-speed manual |
| **Weight:** | 595kg |

**PRICE GUIDE**

| | |
|---|---|
| **Launch price:** | £990 |
| **Excellent:** | £2500 |
| **Good:** | £1500 |
| **Average:** | £700 |
| **Project:** | £300 |

## RELIANT Scimitar GTE SE6/a/b

The revamped GTE was made wider and given a longer wheelbase, while new chassis settings erred on the side of comfort. It continued to sell handsomely and remained Reliant's main money earner. In 1979, the 2.8-litre V6 Ford 'Cologne' engine was introduced, adding little to the mix other than continued supply. After Reliant finally ended production, the GTE was briefly resurrected by Nottingham company Middlebridge in the late 1980s. These improved cars command a significant premium, the very best fetching as much as £25k.

**SPECIFICATIONS (SE6b)**

| | |
|---|---|
| **Years produced:** | 1976-1986 (4420/437 in total) |
| **Performance:** | 0-60mph: 10.0sec<br>Top speed: 119mph |
| **Power & torque:** | 135bhp/152lb ft |
| **Engine:** | Normally aspirated 2792cc four cylinder, petrol, carburettor, 12 valves |
| **Drivetrain:** | Front-engine RWD |
| **Structure:** | Steel chassis/glassfibre body |
| **Transmission:** | Four-speed manual with overdrive |
| **Weight:** | 1293kg |

**PRICE GUIDE**

| | |
|---|---|
| **Launch price:** | £10,324 |
| **Excellent:** | £6000 |
| **Good:** | £4400 |
| **Average:** | £1750 |
| **Project:** | £700 |

## RELIANT Scimitar GTC

This should have been another money-spinner for Reliant. When it emerged in 1980, it had the market all to itself – Triumph's Stag had been dead three years. The Stag had clearly provided inspiration with its T-piece targa arrangement and removable hardtop, and, just like its fellow British marque, Reliant struggled to meet sales expectations. The main problem wasn't the product at all, but the fact the car was launched in the middle of a recession. By the time the economy had recovered, the GTC was old hat. Has quite a following today, though.

**SPECIFICATIONS**

| | |
|---|---|
| **Years produced:** | 1980-1985 (442 in total) |
| **Performance:** | 0-60mph: 8.7sec<br>Top speed: 114mph |
| **Power & torque:** | 135bhp/152lb ft |
| **Engine:** | Normally aspirated 2792cc V6, petrol, carburettor, 12 valves |
| **Drivetrain:** | Front-engine RWD |
| **Structure:** | Steel chassis/glassfibre body |
| **Transmission:** | Four-speed manual with overdrive |
| **Weight:** | 1265kg |

**PRICE GUIDE**

| | |
|---|---|
| **Launch price:** | £11,600 |
| **Excellent:** | £9250 |
| **Good:** | £5500 |
| **Average:** | £3400 |
| **Project:** | £1800 |

## RELIANT Scimitar SS1/SST

A brave experiment that didn't quite make the grade despite being ahead of its time. The SS1 was designed to plug the gap in the market vacated by the MGB and TR7 when they went out of production, and should have been a massive success. It was simple, cheap and fun – and handled well with all-independent suspension. However, the Michelotti styling was a mess, the Ford CVH engines were underpowered and panel fit of the glassfibre body was terrible. A 135bhp Nissan-engined version was nippier but still only sold in tiny numbers.

**SPECIFICATIONS**

| | |
|---|---|
| **Years produced:** | 1984-1990 (1507 in total) |
| **Performance:** | 0-60mph: 11.2sec<br>Top speed: 111mph |
| **Power & torque:** | 95bhp/97lb ft |
| **Engine:** | Normally aspirated 1597cc four cylinder, petrol, carburettor, 8 valves |
| **Drivetrain:** | Front-engine RWD |
| **Structure:** | Steel chassis, plastic body |
| **Transmission:** | Five-speed manual |
| **Weight:** | 887kg |

**PRICE GUIDE**

| | |
|---|---|
| **Launch price:** | £6995 |
| **Excellent:** | £4500 |
| **Good:** | £3250 |
| **Average:** | £1250 |
| **Project:** | £500 |

RENAULT

# RENAULT

LOUIS RENAULT'S first vehicle was knocked up in the back garden of his parents' house in 1898. It led to the formation of the self-named marque with his two brothers, with much of the company's early profit coming from the manufacture of taxis. In the inter-war years it lost ground to rivals because of its old-fashioned engineering. Post-WW2, though, its range showed true imagination with cars like the 4CV, R4, Floride and Caravelle, and the landmark 16 of 1964 – regarded as the first modern-format hatch. In the 1980s and '90s it won the hearts of keen drivers with a succession of brilliant 'hot hatches'. Today, with partner Nissan, it is a market leader in affordable electric cars.

# RENAULT
## 4CV

Developed in occupied France during the war, it's tempting to believe that this rear-engined car was influenced by certain German machines. The 4CV was launched postwar with an 18bhp 760cc four-cylinder engine, all-independent suspension plus very chic and cuddly styling. More power – albeit from a smaller 747cc engine – came in 1950, and the gradual advancements continued until 1961. Most intriguing was the R1063 Sport, with 42bhp. Not that much, but in a car this light and small, enough to turn it into a real terrier. Values of all versions are holding firm.

**SPECIFICATIONS**

| | |
|---|---|
| **Years produced:** | 1947-1961 (1,105,547 in total) |
| **Performance:** | 0-60mph: N/A<br>Top speed: 57mph |
| **Power & torque:** | 19bhp/33lb ft |
| **Engine:** | Normally aspirated 760cc four cylinder, petrol, carburettor, 8 valves |
| **Drivetrain:** | Rear-engine RWD |
| **Structure:** | Monocoque |
| **Transmission:** | Three-speed manual |
| **Weight:** | 560kg |

**PRICE GUIDE**

| | |
|---|---|
| **Launch price:** | £474 |
| **Excellent:** | £7500 |
| **Good:** | £4700 |
| **Average:** | £2350 |
| **Project:** | £1000 |

# RENAULT
## Dauphine

The 4CV lived on in the stylish Dauphine. Born in 1956, this was a development of the 4CV with a bigger rear engine, chassis and bodywork. It sold almost twice as many examples as the car it grew out of. Intriguing features were the Ferlec transmission – giving finger-touch changes – and Aerostable semi-pneumatic variable suspension, plus disc brakes on all four wheels from 1964. The 37-40bhp Gordini (add 75% to the prices here) and the 49bhp racing-striped 1093cc Rallye (not imported to UK) gave Mini-Cooper-esque performance.

**SPECIFICATIONS**

| | |
|---|---|
| **Years produced:** | 1956-1967 (2,150,738 in total) |
| **Performance:** | 0-60mph: 45.7sec<br>Top speed: 70mph |
| **Power & torque:** | 30bhp/43lb ft |
| **Engine:** | Normally aspirated 845cc four cylinder, petrol, carburettor, 8 valves |
| **Drivetrain:** | Rear-engine RWD |
| **Structure:** | Monocoque |
| **Transmission:** | 3/4-speed manual or 3-speed auto |
| **Weight:** | 650kg |

**PRICE GUIDE**

| | |
|---|---|
| **Launch price:** | £769 |
| **Excellent:** | £5800 |
| **Good:** | £3500 |
| **Average:** | £1650 |
| **Project:** | £700 |

# RENAULT
## 4

If any Renault was a true 2CV rival, then this was it. Long-lived – built from 1961 to 1992 – and utterly simple in some places yet complex in others, it was Renault's first front-wheel-drive car. Quirks included the gearlever sprouting from the dashboard – necessary because the transmission was mounted in front of the engine – plus a different wheelbase on each side. The six engines available ranged from 603cc to 1108cc, but power stayed between the limits of 23bhp and 34bhp. As well as the saloon, there was also a 4x4 and a beach car known as the Plein Air.

**SPECIFICATIONS**

| | |
|---|---|
| **Years produced:** | 1961-1992 (8,135,424 in total) |
| **Performance:** | 0-60mph: 38.1sec<br>Top speed: 70mph |
| **Power & torque:** | 30bhp/41lb ft |
| **Engine:** | Normally aspirated 845cc four cylinder, petrol, carburettor, 8 valves |
| **Drivetrain:** | Front-engine FWD |
| **Structure:** | Monocoque |
| **Transmission:** | Three-speed manual |
| **Weight:** | 597kg |

**PRICE GUIDE**

| | |
|---|---|
| **Launch price:** | £539 |
| **Excellent:** | £4750 |
| **Good:** | £2000 |
| **Average:** | £900 |
| **Project:** | £450 |

# RENAULT
## Caravelle

America knew the Floride as the Caravelle. Yet from 1962, the name was used in Europe for a facelifted version, available as a coupé and convertible. The shape was largely the same, although some of the over-fussy ornamentation was dispensed with and passengers in the coupé had more headroom. The 956cc engine of the Floride S was initially used, still rear-mounted, but after a year capacity was boosted to 1108cc. With 54bhp on tap, top speed rose to within a whisper of 90mph, yet Renault never managed to resolve the handling issues. Add 25% for convertibles.

**SPECIFICATIONS**

| | |
|---|---|
| **Years produced:** | 1962-1968 |
| **Performance:** | 0-60mph: 17.6sec<br>Top speed: 89mph |
| **Power & torque:** | 54bhp/65lb ft |
| **Engine:** | Normally aspirated 1108cc four cylinder, petrol, carburettor, 8 valves |
| **Drivetrain:** | Rear-engine RWD |
| **Structure:** | Monocoque |
| **Transmission:** | Four-speed manual |
| **Weight:** | 800kg |

**PRICE GUIDE (Coupé)**

| | |
|---|---|
| **Launch price:** | £1168 |
| **Excellent:** | £9500 |
| **Good:** | £5000 |
| **Average:** | £2350 |
| **Project:** | £1300 |

# RENAULT
## 8

Renault persisted with a rear-engined layout for the 8, the successor to the Dauphine. First unveiled in 1962, it was an altogether more angular car. The 956cc engine was larger than before, suspension was independent all round, and there were disc brakes on each wheel... which certainly wasn't usual for most cars of this class at the time. They were more justified on faster, more powerful versions such as 1964's 8-1100 – also known as the 8 Major – with 1108cc, and the 8S of 1968, which could boast 53bhp and had a quad-headlamp front to show off sportier pretensions. Pay double for these.

**SPECIFICATIONS**

| | |
|---|---|
| **Years produced:** | 1964-1972 (1,316,134 in total) |
| **Performance:** | 0-60mph: 16.5sec<br>Top speed: 81mph |
| **Power & torque:** | 45bhp/65lb ft |
| **Engine:** | Normally aspirated 1108cc four cylinder, petrol, carburettor, 8 valves |
| **Drivetrain:** | Rear-engine RWD |
| **Structure:** | Monocoque |
| **Transmission:** | Four-speed manual |
| **Weight:** | 767kg |

**PRICE GUIDE**

| | |
|---|---|
| **Launch price:** | £764 |
| **Excellent:** | £4000 |
| **Good:** | £2800 |
| **Average:** | £1350 |
| **Project:** | £550 |

## RENAULT
### 8 Gordini 1100/1300

When it comes to mad Renaults, the 8 Gordini takes some beating. Launched in 1964, this rear-engined car was tuned to more than 90bhp – rather more than its chassis could cope with despite the lowered suspension. The servo-assisted disc brakes at least gave it the ability to stop quickly. More madness was to follow, though, for in 1967 the engine was upped to 1255cc, giving it 103bhp and the ability to easily top the ton. Originally, Gordinis were available only in blue with white stripes; other identifiers were spotlamps and four headlamps on the 1255cc R1135.

**SPECIFICATIONS**

**Years produced:** 1964-1970 (12,203 in total)
**Performance:** 0-60mph: 12.3sec
Top speed: 100mph
**Power & torque:** 95bhp/72lb ft
**Engine:** Normally aspirated 1108cc four cylinder, petrol, carburettor, 8 valves
**Drivetrain:** Rear-engine RWD
**Structure:** Monocoque
**Transmission:** Four-speed manual
**Weight:** 853kg

**PRICE GUIDE**

**Launch price:** £984
**Excellent:** £33,000
**Good:** £24,000
**Average:** £16,000
**Project:** £9250

## RENAULT
### 16

The 16 can lay major claim to being the first modern hatchback. Its design seems to be a blueprint for much that came after it, with a lifting tailgate, two-box shape with a roomy interior, front-wheel drive, lively alloy engine and disc brakes up front. There was even what could be regarded as a hot hatch from 1973, two years before the Golf GTi popularised the genre. This was the TX with a 1647cc 93bhp engine, five-speed transmission and quad headlights. A very forward-thinking and well-behaved machine with a lot of typically French quirks to make it even more intriguing.

**SPECIFICATIONS**

**Years produced:** 1965-1979 (1,846,000 in total)
**Performance:** 0-60mph: 12.3sec
Top speed: 101mph
**Power & torque:** 83bhp/88lb ft
**Engine:** Normally aspirated 1470cc four cylinder, petrol, carburettor, 8 valves
**Drivetrain:** Front-engine FWD
**Structure:** Monocoque
**Transmission:** Four-speed manual
**Weight:** 980kg

**PRICE GUIDE**

**Launch price:** £949
**Excellent:** £5000
**Good:** £3000
**Average:** £1400
**Project:** £650

## RENAULT
### 6

When did you last see a Renault 6? It's difficult to believe that almost two million of these forgettable hatchbacks were sold. The theory behind the 6 was simple – to turn the 4 into something more habitable, and, in doing so, add higher equipment levels and a more sober-suited bodystyle. This all combined elements of the 4 and 16, without capturing any of their charisma. Good to drive in a loping kind of way, with soft ride, door-handle cornering and a buzzy engine with little performance. Pretty rare today, as these cars could rot for England... or France.

**SPECIFICATIONS**

**Years produced:** 1965-1979 (1,773,000 in total)
**Performance:** 0-60mph: 38.1sec
Top speed: 70mph
**Power & torque:** 38bhp/42lb ft
**Engine:** Normally aspirated 845cc four cylinder, petrol, carburettor, 8 valves
**Drivetrain:** Front-engine FWD
**Structure:** Monocoque
**Transmission:** Four-speed manual
**Weight:** 750kg

**PRICE GUIDE**

**Launch price:** £669
**Excellent:** £2500
**Good:** £1800
**Average:** £950
**Project:** £400

## RENAULT
### 10

Renault stuck extra length onto the boot and bonnet of the 8 to create the 10. Quite what the reason for this was is unclear, and perhaps even the company didn't know, for the model lasted only three years from 1969 to 1971, and was still tagged as the 8 in some markets. However, in its homeland it was the 10, as it was in the UK. Aside from the big nose and plumper rump, changes from the 8 were minimal save for the fitment of the new five-bearing 1289cc engine (shared with the 12) at the rear to give an unremarkable top speed. Handling was better, too.

**SPECIFICATIONS**

**Years produced:** 1969-1971 (699,490 in total)
**Performance:** 0-60mph: 17.0sec
Top speed: 88mph
**Power & torque:** 52bhp/72lb ft
**Engine:** Normally aspirated 1289cc four cylinder, petrol, carburettor, 8 valves
**Drivetrain:** Rear-engine RWD
**Structure:** Monocoque
**Transmission:** Four-speed manual
**Weight:** 792kg

**PRICE GUIDE**

**Launch price:** £776
**Excellent:** £3800
**Good:** £2650
**Average:** £1550
**Project:** £650

## RENAULT
### 12

Renault's new mid-sized saloon was designed to bridge the gap between the 8/10 and the 16. The smaller car's rear-engined layout gave way to a far more orthodox (in future years) longitudinal front-driver. For a 1969 saloon, this was almost state of the art, as was the near-fastback styling, which hinted at a hatch layout. It was built in various locations, most notably in Turkey and Romania, where the Dacia pick-up version remained in production until 2006. Very few 12s survive in the UK (or France, for that matter) – rust and mechanical fragility were its weaknesses.

**SPECIFICATIONS**

**Years produced:** 1969-1980 (2,865,079 in total)
**Performance:** 0-60mph: 16.5sec
Top speed: 89mph
**Power & torque:** 54bhp/69lb ft
**Engine:** Normally aspirated 1289cc four cylinder, petrol, carburettor, 8 valves
**Drivetrain:** Front-engine FWD
**Structure:** Monocoque
**Transmission:** Four-speed manual
**Weight:** 840kg

**PRICE GUIDE**

**Launch price:** £870
**Excellent:** £3000
**Good:** £2000
**Average:** £1200
**Project:** £500

## RENAULT
### 5

Michel Boué's legacy to the automotive world was one he would never see bear fruit, as he died months before the Renault 5 was launched. The three-door hatchback was based on the utilitarian 4, but the styling was super-chic – and when it went on sale in 1972, the 5 caused a sensation. Wraparound plastic bumpers made the car Paris-friendly, and a wide range of engines gave the driver plenty of options. Through the years the car received ever more power, and in 1979 a five-door version added even more practicality. An all-time design classic.

**SPECIFICATIONS**

**Years produced:** 1972-1984 (5,471,079 in total)
**Performance:** 0-60mph: 18.9sec
Top speed: 85mph
**Power & torque:** 42bhp/61lb ft
**Engine:** Normally aspirated 1289cc four cylinder, petrol, carburettor, 8 valves
**Drivetrain:** Front-engine, FWD
**Structure:** Monocoque
**Transmission:** Four-speed manual
**Weight:** 785kg

**PRICE GUIDE**

**Launch price:** £854
**Excellent:** £2500
**Good:** £1400
**Average:** £700
**Project:** £350

## RENAULT
### 5 Gordini/Turbo

Known as the Renault 5 Alpine in Continental Europe, the Gordini was one of the first generation hot hatches, predating the Golf GTi by a year. The car's 1397cc engine produced 93bhp, more than double the power of the standard 5. However, this was a time of rapidly expanding power figures, and the Gordini was quickly outgunned by its new-found rivals. Renault's solution to this problem, as with its F1 car, was forced induction. Bolting on a Garrett T3 turbo instantly gave the car a handy increase in power and torque. A really nice Turbo could be £9k+.

**SPECIFICATIONS (Gordini)**

**Years produced:** 1976-1984
**Performance:** 0-60mph: 10.7sec
Top speed: 107mph
**Power & torque:** 93bhp/85lb ft
**Engine:** Normally aspirated 1397cc four cylinder, petrol, carburettor, 8 valves
**Drivetrain:** Front-engine, FWD
**Structure:** Monocoque
**Transmission:** Five-speed manual
**Weight:** 850kg

**PRICE GUIDE**

**Launch price:** £4149
**Excellent:** £7500
**Good:** £5500
**Average:** £2500
**Project:** £1500

## RENAULT
### 5 Turbo/Turbo 2

The first 400 5 Turbos were built in line with Group 4 regulations with the intention of going rallying. However, this homologation special would have cost Renault too much money to put into full-scale production, as there were so many lightweight aluminium parts unique to the mid-engined rally car. That is why the firm brought out the 5 Turbo 2. This more production-friendly model shared more of its components with the front-engined Gordini Turbo. The Turbo 2 was almost as fast as the original car, if a little more mainstream in ambience. All values holding.

**SPECIFICATIONS**

**Years produced:** 1980-1986 (3576 in total)
**Performance:** 0-60mph: 6.6sec
Top speed: 124mph
**Power & torque:** 160bhp/163lb ft
**Engine:** Turbocharged 1397cc four cylinder, petrol, electronic fuel injection, 8 valves
**Drivetrain:** Mid-engine RWD
**Structure:** Steel monocoque with glassfibre panels
**Transmission:** Five-speed manual
**Weight:** 970kg

**PRICE GUIDE (Turbo 2 in brackets)**

**Launch price:** £N/A
**Excellent:** £90,000 (£65,000)
**Good:** £67,000 (£48,000)
**Average:** £48,500 (£35,000)
**Project:** £32,500 (£22,000)

## RENAULT
### Fuego/Turbo

After eight years of moderate coupé sales with the 15/17, Renault needed something fresh – and despite being based on the 18 the Fuego was certainly distinctive. As the first car ever to be fitted with a 'plip', or remote central locking, it was novel, too. In 1982, after two years at the top of the sales charts in Europe, Renault introduced a 132bhp Fuego Turbo which could sprint from 0-60mph in 9.5 seconds. Wearing Turbo decals and BBS alloys, it was less than subtle, but UK sales proved surprisingly strong. British imports stopped in 1986.

**SPECIFICATIONS**

**Years produced:** 1980-1987
**Performance:** 0-60mph: 8.9sec
Top speed: 120mph
**Power & torque:** 132bhp/147lb ft
**Engine:** Turbocharged 1565cc four cylinder, petrol, carburettor, 8 valves
**Drivetrain:** Front-engine FWD
**Structure:** Monocoque
**Transmission:** Five-speed manual
**Weight:** 1050kg

**PRICE GUIDE**

**Launch price:** £8700
**Excellent:** £3000
**Good:** £1800
**Average:** £1000
**Project:** £500

## RENAULT
### Espace

In reality the Espace is far from being the first MPV, but it was a massive hit for Renault and went a long way towards popularising the concept in Europe. The innovative car was developed and built by Matra, and was initially offered to Peugeot as the replacement for the Rancho. The company refused it, so Renault took it wholescale – Chrysler Alpine front end and all – and the firm has never looked back. Unfortunately, the adaptable interior wasn't well made, and the exterior panels damaged easily, so finding a minter is never easy... the perfect recipe for future classic status!

**SPECIFICATIONS**

**Years produced:** 1984-1991
**Performance:** 0-60mph: 12.5sec
Top speed: 109mph
**Power & torque:** 106bhp/118lb ft
**Engine:** Turbocharged 1995cc four cylinder, petrol, carburettor, 8 valves
**Drivetrain:** Front-engine FWD
**Structure:** Spaceframe
**Transmission:** Five-speed manual
**Weight:** 1200kg

**PRICE GUIDE**

**Launch price:** £8878
**Excellent:** £2000
**Good:** £1300
**Average:** £850
**Project:** £400

## RENAULT
## 5 GT Turbo

When the Gordini Turbo was phased out in 1984 with the arrival of the 'Supercinq', Renault had to up the ante. The GT Turbo used the same basic engine as the Gordini, but a Garrett T2 turbocharger and a few other induction system modifications raised the power to 115bhp, and again to 118bhp in 1987. This power figure on its own isn't that impressive, but the Renault 5 tipped the scales at only 820kg, giving the tiny hot hatch truly vigorous acceleration – not to mention fun, rear-inside-wheel-lifting handling. Grab a standard car before values takes off again.

**SPECIFICATIONS**

| | |
|---|---|
| **Years produced:** | 1985-1991 |
| **Performance:** | 0-60mph: 7.1sec<br>Top speed: 123mph |
| **Power & torque:** | 115bhp/121lb ft |
| **Engine:** | Turbocharged 1397cc four cylinder, petrol, carburettor, 8 valves |
| **Drivetrain:** | Front-engine FWD |
| **Structure:** | Monocoque |
| **Transmission:** | Five-speed manual |
| **Weight:** | 820kg |

**PRICE GUIDE**

| | |
|---|---|
| **Launch price:** | £7630 |
| **Excellent:** | £9000 |
| **Good:** | £5750 |
| **Average:** | £3000 |
| **Project:** | £1600 |

## RENAULT
## 21 Turbo

Renault's Giugiaro-styled 21 was a pretty but forgettable repmobile. Its only technical novelty was a mixture of transverse and longitudinal engines, which betrayed the car's mixed parentage. However, when *La Regie* bolted a turbo onto the 2.0-litre model, the 21 was transformed into an entertaining sports saloon that could eat BMW 325is for breakfast. And if 175bhp doesn't sound that much these days, consider the car's 0-60mph time of 6.5 seconds, along with all the wheelspin you could ever want. Many examples are still going strong – and making decent money.

**SPECIFICATIONS**

| | |
|---|---|
| **Years produced:** | 1988-1992 |
| **Performance:** | 0-60mph: 8.1sec<br>Top speed: 141mph |
| **Power & torque:** | 175bhp/199lb ft |
| **Engine:** | Turbocharged 1995cc four cylinder, petrol, fuel injection, 8 valves |
| **Drivetrain:** | Front-engine FWD |
| **Structure:** | Monocoque |
| **Transmission:** | Five-speed manual |
| **Weight:** | 1190kg |

**PRICE GUIDE (Add 20% for Quadra)**

| | |
|---|---|
| **Launch price:** | £16,500 |
| **Excellent:** | £3700 |
| **Good:** | £2000 |
| **Average:** | £1200 |
| **Project:** | £600 |

## RENAULT
## Clio Williams

The first 'hot' Clio was the 16V that arrived in 1991, complete with flared wheelarches and a peppy 137bhp 1.8. The limited-edition Williams launched in 1993 was the real superstar, though, with its Sports Blue paint and gold Speedline alloy wheels. In fact it was developed by Renaultsport, not the F1 team, but thanks to a torquier 2.0 and chassis tweaks it was a riot to drive. Renault famously extended the initial production run of 3800 cars (500 for the UK) to over 12,100 by 1996, to the dismay of many original Willy owners.

**SPECIFICATIONS**

| | |
|---|---|
| **Years produced:** | 1993-1996 (12,100 in total) |
| **Performance:** | 0-60mph: 7.7sec (Williams)<br>Top speed: 130mph |
| **Power & torque:** | 145bhp/129lb ft |
| **Engine:** | Normally aspirated 1998cc four cylinder, petrol, injection, 16 valves |
| **Drivetrain:** | Front-engine FWD |
| **Structure:** | Monocoque |
| **Transmission:** | Five-speed manual |
| **Weight:** | 1010kg (Williams 1) |

**PRICE GUIDE Williams 1 (2&3 in brackets)**

| | |
|---|---|
| **Launch price:** | £15,000 |
| **Excellent:** | £9000 (£6750) |
| **Good:** | £4800 (£4000) |
| **Average:** | £2200 (£1750) |
| **Project:** | £1350 (£1100) |

## RENAULT
## Clio V6

Taking inspiration from the mid-engined 5 Turbo – a true motorsport homologation special – Renault created an equally wide-hipped mid-engined 'baby supercar' in the Clio V6. Most of the engineering work was undertaken by motorsport specialists TWR, with a tweaked 3.0-litre V6 from the Laguna saloon in place of the rear seats. TWR built the Phase 1 V6s at its Swedish Uddevalla facility, but production of the improved (less lairy) Phase 2 moved to the Alpine factory at Dieppe. Buy a Phase 2 if you can afford it.

**SPECIFICATIONS**

| | |
|---|---|
| **Years produced:** | 2001-2005 (1513 Phase 1, 1309 Phase 2) |
| **Performance:** | 0-60mph: 6.6sec<br>Top speed: 145mph |
| **Power & torque:** | 226bhp/221lb ft |
| **Engine:** | Normally aspirated 2946cc V6, petrol, injection, 24 valves |
| **Drivetrain:** | Mid-engine RWD |
| **Structure:** | Monocoque |
| **Transmission:** | Six-speed manual |
| **Weight:** | 1410kg |

**PRICE GUIDE (Phase 2 in brackets)**

| | |
|---|---|
| **Launch price:** | £25,995 |
| **Excellent:** | £25,000 (£40,000) |
| **Good:** | £21,000 (£32,500) |
| **Average:** | £17,000 (£25,000) |
| **Project:** | £10,000 N/A |

## RENAULT
## Sport Spider

Despite the relative affordability, availability and track suitability of the Lotus Elise, there's something seriously cool about the slightly more oddball Spider. Built at the old Alpine factory in Dieppe, the mid-engined Spider uses the same F7R engine as the Clio Williams. Early cars did without a windscreen, but all 96 right-hand-drive UK cars had one fitted. At 930kg, it's not actually that lightweight, but performance and handling are good. A good long-term bet due to limited numbers and those dramatic looks.

**SPECIFICATIONS**

| | |
|---|---|
| **Years produced:** | 1996-1999 (1685 produced) |
| **Performance:** | 0-60mph: 6.5sec<br>Top speed: 131mph |
| **Power & torque:** | 147bhp/129lb ft |
| **Engine:** | Normally aspirated 1998cc four, petrol, injection, 16 valves |
| **Drivetrain:** | Mid-engine RWD |
| **Structure:** | Aluminium chassis, composite body |
| **Transmission:** | Five-speed manual |
| **Weight:** | 930kg |

**PRICE GUIDE**

| | |
|---|---|
| **Launch price:** | £25,950 |
| **Excellent:** | £23,000 |
| **Good:** | £19,000 |
| **Average:** | £16,000 |
| **Project:** | £10,000 |

## RENAULT SPORT
### Clio 172/182/Trophy

Providing a much-needed shot in the arm for the hot hatch market, Renault Sport's Clio 172 was an absolute riot, with low weight, stiff suspension and a highly tuned 16v engine, while stripped-out Cup amplified the formula even further. Later 182 slightly better all-rounder with a slight increase in power. Run-out Trophy, featuring trick remote reservoir Sachs dampers and Speedline Turini wheels, is the most valuable today, with the best commanding up to £8k. Many have been turned into cheap track toys, meaning values of clean, original cars are on the up.

**SPECIFICATIONS**

| | |
|---|---|
| **Years produced:** | 2000-2005 |
| **Performance:** | 0-60mph: 6.8sec<br>Top speed: 138mph |
| **Power & torque:** | 170bhp/148lb ft |
| **Engine:** | Normally aspirated 1998cc four cylinder, petrol, electronic fuel injection, 16 valves |
| **Drivetrain:** | Front-engine FWD |
| **Structure:** | Monocoque |
| **Transmission:** | Five-speed manual |
| **Weight:** | 1021kg |

**PRICE GUIDE (172)**

| | |
|---|---|
| **Launch price:** | £15,495 |
| **Excellent:** | £3500 |
| **Good:** | £2200 |
| **Average:** | £1250 |
| **Project:** | £500 |

# RILEY

AFTER MAINLY building tricars, Riley – established in 1898 – moved onto four wheels from 1907. As the firm matured, it was responsible for some very rakish designs, and soon became a competition favourite. Unfortunately, sporting prowess was no substitute for cold, hard cash, and the ailing company was taken over by Morris to form the Nuffield Organisation. While this saved the name, it ended Riley's independence, and the firm's cars became more reliant on Morris (and, from 1952, BMC) in their make-up. The last model to feature any Riley individuality was the 1953-1957 Pathfinder; after that, the models became just badge-engineered BMC variants. The Riley name was killed off in 1969.

## RILEY
### RMA/RME

The immediate post-war Rileys continued with their traditional method of a separate chassis and ash-frame construction. The RMA was a handsome, streamlined saloon, with a lively twin-camshaft 1496cc engine giving effective performance while the independent front suspension meant effective handling as well. The RMA metamorphosed into the RME in 1952, with hydraulic brakes – one of the areas where its predecessor's had been weak – plus a larger rear window. A year before production end, wheel spats were added and the running boards dispensed with.

**SPECIFICATIONS**

| | |
|---|---|
| **Years produced:** | 1946-1955 (13,950 in total) |
| **Performance:** | 0-60mph: 25.1sec<br>Top speed: 81mph |
| **Power & torque:** | 55bhp/76lb ft |
| **Engine:** | Normally aspirated 1496cc four cylinder, petrol, carburettor, overhead valves |
| **Drivetrain:** | Front-engine RWD |
| **Structure:** | Separate chassis |
| **Transmission:** | Four-speed manual |
| **Weight:** | 1422kg |

**PRICE GUIDE**

| | |
|---|---|
| **Launch price:** | £710 |
| **Excellent:** | £13,500 |
| **Good:** | £10,000 |
| **Average:** | £5500 |
| **Project:** | £2000 |

## RILEY
### RMB/RMF

A step upwards from the RMA was the RMB, with its 2443cc engine offering enhanced potential. The 'B kept the same basic look as the 'A, but had a longer wheelbase and bonnet. When launched in 1946 90bhp was available, but this went up to 100bhp in 1948. By happy coincidence, this brought top speed up to 100mph as well. The RMF of 1952 was an almost identical-looking replacement with improved suspension, hydraulic brakes in place of the previous hydromechanical ones, and a larger, curved rear screen. Manufacture continued until 1953.

**SPECIFICATIONS**

| | |
|---|---|
| **Years produced:** | 1946-1953 (8959 in total) |
| **Performance:** | 0-60mph: 15.2sec<br>Top speed: 95mph |
| **Power & torque:** | 90bhp/N/A |
| **Engine:** | Normally aspirated 2443cc four cylinder, petrol, carburettor, 8 valves |
| **Drivetrain:** | Front-engine RWD |
| **Structure:** | Separate chassis |
| **Transmission:** | Four-speed manual |
| **Weight:** | 1211kg |

**PRICE GUIDE**

| | |
|---|---|
| **Launch price:** | £1125 |
| **Excellent:** | £17,000 |
| **Good:** | £13,250 |
| **Average:** | £6750 |
| **Project:** | £3000 |

## RILEY
### RMC Roadster

The rarest of the RM variants, especially in Britain, was the RMC – a three-seater, two-door roadster version of the RMB. The sleek lines were even more attractive sans roof, especially with the windscreen folded flat, and the more compact interior meant a larger boot could be fitted. The engine was the same as that of the RMB – a 2443cc overhead-valve unit – and was also tuned to give 100bhp. The RMC was intended for overseas markets, with most going to North America. Only 507 were constructed up until the end of the line in 1950. Values rising steadily.

**SPECIFICATIONS**

| | |
|---|---|
| **Years produced:** | 1948-1950 (507 in total) |
| **Performance:** | 0-60mph: 19.0sec<br>Top speed: 98mph |
| **Power & torque:** | 100bhp/N/A |
| **Engine:** | Normally aspirated 2443cc four cylinder, petrol, carburettor, 8 valves |
| **Drivetrain:** | Front-engine RWD |
| **Structure:** | Separate chassis |
| **Transmission:** | Four-speed manual |
| **Weight:** | 1219kg |

**PRICE GUIDE**

| | |
|---|---|
| **Launch price:** | £1225 |
| **Excellent:** | £38,000 |
| **Good:** | £26,000 |
| **Average:** | £16,500 |
| **Project:** | £7500 |

# RILEY
## RMD Convertible

More practical than the RMC Roadster was the four-seater RMD. Introduced at the same time as the RMC, this elegant drophead coupé would turn out to be the final open-top car to wear the Riley name, aside from the specially-converted Elf convertibles of the 1960s. The RMD kept much the same lines as the RMB, so no fold-flat one-piece windscreen or enlarged boot. It did have distinctive grab irons on its hood though. Production continued one year past the RMC until 1951 but, by the end of its three-year life, only 502 had found homes. Values holding firm.

**SPECIFICATIONS**
**Years produced:** 1948-1951 (502 in total)
**Performance:** 0-60mph: 15.2sec
Top speed: 95mph
**Power & torque:** 100bhp/N/A
**Engine:** Normally aspirated 2443cc four cylinder, petrol, carburettor, 8 valves
**Drivetrain:** Front-engine RWD
**Structure:** Separate chassis
**Transmission:** Four-speed manual
**Weight:** 1239kg

**PRICE GUIDE**
**Launch price:** £1382
**Excellent:** £26,000
**Good:** £18,500
**Average:** £12,500
**Project:** £5000

# RILEY
## Pathfinder/2.6

The sleek Pathfinder brought Riley into the modern age, although its twin-cam four-cylinder engine was carried over from the traditional and upright RMF. Its right-hand floorshift gearstick can take some getting used to, as can the handling. Later cars got leaf rather than coil rear springs, and the improvement was clear. The 2.6 that replaced the Pathfinder was of similar style but was really a Wolseley 6/90 with a Riley grille and an extra 4bhp from its BMC C-series six-cylinder engine. Both offer a large slice of 1950s British wood and leather luxury, and values have been edging up.

**SPECIFICATIONS**
**Years produced:** 1953-1958 (8959/2000 in total)
**Performance:** 0-60mph: 16.7sec
Top speed: 100mph
**Power & torque:** 110bhp/135lb ft
**Engine:** Normally aspirated 2443cc four cylinder, petrol, carburettor, 8 valves
**Drivetrain:** Front-engine RWD
**Structure:** Separate chassis
**Transmission:** Four-speed manual
**Weight:** 1500kg

**PRICE GUIDE**
**Launch price:** £1382
**Excellent:** £9500
**Good:** £6000
**Average:** £2750
**Project:** £1300

# RILEY
## One-Point-Five

Originally intended as a Morris Minor successor, the One-Point-Five instead emerged in 1957 as the sassier sister to the Wolseley 1500. The shell was the same, albeit with differences in trim and the front end, which sported Riley's traditional grille. It was under the bonnet where the real fun lay, though, for the BMC B-series 1489cc had an extra carburettor fitted, boosting output to 62bhp over the Wolseley's 43bhp. Coupled with Morris Minor running gear, the One-Point-Five was a nimble and entertaining car to drive. The luxurious interior also befitted the Riley image.

**SPECIFICATIONS**
**Years produced:** 1957-1965 (39,568 in total)
**Performance:** 0-60mph: 17.4sec
Top speed: 84mph
**Power & torque:** 62bhp/82lb ft
**Engine:** Normally aspirated 1489cc four cylinder, petrol, carburettor, 8 valves
**Drivetrain:** Front-engine RWD
**Structure:** Monocoque
**Transmission:** Four-speed manual
**Weight:** 864kg

**PRICE GUIDE**
**Launch price:** £864
**Excellent:** £5500
**Good:** £3300
**Average:** £1500
**Project:** £550

# RILEY
## 4/68, 4/72

Or, as Shakespeare might have said, a Farina by any other name... The Riley-badged version of BMC's mid-sized Farina-penned saloons of 1959 to 1969 was arguably the most desirable, for it blended the performance and cabin luxury of its MG and Wolseley rivals respectively. The car was based on the MG Magnette, so had cut-back fins from its birth plus the same 66bhp twin-carburettor, four-cylinder engine. The 4/72 in 1961 put that figure at 68bhp; there was also a wider track, increased wheelbase and anti-roll bars to combat the body roll all Farinas suffered from.

**SPECIFICATIONS**
**Years produced:** 1959-1969 (10,940/14,151 in total)
**Performance:** 0-60mph: 20.6sec
Top speed: 84mph
**Power & torque:** 66bhp/85lb ft
**Engine:** Normally aspirated 1489cc four cylinder, petrol, carburettor, 8 valves
**Drivetrain:** Front-engine RWD
**Structure:** Monocoque
**Transmission:** Four-speed manual
**Weight:** 1092kg

**PRICE GUIDE**
**Launch price:** £1028
**Excellent:** £5500
**Good:** £2850
**Average:** £1750
**Project:** £650

# RILEY
## Elf

Continuing Riley's adventures in badge engineering was the Elf of 1961 to 1969. It looked like a Mini on steroids, with an extended rump framed by fins and an old-school Riley front end. Occupants could delight in a less spartan interior with a full-length burr walnut dash. The MkII in 1963 made use of the bigger 998cc A-series engine, Hydrolastic suspension arrived in 1964 and the MkIII introduced winding windows, better ventilation and a 'remote-control' gearbox. Despite selling well, the Elf was discontinued when British Leyland killed off Riley.

**SPECIFICATIONS**
**Years produced:** 1961-1969 (30,912 in total)
**Performance:** 0-60mph: 32.3sec
Top speed: 71mph
**Power & torque:** 34bhp/N/A
**Engine:** Normally aspirated 848cc four cylinder, petrol, carburettor, 8 valves
**Drivetrain:** Front-engine FWD
**Structure:** Monocoque
**Transmission:** Four-speed manual
**Weight:** 660kg

**PRICE GUIDE**
**Launch price:** £694
**Excellent:** £7500
**Good:** £4750
**Average:** £2500
**Project:** £1000

## RILEY Kestrel

The last Riley of all was the Kestrel (and subsequent 1300 upgrade). It wasn't really a Riley, though, being just a rebadged BMC 1100 with the 55bhp specification of the MG plus the now-expected individual grille and side whiskers. A walnut veneer dashboard upgraded the interior. When the 1275cc A-series was installed under the bonnet in 1967, power rose first to 65bhp, then 70bhp a year later. The car was de-named in 1968, becoming just the Riley 1300. This suggested the writing was on the wall for the marque. It was, for the car and the life of Riley ended only a year later.

**SPECIFICATIONS**

| | |
|---|---|
| **Years produced:** | 1965-1969 (21,529 in total) |
| **Performance:** | 0-60mph: 18.4sec<br>Top speed: 85mph |
| **Power & torque:** | 55bhp/62lb ft |
| **Engine:** | Normally aspirated 1098cc four cylinder, petrol, carburettor, 8 valves |
| **Drivetrain:** | Front-engine FWD |
| **Structure:** | Monocoque |
| **Transmission:** | Four-speed manual |
| **Weight:** | 832kg |

**PRICE GUIDE**

| | |
|---|---|
| **Launch price:** | £781 |
| **Excellent:** | £4500 |
| **Good:** | £2750 |
| **Average:** | £2000 |
| **Project:** | £800 |

# ROCHDALE

THE BODYWORK repair business, Rochdale Motor Panels, was formed in 1948 by Harry Smith and Frank Butterworth. They were both keen racers – and specials enthusiasts – and it was inevitable that they would end up building their own. The were soon creating bespoke cars to customers' specifications, and by 1952 had abandoned aluminium in favour of glassfibre. The GT and Olympic picked up useful sales, but the company was badly affected by a factory fire in 1961. Sales continued until 1963, but by then they had slowed to a trickle, and Rochdale refocused its efforts, concentrating on making heating equipment. It did, however, continue selling cars as one-offs until 1972.

## ROCHDALE GT

Rochdale made a success of supplying bodies for the specialist auto industry. Its glassfibre shells were found adorning a number of specials – so much so that it started making complete cars. The best-selling GT (a coupé version of the Rochdale F racing body), was designed specifically to work with Ford Popular running gear. It was an advanced design, with sleek styling, a curved screen, plus ready-fitted doors and bonnet. One of the main bonuses of the coupé roof was the reduction of chassis flex – a lesson learned for subsequent models.

**SPECIFICATIONS**

| | |
|---|---|
| **Years produced:** | 1957-1961 (1350 in total) |
| **Performance:** | 0-60mph: N/A<br>Top speed: N/A |
| **Power & torque:** | N/A |
| **Engine:** | Normally aspirated 1172cc four cylinder, petrol, carburettor, 8 valves |
| **Drivetrain:** | Front-engine RWD |
| **Structure:** | Separate chassis |
| **Transmission:** | Four-speed manual |
| **Weight:** | 650kg |

**PRICE GUIDE**

| | |
|---|---|
| **Launch price:** | N/A |
| **Excellent:** | £7500 |
| **Good:** | £3500 |
| **Average:** | £1900 |
| **Project:** | £700 |

## ROCHDALE Olympic

When it appeared in 1960, the Olympic was only the second car to feature a glassfibre monocoque – following hot on the heels of the Lotus Elite. The 1.5-litre Riley-engined Rochdale lacked the glamour of its rival, but it was well-engineered and handled assuredly thanks to its coil spring suspension. Production endured a setback following a fire at the factory a year after launch, but it picked up slowly afterwards with the car being offered in component form or as a complete package. The 1963 Olympic II moved to Ford power. All enjoy a following today.

**SPECIFICATIONS**

| | |
|---|---|
| **Years produced:** | 1960-1973 (400 in total) |
| **Performance:** | 0-60mph: 11.9sec<br>Top speed: 102mph |
| **Power & torque:** | 60bhp/N/A |
| **Engine:** | Normally aspirated 1498cc four cylinder, petrol, carburettor, 8 valves |
| **Drivetrain:** | Front-engine RWD |
| **Structure:** | Glassfibre monocoque |
| **Transmission:** | Four-speed manual |
| **Weight:** | 700kg |

**PRICE GUIDE**

| | |
|---|---|
| **Launch price:** | £670 |
| **Excellent:** | £9500 |
| **Good:** | £4750 |
| **Average:** | £2500 |
| **Project:** | £1000 |

# ROLLS-ROYCE

THE PARTNERSHIP of engineer Henry Royce and rich gentleman Charles Rolls resulted in the 1906 formation of the world's most prestigious marque. The Silver Ghost was dubbed 'The Best Car in the World' and RR tried to stick to this creed with all subsequent models. Magnificent leviathans followed, each unstinting in their luxury and price. The postwar Silver Cloud models were perhaps the zenith of RR's accomplishments, but the succeeding Silver Shadow became a common sight because so many were built. Nationalised amid financial woes in 1971, the company was sold off again in 1973. BMW and Volkswagen competed to buy it in 1998, with BMW the eventual winner.

## ROLLS-ROYCE Silver Wraith

Rolls-Royce re-emerged after WW2 with the Silver Wraith, based on the Wraith model sold in 1939. At first it was available only for export, Great Britain having to wait until 1948 before home sales started. As was traditional, the Wraith was offered as a bare chassis only; it was up to the affluent owner to have a coachbuilder construct the body, with Mulliner proving the most popular option. Initially, motive power was a 4257cc straight-six, but this rose to 4566cc in 1951 and then jumped to 4887cc in 1954. Values holding firm, say specialists Hillier Hill.

**SPECIFICATIONS**

| | |
|---|---|
| **Years produced:** | 1946-1959 (1783 in total) |
| **Performance:** | 0-60mph: 16.2sec<br>Top speed: 88mph |
| **Power & torque:** | N/A |
| **Engine:** | Normally aspirated 4566cc straight six, petrol, carburettor, 12 valves |
| **Drivetrain:** | Front-engine RWD |
| **Structure:** | Separate chassis |
| **Transmission:** | Four-speed automatic |
| **Weight:** | 2359kg |

**PRICE GUIDE (standard steel saloons)**

| | |
|---|---|
| **Launch price:** | £4190 |
| **Excellent:** | £75,000 |
| **Good:** | £45,000 |
| **Average:** | £20,000 |
| **Project:** | £10,000 |

## ROLLS-ROYCE Silver Dawn

Before WW2, most Rolls-Royces had been large and imposing chauffeur-driven palaces on wheels. But the world was changing, and the marque felt the need to change with it. Thus the Silver Dawn was a more compact Rolls, based on the Bentley MkVI and aimed at owners who also drove themselves. Engines were less powerful than their Bentley counterparts, and Rolls-Royce never let on the power output figures – at least not to the public. Most cars had standard Pressed Steel bodies, but there were some coachbuilt specials. The best are now quite sough-after.

**SPECIFICATIONS**

| | |
|---|---|
| **Years produced:** | 1949-1955 (761 in total) |
| **Performance:** | 0-60mph: 16.2sec<br>Top speed: 87mph |
| **Power & torque:** | N/A |
| **Engine:** | Normally aspirated 4556cc straight six, petrol, carburettor, 12 valves |
| **Drivetrain:** | Front-engine RWD |
| **Structure:** | Separate chassis |
| **Transmission:** | Four-speed automatic |
| **Weight:** | 1842kg |

**PRICE GUIDE (standard steel saloons)**

| | |
|---|---|
| **Launch price:** | £3250 |
| **Excellent:** | £65,000 |
| **Good:** | £45,000 |
| **Average:** | £25,000 |
| **Project:** | £10,000 |

## ROLLS-ROYCE Silver Cloud I

A new era for Rolls-Royce was ushered in with the Silver Cloud in 1955. The company started making bodies in-house, although many customers still preferred to have their favourite coachbuilder construct something special. But such was the imposing elegance of the Cloud's standard body that many buyers never felt the need to shop elsewhere. The 4887cc engine was an enlargement of that which had been used in previous models. In addition to the standard 123in wheelbase cars, a 127in limousine was offered with bodywork by Park Ward.

**SPECIFICATIONS**

| | |
|---|---|
| **Years produced:** | 1955-1959 (2359 in total) |
| **Performance:** | 0-60mph: 13.0sec<br>Top speed: 106mph |
| **Power & torque:** | N/A |
| **Engine:** | Normally aspirated 4887cc straight six, petrol, carburettor, 12 valves |
| **Drivetrain:** | Front-engine RWD |
| **Structure:** | Separate chassis |
| **Transmission:** | Four-speed automatic |
| **Weight:** | 2032kg |

**PRICE GUIDE (standard steel saloons)**

| | |
|---|---|
| **Launch price:** | £3385 |
| **Excellent:** | £70,000 |
| **Good:** | £45,000 |
| **Average:** | £20,000 |
| **Project:** | £10,000 |

## ROLLS-ROYCE Silver Cloud II

V8 power reached Rolls-Royce with the Silver Cloud II of 1959. The firm's new 6230cc eight cylinder brought muscle, flexibility and smoothness to this commanding heavyweight. Although the actual power figure was never revealed, it was estimated to be around 200bhp – or 25 per cent greater than in the six-cylinder Cloud. Other changes included the adoption of power-assisted steering and a new facia. The standard saloons and Park Ward limousines were now complemented by the choice of a Mulliner drophead coupé, although its price was just as fabulous as its looks.

**SPECIFICATIONS**

| | |
|---|---|
| **Years produced:** | 1959-1965 (5013 in total) |
| **Performance:** | 0-60mph: 11.5sec<br>Top speed: 113mph |
| **Power & torque:** | N/A |
| **Engine:** | Normally aspirated 6230cc V8, petrol, carburettor, 16 valves |
| **Drivetrain:** | Front-engine RWD |
| **Structure:** | Separate chassis |
| **Transmission:** | Four-speed automatic |
| **Weight:** | 2109kg |

**PRICE GUIDE (standard steel saloons)**

| | |
|---|---|
| **Launch price:** | £5802 |
| **Excellent:** | £70,000 |
| **Good:** | £45,000 |
| **Average:** | £20,000 |
| **Project:** | £10,000 |

## ROLLS-ROYCE Phantom V limousine

Boy, did the Phantom V need the company's new V8 engine! This ultra-luxurious leviathan weighed just under three tonnes, and the huge rear passenger compartment was made possible by the elongated 12-foot wheelbase. Everything about the Phantom was designed to pamper its occupants; aside from the acres of wood trim and leather upholstery, power steering and an automatic transmission came as standard. As each car was essentially a personal commission, values can vary widely according to the spec; some will be worth considerably more.

**SPECIFICATIONS**

| | |
|---|---|
| **Years produced:** | 1959-1968 (516 in total) |
| **Performance:** | 0-60mph: 13.8sec<br>Top speed: 101mph |
| **Power & torque:** | N/A |
| **Engine:** | Normally aspirated 6223cc V8, petrol, carburettor, 16 valves |
| **Drivetrain:** | Front-engine, RWD |
| **Structure:** | Separate chassis |
| **Transmission:** | Four-speed automatic |
| **Weight:** | 2540kg |

**PRICE GUIDE**

| | |
|---|---|
| **Launch price:** | £8905 |
| **Excellent:** | £150,000 |
| **Good:** | £80,000 |
| **Average:** | £45,000 |
| **Project:** | £25,000 |

## ROLLS-ROYCE
### Silver Cloud III

The adoption of the V8 engine for the Cloud II was universally regarded as an improvement. Not everybody was convinced by the 1962 facelift that created the Cloud III, though. It modernised the looks, but old-school aficionados bemoaned the loss of the traditional 'face'. However, it didn't offend the 'new money' celebrities who were now buying into the Rolls-Royce dream; John Lennon even had his Cloud III painted in a psychedelic colour scheme. A raised compression ratio resulted in more power although, predictably, how much more remained a secret.

**SPECIFICATIONS**

**Years produced:** 1962-1965 (2359 in total)
**Performance:** 0-60mph: 10.8sec
Top speed: 116mph
**Power & torque:** N/A
**Engine:** Normally aspirated 6230cc V8, petrol, carburettor, 16 valves
**Drivetrain:** Front-engine, RWD
**Structure:** Separate chassis
**Transmission:** Four-speed automatic
**Weight:** 2109kg

**PRICE GUIDE**

**Launch price:** £5517
**Excellent:** £75,000
**Good:** £40,000
**Average:** £25,000
**Project:** £15,000

## ROLLS-ROYCE
### Silver Shadow

If ever there was a Rolls-Royce for the masses, then the Shadow was it. It was revolutionary for the company, with unitary construction, all-round disc brakes and self-levelling suspension. The modern lines reflected contemporary car design, yet also managed to retain Rolls-Royce's upper-class air. The 6230cc V8 rose in capacity to 6750cc in 1970, and the Shadow II fell victim to rubber-faced bumpers and a front air dam in 1977. The Silver Wraith name was used from the same year to distinguish the long-wheelbase version.

**SPECIFICATIONS**

**Years produced:** 1965-1980 (27,915 in total)
**Performance:** 0-60mph: 10.9sec
Top speed: 118mph
**Power & torque:** N/A
**Engine:** Normally aspirated 6230cc V8, petrol, carburettor, 16 valves
**Drivetrain:** Front-engine, RWD
**Structure:** Monocoque
**Transmission:** Three-speed automatic
**Weight:** 2114kg

**PRICE GUIDE**

**Launch price:** £6670
**Excellent:** £40,000+
**Good:** £25,000
**Average:** £15,000
**Project:** £5000

## ROLLS-ROYCE
### Phantom VI Limousine

The existing Phantom metamorphosed into the even more magnificent Phantom VI in 1968, a car that Rolls-Royce would continue to build – to special order only – right up until 1992. Despite this, and its V8's capacity boost to 6750cc in 1978, it had drum brakes right until the end. However, this most stately of British limousines wasn't intended for speed, more for cruising along gently while those inside basked in the glory of being incredibly rich. During its quarter-of-a-century existence, a mere 373 were constructed, ownership reading like a 'who's who' of the global elite.

**SPECIFICATIONS**

**Years produced:** 1968-1992 (373 in total)
**Performance:** 0-60mph: 13.2sec
Top speed: 112mph
**Power & torque:** N/A
**Engine:** Normally aspirated 6750cc V8, petrol, carburettor, 16 valves
**Drivetrain:** Front-engine, RWD
**Structure:** Separate chassis
**Transmission:** Three-speed automatic
**Weight:** 2722kg

**PRICE GUIDE**

**Launch price:** £8905
**Excellent:** £175,000
**Good:** £100,000
**Average:** £55,000
**Project:** £35,000

## ROLLS-ROYCE
### Corniche I

One of the few coachbuilders to create special versions of the Shadow was Mulliner Park Ward – although, as it was owned by Rolls-Royce, it was well placed to do so. Its two-door coupé and convertible had been around since 1965, but became known officially as Corniches in 1971. Britain's most expensive car at the time had the mechanical layout of the Shadow, but with even more lavish levels of equipment. Values are firming up nicely, says specialists Hillier-Hill, and steadily pulling away from the Shadow itself. Dropheads nowadays command a premium of up to a third more.

**SPECIFICATIONS**

**Years produced:** 1971-1987
**Performance:** 0-60mph: 9.7sec
Top speed: 126mph
**Power & torque:** N/A
**Engine:** Normally aspirated 6750cc V8, petrol, carburettor, 16 valves
**Drivetrain:** Front-engine RWD
**Structure:** Monocoque
**Transmission:** Three-speed automatic
**Weight:** 2184kg

**PRICE GUIDE**

**Launch price:** £11,556
**Excellent:** £85,000+
**Good:** £50,000
**Average:** £25,000
**Project:** £12,000

## ROLLS-ROYCE
### Camargue

Rolls-Royce tried to pull something special out of the bag with the Camargue, which, at £29,250 in 1975, took over from the Corniche as the UK's most expensive car. Using the Shadow platform, Italian styling house Pininfarina produced the car's razor-edged silhouette. The 6750cc V8 had extra (undisclosed) power, too, but in just over ten years of production just 530 Camargues were made, including one Bentley-badged sister. The looks, widely criticised at the time, are gaining more acceptance now, and rising values of the best examples reflect that.

**SPECIFICATIONS**

**Years produced:** 1975-1986 (530 in total)
**Performance:** 0-60mph: 10.9sec
Top speed: 118mph
**Power & torque:** 220bhp/330lb ft
**Engine:** Normally aspirated 6750cc V8, petrol, carburettor, 16 valves
**Drivetrain:** Front-engine RWD
**Structure:** Monocoque
**Transmission:** Three-speed automatic
**Weight:** 2390kg

**PRICE GUIDE**

**Launch price:** £29,250
**Excellent:** £80,000+
**Good:** £45,000
**Average:** £25,000
**Project:** £15,000

## ROLLS-ROYCE
## Silver Spirit/Silver Spur

In 1980, Rolls-Royce pensioned off the 15-year-old Shadow and replaced it with the Silver Spirit – although the Shadow really did live on in spirit, because the new car was effectively the old one with a fresh skin. The angular body was completely new, while an update in 1989 resulted in fuel injection, more power, anti-lock brakes and a revised interior. The Silver Spur was a long-wheelbase offshoot and outlasted the short-wheelbase cars on which it was based. In 1994, the Flying Spur was added to the range, complete with Bentley-esque turbocharging.

**SPECIFICATIONS**

| | |
|---|---|
| **Years produced:** | 1980-1998 |
| **Performance:** | 0-60mph: 10.4sec<br>Top speed: 126mph |
| **Power & torque:** | N/A |
| **Engine:** | Normally aspirated 6750cc V8, petrol, carburettor, overhead valves |
| **Drivetrain:** | Front-engine RWD |
| **Structure:** | Monocoque |
| **Transmission:** | Four-speed automatic |
| **Weight:** | 2285kg |

**PRICE GUIDE**

| | |
|---|---|
| **Launch price:** | £85,609 |
| **Excellent:** | £30,000 |
| **Good:** | £20,000 |
| **Average:** | £10,000 |
| **Project:** | £3000 |

## ROLLS-ROYCE
## Corniche II-IV

The Corniche lived on beyond the Silver Shadow saloon on which it was based, and survived well into the Silver Spirit era. Although coupés were discontinued in 1982, the convertibles were updated enough for 1987 to justify a small change of name to Corniche II. Alloy and rubber bumpers replaced the chrome items and fuel injection became standard for all markets, as did ABS. Subsequent incarnations remained largely unchanged: 1989's Corniche III had colour-coded bumpers and better suspension, while the end-of-the-line Corniche S in 1995 incorporated a turbocharger.

**SPECIFICATIONS**

| | |
|---|---|
| **Years produced:** | 1987-1995 (452 in total) |
| **Performance:** | 0-60mph: 17.1sec<br>Top speed: 120mph |
| **Power & torque:** | 215bhp/325lb ft |
| **Engine:** | Normally aspirated 6750cc V8, petrol, electronic fuel injection, 16 valves |
| **Drivetrain:** | Front-engine RWD |
| **Structure:** | Monocoque |
| **Transmission:** | Three-speed automatic |
| **Weight:** | 1430kg |

**PRICE GUIDE**

| | |
|---|---|
| **Launch price:** | £115,660 |
| **Excellent:** | £95,000+ |
| **Good:** | £60,000 |
| **Average:** | £40,000 |
| **Project:** | £20,000 |

## ROLLS-ROYCE
## Silver Seraph

Marking both a fresh start and the end of an era, the Silver Seraph replaced the Silver Spirit in 1998. It featured a completely new body, shared with its Bentley Arnage sister, but while the Bentley had a BMW twin-turbo V8, the softer-riding Seraph was powered by a 5.4-litre V12, also a BMW unit, making it the first 12-cylinder Rolls-Royce since the pre-war Phantom III. It was also the last Rolls-Royce to be built at Crewe before BMW bought the production rights and moved assembly to Goodwood. Values holding steady.

**SPECIFICATIONS**

| | |
|---|---|
| **Years produced:** | 1998-2002 (1570 in total) |
| **Performance:** | 0-60mph: 7.1sec<br>Top speed: 140mph |
| **Power & torque:** | 322bhp/361lb ft |
| **Engine:** | Normally aspirated 5379cc V12, petrol, electronic fuel injection, 48 valves |
| **Drivetrain:** | Front-engine RWD |
| **Structure:** | Monocoque |
| **Transmission:** | Five-speed automatic |
| **Weight:** | 2350kg |

**PRICE GUIDE**

| | |
|---|---|
| **Launch price:** | £155,175 |
| **Excellent:** | £60,000 |
| **Good:** | £40,000 |
| **Average:** | £25,000 |
| **Project:** | £16,000 |

## ROLLS-ROYCE
## Phantom VII

First product of a whole new era for Rolls-Royce, with BMW now owning the name and having built a new factory at Goodwood. The structure was all-new but the engine was a reworking of the V12 from the contemporary BMW 7-series, its 6.75-litre capacity a nod to the classic R-R V8, its outputs a very modern 453bhp and 531lb ft, enough to whisk this 2.5-tonne giant along at a very brisk pace and in almost total silence. Produced in greater numbers than any previous Phantom, there are plenty around. Buy very, *very* carefully to avoid ruinous running costs.

**SPECIFICATIONS**

| | |
|---|---|
| **Years produced:** | 2003-2017 (10,327 in total) |
| **Performance:** | 0-60mph: 5.7sec<br>Top speed: 149mph (limited) |
| **Power & torque:** | 453bhp/531lb ft |
| **Engine:** | Normally aspirated 6749cc V12, petrol, electronic fuel injection, 16 valves |
| **Drivetrain:** | Front-engine RWD |
| **Structure:** | Monocoque |
| **Transmission:** | Six-speed automatic |
| **Weight:** | 2485g |

**PRICE GUIDE (models up to 2010)**

| | |
|---|---|
| **Launch price:** | £252,038 |
| **Excellent:** | £110,000 |
| **Good:** | £90,000 |
| **Average:** | £60,000 |
| **Project:** | N/A |

# ROVER

ROVER STARTED car production in 1908 and made its name with robust, middle-class vehicles – an image that was consolidated after World War Two with models such as the P4 and P5, which earned the marque its 'Auntie' nickname. Slighty racier was the P6 of 1963, especially when it gained a V8 in 1968. Around that time it became part of British Leyland, and troubled years followed, although it still captured headlines with its SD1 in 1976. The company was sold to British Aerospace in 1988, and thence to BMW in 1994. Though the resulting 75 was a fine car, in 2000 BMW sold MG and Rover to a consortium, under which MG Rover struggled on until 2005 before going into administration.

## ROVER
## P4 75 'Cyclops'

The 1948 P3 had been a prewar hangover. With the new P4, Rover wiped its slate clean and presented a confident Studebaker-inspired – if rather upright – façade for the 1950s. The original P4 shared its chassis and engines with the P3, but it appeared radically different. Its most striking feature (up to 1952) was the centrally mounted headlight in the radiator grille – hence the 'Cyclops' nickname. The 2.1-litre straight-six was noted for its smoothness, and this was allied to a four-speed column-shift manual transmission. Values have levelled off.

**SPECIFICATIONS**

| | |
|---|---|
| **Years produced:** | 1949-1954 (33,267 in total) |
| **Performance:** | 0-60mph: 23.1sec<br>Top speed: 82mph |
| **Power & torque:** | 75bhp/111lb ft |
| **Engine:** | Normally aspirated 2103cc straight six, petrol, carburettor, 12 valves |
| **Drivetrain:** | Front-engine RWD |
| **Structure:** | Separate chassis |
| **Transmission:** | Four-speed manual |
| **Weight:** | 1451kg |

**PRICE GUIDE**

| | |
|---|---|
| **Launch price:** | £1106 |
| **Excellent:** | £14,500 |
| **Good:** | £7800 |
| **Average:** | £3700 |
| **Project:** | £1600 |

## ROVER
## P4 60/80

In 1953, the sales potential of the P4 was widened considerably by the arrival of the four-cylinder model. The 2.0-litre engine was also used in the Land Rover, and after the smoothness of the straight-six it proved something of a disappointment. However, in practice it wasn't much slower than the standard car, and proved slightly more economical, too. The 60bhp engine remained in the P4 until 1959, when it made way for the more powerful 2.2-litre 80bhp engine – reason enough to re-designate the car the P4 80 in its final three seasons.

**SPECIFICATIONS**

| | |
|---|---|
| **Years produced:** | 1953-1962 |
| **Performance:** | 0-60mph: 19.3sec<br>Top speed: 88mph |
| **Power & torque:** | 60bhp/101lb ft |
| **Engine:** | Normally aspirated 1997cc four cylinder, petrol, carburettor, 8 valves |
| **Drivetrain:** | Front-engine RWD |
| **Structure:** | Separate chassis |
| **Transmission:** | Four-speed manual |
| **Weight:** | 1481kg |

**PRICE GUIDE**

| | |
|---|---|
| **Launch price:** | £1163 |
| **Excellent:** | £7000 |
| **Good:** | £4250 |
| **Average:** | £2000 |
| **Project:** | £1000 |

## ROVER
## P4 90/100/110

The six-cylinder P4 was offered in a wide variety of forms. After its first facelift, the 2.6-litre IOE engine producing 90bhp was installed, giving it a 90mph top speed and effortless motorway cruising. That made way for the more powerful P4 100 in 1960. The new engine was a short-stroke version of the P5 3.0-litre, and even smoother in service. Performance was up and overdrive improved refinement at speed. Also look out for the 105 R and S: with 108bhp, they could easily top the 'ton'. All are refined, high-quality classics and values are holding firm.

**SPECIFICATIONS**

| | |
|---|---|
| **Years produced:** | 1954-1964 (60,724 in total) |
| **Performance:** | 18.4sec<br>Top speed: 90mph |
| **Power & torque:** | 93bhp/138lb ft |
| **Engine:** | Normally aspirated 2638cc straight six, petrol, carburettor, 12 valves |
| **Drivetrain:** | Front-engine RWD |
| **Structure:** | Separate chassis |
| **Transmission:** | Four-speed manual |
| **Weight:** | 1486kg |

**PRICE GUIDE**

| | |
|---|---|
| **Launch price:** | £1297 |
| **Excellent:** | £10,000 |
| **Good:** | £6500 |
| **Average:** | £3300 |
| **Project:** | £1200 |

## ROVER
## P5 & P5 Coupé

Introduced in 1958, the Rover P5 established itself as the company's flagship, easily slotting in above the P4 105 models. In the process, it became the favoured transport of British prime ministers and royalty. The new styling had been penned by David Bache, while the monocoque body (Rover's first) had been engineered by Spen King and Gordon Bashford. Power was from a 2995cc version of the IOE that had first seen service in the P3, but which continued to deliver supreme smoothness and refinement. The Coupé with its lower roofline joined the range in 1962.

**SPECIFICATIONS**

| | |
|---|---|
| **Years produced:** | 1958-1967 (48,541 in total) |
| **Performance:** | 0-60mph: 16.2sec<br>Top speed: 96mph |
| **Power & torque:** | 115bhp/164lb ft |
| **Engine:** | Normally aspirated 2995cc straight six, petrol, carburettor, 12 valves |
| **Drivetrain:** | Front-engine RWD |
| **Structure:** | Monocoque |
| **Transmission:** | Four-speed manual |
| **Weight:** | 1613kg |

**PRICE GUIDE (add 20% for Coupé)**

| | |
|---|---|
| **Launch price:** | £1764 |
| **Excellent:** | £8500 |
| **Good:** | £5000 |
| **Average:** | £2400 |
| **Project:** | £1000 |

## ROVER
## P5B & P5B Coupé

The P5 was continuously developed during its life, first with the arrival of the more powerful 'Weslake Head' version, and then with the arrival of the handsome coupé. Nevertheless, the most exciting addition to the range came in 1967, when an ex-Buick V8 engine was squeezed under the bonnet to create the P5B. The gutsy new motor improved performance, and economy, too, while the appealing straight-six soundtrack had been replaced by a charismatic V8 rumble. For many, this was Rover's high-water mark, never to be topped.

**SPECIFICATIONS**

| | |
|---|---|
| **Years produced:** | 1967-1973 (20,600 in total) |
| **Performance:** | 0-60mph: 12.4sec<br>Top speed: 108mph |
| **Power & torque:** | 161bhp/201lb ft |
| **Engine:** | Normally aspirated 3528cc V8, petrol, carburettor, 16 valves |
| **Drivetrain:** | Front-engine RWD |
| **Structure:** | Monocoque |
| **Transmission:** | Three-speed automatic |
| **Weight:** | 1586kg |

**PRICE GUIDE (Coupé in brackets)**

| | |
|---|---|
| **Launch price:** | £2009 |
| **Excellent:** | £12,000 (£17,000) |
| **Good:** | £8000 (£9500) |
| **Average:** | £3500 (£3800) |
| **Project:** | £1350 (£1650) |

## ROVER
## P6 2000/2200

In the UK, the Rover 2000 and Triumph 2000 pairing created the executive car class as we know it today. Less bulky than the luxury models of old, but just as comfortable and a whole lot more economical. When it first appeared, the P6 was rather radical, with its skeleton structure and modern styling. The company gambled that it would appeal to traditionally conservative Rover customers, as well as attracting new ones. The strategy worked, and the P6 went on to become a huge success. It was a none-too-shabby, if improbable, rally car, too.

**SPECIFICATIONS**

| | |
|---|---|
| **Years produced:** | 1963-1977 (213,890 in total) |
| **Performance:** | 0-60mph: 11.9sec<br>Top speed: 112mph |
| **Power & torque:** | 113bhp/126lb ft |
| **Engine:** | Normally aspirated 1978cc four cylinder, petrol, carburettor, 8 valves |
| **Drivetrain:** | Front-engine RWD |
| **Structure:** | Monocoque |
| **Transmission:** | Four-speed manual |
| **Weight:** | 1222kg |

**PRICE GUIDE**

| | |
|---|---|
| **Launch price:** | £1264 |
| **Excellent:** | £7500 |
| **Good:** | £3400 |
| **Average:** | £2000 |
| **Project:** | £800 |

## ROVER
## P6B 3500

Although the Rover 2000 was capable, in no way could it be described as quick. Yet with the installation of the ex-Buick V8 it became Rover's first Q-car, offering Jaguar-matching pace and poise. The P6B caught on rapidly, selling in huge numbers despite its loftier price tag than the four-cylinder models. It was initially offered in automatic guise only, but the balance was redressed in 1971 with the arrival of the more sporting, four-speed manual 3500S. Take care when buying, as clean body panels can hide many horrors beneath. Values creeping up.

**SPECIFICATIONS**

| | |
|---|---|
| **Years produced:** | 1968-1976 (79,057 in total) |
| **Performance:** | 0-60mph: 9.5sec<br>Top speed: 117mph |
| **Power & torque:** | 144bhp/197lb ft |
| **Engine:** | Normally aspirated 3528cc V8, petrol, carburettor, 16 valves |
| **Drivetrain:** | Front-engine RWD |
| **Structure:** | Monocoque |
| **Transmission:** | Three-speed auto/four-speed manual |
| **Weight:** | 1272kg |

**PRICE GUIDE (add 20% for 3500S)**

| | |
|---|---|
| **Launch price:** | £1801 |
| **Excellent:** | £10,000 |
| **Good:** | £5000 |
| **Average:** | £2500 |
| **Project:** | £1100 |

## ROVER
## SD1 3500/VDP

The SD1 was the final flowering of the Rover V8 line first masterminded by Spen King, Gordon Bashford and David Bache – although looking at its swooping Ferrari Daytona-inspired styling and BL build quality, it's hard to see the connection. Initially it sold like hot cakes, yet the shoddy quality soon started putting buyers off. The car was improved during its life, so the final models were fast, appealing and genuinely desirable, but the SD1 was always tarnished by the BL connection. Nowadays, there's excellent parts availability and club support.

**SPECIFICATIONS**

| | |
|---|---|
| **Years produced:** | 1976-1986 (303,345 in total) |
| **Performance:** | 0-60mph: 8.6sec<br>Top speed: 126mph |
| **Power & torque:** | 155bhp/198lb ft |
| **Engine:** | Normally aspirated 3528cc V8, petrol, carburettor, 16 valves |
| **Drivetrain:** | Front-engine RWD |
| **Structure:** | Monocoque |
| **Transmission:** | Five-speed manual |
| **Weight:** | 1313kg |

**PRICE GUIDE**

| | |
|---|---|
| **Launch price:** | £4750 |
| **Excellent:** | £5000 |
| **Good:** | £3000 |
| **Average:** | £1500 |
| **Project:** | £750 |

## ROVER
## SD1 2000/2300/2600

As good as they are to drive, the six-cylinder Rover SD1s are always going to have two things going against them: a reputation for unreliability from their Triumph-designed engines, and the fact they are not V8-powered. And that's a shame, because the 2300 and 2600 are refined, relatively economical and punchy. The O-series-powered 2000 appeared in 1982 with the Series 2 facelift, and goes better than you might imagine, too. There's also enough room in the engine bay to climb in while servicing – and, as with all SD1s, that's still facilitated by plentiful parts supply.

**SPECIFICATIONS**

| | |
|---|---|
| **Years produced:** | 1977-1986 (303,345 in total) |
| **Performance:** | 0-60mph: 9.5sec<br>Top speed: 117mph |
| **Power & torque:** | 136bhp/152lb ft |
| **Engine:** | Normally aspirated 2597cc straight six, carburettor, 12 valves |
| **Drivetrain:** | Front-engine RWD |
| **Structure:** | Monocoque |
| **Transmission:** | Five-speed manual |
| **Weight:** | 1351kg |

**PRICE GUIDE**

| | |
|---|---|
| **Launch price:** | £7450 |
| **Excellent:** | £4000 |
| **Good:** | £2000 |
| **Average:** | £700 |
| **Project:** | £500 |

## ROVER
## SD1 Vitesse

Once referred to as 'the poor man's Aston Martin' by *Motor* magazine, the Vitesse remains a fast and effective bruiser of a sports saloon, despite the relatively paltry horsepower figure. Extrovert spoilers and racy trim completed the Vitesse's transformation, and, despite the SD1 having been around for six years when it first appeared, it was a surprise success for Rover. Later twin-plenum version homologation special, developed with Lotus, was more powerful (add 20% for these), while TWR race versions were Touring Car favourites.

**SPECIFICATIONS**

| | |
|---|---|
| **Years produced:** | 1982-1986 |
| **Performance:** | 0-60mph: 7.1sec<br>Top speed: 135mph |
| **Power & torque:** | 190bhp/220lb ft |
| **Engine:** | Normally aspirated 3528cc V8, petrol, electronic fuel injection, 16 valves |
| **Drivetrain:** | Front-engine RWD |
| **Structure:** | Monocoque |
| **Transmission:** | Five-speed manual |
| **Weight:** | 1440kg |

**PRICE GUIDE**

| | |
|---|---|
| **Launch price:** | £14,950 |
| **Excellent:** | £8500 |
| **Good:** | £4000 |
| **Average:** | £1650 |
| **Project:** | £800 |

## ROVER
### 800/Vitesse/Sterling

As a replacement for the Rover SD1, the 800 should have hit the spot perfectly – it was sophisticated, powered by a range of multi-valve engines, and looked bang up to date. But those shiny new motors failed to deliver, and early build issues soon tarnished the car's reputation. The 2.5-litre Honda V6 was soon replaced by a torquier 2.7, and that transformed the Sterling luxury model and its new Vitesse stablemate into fast and effortless sporting saloons. Smart examples of the Honda-engined cars are quite sought-after; there's not the same following for the smaller fours.

**SPECIFICATIONS**

| | |
|---|---|
| **Years produced:** | 1988-1991 (49,496 827s in total) |
| **Performance:** | 0-60mph: 7.7sec<br>Top speed: 139mph |
| **Power & torque:** | 177bhp/168lb ft |
| **Engine:** | Normally aspirated 2675cc V6, petrol, fuel injection, 24 valves |
| **Drivetrain:** | Front-engine FWD |
| **Structure:** | Monocoque |
| **Transmission:** | Five-speed manual/four-speed auto |
| **Weight:** | 1427kg |

**PRICE GUIDE**

| | |
|---|---|
| **Launch price:** | £23,950 |
| **Excellent:** | £3500 |
| **Good:** | £2000 |
| **Average:** | £1200 |
| **Project:** | £500 |

## ROVER
### 200/220 Coupe

Rover launched its two-door 200 Coupe in 1992, boasting a unique bodyshell, an innovative two-piece lift-out glass sunroof, and even a splash of walnut veneer and leather trim on the top versions. There were normally aspirated 1.6 and 2.0 engines, but the driver's choice was the 220 Coupe Turbo (or Tomcat), forced induction lifting the output of the 2-litre 16v T-series engine to 200PS (197bhp). This gave the driven front wheels quite a workout, even with Torsen traction control. Still, its 149mph top speed made it the fastest ever production Rover and a bit of a Q-car.

**SPECIFICATIONS**

| | |
|---|---|
| **Years produced:** | 1992-1998 |
| **Performance:** | 0-60mph: 6.3sec (Turbo)<br>Top speed: 149mph |
| **Power & torque:** | 197bhp/174lb ft |
| **Engine:** | Turbocharged 1994cc four cylinder, petrol, electronic fuel injection, 16v |
| **Drivetrain:** | Front-engine FWD |
| **Structure:** | Monocoque |
| **Transmission:** | Five-speed manual |
| **Weight:** | 1240kg |

**PRICE GUIDE**

| | |
|---|---|
| **Launch price:** | £18,315 |
| **Excellent:** | £3500 |
| **Good:** | £1750 |
| **Average:** | £1000 |
| **Project:** | £300 |

## ROVER
### 75

When it was launched in 1999, the 75 represented a bright new future for the Great British brand, but sadly this was Rover's last ever big saloon. The company, with significant help from BMW, put a lot of time and effort into getting the 75 right, the retro styling was well judged, and its road manners are excellent. The 1.8 K-Series and 2.0-litre KV6 petrol versions are gutless, but the BMW-engined diesel and Rover 2.5-litre KV6 units are strong and long-lasting if looked after. Rare rear-wheel-drive V8 models can fetch up to £10k.

**SPECIFICATIONS**

| | |
|---|---|
| **Years produced:** | 1998-2005 (211,175 produced) |
| **Performance:** | 0-60mph: 8.8sec (2.5 V6)<br>Top speed: 137mph |
| **Power & torque:** | 175bhp/177lb ft |
| **Engine:** | Normally aspirated 2497cc V6, petrol, fuel injection, 24 valves |
| **Drivetrain:** | Front-engine FWD |
| **Structure:** | Monocoque |
| **Transmission:** | Five-speed manual/four-speed auto |
| **Weight:** | 1425kg |

**PRICE GUIDE**

| | |
|---|---|
| **Launch price:** | £25,625 |
| **Excellent:** | £3000 |
| **Good:** | £1500 |
| **Average:** | £1250 |
| **Project:** | £500 |

# SAAB

SWEDISH AERONAUTICS firm Svenska Aeroplan Aktiebolaget thankfully shortened its name to SAAB when it started building cars in 1949. The 92 made great use of aviation principles in its design and was very advanced for its era. Subsequent developments built on the foundations of the 92 and kept much of its styling, right up until the 1968 launch of the 99, which in turn grew into the 900. These cars brought Saab much acclaim, thanks partly to their innovative use of turbocharging. Following a 1980s partnership with Fiat, General Motors took over in 1989, managing to destroy the cars' individual character – and ultimately the marque itself, with Saab ceasing trading in 2012.

## SAAB
### 95/96 two-stroke

The Saab 96 was marketed as a new car when launched in 1960, but it was very closely related to the original two-stroke, front-wheel-drive 92 that had been around since 1949 and had proved to be a massive breakthrough in design. More than 10 years on, the 96, with its aerodynamic styling, independent suspension and tenacious roadholding, still seemed ultra-modern despite being a facelift. The 841cc two-stroke developed enough power to push the 96 to nearly 80mph. The 95 is the quirkily-styled estate version of the 96.

**SPECIFICATIONS**

| | |
|---|---|
| **Years produced:** | 1960-1968 (253,305 in total) |
| **Performance:** | 0-60mph: 24.1sec<br>Top speed: 79mph |
| **Power & torque:** | 38bhp/60lb ft |
| **Engine:** | Normally aspirated 841cc two-stroke triple, petrol, carburettor |
| **Drivetrain:** | Front-engine FWD |
| **Structure:** | Monocoque |
| **Transmission:** | Three/four-speed manual |
| **Weight:** | 803kg |

**PRICE GUIDE (Add 10% for '60-65 cars)**

| | |
|---|---|
| **Launch price:** | £885 |
| **Excellent:** | £7500 |
| **Good:** | £4500 |
| **Average:** | £2200 |
| **Project:** | £1200 |

## SAAB
## 96 Sport/Monte Carlo

Introduced in 1962, the 96 Sport model was the raciest of the breed and reflected its competition breeding. The shrieking two-stroke pushed out a heady 57bhp and the model soon proved its mettle in rallying. Factory driver Erik Carlsson won the 1960, 1961 and 1962 RAC rallies in addition to the 1962 and '63 Monte Carlo classics. Three years later, the Sport was renamed Monte Carlo to reflect its top-level success. As marketing opportunities went, it was a case of too little too late, although this special edition is highly prized today.

**SPECIFICATIONS**

**Years produced:** 1962-1968 (2412/2453 in total)
**Performance:** 0-60mph: 19.3sec
Top speed: 88mph
**Power & torque:** 57bhp/67lb ft
**Engine:** Normally aspirated 841cc two-stroke triple, petrol, carburettor
**Drivetrain:** Front-engine FWD
**Structure:** Monocoque
**Transmission:** Four-speed manual
**Weight:** 888kg

**PRICE GUIDE**

**Launch price:** £1059
**Excellent:** £11,000
**Good:** £7200
**Average:** £4000
**Project:** £2000

## SAAB
## Sonett II/III

The Sonett was an unusual addition to the Saab line-up. This Björn Karlström-penned two-seater coupé was powered initially by the 96's two-stroke, but then received Ford's V4 power unit for increased performance. The Sonett II made way for the heavily-revised, Sergio Coggiola-styled Sonett III (pictured) in 1970: this retained the same centre section and, despite a more powerful 1.7-litre V4, delivered near-identical performance due to its extra weight. In 1974 the Sonett was phased out, having failed to find favour in the lucrative Stateside market.

**SPECIFICATIONS**

**Years produced:** 1967-1974 (10,236 in total)
**Performance:** 0-60mph: 14.4sec
Top speed: 100mph
**Power & torque:** 75bhp/94lb ft
**Engine:** Normally aspirated 1699cc V4, petrol, carburettor, 8 valves
**Drivetrain:** Front-engine FWD
**Structure:** Steel box chassis, glassfibre body
**Transmission:** Four-speed manual
**Weight:** 810kg

**PRICE GUIDE**

**Launch price:** N/A in UK
**Excellent:** £15,000
**Good:** £9000
**Average:** £5000
**Project:** £2250

## SAAB
## 95/96 V4

In 1967, the two-stroke that had served so well for so long was joined by a V4. The four-stroke 1498cc Ford Taunus engine had been installed to take the 96 (and estate 95) further upmarket, but it also acted as an insurance against the threat of emissions regulations in Europe. The first V4 96s produced 55bhp – rising to 65bhp – and usefully boosted performance, with top speed climbing to over 90mph. It was in this form that the 96 remained to the end, gaining more equipment and impact-absorbing bumpers before finally being retired in 1980.

**SPECIFICATIONS**

**Years produced:** 1967-1980 (326,570/77,873 in total)
**Performance:** 0-60mph: 16.5sec
Top speed: 96mph
**Power & torque:** 65bhp/85lb ft
**Engine:** Normally aspirated 1498cc V4, petrol, carburettor, 8 valves
**Drivetrain:** Front-engine FWD
**Structure:** Monocoque
**Transmission:** Four-speed manual
**Weight:** 873kg

**PRICE GUIDE**

**Launch price:** £801
**Excellent:** £5500
**Good:** £3350
**Average:** £1500
**Project:** £600

## SAAB
## 99

Although the 92 and 96 had done well for Saab, the firm's bosses knew that in order to retain customers, it would need to introduce a larger car. The 99 ended up being the perfect model to head the range as it was also innovative, quirky and individual. The wraparound screen and impressive aerodynamics headed up a front-wheel-drive car of commendable dynamic prowess. Its 1.7-litre engine had been developed in tandem with Triumph and UK engineering company Ricardo, although Saab developed the unit further to overcome some design faults. Prices on the up.

**SPECIFICATIONS**

**Years produced:** 1968-1984 (588,643 in total)
**Performance:** 0-60mph: 15.2sec
Top speed: 97mph
**Power & torque:** 80bhp/N/A
**Engine:** Normally aspirated 1709cc four cylinder, petrol, carburettor, 8 valves
**Drivetrain:** Front-engine FWD
**Structure:** Monocoque
**Transmission:** Four-speed manual
**Weight:** 925kg

**PRICE GUIDE**

**Launch price:** £1288
**Excellent:** £5000
**Good:** £2600
**Average:** £1350
**Project:** £700

## SAAB
## 99 Turbo

During its lifetime, the 99 had received regular upgrades: first a larger version of its slant-four engine, then fuel injection to create the effective EMS sports saloon. However, in 1978, Saab created a legend – the 145bhp 99 Turbo. An early adopter of forced induction, the firm's fast but laggy 99 Turbo hit the market at just the right time – the second energy crisis of 1979 witnessed many people trading down from larger cars, and the seemingly economical new model offered all of the pace without the fuel consumption of the multi-cylinder opposition. Values rising.

**SPECIFICATIONS**

**Years produced:** 1978-1981 (10,607 in total)
**Performance:** 0-60mph: 8.9sec
Top speed: 121mph
**Power & torque:** 145bhp/174lb ft
**Engine:** Turbocharged 1985cc four cylinder, petrol, electronic fuel injection, 8 valves
**Drivetrain:** Front-engine FWD
**Structure:** Monocoque
**Transmission:** Four-speed manual
**Weight:** 1130kg

**PRICE GUIDE**

**Launch price:** £7850
**Excellent:** £11,500
**Good:** £7000
**Average:** £4000
**Project:** £1750

## SAAB
### 900

Saab cleverly evolved its models and augmented platforms, so when it launched the 900 in 1979 the newcomer was clearly based heavily on the decade-old 99. But given that car's continued popularity, this was no handicap. The 900 majored on safety, and its impact-absorbing bumpers, crumple zones and padded interior were touted as major selling points. It was developed through its life to keep pace with contemporary technology – and that maintained a healthy demand. Overshadowed by the Turbo, but considerably more durable due to being less stressed.

**SPECIFICATIONS**

**Years produced:** 1979-1993 (202,284 in total)
**Performance:** 0-60mph: 13.3sec
Top speed: 105mph
**Power & torque:** 108bhp/121lb ft
**Engine:** Normally aspirated 1985cc four cylinder, petrol, carburettor, 8 valve
**Drivetrain:** Front-engine FWD
**Structure:** Monocoque
**Transmission:** Five-speed manual
**Weight:** 1214kg

**PRICE GUIDE**

**Launch price:** £8675
**Excellent:** £3500
**Good:** £1800
**Average:** £1200
**Project:** £500

## SAAB
### 900 Turbo

Star of the 900 range was the Turbo – earliest models pushed out 145bhp and delivered rapid (if laggy) performance. This was soon improved, first by the fitment of APC and engine management, and then with the arrival of the 175bhp 16-valve T16S model in 1984. Three-doors were the most popular, and have a near-cult following now – especially in Aero form. Can suffer from rust around the edges and the weak gearbox is an issue but, otherwise, the cars will take 200,000 miles, and more, in their stride. Pay c50% more for uprated (185bhp) Carlsson model (pictured). All are on the up.

**SPECIFICATIONS**

**Years produced:** 1979-1993 (202,284 in total)
**Performance:** 0-60mph: 7.5sec
Top speed: 135mph
**Power & torque:** 175bhp/205lb ft
**Engine:** Turbocharged 1985cc four cylinder, petrol, fuel injection, 16 valves
**Drivetrain:** Front-engine FWD
**Structure:** Monocoque
**Transmission:** Five-speed manual
**Weight:** 1340kg

**PRICE GUIDE**

**Launch price:** £8675
**Excellent:** £7250
**Good:** £3500
**Average:** £1500
**Project:** £750

## SAAB
### 9000/Turbo/Carlsson

For its first all-new car since the 99, Saab went down the collaborative route with the Italians. The 9000 was one of the 'Type 4' gang and, like its Lancia and Fiat cousins, was styled by Giorgetto Giugiaro. The engine was the familiar 2.0-litre Saab 99 unit, but mounted transversally, and the interior was ergonomically styled to make upgrading 99 and 900 owners feel right at home. Constantly improved throughout its life, the 9000 stayed on the pace right to the end of its production. Carlssons ended up with 225bhp and were 150mph flying machiines.

**SPECIFICATIONS (Turbo)**

**Years produced:** 1985-1992 (153,469 in total)
**Performance:** 0-60mph: 7.2sec
Top speed: 141mph
**Power & torque:** 175bhp/201lb ft
**Engine:** Turbocharged 1985cc four cylinder, petrol, fuel injection, 16 valves
**Drivetrain:** Front-engine FWD
**Structure:** Monocoque
**Transmission:** Five-speed manual
**Weight:** 1316kg

**PRICE GUIDE (Carlsson in brackets)**

**Launch price:** £18,700
**Excellent:** £2500 (£5000)
**Good:** £1500 (£3400)
**Average:** £800 (£2350)
**Project:** £350 (£1200)

# SEAT

SEAT STARTED life as a Fiat subsidiary in 1919, with its cars known as Fiat-Hispania. It became SEAT – Sociedad Española de Automóviles de Turismo – in 1950 when the Spanish state took over. Fiat stayed very involved though, to the degree that most SEATS were simply Spanish-built copies of Fiat models such as the 600, 850, 1400 and Panda (which was known as the Marbella), although there were one or two unique models. Fiat's involvement came to an abrupt end in 1981, leaving Volkswagen to snatch control in 1986. Since then, SEAT has built its own individually-styled models, albeit using Volkswagen floorpans and engines, with the Ibiza the best-selling car in its range.

## SEAT
### 600

The SEAT Seiscientos kick-started the Spanish car industry, as a result of a tie-up between Franco's government, the Spanish banks and Fiat. It was effectively a badge-engineered Fiat 600, which ended up enjoying a long production run and becoming a Spanish legend in the process (earning the nicknames *pelotilla* and *seílla*). The 600 was an integral part of the country's post-Civil War economic boom – although, like its donor car, it was far from inspiring to drive. The SEAT-only four-door was an interesting derivative. Rare in the UK.

**SPECIFICATIONS**

**Years produced:** 1957-1973 (797,350 in total)
**Performance:** 0-60mph: N/A
Top speed: 66mph
**Power & torque:** 29bhp/40lb ft
**Engine:** Normally aspirated 767cc four cylinder, petrol, carburettor, 8 valves
**Drivetrain:** Rear-engine RWD
**Structure:** Monocoque
**Transmission:** Four-speed manual
**Weight:** 585kg

**PRICE GUIDE**

**Launch price:** N/A in UK
**Excellent:** £5000
**Good:** £4000
**Average:** £2000
**Project:** £850

## SEAT
### 133

The 133 was a strange mixture of old and new that was actually briefly imported into the UK and sold by Fiat dealerships. The floorpan, engine and gearbox were taken from the SEAT 850, but the body styling was all-new, and looked like a cross between the Fiat 126 and 127. But compared with the cream of the '70s supermini crop, the 133 didn't stand a chance – and it flopped outside of its home market. In Spain, where tough import barriers had been erected and money was tight, its excellent fuel consumption and trusted mechanicals were positive selling points.

**SPECIFICATIONS**

| | |
|---|---|
| **Years produced:** | 1974-1980 |
| **Performance:** | 0-60mph: 18.5sec<br>Top speed: 81mph |
| **Power & torque:** | 39bhp/42lb ft |
| **Engine:** | Normally aspirated 903cc four cylinder, petrol, carburettor, 8 valves |
| **Drivetrain:** | Rear-engine RWD |
| **Structure:** | Monocoque |
| **Transmission:** | Four-speed manual |
| **Weight:** | 780kg |

**PRICE GUIDE**

| | |
|---|---|
| **Launch price:** | N/A in UK |
| **Excellent:** | £2000 |
| **Good:** | £1300 |
| **Average:** | £650 |
| **Project:** | £400 |

## SEAT
### 1200/1430 Sport

There's no doubting the SEAT 1200 Sport's good looks, yet its creation was a hard-nosed business decision. The Spanish carmaker decided that it wasn't going to licence-build the Fiat 128 3P, and pledged to build its own instead. The car was known as the *Bocanegra* (Spanish for 'Black Mouth') because of its black polymer bumpers – perfect for Mediterranean driving conditions. The locally produced engine was shared with the Fiat 124, and the car's underpinnings were from the 127, so it was a real 'bitza' – but an appealing one. Body not suited to northern climes...

**SPECIFICATIONS**

| | |
|---|---|
| **Years produced:** | 1975-1980 |
| **Performance:** | 0-60mph: 12.5sec<br>Top speed: 102mph |
| **Power & torque:** | 77bhp/82lb ft |
| **Engine:** | Normally aspirated 1438cc four cylinder, petrol, carburettor, 8 valves |
| **Drivetrain:** | Front-engine FWD |
| **Structure:** | Monocoque |
| **Transmission:** | Four-speed manual |
| **Weight:** | 815kg |

**PRICE GUIDE**

| | |
|---|---|
| **Launch price:** | N/A in UK |
| **Excellent:** | £4000 |
| **Good:** | £2600 |
| **Average:** | £1800 |
| **Project:** | £1000 |

## SEAT
### Ibiza Cupra

The second-gen Ibiza was launched after SEAT's takeover by the VW group, so it shares many parts with VWs, the Polo in particular. What makes it interesting is a plethora of sporting versions with real driver appeal: the launch of the Cupra models with punchy turbo engines and keen handling, allied with much success in rallying, transformed SEAT's image. Post-1999-facelift models are best; distinguished by the 'S' badge doubling as the bootlid release. As mk1 Golf GTI prices soar, here's an affordable alternative.

**SPECIFICATIONS**

| | |
|---|---|
| **Years produced:** | 1993-2002 (c1.5 million in total) |
| **Performance:** | 0-60mph: 7.8sec (1.8T Cupra)<br>Top speed: 135mph |
| **Power & torque:** | 156bhp/152lb ft |
| **Engine:** | Turbocharged 1781cc four cylinder, petrol, electronic injection, 20 valves |
| **Drivetrain:** | Front-engine FWD |
| **Structure:** | Monocoque |
| **Transmission:** | Five-speed manual |
| **Weight:** | 1119kg |

**PRICE GUIDE**

| | |
|---|---|
| **Launch price:** | £14,000 |
| **Excellent:** | £3000 |
| **Good:** | £2000 |
| **Average:** | £1500 |
| **Project:** | £600 |

# SIMCA

THE SOCIÉTÉ Industrielle de Mécanique et de Carrosserie Automobile was founded in France in 1935, building rebadged Fiats. This it did so well that, during the 1950s, it was able to take over a number of other manufacturers, including Ford France, and put that company's V8 into production, as well as constructing its own rather distinctive designs. Chrysler, which was seeking a European toehold, took over in 1963, but it had similar problems running the marque as it suffered in the UK with Rootes. In 1970, Simca became Chrysler France, before being sold to Peugeot in 1978. It soon renamed all the models Talbot; the last 'Simca', a Solara, came out in 1980.

## SIMCA
### Aronde

The conventionally-engineered Aronde was the car that carried Simca into the world of constructors, the French firm having hitherto assembled licence-built Fiats (the Aronde retained a Fiat-conceived engine). The model proved popular in its home market, competing strongly with the Peugeot 203, and paved the way for a long line of middle-market Simcas. It was of monocoque construction with a typically soft Gallic ride. Rare even in France, especially as rust is a major enemy of these cars, so finding one won't be the work of a moment.

**SPECIFICATIONS**

| | |
|---|---|
| **Years produced:** | 1951-1964 (1,104,315 in total) |
| **Performance:** | 0-60mph: 29.4sec<br>Top speed: 73mph |
| **Power & torque:** | 45bhp/61lb ft |
| **Engine:** | Normally aspirated 1221cc four cylinder, petrol, carburettor, 8 valves |
| **Drivetrain:** | Front-engine RWD |
| **Structure:** | Monocoque |
| **Transmission:** | Four-speed manual |
| **Weight:** | 1140kg |

**PRICE GUIDE**

| | |
|---|---|
| **Launch price:** | £896 |
| **Excellent:** | £5000 |
| **Good:** | £3100 |
| **Average:** | £1300 |
| **Project:** | £750 |

## SIMCA
### Océane/Plein Ciel

The convertible Océane and its coupé Plein Ciel sibling are very effectively based on the frumpy Aronde saloon. Solid and dependable mechanicals underneath won't set the world alight, but these delicately styled and likeable cars are pleasant to drive in an *olde worlde* way. More powerful engines were introduced along the way, including the charmingly named 70bhp Flash super special. Rust has diminished numbers but the cars have a ready following in France, and are developing one in the UK, too, thanks to the Simca Club. Values rising.

**SPECIFICATIONS**

| | |
|---|---|
| **Years produced:** | 1957-1961 (11,500 in total) |
| **Performance:** | 0-60mph: 18.5sec<br>Top speed: 80mph |
| **Power & torque:** | 56bhp/67lb ft |
| **Engine:** | Normally aspirated 1290cc four cylinder, petrol, carburettor, 8 valves |
| **Drivetrain:** | Front-engine RWD |
| **Structure:** | Monocoque |
| **Transmission:** | Four-speed manual |
| **Weight:** | 1000kg |

**PRICE GUIDE**

| | |
|---|---|
| **Launch price:** | N/A in UK |
| **Excellent:** | £15,000 |
| **Good:** | £12,000 |
| **Average:** | £5000 |
| **Project:** | £2500 |

## SIMCA
### 1000/1200 Coupé

In its desire to create a sporting version of its 1000 saloon, Simca turned to Bertone – and chief stylist Giorgetto Giugiaro – to fashion this chic coupé's outline. Under the skin, changes from the saloon were limited to the adoption of all-round disc brakes, with the donor car's robust 944cc engine/gearbox package being carried straight over. The model was upgraded to 1200S specification in 1967, by now packing an 80bhp 1204cc engine. This pert machine achieved little success outside of its homeland, due largely to a near total lack of promotion. On the up.

**SPECIFICATIONS**

| | |
|---|---|
| **Years produced:** | 1963-1971 |
| **Performance:** | 0-60mph: 13.6sec<br>Top speed: 107mph |
| **Power & torque:** | 80bhp/76lb ft |
| **Engine:** | Normally aspirated 1204cc four cylinder, petrol, carburettor, 8 valves |
| **Drivetrain:** | Rear-engine RWD |
| **Structure:** | Monocoque |
| **Transmission:** | Four-speed manual |
| **Weight:** | 891kg |

**PRICE GUIDE (add 25% for 1200 Coupé)**

| | |
|---|---|
| **Launch price:** | £1493 |
| **Excellent:** | £12,000 |
| **Good:** | £6500 |
| **Average:** | £2350 |
| **Project:** | £1300 |

## SIMCA
### 1000 GLS/Special

The Simca Mille was more than a baby car for a generation of young French families; it was a way of life. The rear-engined saloon boasted four doors, reasonable cabin space plus a large front luggage compartment. However, handling was 'interesting' due to its rearward weight bias. Later GLS and Special models had additional equipment and were powered by 1.1- and 1.3-litre engines. The improved performance made them easier to live with as a result. These cars suffer from widespread rust but are bulletproof mechanically.

**SPECIFICATIONS**

| | |
|---|---|
| **Years produced:** | 1969-1978 |
| **Performance:** | 0-60mph: 16.4sec<br>Top speed: 88mph |
| **Power & torque:** | 40bhp/47lb ft |
| **Engine:** | Normally aspirated 944cc four cylinder, petrol, carburettor, 8 valves |
| **Drivetrain:** | Rear-engine RWD |
| **Structure:** | Monocoque |
| **Transmission:** | Four-speed manual |
| **Weight:** | 796kg |

**PRICE GUIDE**

| | |
|---|---|
| **Launch price:** | £758 |
| **Excellent:** | £3000 |
| **Good:** | £1750 |
| **Average:** | £1200 |
| **Project:** | £500 |

# SINGER

GRADUATING FROM bicycles and motorcycles, Singer built its first car in 1905, found success with the Ten in 1912, and during the 1920s rose to be Britain's third largest car maker. A certain Billy Rootes bought 50 Tens and used the profits from selling them on to start his own firm, but we'll talk about that elsewhere. The '30s recession hit Singer hard, and the firm had barely recovered when war broke out. Things were no better afterwards, and in 1955 it became another badge picked up by the Rootes empire. The cars retained their overhead-cam engines for a few years, then became Hillmans with a fancy grille and interior. Chrysler canned the marque in 1970.

## SINGER
### Nine Roadster/4A/4B

Inhabiting the same territory as MG's T-series, Singer's Nine Roadster used the beam axle and leaf spring suspension as found on the Ten and Twelve. It featured a vintage-looking open body with flowing wings and running boards. The 1074cc overhead-camshaft engine of 36bhp was lively enough in this wood-framed tourer, although the mechanical brakes left a lot to be desired. The 4A of 1949 changed the three-speed transmission for one with four ratios, while a year later the 4AB arrived with more compliant coil-sprung independent front suspension and better brakes.

**SPECIFICATIONS**

| | |
|---|---|
| **Years produced:** | 1939-1952 (7623 in total) |
| **Performance:** | 0-60mph: 37.6sec<br>Top speed: 65mph |
| **Power & torque:** | 36bhp/48lb ft |
| **Engine:** | Normally aspirated 1074cc four cylinder, petrol, carburettor, 8 valves |
| **Drivetrain:** | Front-engine RWD |
| **Structure:** | Separate chassis |
| **Transmission:** | Three/four-speed manual |
| **Weight:** | 840kg |

**PRICE GUIDE**

| | |
|---|---|
| **Launch price:** | £493 |
| **Excellent:** | £14,000 |
| **Good:** | £9500 |
| **Average:** | £5500 |
| **Project:** | £3750 |

## SINGER
## SM1500/Hunter

For a small company like Singer the SM1500 saloon was a brave step, its blocky and slab-sided styling reflecting contemporary American trends. However, whatever the good intentions, the result was a very unappealing car with a rather plain appearance and a row of slats in place of a front grille. The 1506cc overhead-cam engine was sprightly enough, as was the 1497cc version fitted from 1951 (but which had more power). The 1954 update for the Hunter brought a more attractive and traditional look, with a proper grille but some glassfibre panels.

**SPECIFICATIONS**

| | |
|---|---|
| **Years produced:** | 1949-1956 (17,382/4772 in total) |
| **Performance:** | 0-60mph: 33.7sec<br>Top speed: 71mph |
| **Power & torque:** | 48bhp/72lb ft |
| **Engine:** | Normally aspirated 1497cc four cylinder, petrol, carburettor, 8 valves |
| **Drivetrain:** | Front-engine RWD |
| **Structure:** | Separate chassis |
| **Transmission:** | Four-speed manual |
| **Weight:** | 1184kg |

**PRICE GUIDE**

| | |
|---|---|
| **Launch price:** | £799 |
| **Excellent:** | £4000 |
| **Good:** | £3000 |
| **Average:** | £1700 |
| **Project:** | £850 |

## SINGER
## SM Roadster 4AD

The SM Roadster – a progression of the Nine Roadster – came along in 1951 to fight against MG's TD model, a car it bore rather a striking resemblance to. With an SM1500 overhead-cam engine reduced in size to 1497cc (to allow it to enter under-1500cc motorsport events), it had less power than the MG but similar performance thanks to its light weight. The battle lines were more evenly drawn from 1952, when twin carburettors became an option. With the extra carb, 58bhp was the more satisfying output. Some cars had bodies by Bertone, but these are very rare.

**SPECIFICATIONS**

| | |
|---|---|
| **Years produced:** | 1951-1955 (3440 in total) |
| **Performance:** | 0-60mph: 23.6sec<br>Top speed: 73mph |
| **Power & torque:** | 48bhp/72lb ft |
| **Engine:** | Normally aspirated 1497cc four cylinder, petrol, carburettor, 8 valves |
| **Drivetrain:** | Front-engine RWD |
| **Structure:** | Separate chassis |
| **Transmission:** | Four-speed manual |
| **Weight:** | 840kg |

**PRICE GUIDE**

| | |
|---|---|
| **Launch price:** | £724 |
| **Excellent:** | £13,250 |
| **Good:** | £9500 |
| **Average:** | £5600 |
| **Project:** | £3350 |

## SINGER
## Gazelle

With the Rootes Group now in control of Singer, the marque was set to become another exercise in badge engineering, pitched between Hillman and Humber in the pecking order. However, in the new Gazelle – a plusher version of the Hillman Minx – Singer's 1497cc OHC engine was used at first, but was replaced in 1958 by Rootes' own OHV unit. Saloons, estates (rare and worth 25% more) and convertibles (pay double for those) were all available. Rootes updated the Gazelle almost every year until production ended in 1967, by which time it had a 1725cc engine and fewer curves.

**SPECIFICATIONS**

| | |
|---|---|
| **Years produced:** | 1955-1967 (83,061 in total) |
| **Performance:** | 0-60mph: 21.4sec<br>Top speed: 82mph |
| **Power & torque:** | 53bhp/87lb ft |
| **Engine:** | Normally aspirated 1592cc four cylinder, petrol, carburettor, 8 valves |
| **Drivetrain:** | Front-engine RWD |
| **Structure:** | Monocoque |
| **Transmission:** | Four-speed manual |
| **Weight:** | 1043kg |

**PRICE GUIDE (Saloon)**

| | |
|---|---|
| **Launch price:** | £898 |
| **Excellent:** | £5000 |
| **Good:** | £3450 |
| **Average:** | £1650 |
| **Project:** | £650 |

## SINGER
## Vogue

In Singer form, Rootes' new medium-sized family model was christened the Vogue. Originally intended as a replacement for the Gazelle, this slightly larger car kept the clan resemblance and was quite comfortably appointed inside. Powered by a 1592cc OHV engine, and due to Rootes' policy of constant change, it got front disc brakes from 1962 and a flatter roof plus changes to the window arrangement from 1964. A year later, the 1725cc engine from the Humber Sceptre found its way under the bonnet, meaning a generous jump in power to 85bhp.

**SPECIFICATIONS**

| | |
|---|---|
| **Years produced:** | 1961-1966 (47,769 in total) |
| **Performance:** | 0-60mph: 14.1sec<br>Top speed: 91mph |
| **Power & torque:** | 85bhp/106lb ft |
| **Engine:** | Normally aspirated 1725cc four cylinder, petrol, carburettor, 8 valves |
| **Drivetrain:** | Front-engine RWD |
| **Structure:** | Monocoque |
| **Transmission:** | Four-speed manual, overdrive optional |
| **Weight:** | 1092kg |

**PRICE GUIDE**

| | |
|---|---|
| **Launch price:** | £929 |
| **Excellent:** | £4500 |
| **Good:** | £2850 |
| **Average:** | £1250 |
| **Project:** | £500 |

## SINGER
## Chamois

To sit alongside its mainstream Hillman Imp, Rootes also launched sportier versions. The Singer variant, from 1964, was dubbed the Chamois and followed the usual marque policy of walnut veneer inside and extra brightwork outside, including, from 1968, quad headlamps. All models had chrome grilles at the front – but these were for appearance's sake only since the Chamois was rear-engined. Still, it looked good! In 1966 a Sport version was launched. It had a 51bhp engine instead of the standard saloon's 39bhp. From '67, there was also a pretty fastback coupé.

**SPECIFICATIONS**

| | |
|---|---|
| **Years produced:** | 1964-1970 (97,567 in total) |
| **Performance:** | 0-60mph: 25.4sec<br>Top speed: 78mph |
| **Power & torque:** | 39bhp/52lb ft |
| **Engine:** | Normally aspirated 875cc four cylinder, petrol, carburettor, 8 valves |
| **Drivetrain:** | Rear-engine RWD |
| **Structure:** | Monocoque |
| **Transmission:** | Four-speed manual |
| **Weight:** | 711kg |

**PRICE GUIDE (add 20% for coupé)**

| | |
|---|---|
| **Launch price:** | £582 |
| **Excellent:** | £4750 |
| **Good:** | £3000 |
| **Average:** | £1700 |
| **Project:** | £550 |

# ŠKODA

ONCE A motoring joke because of their poor quality and cheap prices, Škodas have enjoyed a major metamorphosis in recent years under the ownership of Volkswagen. Formed in 1924 in Czechoslovakia, the firm's pre-war cars proved popular and sold well. After the war, Škoda found itself behind the Iron Curtain, which meant it concentrated on low-cost machines. During the 1960s, it moved over to building somewhat quirky rear-engined cars – at a time when many others were abandoning the layout – and continued for the next quarter of a century. VW took control in 1990 and revamped the range; Škoda today is a high-quality budget brand with a much-improved image.

## ŠKODA Felicia Convertible

The Felicia might not have been the most exciting technical package around, being based on the Octavia saloon, and it wasn't exactly quick, with just 53bhp on tap. But that didn't stop it being one of the most desirable cars produced in the Soviet Pact countries. Swing axle suspension meant that handling could be unpredictable, yet its styling largely made up for the lack of dynamic fizz. It was sold in the UK – the first Škoda to find its way over here – and was met with an apathetic response. Climbing values have recently levelled off.

**SPECIFICATIONS**

| | |
|---|---|
| **Years produced:** | 1959-1964 |
| **Performance:** | 0-60mph: 24.5sec<br>Top speed: 85mph |
| **Power & torque:** | 53bhp/55lb ft |
| **Engine:** | Normally aspirated 1089cc four cylinder, petrol, carburettor, 8 valves |
| **Drivetrain:** | Front-engine RWD |
| **Structure:** | Separate chassis |
| **Transmission:** | Four-speed manual |
| **Weight:** | 863kg |

**PRICE GUIDE**

| | |
|---|---|
| **Launch price:** | £809 |
| **Excellent:** | £8000 |
| **Good:** | £4800 |
| **Average:** | £2200 |
| **Project:** | £1000 |

## ŠKODA Octavia

So-called because it was the eighth model line to be produced by the Czech manufacturer, the Octavia was a rugged, dependable and tough family car. Thoroughly conventional in its engineering, it was a development of the 1954 440 model. The vehicle was improved during its five-year production run, with the 50bhp 1221cc engines in the Super and TS models giving a welcome performance lift over the standard variant. Today, there are a surprising number of Octavias on the road in the UK, and they have an enthusiastic following.

**SPECIFICATIONS**

| | |
|---|---|
| **Years produced:** | 1959-1964 |
| **Performance:** | 0-60mph: 29sec<br>Top speed: 78mph |
| **Power & torque:** | 43bhp/51lb ft |
| **Engine:** | Normally aspirated 1089cc four cylinder, petrol, carburettor, 8 valves |
| **Drivetrain:** | Front-engine RWD |
| **Structure:** | Separate chassis |
| **Transmission:** | Four-speed manual |
| **Weight:** | 920kg |

**PRICE GUIDE**

| | |
|---|---|
| **Launch price:** | £745 |
| **Excellent:** | £4200 |
| **Good:** | £3000 |
| **Average:** | £1750 |
| **Project:** | £800 |

## ŠKODA 1000MB/1100MB

The rear-engined Škoda 1000MB represented the beginning of a very dark period in Škoda's history. It was considered a joke by many in the West, but in its home land the practical, reliable and easy-to-work-on machine had a waiting list. What is easily forgotten today is that the car, which was essentially a reskinned Renault Dauphine, was cheap to buy, cheap to run, and motorised a generation of Czechs and Slovaks. The 1000MB was one of the least expensive new motors you could purchase in the UK – and plenty of people did. Edging slowly up.

**SPECIFICATIONS**

| | |
|---|---|
| **Years produced:** | 1965-1977 |
| **Performance:** | 0-60mph: 30.8sec<br>Top speed: 78mph |
| **Power & torque:** | 48bhp/55lb ft |
| **Engine:** | Normally aspirated 988cc four cylinder, petrol, carburettor, 8 valves |
| **Drivetrain:** | Rear-engine RWD |
| **Structure:** | Monocoque |
| **Transmission:** | Four-speed manual |
| **Weight:** | 787kg |

**PRICE GUIDE**

| | |
|---|---|
| **Launch price:** | £580 |
| **Excellent:** | £3500 |
| **Good:** | £2250 |
| **Average:** | £1400 |
| **Project:** | £600 |

## ŠKODA S110R

Based on the S100 saloon, which itself was a revised 1000MB, the S110R coupé probably shouldn't have excited too many enthusiasts. Yet its introduction in the West coincided with a long rallying career that resulted in class wins on the RAC Rally on an almost annual basis. Powered by a 1107cc water-cooled four, mounted in the rear, the pretty S110R was also great value – even if its swing-axle rear suspension caused a few white knuckles on wet roundabouts. These models have a strong following on the classic scene today.

**SPECIFICATIONS**

| | |
|---|---|
| **Years produced:** | 1970-1980 |
| **Performance:** | 0-60mph: 17.7sec<br>Top speed: 90mph |
| **Power & torque:** | 52bhp/64lb ft |
| **Engine:** | Normally aspirated 1107cc four cylinder, petrol, carburettor, 8 valves |
| **Drivetrain:** | Rear-engine RWD |
| **Structure:** | Monocoque |
| **Transmission:** | Four-speed manual |
| **Weight:** | 840kg |

**PRICE GUIDE**

| | |
|---|---|
| **Launch price:** | £1050 |
| **Excellent:** | £5000 |
| **Good:** | £3700 |
| **Average:** | £1600 |
| **Project:** | £750 |

## ŠKODA
## Estelle 105/120/Rapid

Škoda's MB1000 replacement was supposed to have front-wheel drive, and had the Estelle received the drivetrain it deserved, it may have been better received in the West. As it was, it ended up becoming the butt of countless bar-room jokes thanks to its total lack of desirability. In the mid-1980s, Škoda introduced a coupé version in the UK. No one expected very much of the car, least of all Škoda: marketing the Rapid strongly as the cheapest coupé in Britain was not a great message. In fact it was quite fun, and the few that remain in the UK are cherished by their owners.

**SPECIFICATIONS**

| | |
|---|---|
| **Years produced:** | 1976-1991 (1,350,250 in total) |
| **Performance:** | 0-60mph: 18.9sec<br>Top speed: 87mph |
| **Power & torque:** | 52bhp/63lb ft |
| **Engine:** | Normally aspirated 1174cc four cylinder, petrol, carburettor, 8 valves |
| **Drivetrain:** | Rear-engine RWD |
| **Structure:** | Monocoque |
| **Transmission:** | Five-speed manual |
| **Weight:** | 880kg |

| | PRICE GUIDE | Rapid |
|---|---|---|
| **Launch price:** | £1050 | £3751 |
| **Excellent:** | £2000 | £4250 |
| **Good:** | £1200 | £3200 |
| **Average:** | £850 | £2000 |
| **Project:** | £300 | £500 |

# STANDARD

WHEN STANDARD was established in 1903, the word denoted quality and superiority; it was also chosen because the cars were made from standard patterns with interchangeable parts. And early cars certainly set a high standard, with the Flying models of the 1930s widely admired. Immediately postwar, it seemed Standard was on a roll; the firm bought Triumph and launched the advanced (in both engineering and looks) Vanguard. But when Leyland Motors took over in 1961, Triumph started to become the dominant partner of the pair. The marque died in 1963, as much a victim of changing language as anything else since the word 'Standard' was no longer as flattering as it had been.

## STANDARD
## Vanguard I

With its modern beetle-back styling, the Vanguard replaced Standard's entire range of pre-war offerings in one go – there would be no more small cars from the marque until 1953. A full six-seater with a split windscreen, it introduced the world to the tough wet-liner four-cylinder engine that would go on to power everything from Triumph TRs to Ferguson tractors. Now-rare estate model was introduced in 1950, and all got a lower bonnet line and larger rear window from October '51. Try to find one with overdrive – it makes a big difference to fuel consumption.

**SPECIFICATIONS**

| | |
|---|---|
| **Years produced:** | 1948-1953 (184,799 in total) |
| **Performance:** | 0-60mph: 22.0sec<br>Top speed: 78mph |
| **Power & torque:** | 68bhp/108lb ft |
| **Engine:** | Normally aspirated 2088cc four cylinder, petrol, carburettor, 8 valves |
| **Drivetrain:** | Front-engine RWD |
| **Structure:** | Separate chassis |
| **Transmission:** | Three-speed manual, optional overdrive |
| **Weight:** | 1188kg |

| | PRICE GUIDE |
|---|---|
| **Launch price:** | £544 |
| **Excellent:** | £7500 |
| **Good:** | £4650 |
| **Average:** | £2250 |
| **Project:** | £1200 |

## STANDARD
## Vanguard II

The revised and more conventional three-box styling of the Phase II Vanguard lacked some of the character of the original, but it did provide better headroom and something in the region of 50% more luggage space. Getting in and out was easier too, as the front doors were longer. Suspension was stiffer, but the anti-roll bar had been deleted, so despite wider tyres the handling was still not a Vanguard strong point. With this car, Standard also became the first British manufacturer to offer a diesel engine (with a claimed 37mpg), although surviving examples are rare.

**SPECIFICATIONS**

| | |
|---|---|
| **Years produced:** | 1953-1955 (81,074 in total) |
| **Performance:** | 0-60mph: 19.9sec<br>Top speed: 80mph |
| **Power & torque:** | 68bhp/108lb ft |
| **Engine:** | Normally aspirated 2088cc four cylinder, petrol, carburettor, 8 valves |
| **Drivetrain:** | Front-engine RWD |
| **Structure:** | Separate chassis |
| **Transmission:** | Three-speed manual, optional overdrive |
| **Weight:** | 1270kg |

| | PRICE GUIDE |
|---|---|
| **Launch price:** | £919 |
| **Excellent:** | £4300 |
| **Good:** | £2850 |
| **Average:** | £1500 |
| **Project:** | £600 |

## STANDARD
## 8/10/Pennant

These were Standard's entries in the popular Minor/A30/Ford 100E market, and they were worthy rivals. The 8 came with an 803cc engine and was very basically equipped: you didn't even get winding windows until 1954, or an opening bootlid until 1957. The better-selling 10 did have these features from its inception in 1954 (except on the rare base-spec Family 10), and also a 948cc engine. The Pennant was a luxury 10 but with lengthened wings, two-tone paint, hooded headlamps and more equipment. They were outnumbered by about five-to-one by the other models.

**SPECIFICATIONS**

| | |
|---|---|
| **Years produced:** | 1953-1961 (351,727 in total) |
| **Performance:** | 0-60mph: 38.3sec<br>Top speed: 69mph |
| **Power & torque:** | 35bhp/48lb ft |
| **Engine:** | Normally aspirated 948cc four cylinder, petrol, carburettor, 8 valves |
| **Drivetrain:** | Front-engine RWD |
| **Structure:** | Monocoque |
| **Transmission:** | Four-speed manual |
| **Weight:** | 762kg |

| | PRICE GUIDE |
|---|---|
| **Launch price:** | £481 |
| **Excellent:** | £4500 |
| **Good:** | £2750 |
| **Average:** | £1650 |
| **Project:** | £650 |

## STANDARD Vanguard III

Not only was there an all-new and much lower body for the Phase III, but at last Standard did away with the separate chassis and embraced the concept of monocoque construction. As a result, the new car was lighter than its predecessors, with taller gearing that made it quicker, too. An 8in-longer wheelbase aided ride and handling, yet otherwise the running gear was pretty much as before. A curved glass windscreen in place of the old split-screen added another touch of modernity, and from 1957 an automatic gearbox option was available.

### SPECIFICATIONS

**Years produced:** 1955-1958 (37,194 in total)
**Performance:** 0-60mph: 22.2sec
Top speed: 77mph
**Power & torque:** 62bhp/113lb ft
**Engine:** Normally aspirated 2088cc four cylinder, petrol, carburettor, 8 valves
**Drivetrain:** Front-engine RWD
**Structure:** Monocoque
**Transmission:** Three-speed manual, optional overdrive
**Weight:** 1194kg

### PRICE GUIDE

**Launch price:** £850
**Excellent:** £4000
**Good:** £2250
**Average:** £1000
**Project:** £400

## STANDARD Vanguard Sportsman

This sporty variation on the Vanguard theme was the most distinctive car in the range. Never mind the standard two-tone paint – the main standout was that small-mouth grille that looked to have been an inspiration for the MG 1100. It was there because this was supposed to have been a new Triumph, but the company changed its plans at the last minute. The car does have a TR3 engine and bigger brakes, though. A real rarity now – the number of survivors in the UK is thought to be in single figures – hence the price difference over the regular Vanguard III.

### SPECIFICATIONS

**Years produced:** 1956-1958 (901 in total)
**Performance:** 0-60mph: 19.2sec
Top speed: 91mph
**Power & torque:** 90bhp/122lb ft
**Engine:** Normally aspirated 2088cc four cylinder, petrol, carburettor, 8 valves
**Drivetrain:** Front-engine RWD
**Structure:** Monocoque
**Transmission:** Three-speed manual
**Weight:** 1283kg

### PRICE GUIDE

**Launch price:** £1231
**Excellent:** £5500
**Good:** £4000
**Average:** £1800
**Project:** £800

## STANDARD Ensign/Ensign De Luxe

The Ensign started out as a stripped-down version of the Vanguard, lacking much of that car's chrome trim and using cheaper materials inside. It was also fitted with a small-bore engine of just 1670cc. After four-cylinder Vanguard production ended in 1961, the Ensign was revitalised as the De Luxe. That kept the cheap Ensign's grille, but had more chrome, a larger-capacity engine than the Vanguard, and all came with a four-speed floor shift. Overdrive was an option, and most cars came with disc brakes, too. Unlike the cheap Ensign, there was an estate option for the De Luxe.

### SPECIFICATIONS

**Years produced:** 1957-1963 (18,852/2318 in total)
**Performance:** 0-60mph: 24.4sec
Top speed: 78mph
**Power & torque:** 60bhp/91lb ft
**Engine:** Normally aspirated 1670cc four cylinder, petrol, carburettor, 8 valves
**Drivetrain:** Front-engine RWD
**Structure:** Monocoque
**Transmission:** Four-speed manual
**Weight:** 762kg

### PRICE GUIDE

**Launch price:** £900
**Excellent:** £3500
**Good:** £2400
**Average:** £1400
**Project:** £500

## STANDARD Vignale/Luxury Six

That Vignale tag adds a hint of glamour, but really this is nothing more than a Vanguard Phase IV. Changes over the previous model were limited to bigger front and rear windows along with a new grille and back lights, although you also got the option of a floor-mounted gearchange. More significant changes came with 1960's Luxury Six. By then it was all over for the old four-cylinder lump, which had been replaced by the smooth twin-carb straight-six heading for the Triumph 2000. Longer rear springs improved the ride, and disc brakes were offered from 1961.

### SPECIFICATIONS

**Years produced:** 1958-1963 (36,229 in total)
**Performance:** 0-60mph: 22.2sec
Top speed: 83mph
**Power & torque:** 62bhp/113lb ft
**Engine:** Normally aspirated 2088cc four cylinder, petrol, carburettor, 8 valves
**Drivetrain:** Front-engine RWD
**Structure:** Monocoque
**Transmission:** Four-speed manual
**Weight:** 1194kg

### PRICE GUIDE

**Launch price:** £1021
**Excellent:** £4000
**Good:** £2400
**Average:** £1350
**Project:** £450

# SUBARU

LONG BEFORE IT became associated with 4x4s and rally homologation specials, Subaru's origins were very different. As a division of Fuji Heavy Industry, its first production car was the tiny and odd-looking 360 microcar of 1958, which stayed in production in Japan for 12 years. Exports of later models worldwide began in the 1970s, but it wasn't until the 1980s that Subaru really started to establish itself, standing out with its permanent-four-wheel-drive passenger cars and competition exploits. The Impreza became as much a legend on the road as it was on the rally track, and remains the company's most revered model, with a large enthusiast following.

## SUBARU
### 360

The 360 was the first Subaru created to compete in Japan's emerging '*Kei*-class' of microcars. Unlike the competition from Honda and Toyota, which were deliberately styled to resemble shrunken versions of the firms' full-scale models, the Subaru had a bug-like style all of its own. It was an interesting mixture of advanced – the independent suspension – and primitive – mechanical brakes and three-speed gearbox. Cramped, slow, utterly baffling to Europeans at the time... and yet the Subaru 360's following among enthusiasts continues to grow, as do values.

**SPECIFICATIONS**

| | |
|---|---|
| **Years produced:** | 1958-1971 |
| **Performance:** | 0-60mph: N/A<br>Top speed: 59mph |
| **Power & torque:** | 25bhp/30lb ft |
| **Engine:** | Normally aspirated 356cc two-stroke twin, petrol, carburettor |
| **Drivetrain:** | Rear-engine RWD |
| **Structure:** | Monocoque |
| **Transmission:** | Three-speed manual |
| **Weight:** | 549kg |

**PRICE GUIDE**

| | |
|---|---|
| **Launch price:** | N/A in UK |
| **Excellent:** | £8500 |
| **Good:** | £5250 |
| **Average:** | £3500 |
| **Project:** | £1600 |

## SUBARU
### Leone

Subaru's first official import into the UK was the mid-sized Leone saloon, although it was known simply as the 1600 in the UK. When it arrived in the mid-1970s, the flat-four-powered saloon (or estate, or coupé) stood apart from all its rivals by being offered with four-wheel-drive transmission alongside the more mainstream FWD models. And the farming set loved it for that, taking the oddball car to its collective heart. Saloons and coupés are rare in the UK as the importers concentrated on bringing in estates, but a number have subsequently been shipped in.

**SPECIFICATIONS**

| | |
|---|---|
| **Years produced:** | 1972-1981 |
| **Performance:** | 0-60mph: 13.0sec<br>Top speed: 95mph |
| **Power & torque:** | 77bhp/83lb ft |
| **Engine:** | Normally aspirated 1595cc flat-four, petrol, carburettor, 8 valves |
| **Drivetrain:** | Front-engine FWD |
| **Structure:** | Monocoque |
| **Transmission:** | Five-speed manual |
| **Weight:** | 855kg |

**PRICE GUIDE**

| | |
|---|---|
| **Launch price:** | N/A |
| **Excellent:** | £3750 |
| **Good:** | £2200 |
| **Average:** | £900 |
| **Project:** | £500 |

## SUBARU
### Leone II/1600/1800

The squarer-cut 1800GLF (as it was known in the UK) kept to the same refreshingly unconventional technical formula as before, but offered more equipment and interior room, and continued to sell well into the '80s. Subaru cleverly overlapped production of the first- and second-generation cars to maximise sales. Stand-out points in the most conservative of market sectors were a signature flat-four engine and frameless side windows. It's a shame so few survive, but the pillarless coupé (left) has picked up a good retro following in the UK.

**SPECIFICATIONS**

| | |
|---|---|
| **Years produced:** | 1979-1989 |
| **Performance:** | 0-60mph: 10.1sec<br>Top speed: 103mph |
| **Power & torque:** | 80bhp/92lb ft |
| **Engine:** | Normally aspirated 1781cc flat four, petrol, carburettor, 8 valves |
| **Drivetrain:** | Front-engine AWD |
| **Structure:** | Monocoque |
| **Transmission:** | Five-speed manual |
| **Weight:** | 977kg |

**PRICE GUIDE**

| | |
|---|---|
| **Launch price:** | £4133 |
| **Excellent:** | £3000 |
| **Good:** | £2300 |
| **Average:** | £1250 |
| **Project:** | £450 |

## SUBARU
### Leone III/XT

The chiselled mid-'80s Leone III expanded on Subaru's policy for sensible quirkiness, but the XT coupé was something else entirely. The wedge-shaped two-door added turbo shove to the thrumming flat-four, and was certainly quick enough. Unfortunately, that styling really was too much for most buyers to stomach, and it sold slowly. Yet for those who could live with the looks, the XT rewarded with great build quality and peerless reliability. It rusted, but nowhere near as badly as its ancestors, and it now has bags of '80s retro appeal. Best XTs can be up to £10k.

**SPECIFICATIONS**

| | |
|---|---|
| **Years produced:** | 1985-1989 |
| **Performance:** | 0-60mph: 8.7sec<br>Top speed: 119mph |
| **Power & torque:** | 134bhp/148lb ft |
| **Engine:** | Turbocharged 1701cc flat-four, petrol, fuel injection, 8 valves |
| **Drivetrain:** | Front-engine AWD |
| **Structure:** | Monocoque |
| **Transmission:** | Five-speed manual |
| **Weight:** | 1130kg |

**PRICE GUIDE**

| | |
|---|---|
| **Launch price:** | £12,000 |
| **Excellent:** | £3500 |
| **Good:** | £2500 |
| **Average:** | £1600 |
| **Project:** | £700 |

## SUBARU
### SVX

Follow-up to the XT, and strikingly styled by Giugiaro, the SVX took proven mechanicals and repackaged them in a most distinctive and extremely aerodynamic bodyshell that included a side window-within-a-window *a la* Countach and McLaren F1. Powered by a non-turbo 3.3-litre flat-six, with auto gearbox and four-wheel drive, the SVX was more cruiser than sports car, but an agreeable steer nonetheless. A rare sight, just 200 were officially imported to the UK. To fans of quirky modern classics, a real collectors' piece.

**SPECIFICATIONS**

| | |
|---|---|
| **Years produced:** | 1991-1996 (24,379 in total) |
| **Performance:** | 0-60mph: 7.3sec<br>Top speed: 154mph |
| **Power & torque:** | 226bhp/228lb ft |
| **Engine:** | Normally aspirated 3318cc flat-six, petrol, fuel injection, 24 valves |
| **Drivetrain:** | Front-engine AWD |
| **Structure:** | Monocoque |
| **Transmission:** | Four-speed automatic |
| **Weight:** | 1590kg |

**PRICE GUIDE**

| | |
|---|---|
| **Launch price:** | £27,999 |
| **Excellent:** | £3800 |
| **Good:** | £2650 |
| **Average:** | £1800 |
| **Project:** | £1000 |

## SUBARU
### Impreza Turbo

The first-generation Impreza Turbo ran from 1992 until 2000 and, driven by success in international rallying, it became a cult car with a devoted following. There are many variations, but all use a four-cylinder 'boxer' engine and permanent four-wheel drive. These rally-inspired Imprezas were marketed in the UK initially as the Turbo 2000, though the WRX and STi badges were both applied to later variants. Generally, the earlier the car the more discreet its appearance, but all have terrific all-weather, all-road pace combined with a distinctive flat-four soundtrack.

**SPECIFICATIONS**

**Years produced:** 1992-2000
**Performance:** 0-60mph: 5.9sec
Top speed: 139mph
**Power & torque:** 218bhp/201lb ft
**Engine:** Turbocharged 1994cc flat-four, petrol, fuel injection, 16 valves
**Drivetrain:** Front-engine AWD
**Structure:** Monocoque
**Transmission:** Five-speed manual
**Weight:** 1235kg

**PRICE GUIDE (Turbo 2000)**
**Launch price:** £17,999
**Excellent:** £6000
**Good:** £4000
**Average:** £2500
**Project:** £1300

# SUNBEAM

FORMER CYCLE manufacturer, Wolverhampton-based Sunbeam, produced cars of great quality and sporting pedigree. It even made history with Britain's first Grand Prix win, at the 1923 French GP. However, in 1920 Sunbeam joined with Talbot and Darracq to form STD Motors Ltd, which proved an effective way to waste a lot of money. By 1935 it was bust, and the Rootes Group picked up the Sunbeam-Talbot bit to create a badge for upmarket Hillmans.

The Talbot part was dropped in 1954 and Sunbeam once again became a more sporting marque, with the Rapier and Alpine. Chrysler killed off the badge in 1976, but shamefully re-used the name for a new small hatchback.

## SUNBEAM-TALBOT
### 80

Introduced in 1948, the Sunbeam-Talbot 80 was the stylish entry-level model in a range that didn't fit easily within the Rootes Group. Effectively, Sunbeam-Talbots were touring versions of Humbers and Hillmans, and ended up being phased out in favour of the standalone Sunbeam. Although it was a stylish vehicle, the 80 was powered by the 1.2-litre engine also found in the Minx – a car not known for its sparkling performance. Despite that, it sold reasonably well to those looking for the style and image of the Sunbeam-Talbot 90 without the price.

**SPECIFICATIONS**

**Years produced:** 1948-1950 (3500 in total)
**Performance:** 0-60mph: 36.4sec
Top speed: 73mph
**Power & torque:** 47bhp/61lb ft
**Engine:** Normally aspirated 1185cc four cylinder, petrol, carburettor, 8 valves
**Drivetrain:** Front-engine RWD
**Structure:** Separate chassis
**Transmission:** Four-speed manual
**Weight:** 1184kg

**PRICE GUIDE (Coupé in brackets)**
**Launch price:** £889
**Excellent:** £6500 (£11,000)
**Good:** £4200 (£6500)
**Average:** £2275 (£3200)
**Project:** £800 (£1500)

## SUNBEAM-TALBOT
### 90

With an uninspiring suspension set-up – a beam-axle front and semi-elliptic springs all round, the Sunbeam-Talbot 90 shouldn't have been memorable to drive, and certainly not worthy of the great marque. However, its reasonably powerful 2.0-litre OHV engine produced enough grunt to allow the well set-up chassis to entertain its driver. The MkII of 1950 was a much better effort thanks to its chassis with coils and wishbone suspension – as was proved in rallying, where the car did rather well.

**SPECIFICATIONS**

**Years produced:** 1948-1954 (22,631 in total)
**Performance:** 0-60mph: 22.5sec
Top speed: 80mph
**Power & torque:** 64bhp/101lb ft
**Engine:** Normally aspirated 1944cc four cylinder, petrol, carburettor, 8 valves
**Drivetrain:** Front-engine RWD
**Structure:** Separate chassis
**Transmission:** Four-speed manual
**Weight:** 1235kg

**PRICE GUIDE (Coupé in brackets)**
**Launch price:** £991
**Excellent:** £8500 (£13,500)
**Good:** £5500 (£7500)
**Average:** £3000 (£3500)
**Project:** £1400 (£1600)

## SUNBEAM
### Alpine

The Alpine was a stylish two-seater convertible version of the Sunbeam-Talbot 90. It shared the saloon's effective suspension set-up, but was powered by an 80bhp 2.3-litre four, also used in the Humber Hawk. It was a heavy car, and didn't offer sparkling performance, yet it proved good enough to take outright victory in the 1955 Monte Carlo Rally. The Alpine was designed with the American market in mind, hence its soft ride, but failed to make the grade there. It eventually dropped out of production after just two years. Prized today.

**SPECIFICATIONS**

**Years produced:** 1953-1955 (3000 in total)
**Performance:** 0-60mph: 18.9sec
Top speed: 95mph
**Power & torque:** 80bhp/120lb ft
**Engine:** Normally aspirated 2267cc four cylinder, petrol, carburettor, 8 valves
**Drivetrain:** Front-engine RWD
**Structure:** Separate chassis
**Transmission:** Four-speed manual
**Weight:** 1270kg

**PRICE GUIDE**
**Launch price:** £1269
**Excellent:** £40,000
**Good:** £28,000
**Average:** £18,000
**Project:** £10,000

## SUNBEAM
# Rapier I-V

In design and engineering terms, the Rapier was a two-door version of the Hillman Minx. But the stylish Sunbeam was definitely that workaday car's glamorous cousin. During its production run, the Rapier went through four facelifts, starting out with 1390cc and ending up as a rapid 1592cc sporting saloon that continues to prove itself in competition. Like all Rootes Group cars of its era, build quality was good and the construction tough – and that's why so many survive today, and why the Rapier is such a popular classic choice.

### SPECIFICATIONS

**Years produced:** 1955-1965 (76,954 in total)
**Performance:** 0-60mph: 21.7sec
Top speed: 85mph
**Power & torque:** 63bhp/74lb ft
**Engine:** Normally aspirated 1390cc four cylinder, petrol, carburettor, 8 valves
**Drivetrain:** Front-engine RWD
**Structure:** Monocoque
**Transmission:** Four-speed manual
**Weight:** 1070kg

### PRICE GUIDE (add 20% for convertible)

**Launch price:** £1044
**Excellent:** £9500
**Good:** £6000
**Average:** £3350
**Project:** £1400

## SUNBEAM
# Alpine Sports

The second car to bear the Sunbeam Alpine name was a very different proposition to its more portly predecessor. The new roadster was designed to compete with the MGA and appeal to US buyers. That meant a comfortable interior and sharp styling, but the Hillman Husky underpinnings and lack of a sporting powerplant were always going to count against the Alpine. Sales were disappointing, and the final nail in the coffin was probably the appearance of the 1.8-litre MGB, which was a far more complete all-round package. Series III and V can be £20k+.

### SPECIFICATIONS

**Years produced:** 1959-1968 (69,251 in total)
**Performance:** 0-60mph: 14.0sec
Top speed: 98mph
**Power & torque:** 78bhp/74lb ft
**Engine:** Normally aspirated 1494cc four cylinder, petrol, carburettor, 8 valves
**Drivetrain:** Front-engine RWD
**Structure:** Monocoque
**Transmission:** Four-speed manual
**Weight:** 966kg

### PRICE GUIDE

**Launch price:** £972
**Excellent:** £14,000
**Good:** £9500
**Average:** £4500
**Project:** £1800

## SUNBEAM
# Harrington Alpine GT

Made famous at the Le Mans 24 Hour race, the Harrington GT was essentially a Sunbeam Alpine GT with a fastback hardtop that turned the roadster into a pretty, convincing-looking coupé. Of course, the reason for that shape was down to aerodynamics – wearing the Harrington GT roof, the Sunbeam Alpine was faster down the Mulsanne Straight than it would have been with the standard steel hardtop. When the Harrington was sold as a standalone model, though, it struggled on the market and failed to dent the MGB's success. Still, much prized today.

### SPECIFICATIONS

**Years produced:** 1961-1963 (425 in total)
**Performance:** 0-60mph: 12.7sec
Top speed: 99mph
**Power & torque:** 93bhp/N/A
**Engine:** Normally aspirated 1592cc four cylinder, petrol, carburettor, 8 valves
**Drivetrain:** Front-engine RWD
**Structure:** Monocoque
**Transmission:** Four-speed manual
**Weight:** 972kg

### PRICE GUIDE

**Launch price:** £1225
**Excellent:** £22,500
**Good:** £16,000
**Average:** £7500
**Project:** £3500

## SUNBEAM
# Tiger 260

Following the example of Caroll Shelby, who had first come up with the idea of stuffing an American V8 under the bonnet of a British sports car to produce the AC Cobra, Rootes fitted a 4.2-litre Ford V8 in the Sunbeam Alpine to produce the Tiger. Sales took off in the US far more than the UK, where the underdeveloped suspension set-up was far more evident, but before the Tiger got into its stride the plug was pulled and the car went out of production. Why? Because Chrysler took a controlling stake in Rootes, and its own engine didn't fit in the Tiger.

### SPECIFICATIONS

**Years produced:** 1964-1968 (7085 in total)
**Performance:** 0-60mph: 7.8sec
Top speed: 117mph
**Power & torque:** 164bhp/258lb ft
**Engine:** Normally aspirated 4261cc V8, petrol, carburettor, 16 valves
**Drivetrain:** Front-engine RWD
**Structure:** Monocoque
**Transmission:** Four-speed manual
**Weight:** 1163kg

### PRICE GUIDE (add 25% for '66-68 models)

**Launch price:** £1446
**Excellent:** £55,000
**Good:** £36,000
**Average:** £27,000
**Project:** £14,000

## SUNBEAM
# Imp Sport

When Rootes decided to build a hot version of the Imp, it was logical to market the model as a Sunbeam, the group's most flamboyant marque. What we got was a car closely related to the original, yet thanks to the fitment of twin carburettors and wider wheels, not only was it faster in a straight line, it was more fun in the corners. Another surprising success given the dominance of the Mini-Cooper in the sector, but the Imp Sport's smooth little engine and beautifully set-up handling made it a rewarding drive for press-on drivers. Well worth seeking out now, and on the up.

### SPECIFICATIONS

**Years produced:** 1966-1976 (10,000 in total)
**Performance:** 0-60mph: 16.3sec
Top speed: 90mph
**Power & torque:** 51bhp/52lb ft
**Engine:** Normally aspirated 875cc four cylinder, petrol, carburettor, 8 valves
**Drivetrain:** Rear-engine RWD
**Structure:** Monocoque
**Transmission:** Four-speed manual
**Weight:** 747kg

### PRICE GUIDE

**Launch price:** £665
**Excellent:** £5750
**Good:** £3000
**Average:** £1350
**Project:** £400

## SUNBEAM Stiletto

Of all the Imp variants offered by the Rootes Group, the Sunbeam Stiletto remains by far the most desirable with collectors. The combination of the Hillman Californian's pretty bodyshell and Imp Sport's engine created a desirable sporting baby. Handling was further improved over the Imp Sport thanks to geometry changes to the front suspension, making this the best of the lot to drive. The jazzed-up interior with bespoke dashboard and reclining seats were further attractions, as was the ever-attractive quad-headlamp nose. Values up.

**SPECIFICATIONS**

| | |
|---|---|
| **Years produced:** | 1967-1973 (10,000 in total) |
| **Performance:** | 0-60mph: 17.6sec<br>Top speed: 87mph |
| **Power & torque:** | 51bhp/52lb ft |
| **Engine:** | Normally aspirated 875cc four cylinder, petrol, carburettor, 8 valves |
| **Drivetrain:** | Rear-engine RWD |
| **Structure:** | Monocoque |
| **Transmission:** | Four-speed manual |
| **Weight:** | 711kg |

**PRICE GUIDE**

| | |
|---|---|
| **Launch price:** | £726 |
| **Excellent:** | £6500 |
| **Good:** | £3250 |
| **Average:** | £1500 |
| **Project:** | £600 |

## SUNBEAM Rapier/Alpine

Although designer Roy Axe said it was pure coincidence that the Rapier looked similar to the Plymouth Barracuda, the resemblance between the half cousins was clear. Based on the Hillman Hunter, but not sharing a single panel, the Rapier (and its cheaper Alpine sister) were striking-looking cars that were well engineered, handled tidily and, in Holbay-tuned H120 form, quick (add £1000 for an H120). The model died when Chrysler rationalised its range. It's overshadowed today by its earlier forebears and rather undervalued as a consequence.

**SPECIFICATIONS**

| | |
|---|---|
| **Years produced:** | 1967-1976 (46,204 in total) |
| **Performance:** | 0-60mph: 13.2sec<br>Top speed: 103mph |
| **Power & torque:** | 79bhp/93lb ft |
| **Engine:** | Normally aspirated 1598cc four cylinder, petrol, carburettor, 8 valves |
| **Drivetrain:** | Front-engine RWD |
| **Structure:** | Monocoque |
| **Transmission:** | Four-speed manual |
| **Weight:** | 1016kg |

**PRICE GUIDE**

| | |
|---|---|
| **Launch price:** | £1200 |
| **Excellent:** | £5000 |
| **Good:** | £2700 |
| **Average:** | £1300 |
| **Project:** | £400 |

# SUZUKI

THE SUZUKI MOTOR Company was formed in June 1954, and introduced its first car – the 360cc Suzulight – the following year, after closely studying a selection of European microcars. It proved a hit in its homeland, and soon gained van and pick-up versions. In 1959, it was also joined by the Suzulight TL, a car that looked eerily similar to BMC's Mini. The company concentrated on *kei-class* (miniature) cars well into the 1980s, producing the Fronte, Cervo and Alto – but it was the arrival of the scaled-down off-roader, the LJ80, that really opened up Suzuki to significant export success. Since then, it's grown into one of the world's leading manufacturers of small hatches and off-roaders.

## SUZUKI SC100GX Whizzkid

Launched as the two-cylinder Cervo in Japan in 1977, the Whizzkid started out as a coupé version of the Fronte Kei-Car, yet ended up being transformed when it came to the UK at the end of 1979 by the fitment of a 970cc four-cylinder powerplant. It was well-equipped and surprisingly sprightly, so it is no surprise that these baby racers have become something of a cult car, even if the values seldom match the interest the models generate. But with a mere 4096 imported into the UK, and rust being a killer, demand for the SC100GX Whizzkid has been rising in recent times.

**SPECIFICATIONS**

| | |
|---|---|
| **Years produced:** | 1977-1982 |
| **Performance:** | 0-60mph: 16.5sec<br>Top speed: 85mph |
| **Power & torque:** | 47bhp/61lb ft |
| **Engine:** | Normally aspirated 970cc four cylinder, petrol, carburettor, 8 valves |
| **Drivetrain:** | Rear-engine RWD |
| **Structure:** | Monocoque |
| **Transmission:** | Four-speed manual |
| **Weight:** | 655kg |

**PRICE GUIDE**

| | |
|---|---|
| **Launch price:** | £3070 |
| **Excellent:** | £3350 |
| **Good:** | £1700 |
| **Average:** | £1150 |
| **Project:** | £500 |

## SUZUKI Cappuccino

An appealing little roadster that emerged during a particularly fertile period in Japanese design. Powered by a mid-mounted 660cc turbocharged three-cylinder engine, the Cappuccino was designed to qualify for Japanese Kei-car regulations that entitled it to low tax and insurance in its home market. Although a niche car, it proved popular in Europe – well over 1000 were sold through UK dealers between 1993 and 1995. Today, these cars remain very much in demand, as buyers switch on to their low running costs, reliability and excellent build quality.

**SPECIFICATIONS**

| | |
|---|---|
| **Years produced:** | 1991-1997 |
| **Performance:** | 0-60mph: 8.2sec<br>Top speed: 93mph |
| **Power & torque:** | 63bhp / 63lb/ft |
| **Engine:** | Turbocharged 657cc in-line three, petrol, electronic fuel injection, 12v |
| **Drivetrain:** | Front-engine RWD |
| **Structure:** | Monocoque |
| **Transmission:** | Five-speed manual |
| **Weight:** | 725kg |

**PRICE GUIDE**

| | |
|---|---|
| **Launch price:** | £11,995 |
| **Excellent:** | £4000 |
| **Good:** | £3000 |
| **Average:** | £2250 |
| **Project:** | £1000 |

# SWALLOW

SWALLOW was born out of William Lyons' SS company. The founder of Jaguar sold his Swallow Coachbuilding Company to the Helliwell Group in 1945 with sidecar production being passed on to Tube Investments the following year. The coachbuilding company worked within the aviation world initially, but branched out into car production in 1954, with the introduction of its Triumph-based Swallow Doretti in 1954. It would prove to be the only car produced by the company – and its supply situation was made more difficult when Standard-Triumph chairman Sir John Black had a crash in one. In 1956, Swallow Coachbuilding was sold to the sidecar manufacturer Watsonian.

## SWALLOW Doretti

The Triumph TR2-based Swallow Doretti is one of the most sought-after British specials of the 1950s because of its combination of simple, elegant style and rugged TR2 mechanicals. The bodyshell had a steel inner structure with aluminium panels attached, mated to an immensely strong tubular frame chassis. The car was as good to drive as the Triumph on which it was based, and the leather-trimmed interior was well made – but advantages over its donor weren't sufficient enough to warrant the hefty premium. Values currently holding.

**SPECIFICATIONS**

| | |
|---|---|
| **Years produced:** | 1954-1955 (250 in total) |
| **Performance:** | 0-60mph: 12.3sec<br>Top speed: 100mph |
| **Power & torque:** | 90bhp/117lb ft |
| **Engine:** | Normally aspirated 1991cc four cylinder, petrol, carburettor, 8 valves |
| **Drivetrain:** | Front-engine RWD |
| **Structure:** | Separate chassis |
| **Transmission:** | Four-speed manual with overdrive |
| **Weight:** | 864kg |

**PRICE GUIDE**

| | |
|---|---|
| **Launch price:** | £1102 |
| **Excellent:** | £60,000 |
| **Good:** | £50,000 |
| **Average:** | £35,000 |
| **Project:** | £15,000 |

# TALBOT

INITIALLY, TALBOT built French Clément cars from 1903, but it gradually moved into constructing its own machines. It became a member of the Sunbeam-Talbot-Darracq partnership in 1920 and forged a reputation as a builder of comprehensively engineered cars with true sporting prowess. In 1935, though, the Rootes Group gained control and renamed the marque Sunbeam-Talbot. That should probably have been the end of the name in its own right, but when Peugeot took over what remained of Rootes in 1978, it decided to resurrect the badge. These 'new' Talbots included the Alpine, Horizon, Solara and Samba, but poor sales prompted Peugeot to kill off Talbot once more in 1986.

## TALBOT Sunbeam Lotus

Chrysler commissioned Lotus to produce an effective entrant for international rallying. The Norfolk firm took a 1.6GLS shell, installed its own slant-four 2.2-litre 16-valve engine and a ZF gearbox, fitted light alloy wheels and uprated the suspension. The result proved effective in rallying, winning the 1980 RAC event. The road-going version was also quick and balanced, although it was priced higher than the comparable Vauxhall Chevette HS – and current values remain ahead of its homologation special-style opposition from Luton.

**SPECIFICATIONS**

| | |
|---|---|
| **Years produced:** | 1979-1983 (2308 in total) |
| **Performance:** | 0-60mph: 7.4sec<br>Top speed: 121mph |
| **Power & torque:** | 150bhp/150lb ft |
| **Engine:** | Normally aspirated 2174cc four cylinder, petrol, carburettor, 16 valves |
| **Drivetrain:** | Front-engine RWD |
| **Structure:** | Monocoque |
| **Transmission:** | Five-speed manual |
| **Weight:** | 960kg |

**PRICE GUIDE**

| | |
|---|---|
| **Launch price:** | £6995 |
| **Excellent:** | £22,500 |
| **Good:** | £16,000 |
| **Average:** | £9000 |
| **Project:** | £4500 |

## TALBOT Samba

The final product of the Talbot marque was a truly Anglo-French effort, with Peugeot 104 underpinnings (on a unique wheelbase) and UK styling. Project T15 was designed to replace the shortlived Sunbeam, and was a very different beast. It had a predictable engine and model line-up, but the arrival of the cabrio in 1983 was a innovative marketing step that added some glamour to the range. The French-built Samba failed to capture the hearts of UK buyers, and despite being good to drive and economical it was overshadowed by the Metro and Fiesta.

**SPECIFICATIONS**

| | |
|---|---|
| **Years produced:** | 1981-1986 |
| **Performance:** | 0-60mph: 11.5sec<br>Top speed: 101mph |
| **Power & torque:** | 80bhp/80lb ft |
| **Engine:** | Normally aspirated 1360cc four cylinder, petrol, carburettor, 8 valves |
| **Drivetrain:** | Front-engine FWD |
| **Structure:** | Monocoque |
| **Transmission:** | Four-speed manual |
| **Weight:** | 810kg |

**PRICE GUIDE**

| | |
|---|---|
| **Launch price:** | £5380 |
| **Excellent:** | £3500 |
| **Good:** | £1750 |
| **Average:** | £1000 |
| **Project:** | £450 |

# TATRA

TATRA CAN trace its origins back to horse-drawn carriages in 1850, but when this Czechoslovakian concern started building cars from 1919, it soon became one of Europe's most imaginative car builders. After early conventionality, its products took an unorthodox turn, featuring streamlining and a rear-mounted V8 engine on 1934's T77. Post-war, under Communist control, this theme continued, and Tatra was responsible for the extraordinary T603 and T613, the latter funded by damages awarded against Volkswagen over the design of the Beetle. In 1996, by which time its designs had become outdated, Tatra withdrew from cars to concentrate on trucks.

## TATRA T603

If you were a senior Communist in any of the Eastern Bloc countries from 1956, the chances are that your vehicular possibilities included the Tatra T603. And if you had any sense of style, you'd have made a beeline straight for this Czech plutocrat with its air-cooled rear-mounted V8 and highly aerodynamic styling. It would have been a wise choice, too, as interior room was massive, the engine note was exceptional, and build quality was first rate. Most survived the Cold War and a great many headed west, where they are now revered by fans. Early tri-lamp cars are £30k+.

**SPECIFICATIONS**

| | |
|---|---|
| **Years produced:** | 1955-1975 (22,422 in total) |
| **Performance:** | 0-60mph: 16.0sec<br>Top speed: 100mph |
| **Power & torque:** | 105bhp/123lb ft |
| **Engine:** | Normally aspirated 2474cc V8, petrol, carburettor, 16 valves |
| **Drivetrain:** | Rear-engine RWD |
| **Structure:** | Monocoque |
| **Transmission:** | Four-speed manual |
| **Weight:** | 1470kg |

**PRICE GUIDE**

| | |
|---|---|
| **Launch price:** | N/A in UK |
| **Excellent:** | £20,000 |
| **Good:** | £14,000 |
| **Average:** | £6000 |
| **Project:** | £3000 |

# TOYOTA

THE FIRST TOYOTAS appeared a few years before the Second World War, but production only really got underway once the conflict was over. Early designs were American-inspired, so it seemed natural when the company started exporting its substantial Crown model to the States in 1957. European sales kicked off in 1962, with the Corona and Corolla proving big money-generators for the Japanese marque. Particularly notable models include the sublime 2000GT, delicate MR2 and cult-classic Corolla AE86. Toyota now vies with VW as the world's biggest car maker, with factories around the globe, while the Corolla is the biggest-selling car, with over 40 million sold since 1966.

## TOYOTA Sports 800

Considering the S800 was Toyota's first sports car, it was an impressive effort. Cast in the mould of the MG Midget, it was based on the Publica mini-car and conceived for the *Kei*-class. Its flat-twin was eager and capable of pushing the Sports 800 to almost 100mph.Unlike its rival, the Honda S800, the Toyota was no technical *tour de force*, with solid rear axle and drum brakes, but the body had been styled with particular attention to aerodynamics, and it featured a useful targa top. Never imported to the UK, but a few have subsequently made the trip. Values holding.

**SPECIFICATIONS**

| | |
|---|---|
| **Years produced:** | 1965-1970 (3131 in total) |
| **Performance:** | 0-60mph: 11.0sec<br>Top speed: 97mph |
| **Power & torque:** | 44bhp/49lb ft |
| **Engine:** | Normally aspirated 791cc twin, petrol, carburettor, four valves |
| **Drivetrain:** | Front-engine RWD |
| **Structure:** | Monocoque |
| **Transmission:** | Four-speed manual |
| **Weight:** | 591kg |

**PRICE GUIDE**

| | |
|---|---|
| **Launch price:** | N/A |
| **Excellent:** | £30,000 |
| **Good:** | £22,000 |
| **Average:** | £15,000 |
| **Project:** | £7500 |

## TOYOTA 2000GT

Thanks to its drop-dead good looks and a guest appearance in *You Only Love Twice*, the 2000GT put Toyota on the world map. Produced in a joint venture with Yamaha, the gorgeous 2000GT was offered to Toyota when Yamaha failed to excite Nissan into producing the car – and a mere 337 were built between 1967 and 1970. And that's a shame given its fantastic technical specification, which boasted a jewel-like twin-cam straight six that pumped out 150bhp to give a 135mph maximum speed. Revered as an absolute classic, and one of Japan's finest ever.

**SPECIFICATIONS**

| | |
|---|---|
| **Years produced:** | 1967-1970 (337 in total) |
| **Performance:** | 0-60mph: 8.4sec<br>Top speed: 137mph |
| **Power & torque:** | 150bhp/129lb ft |
| **Engine:** | Normally aspirated 1988cc six cylinder, petrol, carburettor, 12 valves |
| **Drivetrain:** | Front-engine RWD |
| **Structure:** | Monocoque |
| **Transmission:** | Five-speed manual |
| **Weight:** | 1125kg |

**PRICE GUIDE**

| | |
|---|---|
| **Launch price:** | N/A |
| **Excellent:** | £500,000 |
| **Good:** | £470,000 |
| **Average:** | £375,000 |
| **Project:** | N/A |

## TOYOTA
### Celica 1600 ST

When new, these sporting coupés were considered the dynamic inferiors of their European rivals, but considering the A20/35-generation Celica was to the Carina what the Capri was to the Cortina, they were very much the same thing. Sold in huge numbers in Japan and the USA, the Celica was a braver choice over here, although bulletproof reliability made ownership a painless experience. Rust and indifference killed most, but their chintzy mid-Atlantic styling has made these cult cars in the burgeoning Japanese car scene. Values nudging up.

**SPECIFICATIONS**

**Years produced:** 1970-1977
**Performance:** 0-60mph: 11.5sec
Top speed: 104mph
**Power & torque:** 105bhp/101lb ft
**Engine:** Normally aspirated 1588cc four cylinder, petrol, carburettor, 8 valves
**Drivetrain:** Front-engine RWD
**Structure:** Monocoque
**Transmission:** Four-speed manual
**Weight:** 1100kg

**PRICE GUIDE**

**Launch price:** £1362
**Excellent:** £10,000
**Good:** £6500
**Average:** £2750
**Project:** £1450

## TOYOTA
### Crown

The third-generation MS60 Crown was a bold leap forward stylistically. Out went conventionally boxy looks, and in their place came swooping flanks and the characteristic double-deck front lights. In the UK, the Crown was offered in saloon and estate form only, and we were denied the stylish coupé (left). Its straight-six engine was lusty and thirsty, the rest reliable and well made. Sloppy to drive compared with European rivals, but that's less of an issue now, and most cars in the UK are personal imports. Definitely a head-turner.

**SPECIFICATIONS**

**Years produced:** 1971-1974
**Performance:** 0-60mph: 12.5sec
Top speed: 110mph
**Power & torque:** 150bhp/164lb ft
**Engine:** Normally aspirated 2563cc straight six, petrol, carburettor, 12 valves
**Drivetrain:** Front-engine RWD
**Structure:** Monocoque
**Transmission:** Five-speed manual/three-speed auto
**Weight:** 1302kg

**PRICE GUIDE**

**Launch price:** £1362
**Excellent:** £5000
**Good:** £3250
**Average:** £1750
**Project:** £1000

## TOYOTA
### Celica GT

The facelifted RA25 and R28 Celicas introduced the popular liftback bodystyle (left), and provided Toyota with the perfect weapon with which to chase Capris. Referred to by many as the 'Mustang-shape' car, the GT version was genuinely quick thanks to its 124bhp twin-cam 1600. Sales were limited due to lack of badge kudos in the UK. Japanese-market cars were also treated to a mighty 2.0-litre Yamaha-headed power unit, dubbed the 18R-GU, that pushed out 134bhp. The spectre of rusty cars has long been banished, and values are on the rise.

**SPECIFICATIONS**

**Years produced:** 1974-1977
**Performance:** 0-60mph: 8.8sec
Top speed: 120mph
**Power & torque:** 124bhp/113lb ft
**Engine:** Normally aspirated 1588cc four cylinder, petrol, carburettor, 8 valves
**Drivetrain:** Front-engine RWD
**Structure:** Monocoque
**Transmission:** Five-speed manual
**Weight:** 1116kg

**PRICE GUIDE**

**Launch price:** £2345
**Excellent:** £12,000
**Good:** £7500
**Average:** £3000
**Project:** £1500

## TOYOTA
### Celica

Along with the Carina A40, the Celica came in for some serious updates in 1977. Sadly, whereas the saloon it was based upon became better-looking and more appealing for western tastes, the new coupé and liftbacks lost their charming mid-Atlantic good looks. But, despite that, the Celica proved popular in the UK and stacked up well against the Capri and Cavalier Sportshatch of the day. Not as highly valued as the baby 'Pony car' predecessor, though, and the six-cylinder Supra version was not brought into European markets.

**SPECIFICATIONS**

**Years produced:** 1977-1981
**Performance:** 0-60mph: 9.5sec
Top speed: 113mph
**Power & torque:** 118bhp/112lb ft
**Engine:** Normally aspirated 1968cc four cylinder, petrol, carburettor, 8 valves
**Drivetrain:** Front-engine RWD
**Structure:** Monocoque
**Transmission:** Five-speed manual
**Weight:** 1100kg

**PRICE GUIDE**

**Launch price:** £2345
**Excellent:** £3500
**Good:** £2000
**Average:** £1250
**Project:** £850

## TOYOTA
### Celica Supra

Known as the Celica XX in Japan, the Celica Supra was heavily based on the Toyota Celica range. The major difference between the two was the use of a six-cylinder engine up front, which gave Toyota a direct rival to the Capri 2.8 Injection and Alfa Romeo GTV6 in Europe. The power output started out at 174bhp and rose to 178bhp. Even so, the Supra was always more of a luxury barge than a sports car. Lairy rear-wheel-drive handling made them popular in the drifting scene, but these cars are now emerging as true classics. Prices edging upwards.

**SPECIFICATIONS**

**Years produced:** 1982-1985 (863,700 in total)
**Performance:** 0-60mph: 8.7sec
Top speed: 131mph
**Power & torque:** 168bhp/169lb ft
**Engine:** Normally aspirated 2759cc six cylinder, petrol, fuel injection, 12 valves
**Drivetrain:** Front-engine RWD
**Structure:** Monocoque
**Transmission:** Five-speed manual
**Weight:** 1265kg

**PRICE GUIDE**

**Launch price:** £9888
**Excellent:** £8500
**Good:** £4750
**Average:** £2250
**Project:** £1200

## TOYOTA
## Corolla GT (FWD)

Although the Tercel was Europe's first FWD Toyota, it was the 1983 Corolla E80 that held the honour of being the first *popular* front-driver here. It was conservatively styled and remains pretty forgettable today, but unfairly so if the excellence of the GT is anything to go by. It's revvy and responsive, handles well and, most importantly for any '80s hot-shoe, it was considerably quicker than the market-leading Ford Escort XR3i. You'll struggle to find one in rust-free condition but, even if you do, chances are it won't be cheap as chips – buyers have cottoned on.

**SPECIFICATIONS**

**Years produced:** 1983-1987 (3,270,000 in total)
**Performance:** 0-60mph: 8.7sec
Top speed: 118mph
**Power & torque:** 130bhp/110lb ft
**Engine:** Normally aspirated 1587cc four cylinder, petrol, fuel injection, 16 valves
**Drivetrain:** Front-engine FWD
**Structure:** Monocoque
**Transmission:** Five-speed manual
**Weight:** 930kg

**PRICE GUIDE**

**Launch price:** £7295
**Excellent:** £2500
**Good:** £1650
**Average:** £900
**Project:** £400

## TOYOTA
## Corolla GT (AE86)

In 1983, there was a very confusing situation in the UK – you could buy a Corolla GT with either front- or rear-wheel drive. Both were exceptional fun. However, it's the RWD AE86 that has captured the hearts of a generation of Playstation fans, drift fanatics and club rally drivers because, with 122bhp of twin-cam power under the bonnet and tail-happy handling, it has become a legend in its own lifetime and values have gone stratospheric, for what is essentially a fairly humdrum Japanese coupé. Rust is an ever-present issue, but most are cherished now. Holding firm.

**SPECIFICATIONS**

**Years produced:** 1983-1987 (958,760 in total)
**Performance:** 0-60mph: 8.7sec
Top speed: 122mph
**Power & torque:** 122bhp/105lb ft
**Engine:** Normally aspirated 1587cc four cylinder, petrol, fuel injection, 16 valves
**Drivetrain:** Front-engine RWD
**Structure:** Monocoque
**Transmission:** Five-speed manual
**Weight:** 915kg

**PRICE GUIDE**

**Launch price:** £6995
**Excellent:** £12,500
**Good:** £8000
**Average:** £4250
**Project:** £2250

## TOYOTA
## Celica GT

Toyota might have been late in adopting front-wheel drive, but it embraced the concept wholeheartedly as the '80s went on. When the Celica moved across, fans of the breed had little to fear – the outgoing model was pretty insipid, while the new one was excellent in all respects. Twin-cam power ensured performance, tidy handling made all that poke accessible and, like all Toyotas until recently, its reliability was bulletproof. Undervalued today, and the survival rate is low, as it's overshadowed by the more radical replacement from 1989. Buy, enjoy, and stock up on rust treatment.

**SPECIFICATIONS**

**Years produced:** 1985-1989
**Performance:** 0-60mph: 8.3sec
Top speed: 130mph
**Power & torque:** 148bhp/133lb ft
**Engine:** Normally aspirated 1998cc four cylinder, petrol, fuel injection, 16 valves
**Drivetrain:** Front-engine FWD
**Structure:** Monocoque
**Transmission:** Five-speed manual
**Weight:** 1250kg

**PRICE GUIDE**

**Launch price:** £12,000
**Excellent:** £2200
**Good:** £1300
**Average:** £750
**Project:** £350

## TOYOTA
## MR2 MkI

A shock to Japan and the rest of the world, Toyota brought the mid-engined MR2 to the market in 1984.No Japanese manufacturer had attempted to sell a mid-engined car before. The standard MR2 came with the 1.6 16-valve engine first seen in the Corolla GT, which gave it brisk performance. Sadly the supercharged MR2 was never officially sold in Europe, but we did get the removable roof panels and improved suspension package from that model. Like most other Toyotas, the MR2 was a very reliable car – the main thing to watch out for is rust.

**SPECIFICATIONS**

**Years produced:** 1984-1989 (166,104 in total)
**Performance:** 0-60mph: 7.7sec
Top speed: 116mph
**Power & torque:** 122bhp/105lb ft
**Engine:** Normally aspirated 1587cc four cylinder, petrol, electronic fuel injection, 16 valves
**Drivetrain:** Mid-engine RWD
**Structure:** Monocoque
**Transmission:** Five-speed manual
**Weight:** 1052kg

**PRICE GUIDE**

**Launch price:** £9295
**Excellent:** £5000
**Good:** £2750
**Average:** £1350
**Project:** £500

## TOYOTA
## Supra/Supra Turbo

This was Toyota's third incarnation of the Supra, but unlike the previous two, this 'New' Supra was not directly related to the Celica. Available with a 200bhp normally aspirated straight six at launch; the turbocharged version arrived in 1987, boasting a more impressive 232bhp. The car was very advanced, and offered (as an expensive optional extra) a clever set of electronically controlled dampers. All the gadgets in the world could not disguise its weight though, and for this reason the Supra was more grand tourer than sports car.

**SPECIFICATIONS**

**Years produced:** 1986-1993
**Performance:** 0-60mph: 6.9sec
Top speed: 144mph
**Power & torque:** 232bhp/254lb ft
**Engine:** Turbocharged 2954cc six cylinder, petrol, fuel injection, 24 valves
**Drivetrain:** Front-engine RWD
**Structure:** Monocoque
**Transmission:** Five-speed manual
**Weight:** 1603kg

**PRICE GUIDE (add 50% for Turbo)**

**Launch price:** £15,299
**Excellent:** £3800
**Good:** £2700
**Average:** £1250
**Project:** £650

## TOYOTA
## MR2 Mk2

The second MR2 looked radically different to the first. Its curvy, exotic lines led some to dub it a 'poor man's Ferrari'. Others, though, focused on its occasionally tricky handling, specifically a readiness to swap ends if the driver backed off the throttle in a corner (a trait addressed by the revised model that appeared in 1994). The UK got the basic MR2 with 119bhp, the GT with 158bhp and the GT T-bar, which added lift-out roof panels. The Turbo version available in some markets was never officially sold here, though some found a way in as 'grey' imports.

**SPECIFICATIONS (GT)**

| | |
|---|---|
| **Years produced:** | 1990-1999 |
| **Performance:** | 0-60mph: 7.6sec<br>Top speed: 137mph |
| **Power & torque:** | 158bhp/140lb ft |
| **Engine:** | Normally aspirated 1998cc four cylinder, petrol, electronic fuel injection, 16v |
| **Drivetrain:** | Mid-engine RWD |
| **Structure:** | Monocoque |
| **Transmission:** | Five-speed manual |
| **Weight:** | 1275kg |

**PRICE GUIDE**

| | |
|---|---|
| **Launch price:** | £17,074 |
| **Excellent:** | £5000 |
| **Good:** | £2700 |
| **Average:** | £1350 |
| **Project:** | £800 |

## TOYOTA
## Celica GT/GT-Four

The fifth generation Celica ushered in 'organic' rounded lines that divided opinion then as now. The UK got a naturally aspirated 2-litre front-wheel-drive 'Liftback' coupe, but the star performer was the GT-Four with its turbocharged 2-litre engine and four-wheel drive. The works rally version took Carlos Sainz to the driver's world title in 1990 and 1992. In August 1991 a facelifted model introduced a raft of detail improvements. The following month the 'Carlos Sainz' limited edition appeared, of which 5000 were made, 3000 of them for Europe.

**SPECIFICATIONS**

| | |
|---|---|
| **Years produced:** | 1989-1993 |
| **Performance:** | 0-60mph: 7.0sec (GT-Four)<br>Top speed: 138mph |
| **Power & torque:** | 201bhp/203lb ft |
| **Engine:** | Turbocharged 1998cc four cylinder, petrol, fuel injection, 16 valves |
| **Drivetrain:** | Front-engine AWD |
| **Structure:** | Monocoque |
| **Transmission:** | Five-speed manual |
| **Weight:** | 1530kg |

**PRICE GUIDE (add 50% for Sainz edition)**

| | |
|---|---|
| **Launch price:** | £24,777 |
| **Excellent:** | £4500 |
| **Good:** | £2800 |
| **Average:** | £1350 |
| **Project:** | £800 |

## TOYOTA
## Supra

The Mk4 Supra was a huge leap forwards over the models that had gone before. The new lines were as clean as they were dramatic, many parts were aluminium to reduce weight, and beneath the long bonnet, twin sequential turbos endowed the 3-litre straight-six with massive torque with little throttle-lag, taking the Supra into junior supercar territory. It handled pretty well, too. In fact when Toyota canned the Supra in 2002 it left a large hole in the market. Unmolested examples are rare and fast gaining in value. Add 25% for manual, UK market cars.

**SPECIFICATIONS**

| | |
|---|---|
| **Years produced:** | 1993-2002 |
| **Performance:** | 0-60mph: 6.2sec<br>Top speed: 155mph (limited) |
| **Power & torque:** | 326bhp/325lb ft |
| **Engine:** | Twin-turbocharged 2997cc six cylinder, petrol, fuel injection, 24 valves |
| **Drivetrain:** | Front-engine RWD |
| **Structure:** | Monocoque |
| **Transmission:** | Six-speed manual |
| **Weight:** | 1582kg |

**PRICE GUIDE**

| | |
|---|---|
| **Launch price:** | £37,500 |
| **Excellent:** | £17,500 |
| **Good:** | £9000 |
| **Average:** | £6000 |
| **Project:** | £2500 |

## TOYOTA
## MR2 Mk3

Known as the MR2 Roadster in Europe, the third-gen MR2 was again an entirely new model, this time a compact, sweet-handling mid-engine soft-top that went head-to-head with Mazda's MX-5 and Lotus's brilliant Elise. It was that good. That it didn't sell in huge numbers was down partly to its rather plain lines, but also to its lack of a boot, though there's useful stowage space behind the seats. In every other regard the MR2 is a more practical car than an Elise, and also more rewarding than an MX-5. Currently a bargain.

**SPECIFICATIONS**

| | |
|---|---|
| **Years produced:** | 1999-2007 (c14,000 UK sales) |
| **Performance:** | 0-60mph: 7.6sec<br>Top speed: 130mph |
| **Power & torque:** | 138bhp/125lb ft |
| **Engine:** | Normally aspirated 1794cc four cylinder, petrol, electronic fuel injection, 16v |
| **Drivetrain:** | Mid-engine RWD |
| **Structure:** | Monocoque |
| **Transmission:** | Five- or six-speed manual |
| **Weight:** | 996kg |

**PRICE GUIDE**

| | |
|---|---|
| **Launch price:** | £17,995 |
| **Excellent:** | £4000 |
| **Good:** | £2500 |
| **Average:** | £1500 |
| **Project:** | £750 |

# TRIDENT

TRIDENT HAD ITS ORIGINS in a mid-1960s TVR prototype designed by Trevor Fiore. In true British specialist car industry fashion, TVR found itself in financial strife and the car ended up in the hands of one of its dealers, WJ (Bill) Last, who created Trident Cars to bring the car to market in 1967. The Suffolk-based company struggled after an initial flurry of interest, and by 1973 was effectively bankrupt. A reorganisation saw production resume from 1976, but by 1978 the original Trident was finished. A new company bearing the Trident name appeared in 1999 with a new sports car called the Iceni, which enjoyed only limited success (possibly as a result of being offered with a 6.6-litre turbo-diesel engine!).

## TRIDENT
### Clipper

The Trident Clipper is one of those fascinating British nearly-cars that could have conquered the world. Could have... It started life as a TVR prototype, but when the Blackpool company was declared bankrupt, the Fissore-styled Clipper project was picked up by Suffolk company Trident. It was blindingly quick with Detroit muscle under the bonnet, but the lengthened Triumph TR6 chassis that underpinned the whole ensemble wasn't really good enough. Despite its handsome lines – which had numerous detail tweaks – sales were elusive. Values seem to have peaked.

**SPECIFICATIONS**

| | |
|---|---|
| **Years produced:** | 1968-1977 (135 in total) |
| **Performance:** | 0-60mph: 5.0sec<br>Top speed: 145mph |
| **Power & torque:** | 270bhp/312lb ft |
| **Engine:** | Normally aspirated 4727cc V8, petrol, carburettor, 16 valves |
| **Drivetrain:** | Front-engine RWD |
| **Structure:** | Glassfibre body/separate chassis |
| **Transmission:** | Four-speed manual |
| **Weight:** | 1200kg |

**PRICE GUIDE**

| | |
|---|---|
| **Launch price:** | £2400 |
| **Excellent:** | £37,500 |
| **Good:** | £24,000 |
| **Average:** | £12,000 |
| **Project:** | £7500 |

## TRIDENT
### Venturer V6/Tycoon

An attempt to find more sales for Trident resulted in Ford V6 power being installed and a new name. It was the same car in essence, with the same all-independent suspension set-up, but with 138bhp instead of 270bhp, making it a much tamer beast. Tycoon was a similar car again, but with Triumph 2500 power. Production halted in 1974, revived in 1976 with a fully Federalised version. Problem was, the required impact bumpers and joke ride height made it look plain silly. The concept was revived – in a way – by the TVR Tasmin in 1980. Values currently holding.

**SPECIFICATIONS**

| | |
|---|---|
| **Years produced:** | 1967-1977 |
| **Performance:** | 0-60mph: 9.2sec<br>Top speed: 120mph |
| **Power & torque:** | 138bhp/192lb ft |
| **Engine:** | Normally aspirated 2994cc V6, petrol, carburettor, 12 valves |
| **Drivetrain:** | Front-engine RWD |
| **Structure:** | Glassfibre body/separate chassis |
| **Transmission:** | Four-speed manual |
| **Weight:** | 1090kg |

**PRICE GUIDE**

| | |
|---|---|
| **Launch price:** | £2400 |
| **Excellent:** | £17,000 |
| **Good:** | £12,000 |
| **Average:** | £7000 |
| **Project:** | £3500 |

# TRIUMPH

TRIUMPH CONCENTRATED on motorcycles until it built its first car in 1923 (the motorbike arm was sold off in 1936 after financial struggles largely due to over-concentration on sporting models). After entering receivership in 1939, Triumph was rescued by Standard and soon began to eclipse its saviour with the TR sports cars and, from 1959, the Herald saloon. That became the basis for the Spitfire and six-cylinder Vitesse and GT6. Triumph became part of Leyland Motors in 1961 and British Leyland in 1968, its notables of that era being the Stag and Dolomite Sprint. The marque disappeared in 1984; for the final three years its sole product was the Acclaim, a thinly disguised Honda Ballade.

## TRIUMPH
### 1800/2000 Roadster

It's impossible to write this without mentioning the *Bergerac* connection, especially as so many that come up for sale claim to have appeared in the Jersey-based TV detective series. There's reasonable evidence to suggest that five cars did, but don't pay a premium for one without checking its provenance. There were 1800 and 2000 versions, the former using a Triumph unit with a four-speed 'box, the latter adopting more powerful Standard Vanguard running gear, though that means you only get a three-speed gearbox. Stiffer chassis and better brakes make up for it, though.

**SPECIFICATIONS**

| | |
|---|---|
| **Years produced:** | 1946-1949 (2501/2000 in total) |
| **Performance:** | 0-60mph: 24.8sec<br>Top speed: 77mph |
| **Power & torque:** | 68bhp/108lb ft |
| **Engine:** | Normally aspirated 2088cc four cylinder, petrol, carburettor, 8 valves |
| **Drivetrain:** | Front-engine RWD |
| **Structure:** | Separate chassis |
| **Transmission:** | Three-speed manual |
| **Weight:** | 1283kg |

**PRICE GUIDE**

| | |
|---|---|
| **Launch price:** | £991 |
| **Excellent:** | £35,000 |
| **Good:** | £25,000 |
| **Average:** | £17,000 |
| **Project:** | £7000 |

## TRIUMPH
### 1800/2000/Renown

Proper coachbuilt cars in the great British tradition, with sharp-edged aluminium bodies on an ash frame, mounted on a steel chassis. The 1800s use a Triumph four-cylinder engine and four-speed gearbox (column-change, as all versions would be) and transverse-leaf front suspension. The 2000 was only produced during 1949 and had switched to the Standard 2088cc engine and three-speed gearbox. The Renown used the same body mounted on a lengthened Standard Vanguard chassis, complete with its coil spring front suspension. From 1952 this was lengthened by three inches.

**SPECIFICATIONS**

| | |
|---|---|
| **Years produced:** | 1946-1954 (4000/2000/9301 in total) |
| **Performance:** | 0-60mph: 25.1sec<br>Top speed: 75mph |
| **Power & torque:** | 68bhp/108lb ft |
| **Engine:** | Normally aspirated 2088cc four cylinder, petrol, carburettor, 8 valves |
| **Drivetrain:** | Front-engine RWD |
| **Structure:** | Separate chassis |
| **Transmission:** | Three-speed manual with overdrive |
| **Weight:** | 1283kg |

**PRICE GUIDE**

| | |
|---|---|
| **Launch price:** | £889 |
| **Excellent:** | £12,000 |
| **Good:** | £8000 |
| **Average:** | £4000 |
| **Project:** | £1500 |

## TRIUMPH
# Mayflower

A peculiar little car with shrunken Rolls-Royce styling that doesn't quite fit the short wheelbase. It is, however, roomy and comfortable, and assembled from good-quality materials. As long as you are in no real hurry, the unique-to-this-model aluminium-headed 1247cc sidevalve engine has enough torque to make decent progress, though its maximum speed is just over 60mph. It is very economical, though, and enthusiastic club back-up is there to keep it on the road. Just as when it was new, this makes an intriguing alternative to a Minor or Austin Devon.

**SPECIFICATIONS**

| | |
|---|---|
| **Years produced:** | 1949-1953 (34,000 in total) |
| **Performance:** | 0-60mph: N/A<br>Top speed: 63mph |
| **Power & torque:** | 38bhp/58lb ft |
| **Engine:** | Normally aspirated 1247cc four cylinder, petrol, carburettor, 8 valves |
| **Drivetrain:** | Front-engine RWD |
| **Structure:** | Separate chassis |
| **Transmission:** | Three-speed manual |
| **Weight:** | 914kg |

**PRICE GUIDE**

| | |
|---|---|
| **Launch price:** | £480 |
| **Excellent:** | £6000 |
| **Good:** | £3500 |
| **Average:** | £2000 |
| **Project:** | £750 |

## TRIUMPH
# TR2

Did Triumph know what it was starting? The TR2 practically defined the new wave of British sports cars that came along in the '50s: quick, basic, admirably strong with, under the bonnet, a well-proven engine from a saloon car with an extra carburettor bolted on. Instantly distinguished from later cars by its deeply recessed grille, the TR2 will easily pass 100mph, won rallies in its day, and is still popular for classic rallying. Care built after October 1954 also got shorter doors so you could at last get out next to kerbs. Concours cars might fetch £40k-plus, but all values have taken a hit.

**SPECIFICATIONS**

| | |
|---|---|
| **Years produced:** | 1953-1955 (8628 in total) |
| **Performance:** | 0-60mph: 11.9sec<br>Top speed: 103mph |
| **Power & torque:** | 90bhp/117lb ft |
| **Engine:** | Normally aspirated 1991cc four cylinder, petrol, carburettor, 8 valves |
| **Drivetrain:** | Front-engine RWD |
| **Structure:** | Separate chassis |
| **Transmission:** | Four-speed with overdrive |
| **Weight:** | 838kg |

**PRICE GUIDE**

| | |
|---|---|
| **Launch price:** | £787 |
| **Excellent:** | £27,500 |
| **Good:** | £22,000 |
| **Average:** | £17,000 |
| **Project:** | £7000 |

## TRIUMPH
# TR3/3A

The TR3 had been in production for almost a year before it gained its great claim to automotive fame. In September 1956 this became the first production car to be fitted as standard with front disc brakes, beating the Jaguar XK150 by four months. Eggcrate grille marks it out over the TR2, and it gained an extra 5bhp thanks to larger carbs. Sales were even better, and 90% were exported. The 3A is easily distinguished by its full-width grille and headlamps recessed further into the front panel. Public demand brought the welcome addition of external door handles. Less 10% for no overdrive.

**SPECIFICATIONS**

| | |
|---|---|
| **Years produced:** | 1955-1961 (13,377/58,236 in total) |
| **Performance:** | 0-60mph: 11.4sec<br>Top speed: 106mph |
| **Power & torque:** | 100bhp/117lb ft |
| **Engine:** | Normally aspirated 1991cc four cylinder, petrol, carburettor, 8 valves |
| **Drivetrain:** | Front-engine RWD |
| **Structure:** | Separate chassis |
| **Transmission:** | Four-speed manual with overdrive |
| **Weight:** | 902kg |

**PRICE GUIDE**

| | |
|---|---|
| **Launch price:** | £976 |
| **Excellent:** | £28,000 |
| **Good:** | £23,000 |
| **Average:** | £17,000 |
| **Project:** | £7000 |

## TRIUMPH
# Herald

One of the new small family-car stars of the 1959 Motor Show, the Herald was a bit more upmarket than the Mini and Anglia. All that really held it back was the lack of power from its 948cc engine, even in the twin-carb form used in the convertible launched in 1960 (worth a 50% premium) and soon offered as an option for the saloon. There was also a Herald S launched in 1961, but don't go thinking that stands for Sport. It was actually a stripped-out budget model that continued for some time after the 1200 arrived and, though rarer, is the least valuable of the range.

**SPECIFICATIONS**

| | |
|---|---|
| **Years produced:** | 1959-1964 (76,860 in total) |
| **Performance:** | 0-60mph: 31.1sec<br>Top speed: 71mph |
| **Power & torque:** | 35bhp/41lb ft |
| **Engine:** | Normally aspirated 948cc four cylinder, petrol, carburettor, 8 valves |
| **Drivetrain:** | Front-engine RWD |
| **Structure:** | Separate chassis |
| **Transmission:** | Four-speed manual |
| **Weight:** | 870kg |

**PRICE GUIDE**

| | |
|---|---|
| **Launch price:** | £702 |
| **Excellent:** | £3750 |
| **Good:** | £2750 |
| **Average:** | £1750 |
| **Project:** | £700 |

## TRIUMPH
# Herald Coupé

By a couple of weeks, this was actually the first Herald model to become available, and was what Michelotti's Herald prototype had looked like. Initially all Coupés were sold with a twin-carb version of the 948cc engine, though this was increased to a single-carb 1147cc along with the rest of the range in 1961. Front disc brakes became optional just before the engine swap. All but very early cars had strengthening ribs on the hardtop behind the side windows. Though undoubtedly pretty and sought after today, the Coupé proved a poor seller and was discontinued in 1964.

**SPECIFICATIONS**

| | |
|---|---|
| **Years produced:** | 1959-1964 (20,472 in total) |
| **Performance:** | 0-60mph: 23.6sec<br>Top speed: 77mph |
| **Power & torque:** | 39bhp/41lb ft |
| **Engine:** | Normally aspirated 948cc four cylinder, petrol, carburettor, 8 valves |
| **Drivetrain:** | Front-engine RWD |
| **Structure:** | Separate chassis |
| **Transmission:** | Four-speed manual |
| **Weight:** | 749kg |

**PRICE GUIDE**

| | |
|---|---|
| **Launch price:** | £731 |
| **Excellent:** | £4500 |
| **Good:** | £3250 |
| **Average:** | £2000 |
| **Project:** | £750 |

# TRIUMPH
## Italia

The Italia was a very successful attempt – stylistically – to turn the very capable Triumph TR3A convertible into a fixed head coupe. Styled by Giovanni Michelotti, who had pretty much defined Triumph's corporate style during the '50s, and built up from rolling chassis at *carrozzeria* Vignale, the Italia was short-lived and now in serious demand. The Italia was never officially imported into the UK, the majority remaining in their home country, but a few have been personally imported since. Production quality isn't all it should be, but enthusiasts would say that adds to the charm.

**SPECIFICATIONS**

| | |
|---|---|
| **Years produced:** | 1959-1963 (329 in total) |
| **Performance:** | 0-60mph: 12.0 secs<br>Top speed: 110mph |
| **Power & torque:** | 100bhp / 117lb ft |
| **Engine:** | Normally aspirated 1991cc in-line four, petrol, carburettor, 8 valves |
| **Drivetrain:** | Front-engine RWD |
| **Bodyframe:** | Chassis and separate body |
| **Transmission:** | Four-speed manual with overdrive |
| **Weight:** | 975kg |

**PRICE GUIDE**

| | |
|---|---|
| **Launch price:** | N/A |
| **Excellent:** | £100,000 |
| **Good:** | £75,000 |
| **Average:** | £50,000 |
| **Project:** | N/A |

# TRIUMPH
## TR4/4A

Michelotti's radical restyle on a widened TR3A chassis so frightened American dealers that they ordered another 3000-odd TR3As for 1962 instead. Everyone else took well to the sharp modern lines, though there were a few purist mutterings about it having gone soft, what with the wind-up windows and face-level air vents (it was the first British car to have them). Other benefits included rack-and-pinion steering, all-synchro gearbox and an extra 150cc in engine capacity. From 1964 the TR4A was more of the same, but with independent rear suspension. Take 10% off for no overdrive.

**SPECIFICATIONS**

| | |
|---|---|
| **Years produced:** | 1961-1967 (40,253/28,465 in total) |
| **Performance:** | 0-60mph: 11.4sec<br>Top speed: 109mph |
| **Power & torque:** | 104bhp/132lb ft |
| **Engine:** | Normally aspirated 2138cc four cylinder, petrol, carburettor, 8 valves |
| **Drivetrain:** | Front-engine RWD |
| **Structure:** | Separate chassis |
| **Transmission:** | Four-speed manual with overdrive |
| **Weight:** | 1016kg |

**PRICE GUIDE**

| | |
|---|---|
| **Launch price:** | £968 |
| **Excellent:** | £27,000 |
| **Good:** | £22,000 |
| **Average:** | £16,000 |
| **Project:** | £5000 |

# TRIUMPH
## Herald 1200 & 12/50

The 1200 joined the Herald range in 1961 and was easily the best-seller. The 1147cc engine was much torquier than the smaller twin-carb engine it replaced, and a higher axle ratio was fitted for easier cruising. This time there was an estate version as well as a convertible (either of those can command up to 50% more than the saloon). Fittings were more luxurious than earlier Heralds and disc brakes were an option. The 12/50 arrived in 1963 with extra power (51bhp), discs as standard and a full-length sunroof. For many the best of all Heralds, so expect to pay a premium.

**SPECIFICATIONS**

| | |
|---|---|
| **Years produced:** | 1961-1970 (284,256 in total) |
| **Performance:** | 0-60mph: 28.6sec<br>Top speed: 74mph |
| **Power & torque:** | 39bhp/51lb ft |
| **Engine:** | Normally aspirated 948cc four cylinder, petrol, carburettor, 8 valves |
| **Drivetrain:** | Front-engine RWD |
| **Structure:** | Separate chassis |
| **Transmission:** | Four-speed manual |
| **Weight:** | 800kg |

**PRICE GUIDE (Convertible in brackets)**

| | |
|---|---|
| **Launch price:** | £708 |
| **Excellent:** | £3750 (£5500) |
| **Good:** | £2250 (£3750) |
| **Average:** | £1250 (£2500) |
| **Project:** | £500 (£950) |

# TRIUMPH
## Vitesse 1600/2-litre

Basically a Herald with an extra two cylinders, twin headlamps and a beefed-up chassis – all of which can be considered improvements. The 1600 was by far the most numerous Vitesse from a production point of view, but the classic car movement came too late to save many and it's now the hardest to find. The 2-litre, which arrived in 1966, had 96bhp, which raised the top speed to 95mph and dropped the 0-60 time to 12.6sec. As ever, convertibles are most sought-after so add up c50% on top of the prices quoted here if you want a soft-top. Really good convertibles now fetch c£10k.

**SPECIFICATIONS**

| | |
|---|---|
| **Years produced:** | 1962-1968 (31,278 and 10,830) |
| **Performance:** | 0-60mph: 17.6sec (1600)<br>Top speed: 91mph |
| **Power & torque:** | 70bhp/92lb ft |
| **Engine:** | Normally aspirated 1596cc six cylinder, petrol, carburettor, 12 valves |
| **Drivetrain:** | Front-engine RWD |
| **Structure:** | Separate chassis |
| **Transmission:** | Four-speed manual with overdrive |
| **Weight:** | 909kg |

**PRICE GUIDE 1600 saloon (2.0 in brackets)**

| | |
|---|---|
| **Launch price:** | £839 |
| **Excellent:** | £5000 (£6000) |
| **Good:** | £3250 (£3750) |
| **Average:** | £2250 (£2750) |
| **Project:** | £500 (£750) |

# TRIUMPH
## Spitfire 4/MkII

Inspired by the success of the Frogeye Sprite, and Triumph's firm belief that it could build something better, the Spitfire was born in 1962, after the Frogeye had gone, but in time to tackle the MG Midget head-to-head. With similar performance and the benefit of independent rear suspension, it fulfilled that task with great success. Overdrive became an option from October '63, and was something else the Midget never got. The MkII arrived in March 1965 with a new grille, improved interior and an extra 4bhp. The very best might be £15k-plus, says Gary Bates of TRGB.

**SPECIFICATIONS**

| | |
|---|---|
| **Years produced:** | 1962-1967 (45,753/37,409 in total) |
| **Performance:** | 0-60mph: 15.5sec<br>Top speed: 92mph |
| **Power & torque:** | 67bhp/67lb ft |
| **Engine:** | Normally aspirated 1147cc four cylinder, petrol, carburettor, 8 valves |
| **Drivetrain:** | Front-engine RWD |
| **Structure:** | Separate chassis |
| **Transmission:** | Four-speed manual with overdrive |
| **Weight:** | 711kg |

**PRICE GUIDE**

| | |
|---|---|
| **Launch price:** | £730 |
| **Excellent:** | £12,000 |
| **Good:** | £7500 |
| **Average:** | £5500 |
| **Project:** | £2500 |

## TRIUMPH 2000

The demise of the Standard brand saw the Vanguard's replacement wearing a Triumph badge – and bearing no relation to its predecessor apart from the 2.0-litre engine that was passed on. Michelotti's styling took a brave leap into the 1960s, and Triumph now had a credible Rover 2000 rival with all-independent suspension in what would become known as the executive saloon class. A MkII arrived in 1969 with more of an edge to the styling, and longer bonnet and boot. Relatively few estates were built, but they make a practical and interesting classic if you can find one.

**SPECIFICATIONS**

| | |
|---|---|
| **Years produced:** | 1963-1977 (219,816 in total) |
| **Performance:** | 0-60mph: 14.9sec<br>Top speed: 96mph |
| **Power & torque:** | 84bhp/100lb ft |
| **Engine:** | Normally aspirated 1998cc six cylinder, petrol, carburettor, 12 valves |
| **Drivetrain:** | Front-engine RWD |
| **Structure:** | Monocoque |
| **Transmission:** | Four-speed manual with overdrive |
| **Weight:** | 1188kg |

**PRICE GUIDE**

| | |
|---|---|
| **Launch price:** | £1412 |
| **Excellent:** | £4500 |
| **Good:** | £2750 |
| **Average:** | £1500 |
| **Project:** | £500 |

## TRIUMPH 1300/1500 FWD

This small, well-appointed front-wheel-drive saloon was another radical departure for Triumph that it subsequently retreated from. Engine is the same as the Herald 13/60's, but it was joined in 1967 by a twin-carb version in the sportier 1300TC. That got an extra 14bhp, plus a brake servo to help cope with it. Both were replaced by the 1500 in 1970, an elegant restyle that saw the car grow seven inches in length and acquire twin headlamps. Wood trim and deep carpets added to the attractions, but its days were numbered as Triumph already had a rear-wheel-drive alternative.

**SPECIFICATIONS**

| | |
|---|---|
| **Years produced:** | 1965-1973 |
| **Performance:** | 0-60mph: 15.9sec<br>Top speed: 93mph |
| **Power & torque:** | 75bhp/75lb ft |
| **Engine:** | Normally aspirated 1296cc four cylinder, petrol, carburettor, 8 valves |
| **Drivetrain:** | Front-engine FWD |
| **Structure:** | Monocoque |
| **Transmission:** | Four-speed manual |
| **Weight:** | 914kg |

**PRICE GUIDE**

| | |
|---|---|
| **Launch price:** | £874 |
| **Excellent:** | £2750 |
| **Good:** | £1750 |
| **Average:** | £900 |
| **Project:** | £500 |

## TRIUMPH TR5/TR250

In the search for greater power and refinement, Triumph dropped a long-stroke version of its six-cylinder engine into the TR4A body and created the 2.5-litre TR5. Most of the world got the 150bhp Lucas fuel-injection engine. America was different. To get around emissions regulations Triumph sent them a twin-carb version with just 104bhp and called it the TR250. It sounds like a terrible idea, but these outsold the TR5 by almost three-to-one. It's not unusual to find examples repatriated to the UK and fitted with the injection engine from the much-less-valuable TR6.

**SPECIFICATIONS**

| | |
|---|---|
| **Years produced:** | 1967-1968 (2947 in total) |
| **Performance:** | 0-60mph: 8.8sec<br>Top speed: 120mph |
| **Power & torque:** | 150bhp/164lb ft |
| **Engine:** | Normally aspirated 2498cc six cylinder, petrol, fuel injection, 12 valves |
| **Drivetrain:** | Front-engine RWD |
| **Structure:** | Separate chassis |
| **Transmission:** | Four-speed with overdrive |
| **Weight:** | 1029kg |

**PRICE GUIDE (TR250 in brackets)**

| | |
|---|---|
| **Launch price:** | £1212 |
| **Excellent:** | £50,000 (£35,000) |
| **Good:** | £40,000 (£28,000) |
| **Average:** | £32,000 (£22,000) |
| **Project:** | £18,000 (£12,000) |

## TRIUMPH Spitfire MkIII

Recognisable by the raised front bumper that adds a hint of Lotus Elan, the MkIII Spitfire may count as the only car in history to have its looks improved by trying to meet US regulations. The hood was also improved, in both looks and ease of operation. But the best change lies under the bonnet: a 1296cc engine with an eight-port cylinder head based on the FWD Triumph 1300 unit. This adds up to a 12% power increase (with better economy), so a stronger clutch, larger brake calipers and stiffer front springs join the party. Values are strong, but take 10% off for no overdrive.

**SPECIFICATIONS**

| | |
|---|---|
| **Years produced:** | 1967-1970 (65,320 in total) |
| **Performance:** | 0-60mph: 14.5sec<br>Top speed: 95mph |
| **Power & torque:** | 75bhp/75lb ft |
| **Engine:** | Normally aspirated 1296cc four cylinder, petrol, carburettor, 8 valves |
| **Drivetrain:** | Front-engine RWD |
| **Structure:** | Separate chassis |
| **Transmission:** | Four-speed with overdrive |
| **Weight:** | 749kg |

**PRICE GUIDE**

| | |
|---|---|
| **Launch price:** | £717 |
| **Excellent:** | £12,000 |
| **Good:** | £8000 |
| **Average:** | £4750 |
| **Project:** | £2000 |

## TRIUMPH Herald 13/60

The final and most powerful Herald got a single-carb version of the 1300 engine. That makes it the most useable of the range, and you'll usually find it in any magazine's list of the top ten starter classics, as they combine driveability with ease of maintenance. There's a new dashboard and more space for rear passengers, but the most noticeable change is to a single-headlamp version of the Vitesse's front end and bonnet. Saloon production ended in 1970, with convertibles and estates lasting another year. Both can be worth 50% more than saloons.

**SPECIFICATIONS**

| | |
|---|---|
| **Years produced:** | 1967-1971 (82,650 in total) |
| **Performance:** | 0-60mph: 17.7sec<br>Top speed: 84mph |
| **Power & torque:** | 58bhp/73lb ft |
| **Engine:** | Normally aspirated 1296cc four cylinder, petrol, carburettor, 8 valves |
| **Drivetrain:** | Front-engine RWD |
| **Structure:** | Separate chassis |
| **Transmission:** | Four-speed manual |
| **Weight:** | 838kg |

**PRICE GUIDE**

| | |
|---|---|
| **Launch price:** | £700 |
| **Excellent:** | £4500 |
| **Good:** | £3000 |
| **Average:** | £1500 |
| **Project:** | £500 |

## TRIUMPH GT6 MkI/II

Conceived as a Spitfire GT, with the same four-cylinder running gear, it was quickly discovered that the extra weight of the fastback resulted in less performance. The solution was the six-cylinder Triumph 2000 engine, creating an instant rival for the MGB GT. An E-type-like bonnet bulge completed the visual move upmarket. Great in a straight line, but that extra power highlights the deficiencies of the MkI's swing-axle rear – lift-off oversteer means they must be driven with respect. Improved suspension makes the MkII much better. Take 10% off for no overdrive.

**SPECIFICATIONS**
**Years produced:** 1968-1970 (15,818/12,066 in total)
**Performance:** 0-60mph: 10.0sec
Top speed: 107mph
**Power & torque:** 104bhp/117lb ft
**Engine:** Normally aspirated 1998cc six cylinder, petrol, carburettor, 12 valves
**Drivetrain:** Front-engine RWD
**Structure:** Separate chassis
**Transmission:** Four-speed manual with overdrive
**Weight:** 864kg

**PRICE GUIDE**
**Launch price:** £1125
**Excellent:** £17,500
**Good:** £12,000
**Average:** £7500
**Project:** £3000

## TRIUMPH TR6

It might look like a new car but all Triumph did was ask Karmann to reshape the front and rear panelwork in a more modern style. The doors and windscreen are still TR4. Wider wheels are now more commonly steel with chrome trim rings, and the seats have a bit more padding, but under the bonnet things continued as with the TR5/TR250, with fuel injection and 150bhp for most of the world and 104bhp with carbs for the US, where most were sold. That differential was reduced in 1972 when the injection cars' output was cut to 125bhp – pay 10% less for these, 35% less for converted US cars.

**SPECIFICATIONS**
**Years produced:** 1968-1976 (91,850 in total)
**Performance:** 0-60mph: 8.2sec
Top speed: 119mph
**Power & torque:** 150bhp/164lb ft
**Engine:** Normally aspirated 2498cc six cylinder, petrol, fuel injection, 12 valves
**Drivetrain:** Front-engine RWD
**Structure:** Separate chassis
**Transmission:** Four-speed manual with overdrive
**Weight:** 1122kg

**PRICE GUIDE**
**Launch price:** £1334
**Excellent:** £24,000
**Good:** £15,000
**Average:** £10,000
**Project:** £4000

## TRIUMPH 2.5PI/2500TC/2500S

Think Triumph 2000 with TR5 engine, which made this Britain's first family car to be fitted with fuel injection. After little over a year it got the MkII bodyshell, but neither had the best reputation for reliability – mostly fuel-injection problems, though you can expect those to have been sorted out by now. This led Triumph back to using carburettors again in 1974 for the 2500TC, which had 99bhp, lower spec, and was cheaper than the 2.5PI. Then in 1975 the 2500S fully replaced the PI with a 106bhp carburettor engine, stiffer suspension and Stag alloys. This is the one to have.

**SPECIFICATIONS**
**Years produced:** 1968-1977 (47,455 in total)
**Performance:** 0-60mph: 11.5sec
Top speed: 106mph
**Power & torque:** 132bhp/153lb ft
**Engine:** Normally aspirated 2498cc six cylinder, petrol, carburettor, 12 valves
**Drivetrain:** Front-engine RWD
**Structure:** Monocoque
**Transmission:** Four-speed manual with overdrive
**Weight:** 1252kg

**PRICE GUIDE**
**Launch price:** £1595
**Excellent:** £6500
**Good:** £3750
**Average:** £2750
**Project:** £1000

## TRIUMPH GT6 MkIII

Visual changes were in line with the MkIV Spitfire, though if anything they are more successful on the GT6, whose fastback styling suits the new cut-off tail. At the front, the bonnet bulge remains, in a flatter and wider form. Rear side windows are reprofiled for a cleaner look. There was no significant change to the 2.0-litre power unit, but switching to the DIN standard of power measurement drops quoted output from 104bhp to 98bhp. The rear axle was changed to the cheaper Spitfire system for 1973 – but you won't notice the difference. Take 10% off for no overdrive.

**SPECIFICATIONS**
**Years produced:** 1970-1973 (13,042 in total)
**Performance:** 0-60mph: 10sec
Top speed: 112mph
**Power & torque:** 104bhp/117lb ft
**Engine:** Normally aspirated 1998cc six cylinder, petrol, carburettor, 12 valves
**Drivetrain:** Front-engine RWD
**Structure:** Separate chassis
**Transmission:** Four-speed manual with overdrive
**Weight:** 921kg

**PRICE GUIDE**
**Launch price:** £1287
**Excellent:** £14,000
**Good:** £9000
**Average:** £6500
**Project:** £2250

## TRIUMPH Spitfire MkIV

Michelotti restyled the Spitfire for the 1970s using many cues from the recently launched Stag – only the sills and doorskins were carried over from the MkIII. A change to 'swing-spring' rear suspension made a vast difference to roadholding. The engine is often said to have been detuned from MkIII spec, but in fact only the system of measuring output changed – from SAE to DIN – so the drop from 75bhp to 63bhp was not a real one. The MkIV was slower though, thanks to both extra weight and the taller gearing fitted to improve economy. Take 20% off for a non-overdrive car.

**SPECIFICATIONS**
**Years produced:** 1970-1974 (70,021 in total)
**Performance:** 0-60mph: 16.2sec
Top speed: 90mph
**Power & torque:** 63bhp/69lb ft
**Engine:** Normally aspirated 1296cc four cylinder, petrol, carburettor, 8 valves
**Drivetrain:** Front-engine RWD
**Structure:** Separate chassis
**Transmission:** Four-speed manual with overdrive
**Weight:** 779kg

**PRICE GUIDE**
**Launch price:** £985
**Excellent:** £8000
**Good:** £4500
**Average:** £2750
**Project:** £1250

## TRIUMPH
# Stag

Triumph's four-seat V8 tourer stumbled at the hurdles marked 'development budget' and 'build quality'. The good news is that all the teething troubles are now well known and a large proportion of surviving Stags have been put together properly, with specialist knowledge. That leaves us free to describe it as a stylish, strong and refined grand tourer that's simple and cheap to maintain and has one of the best exhaust notes this side of a street rod event. Common with a three-speed auto, but the manual/overdrive version is preferred, not just because it uses less fuel. Very best can be c£25k.

### SPECIFICATIONS

| | |
|---|---|
| **Years produced:** | 1970-1977 (25,939 in total) |
| **Performance:** | 0-60mph: 9.7sec<br>Top speed: 117mph |
| **Power & torque:** | 145bhp/170lb ft |
| **Engine:** | Normally aspirated 2997cc V8, petrol, carburettor, 16 valves |
| **Drivetrain:** | Front-engine RWD |
| **Structure:** | Monocoque |
| **Transmission:** | Four-speed manual with overdrive |
| **Weight:** | 1273kg |

### PRICE GUIDE

| | |
|---|---|
| **Launch price:** | £1996 |
| **Excellent:** | £19,500 |
| **Good:** | £15,000 |
| **Average:** | £9000 |
| **Project:** | £4000 |

## TRIUMPH
# Toledo/1500TC/Dolomite

Are you sitting comfortably? The Toledo was a 1300cc rear-wheel-drive car that used the front-wheel-drive 1500's body with a shorter nose and tail, but was launched at the same time. These rear-drive underpinning were used in the 1500's replacement, the 1500TC, in 1973. That got the 1500's full-length body. Both were renamed Dolomite in 1976, when you could have either 1300 or 1500 engines and rectangular headlamps, or, for driveway one-upmanship, the 1500HL with twin headlamps, more gauges and a better standard of trim. An excellent starter classic.

### SPECIFICATIONS

| | |
|---|---|
| **Years produced:** | 1970-1981 (220,017 in total) |
| **Performance:** | 0-60mph: 14.2sec<br>Top speed: 91mph |
| **Power & torque:** | 71bhp/84lb ft |
| **Engine:** | Normally aspirated 1493cc four cylinder, petrol, carburettor, 8 valves |
| **Drivetrain:** | Front-engine RWD |
| **Structure:** | Monocoque |
| **Transmission:** | Four-speed manual |
| **Weight:** | 980kg |

### PRICE GUIDE

| | |
|---|---|
| **Launch price:** | £2441 |
| **Excellent:** | £3250 |
| **Good:** | £1750 |
| **Average:** | £1250 |
| **Project:** | £500 |

## TRIUMPH
# Dolomite 1850

A woefully under-rated sporting saloon that was a genuine BMW contender in its day, but has come to be overshadowed by the Sprint. In essence it's a 1500TC fitted with an 1854cc version of the overhead-cam slant-four engine Triumph had been building for the Saab 99. Wishbone front suspension and live rear axle was all very conventional, but tightened up for the 1850 it created a sweet-handling and friendly machine that could be driven hard. Plusher 1850HL from 1976, and from 1973 all could be had with automatic transmission or manual with overdrive.

### SPECIFICATIONS

| | |
|---|---|
| **Years produced:** | 1972-1980 (79,010 in total) |
| **Performance:** | 0-60mph: 11.6sec<br>Top speed: 100mph |
| **Power & torque:** | 91bhp/105lb ft |
| **Engine:** | Normally aspirated 1854cc four cylinder, petrol, carburettor, 8 valves |
| **Drivetrain:** | Front-engine RWD |
| **Structure:** | Monocoque |
| **Transmission:** | Four-speed manual with overdrive |
| **Weight:** | 965kg |

### PRICE GUIDE

| | |
|---|---|
| **Launch price:** | £1399 |
| **Excellent:** | £3500 |
| **Good:** | £2000 |
| **Average:** | £1250 |
| **Project:** | £500 |

## TRIUMPH
# Dolomite Sprint

With a strong background in touring car racing winning it the accolade of BL's most successful competition car of the 1970s, by rights the Dolomite Sprint should be valued as highly as its old rivals: Alfa GTV, BMW 2002tii or Escort RS2000. But it's not, which must make it a bargain. Those others may all be two-doors, but the Dolly is the only one with a 16-valve head. Well equipped as standard, they come with plenty of wood trim and tinted glass plus that most 1970s of items, a vinyl roof. Overdrive too, from May 1975. With around 400 UK survivors, choice is good. Values holding firm.

### SPECIFICATIONS

| | |
|---|---|
| **Years produced:** | 1973-1980 (22,941 in total) |
| **Performance:** | 0-60mph: 8.7sec<br>Top speed: 115mph |
| **Power & torque:** | 127bhp/124lb ft |
| **Engine:** | Normally aspirated 1998cc four cylinder, petrol, carburettor, 16 valves |
| **Drivetrain:** | Front-engine RWD |
| **Structure:** | Monocoque |
| **Transmission:** | Four-speed manual with overdrive |
| **Weight:** | 1004kg |

### PRICE GUIDE

| | |
|---|---|
| **Launch price:** | £1740 |
| **Excellent:** | £12,000 |
| **Good:** | £8000 |
| **Average:** | £5000 |
| **Project:** | £1500 |

## TRIUMPH
# Spitfire 1500

Aside from the very obvious Spitfire 1500 decals on the nose and tail, you'd need to be a devout anorak-wearer to spot the external differences between this and a MkIV. Silver rather than black wheel centres are probably the most obvious. The real change comes under the bonnet. The new capacity came from a longer-stroke crankshaft which rather blunted the engine's will to rev, and made life tougher for the crank bearings, but it punches out a lot more mid-range power and taller gearing made the Spitfire a genuine 100mph car at last. Values currently static.

### SPECIFICATIONS

| | |
|---|---|
| **Years produced:** | 1974-1980 (91,137 in total) |
| **Performance:** | 0-60mph: 13.2sec<br>Top speed: 100mph |
| **Power & torque:** | 71bhp/82lb ft |
| **Engine:** | Normally aspirated 1493cc four cylinder, petrol, carburettor, 8 valves |
| **Drivetrain:** | Front-engine RWD |
| **Structure:** | Separate chassis |
| **Transmission:** | Four-speed with overdrive |
| **Weight:** | 794kg |

### PRICE GUIDE

| | |
|---|---|
| **Launch price:** | £1360 |
| **Excellent:** | £8500 |
| **Good:** | £5500 |
| **Average:** | £4250 |
| **Project:** | £2000 |

## TRIUMPH
## TR7

After the TR6 this was a disappointment for purists, having gained a roof but lost two cylinders, 500cc and independent rear suspension. It really wasn't a true TR, until the convertible version arrived in 1979 – those initials simply meant Triumph Roadster. But for all the criticism over these points and the still controversial 'wedge' styling, it sold faster than the TR6 ever had. It's a much easier car to live with too, driving more like a two-seater saloon than a sports car. It's also by far the cheapest way to join the ranks of Triumph TR ownership. Add 25% or more for the drophead.

**SPECIFICATIONS**

**Years produced:** 1975-1981 (112,375 in total)
**Performance:** 0-60mph: 9.1sec
Top speed: 109mph
**Power & torque:** 105bhp/119lb ft
**Engine:** Normally aspirated 1998cc four cylinder, petrol, carburettor, 8 valves
**Drivetrain:** Front-engine RWD
**Structure:** Monocoque
**Transmission:** 4/5-speed manual or 3-speed auto
**Weight:** 1000kg

**PRICE GUIDE (coupé)**

**Launch price:** £3000
**Excellent:** £4500
**Good:** £3000
**Average:** £2000
**Project:** £600

## TRIUMPH
## TR8

This was the car the TR7 should have been – it was designed to accept the Rover V8 engine from the outset. Sadly it arrived too late, was in production for less than two years and nearly all were left-hand drive examples for the US market. A handful of UK cars escaped into the wild (these fetch more) – many more have since been created on a DIY basis from TR7s (you can buy a kit from Rimmer Bros). There are few other differences apart from bigger brakes, radiator and modified crossmember. They might not be original, but they are a pretty good proposition for UK buyers.

**SPECIFICATIONS**

**Years produced:** 1979-1981 (2722 in total)
**Performance:** 0-60mph: 8.4sec
Top speed: 120mph
**Power & torque:** 137bhp/168lb ft
**Engine:** Normally aspirated 3528cc V8, petrol, mechanical fuel injection, 16 valves
**Drivetrain:** Front-engine RWD
**Structure:** Monocoque
**Transmission:** Five-speed manual
**Weight:** 1163kg

**PRICE GUIDE**

**Launch price:** £N/A
**Excellent:** £11,000
**Good:** £9000
**Average:** £7000
**Project:** £3000

# TURNER

JOHN TURNER Sports Cars was created in 1949 to build specials and racing engines: Turner's 500cc Formula 3 engine proved effective, and would have starred in the Egyptian-made Phoenix sports car, had it survived the Suez Crisis. In 1954, Turner moved into the production of its own cars from its factory near Wolverhampton, and the first sports car was available either with 803cc BMC A-series power, or Coventry-Climax for competition use. The cars were developed throughout the 1960s, after picking up the nickname 'Tatty Turner' in racing circles. Despite apparent sales success (600 cars were sold in total), the company went into liquidation in 1966 and production ceased.

## TURNER
## 803/950 Sports

Jack Turner started out making specials, but such was the quality of his work that others would ask him to make cars for them. Before he knew it, he'd become a car constructor. The 803 and 950 Sports were powered by Austin A30 and A35 A-series engines, and suspension was by torsion bars and trailing arms. It was a simple but effective recipe that appeared a while before the Austin-Healey Sprite. BMC ended up refusing to supply parts directly, pushing up the price of the final product but, like all Turners, it was available in kit form.

**SPECIFICATIONS**

**Years produced:** 1955-1959 (260 in total)
**Performance:** 0-60mph: 12.0sec
Top speed: 94mph
**Power & torque:** 34bhp/50lb ft
**Engine:** Normally aspirated 803cc four cylinder, petrol, carburettor, 8 valves
**Drivetrain:** Front-engine RWD
**Structure:** Spaceframe
**Transmission:** Four-speed manual
**Weight:** 560kg

**PRICE GUIDE**

**Launch price:** £789
**Excellent:** £11,000
**Good:** £6500
**Average:** £4000
**Project:** £2000

## TURNER
## Climax

All Turners shared the same ingredients as the original 803 Sports and, from the 950 Sports onwards, the excellent Climax FWA and 1220cc 90bhp FWE engines were made an optional extra to create the Turner-Climax. Considering it was a low-volume special, the Turner-Climax was very well finished, and drove every bit as well as the Austin-Healey Sprite that it was often compared with. In truth, the special car was far quicker, but because it cost at least a third more than its BMC rival, sales were slow. Values have been rising, albeit slowly.

**SPECIFICATIONS**

**Years produced:** 1959-1966
**Performance:** 0-60mph: 12.8sec
Top speed: 99mph
**Power & torque:** 85bhp/75lb ft
**Engine:** Normally aspirated 1216cc four cylinder, petrol, carburettor, 8 valves
**Drivetrain:** Front-engine RWD
**Structure:** Spaceframe
**Transmission:** Four-speed manual
**Weight:** 600kg

**PRICE GUIDE**

**Launch price:** £N/A
**Excellent:** £17,000
**Good:** £14,000
**Average:** £9000
**Project:** £4250

# TVR

TVR GREW OUT of Trevcar Motors, run by young Blackpool engineer Trevor Wilkinson, whose original idea was to badge the cars 'Trevors'. The first was sold in 1949, and the firm soon settled on the glassfibre body over steel frame that would form the structure of all TVRs. After several changes of management, Martin Lilley bought the company in 1965 and revitalised it. However, its Tasmin 'wedge' range strained finances and in 1981 the company was sold to Peter Wheeler, who turned TVR into a serious car-maker, even producing its own engines. He sold out to Nikolai Smolensky in 2004, but the factory closed two years later. A new TVR company is now developing an all-new Griffith.

## TVR
## Grantura I-1800S

Trevor Wilkinson's company started out like so many others – marrying lightweight special bodies with tried-and- tested mechanicals to produce affordable kit cars that could be enjoyed by many. What set TVR apart was its staying power, and most of that was down to the appeal of early models like the Grantura, and the sheer number of permutations you could buy it in – with engines ranging from the 1172cc Ford Popular engine to the 1798cc twin-carburettor MGB engine, there was bound to be a TVR for you. Values have softened in last 12 months, say Fernhurst TVR.

### SPECIFICATIONS

**Years produced:** 1958-1967 (800 approx in total)
**Performance:** 0-60mph: 10.0sec
Top speed: 111mph
**Power & torque:** 95bhp/N/A
**Engine:** Normally aspirated 1799cc four cylinder, petrol, carburettor, 8 valves
**Drivetrain:** Front-engine RWD
**Structure:** Tubular steel chassis/GRP body
**Transmission:** Four-speed manual
**Weight:** 864kg

### PRICE GUIDE

**Launch price:** £1426
**Excellent:** £30,000
**Good:** £20,000
**Average:** £10,000
**Project:** £5000

## TVR
## Griffith V8

American racing driver Jack Griffith approached TVR with a proposal to produce a V8-engined Grantura for competition. TVR agreed and supplied Grantura bodies and chassis for Griffith to fit 4727cc Ford V8s into. These cars were badged as the Griffith in the USA and were offered with either a manual or automatic gearbox. Performance was predictably swift. Some models could top 150mph and hit 60mph in around six seconds. They were overpowered, and only remained in production for a couple of years, but that rarity adds £s.

### SPECIFICATIONS

**Years produced:** 1963-1965 (300 in total)
**Performance:** 0-60mph: 6.9sec
Top speed: 140mph
**Power & torque:** 195bhp/282lb ft
**Engine:** Normally aspirated 4727cc V8, petrol, carburettor, 16 valves
**Drivetrain:** Front-engine RWD
**Structure:** Tubular steel chassis/GRP body
**Transmission:** Four-speed manual
**Weight:** 922kg

### PRICE GUIDE

**Launch price:** £1620
**Excellent:** £90,000
**Good:** £60,000
**Average:** £40,000
**Project:** £20,000

## TVR
## Vixen S1-S4

Early Vixens were really just Granturas with a Cortina GT engine in place of the old MGB unit. The improved S2 from October 1968 came with a longer wheelbase - and longer doors to go with it. It is easily distinguishable by its Cortina MkII tail-lights. A year later the S3 brought further upgrades, including a Capri-spec engine, cast alloy wheels, and grilles to cover the engine bay cooling vents. To use up old bodies, 23 Vixen S4s were built on the new M-series chassis. Quite quick, but with a hard ride and quite twitchy handling. Values currently holding steady.

### SPECIFICATIONS

**Years produced:** 1967-1973 (746 in total)
**Performance:** 0-60mph: 10.5sec
Top speed: 109mph
**Power & torque:** 88bhp/96lb ft
**Engine:** Normally aspirated 1599cc four cylinder, petrol, carburettor, 8 valves
**Drivetrain:** Front-engine RWD
**Structure:** Tubular steel chassis/GRP body
**Transmission:** Four-speed manual
**Weight:** 762kg

### PRICE GUIDE

**Launch price:** £1387
**Excellent:** £25,000
**Good:** £15,000
**Average:** £10,000
**Project:** £5000

## TVR
## Tuscan V6/V8/V8 SE

Here's a car that is finally gaining the respect and collector interest that it always should have received, especially with such low build numbers. If the Tuscan looks rather like the Vixen, that's because in effect it is one, but fitted with a selection of US Ford V8s (like the Griffith), and with two body widths – although the UK only saw two wide-bodied Tuscan V8s. The Capri-engined V6 Tuscan was a precursor for the mainstream TVR range of the 1970s. Quality was vastly improved over early cars, but can be hard to find these days. Worth the effort.

### SPECIFICATIONS (V6)

**Years produced:** 1969-1971 (174 in total)
**Performance:** 0-60mph: 8.3sec
Top speed: 125mph
**Power & torque:** 128bhp/173lb ft
**Engine:** Normally aspirated 2994cc V6, petrol, carburettor, 12 valves
**Drivetrain:** Front-engine RWD
**Structure:** Tubular steel chassis/GRP body
**Transmission:** Four-speed manual with overdrive
**Weight:** 907kg

### PRICE GUIDE

**Launch price:** £1930
**Excellent:** £40,000
**Good:** £28,000
**Average:** £20,000
**Project:** £6000

## TVR 2500/3000M

The need for two different engines in the Tuscan's replacement was due to the UK market's 3.0-litre Ford V6 not meeting US emissions standards. So cars heading that way were fitted with the already-approved TR6 engine, with carburettors and smog gear, and quite a few bhp less than the fuel-injection versions the UK was used to. Though most of those went to America, a few found British homes, but 3000Ms are what you will mostly find. Thanks to the TR6's demise, 2500M production ended in 1977. The 3000M soldiered on for another two years. Values static, say Fernhurst TVR.

**SPECIFICATIONS**

| | |
|---|---|
| Years produced: | 1971-1979 (947/654 in total) |
| Performance: | 0-60mph: 7.7sec (3000M)<br>Top speed: 121mph |
| Power & torque: | 138bhp/174lb ft |
| Engine: | Normally aspirated 2994cc V6, petrol, carburettor, 12 valves |
| Drivetrain: | Front-engine RWD |
| Structure: | Tubular steel chassis/GRP body |
| Transmission: | Four-speed manual |
| Weight: | 925kg |

**PRICE GUIDE**

| | |
|---|---|
| Launch price: | £2170 |
| Excellent: | £15,000 |
| Good: | £10,000 |
| Average: | £6000 |
| Project: | £3000 |

## TVR 1600M

Cleverly restyled from the waist down, the M-series TVRs (the M is for TVR boss Martin Lilley) were wider and nine inches longer, mostly in the nose, and built on a dynamically improved, stronger and better protected chassis. Still using the Capri GT 'Kent' engine, the 1600M was a poor seller compared with its more powerful brethren and was dropped in 1973 after less than a year on sale, but reintroduced with a mild restyle and bigger alloys in 1975 in the wake of an energy crisis. If you're not fussed about a big V6 or V8, the 1600M is an interesting alternative.

**SPECIFICATIONS**

| | |
|---|---|
| Years produced: | 1972-1977 (148 in total) |
| Performance: | 0-60mph: 10.4sec<br>Top speed: 106mph |
| Power & torque: | 86bhp/92lb ft |
| Engine: | Normally aspirated 1599cc four cylinder, petrol, carburettor, 8 valves |
| Drivetrain: | Front-engine RWD |
| Structure: | Tubular steel chassis/GRP body |
| Transmission: | Four-speed manual |
| Weight: | 910kg |

**PRICE GUIDE**

| | |
|---|---|
| Launch price: | £1886 |
| Excellent: | £15,000 |
| Good: | £9000 |
| Average: | £5000 |
| Project: | £3000 |

## TVR Taimar

Sold alongside the 3000M for three years, the Taimar finally answered a long-asked question of TVRs and provided proper external access to the boot via a large hatchback. A vast improvement compared with leaning over the seats. This added a mere 9kg in extra weight, and otherwise the cars were identical. Their appeal was obvious and, despite a price premium, the Taimar was a strong seller. Of special note is the Taimar Turbo, of which around 30 were built. Alongside a handful of 3000Ms, these were the first British production cars to be turbo'd, and a good one today will fetch up to £20k.

**SPECIFICATIONS**

| | |
|---|---|
| Years produced: | 1976-1979 (395 in total) |
| Performance: | 0-60mph: 7.7sec<br>Top speed: 121mph |
| Power & torque: | 142bhp/174lb ft |
| Engine: | Normally aspirated 2994cc V6, petrol, carburettor, 12 valves |
| Drivetrain: | Front-engine RWD |
| Structure: | Tubular steel chassis/GRP body |
| Transmission: | Four-speed manual |
| Weight: | 1025kg |

**PRICE GUIDE**

| | |
|---|---|
| Launch price: | £4260 |
| Excellent: | £15,000 |
| Good: | £11,000 |
| Average: | £7500 |
| Project: | £3250 |

## TVR 3000S

Soft-top version of the 3000M, called simply the Convertible at the time, but it was no simple roof-chop. In fact not much more than the chassis, engine and bonnet are shared. The windscreen is new, and the roof detaches completely to stow in the boot. Removing the side windows leaves cutaways in the doors at comfortable elbow height. Even the dashboard joins in the game, with centrally-mounted instruments. Underneath, all Convertibles got a much stronger, Jaguar XJ6 rear axle. Specialists the Fernhurst Motor Co say values have been static for some time now.

**SPECIFICATIONS**

| | |
|---|---|
| Years produced: | 1978-1979 (258 in total) |
| Performance: | 0-60mph: 7.7sec<br>Top speed: 125mph |
| Power & torque: | 142bhp/174lb ft |
| Engine: | Normally aspirated 2994cc V6, petrol, carburettor, 12 valves |
| Drivetrain: | Front-engine RWD |
| Structure: | Tubular steel chassis/GRP body |
| Transmission: | Four-speed manual |
| Weight: | 1098kg |

**PRICE GUIDE**

| | |
|---|---|
| Launch price: | £6390 |
| Excellent: | £25,000 |
| Good: | £15,000 |
| Average: | £8000 |
| Project: | £5000 |

## TVR Tasmin/280i

All change for the 1980s as TVR adopts radical new wedge-shaped bodies from the pen of former Lotus designer Oliver Winterbottom. Launched as a two-seater coupé, the range expanded with a 2+2 and convertible in 1981. The former was shortlived but, when it was dropped, the larger body, without rear seats, was used for the coupé. Engine was from Ford again: the Cologne V6 from the Capri 2.8i. A five-speed gearbox was introduced in 1983; the following year the Tasmin was rebadged 280i. There was a Pinto-powered Tasmin 200 for a short time; not popular. Cheap today.

**SPECIFICATIONS**

| | |
|---|---|
| Years produced: | 1980-1988 |
| Performance: | 0-60mph: 9.7sec<br>Top speed: 134mph |
| Power & torque: | 150bhp/150lb ft |
| Engine: | Normally aspirated 2792cc V6, petrol, mechanical fuel injection, 12 valves |
| Drivetrain: | Front-engine RWD |
| Structure: | Tubular steel chassis/GRP body |
| Transmission: | Five-speed manual |
| Weight: | 1143kg |

**PRICE GUIDE**

| | |
|---|---|
| Launch price: | £11,995 |
| Excellent: | £7500 |
| Good: | £4500 |
| Average: | £2500 |
| Project: | £1300 |

## TVR
## 350i

The arrival of Peter Wheeler at the helm of TVR brought excitement to the marque. He started by bolting a Rover V8 into the Tasmin (it was known as the Tasmin V8 at first, then simplified to 350i). Tubular exhaust manifolds turned up the volume to what would become a TVR trademark, while the much lighter engine, along with revisions to the suspension, brought a significant handling improvement. Series II from 1985 had larger rear lights and no bonnet vents. Rarity of the FHC version (fewer than 40) means only a 10% premium for the convertible. On the up recently.

**SPECIFICATIONS**

| | |
|---|---|
| **Years produced:** | 1983-1986 |
| **Performance:** | 0-60mph: 6.5sec<br>Top speed: 134mph |
| **Power & torque:** | 197bhp/220lb ft |
| **Engine:** | Normally aspirated 3528cc V8, petrol, electronic fuel injection, 16 valves |
| **Drivetrain:** | Front-engine RWD |
| **Structure:** | Tubular steel chassis/GRP body |
| **Transmission:** | Five-speed manual |
| **Weight:** | 1004kg |

**PRICE GUIDE**

| | |
|---|---|
| **Launch price:** | £15,540 |
| **Excellent:** | £17,000 |
| **Good:** | £11,000 |
| **Average:** | £5000 |
| **Project:** | £3000 |

## TVR
## 390/420SE

With the Rover V8 bored out to 3.9 litres and expertly tuned by racer Andy Rouse to extract serious bhp, TVR's wedge really staked its claim as a performance car. To prevent it being too much of a handful, the rear axle received a TorSen limited-slip diff, ducts were added for brake cooling, and the aerodynamics were tweaked to keep the wheels in better touch with the tarmac. The result was raved about in the press, but 390SE sales were restricted by it being more expensive than a Lotus Esprit, without the heritage. All bar one 390 were convertibles. Values edging upwards.

**SPECIFICATIONS**

| | |
|---|---|
| **Years produced:** | 1985-1988 |
| **Performance:** | 0-60mph: 4.9sec<br>Top speed: 144mph |
| **Power & torque:** | 275bhp/270lb ft |
| **Engine:** | Normally aspirated 3905cc V8, petrol, electronic fuel injection, 16 valves |
| **Drivetrain:** | Front-engine RWD |
| **Structure:** | Tubular steel chassis/GRP body |
| **Transmission:** | Five-speed manual |
| **Weight:** | 1107kg |

**PRICE GUIDE**

| | |
|---|---|
| **Launch price:** | £19,700 |
| **Excellent:** | £22,000 |
| **Good:** | £17,000 |
| **Average:** | £9000 |
| **Project:** | £5000 |

## TVR
## 420/450 SEAC

The AC on the end stands for Aramid Composite, which translates to mean a body created using carbonfibre and Kevlar to shave off a lot of weight. The racing version cemented TVR's bad-boy image: it was allegedly banned for being too fast, a marketing man's dream ticket. Around 40 of the 300bhp 420SEACs were built, along with 17 of the 450 version, which added 25bhp. The huge rear wing does nothing for the car's appearance, but an awful lot for high-speed stability. Rarity has led to rumours abounding of upgraded SEs, so make sure you buy the real thing.

**SPECIFICATIONS**

| | |
|---|---|
| **Years produced:** | 1986-1988 (37/18 in total) |
| **Performance:** | 0-60mph: 5.0sec<br>Top speed: 165mph |
| **Power & torque:** | 300bhp/290lb ft |
| **Engine:** | Normally aspirated 4228cc V8, petrol, electronic fuel injection, 16 valves |
| **Drivetrain:** | Front-engine RWD |
| **Structure:** | Tubular steel chassis/composite body |
| **Transmission:** | Five-speed manual |
| **Weight:** | 1130kg |

**PRICE GUIDE**

| | |
|---|---|
| **Launch price:** | £29,550 |
| **Excellent:** | £40,000 |
| **Good:** | £20,000 |
| **Average:** | £14,000 |
| **Project:** | £8000 |

## TVR
## S1-S3

The convertible S range was introduced as an entry-level trad sports car, specifically aimed at those who thought TVRs had grown too fast and too expensive. Pitched 30% cheaper than the 350i, they found a ready market. Early versions used the same Ford 2.8-litre Cologne V6 as the 280i, but this was replaced from 1988 in the S2 by Ford's new 2.9-litre Granada V6. For 1990, the S3 got a better interior and four-inch longer doors for easier access. The ultimate version was the V8S (pay £4k-£6k more), and there were also around 40 S4Cs – basically a V8S with the V6 engine.

**SPECIFICATIONS (S1)**

| | |
|---|---|
| **Years produced:** | 1986-1994 |
| **Performance:** | 0-60mph: 7.6sec<br>Top speed: 128mph |
| **Power & torque:** | 160bhp/162lb ft |
| **Engine:** | Normally aspirated 2792cc V6, petrol, mechanical fuel injection, 12 valves |
| **Drivetrain:** | Front-engine RWD |
| **Structure:** | Tubular steel chassis/GRP body |
| **Transmission:** | Five-speed manual |
| **Weight:** | 987kg |

**PRICE GUIDE (V8S in brackets)**

| | |
|---|---|
| **Launch price:** | £12,995 |
| **Excellent:** | £12,000 (£20,000) |
| **Good:** | £8000 (£15,000) |
| **Average:** | £6000 (£11,000) |
| **Project:** | £3000 (£5000) |

## TVR
## 400/450SE

These bigger-engined TVRs succeeded the 390/420SE and were, in effect, glassfibre versions of the lightweight SEAC cars, aimed at those with a little less money and a little more sanity. Not that they were that much slower, as you can see from the figures. They can prove to be quite a handful on a wet road too, so it's not a bad idea to check the car and its history for past accident damage. Interiors were improved, with better seats and materials, and more curves. TVRs were getting away from the hint of kit-car that had affected their earlier offerings.

**SPECIFICATIONS**

| | |
|---|---|
| **Years produced:** | 1988-1991 |
| **Performance:** | 0-60mph: 5.0sec<br>Top speed: 150mph |
| **Power & torque:** | 275bhp/270lb ft |
| **Engine:** | Normally aspirated 3998cc V8, petrol, electronic fuel injection, 16 valves |
| **Drivetrain:** | Front-engine RWD |
| **Structure:** | Tubular steel chassis/GRP body |
| **Transmission:** | Five-speed manual |
| **Weight:** | 1150kg |

**PRICE GUIDE**

| | |
|---|---|
| **Launch price:** | £24,995 |
| **Excellent:** | £18,000 |
| **Good:** | £15,000 |
| **Average:** | £8500 |
| **Project:** | £3500 |

# TVR Griffith

One of the purest sports car shapes ever, the Griffith transformed TVR's image almost overnight. Using a spaceframe chassis based on that developed for the Tuscan racecar, the first run of Griffiths used the Rover V8 in either 240bhp 4.0 or 280bhp 4.3 form. Production was halted in 1992 to allow the Chimaera to be put into production, and when the Griffith returned the following year it had a 340bhp 5-litre V8 and was now badged Griffith 500. Final run of SE cars can command over £40k. All values have taken a bit of a hit in the last 12 months.

**SPECIFICATIONS**

| | |
|---|---|
| **Years produced:** | 1991-2002 (c2300 of all variants) |
| **Performance:** | 0-60mph: 4.8sec (Griffith 500)<br>Top speed: 151mph |
| **Power & torque:** | 340bhp/350lb ft |
| **Engine:** | Normally aspirated 4998cc V8, petrol, fuel injection, 16 valves |
| **Drivetrain:** | Front-engine RWD |
| **Structure:** | Tubular steel chassis/GRP body |
| **Transmission:** | Five-speed manual |
| **Weight:** | 1060kg |

**PRICE GUIDE Griffith 500 (pre-cat in brackets)**

| | |
|---|---|
| **Launch price:** | £26,000 (4.0) |
| **Excellent:** | £35,000 (£25,000) |
| **Good:** | £25,000 (£18,000) |
| **Average:** | £18,000 (£10,000) |
| **Project:** | £8000 (£7000) |

# TVR Chimaera

Though sharing much with the Griffith, the Chimaera was a slightly bigger, more commodious touring car, though you'll never mistake it for a Jaguar: these are still full-on sports cars. Engines were shared with the Griffith, starting out with the 4.0, but soon adding the 4.3. Later versions even adopted 4.5 and 5-litre versions of the Rover V8. Chimaera 450 ('98-00) is arguably the sweet-spot in the range. Sadly, the tale about Peter Wheeler's dog, Ned, styling the sidelight opening by biting the styling buck was a typical Wheeler wind-up.

**SPECIFICATIONS**

| | |
|---|---|
| **Years produced:** | 1993-2003 (c6500 all variants) |
| **Performance:** | 0-60mph: 5.2sec (4.0)<br>Top speed: 148mph |
| **Power & torque:** | 240bhp/270lb ft |
| **Engine:** | Normally aspirated 3998cc V8, petrol, fuel injection, 16 valves |
| **Drivetrain:** | Front-engine RWD |
| **Structure:** | Tubular steel chassis/GRP body |
| **Transmission:** | Five-speed manual |
| **Weight:** | 1050kg |

**PRICE GUIDE**

| | |
|---|---|
| **Launch price:** | £26,250 |
| **Excellent:** | £25,000 (up to £35k for late '500') |
| **Good:** | £20,000 |
| **Average:** | £14,000 |
| **Project:** | £8000 |

# TVR Cerbera

The Cerbera was the first TVR to feature the company's own engines. It was also notable for being a fixed-head coupé and a 2+2. Early cars had a 360bhp 4.2-litre V8, soon supplemented by a 420bhp 4.5. Performance from both was vivid, with 0-60 in c4sec and a top speed of 170mph+. In 1998 a new 350bhp 4-litre straight-six was introduced for the Speed Six, with hardly any less performance. All had early reliability issues; the six in particular requires costly servicing. Lighter, post-2000 4.5s the ones to have, say Fernhurst.

**SPECIFICATIONS**

| | |
|---|---|
| **Years produced:** | 1996-2003 (c1500 in total) |
| **Performance:** | 0-60mph: 4.0sec (4.5 V8)<br>Top speed: 170mph+ |
| **Power & torque:** | 420bhp/380lb ft |
| **Engine:** | Normally aspirated 4475cc V8, petrol, fuel injection, 16 valves |
| **Drivetrain:** | Front-engine RWD |
| **Structure:** | Tubular steel chassis/GRP body |
| **Transmission:** | Five-speed manual |
| **Weight:** | 1100kg |

**PRICE GUIDE 4.2/4.5/4.0**

| | |
|---|---|
| **Launch price:** | £46,500 |
| **Excellent:** | £32,000/£40,000/£23,000 |
| **Good:** | £22,000/£28,000/£16,000 |
| **Average:** | £14,000/£20,000/£10,000 |
| **Project:** | £9000/£12,000/£7000 |

# TVR Tuscan Speed Six

TVR resurrected the Tuscan name for its next car, a riotously curvaceous two-seater coupé with a lift-out 'targa' roof panel and removable rear window (both of which could be stowed in the boot). Power came from 3.6- and 4-litre versions of TVR's 'Speed Six' straight-six engine, in states of tune from 350 to 400bhp. Mk2 from '05 was usefully improved, but all require fastidious and pricey servicing. A Convertible was also introduced towards the end of the run, reckoned by many to be one of the best TVRs of them all.

**SPECIFICATIONS**

| | |
|---|---|
| **Years produced:** | 1999-2006 (c1700 in total) |
| **Performance:** | 0-60mph: 4.2sec (4.0)<br>Top speed: 170mph+ |
| **Power & torque:** | 360bhp/310lb ft |
| **Engine:** | Normally aspirated 3996cc six cylinder, petrol, fuel injection, 24 valves |
| **Drivetrain:** | Front-engine RWD |
| **Structure:** | Tubular steel chassis/GRP body |
| **Transmission:** | Five-speed manual |
| **Weight:** | 1100kg |

**PRICE GUIDE Mk1/Mk2**

| | |
|---|---|
| **Launch price:** | £39,750 |
| **Excellent:** | £35,000/£45,000 |
| **Good:** | £25,000/£35,000 |
| **Average:** | £15,000/£25,000 |
| **Project:** | £8000/N/A |

# TVR Tamora

Designed to fill the gap left by the end of Griffith and Chimaera production and act as the entry-level TVR, the Tamora was a two-seater convertible fitted with the 3.6-litre Speed Six engine in 350bhp tune: enough to give it a top speed of around 160mph with 0-60mph in 4.2sec and a visceral soundtrack to match. The looks were a touch awkward compared with earlier TVRs and, largely as a consequence, sales were comparitively slow. The resulting rarity – and the fact that it's one of the better TVRs in pure driving terms – helps keep values strong today.

**SPECIFICATIONS**

| | |
|---|---|
| **Years produced:** | 2002-2006 (300-400 in total) |
| **Performance:** | 0-60mph: 4.2sec<br>Top speed: 160mph+ |
| **Power & torque:** | 350bhp/290lb ft |
| **Engine:** | Normally aspirated 3605cc six cylinder, petrol, fuel injection, 24 valves |
| **Drivetrain:** | Front-engine RWD |
| **Structure:** | Tubular steel chassis/GRP body |
| **Transmission:** | Five-speed manual |
| **Weight:** | 1060kg |

**PRICE GUIDE**

| | |
|---|---|
| **Launch price:** | £36,500 |
| **Excellent:** | £35,000 |
| **Good:** | £28,000 |
| **Average:** | £22,000 |
| **Project:** | £12,000 |

## TVR
## T350

Based on the Tamora, so the familiar TVR steel backbone and glassfibre bodywork and the 350bhp version of the Speed Six engine, but here dressed in aerodynamic coupé form with a glass hatchback to give access to the luggage space. If you wanted the sky above your head, there was also a Targa version with two lift-out roof panels that could be stowed behind the seats. No official factory record of sales numbers, but the TVR Car Club reckons around 390 coupés were built, but only around 70 Targas. Post-2004 engines tend to be more robust.

**SPECIFICATIONS**

| | |
|---|---|
| **Years produced:** | 2002-2006 (c460 in total) |
| **Performance:** | 0-60mph: 4.3sec<br>Top speed: 175mph |
| **Power & torque:** | 350bhp/290lb ft |
| **Engine:** | Normally aspirated 3605cc six cylinder, petrol, fuel injection, 24 valves |
| **Drivetrain:** | Front-engine RWD |
| **Structure:** | Tubular steel chassis/GRP body |
| **Transmission:** | Five-speed manual |
| **Weight:** | 1187kg |

**PRICE GUIDE pre/post 2004**

| | |
|---|---|
| **Launch price:** | £38,500 |
| **Excellent:** | £34,000/£37,000 |
| **Good:** | £28,000/£32,000 |
| **Average:** | £22,000/£22,000 |
| **Project:** | £15,000/£15,000 |

## TVR
## Sagaris

Conceived as the basis for an endurance racer (the serrations in the front wings were orginally intended to be open vents to release air pressure at high speed), the Sagaris was the last – and many believe the best – of the Blackpool TVRs. The wild bodywork was matched by savage performance from the 4-litre 406bhp Speed Six, but there was an underlying quality and feeling of thorough development that hadn't always been TVR hallmarks. Sadly the closure of the factory brought a premature end to production. Today, the most prized of all modern TVRs.

**SPECIFICATIONS**

| | |
|---|---|
| **Years produced:** | 2005-2007 (c200 in total) |
| **Performance:** | 0-60mph: 3.7sec<br>Top speed: 185mph |
| **Power & torque:** | 406bhp/349lb ft |
| **Engine:** | Normally aspirated 3996cc six cylinder, petrol, fuel injection, 24 valves |
| **Drivetrain:** | Front-engine RWD |
| **Structure:** | Tubular steel chassis/GRP body |
| **Transmission:** | Five-speed manual |
| **Weight:** | 1078kg |

**PRICE GUIDE**

| | |
|---|---|
| **Launch price:** | £49,995 |
| **Excellent:** | £70,000 |
| **Good:** | £60,000 |
| **Average:** | £50,000 |
| **Project:** | N/A |

# VANDEN PLAS

EARLY IN ITS life, Vanden Plas built coachwork, mainly for Bentley. But in 1946 it was bought by Austin, which used the firm to build its luxury Princess model. The cachet of the name prompted Austin – now part of the British Motor Corporation – to set Vanden Plas up as a separate marque in 1960. A series of large and well-appointed machines followed, although the offshoot also produced its own version of small machines based on BMC's 1100/1300 range and British Leyland's Allegro, the latter not an aesthetic success (to put it politely). After its London plant closed in 1979, Vanden Plas became a mere trim level on certain Austins, Rovers and Jaguars.

## VANDEN PLAS
## Princess 4-Litre Limo

What had been the Austin A135 Princess in 1952 became a Vanden Plas model in 1957, the prestigious badge being regarded as a way of making it seem even more upmarket. This cut-price Rolls-Royce had much to recommend it, becoming a particular favourite of mayors and successful businessman across Britain. Its 3993cc six-cylinder 122bhp engine made it a capable cruiser, and it could be had in three body styles; saloon, six-seater limousine or landaulette. An offshoot was the Princess IV of 1956, an expensive grand touring version intended to compete with Jaguar.

**SPECIFICATIONS**

| | |
|---|---|
| **Years produced:** | 1957-1968 (3344 in total) |
| **Performance:** | 0-60mph: 26.0sec<br>Top speed: 75mph |
| **Power & torque:** | 120bhp/185lb ft |
| **Engine:** | Normally aspirated 3990cc six cylinder, petrol, carburettor, 12 valves |
| **Drivetrain:** | Front-engine RWD |
| **Structure:** | Separate chassis |
| **Transmission:** | Four-speed manual/three-speed auto |
| **Weight:** | 2121kg |

**PRICE GUIDE**

| | |
|---|---|
| **Launch price:** | £3047 |
| **Excellent:** | £12,000 |
| **Good:** | £8750 |
| **Average:** | £4750 |
| **Project:** | £2250 |

## VANDEN PLAS
## 3-Litre

Farina styling reached Vanden Plas in 1959 with the 3-Litre model. The VP was top dog of the trio that also included the Austin Westminster and Wolseley 6/99. It was packed with even more wood and leather and offered silent refinement from its extensive soundproofing, which successfully drowned the burble of the six-cylinder 2912cc C-series engine. The MkII of 1961 gave more power – 120bhp – and the ability to sail past 100mph at last, plus a four-speed floor-mounted transmission. As well as the standard saloon, a touring limousine could also be specified. Values rising gently.

**SPECIFICATIONS**

| | |
|---|---|
| **Years produced:** | 1959-1964 (12,703 in total) |
| **Performance:** | 0-60mph: 17.9sec<br>Top speed: 97mph |
| **Power & torque:** | 108bhp/165lb ft |
| **Engine:** | Normally aspirated 2912cc six cylinder, petrol, carburettor, 12 valves |
| **Drivetrain:** | Front-engine RWD |
| **Structure:** | Monocoque |
| **Transmission:** | Three-speed manual |
| **Weight:** | 1530kg |

**PRICE GUIDE**

| | |
|---|---|
| **Launch price:** | £1396 |
| **Excellent:** | £9000 |
| **Good:** | £5200 |
| **Average:** | £2600 |
| **Project:** | £1200 |

## VANDEN PLAS
### Princess 1100/1300

BMC badge engineering ran amok with the 1100 and 1300 range, but the flagship Vanden Plas Princess was quite a superior machine. For its size, it managed to pack in a lot of luxury. All the trimming was done at the Vanden Plas factory in London and, as well as all the expected wood and leather touches, VP also fitted extra sound-deadening – and picnic tables for rear seat passengers. The initial 1098cc engine gave 55bhp, which rose to 65bhp with the MkII of 1967 (but only after BMC upgraded it from single- to twin-carb in 1968). Probably the most desirable of all BMC 1100s.

**SPECIFICATIONS**

| | |
|---|---|
| **Years produced:** | 1963-1974 (43,741 in total) |
| **Performance:** | 0-60mph: 21.1sec<br>Top speed: 85mph |
| **Power & torque:** | 55bhp/60lb ft |
| **Engine:** | Normally aspirated 1098cc four cylinder, petrol, carburettor, 8 valves |
| **Drivetrain:** | Front-engine FWD |
| **Structure:** | Monocoque |
| **Transmission:** | Four-speed manual |
| **Weight:** | 832kg |

**PRICE GUIDE**

| | |
|---|---|
| **Launch price:** | £895 |
| **Excellent:** | £4750 |
| **Good:** | £3500 |
| **Average:** | £1450 |
| **Project:** | £600 |

## VANDEN PLAS
### 4-Litre R

A brief encounter between Rolls-Royce and BMC led to the Vanden Plas 4-Litre R of 1964. The 'R' of the name was shorthand for the 3909cc Rolls-Royce six-cylinder engine under the bonnet of a modified 3-Litre bodyshell. The 175bhp of the all-alloy unit meant an easy car to drive – even without the extra refinement from the Borg Warner automatic transmission, power steering and servo-assisted front disc brakes. There was even more wood and leather inside than in the 3-Litre cars. Rolls-Royce even considered building its own version as a Bentley. Prices are on the up.

**SPECIFICATIONS**

| | |
|---|---|
| **Years produced:** | 1964-1968 (6999 in total) |
| **Performance:** | 0-60mph: 12.7sec<br>Top speed: 106mph |
| **Power & torque:** | 175bhp/218lb ft |
| **Engine:** | Normally aspirated 3909cc six cylinder, petrol, carburettor, 12 valves |
| **Drivetrain:** | Front-engine RWD |
| **Structure:** | Monocoque |
| **Transmission:** | Three-speed automatic |
| **Weight:** | 1575kg |

**PRICE GUIDE**

| | |
|---|---|
| **Launch price:** | £1994 |
| **Excellent:** | £10,500 |
| **Good:** | £6000 |
| **Average:** | £3000 |
| **Project:** | £1400 |

## VANDEN PLAS
### 1500/1750

Yes, it's an Allegro. With a faux-Bentley grille and a rather pretentious air. When the Allegro superseded the 1300 range, it seemed only logical that a posh version would follow to satisfy British Leyland devotees who prized luxury motoring in a small package. The disproportionate grille did little for the Allegro's already inelegant looks but it had a great interior. Those picnic tables were there, alongside the walnut veneer and hide. Most cars had 1485cc ohc engines of 68bhp but in the final couple of years there was a 90bhp 1748cc unit, mated to an automatic transmission only.

**SPECIFICATIONS**

| | |
|---|---|
| **Years produced:** | 1974-1980 (11,840 in total) |
| **Performance:** | 0-60mph: 16.7sec<br>Top speed: 90mph |
| **Power & torque:** | 69bhp/77lb ft |
| **Engine:** | Normally aspirated 1485cc four cylinder, petrol, carburettor, 8 valves |
| **Drivetrain:** | Front-engine FWD |
| **Structure:** | Monocoque |
| **Transmission:** | Five-speed manual |
| **Weight:** | 850kg |

**PRICE GUIDE**

| | |
|---|---|
| **Launch price:** | £1951 |
| **Excellent:** | £2700 |
| **Good:** | £2000 |
| **Average:** | £1250 |
| **Project:** | £500 |

# VAUXHALL

BUILDING ITS FIRST car in 1903, Vauxhall Ironworks started out as a manufacturer of sports and touring cars, becoming Vauxhall Motors in 1907. Its early models were Bentley rivals in their day, but the takeover by General Motors in 1925 saw it refocus more profitably on the mass market that was just starting to emerge. In 1932, the milestone Cadet became the first British car with a synchromesh gearbox. Another first came in 1938 with unitary construction for the Vauxhall 10. Post-war, subsequent rationalisation gradually pushed Vauxhall closer to its German counterpart Opel and, after Viva production ended in 1979, all subsequent Vauxhalls were little more than rebadged Opels.

## VAUXHALL
### Velox/Cresta E

Moving upmarket from the Wyvern were Vauxhall's Velox and Cresta, six-cylinder models with considerably enhanced creature comforts. Launched in 1951, the monocoque-construction Velox had a 2275cc engine and Chevrolet-inspired looks, with a significant amount of chrome on its body. After one year, a 2262cc engine made an appearance; although smaller in capacity, it had more power (from 58bhp to 64 or 69bhp). The Cresta joined the line-up in 1954 as an even more prestigious model; from the outside it could be distinguished by its two-tone paint. Edging up.

**SPECIFICATIONS**

| | |
|---|---|
| **Years produced:** | 1951-1957 (251,800 in total) |
| **Performance:** | 0-60mph: 20.9sec<br>Top speed: 80mph |
| **Power & torque:** | 58bhp/106lb ft |
| **Engine:** | Normally aspirated 2275cc six cylinder, petrol, carburettor, 12 valves |
| **Drivetrain:** | Front-engine RWD |
| **Structure:** | Monocoque |
| **Transmission:** | Three-speed manual |
| **Weight:** | 1021kg |

**PRICE GUIDE**

| | |
|---|---|
| **Launch price:** | £803 |
| **Excellent:** | £9000 |
| **Good:** | £5700 |
| **Average:** | £2800 |
| **Project:** | £1250 |

## VAUXHALL
### Wyvern E

Along with the closely-related Velox and Cresta, the Wyvern EIX was the first completely new post-war Vauxhall. The 1442cc engine was carried over from the previous Wyvern but the bodywork was thoroughly modern and very American in its look, with a lot of flashy chrome up-front and a curved windscreen, something unusual for the era. The increased weight of the new styling blunted performance so, from 1952, a 1507cc engine was fitted. This increased power from 35bhp to 40 or 48bhp. Aside from tweaks to its exterior, the Wyvern continued in this form until 1957.

**SPECIFICATIONS**

| | |
|---|---|
| **Years produced:** | 1951-1957 (5315 in total) |
| **Performance:** | 0-60mph: 37.2sec<br>Top speed: 71mph |
| **Power & torque:** | 35bhp/68lb ft |
| **Engine:** | Normally aspirated 1442cc four cylinder, petrol, carburettor, 8 valves |
| **Drivetrain:** | Front-engine RWD |
| **Structure:** | Monocoque |
| **Transmission:** | Three-speed manual |
| **Weight:** | 1001kg |

**PRICE GUIDE**

| | |
|---|---|
| **Launch price:** | £495 |
| **Excellent:** | £7500 |
| **Good:** | £5200 |
| **Average:** | £2300 |
| **Project:** | £1100 |

## VAUXHALL
### Velox/Cresta PA

British restraint went completely out of the window with the Velox and Cresta of 1957. Flamboyant American design was wholeheartedly embraced, with fins, a dogleg wraparound windscreen, two-tone paint schemes (on the Cresta) and cascades of chrome. The 2262cc six-cylinder engine was shared by both, so the Cresta only stood out from the cheaper Velox by its greater levels of luxury and equipment inside. In 1960, engine size went up to 2651cc and front disc brakes became available to cope with the extra power; the fins also grew in stature. Has a strong following today.

**SPECIFICATIONS**

| | |
|---|---|
| **Years produced:** | 1957-1962 (173,759 in total) |
| **Performance:** | 0-60mph: 18.0sec<br>Top speed: 87mph |
| **Power & torque:** | 83bhp/124lb ft |
| **Engine:** | Normally aspirated 2651cc six cylinder, petrol, carburettor, 12 valves |
| **Drivetrain:** | Front-engine RWD |
| **Structure:** | Monocoque |
| **Transmission:** | Three-speed manual |
| **Weight:** | 1193kg |

**PRICE GUIDE**

| | |
|---|---|
| **Launch price:** | £984 |
| **Excellent:** | £11,000 |
| **Good:** | £7250 |
| **Average:** | £4200 |
| **Project:** | £1400 |

## VAUXHALL
### Victor FB

More restrained (though also arguably rather less interesting) styling marked the 1961-64 FB Victor incarnation, albeit still with leanings across the Atlantic. The new look was neat, handsome and inoffensive and helped make this mid-sized family car one of Vauxhall's big successes of the 1960s. Four-door saloons and five-door estates were available, with the first cars (1961-63) sporting the same 1507cc engine as the F-type, but those from September 1963 until the end of production had a 1595cc engine of 58.5bhp, and front disc brakes were also adopted.

**SPECIFICATIONS**

| | |
|---|---|
| **Years produced:** | 1961-1964 (328,640 in total) |
| **Performance:** | 0-60mph: 22.6sec<br>Top speed: 76mph |
| **Power & torque:** | 55bhp/80lb ft |
| **Engine:** | Normally aspirated 1507cc four cylinder, petrol, carburettor, 8 valves |
| **Drivetrain:** | Front-engine RWD |
| **Structure:** | Monocoque |
| **Transmission:** | Three-speed manual |
| **Weight:** | 953kg |

**PRICE GUIDE**

| | |
|---|---|
| **Launch price:** | £574 |
| **Excellent:** | £4000 |
| **Good:** | £2500 |
| **Average:** | £1250 |
| **Project:** | £600 |

## VAUXHALL
### VX4/90 FB

As well as the standard Victor FB there was, for the first time, a performance-oriented version of the type, dubbed the VX4/90. Twin carburettors and a high-compression 1507cc engine boosted power from 50bhp to 71bhp, while a floor-mounted transmission and servo front disc brakes allowed the sporty Vauxhall driver to make the most of this extra potential. Spotters could recognise a VX4/90 by its contrasting colour side stripe and a vertical bar grille. When a 1595cc engine was fitted in 1963, power rose to 74bhp, with a wood-panelled dash to make up for this meagre increase.

**SPECIFICATIONS**

| | |
|---|---|
| **Years produced:** | 1961-1964 |
| **Performance:** | 0-60mph: 16.4sec<br>Top speed: 90mph |
| **Power & torque:** | 71bhp/92lb ft |
| **Engine:** | Normally aspirated 1508cc four cylinder, petrol, carburettor, 8 valves |
| **Drivetrain:** | Front-engine RWD |
| **Structure:** | Monocoque |
| **Transmission:** | Three-speed manual |
| **Weight:** | 990kg |

**PRICE GUIDE**

| | |
|---|---|
| **Launch price:** | £674 |
| **Excellent:** | £5500 |
| **Good:** | £3700 |
| **Average:** | £1700 |
| **Project:** | £900 |

## VAUXHALL
### Velox/Cresta PB

Vauxhall toned things down for the 1962-65 PB generation of Velox and Cresta. There was still a US influence and imposing size, but with a more British flavour. Front disc brakes were standard but the traditional three-speed column-mounted transmission persisted; there was also a three-speed Hydramatic automatic which changed to a two-speed Powerglide in 1965. Futuristic names were then all the rage of course. Initially, the 2651cc six-cylinder engine was carried over from the PA, but this jumped to 3294cc in 1964, its 115bhp providing a much-needed shot of adrenalin.

**SPECIFICATIONS**

| | |
|---|---|
| **Years produced:** | 1962-1965 (87,047 in total) |
| **Performance:** | 0-60mph: 19.5sec<br>Top speed: 92mph |
| **Power & torque:** | 95bhp/149lb ft |
| **Engine:** | Normally aspirated 2651cc six cylinder, petrol, carburettor, 12 valves |
| **Drivetrain:** | Front-engine RWD |
| **Structure:** | Monocoque |
| **Transmission:** | Three-speed manual or auto |
| **Weight:** | 1220kg |

**PRICE GUIDE**

| | |
|---|---|
| **Launch price:** | £805 |
| **Excellent:** | £5000 |
| **Good:** | £3350 |
| **Average:** | £1550 |
| **Project:** | £750 |

# VAUXHALL
## Viva HA

The British small-car market was swelled in 1963 by the belated entry of Vauxhall with its Viva HA. Stylistically it was nothing to get excited about; the angular looks were bland by comparison with rivals. However, the mechanical package was neat enough with a four-speed all-synchromesh gearbox, sharp rack-and-pinion steering and front disc brakes as an option. The more desirable variants – the De Luxe and the SL90 – boasted 54bhp from their 1057cc engines, but the Viva's main claim to fame was in being the first UK car with acrylic lacquer paint. Not memorable.

### SPECIFICATIONS

**Years produced:** 1963-1966 (309,538 in total)
**Performance:** 0-60mph: 19.6sec
Top speed: 78mph
**Power & torque:** 44bhp/56lb ft
**Engine:** Normally aspirated 1057cc four cylinder, petrol, carburettor, 8 valves
**Drivetrain:** Front-engine RWD
**Structure:** Monocoque
**Transmission:** Four-speed manual
**Weight:** 709kg

### PRICE GUIDE

**Launch price:** £578
**Excellent:** £3750
**Good:** £2500
**Average:** £1350
**Project:** £650

# VAUXHALL
## Victor FC 101

Marketed as the 101, the third incarnation of Victor was a spacious car with a number of novel design features such as curved side windows, ridged wing tops and front indicators/sidelights incorporated in the bumper. The 1594cc engine was carried over from the preceding type, although there was more power for the FC. As before, the VX4/90 did duty as the racier model, with twin carburettors, higher compression, enhanced suspension and more instrumentation inside, as well as a wood-panelled dashboard. This extra appeal means 25% can be added onto standard FC prices.

### SPECIFICATIONS

**Years produced:** 1964-1967 (219,814 in total)
**Performance:** 0-60mph: 17.1sec
Top speed: 85mph
**Power & torque:** 60bhp/86lb ft
**Engine:** Normally aspirated 1594cc four cylinder, petrol, carburettor, 8 valves
**Drivetrain:** Front-engine RWD
**Structure:** Monocoque
**Transmission:** Four-speed manual
**Weight:** 1086kg

### PRICE GUIDE

**Launch price:** £655
**Excellent:** £3300
**Good:** £2200
**Average:** £1100
**Project:** £450

# VAUXHALL
## Cresta PC/Viscount

The PC was only available with a 3294cc six-cylinder engine. At first, the Cresta De Luxe, with its four headlamps and extra brightwork, did service as the most luxurious model, but then came the 1966 Viscount with its vinyl roof, power steering and windows, plus those essential plush touches of wood and leather inside. Most Viscounts came with automatic transmission, which was improved considerably once the two-speed Powerglide gearbox was ditched in favour of a General Motors three-speeder. A lot of car for the money.

### SPECIFICATIONS

**Years produced:** 1965-1972 (66,937 in total)
**Performance:** 0-60mph: 12.6sec
Top speed: 97mph
**Power & torque:** 123bhp/175lb ft
**Engine:** Normally aspirated 3294cc six cylinder, petrol, carburettor, 12 valves
**Drivetrain:** Front-engine RWD
**Structure:** Monocoque
**Transmission:** Two/three-speed automatic
**Weight:** 1179kg

### PRICE GUIDE

**Launch price:** £956
**Excellent:** £4600
**Good:** £2500
**Average:** £1400
**Project:** £600

# VAUXHALL
## Viva HB

The Viva got more attractive and trendy in HB form. Not only was it larger, but it also featured distinctive 'Coke bottle' side styling, one of the first UK cars to do so. Aside from the engine, an enlarged (to 1159cc) version of the HA unit, little was carried over from the previous model. The suspension was totally new and quite advanced, resulting in impressive handling. This could be better enjoyed in the high compression SL90, with 59.5bhp. When the Viva started to lag behind rivals in the late 1960s, the overhead-cam 1599cc engine from the Victor was added to the mix. Edging up.

### SPECIFICATIONS

**Years produced:** 1966-1970 (566,391 in total)
**Performance:** 0-60mph: 19.7sec
Top speed: 80mph
**Power & torque:** 47bhp/62lb ft
**Engine:** Normally aspirated 1159cc four cylinder, petrol, carburettor, 8 valves
**Drivetrain:** Front-engine RWD
**Structure:** Monocoque
**Transmission:** Four-speed manual
**Weight:** 777kg

### PRICE GUIDE

**Launch price:** £508
**Excellent:** £3700
**Good:** £2400
**Average:** £1500
**Project:** £550

# VAUXHALL
## Viva Brabham HB

If BMC could do it with Cooper and Ford with Lotus, then why notVauxhall with Brabham? That was the thinking behind 1967's Brabham HB Viva, developed with world champ Jack Brabham. The hotted-up 1159cc engine had twin Stromberg carburettors, reworked exhaust manifolds and an uprated camshaft, combining to give 69bhp. Interior trim was improved, and the bodywork embellished with stripes running from the bonnet and around the front wings to the doors. It was in production for just a year before being replaced by the Viva 1600. Continues to creep up in value.

### SPECIFICATIONS

**Years produced:** 1967-1968
**Performance:** 0-60mph: 14.4sec
Top speed: 90mph
**Power & torque:** 68bhp/66lb ft
**Engine:** Normally aspirated 1159cc four cylinder, petrol, carburettor, 8 valves
**Drivetrain:** Front-engine RWD
**Structure:** Monocoque
**Transmission:** Four-speed manual
**Weight:** 777kg

### PRICE GUIDE

**Launch price:** £690
**Excellent:** £6000
**Good:** £3650
**Average:** £2300
**Project:** £1350

## VAUXHALL
### Victor FD

The FD Victor's 'Coke bottle' kink on its rear doors reflected contemporary American trends, just as previous Victors before it had done. Thus the looks were bold and brash, with quad-headlamp styling and the continuation (on some models) of the three-speed column-mounted gearchange and front bench seating that Vauxhall had persisted with for years. Two new hemispherical-head overhead-cam engines of 1599cc and 1975cc were introduced, with servo-assisted front brakes for the latter. The VX4/90 was the sporty model, with twin carburettors, overdrive and Rostyle wheels.

**SPECIFICATIONS**

| | |
|---|---|
| **Years produced:** | 1967-1972 (198,085 in total) |
| **Performance:** | 0-60mph: 14.0sec<br>Top speed: 95mph |
| **Power & torque:** | 83bhp/90lb ft |
| **Engine:** | Normally aspirated 1599cc four cylinder, petrol, carburettor, 8 valves |
| **Drivetrain:** | Front-engine RWD |
| **Structure:** | Monocoque |
| **Transmission:** | Four-speed manual/three-speed auto |
| **Weight:** | 1066kg |

**PRICE GUIDE**

| | |
|---|---|
| **Launch price:** | £819 |
| **Excellent:** | £3000 |
| **Good:** | £1700 |
| **Average:** | £800 |
| **Project:** | £300 |

## VAUXHALL
### Viva GT

The Viva Brabham was a half-hearted effort at injecting some vigour into the HB range but the same couldn't be said of the 1968 Viva GT. This was a storming machine that gave the Viva a heady degree of sportiness that was absent before. To achieve this, Vauxhall dropped in the 1975cc engine from the Victor, adorned with twin carburettors and mated with a close-ratio gearbox. This unleashed 104 horses, giving 100mph. The suspension was uprated, while bonnet scoops, a black grille and contrasting bonnet made it look the part. Vauxhall's equivalent of the Lotus Cortina.

**SPECIFICATIONS**

| | |
|---|---|
| **Years produced:** | 1968-1970 (4606 in total) |
| **Performance:** | 0-60mph: 11.4sec<br>Top speed: 100mph |
| **Power & torque:** | 104bhp/117lb ft |
| **Engine:** | Normally aspirated 1975cc four cylinder, petrol, carburettor, 8 valves |
| **Drivetrain:** | Front-engine RWD |
| **Structure:** | Monocoque |
| **Transmission:** | Four-speed manual |
| **Weight:** | 925kg |

**PRICE GUIDE**

| | |
|---|---|
| **Launch price:** | £1062 |
| **Excellent:** | £7000 |
| **Good:** | £3400 |
| **Average:** | £1600 |
| **Project:** | £750 |

## VAUXHALL
### Ventora FD/FE

Vauxhall continued its obsession with the letter 'V' in 1968, with the launch of the Ventora. It wasn't a new car though, just the amalgam of two existing machines; the Victor FD and the Cresta PC. The body was taken from the former, the 3294cc six-cylinder 123bhp engine came from the latter, while enhanced trim levels raised the car above normal Victor standards of comfort and equipment. The car continued as an FE model from 1972, using the same engine with the same level of power. Slightly bizarrely, estate versions were badged as Victor 3300s rather than Ventoras until 1973.

**SPECIFICATIONS**

| | |
|---|---|
| **Years produced:** | 1970-1975 (25,185 in total) |
| **Performance:** | 0-60mph: 12.1sec<br>Top speed: 107mph |
| **Power & torque:** | 123bhp/176lb ft |
| **Engine:** | Normally aspirated 3294cc six cylinder, petrol, carburettor, 12 valves |
| **Drivetrain:** | Front-engine RWD |
| **Structure:** | Monocoque |
| **Transmission:** | Four-speed manual |
| **Weight:** | 1124kg |

**PRICE GUIDE**

| | |
|---|---|
| **Launch price:** | £1102 |
| **Excellent:** | £4200 |
| **Good:** | £2750 |
| **Average:** | £1800 |
| **Project:** | £600 |

## VAUXHALL
### Firenza

The success of Ford's Capri prompted other manufacturers to offer similar models. The Firenza coupé was Vauxhall's effort, launched in 1971. It bore a family resemblance to the Viva HC it was based on, but had more rounded fastback styling; arguably, it was a more attractive creation than the Capri. Engines ranged from an insipid 1159cc to a rather enjoyable 1975cc, but changes in 1972 introduced 1256cc, 1759cc units, as well as the thoroughly entertaining 2279cc powerhouse of 110bhp. In 1973, the coupés became known as Magnums instead. Climbing up in value.

**SPECIFICATIONS**

| | |
|---|---|
| **Years produced:** | 1971-1973 (18,352 in total) |
| **Performance:** | 0-60mph: 22.0sec<br>Top speed: 84mph |
| **Power & torque:** | 62bhp/65lb ft |
| **Engine:** | Normally aspirated 1159cc four cylinder, petrol, carburettor, 8 valves |
| **Drivetrain:** | Front-engine RWD |
| **Structure:** | Monocoque |
| **Transmission:** | Four-speed manual |
| **Weight:** | 856kg |

**PRICE GUIDE**

| | |
|---|---|
| **Launch price:** | £1017 |
| **Excellent:** | £5200 |
| **Good:** | £2850 |
| **Average:** | £1450 |
| **Project:** | £750 |

## VAUXHALL
### Victor FE/VX1800/2300

British Vauxhalls started to lose their individuality with the Victor FE of 1972, for this car also shared some of its underpinnings with the Opel Rekord, albeit with different suspension and engines. The latter were 1759cc and 2279cc four-cylinder overhead-cam units, giving these mid-sized models effective performance, while front disc brakes meant they stopped well too. The sportier Rostyle wheel-decorated variant was known as the VX4/90 and managed 116bhp from its twin-carb 2.3-litre engine. From 1976, the cars became known as VX1800s or VX2300s.

**SPECIFICATIONS**

| | |
|---|---|
| **Years produced:** | 1972-1978 (80,610 in total) |
| **Performance:** | 0-60mph: 12.4sec<br>Top speed: 97mph |
| **Power & torque:** | 110bhp/138lb ft |
| **Engine:** | Normally aspirated 2279cc four cylinder, petrol, carburettor, 8 valves |
| **Drivetrain:** | Front-engine RWD |
| **Structure:** | Monocoque |
| **Transmission:** | Four-speed manual |
| **Weight:** | 1178kg |

**PRICE GUIDE**

| | |
|---|---|
| **Launch price:** | £1299 |
| **Excellent:** | £3400 |
| **Good:** | £2000 |
| **Average:** | £1000 |
| **Project:** | £600 |

## VAUXHALL Firenza Droopsnoot

The Firenza departed even further from the standard Viva HC formula with the unveiling of the Firenza HP – nicknamed the Droopsnoot – in 1973. This was the HC coupé body with a glassfibre nosecone and injected with 131bhp courtesy of its tweaked 2279cc engine. The streamlined front was more than just show as top speed was raised to 120mph, yet the car wasn't a success. Just 204 had been built when it was dropped in 1975, against estimates of 1000 a year. Resourcefully, Vauxhall then used the left-over noses on 197 HC estate cars, dubbed Sportshatches. Values rising.

**SPECIFICATIONS**

**Years produced:** 1973-1975 (204 in total)
**Performance:** 0-60mph: 9.4sec
Top speed: 120mph
**Power & torque:** 131bhp/145lb ft
**Engine:** Normally aspirated 2279cc four cylinder, petrol, carburettor, 8 valves
**Drivetrain:** Front-engine RWD
**Structure:** Monocoque
**Transmission:** Five-speed manual
**Weight:** 1015kg

**PRICE GUIDE**

**Launch price:** £2625
**Excellent:** £13,500
**Good:** £8750
**Average:** £4350
**Project:** £2200

## VAUXHALL Chevette

When launched in 1975, the Chevette combined the GM T-Car platform that had proved so successful in Germany as the Opel Kadett, and the willing Viva engine/transmission package. It was a very competent small car that was offered in saloon, hatchback and estate car form. The 'droopsnoot' styling proved to be a Vauxhall styling signature for a decade, and set them apart from their German counterparts. Easy to drive and a tidy handler, the Chevette proved popular enough to stay in production until 1984 – long after it was supposed to have been replaced by the Astra.

**SPECIFICATIONS**

**Years produced:** 1975-1984 (415,608 in total)
**Performance:** 0-60mph: 15.5sec
Top speed: 90mph
**Power & torque:** 56bhp/66lb ft
**Engine:** Normally aspirated 1256cc four cylinder, petrol, carburettor, 8 valves
**Drivetrain:** Front-engine RWD
**Structure:** Monocoque
**Transmission:** Four-speed manual
**Weight:** 860kg

**PRICE GUIDE**

**Launch price:** £2000
**Excellent:** £2250
**Good:** £1350
**Average:** £800
**Project:** £450

## VAUXHALL Cavalier/Sportshatch

The Cavalier proved to be a major turning point for Vauxhall – the Opel Ascona-based saloon proved the perfect weapon for the Luton firm to go Cortina fighting. Like the Chevette, it was well-engineered, handled well and was great on the motorway, but the larger car also had the benefit of being offered with engines from 1.3 to 2.0 litres. Luton-built cars were more prone to rust than their Belgian counterparts, but all were leagues ahead of earlier models – even if it was at the expense of their 'Britishness'. Coupe/ Sportshatch can fetch double these prices.

**SPECIFICATIONS (1.6GL)**

**Years produced:** 1975-1981 (238,980 in total)
**Performance:** 0-60mph: 13.0sec
Top speed: 100mph
**Power & torque:** 75bhp/85lb ft
**Engine:** Normally aspirated 1584cc four cylinder, petrol, carburettor, 8 valves
**Drivetrain:** Front-engine RWD
**Structure:** Monocoque
**Transmission:** Four-speed manual
**Weight:** 980kg

**PRICE GUIDE**

**Launch price:** £2749
**Excellent:** £2750
**Good:** £1650
**Average:** £1100
**Project:** £400

## VAUXHALL Chevette 2300HS

The Chevette, of course, was pure family car. The HS and HSR versions were very different beasts though. Built for rally homologation purposes, road versions went on sale in 1978, equipped with a 2279cc twin-cam engine and Getrag five-speed transmission. With 135bhp on tap and the potential for 117mph, this put it head-to-head with Ford's RS Escorts. Front and rear spoilers and wide alloy wheels marked it out from the Chevette herd. The HSR Evolution in 1979 went the whole hog with flared wheelarches and a bodykit, plus 150bhp. You'll pay a hefty premium for one of those.

**SPECIFICATIONS**

**Years produced:** 1976-1980 (450 in total)
**Performance:** 0-60mph: 8.8sec
Top speed: 117mph
**Power & torque:** 135bhp/134lb ft
**Engine:** Normally aspirated 2279cc four cylinder, petrol, carburettor, 16 valves
**Drivetrain:** Front-engine RWD
**Structure:** Monocoque
**Transmission:** Five-speed manual
**Weight:** 970kg

**PRICE GUIDE (HSR in brackets)**

**Launch price:** £5107
**Excellent:** £16,000 (£22,500)
**Good:** £9500 (£15,500)
**Average:** £7000 (£8000)
**Project:** £4000 (£5000)

## VAUXHALL Carlton/Viceroy

The rapid Opelisation of Vauxhall continued apace throughout the 1970s and, with the arrival of the Carlton – a rebranded Opel Rekord – in 1978, it heralded the end of the long-lived Victor range. The 2.0-litre saloon was solidly engineered and competent to drive, but lacked the glamour to take the fight to the Ford Granada and Rover SD1. Six-cylinder Viceroy model (the UK-badged Opel Commodore) followed in 1980, and proved even less popular. Find either now, and you'll be rewarded with a prime slice of German solidity, with a dash of Luton homeliness.

**SPECIFICATIONS**

**Years produced:** 1978-1986 (86,000 in total)
**Performance:** 0-60mph: 12.3sec (2000)
Top speed: 104mph
**Power & torque:** 100bhp/109lb ft
**Engine:** Normally aspirated 1979cc four cylinder, petrol, carburettor, 8 valves
**Drivetrain:** Front-engine RWD
**Structure:** Monocoque
**Transmission:** Four-speed manual
**Weight:** 1120kg

**PRICE GUIDE**

**Launch price:** £6496
**Excellent:** £2250
**Good:** £1300
**Average:** £800
**Project:** £300

## VAUXHALL
### Royale

Topping off the Vauxhall tree in the late-1970s were the Royale saloons and coupés, Anglicised versions of Opel's Senator and Monza models. Aside from the front grille and badges, they were identical to their Opel counterparts and were even built in Germany. The saloons were four-door, coupés had two and a hatchback. The 2784cc six-cylinder engine gave a reassuring 138bhp, but the big bruiser was 1980's 2969cc fuel-injection version, with a dramatic rise in power to 180bhp and, with it, the ability to top 130mph. Less kudos than an Opel but still has its fans.

**SPECIFICATIONS**

| | |
|---|---|
| Years produced: | 1978-1982 (7119 in total) |
| Performance: | 0-60mph: 11.4sec (2.8)<br>Top speed: 118mph |
| Power & torque: | 140bhp/161lb ft |
| Engine: | Normally aspirated 2784cc six cylinder, petrol, carburettor, 12 valves |
| Drivetrain: | Front-engine RWD |
| Structure: | Monocoque |
| Transmission: | Four-speed manual |
| Weight: | 1370kg |

**PRICE GUIDE**

| | |
|---|---|
| Launch price: | £8248 |
| Excellent: | £3000 |
| Good: | £2350 |
| Average: | £1200 |
| Project: | £450 |

## VAUXHALL
### Cavalier Mk2 SRi/130

When the Cavalier Mk2 arrived in August 1981, it marked the point when the mantle of the UK's favourite repmobile passed from Dagenham to Luton. Underneath its conservative styling was an up-to-the-minute FWD platform that proved durable and reliable, and resulted in a fine driver's car. When the 115bhp 1.8-litre engine was installed, the Cav was turned into a real wolf in sheep's clothing, and the ultimate overtaking lane tool. The 1987 SRi 130 was even quicker, and more desirable. Rare now, in some demand, and excellent value for money.

**SPECIFICATIONS**

| | |
|---|---|
| Years produced: | 1981-1988 (806,359 in total) |
| Performance: | 0-60mph: 9.1sec<br>Top speed: 115mph |
| Power & torque: | 115bhp/111lb ft |
| Engine: | Normally aspirated 1796cc four cylinder, petrol, fuel injection, 8 valves |
| Drivetrain: | Front-engine FWD |
| Structure: | Monocoque |
| Transmission: | Five-speed manual |
| Weight: | 1060kg |

**PRICE GUIDE**

| | |
|---|---|
| Launch price: | £6588 |
| Excellent: | £4250 |
| Good: | £2500 |
| Average: | £1400 |
| Project: | £600 |

## VAUXHALL
### Astra GTE Mk1

Vauxhall was a late entrant to the hot-hatch market, but when it finally arrived, it headed straight to the head of the pile. The Astra was always a great-handling car, but when fitted with wide, low-profile tyres and the excellent 115bhp 1.8-litre 'Family Two' engine, it was transformed into a flying machine. The GTE arrived in 1983, and within a few months received a close-ratio gearbox – yet, not long after, it made way for the aerodynamic Mk2 version. Not many survive now, and rust claimed many, which is one factor that's helping see values climb in recent years.

**SPECIFICATIONS**

| | |
|---|---|
| Years produced: | 1983-1984 |
| Performance: | 0-60mph: 8.7sec<br>Top speed: 118mph |
| Power & torque: | 115bhp/111lb ft |
| Engine: | Normally aspirated 1796cc four cylinder, petrol, fuel injection, 8 valves |
| Drivetrain: | Front-engine FWD |
| Structure: | Monocoque |
| Transmission: | Five-speed manual |
| Weight: | 930kg |

**PRICE GUIDE**

| | |
|---|---|
| Launch price: | £6412 |
| Excellent: | £7500 |
| Good: | £4200 |
| Average: | £1750 |
| Project: | £100 |

## VAUXHALL
### Astra GTE/16V Mk2

During the hot-hatch wars of the 1980s, the Astra GTE was usually a pace-setter. The original 115bhp car boasted a top speed of 126mph, but this was soon upped when the 130bhp 2.0-litre arrived in 1987. But less than two years later, the ultimate Astra arrived – the 150bhp GTE 16V, which used its red-top twin-cam to power way beyond 130mph. The rivals could only sit and watch. But straight-line speed wasn't everything – the 16V's road manners lacked breeding, with a combination of torque-steer and poor traction. That said, values of good ones are slowly climbing.

**SPECIFICATIONS**

| | |
|---|---|
| Years produced: | 1984-1991 |
| Performance: | 0-60mph: 6.9sec<br>Top speed: 135mph |
| Power & torque: | 150bhp/144lb ft |
| Engine: | Normally aspirated 1998cc four cylinder, petrol, fuel injection, 16 valves |
| Drivetrain: | Front-engine FWD |
| Structure: | Monocoque |
| Transmission: | Five-speed manual |
| Weight: | 1007kg |

**PRICE GUIDE**

| | |
|---|---|
| Launch price: | £9499 |
| Excellent: | £6000 |
| Good: | £3200 |
| Average: | £1600 |
| Project: | £800 |

## VAUXHALL
### Carlton GSi 3000

The 1986 Vauxhall Carlton/Opel Omega was an impressive leap into the 1980s. The slippery new car boasted an Audi-beating drag co-efficient of 0.28, and a well-sorted RWD chassis that challenged BMW's overall ability. But it was a little dull – until the good men at GM shoehorned in the Senator's 3.0-litre straight six. With 177bhp on tap, the bespoilered GSi was capable of topping 135mph, and doing it all day long. The best was to come in 1990, though, when the 24V version was installed, producing Luton's first genuine BMW 535i-baiter in the process.

**SPECIFICATIONS (12v)**

| | |
|---|---|
| Years produced: | 1986-1994 (241,041 in total) |
| Performance: | 0-60mph: 8.2sec<br>Top speed: 134mph |
| Power & torque: | 177bhp/177lb ft |
| Engine: | Normally aspirated 2969cc six cylinder, petrol, electronic fuel injection, 12 valves |
| Drivetrain: | Front-engine RWD |
| Structure: | Monocoque |
| Transmission: | Five-speed manual |
| Weight: | 1370kg |

**PRICE GUIDE**

| | |
|---|---|
| Launch price: | £16,999 |
| Excellent: | £4200 |
| Good: | £2250 |
| Average: | £1300 |
| Project: | £500 |

## VAUXHALL Senator

And here it was, the ultimate Vauxhall for the ultimate businessman in a hurry. The Senator might have been largely Carlton under the skin, but the imposing new body with cheesegrater grille gave it a presence all of its own. So, it's no wonder that traffic police took the big Vauxhall to their bosom, happy that they'd finally found a replacement for their ageing Rover SD1s. Digital dashboards were an acquired taste, and the 2.5-litre model was a little sluggish. Pick of the range is the 200bhp 24V model that, in manual form, will hit 150mph given a long enough run.

**SPECIFICATIONS (24v)**

| | |
|---|---|
| **Years produced:** | 1987-1994 (33,125 in total) |
| **Performance:** | 0-60mph: 7.5sec<br>Top speed: 149mph |
| **Power & torque:** | 200bhp/199lb ft |
| **Engine:** | Normally aspirated 2969cc six cylinder, petrol, electronic injection, 24 valves |
| **Drivetrain:** | Front-engine RWD |
| **Structure:** | Monocoque |
| **Transmission:** | Five-speed manual/four-speed auto |
| **Weight:** | 1530kg |

**PRICE GUIDE**

| | |
|---|---|
| **Launch price:** | £26,975 |
| **Excellent:** | £3000 |
| **Good:** | £1850 |
| **Average:** | £1150 |
| **Project:** | £400 |

## VAUXHALL Lotus Carlton

A family saloon that was faster than many contemporary supercars – that was the truly extraordinary Lotus Carlton/Omega. With its 24v straight-six expanded to 3.6 litres and fitted with twin turbochargers, it produced a mighty 377bhp and 419lb ft of torque, enough to take this rear-wheel-drive monster from 0-60 in 4.8sec, to 100 in 10.6, and on to a claimed top speed of 176mph. The chassis was thoroughly well sorted too, and the fact that it still offered all the refinement of the donor car made it one of the most remarkable cars of the '90s. Values flying.

**SPECIFICATIONS**

| | |
|---|---|
| **Years produced:** | 1990-1992 (950 in total, 320 RHD) |
| **Performance:** | 0-60mph: 4.8sec<br>Top speed: 176mph |
| **Power & torque:** | 377bhp/419lb ft |
| **Engine:** | Twin-turbocharged 3615cc six cylinder, petrol, electronic fuel injection, 24v |
| **Drivetrain:** | Front-engine RWD |
| **Structure:** | Monocoque |
| **Transmission:** | Six-speed manual |
| **Weight:** | 1660kg |

**PRICE GUIDE**

| | |
|---|---|
| **Launch price:** | £48,000 |
| **Excellent:** | £42,500 |
| **Good:** | £35,000 |
| **Average:** | £25,000 |
| **Project:** | N/A |

## VAUXHALL VX220

The VX220 was a Lotus Elise in a sharper set of clothes, with a (slightly) less Spartan interior and a torquier engine: the 2.2-litre Ecotec motor developed 145bhp compared with 118bhp from the S1 Elise's K-series (the later 197bhp VX Turbo version was a pocket supercar). Although it had airbags, ABS and carpets, in truth it was still pretty hardcore (no PAS, electric windows, aircon or central locking). But a well-cared-for example is one of the finest driving machines of the last 20 years and good value compared with an Elise.

**SPECIFICATIONS**

| | |
|---|---|
| **Years produced:** | 2000-2005 (1214 in total) |
| **Performance:** | 0-60mph: 5.6sec<br>Top speed: 130mph |
| **Power & torque:** | 145bhp/150lb ft |
| **Engine:** | Normally aspirated 2198cc four cylinder, petrol, fuel injection, 16 valves |
| **Drivetrain:** | Mid-engine RWD |
| **Structure:** | Aluminium tub, GRP body |
| **Transmission:** | Five-speed manual |
| **Weight:** | 875kg |

**PRICE GUIDE (add 50% for Turbo)**

| | |
|---|---|
| **Launch price:** | £22,995 |
| **Excellent:** | £12,000 |
| **Good:** | £9000 |
| **Average:** | £7000 |
| **Project:** | £4000 |

# VOLKSWAGEN

THE BEETLE, as conceived in 1938, was simply known as the Volkswagen ('people's car'); the company set up to produce it also adopted the same name. The durable simplicity of Volkswagen's products – the Beetle and the Type 2 bus/van/camper series especially – made the marque phenomenally successful across the globe. It took until the mid-1970s for VW's reliance on the Beetle to end, but it enjoyed similar universal acclaim with the handsome Golf replacement. Today's VW group is a vast conglomerate, embracing Audi, Skoda, SEAT, Bentley, Lamborghini, Porsche, Bugatti and other brands, with a reputation for quality (if not always honesty!).

## VOLKSWAGEN Beetle (split-screen)

Adolf Hitler had the idea for the 'Volkswagen' (People's Car) and Ferdinand Porsche designed it, for the purposes of getting Nazi Germany mobile. Who would have thought that from such a troubled birth, the Beetle would go on to conquer the world? After the war, the British army restarted production and gradually the car started to grow more refined, finding itself exported globally. The original split-rear window models were built until 1953 and featured an 1131cc rear-mounted air-cooled engine of just 25bhp. A simple, charming and ruggedly reliable motoring legend.

**SPECIFICATIONS**

| | |
|---|---|
| **Years produced:** | 1946-1953 |
| **Performance:** | 0-60mph: N/A<br>Top speed: 62mph |
| **Power & torque:** | 24bhp/49lb ft |
| **Engine:** | Normally aspirated 1131cc flat four, petrol, carburettor, 8 valves |
| **Drivetrain:** | Rear-engine RWD |
| **Structure:** | Separate chassis |
| **Transmission:** | Four-speed manual |
| **Weight:** | 749kg |

**PRICE GUIDE**

| | |
|---|---|
| **Launch price:** | £690 |
| **Excellent:** | £24,500 |
| **Good:** | £13,500 |
| **Average:** | £9500 |
| **Project:** | £6000 |

## VOLKSWAGEN
### Beetle (Oval)

Poor visibility was always an issue with the original Beetle and its split back window. Volkswagen addressed this in March 1953 when the screen was replaced by a larger single-piece oval one. This important change coincided with the beginning of sales in the UK, and all but the very first of the 'Oval Beetles' benefited from the first increase in engine size since 1945 when an 1192cc unit added 5bhp. With 30bhp to play with now, 66mph was possible... not much on paper but, of course, a Beetle could happily cruise at that speed all day. All on the up; add 30% for Cabrio.

**SPECIFICATIONS**

| | |
|---|---|
| **Years produced:** | 1953-1957 |
| **Performance:** | 0-60mph: 47.6sec<br>Top speed: 66mph |
| **Power & torque:** | 24.5bhp/49lb ft |
| **Engine:** | Normally aspirated 1131cc flat four, petrol, carburettor, 8 valves |
| **Drivetrain:** | Rear-engine RWD |
| **Structure:** | Separate chassis |
| **Transmission:** | Four-speed manual |
| **Weight:** | 711kg |

**PRICE GUIDE**

| | |
|---|---|
| **Launch price:** | £690 |
| **Excellent:** | £17,000 |
| **Good:** | £10,000 |
| **Average:** | £6500 |
| **Project:** | £3750 |

## VOLKSWAGEN
### Kombi/Camper

The initial idea for a VW-based van was in 1947, but it wasn't until 1950 that the officially designated Type 2 appeared. Many different variants were available but the most popular and numerous were the Kombi (Kombinationskraftwagen – a windowed combination of passenger and cargo vehicle, usually referred to as a 'bus') and the Camper. Westfalia created most of the latter. Nicknamed 'Split' or 'Splittie' due to their divided windscreen, VW updated the mechanical side of the vehicles constantly while leaving their looks mostly untouched... at least until 1968. Values still rising fast.

**SPECIFICATIONS**

| | |
|---|---|
| **Years produced:** | 1950-1968 |
| **Performance:** | 0-60mph: N/A<br>Top speed: 65mph |
| **Power & torque:** | 30bhp/56lb ft |
| **Engine:** | Normally aspirated 1192cc flat four, petrol, carburettor, 8 valves |
| **Drivetrain:** | Rear-engine RWD |
| **Structure:** | Separate chassis |
| **Transmission:** | Four-speed manual |
| **Weight:** | 1105kg |

**PRICE GUIDE**

| | |
|---|---|
| **Launch price:** | N/A |
| **Excellent:** | £55,000 |
| **Good:** | £37,500 |
| **Average:** | £19,000 |
| **Project:** | £12,000 |

## VOLKSWAGEN
### Karmann-Ghia Coupé

With the Beetle so easy to put different bodies on – after all, this was how Porsche started out – it was almost inevitable that Volkswagen would come up with a sports car. Actually, it was coachbuilder Karmann which had the idea and VW jumped at the chance when it saw the pretty coupé body that Ghia designed. The public liked it too, and this sleeker Beetle sold well. However, it was a sheep in wolf's clothing, for its underpinnings were pure Beetle, with anaemic performance. The original 1192cc engine was increased in stages up to 1584cc by 1974.

**SPECIFICATIONS**

| | |
|---|---|
| **Years produced:** | 1955-1974 (364,401 in total) |
| **Performance:** | 0-60mph: 26.5sec<br>Top speed: 77mph |
| **Power & torque:** | 30bhp/56lb ft |
| **Engine:** | Normally aspirated 1192cc flat four, petrol, carburettor, 8 valves |
| **Drivetrain:** | Rear-engine RWD |
| **Structure:** | Separate chassis |
| **Transmission:** | Four-speed manual |
| **Weight:** | 730kg |

**PRICE GUIDE**

| | |
|---|---|
| **Launch price:** | £1235 |
| **Excellent:** | £16,000 |
| **Good:** | £9000 |
| **Average:** | £5750 |
| **Project:** | £2850 |

## VOLKSWAGEN
### Beetle 1200/1300/1500

For the 1200, Volkswagen finally fitted a proper rectangular back window to the Beetle, almost twice the size of what had been there before. With a bigger windscreen too, visibility was much improved. The basic car was constantly updated in detail until 1968 when it was thoroughly revised again. New headlamps and thicker bumpers were fitted, and uprated safety kit appeared inside. Mechanical changes included – at last – 12-volt electrics and dual-circuit brakes, plus a fuel tank that didn't have to be filled by via the front boot. Building continued in Mexico until 2003. All on the up.

**SPECIFICATIONS**

| | |
|---|---|
| **Years produced:** | 1957-1978 |
| **Performance:** | 0-60mph: 32.1sec<br>Top speed: 72mph |
| **Power & torque:** | 40bhp/65lb ft |
| **Engine:** | Normally aspirated1192cc flat four, petrol, carburettor, 8 valves |
| **Drivetrain:** | Rear-engine RWD |
| **Structure:** | Separate chassis |
| **Transmission:** | Four-speed manual |
| **Weight:** | 739kg |

**PRICE GUIDE**

| | |
|---|---|
| **Launch price:** | £617 |
| **Excellent:** | £12,000 |
| **Good:** | £7000 |
| **Average:** | £3750 |
| **Project:** | £1350 |

## VOLKSWAGEN
### Karmann-Ghia Convertible

After the hardtop version of the Karmann-Ghia proved such a success, Volkswagen and Karmann didn't take long to come up with a convertible version. It was unveiled in late 1957 to much the same level of appreciation as its tin-lid sister. Extra strengthening made the convertible heavier and therefore slower than the coupé, but that didn't matter to those who admired this fresh-air fashion statement; America loved it, of course. The car started life with a rear-mounted air-cooled 1192cc engine, which gradually increased in size through 1285cc and 1493cc to 1584cc. Still on the up.

**SPECIFICATIONS**

| | |
|---|---|
| **Years produced:** | 1958-1974 (80,899 in total) |
| **Performance:** | 0-60mph: 27.0sec<br>Top speed: 80mph |
| **Power & torque:** | 39bhp/68lb ft |
| **Engine:** | Normally aspirated 1285cc flat four, petrol, carburettor, 8 valves |
| **Drivetrain:** | Rear-engine RWD |
| **Structure:** | Separate chassis |
| **Transmission:** | Four-speed manual |
| **Weight:** | 830kg |

**PRICE GUIDE**

| | |
|---|---|
| **Launch price:** | £1196 |
| **Excellent:** | £20,000 |
| **Good:** | £13,500 |
| **Average:** | £8000 |
| **Project:** | £4200 |

## VOLKSWAGEN
### 1500/1600 Type 3

The Type 3 was a spin-off from the Beetle, intended to address some of its perceived shortcomings of being old-fashioned, cramped and having poor luggage capacity. And it was a more modern-looking machine, with extra space inside and a boot front and rear. Initially available as a two-door saloon with a 1493cc engine, a two-door estate – known as the Variant – came along in 1962, with a fastback saloon in 1965. By this time there was also a 1584cc engine. All are highly prized these days by air-cooled VW modifiers. Prices have been creeping up recently.

**SPECIFICATIONS**
**Years produced:** 1961-1973 (1,813,600 in total)
**Performance:** 0-60mph: 25.3sec
Top speed: 78mph
**Power & torque:** 44bhp/72lb ft
**Engine:** Normally aspirated 1493cc flat four, petrol, carburettor, 8 valves
**Drivetrain:** Rear-engine RWD
**Structure:** Separate chassis
**Transmission:** Four-speed manual
**Weight:** 860kg

**PRICE GUIDE**
**Launch price:** £998
**Excellent:** £6500
**Good:** £4600
**Average:** £2150
**Project:** £800

## VOLKSWAGEN
### Karmann-Ghia Type 34

From 1961, there was another Karmann-Ghia coupé alongside the more familiar type. An offshoot of VW's Type 3, Ghia styled the vaguely BMW-ish machine while coachbuilder Karmann built it. Although less pretty than its stablemate, it was still very attractive and the wider floorpan and 1493cc engine gave it more practicality and performance too. However, it was never a big seller, even when a 1584cc engine of 54bhp was added, along with front disc brakes, in 1965. A high price, thirst for fuel and not being sold in the USA were the main reasons for this. Values currently static.

**SPECIFICATIONS**
**Years produced:** 1962-1969 (42,563 in total)
**Performance:** 0-60mph: 21.3sec
Top speed: 85mph
**Power & torque:** 65bhp/87lb ft
**Engine:** Normally aspirated 1585cc flat four, petrol,carburettor, 8 valves
**Drivetrain:** Rear-engine RWD
**Structure:** Separate chassis
**Transmission:** Four-speed manual
**Weight:** 920kg

**PRICE GUIDE**
**Launch price:** £1330
**Excellent:** £14,250
**Good:** £11,000
**Average:** £5500
**Project:** £2500

## VOLKSWAGEN
### 411/412

One of the main issues with Volkswagen's passenger cars of the 1960s was that none had four doors. The 411 of 1968 changed all this; it managed to squeeze all the requisite doors onto a Beetle chassis (with a wheelbase stretched by 4in) but kept the faith with the rear-engined layout. However, at the front were MacPherson struts and disc brakes, meaning the 411 was a better-behaved machine than the Beetle. The 1679cc engine received fuel injection in 1969 and the gawky styling was reworked in 1972 for the 412. A 1795cc engine was adopted in 1973. Edging up.

**SPECIFICATIONS**
**Years produced:** 1968-1974 (367,728 in total)
**Performance:** 0-60mph: 16.8sec
Top speed: 96mph
**Power & torque:** 80bhp/97lb ft
**Engine:** Normally aspirated 1679cc flat four, petrol, electronic fuel injection, 8 valves
**Drivetrain:** Rear-engine RWD
**Structure:** Separate chassis
**Transmission:** Four-speed manual
**Weight:** 1030kg

**PRICE GUIDE**
**Launch price:** £1290
**Excellent:** £5200
**Good:** £3250
**Average:** £1450
**Project:** £950

## VOLKSWAGEN
### Beetle 1302/1303

Although they looked the same as previous models, the 1302 and 1303 'Super' Beetles were the most radical reworks of the car during its long life. MacPherson strut front suspension allowed more front boot space and improved handling. The struts also allowed front disc brakes to be fitted. The 1303, from 1972, had a more safety-conscious padded dashboard and wraparound windscreen, plus bigger tail lights. Engines were the usual air-cooled units of 1285cc and 44bhp, and 1584cc and 50bhp. Not quite as liked as other Bugs, but values have been rising slowly.

**SPECIFICATIONS**
**Years produced:** 1970-1975
**Performance:** 0-60mph: 18.3sec
Top speed: 81mph
**Power & torque:** 50bhp/78lb ft
**Engine:** Normally aspirated 1584cc flat four, petrol, carburettor, 8 valves
**Drivetrain:** Rear-engine RWD
**Structure:** Separate chassis
**Transmission:** Four-speed manual
**Weight:** 870kg

**PRICE GUIDE**
**Launch price:** £875
**Excellent:** £7500
**Good:** £4200
**Average:** £2200
**Project:** £700

## VOLKSWAGEN
### K70

Often overlooked, the K70 remains significant in Volkswagen's history for being its first FWD car – even if it was going to be an NSU. The boxy saloon was designed to be the Ro80's smaller brother, but, weeks before its launch, VW pulled the plug on NSU, and took the car for itself. The fact that Wolfsburg desperately needed a new generation of models to replace the Beetle-derived cars had absolutely nothing to do with its decision... It was a poor seller but, in the classic market, the K70 has picked up a small yet enthusiastic following.

**SPECIFICATIONS**
**Years produced:** 1970-1974 (211,127 in total)
**Performance:** 0-60mph: 13.5sec
Top speed: 104mph
**Power & torque:** 75bhp/91lb ft
**Engine:** Normally aspirated 1605cc four cylinder, petrol, carburettor, 8 valves
**Drivetrain:** Front-engine FWD
**Structure:** Monocoque
**Transmission:** Four-speed manual
**Weight:** 1015kg

**PRICE GUIDE**
**Launch price:** £1570
**Excellent:** £3850
**Good:** £2400
**Average:** £1500
**Project:** £700

## VOLKSWAGEN Camper

In 1968, the second generation of Type 2 (some might say, belatedly) had thoroughly modernised looks with a single-piece windscreen, which earned the model the nickname of the 'Bay Window.' Although with less character to its styling, this version was easier to drive with improved suspension and larger engines; at introduction there was a 1584cc unit with a 1679cc one from 1971, when disc brakes also appeared. By the time European assembly came to an end in 1978, the Camper sported a 1970cc engine. Endowed with 70bhp, it was almost speedy. Values have levelled off for now.

### SPECIFICATIONS

**Years produced:** 1968-1979
**Performance:** 0-60mph: N/A
Top speed: 75mph
**Power & torque:** 70bhp/90lb ft
**Engine:** Normally aspirated 1970cc flat four, petrol, carburettor, 8 valves
**Drivetrain:** Rear-engine RWD
**Structure:** Separate chassis
**Transmission:** Four-speed manual
**Weight:** 1105kg

### PRICE GUIDE

**Launch price:** £N/A
**Excellent:** £23,000
**Good:** £9750
**Average:** £3750
**Project:** £1500

## VOLKSWAGEN Passat MkI

Volkswagen's *real* FWD future started here. After the K70 false start, the Audi-engineered Passat proved to be the perfect product at the right time. Although VW's big sellers were the smaller cars in its range, the Passat offered the perfect upgrade path, as it looked and felt so familiar to drive. Its EA827 1.6-litre was a revelation, being smooth, revvy and powerful – providing the mainstay for VW's mid-range models for generations to come. A little clinical compared with rivals, yet more than capable of entertaining. But it had a serious capacity for rusting.

### SPECIFICATIONS

**Years produced:** 1973-1980 (2,000,000 in total)
**Performance:** 0-60mph: 11.0sec
Top speed: 104mph
**Power & torque:** 75bhp/70lb ft
**Engine:** Normally aspirated 1588cc four cylinder, petrol, carburettor, 8 valves
**Drivetrain:** Front-engine FWD
**Structure:** Monocoque
**Transmission:** Four-speed manual
**Weight:** 855kg

### PRICE GUIDE

**Launch price:** £1495
**Excellent:** £2700
**Good:** £1200
**Average:** £600
**Project:** £300

## VOLKSWAGEN Polo MkI

Like the Passat, this Volkswagen started life as an Audi. Yes, forget the 1990s A3 or A2, the first small Audi was actually the 50, which begat the Polo in 1976. It was a great supermini, too, especially when one considers the lack of experience the company had with small cars. Great build, a functional interior, and stylish Bertone bodywork made these cars practically irresistible to small-car buyers in Germany. Some would say the Polo is perhaps a little too rational compared with the fabulous Renault 5 and Fiat 127, but sometimes it's good to be sensible.

### SPECIFICATIONS

**Years produced:** 1975-1981 (1,200,000 in total)
**Performance:** 0-60mph: 16.0sec
Top speed: 90mph
**Power & torque:** 40bhp/55lb ft
**Engine:** Normally aspirated 1043cc four cylinder, petrol, carburettor, 8 valves
**Drivetrain:** Front-engine FWD
**Structure:** Monocoque
**Transmission:** Four-speed manual
**Weight:** 700kg

### PRICE GUIDE

**Launch price:** £1798
**Excellent:** £3000
**Good:** £1400
**Average:** £800
**Project:** £400

## VOLKSWAGEN Scirocco MkI

The first in Volkswagen's new front-wheel-drive generation, the Scirocco emerged as a smart and desirable Capri alternative. Styled by Giorgetto Giugiaro and engineered by Audi, it was a major departure for the Wolfsburg company that previewed the ultra-successful Golf's front-wheel drive platform. In injection form (it shared its engine with the Golf GTI), it was quick and flighty, and handled in a tidy fashion. Cramped interior was not such a problem for coupé buyers, but rot-prone body would prove to be a major bugbear later. Values appear to have peaked for now.

### SPECIFICATIONS (GLi)

**Years produced:** 1973-1988 (504,200)
**Performance:** 0-60mph: 8.5sec
Top speed: 113mph
**Power & torque:** 110bhp/96lb ft
**Engine:** Normally aspirated 1588cc four cylinder, petrol, electronic fuel injection, 8 valves
**Drivetrain:** Front-engine FWD
**Structure:** Monocoque
**Transmission:** Four-speed manual
**Weight:** 865kg

### PRICE GUIDE

**Launch price:** £1995
**Excellent:** £7250
**Good:** £3600
**Average:** £1400
**Project:** £600

## VOLKSWAGEN Golf MkI/GTI

Having scored such huge global success with the Beetle, VW then annoyed its rivals by repeating the trick with its small hatchback Golf. This Giugiaro-designed masterpiece was exactly the right car at the right time, but it was in GTI form, from 1975, that it was most impressive. The car that first earned the term 'hot hatch' used a Bosch fuel-injection 1588cc engine to pump 110bhp through its front wheels and the tight and nimble handling meant all this could be used to the max. A 1781cc engine and quad headlamps marked out 1982's 1800 model. Values holding firm.

### SPECIFICATIONS

**Years produced:** 1976-1984 (600,000 in total)
**Performance:** 0-60mph: 8.7sec (GTI)
Top speed: 112mph
**Power & torque:** 110bhp/96lb ft
**Engine:** Normally aspirated 1588cc four cylinder, petrol, electronic fuel injection, 8 valves
**Drivetrain:** Front-engine FWD
**Structure:** Monocoque
**Transmission:** Four-speed manual
**Weight:** 830kg

### PRICE GUIDE (GTI in brackets)

**Launch price:** £3707
**Excellent:** £3500 (£15,500)
**Good:** £2350 (£6750)
**Average:** £1250 (£3200)
**Project:** £700 (£1350)

# VOLKSWAGEN
## Golf Cabriolet

The MkI Cabriolet was a latecomer to the Golf scene, not seeing the light of day until 1979. However, it would far outlast the saloon on which it was based. Built by Karmann, the four-seater Cabriolet had body strengthening, a transverse roll bar and enhanced trim. Earlier cars had manually-operated hoods but they eventually graduated to powered operation. The GTI equivalent was known as the GLi until 1984 but proved slower and less rigid than the hatch. Because of the high costs of building a MkII version, the roofless MkI continued through until 1993.

**SPECIFICATIONS**

**Years produced:** 1979-1993 (400,871 in total)
**Performance:** 0-60mph: 14.2sec
Top speed: 94mph
**Power & torque:** 54bhp/71lb ft
**Engine:** Normally aspirated 1272cc four cylinder, petrol, carburettor, 8 valves
**Drivetrain:** Front-engine FWD
**Structure:** Monocoque
**Transmission:** Four-speed manual
**Weight:** 845kg

**PRICE GUIDE**

**Launch price:** £6985
**Excellent:** £6500
**Good:** £3300
**Average:** £1500
**Project:** £500

# VOLKSWAGEN
## Passat/Santana GX5

The 1980 Passat retained much of the earlier car's engineering, but was clothed in a larger, more maturely styled body. Offered in three-box saloon form – and called the Santana in the UK – as well hatchback and estate guises, there was a version for everyone. The most interesting model by far was the Santana GX5, which was powered by Audi's warbling five-pot in 1.9-litre form. Pretty much a forgotten entity today, though, and if you find one, it's unlikely to have been cared for. But bag a GX5 for a bargain price, and enjoy the Quattro fantasy.

**SPECIFICATIONS (GX5)**

**Years produced:** 1980-1988 (1,978,200 in total)
**Performance:** 0-60mph: 9.5sec
Top speed: 113mph
**Power & torque:** 115bhp/122lb ft
**Engine:** Normally aspirated 1921cc five cylinder, petrol, carburettor, 10 valves
**Drivetrain:** Front-engine FWD
**Structure:** Monocoque
**Transmission:** Five-speed manual
**Weight:** 1085kg

**PRICE GUIDE**

**Launch price:** £5315
**Excellent:** £1700
**Good:** £1100
**Average:** £550
**Project:** £250

# VOLKSWAGEN
## Polo/Polo Coupé

The 1981 Polo was effectively a rebody of the original car – but where the older car was elegant and delicate, the newer car was practical and rational. Fans have long since been calling it the 'breadvan' and, with that vertical tailgate, it's easy to see why. The older car's look came back in 1983 when the Coupé arrived, with its sloping rear end. More power arrived, although this was no GTi in miniature, whatever VW might have told you. After the facelift in 1991, the mad-cap supercharged G40 was added to the range, and that really did earn its cult status.

**SPECIFICATIONS**

**Years produced:** 1981-1995 (2,200,000 in total)
**Performance:** 0-60mph: 12.5sec
Top speed: 95mph
**Power & torque:** 55bhp/71lb ft
**Engine:** Normally aspirated 1272cc four cylinder, petrol, carburettor, 8 valves
**Drivetrain:** Front-engine FWD
**Structure:** Monocoque
**Transmission:** Four-speed manual
**Weight:** 740kg

**PRICE GUIDE (double these prices for G40)**

**Launch price:** £3799
**Excellent:** £2250
**Good:** £1250
**Average:** £600
**Project:** £300

# VOLKSWAGEN
## Scirocco MkII

Volkswagen went in-house for the second-generation Scirocco, and many would say that without its delicate Italian styling, it lost a fair chunk of appeal. But what the new car lost in style, it gained in practicality – and pace. It benefited from the rising power of the Golf GTi – initially its 112bhp 1.8-litre 8-valve, and then the 136bhp 16-valve engines. So equipped, the Scirocco was a flying machine. Eventually replaced by the Corrado (which was planned to be called Scirocco), and now overlooked compared with what came before and after. Still fun to drive, but watch out for rust!

**SPECIFICATIONS**

**Years produced:** 1982-1992 (340,700 in total)
**Performance:** 0-60mph: 9.1sec
Top speed: 120mph
**Power & torque:** 112bhp/113lb ft
**Engine:** Normally aspirated 1781cc four cylinder, petrol, electronic fuel injection, 8 valves
**Drivetrain:** Front-engine FWD
**Structure:** Monocoque
**Transmission:** Five-speed manual
**Weight:** 920kg

**PRICE GUIDE**

**Launch price:** £5424
**Excellent:** £4250
**Good:** £2100
**Average:** £1200
**Project:** £400

# VOLKSWAGEN
## Golf Mk2/GTI/GTI 16V

Volkswagen's update of the Giugiaro-penned original was an improvement over the 1974 original in every way. It was roomier, easier to service, more rust-resistant and generally faster. If its lines weren't quite as sharp, this didn't dent sales in the slightest. GTI used carry-over 1.8-litre engine, but lacked a little of the fizz of the original. That was restored by the arrival of the 16V in 1986, which pushed power to 136bhp and dropped the 0-60mph time to under 8 seconds. The classiest and most complete hot hatch of its era, and that's reflected by its popularity today

**SPECIFICATIONS**

**Years produced:** 1983-1992 (6,300,000 in total)
**Performance:** 0-60mph: 8.5sec
Top speed: 115mph
**Power & torque:** 112bhp/113lb ft
**Engine:** Normally aspirated 1781cc four cylinder, petrol, electronic fuel injection, 8 valves
**Drivetrain:** Front-engine FWD
**Structure:** Monocoque
**Transmission:** Five-speed manual
**Weight:** 907kg

**PRICE GUIDE (GTI in brackets)**

**Launch price:** £7800
**Excellent:** £2000 (£8000)
**Good:** £1200 (£3500)
**Average:** £700 (£1200)
**Project:** £300 (£500)

## VOLKSWAGEN
## Corrado 16V/G60

Volkswagen's 1988 replacement for the Scirocco successfully updated its predecessor's three-door hatchback style with a brooding and imposing persona. Closely related to the Golf Mk2, it debuted with a 1781cc engine. Topping the range initially was the G60, a supercharged monster of 158bhp that took just 7.8 seconds to reach 60mph and ultimately reached 140mph. And then came the VR6 version, a 187bhp fire-breather with a maximum speed of 143mph and the dash from zero to 60mph taking a mere 6.5 seconds. Add 20% for the VR6.

### SPECIFICATIONS

**Years produced:** 1988-1993
**Performance:** 0-60mph: 7.8sec
Top speed: 140mph
**Power & torque:** 160bhp/166lb ft
**Engine:** Supercharged 1781cc four cylinder, petrol, electronic fuel injection, 8 valves
**Drivetrain:** Front-engine FWD
**Structure:** Monocoque
**Transmission:** Five-speed manual
**Weight:** 1115kg

**PRICE GUIDE (G60)**
**Launch price:** £19,907
**Excellent:** £6000
**Good:** £4350
**Average:** £2400
**Project:** £1200

## VOLKSWAGEN
## Golf Mk3/GTI/VR6

Based on mk2 underpinnings, the third incarnation of the ever-popular hatch was not Volkswagen's finest hour. It was heavy, slow and suffered from some serious build-quality issues, although this did get better with the later post-1996 cars. The 8v GTI was hampered by a real lack of performance; thankfully the 150bhp 16v – only very subtly different to look at – was better. The 2.8-litre VR6 version is the one to have: a large engine in a compact hatchback makes a tempting package, but few remain unmodified.

### SPECIFICATIONS

**Years produced:** 1992-1997
**Performance:** 0-60mph: 7.1sec (VR6)
Top speed: 137mph
**Power & torque:** 174bhp/173lb ft
**Engine:** Normally aspirated 2792cc V6, petrol, electronic fuel injection, 12v
**Drivetrain:** Front-engine FWD
**Structure:** Monocoque
**Transmission:** Five-speed manual
**Weight:** 1155kg

**PRICE GUIDE: GTI (VR6 in brackets)**
**Launch price:** £15,095 (£18,740)
**Excellent:** £2300 (£4000)
**Good:** £1300 (£2200)
**Average:** £700 (£1300)
**Project:** £350 (£800)

## VOLKSWAGEN
## Golf Mk4/GTI

VW got its act together with the mk4 Golf, producing a world-beating hatchback that was solidly built with an air of sophistication about it. The GTI name was however muddied with various different versions, none with any particular sporting ability. The turbocharged 1.8-litre wasn't too shabby, but the limited edition Anniversary model, with uprated suspension, bigger BBS alloy wheels and a new body kit is the real gem. Higher-output TDIs offer brutish in-gear power delivery and more than 50mpg.

### SPECIFICATIONS

**Years produced:** 1997-2004
**Performance:** 0-60mph: 7.9sec (GTI)
Top speed: 138mph
**Power & torque:** 178bhp/173lb ft
**Engine:** Turbocharged 1781cc four cylinder, petrol, electronic fuel injection, 20v
**Drivetrain:** Front-engine FWD
**Structure:** Monocoque
**Transmission:** Six-speed manual
**Weight:** 1279kg

**PRICE GUIDE (GTI)**
**Launch price:** £16,245
**Excellent:** £3400
**Good:** £2000
**Average:** £1000
**Project:** £500

## VOLKSWAGEN
## Golf R32

Squeezing a 3.2-litre V6 and Haldex four-wheel-drive system into a Mk4 Golf was a revelation, creating a very potent but grown-up hot hatch. Externally the R32 got side-skirts, 18in multi-spoke wheels and deeper bumpers – with huge air intakes up front and a pair of tailpipes at the rear. It handled far better than anyone expected, too, though the fact it was a big V6 in a Golf was the main draw. It was also the first production car to offer a dual-clutch 'DSG' gearbox, although the manual is now considered the one to buy. Low UK numbers mean prices are solid.

### SPECIFICATIONS

**Years produced:** 2002-2004
**Performance:** 0-60mph: 6.4sec
Top speed: 154mph
**Power & torque:** 237bhp/236lb ft
**Engine:** Normally aspirated 3189cc V6, petrol, electronic fuel injection, 24 valves
**Drivetrain:** Front-engine AWD
**Structure:** Monocoque
**Transmission:** Six-speed manual
**Weight:** 1477kg

**PRICE GUIDE**
**Launch price:** £22,340
**Excellent:** £10,000
**Good:** £7500
**Average:** £5000
**Project:** N/A

## VOLKSWAGEN
## Golf Mk5 GTI

With a 197bhp 2-litre turbo engine, tartan seats and a red-striped grille, the Mk5 Golf signalled a much-needed return to form for the GTI. With the option of a snappy manual or DSG gearbox and either three or five doors, it was the perfect all-rounder, but it was the outstanding chassis that secured instant classic status. Prices have remained strong for a long time, and demand for the best low-mileage examples remains very high. Most collectible are the limited-run 230bhp Edition 30 (BBS wheels and dimpled 'golf ball' gearknob) and Pirelli special edition models.

### SPECIFICATIONS

**Years produced:** 2004-2009
**Performance:** 0-60mph: 6.7sec
Top speed: 145mph
**Power & torque:** 197bhp/207lb ft
**Engine:** Turbocharged 1984cc four cylinder petrol, electronic fuel injection, 16 valves
**Drivetrain:** Front-engine FWD
**Structure:** Monocoque
**Transmission:** Six-speed manual/Dual-clutch auto
**Weight:** 1336kg

**PRICE GUIDE**
**Launch price:** £19,995
**Excellent:** £8500
**Good:** £5500
**Average:** £3500
**Project:** £1500

# VOLVO

FOR MUCH OF its life, Volvo – derived from the Latin for 'I roll' – has been a byword for safety and solidity. Its first car left the Swedish factory in 1927, and all proved tough in more hospitable climates than the Arctic environment it was designed for. Volvo also placed great store in passenger protection. Its robust, no-nonsense approach was exemplified by the 140 and 240-series, which kept the same basic style from 1967 to 1993, but still sold in huge volumes across the globe. Volvos started to become sexier from the 1990s onwards and moved upmarket under Ford ownership from 1998. The company was bought by Chinese car manufacturer Geely in 2010.

## VOLVO 121/122S/131/132

The 120-series brought Volvo cars to Britain as well as raising the marque's profile elsewhere. Rugged and reliable, with handsome but traditional looks, the 120's unburstable reputation put it in the same category as the Beetle on the worldwide stage. The 121 was the lower-spec four-door machine with less powerful engines, 122S versions had better performance and equipment levels, and were initially intended for export only. Two-door cars (131 and 132) outlived the four-door, as Volvo discontinued the more useful car to make way for the 140-series cars. Values holding.

**SPECIFICATIONS**

| | |
|---|---|
| **Years produced:** | 1955-1970 |
| **Performance:** | 0-60mph: 17sec<br>Top speed: 85mph |
| **Power & torque:** | 66bhp/76lb ft |
| **Engine:** | Normally aspirated 1582cc four cylinder, petrol, carburettor, 8 valves |
| **Drivetrain:** | Front-engine RWD |
| **Structure:** | Monocoque |
| **Transmission:** | Four-speed manual |
| **Weight:** | 1000kg |

**PRICE GUIDE**

| | |
|---|---|
| **Launch price:** | £1197 |
| **Excellent:** | £10,000 |
| **Good:** | £7000 |
| **Average:** | £3500 |
| **Project:** | £1000 |

## VOLVO PV544

Volvo's first model to be exported in any great numbers was the PV444 of 1947. When the time came to replace it, in 1958, Volvo simply modified the curvaceous and sturdy bodyshell slightly – with bigger front and rear windows – and dubbed the new model the PV544 (to signify that this *personvagn* could now seat five instead of four). Two engines were used; a 1584cc unit and, from 1960, a 1778cc one. Sport models boasted twin carbs and extra equipment. The PV was meant to be superseded by the 120 but lasted seven years alongside it. Values currently on the rise.

**SPECIFICATIONS**

| | |
|---|---|
| **Years produced:** | 1959-1965 |
| **Performance:** | 0-60mph: 19sec<br>Top speed: 87mph |
| **Power & torque:** | 66bhp/86lb ft |
| **Engine:** | Normally aspirated 1584cc four cylinder, petrol, carburettor, 8 valves |
| **Drivetrain:** | Front-engine RWD |
| **Structure:** | Monocoque |
| **Transmission:** | Four-speed manual |
| **Weight:** | 940kg |

**PRICE GUIDE**

| | |
|---|---|
| **Launch price:** | £N/A in UK |
| **Excellent:** | £14,000 |
| **Good:** | £9000 |
| **Average:** | £5000 |
| **Project:** | £2000 |

## VOLVO P1800/S/E

Volvo gets racy! Or at least looked it. The P1800, designed by Frua and launched in 1960, was a startling-looking creation and British eyebrows were raised when Roger Moore drove one in *The Saint*. But that sweptback glamour disguised little more than 120 mechanicals, which gave reasonable enough performance but fell short of being exhilarating. Post-1963, the name was changed to 1800S as power increased to 108 and 115bhp. A bit more wolf and less sheepish was the fuel-injection 1800E (1969-1972) with a more interesting 130bhp. Values climbing steadily.

**SPECIFICATIONS**

| | |
|---|---|
| **Years produced:** | 1961-1972 |
| **Performance:** | 0-60mph: 13.2sec<br>Top speed: 104mph |
| **Power & torque:** | 115bhp/108lb ft |
| **Engine:** | Normally aspirated 1780cc four cylinder, petrol, carburettor, 8 valves |
| **Drivetrain:** | Front-engine RWD |
| **Structure:** | Monocoque |
| **Transmission:** | Four-speed manual |
| **Weight:** | 1070kg |

**PRICE GUIDE**

| | |
|---|---|
| **Launch price:** | £1836 |
| **Excellent:** | £25,500 |
| **Good:** | £18,000 |
| **Average:** | £9000 |
| **Project:** | £3750 |

## VOLVO 122 B18

In 1961, Volvo gave the 120-series cars more power to cope with their heavyweight engineering. The B18 engine was a fresh design, which would soon earn a reputation for longevity. Sized at 1778cc, it provided the single-carburettor 121 with 75 or 85bhp, while 122 cars, with their twin carburettors, enjoyed fruitier 90, 95 and 100bhp outputs. Even more power and performance was supplied courtesy of the B20 engine. This was a bored-out version of the B18 with a capacity of 1998cc, and resulted in the most powerful 120 of all, the 1968-1970 122S with 115bhp and 100mph potential.

**SPECIFICATIONS (122S)**

| | |
|---|---|
| **Years produced:** | 1962-1967 |
| **Performance:** | 0-60mph: 13.8sec<br>Top speed: 104mph |
| **Power & torque:** | 115bhp/112lb ft |
| **Engine:** | Normally aspirated 1778cc four cylinder, petrol, carburettor, 8 valves |
| **Drivetrain:** | Front-engine RWD |
| **Structure:** | Monocoque |
| **Transmission:** | Four-speed manual |
| **Weight:** | 1090kg |

**PRICE GUIDE**

| | |
|---|---|
| **Launch price:** | £1022 |
| **Excellent:** | £11,000 |
| **Good:** | £8000 |
| **Average:** | £4000 |
| **Project:** | £1200 |

# VOLVO 123GT

Thanks to their inherent strength and reliability, Amazons proved natural rally cars. To capitalise on this, Volvo gave the go-faster world of 1966 the 123GT. Its twin-carburettor 1778cc engine came from the more sporty 1800S coupé and it had servo-assisted front disc brakes and bumper-mounted spotlamps while, inside, the driver could revel in his special steering wheel and dash-mounted rev-counter. Only available as a two-door, this Swedish grand tourer proved a potent tool. British tuner Ruddspeed offered a 132bhp upgrade, too. Values are climbing fast.

### SPECIFICATIONS

**Years produced:** 1967-1968
**Performance:** 0-60mph: 12.5sec
Top speed: 109mph
**Power & torque:** 115bhp/107lb ft
**Engine:** Normally aspirated 1778cc four cylinder, petrol, carburettor, 8 valves
**Drivetrain:** Front-engine RWD
**Structure:** Monocoque
**Transmission:** Four-speed manual
**Weight:** 1050kg

### PRICE GUIDE

**Launch price:** £1372
**Excellent:** £16,500
**Good:** £10,000
**Average:** £4500
**Project:** £2000

# VOLVO 144/145/142

Volvo's reputation for safety first, style second started in earnest with the 140-series. These big and boxy cars, built from 1967 to 1974, were uncompromising in their looks but thoroughly protected their occupants. The third figure of the model designation denoted the number of doors; thus the 142 had two, the 144 had four, and the 145 was the five-door estate. At first, the 1778cc engine was all that was available, albeit with twin carburettors on the S models, but 1986cc engines became standard in 1968. Best was the 1970s GL, with fuel injection and leather trim. Has a following.

### SPECIFICATIONS

**Years produced:** 1967-1974
**Performance:** 0-60mph: 10.1sec
Top speed: 106mph
**Power & torque:** 124bhp/123lb ft
**Engine:** Normally aspirated 1986cc four cylinder, petrol, mechanical fuel injection, 8 valve
**Drivetrain:** Front-engine RWD
**Structure:** Monocoque
**Transmission:** Four-speed manual
**Weight:** 1290kg

### PRICE GUIDE

**Launch price:** £1354
**Excellent:** £4000
**Good:** £2650
**Average:** £1400
**Project:** £650

# VOLVO 164

Seeking to enter the luxury realms of Jaguar and Mercedes-Benz, Volvo unveiled the 164 in 1968. It was based on the 140-series, with a longer body and a 2978cc six-cylinder engine lurking behind its much grander grille, plus generous equipment. With the TE, owners got leather, air conditioning and power steering. The cars started with 145bhp, but that rose to 175bhp when fuel injection arrived in 1971. The fitment of built-in foglamps from 1969 was a very Jaguar touch, but the 164 failed to appeal as much as the prettier Jags it wanted to emulate, despite the better build quality.

### SPECIFICATIONS

**Years produced:** 1968-1975
**Performance:** 0-60mph: 11sec
Top speed: 110mph
**Power & torque:** 145bhp/163lb ft
**Engine:** Normally aspirated 2978cc six cylinder, petrol, carburettor, 12 valves
**Drivetrain:** Front-engine RWD
**Structure:** Monocoque
**Transmission:** Four-speed manual
**Weight:** 1320kg

### PRICE GUIDE

**Launch price:** £1791
**Excellent:** £4650
**Good:** £3000
**Average:** £1600
**Project:** £800

# VOLVO 1800ES

One of the most intriguing of all Volvos appeared in 1971, with the 1800ES. Cast in the mould of Reliant's Scimitar GTE, this was the 1800 given an estate rear as a way of updating its dated appearance for the 1970s. It was a gamble that worked, for this idiosyncratic load-lugger proved very popular, despite its nickname of 'Snow White's hearse'. The 130bhp fuel-injection engine still gave good performance – 115mph was possible for the boutique shopper in a hurry – while the trademark frameless glass hatchback was a theme that Volvo would return to again. Values holding.

### SPECIFICATIONS

**Years produced:** 1971-1973 (8077 in total)
**Performance:** 0-60mph: 9.7sec
Top speed: 112mph
**Power & torque:** 130bhp/123lb ft
**Engine:** Normally aspirated 1986cc four cylinder, petrol, carburettor, 8 valves
**Drivetrain:** Front-engine RWD
**Structure:** Monocoque
**Transmission:** Four-speed manual
**Weight:** 1130kg

### PRICE GUIDE

**Launch price:** £2650
**Excellent:** £22,000
**Good:** £16,000
**Average:** £8000
**Project:** £3250

# VOLVO 264/265

Alongside the four-cylinder 240-series cars, Volvo weighed in with six-cylinder variants using the same bodyshell. The 264 saloon was launched at the same time; the 265 estate followed a year later. Both used the brand new 2664cc V6 engine developed with Peugeot and Renault; a smooth and mighty motor especially in 140bhp fuel-injection form. This went up to 2849cc in 1981, which added an extra 14bhp. Flagship was the 264TE, a Bertone-built stretched limousine, complete with a telephone and a fridge. As ABBA used one, it must have been special! Values creeping up.

### SPECIFICATIONS

**Years produced:** 1974-1979 (169,127 in total)
**Performance:** 0-60mph: 12.7sec
Top speed: 108mph
**Power & torque:** 148bhp/161lb ft
**Engine:** Normally aspirated 2664cc V6, petrol, electronic fuel injection, 12 valves
**Drivetrain:** Front-engine RWD
**Structure:** Monocoque
**Transmission:** Four-speed manual with overdrive
**Weight:** 1456kg

### PRICE GUIDE

**Launch price:** £3799
**Excellent:** £3250
**Good:** £2350
**Average:** £1450
**Project:** £500

## VOLVO 244/245

The Flying Brick, Swedish Tank... nicknames for Volvo's Lego-like 244/245 were hardly complimentary. But what this tough-mobile lacked in style, it more than made up for in safety and sales. The cars – the 244 was the four-door saloon, the 245 the estate – were based on the 140. However, the fronts were re-engineered for MacPherson strut suspension and a new nose. Aside from Volvo's existing 1986cc engine, a new overhead-cam 2127cc unit featured; this rose to 2315cc in 1978. The last were built in 1993; as durable in lifespan as they were in quality and strength. Prices edging up.

### SPECIFICATIONS

| | |
|---|---|
| **Years produced:** | 1974-1993 (3,000,000+ in total) |
| **Performance:** | 0-60mph: 11.4sec<br>Top speed: 106mph |
| **Power & torque:** | 123bhp/125lb ft |
| **Engine:** | Normally aspirated 2127cc four cylinder, petrol, electronic fuel injection, 8 valves |
| **Drivetrain:** | Front-engine RWD |
| **Structure:** | Monocoque |
| **Transmission:** | Four-speed manual with overdrive |
| **Weight:** | 1404kg |

### PRICE GUIDE

| | |
|---|---|
| **Launch price:** | £2155 |
| **Excellent:** | £3000 |
| **Good:** | £2200 |
| **Average:** | £1250 |
| **Project:** | £400 |

## VOLVO 340/360

The Volvo 300 actually started life as DAF's P900 project, a car that was supposed to replace the quirky 66 model. The Dutch company needed help to get it into production, and in the end Volvo ended up buying a majority stake and rebranding it. Known as the 343, the new small Volvo retained DAF's Variomatic transmission (a manual came later), mounted at the rear. Sales were slow initially, but picked up throughout the 1980s, the 340 eventually becoming a UK top ten seller. Younger classic car fans are drawn to its RWD layout and low running costs.

### SPECIFICATIONS

| | |
|---|---|
| **Years produced:** | 1976-1991 (1,086,405 in total) |
| **Performance:** | 0-60mph: 13.5sec<br>Top speed: 104mph |
| **Power & torque:** | 70bhp/79lb ft |
| **Engine:** | Normally aspirated 1397cc four cylinder, petrol, carburettor, 8 valves |
| **Drivetrain:** | Front-engine RWD |
| **Structure:** | Monocoque |
| **Transmission:** | Variomatic CVT |
| **Weight:** | 943kg |

### PRICE GUIDE

| | |
|---|---|
| **Launch price:** | £3455 |
| **Excellent:** | £2000 |
| **Good:** | £1250 |
| **Average:** | £800 |
| **Project:** | £350 |

## VOLVO 262C

The 262C was a wild card in the Volvo pack, as an attempt to build a luxury coupé. It was distinctive, although the lowered black-vinyl clad roof with swept-back and chunky rear pillars plonked on top of a 260 lower body gave a distinctly tank-like appearance, but the sumptuous leather-bound interior certainly pampered its occupants. Engines were the same as the standard 260's; thus a 140bhp 2664cc V6 at first, followed by a 155bhp 2849cc V6 towards the end of production. Definitely mean and moody but not all that magnificent, although Volvo aficionados adore them.

### SPECIFICATIONS

| | |
|---|---|
| **Years produced:** | 1978-1981 (5622 in total) |
| **Performance:** | 0-60mph: 11.1sec<br>Top speed: 109mph |
| **Power & torque:** | 148bhp/161lb ft |
| **Engine:** | Normally aspirated 2664cc V6, petrol, electronic fuel injection, 12 valves |
| **Drivetrain:** | Front-engine RWD |
| **Structure:** | Monocoque |
| **Transmission:** | Three-speed automatic |
| **Weight:** | 1450kg |

### PRICE GUIDE

| | |
|---|---|
| **Launch price:** | £13,000 |
| **Excellent:** | £8000 |
| **Good:** | £4500 |
| **Average:** | £2500 |
| **Project:** | £1250 |

## VOLVO 740/760/780

The 760 and 740 saloons and estates weren't particularly groundbreaking, but these sensible-looking family cars combined excellent safety with almost unburstable reliability and practicality, making them an instant hit in the UK. Turbocharged GLT models were rapid in a straight line, and have started to attract a cult following. Volvo also made a short-lived return to the coupé scene in 1986 with the Bertone-styled (and built) 780. It failed to make much of an impact at the time and is now very rare.

### SPECIFICATIONS

| | |
|---|---|
| **Years produced:** | 1982–1992 (1,228,500 in total) |
| **Performance:** | 0-60mph: 8.0sec (760 CLT)<br>Top speed: 124mph |
| **Power & torque:** | 179bhp/192lb ft |
| **Engine:** | Turbocharged 2316cc four, petrol, electronic fuel injection, 8 valves |
| **Drivetrain:** | Front-engine RWD |
| **Structure:** | Monocoque |
| **Transmission:** | Five-speed manual |
| **Weight:** | 1280kg |

### PRICE GUIDE (780 in brackets)

| | |
|---|---|
| **Excellent:** | £2500 (£5000) |
| **Good:** | £1600 (£3000) |
| **Average:** | £800 (£1500) |
| **Project:** | £350 (£750) |

## VOLVO 480 ES/Turbo

As a belated successor to the 1800ES, the quirky 480ES echoed its predecessor's frameless glass hatchback but, from the front, looked like no Volvo before. The design was a dramatic and sleek wedge with pop-up headlamps and a tiny Volvo-badged grille hiding under the front bumper. Front-wheel drive was a first for the marque and there were faddish features such as door pillar-mounted locks and an electronic information centre. 1721cc and 1998cc engines featured and there was a turbocharged version from 1989. An oddball in the Volvo canon but an intriguing creation.

### SPECIFICATIONS

| | |
|---|---|
| **Years produced:** | 1986-1995 (80,463 in total) |
| **Performance:** | 0-60mph: 8.6sec<br>Top speed: 124mph |
| **Power & torque:** | 120bhp/129lb ft |
| **Engine:** | Turbocharged 1721cc four cylinder, petrol, electronic fuel injection, 8 valves |
| **Drivetrain:** | Front-engine FWD |
| **Structure:** | Monocoque |
| **Transmission:** | Five-speed manual |
| **Weight:** | 900kg |

### PRICE GUIDE

| | |
|---|---|
| **Launch price:** | £10,850 |
| **Excellent:** | £2500 |
| **Good:** | £1700 |
| **Average:** | £1000 |
| **Project:** | £600 |

## VOLVO
### 850 T5/T5-R

The launch of the 850 range in 1992 marked a turning point for Volvo. Although it kept a family resemblance, its lines were smoother and more modern, while high equipment levels and improved driving dynamics helped find a wider audience. The turbocharged T5 delivered serious performance, but it was the T5-R of 1994 that really caused enthusiasts to take notice. With a tyre-shredding 240bhp pumped through the front wheels, here was a Volvo that was both safe and practical yet also fast and just a bit sexy. The estate version even became a star in Touring Car racing!

**SPECIFICATIONS**

| | |
|---|---|
| **Years produced:** | 1994-1996 (5500 T5-Rs produced) |
| **Performance:** | 0-60mph: 5.8sec (R)<br>Top speed: 155mph (limited) |
| **Power & torque:** | 240bhp/243lb ft |
| **Engine:** | Turbocharged 2319cc in-line five, petrol, electronic fuel injection, 20 valves |
| **Drivetrain:** | Front-engine FWD |
| **Structure:** | Monocoque |
| **Transmission:** | Five-speed manual |
| **Weight:** | 1450kg |

**PRICE GUIDE (T5/T5-R)**

| | |
|---|---|
| **Launch price:** | £26,995 |
| **Excellent:** | £6500/£10,000 |
| **Good:** | £4500/£7500 |
| **Average:** | £3250/£4500 |
| **Project:** | £1250/£3000 |

## VOLVO
### C70/C70 T5/Convertible

Launched towards the end of the golden era for the coupé market, the C70 was arguably the most stylish Volvo since the P1800. It also represented a return to the convertible market for the Swedish company. Developed in conjunction with TWR, the car was based around the old 850 architecture, with the cabriolets criticised for their excessive scuttle-shake when new. As with the saloons, the high-performance T5 models are astonishingly quick, but the chassis wasn't built to inspire. Capable and comfortable just about sums it up.

**SPECIFICATIONS**

| | |
|---|---|
| **Years produced:** | 1997-2004 |
| **Performance:** | 0-60mph: 6.3sec (T5)<br>Top speed: 155mph (limited) |
| **Power & torque:** | 240bhp/243lb ft |
| **Engine:** | Turbocharged 2319cc in-line five, petrol, electronic fuel injection, 20 valves |
| **Drivetrain:** | Front-engine FWD |
| **Structure:** | Monocoque |
| **Transmission:** | Five-speed manual |
| **Weight:** | 1490kg |

**PRICE GUIDE: C70 (add 25% for Convertible)**

| | |
|---|---|
| **Launch price:** | £32,455 |
| **Excellent:** | £3500 |
| **Good:** | £1800 |
| **Average:** | £1000 |
| **Project:** | £500 |

## VOLVO
### S70R/V70R AWD

Picking up where the special edition 850 T5-R left off, the 250bhp V70R endowed the surprisingly quick five-cylinder Volvo wagon with the very welcome option of four-wheel drive. This didn't magically transform the V70 into a sports car, but it could now put its copious power and torque down cleanly in all weathers. The saloon S70R was only offered with front-wheel drive, but lower sports suspension and a viscous limited-slip diff help keep it tied down. The lower weight actually makes this the quicker car. Huge Q-car appeal.

**SPECIFICATIONS**

| | |
|---|---|
| **Years produced:** | 1997-2000 |
| **Performance:** | 0-60mph: 6.2sec (S70R)<br>Top speed: 155mph (limited) |
| **Power & torque:** | 247bhp/258lb ft |
| **Engine:** | Turbocharged 2319cc in-line five, petrol, electronic fuel injection, 20 valves |
| **Drivetrain:** | Front-engine FWD (V70 AWD) |
| **Structure:** | Monocoque |
| **Transmission:** | Five-speed manual |
| **Weight:** | 1424kg |

**PRICE GUIDE**

| | |
|---|---|
| **Launch price:** | £34,055 |
| **Excellent:** | £4250 |
| **Good:** | £3000 |
| **Average:** | £1750 |
| **Project:** | £500 |

# WOLSELEY

THE WOLSELEY SHEEP Shearing Company decided to experiment with cars in 1895 and brought in Herbert Austin as designer. He left in 1906 to start his own company, but Wolseley persisted until 1927, when it went bankrupt and was purchased by William Morris. He positioned Wolseley as a luxury marque, with its own, lively overhead-cam engine to distinguish its models from the Morris cars on which they were based. Post-war rationalisation reduced most of the marque's output to little more than better-equipped Austins or Morrises; there was even a Mini variant called the Hornet. The Wolseley illuminated grille badge was extinguished forever in 1975.

## WOLSELEY
### Eight

At first glance, the Wolseley Eight of 1946 looked like nothing more than a Morris Eight with a Wolseley bonnet and grille transplant. However, it was more than just that, for a smoother 918cc overhead-valve engine of 33bhp was installed in place of the pedestrian 30bhp sidevalve engine of the Morris. A four-speed transmission and hydraulic brakes also featured. A plusher wood and leather interior helped to raise the Wolseley above its humbler Morris sibling and make any passengers feel they were in something a bit special. Values seem to be holding steady.

**SPECIFICATIONS**

| | |
|---|---|
| **Years produced:** | 1946-1948 (5344 in total) |
| **Performance:** | 0-60mph: N/A<br>Top speed: 63mph |
| **Power & torque:** | 33bhp/45lb ft |
| **Engine:** | Normally aspirated 918cc four cylinder, petrol, carburettor, 8 valves |
| **Drivetrain:** | Front-engine RWD |
| **Structure:** | Separate chassis |
| **Transmission:** | Four-speed manual |
| **Weight:** | 864kg |

**PRICE GUIDE**

| | |
|---|---|
| **Launch price:** | £416 |
| **Excellent:** | £5000 |
| **Good:** | £3250 |
| **Average:** | £1700 |
| **Project:** | £1000 |

## WOLSELEY 6/80

While the closely related Wolseley 4/50 was a Morris Oxford MO in drag, the 6/80 was a Morris Six in an evening dress with a Pinocchio nose. The prominent snout was needed to accommodate the hefty 2215cc six-cylinder engine which offered more power than its Morris equivalent (72bhp versus 66bhp) thanks to an extra carburettor. The engineering – independent front suspension and unitary construction – was also modern for its day. Obviously, as befitted a Wolseley, the cabin featured sufficient wood and leather to justify its illuminated grille badge and higher price tag.

**SPECIFICATIONS**

| | |
|---|---|
| **Years produced:** | 1948-1954 (25,281 in total) |
| **Performance:** | 0-60mph: 27.8sec<br>Top speed: 81mph |
| **Power & torque:** | 72bhp/102lb ft |
| **Engine:** | Normally aspirated 2215cc six cylinder, petrol, carburettor, 12 valves |
| **Drivetrain:** | Front-engine RWD |
| **Structure:** | Monocoque |
| **Transmission:** | Four-speed manual |
| **Weight:** | 1308kg |

**PRICE GUIDE**

| | |
|---|---|
| **Launch price:** | £767 |
| **Excellent:** | £8000 |
| **Good:** | £4500 |
| **Average:** | £2300 |
| **Project:** | £1150 |

## WOLSELEY 4/44, 15/50

This time, it was the Wolseley that was built before any other badge-engineering took place; the equivalent MG Magnette ZA didn't appear for a year after the 4/44's 1952 birth. The Wolseley focused more on opulence than performance, with just a single carburettor for its MG-derived 1250cc overhead valve engine. Nevertheless, its handling was adept thanks to the independent front suspension and rack-and-pinion steering and the sleek lines gave it a rakish persona. In 1956, it was upgraded into the 15/50; identical in looks but with a 1489cc B-series engine.

**SPECIFICATIONS**

| | |
|---|---|
| **Years produced:** | 1953-1958 (42,198 in total) |
| **Performance:** | 0-60mph: 24.3sec<br>Top speed: 78mph |
| **Power & torque:** | 50bhp/78lb ft |
| **Engine:** | Normally aspirated 1250cc four cylinder, petrol, carburettor, 8 valves |
| **Drivetrain:** | Front-engine RWD |
| **Structure:** | Monocoque |
| **Transmission:** | Four-speed manual |
| **Weight:** | 1118kg |

**PRICE GUIDE**

| | |
|---|---|
| **Launch price:** | £997 |
| **Excellent:** | £6500 |
| **Good:** | £4200 |
| **Average:** | £1850 |
| **Project:** | £850 |

## WOLSELEY 6/90 Saloon

Riley introduced its Pathfinder in 1953; Wolseley followed suit in 1954 with the visually-similar 6/90. Aside from minor trim, the two cars looked one and the same. However, the Wolseley boasted two extra cylinders from its 2.6-litre six-pot C-series engine, borrowed from the Austin Westminster. This gave 95bhp as well as 90mph. The Series II of 1956 brought in semi-elliptic rear suspension and a floor-mounted gearchange, but only lasted a year before the Series III added a larger rear window and servo-assisted brakes. Overall, an elegant large saloon.

**SPECIFICATIONS**

| | |
|---|---|
| **Years produced:** | 1954-1959 (11,852 in total) |
| **Performance:** | 0-60mph: 18.1sec<br>Top speed: 94mph |
| **Power & torque:** | 95bhp/133lb ft |
| **Engine:** | Normally aspirated 2639cc six cylinder, petrol, carburettor, 12 valves |
| **Drivetrain:** | Front-engine RWD |
| **Structure:** | Monocoque |
| **Transmission:** | Four-speed manual |
| **Weight:** | 1492kg |

**PRICE GUIDE**

| | |
|---|---|
| **Launch price:** | £1064 |
| **Excellent:** | £7000 |
| **Good:** | £4250 |
| **Average:** | £2200 |
| **Project:** | £900 |

## WOLSELEY 1500

After the Morris Minor replacement project was aborted, the resultant small car became the Riley 1.5 and Wolseley 1500 in 1957. The Minor's floorpan and suspension were retained, but with a new, well-rounded and smart-looking body. The Wolseley was the comfortable cruiser of the pair and thus gave a lower 43bhp from its single-carburettor BMC B-series 1489cc engine. The 1960 MkII hid its bonnet and boot hinges, while the 1961 MkIII had lowered suspension, new tail lamps and tweaks to the grille. Quite a characterful small classic today. On the rise.

**SPECIFICATIONS**

| | |
|---|---|
| **Years produced:** | 1957-1965 (100,722 in total) |
| **Performance:** | 0-60mph: 24.4sec<br>Top speed: 78mph |
| **Power & torque:** | 43bhp/71lb ft |
| **Engine:** | Normally aspirated 1489cc four cylinder, petrol, carburettor, 8 valves |
| **Drivetrain:** | Front-engine RWD |
| **Structure:** | Monocoque |
| **Transmission:** | Four-speed manual |
| **Weight:** | 1129kg |

**PRICE GUIDE**

| | |
|---|---|
| **Launch price:** | £759 |
| **Excellent:** | £5250 |
| **Good:** | £3000 |
| **Average:** | £1650 |
| **Project:** | £750 |

## WOLSELEY 6/99, 6/110

The sharp lines of the BMC Farina range worked well on the large Wolseley 6/99 and 6/110, a favourite with British police forces. Sharing the same engine and bodyshell as the Austin Westminster and the Vanden Plas 3-Litre, the 6/99 was a prestigious machine with its big 2912cc C-series engine giving a lazy but smooth 103bhp. All the extra Wolseley trim and interior touches were in place to pamper occupants. In 1961, a revamp saw the car become the 6/110, with more power (120bhp) and improved handling from a Panhard rod rear end and power-assisted steering.

**SPECIFICATIONS (6/99)**

| | |
|---|---|
| **Years produced:** | 1959-1968 (37,209 in total) |
| **Performance:** | 0-60mph: 14.4sec<br>Top speed: 98mph |
| **Power & torque:** | 103bhp/158lb ft |
| **Engine:** | Normally aspirated 2912cc six cylinder, petrol, carburettor, 12 valves |
| **Drivetrain:** | Front-engine RWD |
| **Structure:** | Monocoque |
| **Transmission:** | Three-speed manual |
| **Weight:** | 1530kg |

**PRICE GUIDE**

| | |
|---|---|
| **Launch price:** | £1255 |
| **Excellent:** | £7000 |
| **Good:** | £5000 |
| **Average:** | £3000 |
| **Project:** | £1250 |

## WOLSELEY
## 15/60, 16/60

BMC badge engineering ran riot with the fintastic family-sized Farinas; there were Austin, Morris, MG, Wolseley and Riley versions. Wolseley, as usual, performed the luxury duties, which meant a higher quality cabin of hide and walnut and the trademark grille. So as not to detract from the MG and Riley versions, it shared the 52bhp single-carburettor 1489cc engine of the Austin and Morris machines. In 1961 came the 16/60, with a 1622cc engine of 61bhp, anti-roll bars to rein in the excessive body roll and cut-down fins. Values slowly creeping up.

**SPECIFICATIONS**

| | |
|---|---|
| **Years produced:** | 1959-1971 (87,661 in total) |
| **Performance:** | 0-60mph: 24.3sec<br>Top speed: 77mph |
| **Power & torque:** | 52bhp/82lb ft |
| **Engine:** | Normally aspirated 1489cc four cylinder, petrol, carburettor, 8 valves |
| **Drivetrain:** | Front-engine RWD |
| **Structure:** | Monocoque |
| **Transmission:** | Four-speed manual |
| **Weight:** | 1118kg |

**PRICE GUIDE**

| | |
|---|---|
| **Launch price:** | £991 |
| **Excellent:** | £5500 |
| **Good:** | £3600 |
| **Average:** | £1700 |
| **Project:** | £800 |

## WOLSELEY
## Hornet

With the Mini a big success, BMC decided to extend its appeal even further in 1961 with the Wolseley Hornet, sister model to the Riley Elf. This was a far less utilitarian version than the original though. So there was a rather flamboyant chrome-laden front, a larger boot framed by small fins, and a three-instrument dashboard surrounded by wood veneer. In 1963, the MkIII Hornet introduced the 998cc A-series engine to the Mini for the first time and Hydrolastic suspension replaced the bouncy rubber-cone type. The MkIII of 1966 had winding windows and improved ventilation.

**SPECIFICATIONS**

| | |
|---|---|
| **Years produced:** | 1961-1969 (28,455 in total) |
| **Performance:** | 0-60mph: 32.3sec<br>Top speed: 71mph |
| **Power & torque:** | 34bhp/44lb ft |
| **Engine:** | Normally aspirated 848cc four cylinder, petrol, carburettor, 8 valves |
| **Drivetrain:** | Front-engine FWD |
| **Structure:** | Monocoque |
| **Transmission:** | Four-speed manual |
| **Weight:** | 624kg |

**PRICE GUIDE**

| | |
|---|---|
| **Launch price:** | £672 |
| **Excellent:** | £6500 |
| **Good:** | £3800 |
| **Average:** | £1800 |
| **Project:** | £750 |

## WOLSELEY
## 1100/1300

BMC badge engineering was rife with the popular 1100/1300 range. The Wolseley was a comparative latecomer to the stable, not being launched until 1965, three years after the first-born Morris. Mechanically it played with the same 55bhp as the Riley and MG versions and also had the option of attractive two-tone paintwork. The 1300 appeared in 1967 with a 1275cc engine instead of 1098cc. This had an all-synchromesh manual gearbox and offered 70bhp thanks to twin carburettors. Automatics stuck with the less powerful single-carb version.

**SPECIFICATIONS**

| | |
|---|---|
| **Years produced:** | 1965-1973 (44,867 in total) |
| **Performance:** | 0-60mph: 18.4sec<br>Top speed: 85mph |
| **Power & torque:** | 55bhp/61lb ft |
| **Engine:** | Normally aspirated 1098cc four cylinder, petrol, carburettor, 8 valves |
| **Drivetrain:** | Front-engine FWD |
| **Structure:** | Monocoque |
| **Transmission:** | Four-speed manual |
| **Weight:** | 832kg |

**PRICE GUIDE**

| | |
|---|---|
| **Launch price:** | £754 |
| **Excellent:** | £4500 |
| **Good:** | £3250 |
| **Average:** | £1800 |
| **Project:** | £1000 |

## WOLSELEY
## 18/85, Six

Top of BMC's 'Landcrab' tree was the Wolseley 18/85, introduced in 1967. This ultimate enlargement of the Issigonis front-wheel-drive theme begun with the Mini was a capacious car and, in Wolseley form, offered a lot to please class-conscious customers with leather, wood and high-quality carpeting. Naturally there was the usual Wolseley grille with its trademark illuminated centre-badge. The 18/85S of 1969 had 96bhp to the standard car's 85bhp. Four cylinders grew to six in 1972 with the fitment of a silky-smooth 2227cc overhead-cam engine. Values slowly rising.

**SPECIFICATIONS (18/85)**

| | |
|---|---|
| **Years produced:** | 1967-1975 (35,597 in total) |
| **Performance:** | 0-60mph: 17.1sec<br>Top speed: 90mph |
| **Power & torque:** | 85bhp/99lb ft |
| **Engine:** | Normally aspirated 1798cc four cylinder, petrol, carburettor, 8 valves |
| **Drivetrain:** | Front-engine FWD |
| **Structure:** | Monocoque |
| **Transmission:** | Four-speed manual |
| **Weight:** | 1155kg |

**PRICE GUIDE**

| | |
|---|---|
| **Launch price:** | £1040 |
| **Excellent:** | £4250 |
| **Good:** | £2650 |
| **Average:** | £1450 |
| **Project:** | £750 |

## WOLSELEY
## 18-22 Series saloon

The 1975 Six was the final Wolseley to be built. Designed by Harris Mann, the car that would forever become known as The Wedge was the upmarket version of its Austin and Morris lookalikes, available only with the 2227cc six-cylinder engine (its humbler siblings were available only with four cylinders). At the front was a shrunken version of the traditional Wolseley grille and lit-up badge, the distinctive shape of the car dictating no room for anything larger. After just six months, the entire range was de-badged and the cars renamed as Princesses.

**SPECIFICATIONS**

| | |
|---|---|
| **Years produced:** | 1975-1975 (3800 in total) |
| **Performance:** | 0-60mph: 13.5sec<br>Top speed: 104mph |
| **Power & torque:** | 110bhp/125lb ft |
| **Engine:** | Normally aspirated 2227cc six cylinder, petrol, carburettor, 12 valves |
| **Drivetrain:** | Front-engine FWD |
| **Structure:** | Monocoque |
| **Transmission:** | Four-speed manual |
| **Weight:** | 1215kg |

**PRICE GUIDE**

| | |
|---|---|
| **Launch price:** | £2838 |
| **Excellent:** | £3000 |
| **Good:** | £1750 |
| **Average:** | £1000 |
| **Project:** | £400 |